Human Rights: An Anthropological Reader

Blackwell Readers in Anthropology

As anthropology moves beyond the limits of so-called area studies, there is an increasing need for texts that do the work of synthesizing the literature while challenging more traditional or subdisciplinary approaches to anthropology. This is the object of this exciting new series, *Blackwell Readers in Anthropology*.

Each volume in the series offers seminal readings on a chosen theme and provides the finest, most thought-provoking recent works in the given thematic area. Many of these volumes bring together for the first time a body of literature on a certain topic. The series thus both presents definitive collections and investigates the very ways in which anthropological inquiry has evolved and is evolving.

Human Rights:
An Anthropological
Reader

Edited by

Mark Goodale

WILEY-BLACKWELL

A John Wiley & Sons, Ltd., Publication

This edition first published 2009
© 2009 Blackwell Publishing Ltd except for editorial material and organization © 2009 Mark Goodale

Blackwell Publishing was acquired by John Wiley & Sons in February 2007. Blackwell's publishing program has been merged with Wiley's global Scientific, Technical, and Medical business to form Wiley-Blackwell.

Registered Office
John Wiley & Sons Ltd, The Atrium, Southern Gate, Chichester, West Sussex, PO19 8SQ, United Kingdom

Editorial Offices
350 Main Street, Malden, MA 02148-5020, USA
9600 Garsington Road, Oxford, OX4 2DQ, UK
The Atrium, Southern Gate, Chichester, West Sussex, PO19 8SQ, UK

For details of our global editorial offices, for customer services, and for information about how to apply for permission to reuse the copyright material in this book please see our website at www.wiley.com/wiley-blackwell.

The right of Mark Goodale to be identified as the author of the editorial material in this work has been asserted in accordance with the Copyright, Designs and Patents Act 1988.

Wiley also publishes its books in a variety of electronic formats. Some content that appears in print may not be available in electronic books.

Designations used by companies to distinguish their products are often claimed as trademarks. All brand names and product names used in this book are trade names, service marks, trademarks or registered trademarks of their respective owners. The publisher is not associated with any product or vendor mentioned in this book. This publication is designed to provide accurate and authoritative information in regard to the subject matter covered. It is sold on the understanding that the publisher is not engaged in rendering professional services. If professional advice or other expert assistance is required, the services of a competent professional should be sought.

Library of Congress Cataloging-in-Publication Data

Human rights : an anthropological reader / edited by Mark Goodale.
    p. cm. – (Blackwell readers in anthropology ; 10)
   Includes bibliographical references and index.
   ISBN 978-1-4051-8334-5 (pbk. : alk. paper) – ISBN 978-1-4051-8335-2 (hardcover : alk. paper)
1. Human rights. 2. Anthropological ethics. I. Goodale, Mark.

   JC571.H6915 2009
   323–dc22
                                 2008002411

A catalogue record for this book is available from the British Library.

Set in 10/12 pt Sabon by SPi Publisher Services, Pondicherry, India
Printed in Singapore by Fabulous Printers Pte Ltd

1 2009

Contents

Acknowledgments

I would first like to thank Rosalie Robertson, whose support and enthusiasm for this reader made it a joy to develop. Deirdre Ilkson, her editorial assistant, provided expert guidance and management throughout the process. I am particularly grateful to the five anonymous reviewers who were willing to consider the book in such detail and offer constructive suggestions for both content and form. My graduate research assistant, Ruth Adriana Salcedo, did excellent work at several stages in the book's development. She was primarily responsible for researching and annotating the appendix of websites on human rights, which I think greatly improves the scope and usefulness of the book. Finally, as always, I must acknowledge the sustaining presence of my muses – Isaiah, Dara, and Romana.

The editor and publisher gratefully acknowledge the permission granted to reproduce the copyright material in this book:

1   "Statement on Human Rights" originally published in *American Anthropologist*, n.s. 49: 4 (1947), 539–43; "Comments on the Statement on Human Rights," by Julian H. Steward, in *American Anthropologist*, n.s. 50: 2 (1948), 351–2. "On Science and Human Rights," by H. G. Barnett, in *American Anthropologist*, n.s. 50: 2 (1948), 352–5.
2   Hannah Arendt, "The Decline of the Nation-State and the End of the Rights of Man," originally published in *The Origins of Totalitarianism*, new edition with added prefaces. Orlando, FL: Harcourt Brace & Company, 1973, pp. 267–302.
3   Will Kymlicka, "The Good, the Bad, and the Intolerable: Minority Group Rights," originally published in *Dissent*, 43: 3 (1996), 22–30.
4   Abdullahi Ahmed An-Na'im, "Toward a Cross-Cultural Approach to Defining International Standards of Human Rights: The Meaning of Cruel, Inhuman, or Degrading Treatment or Punishment," originally published in *Human Rights in Cross-Cultural Perspectives: A Quest for Consensus*, ed. Abdullahi Ahmed An-Na'im. Philadelphia: University of Pennsylvania Press, 1992, pp. 19–43. Reprinted with permission of the University of Pennsylvania Press.
5   Amartya Sen, "Human Rights and Capabilities," originally published in *Journal of Human Development*, 6: 2 (2005), 151–66.

6 Committee for Human Rights, American Anthropological Association, "Declaration on Anthropology and Human Rights (1999)." Retrieved August 29, 2007 from www.aaanet.org/stmts/humanrts.htm. American Anthropological Association, Copyright © 1996–2006.

7 Ellen Messer, "Anthropology, Human Rights, and Social Transformation," originally published in *Transforming Societies, Transforming Anthropology*, ed. Emilio F. Moran. Ann Arbor: University of Michigan Press, 1996, pp. 165–210. Reprinted by permission of the University of Michigan Press.

8 Victoria Sanford, "Excavations of the Heart: Healing Fragmented Communities," originally published in *Buried Secrets: Truth and Human Rights in Guatemala*. New York: Palgrave Macmillan, 2003, pp. 232–47.

9 Paul Farmer and Nicole Gastineau, "Rethinking Health and Human Rights: Time for a Paradigm Shift," originally published in *Journal of Law, Medicine & Ethics*, 30: 4 (2002). American Society of Law and Medicine. Reprinted by permission of the *Journal of Law, Medicine & Ethics*.

10 Nancy Scheper-Hughes, "Rotten Trade: Millennial Capitalism, Human Values and Global Justice in Organs Trafficking," originally published in *Journal of Human Rights*, 2: 2 (2003), 197–226.

11 Terry Turner, Laura R. Graham, Carolyn Fluehr-Lobban, and Jane K. Cowan, "Anthropology and Human Rights: Do Anthropologists Have an Ethical Obligation to Promote Human Rights?" Retrieved August 29, 2007 from www.aaanet.org/press/an/1006/human_rights_oct.html#goodale. American Anthropological Association, 2006.

12 Richard. A. Wilson, "Representing Human Rights Violations: Social Contexts and Subjectivities," originally published in *Human Rights, Culture and Context: Anthropological Perspectives*, ed. Richard A. Wilson. London and Sterling, VA: Pluto Press, 1997, pp. 134–60. Reprinted by permission of Pluto Press.

13 Shannon Speed, "Gendered Intersections: Collective and Individual Rights in Indigenous Women's Experience," originally published in *Rights in Rebellion: Indigenous Struggle and Human Rights in Chiapas*. Stanford, CA: Stanford University Press, 2008, pp. 118–36.

14 Harri Englund, "Human Rights and Moral Panics: Listening to Popular Grievances," originally published in *Prisoners of Freedom: Human Rights and the African Poor*. Berkeley: University of California Press, 2006, pp. 170–92. Reprinted by permission of the University of California Press.

15 Sally Engle Merry, "Legal Transplants and Cultural Translation: Making Human Rights in the Vernacular," originally published in *Human Rights and Gender Violence: Translating International Law into Local Justice*, ed. Sally Engle Merry. Chicago: University of Chicago Press, 2006, pp. 134–78. Reprinted by permission of the University of Chicago Press.

16 Jane K. Cowan, "Culture and Rights after *Culture and Rights*," originally published in *American Anthropologist*, n.s. 108: 1 (2006), 9–24.

17 Ann-Belinda S. Preis, "Human Rights as Cultural Practice: An Anthropological Critique," originally published in *Human Rights Quarterly*, 18: 2 (1996), 286–315. © The Johns Hopkins University Press. Reprinted with permission of The Johns Hopkins University Press.

18 Thomas Hylland Eriksen, "Between Universalism and Relativism: A Critique of the UNESCO Concept of Culture," originally published in *Culture and Rights: Anthropological Perspectives*, ed. Jane K. Cowan, Marie-Bénédicte Dembour, and

Richard A. Wilson. Cambridge and New York: Cambridge University Press, 2001, pp. 127–48. © Cambridge University Press. Reprinted with permission.

19 Mark Goodale, "Toward a Critical Anthropology of Human Rights," originally published in *Current Anthropology*, 47: 3 (2006), 485–511. University of Chicago Press. © by The Wenner-Gren Foundation for Anthropological Research.

Introduction: Human Rights and Anthropology

Mark Goodale

The relationship between anthropology and human rights has been marked by confusion and ethical clarity, passion and reticence, historiographical debate and methodological creativity, and, above all, a sense that anthropology's most important contributions to human rights theory and practice are yet to come. This book brings together many of the key expressions of this ever fraught relationship between a discipline that finds itself in a constant state of becoming and the most enduring and compelling of the cosmopolitan visions to (re)emerge from the paroxysm of violence and suffering of the mid century last.

A certain irony infuses the contested political and intellectual histories within which anthropology and anthropologists have alternately danced on both tip-toes and heavy heels around human rights. As a modern academic discipline, anthropology has never fully relinquished its claim to being the "science of mankind" *par excellence*, the discipline whose knowledge practices, ethical sensitivities, and professional commitments seek to most comprehensively apprehend and inform the complexities of the human experience itself. This is a "holism" of the most clear-eyed and ambitious kind: the recognition that the comparative practice of everyday life must be understood, however selectively, in both the conjunctive and the disjunctive, as both an expression of certain vague universal patterns and a reflection of what is absolutely irreducible about *this* practice in *this* place at *this* particular moment in time. And if anthropology has been at all successful in its efforts to holistically document and analyze the human experience, it is odd indeed to have to acknowledge that the findings of anthropological research, and the theoretical frameworks that anthropologists have derived from these findings, played at best a marginal role in the development of the modern idea of human rights and the international legal and political system that was constructed to give effect to the idea.

The normative claims and underlying assumptions of the contemporary idea of human rights are both simple to understand and radically provocative, particularly when we remember that they were foisted onto a wounded world at precisely that historical moment in which the trajectory of Western civilization in which they were – in earlier versions – a constant presence had come to a crashing and dark standstill. All the pretensions of scientific progress, Western rationality, and the modern bureaucratic state perished right along with the victims of the Nazis' murderous regime, yet these were as integral to Western intellectual history as were ideas about the nature of the individual, ideas that formed the basis of the pioneering human rights declarations and political constitutions of late eighteenth-century France and the United States and early nineteenth-century Latin America. So it was a remarkable and perhaps desperate act of moral and political courage for those who were charged with picking up the pieces at the end of World War II to make the multiple assertions of human rights the centerpiece of the postwar settlement: that all human beings are essentially the same; that this essential sameness has normative implications; that this essential sameness must be recognized and protected through a regime of rights (among many other normative possibilities); and that to recognize – and act on – the essential sameness of humanity is an unqualified moral good.

It is not hyperbole to say that the set of interlocking assertions that are brought together within the rubric of human rights is, if true in any meaningful sense, the most potentially important fact about our troubled species, a truth that will be waiting for our disintegrative world when it is – if ever – ready to receive it. Yet it has historically been an unanthropological truth, one unsupported by any systematic cross-cultural empirical analysis of either human nature or legal and moral practice. How the most anthropologically significant of facts emerged in the absence of anthropology, and, more important, what anthropology has done to make up for its ironic absence, are the two thematic pillars on which this reader rests. For if anthropology was forced – willingly or not – to watch from the sidelines as the postwar idea of human rights was refined and debated by legions of political philosophers, legal scholars, and (somewhat later) postcolonial critics, the major international human rights institutions were created within a Cold War world that rendered them impotent, and human rights discourse became, in Richard A. Wilson's words, "the archetypal language of democratic transition" (2001:1), all of this began to change in the 1980s. And by 2008, as we shall see, the relationship between anthropology and human rights had been so fundamentally transformed theoretically, politically, and methodologically that it was possible to say that an anthropology *of* human rights had emerged as a leading-edge area of research, critical scholarship, and political engagement.

It would be more satisfying to be able to say that this transformation in the relationship between anthropology and human rights was the result of the discovery of some epistemological or ethical treasure buried deep within anthropology itself. As it turns out, however, the profound shift was the result of timing more than anything else: anthropology was ready for human rights, and human rights was (more or less) ready for anthropology. And this mutual receptivity was itself made possible by the end of the Cold War, which dissolved the realpolitik logics of the bipolar international system and opened the way for the development of both the international human rights system and the transnational networks through which coursed a globalizing discourse of human rights. Anthropologists found themselves in different ways at the vanguard of this rapid expansion. At times, the encounter was serendipitous: an anthropologist studying international development, or post-conflict reconstruction, or diasporic communities was confronted with the fact that "human rights" had suddenly become a discursive framework bracketing ongoing political, legal, and moral practice; other anthropologists were more foresighted and set out specifically to track this new and increasingly hegemonic discourse as it became what Arjun Appadurai (1996) would call a global "ideoscape." But regardless of the preconditions and contingencies, by the early 2000s anthropologists had made a series of important contributions to both the understanding and praxis of human rights, even if the discipline's characteristic skepticism and pursuit of the ironic meant that the relationship between human rights and anthropology would remain burdened by the dilemmas at the heart of the postwar human rights project.

Thinking of Human Rights Anthropologically

It is of particular importance to begin this reader with a selection of readings on the "conceptual and historical foundations" that inform anthropology's engagement with human rights not – as one might assume – because these foundations are so deep or well established, but because they have only recently and precipitously been laid. If disciplinary relationships to human rights can be compared to mountain ranges, then anthropology's would be the Himalayas, in chronological terms a mere infant compared with, say, philosophy, whose relationship to natural/human rights could compare in agedness and epistemological grandeur to a well-worn range like the Appalachians. (Of course we might also extend this metaphor by noting that the youngest mountain ranges are also the tallest – and still growing!) Even though anthropologists like Franz Boas engaged in what we would today describe as a "public anthropology" that was fundamentally concerned with what we would today describe as "human rights concerns" – especially through his research and public advocacy around immigration and what was called at the time the "race question" (see Salyer 2006; Stocking 1989) – it was only in the years immediately after World War II that anthropologists first formally confronted the idea of human rights and the possibility of its realization in political and legal practice.

As Johannes Morsink (1999) explains in detail, in his authoritative history of the drafting of what became the Universal Declaration of Human Rights (UDHR), the United Nations Educational, Scientific and Cultural Organization (UNESCO) was charged with soliciting expert advisory opinions on the possibility of an official declaration of universal rights. These opinions were indeed solicited and received from a wide range of actors, including national governments, educational organizations, artistic foundations, prominent individuals, and professional associations, among others. Although much of the world of the late 1940s was still laboring under the yoke of colonialism, and the grip of postwar shock and moral devastation made questions of human dignity hollow at best, UNESCO did make an attempt to gather together a body of advice and consent that had some claim to cross-cultural legitimacy. At the very least, the opinions – taken as a whole – contained enough non-Western voices to complicate later claims about the essential Westernness of human rights.

Be that as it may, it appears that anthropology, as a discipline, was solicited by UNESCO through the person of a well known mid-century anthropologist, Melville Herskovits, in his capacity as chairman of the Committee for International Cooperation in Anthropology of the National Research Council, a post which he assumed in 1945.[1] Herskovits was a prominent American anthropologist, a member of the American Anthropological Association's Executive Board, and chairman of the Department of Anthropology at Northwestern University. He had been a student of Franz Boas at Columbia University, where he earned his PhD in anthropology in 1923.[2] After considering the documents sent to him by UNESCO on behalf of the Commission on Human Rights (whose chair was Eleanor Roosevelt), Herskovits wrote on his own what became known as the "Statement on Human Rights," which was sent to the Executive Board of the American Anthropological Association (AAA), which then arranged for it to be published by the Association's journal, *American Anthropologist*, in 1947, the year before the UDHR was ratified by the UN's General Assembly.[3]

Herskovits's – and then the AAA's – "Statement on Human Rights" is the first selection in the reader and it marks a convenient beginning of anthropology's engagement with the modern doctrine of human rights. The Statement expresses grave concerns with the declaration that the Commission on Human Rights was in the process of drafting. Its critique cuts along two axes – one epistemological, the other ethical. It argues that the findings of anthropology, the discipline responsible for producing the "scientific knowledge of Man," do not support the universalizing claims of a declaration of the "rights of man," insofar as these claims gloss over the differences in values between cultures that anthropologists had amply documented. This was a provocative assertion, especially since the recent horrors of World War II were justified by a doctrine of cultural difference taken to its murderous, if not logical, conclusion.

But beyond the "scientific" objections to the proposed declaration of human rights, the Statement also focuses on the historical contexts in which similar declarations were formulated and then made the foundation for experiments in political and social organization. In this way, it links what would become the UDHR to the great rights-of-man documents of eighteenth-century France and the United States. As the Statement argues, the problem is that, as with these earlier historical monuments to universalist idealism, the current declaration of human rights was closely linked to the political fortunes not of the nation-states of the world as a whole, but to the powerful Western nations whose cultural values are both expressed and celebrated in the modern doctrine of human rights. On the basis of both of these interconnected lines of critique, the Statement on Human Rights rejected the legitimacy of the UDHR.

Official AAA correspondence and related documents in the months after the Statement was published do not reveal any reaction at all among the membership, or more broadly (for example, by UNESCO or the UN Commission on Human Rights), to what had become the official (American) anthropological statement on the noblest – if most utopian – symbol of the postwar settlement. In the next two years, three reactions to the Statement were published in the "brief communications" section of *American Anthropologist*, two of which (by Steward and Barnett) are included here. As can be seen, the debate they briefly engendered had nothing to do with the underlying intent and claims of a universal declaration of human rights; instead, it revolved around claims in the Statement about the proper boundaries of anthropology as science. So despite assertions by some scholars that the Statement shocked the collective conscience of anthropology, and would serve as an ever present black mark against the discipline in the decades following its publication (see especially Engle 2001), in fact it would be more accurate to describe the impact of the Statement on anthropology in the early postwar years as negligible.[4]

In a book of this kind, it is not possible or necessary to include readings that give a full account of the intellectual history of human rights, which extends deep into Western antiquity. What is important, however, is to provide enough context to locate anthropology's appearance in this history. The Statement on Human Rights was a response to a process that was under way within a working body of the new

United Nations; the United Nations was the most important institution of postwar reconstruction; and the war itself represented the tragic failure of the sovereignty-based system of international relations that had emerged as a response to an earlier, more regionalized, period of darkness in human history (the Thirty Years War). But World War II was intimately connected to both World War I and the disintegration of the centuries-old Austro-Hungarian and Ottoman Empires that preceded it. In a selection reproduced here from her monumental *Origins of Totalitarianism*, Hannah Arendt describes this tragic connection in the following way:

> The days before and the days after the first World War are separated not like the end of an old and the beginning of a new period, but like the day before and the day after an explosion. Yet this figure of speech is as inaccurate as are all others, because the quiet of sorrow which settles down after a catastrophe has never come to pass. The first explosion seems to have touched off a chain reaction in which we have been caught ever since and which nobody seems to be able to stop (1973:276).

Part of this chain reaction in the interwar period included violence against what were understood as "minority populations," the groups of people who suddenly found themselves confronting the fury of dominant ethnic groups at the reins of power of the new nation-states created in the postimperial landscape. As Arendt demonstrates in elegant and persuasive detail, the systematic violations of human dignity of World War II had their origins in a series of legal and political steps taken against particular *groups* (not individuals) of people after World War I, steps that incrementally narrowed citizenship rights and eventually the perceived humanness of the targeted populations. Beyond merely providing context and a sense of histor-ical linkage between the UDHR and legal, political, and ideological developments in the interwar years, the selection from Arendt also serves as a foreshadowing of a much later anthropological re-engagement with human rights, since (as we shall soon see) it was the ever present threat to "minority populations" that was the basis for mobilization.[5]

In the decades after the 1940s, the international human rights system was halt-ingly constructed by diplomats, international lawyers, and national political leaders. The *idea* of human rights, which the primary architects of the UDHR (Humphrey, Cassin, to a lesser extent Chang) had adopted in only a slightly modified form from its Enlightenment iteration, was debated, refined, and elaborated by growing num-bers of political philosophers, legal theorists, and social critics.[6] When anthropolo-gists were finally ready institutionally to take up human rights as a basis for both political action and ethnographic study, only certain subsets of this much larger human rights scholarship proved initially relevant. Important examples from three of these subsets are included here. A much read work from the liberal Canadian political theorist Will Kymlicka takes on the difficult problem of the political and theoretical relationship between individual rights and collective rights. Here, as elsewhere (Kymlicka 1995a; 1995b; 2007), Kymlicka develops a framework through which the essentially liberal protections of human rights can be extended to collectivities. In order to make this possible, however, it is necessary, according to Kymlicka, that nation-states tolerate certain "unjust practices" within minority groups in order to preserve their group autonomy and right to practice at least some cultural traditions that – taken in isolation – appear to violate the *individual* rights of particular group members.

Since anthropologists took a keen interest in the relationship between "culture" and human rights, they have also had to grapple with the wider body of scholarship that seeks to use variations on hermeneutics in order to "translate" human rights between distinct cultural and religious traditions.[7] The Sudanese legal scholar Abdullahi Ahmed An-Na'im has played an influential role in shaping the terms of debate over intercultural human rights dialogue, especially with regard to the doctrinal relationship between international human rights law and shari'a, or Islamic religious law (see, most recently, An-Na'im 2006; 2008). In the selection reproduced here, which is the introductory essay from his widely used edited volume *Human Rights in Cross-Cultural Perspectives* (1992), An-Na'im makes an extended argument for a "cross-cultural approach" to human rights, one that uses expansive dialogue in order to achieve cross-cultural consensus around common normative standards, those points of ethical connection that interweave through international human rights norms and the world's many moral, legal, and religious systems. The interculturalism of An-Na'im has guided many subsequent anthropologists, especially those who seek a middle ground between the questionable universality of many human rights claims, and the equally questionable irreducibility of many claims of cultural (and thus normative) difference (see, e.g., Cowan et al. 2001; Eberhard 2003).

Part I ends with a final example from the wider body of human rights scholarship that has shaped at least some strains of anthropological research and practice around issues that implicate fundamental human well-being and dignity. The development economist Amartya Sen, along with the political philosopher Martha Nussbaum (1997; 2000), has developed an innovative approach to human rights, one that is meant to achieve the goals of the postwar human rights project by political and normative means that go well beyond the boundaries of international human rights law and institutions. As Sen argues in a 2005 article that appears here, "human rights" should not be understood primarily as a set of "intellectually frail" abstract norms supposedly derived from the "self-evident" fact of common humanness (p. 86). Instead, human rights should be understood as "entitlements to capabilities," which Nussbaum defines as "[human] abilities to do and be certain things deemed valuable" (1997:275). To focus on capabilities in this sense is to decentralize human rights, to view human rights as merely the most significant among a range of *means* to the enablement and protection of full human functioning. This naturally appeals to anthropologists, whose research brings them face to face with the wide variety of ways in which human functioning is tragically and often systematically curtailed. And indeed, this concern with "capabilities" and their relation to human rights can be found in the 1947 Statement on Human Rights itself, which worries at some length about the "full development of the individual personality" and the "problem of human capacity."

Anthropology and Human Rights Activism

Part I of this reader provides an overview of – and makes an argument about – the historical context of anthropology's engagement with human rights, and selectively draws from sources through which scholars have begun to think anthropologically about different problems in the postwar human right project. Parts II to IV pick up the narrative of this intellectual and political history in the late 1980s, which proved to be a watershed moment in the discipline's orientation to human rights. Although the anthropologist David Maybury-Lewis had founded (with his wife Pia Maybury-Lewis) the organization Cultural Survival in the early 1970s, there is some dispute about whether it was originally what we would describe today as a human rights NGO, or whether it was rather an organization whose main focus was the survival of indigenous cultures.[8] In any event, we can point with some certainty to developments in the late 1980s within the American Anthropological Association as marking a profound shift in the way anthropologists understood their individual and disciplinary obligations to promote and advocate for human rights.[9]

Throughout the 1980s and into the early 1990s, anthropologists began to chafe against the legacy of the "Statement on Human Rights," especially as the end of the Cold War had made possible a wave of human rights legislation and transnational advocacy. This dramatic emergence of international and transnational human rights meant that for the first time "human rights" became a pervasive part of the logic of political and social resistance, particularly in parts of the world that had been the sites of the most intensive transnational development work, which was reborn under the sign of human rights and subsequently marked by a new kind of moral urgency. Although biological anthropologists and archaeologists found themselves confronting human rights issues during this time, it was in fact a relatively small group of sociocultural anthropologists that undertook to transform the discipline's official statement of its relationship to human rights. The 1999 "Declaration on Anthropology and Human Rights," which is reproduced here, *was* voted on and approved by the general membership of the American Anthropological Association (in contradistinction to the 1947 Statement). It stands as a definitive and unequivocal repudiation of the 1947 Statement, which the Declaration – revealingly – does not mention.

Far from expressing any hesitation about either the politics or ontology of the UDHR, the Declaration – and thus the largest professional anthropological association in the world – creates a formal ethical obligation for anthropologists to start "from the base line of the Universal Declaration of Human Rights" and move expansively on from there. As the Declaration says, it "reflects a commitment to human rights consistent with international principles but not limited by them.... It is therefore incumbent on anthropologists to be involved in the debate on enlarging our understanding of human rights on the basis of anthropological knowledge and research." In other words, anthropologists are to advocate for the growing body of international human rights law, and create a new category of human rights scholarship, one that combines the findings from anthropology's different methodologies with a commitment to critical social and political engagement.

The 1999 Declaration was in many ways as much a culmination of a decade-long process of reorientation as it was the beginning of a new chapter in anthropology's relationship to human rights. From the establishment of a Commission on Human Rights within the AAA in the early 1990s – later made into a permanent standing Committee on Human Rights – to the increasingly wide-ranging and public human rights activism by anthropologists in the course of their research and writing, anthropology had by 1999 already emerged as a passionate, if not always influential, disciplinary voice on certain problems of concern to the wider human rights community. Particularly fine examples of this passionate combination of anthropological scholarship and human rights activism comprise the heart of Part II. Ellen Messer, who was one of eight founding members of the AAA Commission on Human Rights,[10] has been a leading advocate in the fight to have a "right to food" recognized within international human rights law (see Messer 1996, 2004).[11] In the selection here, Messer provides an overview of anthropology's relationship to human rights and makes a series of arguments for how the work of anthropologists can and should contribute to a transformed human rights practice by "identify[ing] and encourag[ing] the contexts that favor the expansion of human rights protections or a widening notion of human community" (p. 115).

The forensic anthropologist Victoria Sanford has been at the forefront of a kind of anthropology of human rights that we might describe as "anthropological witnessing" (Malkki 1995; Pieke 1995; Scheper-Hughes 1997). Her fieldwork in Guatemala first documented the exhumation of secret mass graves that contained the victims of Guatemala's civil war. But her work subsequently went much further: she also participated in the public analysis of the genocide and has, importantly, focused her scholarship on debates and the truth and reconciliation process within Guatemala itself (Sanford 2000; 2003a; 2003b; 2006). In the chapter from her 2003 book *Buried Secrets* included here, Sanford's account and analysis of her work with a Guatemalan forensic team become her own form of *testimonio*, her own "excavation of the heart."

Paul Farmer's research, medical practice, and public health advocacy have brought medical anthropology together with human rights activism in innovative and powerful ways (see, e.g., Farmer 1992; 1999; 2003). Farmer was one of the cofounders of Partners in Health, an international charity organization that began its work in Haiti by providing free medical care as a form of social justice.[12] As he argues in "Rethinking Health and Human Rights" (with coauthor Nicole Gastineau), anthropologists and health professionals should work toward a "practical solidarity" by deploying "tools and resources to improve the health and well-being of those who suffer [from structural] violence" (p. 151). And *deployment* here is very much central to Farmer's project to make community-based health care a form of human rights activism. Neither "Ivory-tower engagement" nor "research and critical assessment" are sufficient for this task. As the authors explain, the medical anthropologist-as-human-rights-worker should be under the same ethical obligations as the medical clinician: once the cause of the disease (or human rights violation) has been identified, the clinician is duty-bound to propose an intervention, even if there is always the chance the intervention will not "cure" the disease.

Nancy Scheper-Hughes's earlier masterpiece, *Death without Weeping* (1993), revealed the ways in which structural violence and the long-term effects of endemic poverty in northeastern Brazil led to a profound transformation in the relationship between mothers and their children, in which the sheer mundaneness of infant and early child mortality caused mothers to inure themselves to the diminishment of their children's humanity. This was an anthropology of human rights violations of the most complicated kind: who were the victims and who were the perpetrators in this account of death without affect and pervasive dehumanization? More recently, Scheper-Hughes has pioneered another kind of anthropology of (and for) human rights, one that tracks and exposes what she call the "biopolitical terrorism of free trade transplant," which takes the form of "networks of organized crime . . . . that are putting into circulation ambulatory organ buyers, itinerant kidney hunters, outlaw surgeons, medical technicians, makeshift transplant units and clandestine laboratories" (p. 169). Like Farmer, Scheper-Hughes has translated her scholarship into institutional nongovernmental action: she, along with her colleague (and fellow anthropologist) Lawrence Cohen, founded Organs Watch in 1999,[13] which brings attention to the "social and economic context of organ transplantation, focusing on the human rights implications of the desperate, world-wide, search for organs."[14]

In her article on this "rotten trade," reproduced in this reader, she shows how a millennial capitalism brings together kidney sellers and consumers within an "occult economy" in which body parts are both commodified and fetishized in the darker transnational landscapes of the global economy.

Part II of the reader is brought to a close with selections from a four-part series that appeared in *Anthropology News* between April and October of 2006. In that series, which was entitled "Anthropology and Human Rights: An Open Exchange," scholars, practitioners, and government officials responded to four questions that were intended to measure the barometer of the relationship of anthropology to human rights in the years after the 1999 Declaration.[15] The last of these four questions – "Do anthropologists have an ethical obligation to promote human rights?" – was meant to gauge the extent to which the formal ethical injunction of the Declaration had taken hold. The responses to this question included here fall on a spectrum. Those of Terence Turner, Carolyn Fluehr-Lobban, and Laura Graham differ only in the extent to which they argue that the obligation to promote human rights should be understood as a professional responsibility (Graham), a moral choice (Fluehr-Lobban), or a "matter of moral and intellectual principle" (Turner). The response of Jane Cowan – revealingly, a British social anthropologist[16] – echoes the critique that the utilitarian political philosopher Jeremy Bentham levied against the "rights of man": that "focusing energies," as Cowan puts it, "on legal formalization of rights and the state's obligations…diverts attention from other domains, like the economy, that may influence people's lives equally profoundly" (p. 205). She argues that the suggestion that anthropologists have an ethical obligation to promote human rights is "misguided moralism," since "[r]ights are notoriously poor instruments for challenging invidious practices and power arrangements in the private sphere, whether in families or the workplaces of multinational corporations" (p. 205).

The Ethnography of Human Rights Practices

As the selections from Part II of this reader demonstrate, anthropologists will continue to find creative ways to use "anthropological knowledge and research" to expose human rights violations, advance the cause of human dignity and well-being among populations anthropologists have "made the subjects of their scientific careers" (Turner, ch. 11), and make the act of anthropological witnessing the basis for intellectual and institutional action. But during the 1990s and into the early 2000s, another form of anthropological engagement with human rights crystallized, one that was even more clearly linked to the end of the logics of the Cold War and the rapid expansion of the parallel international and transnational human rights regimes. Here anthropologists found themselves confronting the globalization of human rights discourse as an increasingly dominant transnational paradigm of moral inquiry and political praxis. These shifts are what Richard A. Wilson has described as a "sea-change in global politics" (2001:1), in which networks of human rights activists and institutions became increasingly professionalized and committed to the production of specific forms of technocratic knowledge (Riles 2000). Wilson himself was a pioneer ethnographer of the rise of human rights discourse in the post-Cold War period, especially since his most well-known study – on the truth and reconciliation process in early postapartheid South Africa – was on one of the earliest and most important examples of the attempt to forge a "culture of human rights" in a society in the throes of post-Cold War democratic transition (Wilson 2001).

One of Wilson's even earlier writings on anthropology and human rights is reproduced here and it reflects the almost accidental quality of much of the ethnography
of human rights practices in the early and mid 1990s.

As he explains, "I originally had no intention of studying human rights in
Guatemala, but instead focused on religious conversions and ethnic identities in
the department of Alta Verapez... Yet I was repeatedly placed in the position
of bystander – witnessing or hearing personal testimonies of violent expressions of
state power within my immediate social network" (p. 210). Wilson subsequently
conducted a parallel ethnography that both captured the reality of political violence
in Guatemala and showcased the potential anthropological contributions to our
understanding of human rights discourse by viewing its moral and legal categories
from the inside out. In particular, Wilson focused on the ways in which human
rights reporting and monitoring produce new forms of subjectivity – while excluding
others – in ways that resist the kind of contextualization that is needed for human
rights regimes to be both effective and locally legitimate.

Shannon Speed has been studying the use of human rights over the last decade by
indigenous political leaders in Chiapas, Mexico (Speed 2006; 2008). Among other
things, her research has shown how indigenous activists have crafted an alternative
theory of human rights, one in which "human rights" are both circumscribed by
indigenous understandings of the person (rather than by the more inclusive, and
abstract, category of "human") and locally legitimate only to the extent to which
they can be exercised in the course of ongoing political and social struggles. As the
selection from her work reproduced here shows, ethnographers of human rights
practices have also built a significant database of information about what Speed
calls "local appropriations," meaning the actual ways in which social actors harness
human rights discourse and invest it with meaning. The act of appropriation is for
Speed also a process of "grounding human rights," of actualizing "global discourses
on the local terrain" (2008). The praxis of grounding is essentially dialogic and
takes places in a "complex space of interaction within which continual struggles
over meaning, culture, and power are always present" (p. 242). And always framing
these dialogic encounters, these local appropriations of human rights discourse, is
the larger, and often violent, backdrop of "conflict, counterinsurgency, and the
renegotiation of power relations with the state" (p. 242).

In his study of "Africa in the neoliberal world order" (2006), James Ferguson
deconstructs the pretensions of "scientific" responses to the continent's many "crises."
As he argues, the technocratic discourse of late-modern capitalism and international
development

> present[s] itself as a non-moral order, in which neutral, technical principles of efficiency
> and pragmatism give "correct" answers to questions of public policy. Yet a whole series
> of moral premises are implicit in these technicizing arguments. Notions of the inviolate
> rights of individuals, the sanctity of private property, the nobility of capitalist accumu-
> lation, and the intrinsic value of "freedom"... lie just below the surface (2006:80).

And in Africa, as elsewhere, the language of human rights has also become a key
"technicizing argument," one whose often unintended consequences have been
analyzed by other ethnographers of neoliberalism's "global shadows." In the selection included here from his book on "human rights and the African poor," Harri
Englund describes a "moral panic" that shook the country of Malawi in 2003. As he
explains, a series of rumors swept through the country about "a perceived rise in

the abductions and abuse of children" in the nation's capital, Lilongwe (p. 246). The elaborateness of these rumors – which involved accounts of trafficking in body parts by the country's jet-setting president, and a process through which the flesh of children was converted to gold inside the bellies of a certain species of Indian Ocean fish – represents for Englund a heightened reaction against the constricting discourse of human rights, which had become by 2003 a dominant framework in neoliberal Malawi (as elsewhere). In Englund's provocative formulation, Malawi's poor had become "prisoners" as much as beneficiaries of the promises – and "moral premises" – of human rights discourse, which both "eclips[ed] the actual diversity of claims and concerns" and foreclosed the possibility that a wider range of social reforms or economic development would be pursued.

The final selection here that illustrates the important ethnographic contributions that anthropologists have made to our understanding of the practice of human rights is from Sally Engle Merry's comparative study of the interconnected international and transnational networks that have emerged to promote and implement the Convention on the Elimination of All Forms of Discrimination against Women (CEDAW). Merry and her different research collaborators were required to engage in a "deterritorialized ethnography" in order to track the horizontalizing flows through which "information, funds, and personnel" are mobilized and transplanted within the CEDAW system. As she demonstrates in rich comparative detail, the international legal and moral norms embedded in human rights discourse must be "vernacularized," which is a constitutive process of cultural translation in which the universalizing rhetorics of human rights are "adjusted." What results, she explains, "is a bricolage of elements in constantly shifting relation to one another made up of elements that do not necessarily fit together smoothly" (p. 266).

Critical Anthropologies of Human Rights

At the same time that anthropologists were demonstrating the renewed possibilities for making anthropological knowledge relevant for human rights activism, while others were developing innovative methodologies in order to reveal the contradictions and unintended consequences in the practice of human rights, yet another distinct mode of anthropological engagement with human rights could be detected. Portents of this third way in anthropology's relationship to human rights could be found in the edited volume *Culture and Rights* (Cowan et al. 2001). Although its formal intent was to bring together anthropologists in order to "explore how universal concepts [like human rights] were being taken up in local struggles" (Cowan, ch. 16), in fact the volume stands as an empirically grounded but thoroughgoing critique of the misapprehensions of "culture" in both human rights theory and practice. The volume's editors direct the critical gaze at both human rights activists, who strategically deploy an essentialized understanding of "culture" within ongoing political struggles, and dominant human rights theorists, whose understanding of the relationship between human rights and culture is shaped by competing "universalized abstraction[s]" (Cowan et al. 2001:17). In both cases, and for quite different reasons, what is "lacking [is] a theory of the relational attributes" of both "human rights" and "culture" (Cowan et al. 2001:19).

This line of analysis foreshadows the development of a critical anthropology *of* human rights in that it uses the ethnography of human rights discourse in order to reflect back on basic theoretical and ethical problems at the heart of the postwar human rights project. The motivations behind this emergent critical anthropology of human rights are diverse: they range from a desire to re-establish the existing international human rights regime on firmer and more legitimate footing (Preis, ch. 17), to skepticism about the effectiveness of a superordinate system of universal norms grounded in the neo-Kantianism of an instrument like the UDHR (see, e.g., Goodale 2009). Regardless of motivation, however, critical anthropologies of human rights extend a more general kind of anthropology – anthropology as cultural critique (Marcus and Fischer 1986) – to a domain of knowledge production and moral practice that has become over the last 20 years one of the most consequential of "global assemblages" (Ong and Collier 2005).

The first selection in Part IV is from Jane Cowan, who continues and updates the critique of dominant theories of culture by human rights theorists that she (along with coeditors Dembour and Wilson) began in *Culture and Rights*. Cowan has been an anthropologist of contingency, of irreducible complexity, and these pervasive concerns shape her study of "rights formulation and claims making on the ground" (p. 324). Yet even though her critical anthropology of human rights has been shadowed by what she calls a "tragic and ambiguous reading of human sociality" (Cowan 2006), here she adopts a more conciliatory position toward the claims and potentialities of human rights. In the struggle to find more "just and creative ways of living together" (p. 325), Cowan argues that a critical anthropology of human rights should be part of a wider search for "common ground," in which the descriptive and the normative are combined in innovative and rigorous ways.

The work of the Danish anthropologist Ann-Belinda Preis is an early example of a kind of critical anthropology of human rights that is both prescriptive and directed squarely at debates within the international human rights community (and not anthropology itself). In the selection here – which originally appeared in the influential *Human Rights Quarterly* – Preis argues that the international human rights system would be more effective cross-culturally if it de-emphasized what she describes as "mechanical, prefabricated, and externalist modes of human behavior and social change" (p. 335). Instead, she urges human rights researchers and practitioners to focus their work on the "everyday life of living and breathing social actors" (p. 351), both victims and perpetrators, as well as the activists in different parts of the world who seek to inculcate a culture of human rights at the grassroots level. Like Cowan, she brings the lessons of critical social theory to bear on problems in human rights theory and practice; and also like Cowan, these lessons lead Preis to emphasize the essential hybridity in processes of contemporary subject-making, which inform her "dynamic approach" to both culture and human rights.

The Norwegian anthropologist Thomas Hylland Eriksen also uses debates over "culture" as a way into a more expansive critique of the relationship between what he calls "locally embedded values" and the cosmopolitan postwar international system of which human rights are an important – and, since 1989, more than symbolic – part (p. 362). His specific targets are *both* the multiple essentialized versions of "culture" that have been codified by UNESCO as part of the organization's efforts to protect the world's "cultural heritage," and those antirelativist critics of UNESCO – in particular the French public intellectual Alain Finkielkraut – who see in the rise of culture talk a return to the dark days when the universalist aspirations of the Enlightenment had seemingly been thrown over for the imperatives of blood-and-soil, moral relativism, and the murderous national cults of *Volksgeist*. As he puts it, in the debate over the relationship between "culture" and "rights," the trick is to be able to navigate the "muddy waters between the Scylla of nihilistic cultural relativism and the Charybdis of supremacist universalism" (p. 356). In other words, the extremes on both sides of the debate are equally inexcusable – as most extremes usually are. As an alternative, Eriksen (quoting from the French Bulgarian theorist Tzvetan Todorov) urges anthropologists of human rights – and others – to understand rights in a world of diversity through the lens of a "well-tempered humanism" (p. 368). The suggestion that human rights should be grounded in humanism and not universalism – and, moreover, that anthropology reinforces the former and not the latter – is both a theoretical and ethical bombshell that Eriksen simply drops at the end of his examination of the uses of "culture" within the international system. But it is a bombshell that clears the ground for a radically different kind of critical anthropology of human rights, in which the findings of anthropology are used to reconfigure the modern idea of human rights itself.

Finally, my own contribution here moves the discussion of the relationship between anthropology and human rights away from the problem (and potential) of "culture." The article is both a reanalysis of the ways in which American anthropology's relationship to human rights has been (mis)represented, and (mis-)self-represented, and a proposal for a different analytical language through which anthropology can contribute to debates over human rights theory and practice. In part, the effort to think beyond the boundaries of ethnography is a response to the political economy of human rights, in which theoretical debate and advocacy are shaped by epistemologies of deductivism on the one hand, and the politics of social transformation on the other. It is not enough for anthropologists of human rights to retreat too comfortably behind the contradictions and contingencies revealed by the close engagement with human rights in practice. Political philosophers, policymakers, international lawyers, transnational activists, and (most importantly) the millions of ordinary social actors around the world who grapple with the idea of human rights as part of ongoing social and political struggles, all want to know of anthropologists: What do these contradictions mean more generally? Does anthropology have anything to contribute to an alternative *theory* of human rights? How would a human rights regime informed by a "well-tempered humanism" be translated into international law? And – this is not an exhaustive list! – does the critique of the existing international human rights system put vulnerable populations at greater risk by undermining the moral and conceptual claims of the best supranational normativity we've got? How persuasively and creatively anthropologists of human rights respond to these (and related) questions, I argue, will shape both the course of human rights in the coming decades, and the relevance of anthropology in broader efforts to conceive of and institutionalize on a global scale "just and creative ways of living together."

NOTES

1   I say "appears" in order to emphasize that the following historical questions (among others) have been a matter of some dispute among the small group of anthropologists (and some others) who are interested in these particular historical questions: which representatives of the anthropological community did UNESCO approach during its consultative work on behalf of the Commission on Human Rights, and how were they approached? See, e.g., Engle 2001, Messer 1993, Preis 1996, Washburn 1987, Wilson and Mitchell 2003.

2   I have in other places grappled with the question of whether or not American anthropol-
    ogy, in a sense, stood in for anthropology itself during the UNESCO solicitation process
    in the years before 1948 (Goodale 2006a; 2006b; 2009). It was unusual that UNESCO
    solicited Herskovits directly and not the AAA, since it was the practice of UNESCO to
    seek official opinions from fields of knowledge through professional associations (see
    Morsink 1999). There is no evidence that Britain's Association of Social Anthropologists
    was solicited on the question of a declaration of human rights, which makes sense if we
    consider that the ASA was founded only in 1946 with 11 original members (www.theasa.
    org/history.htm). With the exception of the Royal Anthropological Institute, according
    to the World Council of Anthropological Associations (www.wcaanet.org/members/), the
    only other major professional association of anthropologists at the time was the Istituto
    Italiano di Antropologia (ISItA), but again, there is no evidence ISItA was solicited by
    UNESCO or otherwise formally contributed the Italian anthropological position on the
    question of human rights.

3   It was this sequence more than any other that has caused the most confusion among
    later commentators. The "Statement on Human Rights" that was published by *American
    Anthropologist* in 1947 carried above it the indication that it was "submitted to the
    Commission on Human Rights, United Nations, by the Executive Board, American
    Anthropological Association." But in the correspondence I have studied between the
    1947 Executive Board and Herskovits, there is no indication that this Statement was
    ever sent to the Commission, or that the Commission was aware that the AAA, and not
    Herskovits – who had been solicited by UNESCO on the Commission's behalf – was
    intending to publish its response. Certainly the Statement was not ratified or voted on by
    the general membership of the AAA at the time, and it is here where the real crux of the
    problem lies. It has generally been assumed that the Statement was an "embarrassment"
    (see, e.g., Engle 2001) to the anthropological community, which was presumably support-
    ive of the idea of human rights. But there is no evidence of this disjuncture between the
    sentiments expressed in the Statement and the wider anthropological community, either
    at the time the Statement was published or in the years that followed.

4   It is of course difficult to demonstrate something like the absence of awareness or a
    negligible impact. But I have shown how "human rights" did not appear as a topic of
    interest – scholarly or otherwise – among anthropologists until well into the 1980s
    (Goodale 2006a; 2009). And Ellen Messer (2006) has written, prominent international
    lawyers who played an important role in the drafting of major international human rights
    legislation in the 1960s and 1970s specifically excluded the voice of anthropology from
    their deliberations, in part because they felt the problem of "culture" did not deserve a
    place at the table. All of this does not mean that anthropologists were not politically active
    on issues that would today fall within the rubric of "human rights" (e.g., the race debates
    of the 1950s and 1960s; civil rights; the war in Vietnam and colonialism more generally;
    and, somewhat later, the plight of indigenous peoples). But it does illustrate the fact that
    compared with other disciplines, anthropology was marginal to the development of the
    postwar international human rights system.

5   For an excellent study of the relationship between Arendt and the modern doctrine of
    human rights, see Birmingham 2006.

6   There is, as one might imagine, a massive body of literature on both the emergence
    and workings of the international human rights system and the development of human
    rights theory in the decades after the promulgation of the UDHR. For surveys of the
    former, see Donnelly 2006, Dunne and Wheeler 1999 and Claude and Weston 2006; for
    surveys of the latter, see Hayden 2001, Kohen 2007, Lauren 2003, Nickel 2007, and Tesón
    1998. Excellent introductions to international human rights law can be found in Martin
    et. al. 2006, Smith 2007, Steiner and Alston 2007, and Weissbrodt and de la Vega 2007.

7   See, e.g., de Bary and Tu 1999; Eberhard 2001a; 2001b; 2003; and the classic Panikkar
    1982.

8 I have addressed the place of Cultural Survival, Inc. in the wider history of anthropology's relationship to human rights in a recent book (Goodale 2009). I conclude, after studying early CS documents, and especially early issues of *Cultural Survival Quarterly* (begun in 1982), that CS refashioned itself as an indigenous *rights* advocacy organization sometime in the mid 1980s.

9 Again, developments within *American* anthropology are used to stand in for developments within anthropology as a whole, which is an ironically ethnocentric move whose utility can be justified only by the fact that (1) the American Anthropological Association is a deeply international organization and the largest professional association by far of "individuals interested in anthropology" in the world ("[o]ver 11,500 individuals from over 100 countries are members of the AAA and its 36 constituent sections," www.aaanet.org/memsrv.htm); and (2) it would be an impossible undertaking to characterize the state of something called "anthropology" at any one moment in time as a function of global commonalities across the traditions of the many different national anthropologies (Austrian, Finnish, South African, Canadian, French, Brazilian, etc.).

10 The other members of the first (1995) AAA Commission on Human Rights were Leslie Sponsel (chair), George Appell, Robert Hitchcock, Patrick Morris, Victor Montejo, Carole Nagengast, and Terence Turner (www.aaanet.org/committees/cfhr/ar95-00.htm).

11 She was formerly Director of the Alan Shawn Feinstein World Hunger Program at Brown University.

12 As of 2007, Partners in Health (PIH) had active community-based care projects in Haiti, Rwanda, Peru, Russia, Mexico, Guatemala, Lesotho, and the United States (www.pih.org/where/Haiti/Haiti.html).

13 It is perhaps not surprising that Organs Watch was founded in the same year the AAA issued its "Declaration on Anthropology and Human Rights."

14 See http://sunsite.berkeley.edu/biotech/organswatch/pages/about.html.

15 A similar but more theoretical exchange (which I also guest-edited) appeared in the March 2006 *American Anthropologist* (vol. 108, no. 1), entitled "Anthropology and Human Rights in a New Key."

16 See n. 2 above.

REFERENCES AND FURTHER READING

American Anthropological Association (1947). Statement on Human Rights. American Anthropologist (49)4:539–543.

American Anthropological Association, Committee on Human Rights (1999). Declaration on Anthropology and Human Rights. Electronic document, www.aaanet.org/stmts/humanrts.htm, accessed on March 18, 2007.

An-Na'im, Abdullahi Ahmed, ed. (1992). Human Rights in Cross-Cultural Perspectives: A Quest for Consensus. Penn Studies in Human Rights. Philadelphia: University of Pennsylvania Press.

An-Na'im, Abdullahi Ahmed (2006). African Constitutionalism and the Role of Islam. Philadelphia: University of Pennsylvania Press.

An-Na'im, Abdullahi Ahmed (2008). Islam and the Secular State: Negotiating the Future of Shari'a. Cambridge, MA: Harvard University Press.

An-Na'im, Abdullahi Ahmed, and F. Deng, eds. (1990). Human Rights in Africa: Cross-Cultural Perspectives. Washington, DC: Brookings Institution.

Appadurai, Arjun (1996). Modernity at Large: Cultural Dimensions of Globalization. Minneapolis: University of Minnesota Press.

Arendt, Hannah (1973). The Origins of Totalitarianism. New York: Harcourt, Brace.

Baxi, Upendra (2002). The Future of Human Rights. New Delhi: Oxford University Press.

Bell, Lynda, Andrew Nathan, and Ilan Peleg, eds. (2001). Negotiating Culture and Human Rights. New York: Columbia University Press.

Birmingham, Peg (2006). Hannah Arendt and Human Rights: The Predicament of Common Responsibility. Bloomington: Indiana University Press.

Brysk, Alison, ed. (2002). Globalization and Human Rights. Berkeley: University of California Press.

Claude, Richard Pierre, and Burns H. Weston (2006). Human Rights in the World Community: Issues and Action. Penn Studies in Human Rights. Philadelphia: University of Pennsylvania Press.

Cowan, Jane (2006). Culture and Rights after *Culture and Rights*. American Anthropologist (108)1:9–24.

Cowan, Jane, Marie-Bénédicte Dembour, and Richard A. Wilson, eds. (2001). Culture and Rights: Anthropological Perspectives. Cambridge: Cambridge University Press.

de Bary, Wm. Theodore, and Tu Wei-ming, eds. (1999). Confucianism and Human Rights. New York: Columbia University Press.

Dembour, Marie-Bénédicte (2006). Who Believes in Human Rights? Reflections on the European Convention. Cambridge: Cambridge University Press.

Donnelly, Jack (2003). Universal Human Rights in Theory and Practice. Ithaca, NY: Cornell University Press.

Donnelly, Jack (2006). International Human Rights. Boulder, CO: Westview Press.

Dundes Renteln, Alison (1988). Relativism and the Search for Human Rights. American Anthropologist 90:56–72.

Dundes Renteln, Alison (1990). International Human Rights: Universalism versus Relativism. Newbury Park, CA: Sage.

Dunne, Tim, and Nicholas J. Wheeler, eds. (1999). Human Rights in Global Politics. Cambridge: Cambridge University Press.

Eberhard, Christophe (2001a). Toward an Intercultural Legal Theory: The Dialogical Challenge. Social and Legal Studies 10:171–201.

Eberhard, Christophe (2001b). Human Rights and Intercultural Dialogue: An Anthropological Perspective. Indian Socio-Legal Studies 23:99–120.

Eberhard, Christophe (2003). Droits de l'homme et dialogue intercultural. Paris: Éditions des Écrivains.

Engle, Karen (2001). From Skepticism to Embrace: Human Rights and the American Anthropological Association from 1947–1999. Human Rights Quarterly 23:536–559.

Englund, Harri (2006). Prisoners of Freedom: Human Rights and the African Poor. Berkeley: University of California Press.

Farmer, Paul (1992). AIDS and Accusation: Haiti and the Geography of Blame. Berkeley: University of California Press.

Farmer, Paul (1999). Infections and Inequalities: The Modern Plagues. Berkeley: University of California Press.

Farmer, Paul (2003). Pathologies of Power: Health, Human Rights, and the New War on the Poor. Berkeley: University of California Press.

Ferguson, James (2006). Global Shadows: Africa in the Neoliberal World Order. Durham, NC: Duke University Press.

Finkielkraut, Alain (1995). The Defeat of the Mind. New York: Columbia University Press.

Galtung, Johann (1994). Human Rights in Another Key. Cambridge: Polity Press.

Goodale, Mark (2006a). Toward a Critical Anthropology of Human Rights. Current Anthropology (47)3:485–511.

Goodale, Mark (2006b). Introduction. Theme issue, "Anthropology and Human Rights in a New Key." American Anthropologist 108(1):1–8.

Goodale, Mark (2006c). Ethical Theory as Social Practice. American Anthropologist 108(1):25–37.

Goodale, Mark (2007a). Locating Rights, Envisioning Law between the Global and the Local. *In* The Practice of Human Rights: Tracking Law between the Global and the Local. Mark Goodale and Sally Engle Merry, eds. Cambridge: Cambridge University Press.

Goodale, Mark (2007b). The Power of Right(s): Tracking Empires of Law and New Forms of Social Resistance in Bolivia (and Elsewhere). *In* The Practice of Human Rights: Tracking Law between the Global and the Local. Mark Goodale and Sally Engle Merry, eds. Cambridge: Cambridge University Press.

Goodale, Mark (2009). The Anthropology of Human Rights: Critical Essays in Ethical Theory and Social Practice. Stanford: Stanford University Press.

Goodale, Mark, and Sally Engle Merry, eds. (2007). The Practice of Human Rights: Tracking Law Between the Global and the Local. Cambridge: Cambridge University Press.

Hayden, Patrick (2001). The Philosophy of Human Rights. St. Paul, MN: Paragon Press.

Hernández-Truyol, Berta Esperanza, ed. (2002). Moral Imperialism: A Critical Anthology. New York: NYU Press.

Ignatieff, Michael (2001). Human Rights as Politics and Idolatry. Princeton, NJ: Princeton University Press.

Keck, Margaret, and Kathryn Sikkink (1998). Activists beyond Borders: Advocacy Networks in International Politics. Ithaca, NY: Cornell University Press.

Kohen, Ari (2007). In Defense of Human Rights: A Non- Religious Grounding in a Pluralistic World. New York: Routledge.

Korey, William (1998). NGOs and the Universal Declaration on Human Rights: "A Curious Grapevine." New York: St. Martin's Press.

Kymlicka, Will (1995a). Multicultural Citizenship: A Liberal Theory of Minority Rights. Oxford: Oxford University Press.

Kymlicka, Will, ed. (1995b). The Rights of Minority Cultures. Oxford: Oxford University Press.

Kymlicka, Will (2007). Multicultural Odysseys: Navigating the New International Politics of Diversity. New York: Oxford University Press.

Lauren, Paul Gordon (2003). The Evolution of International Human Rights: Visions Seen. Penn Studies in Human Rights. Philadelphia: University of Pennsylvania Press.

Malkki, Liisa (1995). Purity and Exile: Violence, Memory, and National Cosmology among Hutu Refugees in Tanzania. Chicago: University of Chicago Press.

Marcus, George, and Michael M. J. Fischer (1986). Anthropology as Cultural Critique: An Experimental Moment in the Human Sciences. Chicago: University of Chicago Press.

Martin, Francisco Forrest, et al. (2006). International Human Rights and Humanitarian Law: Treaties, Cases, and Analysis. Cambridge: Cambridge University Press.

Merry, Sally Engle (2001). Changing Rights, Changing Culture. *In* Culture and Rights: Anthropological Perspectives. Jane Cowan, Marie-Bénédicte Dembour, and Richard A. Wilson, eds. Cambridge: Cambridge University Press.

Merry, Sally Engle (2006a). Human Rights and Gender Violence: Translating International Law into Local Justice. Chicago: University of Chicago Press.

Merry, Sally Engle (2006b). Transnational Human Rights and Local Activism: Mapping the Middle. American Anthropologist 108(1):38–51.

Messer, Ellen (1993). Anthropology and Human Rights. Annual Review of Anthropology 22:221–249.

Messer, Ellen (1996). Hunger and Human Rights (1989–1994). *In* The Hunger Report: 1995. E. Messer and P. Uvin, eds. Amsterdam: Gordon & Breach.

Messer, Ellen (2002). Anthropologists in a World with and without Human Rights. *In* Exotic No More: Anthropology on the Front Lines. Jeremy MacClancy, ed. Chicago: University of Chicago Press. pp. 319–334.

Messer, Ellen (2004). Hunger and Human Rights: Old and New Roles for Anthropologists. *In* Human Rights: The Scholar as Activist. C. Nagengast and C. G. Vélez-Ibañez, eds. Oklahoma City: Society for Applied Anthropology.

Messer, Ellen (2006). Comment on "Toward a Critical Anthropology of Human Rights." Current Anthropology 47(3):502–503.

Morsink, Johannes (1999). The Universal Declaration of Human Rights: Origins, Drafting, Intent. Philadelphia: University of Pennsylvania Press.

Nader, Laura (1997). Controlling Processes: Tracing the Dynamic Components of Power. Current Anthropology 38(5):711–737.

Nickel, James (2007). Making Sense of Human Rights. Oxford: Blackwell.

Nussbaum, Martha (1997). Capabilities and Human Rights. Fordham Law Review 66:273–300.

Nussbaum, Martha (2000). Women and Human Development: The Capabilities Approach. Cambridge: Cambridge University Press.

Ong, Aihwa, and Stephen Collier, eds. (2005). Global Assemblages: Technology, Politics, and Ethics as Anthropological Problems. Oxford: Blackwell.

Panikkar, Raimon (1982). Is the Notion of Human Rights a Western Concept? Diogenes 120:75–102.

Perry, Michael (1998). The Idea of Human Rights: Four Inquiries. Oxford: Oxford University Press.

Pieke, Frank (1995). Accidental Anthropology: Witnessing the 1989 Chinese People's Movement. In Fieldwork under Fire: Contemporary Studies of Violence and Survival. Carolyn Nordstrom and Antonius Robben, eds. Berkeley: University of California Press. pp. 62–79.

Preis, Ann-Belinda (1996). Human Rights as Cultural Practice: An Anthropological Critique. Human Rights Quarterly 18:286–315.

Rajagopal, Balakrishnan (2003). International Law from Below: Development, Social Movements, and Third World Resistance. Cambridge: Cambridge University Press.

Riles, Annelise (2000). The Network Inside Out. Ann Arbor: University of Michigan Press.

Riles, Annelise (2006). Anthropology, Human Rights, and Legal Knowledge: Culture in an Iron Cage. American Anthropologist 108(1):52–65.

Risse, Thomas, Stephen C. Ropp, and Kathryn Sikkink, eds. (1999). The Power of Human Rights: International Norms and Domestic Change. Cambridge: Cambridge University Press.

Salyer, J. C. (2006). Anthropologists Should Participate in the Current Immigration Debate. Anthropology News 47(5):36–37.

Sanford, Victoria (2000). Informe de la Fundación de Antropología Forense de Guatemala: Cuatro Casos Paradigmaticos Solicitados por La Comisión para el Esclarecimiento Historico de Guatemala Realizadas en las Comunidades de Panzós, Acul, Chel y Belén. Guatemala City: FAFG.

Sanford, Victoria (2003a). Buried Secrets: Truth and Human Rights in Guatemala. New York: Palgrave.

Sanford, Victoria (2003b). Violencia y Genocidio en Guatemala. Guatemala City: F. & G. Editores.

Sanford, Victoria (2006). La Masacre de Panzós: Etnicidad, tierra y violencia en Guatemala. Guatemala City: F. & G. Editores.

Scheper-Hughes, Nancy (1993). Death without Weeping: The Violence of Everyday Life in Brazil. Berkeley: University of California Press.

Scheper-Hughes, Nancy (1997). Demography without Numbers. In Anthropological Demography: Toward a New Synthesis. David I. Kertzer and Tom Fricke, eds. Chicago: University of Chicago Press. pp. 201–222.

Smith, Rhona K. M. (2007). Textbook on International Human Rights. New York: Oxford University Press.

Speed, Shannon (2006). At the Crossroads of Human Rights and Anthropology: Toward a Critically-Engaged Activist Research. American Anthropologist 108(1):66–76.

Speed, Shannon (2008). Rights in Rebellion: Indigenous Struggle and Human Rights in Chiapas. Stanford, CA: Stanford University Press.

Spiro, Melford (1986). Cultural Relativism and the Future of Anthropology. Cultural Anthropology 1(3):259–286.

Steiner, Henry J., and Philip Alston (2007). International Human Rights in Context: Law, Politics, Morals. Oxford: Oxford University Press.

Stocking, George, ed. (1989). A Franz Boas Reader: The Shaping of American Anthropology, 1883–1911. Chicago: University of Chicago Press.

Tesón, Fernando R. (1998). The Philosophy of International Law: A Human Rights Approach. Boulder, CO: Westview Press.

Turner, Terence (1997). Human Rights, Human Difference: Anthropology's Contribution to an Emancipatory Cultural Politics. Journal of Anthropological Research 53:273–291.

Washburn, Wilcomb (1987). Cultural Relativism, Human Rights, and the AAA. American Anthropologist 89(4):939–43.

Weissbrodt, David, and Connie de la Vega (2007). International Human Rights Law: An Introduction. Penn Studies in Human Rights. Philadelphia: University of Pennsylvania Press.

Wilson, Richard A., ed. (1997). Human Rights, Culture and Context: Anthropological Perspectives. London: Pluto Press.

Wilson, Richard A. (2001). The Politics of Truth and Reconciliation in South Africa. Cambridge: Cambridge University Press.

Wilson, Richard A., ed. (2005). Human Rights in the "War on Terror." New York: Cambridge University Press.

Wilson, Richard Ashby, and Jon P. Mitchell, eds. (2003). Human Rights in Global Perspective: Anthropological Studies of Rights, Claims, and Entitlements. London: Routledge.

Part I

Conceptual and Historical Foundations

1

Statement on Human Rights (1947) and Commentaries

American Anthropological Association, Julian H. Steward, and H. G. Barnett

Statement on Human Rights
Submitted to the Commission on Human Rights, United Nations by the Executive Board, American Anthropological Association

The problem faced by the Commission on Human Rights of the United Nations in preparing its Declaration on the Rights of Man must be approached from two points of view. The first, in terms of which the Declaration is ordinarily conceived, concerns the respect for the personality of the individual as such, and his right to its fullest development as a member of his society. In a world order, however, respect for the cultures of differing human groups is equally important.

These are two facets of the same problem, since it is a truism that groups are composed of individuals, and human beings do not function outside the societies of which they form a part. The problem is thus to formulate a statement of human rights that will do more than just phrase respect for the individual as an individual. It must also take into full account the individual as a member of the social group of which he is a part, whose sanctioned modes of life shape his behavior, and with whose fate his own is thus inextricably bound.

Because of the great numbers of societies that are in intimate contact in the modern world, and because of the diversity of their ways of life, the primary task confronting those who would draw up a Declaration on the Rights of Man is thus, in essence, to resolve the following problem: How can the proposed Declaration be applicable to all human beings, and not be a statement of rights conceived only in terms of the values prevalent in the countries of Western Europe and America?

"Statement on Human Rights" was originally published in *American Anthropologist*, n.s. 49: 4 (1947), 539–43; "Comments on the Statement on Human Rights," by Julian H. Steward, in *American Anthropologist*, n.s. 50: 2 (1948), 351–2; "On Science and Human Rights," by H. G. Barnett, in *American Anthropologist*, n.s. 50: 2 (1948), 352–5.

Before we can cope with this problem, it will be necessary for us to outline some of the findings of the sciences that deal with the study of human culture, that must be taken into account if the Declaration is to be in accord with the present state of knowledge about man and his modes of life.

If we begin, as we must, with the individual, we find that from the moment of his birth not only his behavior, but his very thought, his hopes, aspirations, the moral values which direct his action and justify and give meaning to his life in his own eyes and those of his fellows, are shaped by the body of custom of the group of which he becomes a member. The process by means of which this is accomplished is so subtle, and its effects are so far-reaching, that only after considerable training are we conscious of it. Yet if the essence of the Declaration is to be, as it must, a statement in which the right of the individual to develop his personality to the fullest is to be stressed, then this must be based on a recognition of the fact that the personality of the individual can develop only in terms of the culture of his society.

Over the past fifty years, the many ways in which man resolves the problems of subsistence, of social living, of political regulation of group life, of reaching accord with the Universe and satisfying his aesthetic drives has been widely documented by the researches of anthropologists among peoples living in all parts of the world. All peoples do achieve these ends. No two of them, however, do so in exactly the same way, and some of them employ means that differ, often strikingly, from one another.

Yet here a dilemma arises. Because of the social setting of the learning process, the individual cannot but be convinced that his own way of life is the most desirable one. Conversely, and despite changes originating from within and without his culture that he recognizes as worthy of adoption, it becomes equally patent to him that, in the main, other ways than his own, to the degree they differ from it, are less desirable than those to which he is accustomed. Hence valuations arise, that in themselves receive the sanction of accepted belief.

The degree to which such evaluations eventuate in action depends on the basic sanctions in the thought of a people. In the main, people are willing to live and let live, exhibiting a tolerance for behavior of another group different than their own, especially where there is no conflict in the subsistence field. In the history of Western Europe and America, however, economic expansion, control of armaments, and an evangelical religious tradition have translated the recognition of cultural differences into a summons to action. This has been emphasized by philosophical systems that have stressed absolutes in the realm of values and ends. Definitions of freedom, concepts of the nature of human rights, and the like, have thus been narrowly drawn. Alternatives have been decried, and suppressed where controls have been established over non-European peoples. The hard core of *similarities* between cultures has consistently been overlooked.

The consequences of this point of view have been disastrous for mankind. Doctrines of the "white man's burden" have been employed to implement economic exploitation and to deny the right to control their own affairs to millions of peoples over the world, where the expansion of Europe and America has not meant the literal extermination of whole populations. Rationalized in terms of ascribing cultural inferiority to these peoples, or in conceptions of their backwardness in development of their "primitive mentality," that justified their being held in the tutelage of their superiors, the history of the expansion of the western world has been marked by demoralization of human personality and the disintegration of human rights among the peoples over whom hegemony has been established.

The values of the ways of life of these peoples have been consistently misunderstood and decried. Religious beliefs that for untold ages have carried conviction, and permitted adjustment to the Universe have been attacked as superstitious, immoral, untrue. And, since power carries its own conviction, this has furthered the process of demoralization begun by economic exploitation and the loss of political autonomy. The white man's burden, the civilizing mission, have been heavy indeed. But their weight has not been borne by those who, frequently in all honesty, have journeyed to the far places of the world to uplift those regarded by them as inferior.

We thus come to the first proposition that the study of human psychology and culture dictates as essential in drawing up a Bill of Human Rights in terms of existing knowledge:

> 1. *The individual realizes his personality through his culture, hence respect for individual differences entails a respect for cultural differences.*

There can be no individual freedom, that is, when the group with which the individual indentifies himself is not free. There can be no full development of the individual personality as long as the individual is told, by men who have the power to enforce their commands, that the way of life of his group is inferior to that of those who wield the power.

This is more than an academic question, as becomes evident if one looks about him at the world as it exists today. Peoples who on first contact with European and American might were awed and partially convinced of the superior ways of their rulers have, through two wars and a depression, come to re-examine the new and the old. Professions of love of democracy, of devotion to freedom have come with something less than conviction to those who are themselves denied the right to lead their lives as seems proper to them. The religious dogmas of those who profess equality and practice discrimination, who stress the virtue of humility and are themselves arrogant in insistence on their beliefs have little meaning for peoples whose devotion to other faiths makes these inconsistencies as clear as the desert landscape at high noon. Small wonder that these peoples, denied the right to live in terms of their own cultures, are discovering new values in old beliefs they had been led to question.

No consideration of human rights can be adequate without taking into account the related problem of human capacity. Man, biologically, is one. *Homo sapiens* is a single species, no matter how individuals may differ in their aptitudes, their abilities, their interests. It is established that any normal individual can learn any part of any culture other than his own, provided only he is afforded the opportunity to do so. That cultures differ in degree of complexity, of richness of content, is due to historic forces, not biological ones. All existing ways of life meet the test of survival. Of those cultures that have disappeared, it must be remembered that their number includes some that were great, powerful, and complex as well as others that were modest, content with the *status quo*, and simple. Thus we reach a second principle:

> 2. *Respect for differences between cultures is validated by the scientific fact that no technique of qualitatively evaluating cultures has been discovered.*

This principle leads us to a further one, namely that the aims that guide the life of every people are self-evident in their significance to that people. It is the principle that emphasizes the universals in human conduct rather than the absolutes that the culture of Western Europe and America stresses. It recognizes that the eternal verities only seem so because we have been taught to regard them as such; that every people, whether it expresses them or not, lives in devotion to verities whose eternal nature is as real to them as are those of Euroamerican culture to Euroamericans. Briefly stated, this third principle that must be introduced into our consideration is the following:

3. *Standards and values are relative to the culture from which they derive so that any attempt to formulate postulates that grow out of the beliefs or moral codes of one culture must to that extent detract from the applicability of any Declaration of Human Rights to mankind as a whole.*

Ideas of right and wrong, good and evil, are found in all societies, though they differ in their expression among different peoples. What is held to be a human right in one society may be regarded as anti-social by another people, or by the same people in a different period of their history. The saint of one epoch would at a later time be confined as a man not fitted to cope with reality. Even the nature of the physical world, the colors we see, the sounds we hear, are conditioned by the language we speak, which is part of the culture into which we are born.

The problem of drawing up a Declaration of Human Rights was relatively simple in the Eighteenth Century, because it was not a matter of *human* rights, but of the rights of men within the framework of the sanctions laid by a single society. Even then, so noble a document as the American Declaration of Independence, or the American Bill of Rights, could be written by men who themselves were slave-owners, in a country where chattel slavery was a part of the recognized social order. The revolutionary character of the slogan "Liberty, Equality, Fraternity" was never more apparent than in the struggles to implement it by extending it to the French slave-owning colonies.

Today the problem is complicated by the fact that the Declaration must be of world-wide applicability. It must embrace and recognize the validity of many different ways of life. It will not be convincing to the Indonesian, the African, the Indian, the Chinese, if it lies on the same plane as like documents of an earlier period. The rights of Man in the Twentieth Century cannot be circumscribed by the standards of any single culture, or be dictated by the aspirations of any single people. Such a document will lead to frustration, not realization of the personalities of vast numbers of human beings.

Such persons, living in terms of values not envisaged by a limited Declaration, will thus be excluded from the freedom of full participation in the only right and proper way of life that can be known to them, the institutions, sanctions and goals that make up the culture of their particular society.

Even where political systems exist that deny citizens the right of participation in their government, or seek to conquer weaker peoples, underlying cultural values may be called on to bring the peoples of such states to a realization of the consequences of the acts of their governments, and thus enforce a brake upon discrimination and conquest. For the political system of a people is only a small part of their total culture.

World-wide standards of freedom and justice, based on the principle that man is free only when he lives as his society defines freedom, that his rights are those he recognizes as a member of his society, must be basic. Conversely, an effective world-order cannot be devised except insofar as it permits the free play of personality of the members of its constituent social units, and draws strength from the enrichment to be derived from the interplay of varying personalities.

The world-wide acclaim accorded the Atlantic Charter, before its restricted applicability was announced, is evidence of the fact that freedom is understood and sought after by peoples having the most diverse cultures. Only when a statement of the right of men to live in terms of their own traditions is incorporated into the proposed Declaration, then, can the next step of defining the rights and duties of human groups as regards each other be set upon the firm foundation of the present-day scientific knowledge of Man.

June 24, 1947

Comments on the Statement on Human Rights
Julian H. Steward

When the Executive Board was instructed to draft a "Statement on Human Rights," it was, I believe, generally understood that any political stand or value judgment should be avoided. The Board has obviously made every effort to limit the Statement to scientifically supportable assertions, but it seems clear now that it was asked to do the impossible. I am led to this conclusion not only by my own thinking, but by discussions which I have heard.

If the plea that cultural values be respected means merely that the primitive peoples, who are on the receiving end of civilizing influences, be treated with greater understanding and tolerance, there can be little objection to it. To be universally valid, however, the Statement must apply equally to the cultural values which underlie the internal policies and motivate the foreign affairs of the civilized nations. I should doubt that, in urging that values be respected because "man is free only when he lives as his society defines freedom," we really mean to approve the social caste system of India, the racial caste system of the United States, or many of the other varieties of social discrimination in the world. I should question that we intend to condone the exploitation of primitive peoples through the Euro-American system of economic imperialism, while merely asking for more understanding treatment of them: or, on the other hand, that we are prepared to take a stand against the values in our own culture which underly such imperialism.

As "respect for cultural differences" certainly does not advocate tolerance of the values in Nazi Germany, where the "individual ... [realized] his personality" through the Youth movement, a qualification is introduced (p. 543) that seems to contradict the basic premise and to be incompatible with anthropological thinking. "Even where political systems exist that deny citizens the right of participation in their government, or seek to conquer weaker peoples, underlying cultural values may be called on to bring the peoples of such states to a realization of the consequences of the acts of their governments, and thus enforce a brake upon discrimination and conquest." This may have been a loophole to exclude Germany from the advocated tolerance, but it looks to me like the fatal breach in the dyke. Either we tolerate everything, and keep hands off, or we fight intolerance and conquest – political and economic as well as military – in all their forms. Where shall the line be drawn? As human beings, we unanimously opposed the brutal treatment of Jews in Hitler Germany, but what stand shall be taken on the thousands of other kinds of racial and cultural discrimination, unfair practices, and inconsiderate attitudes found throughout the world?

What are these "underlying cultural values" that can be used to suppress intolerance and promote political freedom in cultures which lack economic or social freedom, or that can be used to halt conquest in a competitive world? Even if there were agreement on objectives, it would take some pretty fancy handling to revamp the portions of cultures which are disapproved. I had thought that anthropologists, of all people, stressed the interrelatedness of cultural values and patterns.

Without committing itself to particulars, the Statement is a value judgment any way it is taken. If it does not advocate tolerance for *all* cultural values, no matter how repugnant some of them may be to us as individuals, then it must imply disapproval of *some* cultural values, though it also says that we have no scientific basis for making any value judgments.

The conclusion seems inescapable that we have gotten out of our scientific role and are struggling with contradictions. During the war, we gladly used our professional techniques and knowledge to advance a cause, but I hope that no one believes that he had a scientific justification for doing so. As individual citizens, members of the Association have every right to pass value judgments, and there are some pretty obvious things that we would all agree on. As a scientific organization, the Association has no business dealing with the rights of man. I am sure that we shall serve science better, and I daresay we shall eventually serve humanity better, if we stick to our purpose. Even now, a declaration about human rights can come perilously close to advocacy of American ideological imperialism.

On Science and Human Rights
H. G. Barnett

In a recent issue of the *Anthropologist* there appeared a copy of the "Statement on Human Rights" authored by the Executive Board of the Anthropological Association and submitted to one of the commissions of the United Nations. In taking this action the Board has exhibited initiative of the sort that was contemplated when the question of the reorganization of the Association was first conceived and discussed. It is to be commended for its energy and alertness, and for accepting the responsibility of forwarding the interests of the Association. It is unfortunate, however, that the first major commitment of the Association should take the form that it has. The document submitted to the United Nations is likely to have an effect the opposite of that which was intended; and, in any event, it places the Association on record in a way that embarrasses its position as a scientific organization. It would be regrettable if it were to establish a precedent.

The import of the Statement is that anthropologists, as trained students of human relations who maintain a disciplined attitude toward their materials, have something scientific to say about the requirements for a charter of human rights. Unfortunately this is not so; and the reason is as obvious as it is well known; namely, that there is no scientific approach to the question of human rights, nor to any other problem that calls for an appraisal of human relations in terms of some absolute value system.

Any right, even the "right" to live, is such only by definition. It is contingent upon some presupposition, no matter how vaguely or precisely this may be appreciated, nor how restricted or universal is its application. Within the areas of their acceptance such presuppositions are regarded as absolutes by the people who adhere to them. They define the good, the true, and the proper; and individual behavior is measured, i.e., valued, in terms of the ultimates that they set up. It is the business of the social scientist to record the existence of these value systems, and to study them in all possible ways. It is not his business, *as a scientist*, to adopt the point of view of the people he studies and declare for the superior merits of the values of any one of them. And since anthropologists aspire to an objective study of our culture along with the rest, and reiterate that it must be treated only as one among many, this detachment with respect to our value system is imperative if we are not to lay ourselves open to charges of bias along with the rest of humanity.

It should not be necessary to remind anthropologists of these elementary precepts in our training, and some may resent my impudence in presuming to do so. There is, nevertheless, a need for such a reminder. There is a growing tendency among anthropologists at the present time to subscribe wholeheartedly to the precept of complete objectivity in the abstract and to violate it in practice. This is especially true in these days when glimpses of the practical uses of our data spur us into unexplored areas. All too frequently nowdays we find the anthropologist assertedly making a scientific study of a social situation and yet making recommendations about what "should" be done to remedy its "defects." Too often we find the anthropologist who has analyzed the culture of a people assuming that he knows what is "best" for them. This, in fact, is a common occupational disability. The line of reasoning is not easy to follow, but it is clear what has happened in such cases: the observer, as a result of his knowing a great deal about a people, comes to believe that he also knows what is "good" for them. Upon reflection it must become obvious that there is no necessary connection between a knowledge of the facts of a people's existence and judgments about the significance of those facts based upon some necessarily arbitrary scheme of values. Proficiency in the one has no bearing upon expertness in the other. An intimate knowledge of a people throws no light upon their "needs" – except by virtue of reference to some standard which must always be assumed to be valid in itself, and which is therefore not dependent upon any scientific findings. And since goods are a matter of convention or convenience only, the anthropologist is no more qualified to make decisions about them than is the executive or the administrator; and he would do well not to jeopardize his professional standing by pretending that he is. In other words, the worth or propriety of human motivations and goals is a matter of opinion, adjudication, and policy; whereas the question of the means that are employed, or that can be employed, to achieve these pre-determined goals is amenable to objective analysis and can yield, some day we hope, a foundation for prediction.

It is an inescapable fact that we cannot at the same time be moralists (or policy makers) and scientists. We all know this; we teach it and practice it – except in the pinches when our private or group interests and prejudices become involved. Then, unhappily, we behave like any undisciplined layman – except that, having more resources at our disposal for rationalization, we are more adept at defending our preconceptions. The Statement on Human Rights is a case in point, and because of the seriousness of the criticism I would like to point out specifically why this is so.

The problem, as stated in this document, is: "How can the proposed Declaration [on the Rights of Man] be applicable to all human beings, and not be a statement of rights conceived only in terms of the values prevalent in the countries of Western Europe and America?" It is difficult to see how the discussion that follows is believed to throw any light on the solution of this difficulty. On the contrary, the facts and "principles" that are offered, when viewed objectively, reveal the confused thinking that commonly accompanies such attempts, and contain within themselves the refutation of the basic proposition that is advanced as a solution. Thus, the third "principle" states: "Standards and values are relative to the culture from which they derive so that any attempt to formulate postulates that grow out of the beliefs or moral codes of one culture must to that extent detract from the applicability of any Declaration of Human Rights to mankind as a whole." Most of us, I believe, can subscribe to this. But what is the conclusion to be drawn from it? For a proposition to lead anywhere there must be a second premise, in this case one involving the basic argument of the authors of the Statement, which is that "man is free only when he lives as his society defines freedom." Surely it must be realized that this concept is a value or a standard that is relative to American tradition. There are a great many people in the world to whom it is not a self-evident fact; and it certainly is not a discovery of science. The conclusion must follow, then, that an attempt to include this postulate in a Declaration on the Rights of Man detracts by so much from the applicability of the declaration to mankind as a whole. Thus, the Statement unwittingly sets up what it aims to attack, namely an absolute in the carnival of values.

The confusion of values with facts in the first and second "principles" makes them ironical in a context that decries the widespread tendency to evaluate differences in cultures. Regardless of our sympathies it must be admitted that these sentences do no more than rationalize a certain point of view. In each instance the "principle" contains a fact that is carried off into the realms of casuistry by a purely verbal linkage with a humanitarian ideal. Thus we can show proof, as the first "principle" implies, that "the individual realizes his personality through his culture." But what researches have shown that "respect for individual differences entail a respect for cultural differences?" If anything, research would probably show the opposite. Obviously, the only meaning this part of the statement can have is that *if* one has respect for individual differences then one *should* have respect for cultural differences. But this has nothing to do with science, and requires an additional premise to meet the requirements of logic.

Much the same can be said of the second "principle." The fact that we cannot qualitatively evaluate cultures in no way calls for the conclusion that this "validates" respect for differences between them. The most that can be said is that *if* respect is due all things that cannot be differentiated then it is due all cultures. But in any event, respect is a measure of value, and science knows no means of determining when and where it *should* function, only when and where it does. Beyond that the philosophers take over.

It is disturbing to find a document of this sort resting upon such a shaky foundation of hidden premises. Only that fact can account for the evaluative descriptions of certain historical situations (e.g., "disastrous for mankind," "demoralization of human personality," etc.); and for such otherwise meaningless statements as: "There can be no full development of the individual personality as long as the individual is told, by men who have the power to enforce their commands, that the way of life of his group is inferior to that of those who wield the power." No matter how we may feel about the situation, it can hardly be denied that the individual Javanese or Samoan, for instance, has a fully developed personality – unless the definition of "full development" rests upon some arbitrary premise that excludes these cases.

The weakness that is inherent in all evaluative approaches to social problems – those that involve preconceptions of what is "good" or "bad" for a people – is evident in the third from the last paragraph of the Statement. In it the question of totalitarian states and their obscurantist policies is raised, and advised upon, apparently without embarrassment, although the doctrine of cultural self-determination, advocated throughout the rest of the argument, seems to suffer in the process. To quote: "Even where political systems exist that deny citizens the right of participation in their government, or seek to conquer weaker peoples, underlying cultural values may be called on to bring the peoples of such states to a realization of the consequences of the acts of their governments, and thus enforce a brake upon discrimination and conquest." In other words, there should be a limit to the application of the doctrine of cultural laissez-faire. The United Nations are advised to allow free choice in cultural, hence individual, development unless a people choose to reject the ideal of individual freedom, an eventuality that we Americans can conceive to happen only because of ignorance. This is, of course, the ultimate dilemma of democracy; but that is no reason why anthropologists should throw themselves on its horns with a "scientific" solution.

At this critical point in the career of the Association it is fitting and necessary for us to take stock of ourselves as professed scientists. We should each of us, and all together, get our bearings and decide where we are going. That much at least can be expected of us immediately. To date our performance in the field of cultural anthropology has not been very promising. We can do an excellent job of reporting and analyzing, but beyond that we are, as a group, badly confused. In our factual accounts we are exacting and tireless in our efforts to be exhaustive and accurate; but in our entirely understandable wishes to put our knowledge to practical use we too often forget that there is a fundamental distinction between social engineering and social planning, between recommending means and recommending ends. And as long as we cannot ourselves divorce our opinions from our facts we cannot expect others to take us at face value as scientists.

We need to do some thinking on this matter before we further commit ourselves on an action program. We cannot afford to jeopardize what little scientific repute we have by advocating predilections disguised as universals. For one thing, the sequel is more than likely to prove us wrong; and, for another, people of all degrees of sophistication will still prefer their opinions to ours despite the quantities of "evidence" that we can bring to bear. If we must support proposals and movements – and I believe that the Association should at times do just that – then let us admit, either tacitly or explicitly, that we have an axe to grind and dispense with the camouflage. Above all, let us not delude ourselves that in defining the right, the true, and the just we are building upon "the firm foundation of the present day scientific knowledge of Man."

2

The Decline of the Nation-State and the End of the Rights of Man

Hannah Arendt

It is almost impossible even now to describe what actually happened in Europe on August 4, 1914. The days before and the days after the first World War are separated not like the end of an old and the beginning of a new period, but like the day before and the day after an explosion. Yet this figure of speech is as inaccurate as are all others, because the quiet of sorrow which settles down after a catastrophe has never come to pass. The first explosion seems to have touched off a chain reaction in which we have been caught ever since and which nobody seems to be able to stop. The first World War exploded the European comity of nations beyond repair, something which no other war had ever done. Inflation destroyed the whole class of small property owners beyond hope for recovery or new formation, something which no monetary crisis had ever done so radically before. Unemployment, when it came, reached fabulous proportions, was no longer restricted to the working class but seized with insignificant exceptions whole nations. Civil wars which ushered in and spread over the twenty years of uneasy peace were not only bloodier and more cruel than all their predecessors; they were followed by migrations of groups who, unlike their happier predecessors in the religious wars, were welcomed nowhere and could be assimilated nowhere. Once they had left their homeland they remained homeless, once they had left their state they became stateless; once they had been deprived of their human rights they were rightless, the scum of the earth. Nothing which was being done, no matter how stupid, no matter how many people knew and foretold the consequences, could be undone or prevented. Every event had the finality of a last judgment, a judgment that was passed neither by God nor by the devil, but looked rather like the expression of some unredeemably stupid fatality.

Before totalitarian politics consciously attacked and partially destroyed the very structure of European civilization, the explosion of 1914 and its severe consequences

Originally published in *The Origins of Totalitarianism*, new edition with added prefaces. Orlando, FL: Harcourt Brace & Company, 1973, pp. 267–302.

of instability had sufficiently shattered the façade of Europe's political system to lay bare its hidden frame. Such visible exposures were the sufferings of more and more groups of people to whom suddenly the rules of the world around them had ceased to apply. It was precisely the seeming stability of the surrounding world that made each group forced out of its protective boundaries look like an unfortunate exception to an otherwise sane and normal rule, and which filled with equal cynicism victims and observers of an apparently unjust and abnormal fate. Both mistook this cynicism for growing wisdom in the ways of the world, while actually they were more baffled and therefore became more stupid than they ever had been before. Hatred, certainly not lacking in the pre-war world, began to play a central role in public affairs everywhere, so that the political scene in the deceptively quiet years of the twenties assumed the sordid and weird atmosphere of a Strindbergian family quarrel. Nothing perhaps illustrates the general disintegration of political life better than this vague, pervasive hatred of everybody and everything, without a focus for its passionate attention, with nobody to make responsible for the state of affairs – neither the government nor the bourgeoisie nor an outside power. It consequently turned in all directions, haphazardly and unpredictably, incapable of assuming an air of healthy indifference toward anything under the sun.

This atmosphere of disintegration, though characteristic of the whole of Europe between the two wars, was more visible in the defeated than in the victorious countries, and it developed fully in the states newly established after the liquidation of the Dual Monarchy and the Czarist Empire. The last remnants of solidarity between the nonemancipated nationalities in the "belt of mixed populations" evaporated with the disappearance of a central despotic bureaucracy which had also served to gather together and divert from each other the diffuse hatreds and conflicting national claims. Now everybody was against everybody else, and most of all against his closest neighbors – the Slovaks against the Czechs, the Croats against the Serbs, the Ukrainians against the Poles. And this was not the result of the conflict between nationalities and the state peoples (or minorities and majorities); the Slovaks not only constantly sabotaged the democratic Czech government in Prague, but at the same time persecuted the Hungarian minority on their own soil, while a similar hostility against the state people on one hand, and among themselves on the other, existed among the dissatisfied minorities in Poland.

At first glance these troubles in the old European trouble spot looked like petty nationalist quarrels without any consequence for the political destinies of Europe. Yet in these regions and out of the liquidation of the two multinational states of pre-war Europe, Russia and Austria-Hungary, two victim groups emerged whose sufferings were different from those of all others in the era between the wars; they were worse off than the dispossessed middle classes, the unemployed, the small *rentiers*, the pensioners whom events had deprived of social status, the possibility to work, and the right to hold property: they had lost those rights which had been thought of and even defined as inalienable, namely the Rights of Man. The stateless and the minorities, rightly termed "cousins-germane,"[1] had no governments to represent and to protect them and therefore were forced to live either under the law of exception of the Minority Treaties, which all governments (except Czechoslovakia) had signed under protest and never recognized as law, or under conditions of absolute lawlessness.

With the emergence of the minorities in Eastern and Southern Europe and with the stateless people driven into Central and Western Europe, a completely new element of disintegration was introduced into postwar Europe. Denationalization became a powerful weapon of totalitarian politics, and the constitutional inability of European nation-states to guarantee human rights to those who had lost nationally guaranteed rights, made it possible for the persecuting governments to impose their standard of values even upon their opponents. Those whom the persecutor had singled out as scum of the earth – Jews, Trotskyites, etc. – actually were received as scum of the earth everywhere; those whom persecution had called undesirable became the *indésirables* of Europe. The official SS newspaper, the *Schwarze Korps*, stated explicitly in 1938 that if the world was not ye convinced that the Jews were the scum of the earth, it soon would be when unidentifiable beggars, without nationality, without money, and without passports crossed their frontiers. And it is true that this kind of factual propaganda worked better than Goebbels' rhetoric, not only because it established the Jews as scum of the earth, but also because the incredible plight of an ever-growing group of innocent people was like a practical demonstration of the totalitarian movements' cynical claims that no such thing as inalienable human rights existed and that the affirmations of the democracies to the contrary were mere prejudice, hypocrisy, and cowardice in the face of the cruel majesty of a new world. The very phrase "human rights" became for all concerned – victims, persecutors, and onlookers alike – the evidence of hopeless idealism or fumbling feeble-minded hypocrisy.

The "Nation of Minorities" and the Stateless People

Modern power conditions which make national sovereignty a mockery except for giant states, the rise of imperialism, and the pan-movements undermined the stability of Europe's nation-state system from the outside. None of these factors, however, had sprung directly from the tradition and the institutions of nation-states themselves. Their internal disintegration began only after the first World War, with the appearance of minorities created by the Peace Treaties and of a constantly growing refugee movement, the consequence of revolutions.

The inadequacy of the Peace Treaties has often been explained by the fact that the peacemakers belonged to a generation formed by experiences in the pre-war era, so that they never quite realized the full impact of the war whose peace they had to conclude. There is no better proof of this than their attempt to regulate the nationality problem in Eastern and Southern Europe through the establishment of nation-states and the introduction of minority treaties. If the wisdom of the extension of a form of government which even in countries with old and settled national tradition could not handle the new problems of world politics had become questionable, it was even more doubtful whether it could be imported into an area which lacked the very conditions for the rise of nation-states: homogeneity of population and rootedness in the soil. But to assume that nation-states could be established by the methods of the Peace Treaties was simply preposterous. Indeed: "One glance at the demographic map of Europe should be sufficient to show that the nation-state principle cannot be introduced into Eastern Europe."[2] The Treaties lumped together many peoples in single states, called some of them "state people" and entrusted them with the government, silently assumed that others (such as the Slovaks in Czechoslovakia, or the Croats and Slovenes in Yugoslavia) were equal partners in the government, which of course they were not,[3] and with equal arbitrariness created out of the remnant a third group of nationalities called "minorities," thereby adding to the many burdens of the new states the trouble of observing special regulations for part of the population.[4] The result was that those peoples to whom states were not conceded, no matter whether they were official minorities or only nationalities, considered the Treaties an arbitrary game which handed out rule to some and servitude to others. The newly created states, on the other hand, which were promised equal status in national sovereignty with the Western nations, regarded the Minority Treaties as an open breach of promise and discrimination because only new states, and not even defeated Germany, were bound to them.

The perplexing power vacuum resulting from the dissolution of the Dual Monarchy and the liberation of Poland and the Baltic countries from Czarist despotism was not the only factor that had tempted the statesmen into this disastrous experiment. Much stronger was the impossibility of arguing away any longer the more than 100 million Europeans who had never reached the stage of national freedom and self-determination to which colonial peoples already aspired and which was being held out to them. It was indeed true that the role of the Western and Central European proletariat, the oppressed history-suffering group whose emancipation was a matter of life and death for the whole European social system, was played in the East by "peoples without a history."[5] The national liberation movements of the East were revolutionary in much the same way as the workers' movements in the West; both represented the "unhistorical" strata of Europe's population and both strove to secure recognition and participation in public affairs. Since the object was to conserve the European status quo, the granting of national self-determination and sovereignty to all European peoples seemed indeed inevitable; the alternative would have been to condemn them ruthlessly to the status of colonial peoples (something the pan-movements had always proposed) and to introduce colonial methods into European affairs.

The point, of course, is that the European status quo could not be preserved and that it became clear only after the downfall of the last remnants of European autocracy that Europe had been ruled by a system which had never taken into account or responded to the needs of at least 25 per cent of her population. This evil, however, was not cured with the establishment of the succession states, because about 30 per cent of their roughly 100 million inhabitants were officially recognized as exceptions who had to be specially protected by minority treaties. This figure, moreover, by no means tells the whole story; it only indicates the difference between peoples with a government of their own and those who supposedly were too small and too scattered to reach full nationhood. The Minority Treaties covered only those nationalities of whom there were considerable numbers in at least two of the succession states, but omitted from consideration all the other nationalities without a government of their own, so that in some of the succession states the nationally frustrated peoples constituted 50 per cent of the total population.[6] The worst factor in this situation was not even that it became a matter of course for the nationalities to be disloyal to their imposed government and for the governments to oppress their nationalities as efficiently as possible, but that the nationally frustrated population was firmly convinced – as was everybody else – that true freedom, true emancipation, and true popular sovereignty could be attained only with full national emancipation, that people without their own national government were deprived of human rights. In this conviction, which could base itself on the fact that the French Revolution had combined the declaration of the Rights of Man with national sovereignty, they were supported by the Minority Treaties themselves, which did not entrust the governments with the protection of different nationalities but charged the League of Nations with the safeguarding of the rights of those who, for reasons of territorial settlement, had been left without national states of their own.

Not that the minorities would trust the League of Nations any more than they had trusted the state peoples. The League, after all, was composed of national statesmen whose sympathies could not but be with the unhappy new governments which were hampered and opposed on principle by between 25 and 50 per cent of their inhabitants. Therefore the creators of the Minority Treaties were soon forced to interpret their real intentions more strictly and to point out the "duties" the minorities owed to the new states;[7] it now developed that the Treaties had been conceived merely as a painless and humane method of assimilation, an interpretation which naturally enraged the minorities. But nothing else could have been expected within a system of sovereign nation-states; if the Minority Treaties had been intended to be more than a temporary remedy for a topsy-turvy situation, then their implied restriction on national sovereignty would have affected the national sovereignty of the older European powers. The representatives of the great nations knew only too well that minorities within nation-states must sooner or later be either assimilated or liquidated. And it did not matter whether they were moved by humanitarian considerations to protect splinter nationalities from persecution, or whether political considerations led them to oppose bilateral treaties between the concerned states and the majority countries of the minorities (after all, the Germans were the strongest of all the officially recognized minorities, both in numbers and economic position); they were neither willing nor able to overthrow the laws by which nation-states exist.

Neither the League of Nations nor the Minority Treaties would have prevented the newly established states from more or less forcefully assimilating their minorities. The strongest factor against assimilation was the numerical and cultural weakness of the so-called state peoples. The Russian or the Jewish minority in Poland did not feel Polish culture to be superior to its own and neither was particularly impressed by the fact that Poles formed roughly 60 per cent of Poland's population.

The embittered nationalities, completely disregarding the League of Nations, soon decided to take matters into their own hands. They banded together in a minority congress which was remarkable in more than one respect. It contradicted the very idea behind the League treaties by calling itself officially the "Congress of Organized National Groups in European States," thereby nullifying the great labor spent during the peace negotiations to avoid the ominous word "national."[8] This had the important consequence that all "nationalities," and not just "minorities," would join and that the number of the "nation of minorities" grew so considerably that the combined nationalities in the succession states outnumbered the state peoples. But in still another way the "Congress of National Groups" dealt a decisive blow to the League treaties. One of the most baffling aspects of the Eastern European nationality problem (more baffling than the small size and great number of peoples involved, or the "belt of mixed populations") was the interregional character of the nationalities which, in case they put their national interests above the interests of their respective governments, made them an obvious risk to the security of their countries. The League treaties had attempted to ignore the interregional character of the minorities by concluding a separate treaty with each country, as though there were no Jewish or German minority beyond the borders of the respective states. The "Congress of National Groups" not only sidestepped the territorial principle of the League; it was naturally dominated by the two nationalities which were represented in all succession states and were therefore in a position, if they wished, to make their weight felt all over Eastern and Southern Europe. These two groups were the Germans and the Jews. The German minorities in Rumania and Czechoslovakia voted of course with the German minorities in Poland and Hungary, and nobody could have expected the Polish Jews, for instance, to remain indifferent to discriminatory practices of the Rumanian government. In other words, national interests and not common interests of minorities as such formed the true basis of membership in the Congress,[9] and only the harmonious relationship between the Jews and the Germans (the Weimar Republic had successfully played the role of special protector of minorities) kept it together. Therefore, in 1933 when the Jewish delegation demanded a protest against the treatment of Jews in the Third Reich (a move which they had no right to make, strictly speaking, because German Jews were no minority) and the Germans announced their solidarity with Germany and were supported by a majority (antisemitism was ripe in all succession states), the Congress, after the Jewish delegation had left forever, sank into complete insignificance.

The real significance of the Minority Treaties lies not in their practical application but in the fact that they were guaranteed by an international body, the League of Nations. Minorities had existed before, but the minority as a permanent institution, the recognition that millions of people lived outside normal legal protection and needed an additional guarantee of their elementary rights from an outside body, and the assumption that this state of affairs was not temporary but that the Treaties were needed in order to establish a lasting *modus vivendi* – all this was something new, certainly on such a scale, in European history. The Minority Treaties said in plain language what until then had been only implied in the working system of nation-states, namely, that only nationals could be citizens, only people of the same national origin could enjoy the full protection of legal institutions, that persons of different nationality needed some law of exception until or unless they were completely assimilated and divorced from their origin. The interpretative speeches on the League treaties by statesmen of countries without minority obligations spoke an even plainer language: they took it for granted that the law of a country could not be responsible for persons insisting on a different nationality. They thereby admitted – and were quickly given the opportunity to prove it practically with the rise of stateless people – that the transformation of the state from an instrument of the law into an instrument of the nation had been completed; the nation had conquered the state, national interest had priority over law long before Hitler could pronounce "right is what is good for the German people." Here again the language of the mob was only the language of public opinion cleansed of hypocrisy and restraint.

Certainly the danger of this development had been inherent in the structure of the nation-state since the beginning. But insofar as the establishment of nation-states coincided with the establishment of constitutional government, they always had represented and been based upon the rule of law as against the rule of arbitrary administration and despotism. So that when the precarious balance between nation and state, between national interest and legal institutions broke down, the disintegration of this form of government and of organization of peoples came about with terrifying swiftness. Its disintegration, curiously enough, started at precisely the moment when the right to national self-determination was recognized for all of Europe and when its essential conviction, the supremacy of the will of the nation over all legal and "abstract" institutions, was universally accepted.

At the time of the Minority Treaties it could be, and was, argued in their favor, as it were as their excuse, that the older nations enjoyed constitutions which implicitly or explicitly (as in the case of France, the *nation par excellence*) were founded upon the Rights of Man, that even if there were other nationalities within their borders they needed no additional law for them, and that only in the newly established succession states was a temporary enforcement of human rights necessary as a compromise and exception. The arrival of the stateless people brought an end to this illusion.

The minorities were only half stateless; *de jure* they belonged to some political body even though they needed additional protection in the form of special treaties and guarantees; some secondary rights, such as speaking one's own language and staying in one's own cultural and social milieu, were in jeopardy and were halfheartedly protected by an outside body; but other more elementary rights, such as the right to residence and to work, were never touched. The framers of the Minority Treaties did not foresee the possibility of wholesale population transfers or the problem of people who had become "undeportable" because there was no country on earth in which they enjoyed the right to residence. The minorities could still be regarded as an exceptional phenomenon, peculiar to certain territories that deviated from the norm. This argument was always tempting because it left the system itself untouched; it has in a way survived the second World War whose peacemakers, convinced of the impracticability of minority treaties, began to "repatriate" nationalities as much as possible in an effort to unscramble "the belt of mixed populations." And this attempted large-scale repatriation was not the direct result of the catastrophic experiences following in the wake of the Minority Treaties; rather, it was hoped that such a step would finally solve a problem which, in the preceding decades, had assumed ever larger proportions and for which an internationally recognized and accepted procedure simply did not exist – the problem of the stateless people.

Much more stubborn in fact and much more far-reaching in consequence has been statelessness, the newest mass phenomenon in contemporary history, and the existence of an ever-growing new people comprised of stateless persons, the most symptomatic group in contemporary politics. Their existence can hardly be blamed on one factor alone, but if we consider the different groups among the stateless it appears that every political event since the end of the first World War inevitably added a new category to those who lived outside the pale of the law, while none of the categories, no matter how the original constellation changed, could ever be renormalized.[10]

Among them, we still find that oldest group of stateless people, the *Heimatlosen* produced by the Peace Treaties of 1919, the dissolution of Austria-Hungary, and the establishment of the Baltic states. Sometimes their real origin could not be determined, especially if at the end of the war they happened not to reside in the city of their birth,[11] sometimes their place of origin changed hands so many times in the turmoil of postwar disputes that the nationality of its inhabitants changed from year to year (as in Vilna which a French official once termed *la capitale des apatrides*); more often than one would imagine, people took refuge in statelessness after the first World War in order to remain where they were and avoid being deported to a "homeland" where they would be strangers (as in the case of many Polish and Rumanian Jews in France and Germany, mercifully helped by the antisemitic attitude of their respective consulates).

Unimportant in himself, apparently just a legal freak, the *apatride* received belated attention and consideration when he was joined in his legal status by the postwar refugees who had been forced out of their countries by revolutions, and were promptly denationalized by the victorious governments at home. To this group belong, in chronological order, millions of Russians, hundreds of thousands of Armenians, thousands of Hungarians, hundreds of thousands of Germans, and more than half a million Spaniards – to enumerate only the more important categories. The behavior of these governments may appear today to be the natural consequence of civil war; but at the time mass denationalizations were something entirely new and unforeseen. They presupposed a state structure which, if it was not yet fully totalitarian, at least would not tolerate any opposition and would rather lose its citizens than harbor people with different views. They revealed, moreover, what had been hidden throughout the history of national sovereignty, that sovereignties of neighboring countries could come into deadly conflict not only in the extreme case of war but in peace. It now became clear that full national sovereignty was possible only as long as the comity of European nations existed; for it was this spirit of unorganized solidarity and agreement that prevented any government's exercise of its full sovereign power. Theoretically, in the sphere of international law, it had always been true that sovereignty is nowhere more absolute than in matters of "emigration, naturalization, nationality, and expulsion";[12] the point, however, is that practical consideration and the silent acknowledgment of common interests restrained national sovereignty until the rise of totalitarian regimes. One is almost tempted to measure the degree of totalitarian infection by the extent to which the concerned governments use their sovereign right of denationalization [...] But one should bear in mind at the same time that there was hardly a country left on the Continent that did not pass between the two wars some new legislation which, even if it did not use this right extensively, was always phrased to allow for getting rid of a great number of its inhabitants at any opportune moment.[13]

No paradox of contemporary politics is filled with a more poignant irony than the discrepancy between the efforts of well-meaning idealists who stubbornly insist on regarding as "inalienable" those human rights, which are enjoyed only by citizens of the most prosperous and civilized countries, and the situation of the rightless themselves. Their situation has deteriorated just as stubbornly, until the internment camp – prior to the second World War the exception rather than the rule for the stateless – has become the routine solution for the problem of domicile of the "displaced persons."

Even the terminology applied to the stateless has deteriorated. The term "stateless" at least acknowledged the fact that these persons had lost the protection of their government and required international agreements for safeguarding their legal status. The postwar term "displaced persons" was invented during the war for the express purpose of liquidating statelessness once and for all by ignoring its existence. Nonrecognition of statelessness always means repatriation, i.e., deportation to a country of origin, which either refuses to recognize the prospective repatriate as a citizen, or, on the contrary, urgently wants him back for punishment. Since non-totalitarian countries, in spite of their bad intentions inspired by the climate of war, generally have shied away from mass repatriations, the number of stateless people – twelve years after the end of the war – is larger than ever. The decision of the statesmen to solve the problem of statelessness by ignoring it is further revealed by the lack of any reliable statistics on the subject. This much is known, however: while there are one million "recognized" stateless, there are more than ten million so-called *"de facto"* stateless; and whereas the relatively innocuous problem of the *"de jure"* stateless occasionally comes up at international conferences, the core of statelessness, which is identical with the refugee question, is simply not mentioned. Worse still, the number of potentially stateless people is continually on the increase. Prior to the last war, only totalitarian or half-totalitarian dictatorships resorted to the weapon of denaturalization with regard to those who were citizens by birth; now we have reached the point where even free democracies, as, for instance, the United States, were seriously considering depriving native Americans who are Communists of their citizenship. The sinister aspect of these measures is that they are being considered in all innocence. Yet, one need only remember the extreme care of the Nazis, who insisted that all Jews of non-German nationality "should be deprived of their citizenship either prior to, or, at the latest, on the day of deportation" (for German Jews such a decree was not needed, because in the Third Reich there existed a law according to which all Jews who had left the territory – including, of course, those deported to a Polish camp – automatically lost their citizenship) in order to realize the true implications of statelessness.

The first great damage done to the nation-states as a result of the arrival of hundreds of thousands of stateless people was that the right of asylum, the only right that had ever figured as a symbol of the Rights of Man in the sphere of international relationships, was being abolished. Its long and sacred history dates back to the very beginnings of regulated political life. Since ancient times it has protected both the refugee and the land of refuge from situations in which people were forced to become outlaws through circumstances beyond their control. It was the only modern remnant of the medieval principle that *quid quid est in territorio est de territorio*, for in all other cases the modern state tended to protect its citizens beyond its own borders and to make sure, by means of reciprocal treaties, that they remained subject to the laws of their country. But though the right of asylum continued to function in a world organized into nation-states and, in individual instances, even survived both World Wars, it was felt to be an anachronism and in conflict with the international rights of the state. Therefore it cannot be found in written law, in no constitution or international agreement, and the Covenant of the League of Nations never even so much as mentioned it. It shares, in this respect, the fate of the Rights of Man, which also never became law but led a somewhat shadowy existence as an appeal in individual exceptional cases for which normal legal institutions did not suffice.[14]

The second great shock that the European world suffered through the arrival of the refugees was the realization that it was impossible to get rid of them or transform them into nationals of the country of refuge. From the beginning everybody had agreed that there were only two ways to solve the problem: repatriation or naturalization. When the example of the first Russian and Armenian waves proved that neither way gave any tangible results, the countries of refuge simply refused to recognize statelessness in all later arrivals, thereby making the situation of the refugees even more intolerable.[15] From the point of view of the governments concerned it was understandable enough that they should keep reminding the League of Nations "that [its] Refugee work must be liquidated with the utmost rapidity"; they had many reasons to fear that those who had been ejected from the old trinity of state-people-territory, which still formed the basis of European organization and political civilization, formed only the beginning of an increasing movement, were only the first trickle from an ever-growing reservoir. It was obvious, and even the Evian Conference recognized it in 1938, that all German and Austrian Jews were potentially stateless; and it was only natural that the minority countries should be encouraged by Germany's example to try to use the same methods for getting rid of some of their minority populations. Among the minorities the Jews and the Armenians ran the greatest risks and soon showed the highest proportion of statelessness; but they proved also that minority treaties did not necessarily offer protection but could also serve as an instrument to single out certain groups for eventual expulsion.

Almost as frightening as these new dangers arising from the old trouble spots of Europe was the entirely new kind of behavior of all European nationals in "ideological" struggles. Not only were people expelled from country and citizenship, but more and more persons of all countries, including the Western democracies, volunteered to fight in civil wars abroad (something which up to then only a few idealists or adventurers had done) even when this meant cutting themselves off from their national communities. This was the lesson of the Spanish Civil War and one of the reasons why the governments were so frightened by the International Brigade. Matters would not have been quite so bad if this had meant that people no longer clung so closely to their nationality and were ready eventually to be assimilated into another national community. But this was not at all the case. The stateless people had already shown a surprising stubbornness in retaining their nationality; in every sense the refugees represented separate foreign minorities who frequently did not care to be naturalized, and they never banded together, as the minorities had done temporarily, to defend common interests. The International Brigade was organized into national battalions in which the Germans felt they fought against Hitler and the Italians against Mussolini, just as a few years later, in the Resistance, the Spanish refugees felt they fought against Franco when they helped the French against Vichy. What the European governments were so afraid of in this process was that the new stateless people could no longer be said to be of dubious or doubtful nationality (*de nationalité indéterminée*). Even though they had renounced their citizenship, no longer had any connection with or loyalty to their country of origin, and did not identify their nationality with a visible, fully recognized government, they retained a strong attachment to their nationality. National splinter groups and minorities, without deep roots in their territory and with no loyalty or relationship to the state, had ceased to be characteristic only of the East. They had by now infiltrated, as refugees and stateless persons, the older nation-states of the West.

The real trouble started as soon as the two recognized remedies, repatriation and naturalization, were tried. Repatriation measures naturally failed when there was no country to which these people could be deported. They failed not because of consideration for the stateless person (as it may appear today when Soviet Russia claims its former citizens and the democratic countries must protect them from a repatriation they do not want); and not because of humanitarian sentiments on the part of the countries that were swamped with refugees; but because neither the country of origin nor any other agreed to accept the stateless person. It would seem that the very undeportability of the stateless person should have prevented a government's expelling him; but since the man without a state was "an anomaly for whom there is no appropriate niche in the framework of the general law" – an outlaw by definition – he was completely at the mercy of the police, which itself did not worry too much about committing a few illegal acts in order to diminish the country's burden of *indésirables*.[16] In other words, the state, insisting on its sovereign right of expulsion, was forced by the illegal nature of statelessness into admittedly illegal acts.[17] It smuggled its expelled stateless into the neighboring countries, with the result that the latter retaliated in kind. The ideal solution of repatriation, to smuggle the refugee back into his country of origin, succeeded only in a few prominent instances, partly because a nontotalitarian police was still restrained by a few rudimentary ethical considerations, partly because the stateless person was as likely to be smuggled back from his home country as from any other, and last but not least because the whole traffic could go on only with neighboring countries. The consequences of this smuggling were petty wars between the police at the frontiers, which did not exactly contribute to good international relations, and an accumulation of jail sentences for the stateless who, with the help of the police of one country, had passed "illegally" into the territory of another.

Every attempt by international conferences to establish some legal status for stateless people failed because no agreement could possibly replace the territory to which an alien, within the framework of existing law, must be deportable. All discussions about the refugee problems revolved around this one question: How can the refugee be made deportable again? The second World War and the DP camps were not necessary to show that the only practical substitute for a nonexistent homeland was an internment camp. Indeed, as early as the thirties this was the only "country" the world had to offer the stateless.

Naturalization, on the other hand, also proved to be a failure. The whole naturalization system of European countries fell apart when it was confronted with stateless people, and this for the same reasons that the right of asylum had been set aside. Essentially naturalization was an appendage to the nation-state's legislation that reckoned only with "nationals," people born in its territory and citizens by birth. Naturalization was needed in exceptional cases, for single individuals whom circumstances might have driven into a foreign territory. The whole process broke down when it became a question of handling mass applications for naturalization: even from the purely administrative point of view, no European civil service could possibly have dealt with the problem. Instead of naturalizing at least a small portion of the new arrivals, the countries began to cancel earlier naturalizations, partly because of general panic and partly because the arrival of great masses of newcomers actually changed the always precarious position of naturalized citizens of the same origin. Cancellation of naturalization or the introduction of new laws which obviously paved the way for mass denaturalization shattered what little confidence the refugees might have retained in the possibility of adjusting themselves to a new normal life; if assimilation to the new country once looked a little shabby or disloyal, it was now simply ridiculous. The difference between a naturalized citizen and a stateless resident was not great enough to justify taking any trouble, the former being frequently deprived of important civil rights and threatened at any moment with the fate of the latter. Naturalized persons were largely assimilated to the status of ordinary aliens, and since the naturalized had already lost their previous citizenship, these measures simply threatened another considerable group with statelessness.

It was almost pathetic to see how helpless the European governments were, despite their consciousness of the danger of statelessness to their established legal and political institutions and despite all their efforts to stem the tide. Explosive events were no longer necessary. Once a number of stateless people were admitted to an otherwise normal country, statelessness spread like a contagious disease. Not only were naturalized citizens in danger of reverting to the status of statelessness, but living conditions for all aliens markedly deteriorated. In the thirties it became increasingly difficult to distinguish clearly between stateless refugees and normal resident aliens. Once the government tried to use its right and repatriate a resident alien against his will, he would do his utmost to find refuge in statelessness. During the first World War enemy aliens had already discovered the great advantages of statelessness. But what then had been the cunning of individuals who found a loophole in the law had now become the instinctive reaction of masses. France, Europe's greatest immigrant-reception area, because she had regulated the chaotic labor market by calling in alien workers in times of need and deporting them in times of unemployment and crisis, taught her aliens a lesson about the advantages of statelessness which they did not readily forget. After 1935, the year of mass repatriation by the Laval government from which only the stateless were saved, so-called "economic immigrants" and other groups of earlier origin – Balkans, Italians, Poles, and Spaniards – mixed with the waves of refugees into a tangle that never again could be unraveled.

Much worse than what statelessness did to the time-honored and necessary distinctions between nationals and foreigners, and to the sovereign right of states in matters of nationality and expulsion, was the damage suffered by the very structure of legal national institutions when a growing number of residents had to live outside the jurisdiction of these laws and without being protected by any other. The stateless person, without right to residence and without the right to work, had of course constantly to transgress the law. He was liable to jail sentences without ever committing a crime. More than that, the entire hierarchy of values which pertain in civilized countries was reversed in his case. Since he was the anomaly for whom the general law did not provide, it was better for him to become an anomaly for which it did provide, that of the criminal.

The best criterion by which to decide whether someone has been forced outside the pale of the law is to ask if he would benefit by committing a crime. If a small burglary is likely to improve his legal position, at least temporarily, one may be sure he has been deprived of human rights. For then a criminal offense becomes the best opportunity to regain some kind of human equality, even if it be as a recognized exception to the norm. The one important fact is that this exception is provided for by law. As a criminal even a stateless person will not be treated worse than another criminal, that is, he will be treated like everybody else. Only as an offender against the law can he gain protection from it. As long as his trial and his sentence last, he will be safe from that arbitrary police rule against which there are no lawyers and no appeals. The same man who was in jail yesterday because of his mere presence in this world, who had no rights whatever and lived under threat of deportation, or who was dispatched without sentence and without trial to some kind of internment because he had tried to work and make a living, may become almost a full-fledged citizen because of a little theft. Even if he is penniless he can now get a lawyer, complain about his jailers, and he will be listened to respectfully. He is no longer the scum of the earth but important enough to be informed of all the details of the law under which he will be tried. He has become a respectable person.[18]

The nation-state, incapable of providing a law for those who had lost the protection of a national government, transferred the whole matter to the police. This was the first time the police in Western Europe had received authority to act on its own, to rule directly over people; in one sphere of public life it was no longer an instrument to carry out and enforce the law, but had become a ruling authority independent of government and ministries. Its strength and its emancipation from law and government grew in direct proportion to the influx of refugees. The greater the ratio of stateless and potentially stateless to the population at large – in prewar France it had reached 10 per cent of the total – the greater the danger of a gradual transformation into a police state.

It goes without saying that the totalitarian regimes, where the police had risen to the peak of power, were especially eager to consolidate this power through the domination over vast groups of people, who, regardless of any offenses committed by individuals, found themselves anyway beyond the pale of the law. In Nazi Germany, the Nuremberg Laws with their distinction between Reich citizens (full citizens) and nationals (second-class citizens without political rights) had paved the way for a development in which eventually all nationals of "alien blood" could lose their nationality by official decree; only the outbreak of the war prevented a corresponding legislation, which had been prepared in detail. On the other hand, the increasing groups of stateless in the nontotalitarian countries led to a form of lawlessness, organized by the police, which practically resulted in a co-ordination of the free world with the legislation of the totalitarian countries. That concentration camps were ultimately provided for the same groups in all countries, even though there were considerable differences in the treatment of their inmates, was all the more characteristic as the selection of the groups was left exclusively to the initiative of the totalitarian regimes: if the Nazis put a person in a concentration camp and if he made a successful escape, say, to Holland, the Dutch would put him in an internment camp. Thus, long before the outbreak of the war the police in a number of Western countries, under the pretext of "national security," had on their own initiative established close connections with the Gestapo and the GPU, so that one might say there existed an independent foreign policy of the police. This police-directed foreign policy functioned quite independently of the official governments; the relations between the Gestapo and the French police were never more cordial than at the time of Leon Blum's popular-front government, which was guided by a decidedly anti-German policy. Contrary to the governments, the various police organizations were never overburdened with "prejudices" against any totalitarian regime; the information and denunciations received from GPU agents were just as welcome to them as those from Fascist or Gestapo agents. They knew about the eminent role of the police apparatus in all totalitarian regimes, they knew about its elevated social status and political importance, and they never bothered to conceal their sympathies. That the Nazis eventually met with so disgracefully little resistance from the police in the countries they occupied, and that they were able to organize terror as much as they did with the assistance of these local police forces, was due at least in part to the powerful position which the police had achieved over the years in their unrestricted and arbitrary domination of stateless and refugees.

Both in the history of the "nation of minorities" and in the formation of a stateless people, Jews have played a significant role. They were at the head of the so-called minority movement because of their great need for protection (matched only by the need of the Armenians) and their excellent international connections, but above all because they formed a majority in no country and therefore could be regarded as the minorité par excellence, i.e., the only minority whose interests could be defended only by internationally guaranteed protection.

The special needs of the Jewish people were the best possible pretext for denying that the Treaties were a compromise between the new nations' tendency forcefully to assimilate alien peoples and nationalities who for reasons of expediency could not be granted the right to national self-determination.

A similar incident made the Jews prominent in the discussion of the refugee and statelessness problem. The first Heimatlose or apatrides, as they were created by the Peace Treaties, were for the most part Jews who came from the succession states and were unable or unwilling to place themselves under the new minority protection of their homelands. Not until Germany forced German Jewry into emigration and statelessness did they form a very considerable portion of the stateless people. But in the years following Hitler's successful persecution of German Jews all the minority countries began to think in terms of expatriating their minorities, and it was only natural that they should start with the *minorité par excellence*, the only nationality that actually had no other protection than a minority system which by now had become a mockery.

The notion that statelessness is primarily a Jewish problem[19] was a pretext used by all governments who tried to settle the problem by ignoring it. None of the statesmen was aware that Hitler's solution of the Jewish problem, first to reduce the German Jews to a nonrecognized minority in Germany, then to drive them as stateless people across the borders, and finally to gather them back from everywhere in order to ship them to extermination camps, was an eloquent demonstration to the rest of the world how really to "liquidate" all problems concerning minorities and stateless. After the war it turned out that the Jewish question, which was considered the only insoluble one, was indeed solved – namely, by means of a colonized and then conquered territory – but this solved neither the problem of the minorities nor the stateless. On the contrary, like virtually all other events of our century, the solution of the Jewish question merely produced a new category of refugees, the Arabs, thereby increasing the number of the stateless and rightless by another 700,000 to 800,000 people. And what happened in Palestine within the smallest territory and in terms of hundreds of thousands was then repeated in India on a large scale involving many millions of people. Since the Peace Treaties of 1919 and 1920 the refugees and the stateless have attached themselves like a curse to all the newly established states on earth which were created in the image of the nation-state.

For these new states this curse bears the germs of a deadly sickness. For the nation-state cannot exist once its principle of equality before the law has broken down. Without this legal equality, which originally was destined to replace the older laws and orders of the feudal society, the nation dissolves into an anarchic mass of over- and underprivileged individuals. Laws that are not equal for all revert to rights and privileges, something contradictory to the very nature of nation-states. The clearer the proof of their inability to treat stateless people as legal persons and the greater the extension of arbitrary rule by police decree, the more difficult it is for states to resist the temptation to deprive all citizens of legal status and rule them with an omnipotent police.

The Perplexities of the Rights of Man

The Declaration of the Rights of Man at the end of the eighteenth century was a turning point in history. It meant nothing more nor less than that from then on Man, and not God's command or the customs of history, should be the source of Law. Independent of the privileges which history had bestowed upon certain strata of society or certain nations, the declaration indicated man's emancipation from all tutelage and announced that he had now come of age.

Beyond this, there was another implication of which the framers of the declaration were only half aware. The proclamation of human rights was also meant to be a much-needed protection in the new era where individuals were no longer secure in the estates to which they were born or sure of their equality before God as Christians.

In other words, in the new secularized and emancipated society, men were no longer sure of these social and human rights which until then had been outside the political order and guaranteed not by government and constitution, but by social, spiritual, and religious forces. Therefore throughout the nineteenth century, the consensus of opinion was that human rights had to be invoked whenever individuals needed protection against the new sovereignty of the state and the new arbitrariness of society.

Since the Rights of Man were proclaimed to be "inalienable," irreducible to and undeducible from other rights or laws, no authority was invoked for their establishment; Man himself was their source as well as their ultimate goal. No special law, moreover, was deemed necessary to protect them because all laws were supposed to rest upon them. Man appeared as the only sovereign in matters of law as the people was proclaimed the only sovereign in matters of government. The people's sovereignty (different from that of the prince) was not proclaimed by the grace of God but in the name of Man, so that it seemed only natural that the "inalienable" rights of man would find their guarantee and become an inalienable part of the right of the people to sovereign self-government.

In other words, man had hardly appeared as a completely emancipated, completely isolated being who carried his dignity within himself without reference to some larger encompassing order, when he disappeared again into a member of a people. From the beginning the paradox involved in the declaration of inalienable human rights was that it reckoned with an "abstract" human being who seemed to exist nowhere, for even savages lived in some kind of a social order. If a tribal or other "backward" community did not enjoy human rights, it was obviously because as a whole it had not yet reached that stage of civilization, the stage of popular and national sovereignty, but was oppressed by foreign or native despots. The whole question of human rights, therefore, was quickly and inextricably blended with the question of national emancipation; only the emancipated sovereignty of the people, of one's own people, seemed to be able to insure them. As mankind, since the French Revolution, was conceived in the image of a family of nations, it gradually became self-evident that the people, and not the individual, was the image of man.

The full implication of this identification of the rights of man with the rights of peoples in the European nation-state system came to light only when a growing number of people and peoples suddenly appeared whose elementary rights were as little safeguarded by the ordinary functioning of nation-states in the middle of Europe as they would have been in the heart of Africa. The Rights of Man, after all, had been defined as "inalienable" because they were supposed to be independent of all governments; but it turned out that the moment human beings lacked their own government and had to fall back upon their minimum rights, no authority was left to protect them and no institution was willing to guarantee them. Or when, as in the case of the minorities, an international body arrogated to itself a nongovernmental authority, its failure was apparent even before its measures were fully realized; not only were the governments more or less openly opposed to this encroachment on their sovereignty, but the concerned nationalities themselves did not recognize a nonnational guarantee, mistrusted everything which was not clear-cut support of their "national" (as opposed to their mere "linguistic, religious, and ethnic") rights, and preferred either, like the Germans or Hungarians, to turn to the protection of the "national" mother country, or, like the Jews, to some kind of interterritorial solidarity.

The stateless people were as convinced as the minorities that loss of national rights was identical with loss of human rights, that the former inevitably entailed the latter.

The more they were excluded from right in any form, the more they tended to look for a reintegration into a national, into their own national community. The Russian refugees were only the first to insist on their nationality and to defend themselves furiously against attempts to lump them together with other stateless people. Since them, not a single group of refugees or Displaced Persons has failed to develop a fierce, violent group consciousness and to clamor for rights as – and only as – Poles or Jews or Germans, etc.

Even worse was that all societies formed for the protection of the Rights of Man, all attempts to arrive at a new bill of human rights were sponsored by marginal figures – by a few international jurists without political experience or professional philanthropists supported by the uncertain sentiments of professional idealists. The groups they formed, the declarations they issued, showed an uncanny similarity in language and composition to that of societies for the prevention of cruelty to animals. No statesman, no political figure of any importance could possibly take them seriously; and none of the liberal or radical parties in Europe thought it necessary to incorporate into their program a new declaration of human rights. Neither before nor after the second World War have the victims themselves ever invoked these fundamental rights, which were so evidently denied them, in their many attempts to find a way out of the barbed-wire labyrinth into which events had driven them. On the contrary, the victims shared the disdain and indifference of the powers that be for any attempt of the marginal societies to enforce human rights in any elementary or general sense.

The failure of all responsible persons to meet the calamity of an ever-growing body of people forced to live outside the scope of all tangible law with the proclamation of a new bill of rights was certainly not due to ill will. Never before had the Rights of Man, solemnly proclaimed by the French and the American revolutions as the new fundament for civilized societies, been a practical political issue. During the nineteenth century, these rights had been invoked in a rather perfunctory way, to defend individuals against the increasing power of the state and to mitigate the new social insecurity caused by the industrial revolution. Then the meaning of human rights acquired a new connotation: they became the standard slogan of the protectors of the underprivileged, a kind of additional law, a right of exception necessary for those who had nothing better to fall back upon.

The reason why the concept of human rights was treated as a sort of stepchild by nineteenth-century political thought and why no liberal or radical party in the twentieth century, even when an urgent need for enforcement of human rights arose, saw fit to include them in its program seems obvious: civil rights – that is the varying rights of citizens in different countries – were supposed to embody and spell out in the form of tangible laws the eternal Rights of Man, which by themselves were supposed to be independent of citizenship and nationality. All human beings were citizens of some kind of political community; if the laws of their country did not live up to the demands of the Rights of Man, they were expected to change them, by legislation in democratic countries or through revolutionary action in despotisms.

The Rights of Man, supposedly inalienable, proved to be unenforceable – even in countries whose constitutions were based upon them – whenever people appeared who were no longer citizens of any sovereign state. To this fact, disturbing enough in itself, one must add the confusion created by the many recent attempts to frame a new bill of human rights, which have demonstrated that no one seems able to define with any assurance what these general human rights, as distinguished from the rights of citizens, really are. Although everyone seems to agree that the plight of these people consists precisely in their loss of the Rights of Man, no one seems to know which rights they lost when they lost these human rights.

The first loss which the rightless suffered was the loss of their homes, and this meant the loss of the entire social texture into which they were born and in which they established for themselves a distinct place in the world. This calamity is far from unprecedented; in the long memory of history, forced migrations of individuals or whole groups of people for political or economic reasons look like everyday occurrences. What is unprecedented is not the loss of a home but the impossibility of finding a new one. Suddenly, there was no place on earth where migrants could go without the severest restrictions, no country where they would be assimilated, no territory where they could found a new community of their own. This, moreover, had next to nothing to do with any material problem of overpopulation; it was a problem not of space but of political organization. Nobody had been aware that mankind, for so long a time considered under the image of a family of nations, had reached the stage where whoever was thrown out of one of these tightly organized closed communities found himself thrown out of the family of nations altogether.

The second loss which the rightless suffered was the loss of government protection, and this did not imply just the loss of legal status in their own, but in all countries. Treaties of reciprocity and international agreements have woven a web around the earth that makes it possible for the citizen of every country to take his legal status with him no matter where he goes (so that, for instance, a German citizen under the Nazi regime might not be able to enter a mixed marriage abroad because of the Nuremberg laws). Yet, whoever is no longer caught in it finds himself out of legality altogether (thus during the last war stateless people were invariably in a worse position than enemy aliens who were still indirectly protected by their governments through international agreements).

By itself the loss of government protection is no more unprecedented than the loss of a home. Civilized countries did offer the right of asylum to those who, for political reasons, had been persecuted by their governments, and this practice, though never officially incorporated into any constitution, has functioned well enough throughout the nineteenth and even in our century. The trouble arose when it appeared that the new categories of persecuted were far too numerous to be handled by an unofficial practice destined for exceptional cases. Moreover, the majority could hardly qualify for the right of asylum, which implicitly presupposed political or religious convictions which were not outlawed in the country of refuge. The new refugees were persecuted not because of what they had done or thought, but because of what they unchangeably were – born into the wrong kind of race or the wrong kind of class or drafted by the wrong kind of government (as in the case of the Spanish Republican Army).

The more the number of rightless people increased, the greater became the temptation to pay less attention to the deeds of the persecuting governments than to the status of the persecuted. And the first glaring fact was that these people, though persecuted under some political pretext, were no longer, as the persecuted had been throughout history, a liability and an image of shame for the persecutors; that they were not considered and hardly pretended to be active enemies (the few thousand Soviet citizens who voluntarily left Soviet Russia after the second World War and found asylum in democratic countries did more damage to the prestige of the Soviet Union than millions of refugees in the twenties who belonged to the wrong class), but that they were and appeared to be nothing but human beings whose very innocence – from every point of view, and especially that of the persecuting government – was their greatest misfortune. Innocence, in the sense of complete lack of responsibility, was the mark of their rightlessness as it was the seal of their loss of political status.

Only in appearance therefore do the needs for a reinforcement of human rights touch upon the fate of the authentic political refugee. Political refugees, of necessity few in number, still enjoy the right to asylum in many countries, and this right acts, in an informal way, as a genuine substitute for national law.

One of the surprising aspects of our experience with stateless people who benefit legally from committing a crime has been the fact that it seems to be easier to deprive a completely innocent person of legality than someone who has committed an offense. Anatole France's famous quip, "If I am accused of stealing the towers of Notre Dame, I can only flee the country," has assumed a horrible reality. Jurists are so used to thinking of law in terms of punishment, which indeed always deprives us of certain rights, that they may find it even more difficult than the layman to recognize that the deprivation of legality, i.e., of *all* rights, no longer has a connection with specific crimes.

This situation illustrates the many perplexities inherent in the concept of human rights. No matter how they have once been defined (life, liberty, and the pursuit of happiness, according to the American formula, or as equality before the law, liberty, protection of property, and national sovereignty, according to the French); no matter how one may attempt to improve an ambiguous formulation like the pursuit of happiness, or an antiquated one like unqualified right to property; the real situation of those whom the twentieth century has driven outside the pale of the law shows that these are rights of citizens whose loss does not entail absolute rightlessness. The soldier during the war is deprived of his right to life, the criminal of his right to freedom, all citizens during an emergency of their right to the pursuit of happiness, but nobody would ever claim that in any of these instances a loss of human rights has taken place. These rights, on the other hand, can be granted (though hardly enjoyed) even under conditions of fundamental rightlessness.

The calamity of the rightless is not that they are deprived of life, liberty, and the pursuit of happiness, or of equality before the law and freedom of opinion – formulas which were designed to solve problems *within* given communities – but that they no longer belong to any community whatsoever. Their plight is not that they are not equal before the law, but that no law exists for them; not that they are oppressed but that nobody wants even to oppress them. Only in the last stage of a rather lengthy process is their right to live threatened; only if they remain perfectly "superfluous," if nobody can be found to "claim" them, may their lives be in danger. Even the Nazis started their extermination of Jews by first depriving them of all legal status (the status of second-class citizenship) and cutting them off from the world of the living by herding them into ghettos and concentration camps; and before they set the gas chambers into motion they had carefully tested the ground and found out to their satisfaction that no country would claim these people. The point is that a condition of complete rightlessness was created before the right to live was challenged.

The same is true even to an ironical extent with regard to the right of freedom which is sometimes considered to be the very essence of human rights. There is no question that those outside the pale of the law may have more freedom of movement than a lawfully imprisoned criminal or that they enjoy more freedom of opinion in the internment camps of democratic countries than they would in any ordinary despotism, not to mention in a totalitarian country. But neither physical safety – being fed by some state or private welfare agency – nor freedom of opinion changes in the least their fundamental situation of rightlessness. The prolongation of their lives is due to charity and not to right, for no law exists which could force the nations to feed them; their freedom of movement, if they have it at all, gives them no right to residence which even the jailed criminal enjoys as a matter of course; and their freedom of opinion is a fool's freedom, for nothing they think matters anyhow.

These last points are crucial. The fundamental deprivation of human rights is manifested first and above all in the deprivation of a place in the world which makes opinions significant and actions effective. Something much more fundamental than freedom and justice, which are rights of citizens, is at stake when belonging to the community into which one is born is no longer a matter of course and not belonging no longer a matter of choice, or when one is placed in a situation where, unless he commits a crime, his treatment by others does not depend on what he does or does not do. This extremity, and nothing else, is the situation of people deprived of human rights. They are deprived, not of the right to freedom, but of the right to action; not of the right to think whatever they please, but of the right to opinion. Privileges in some cases, injustices in most, blessings and doom are meted out to them according to accident and without any relation whatsoever to what they do, did, or may do.

We became aware of the existence of a right to have rights (and that means to live in a framework where one is judged by one's actions and opinions) and a right to belong to some kind of organized community, only when millions of people emerged who had lost and could not regain these rights because of the new global political situation. The trouble is that this calamity arose not from any lack of civilization, backwardness, or mere tyranny, but, on the contrary, that it could not be repaired, because there was no longer any "uncivilized" spot on earth, because whether we like it or not we have really started to live in One World. Only with a completely organized humanity could the loss of home and political status become identical with expulsion from humanity altogether.

Before this, what we must call a "human right" today would have been thought of as a general characteristic of the human condition which no tyrant could take away. Its loss entails the loss of the relevance of speech (and man, since Aristotle, has been defined as a being commanding the power of speech and thought), and the loss of all human relationship (and man, again since Aristotle, has been thought of as the "political animal," that is one who by definition lives in a community), the loss, in other words, of some of the most essential characteristics of human life. This was to a certain extent the plight of slaves, whom Aristotle therefore did not count among human beings. Slavery's fundamental offense against human rights was not that it took liberty away (which can happen in many other situations), but that it excluded a certain category of people even from the possibility of fighting for freedom – a fight possible under tyranny, and even under the desperate conditions of modern terror (but not under any conditions of concentration-camp life). Slavery's crime against humanity did not begin when one people defeated and enslaved its enemies (though of course this was bad enough), but when slavery became an institution in which some men were "born" free and others slave, when it was forgotten that it was man who had deprived his fellow-men of freedom, and when the sanction for the crime was attributed to nature. Yet in the light of recent events it is possible to say that even slaves still belonged to some sort of human community; their labor was needed, used, and exploited, and this kept them within the pale of humanity. To be a slave was after all to have a distinctive character, a place in society – more than the abstract nakedness of being human and nothing but human. Not the loss of specific rights, then, but the loss of a community willing and able to guarantee any rights whatsoever, has been the calamity which has befallen ever-increasing numbers of people. Man, it turns out, can lose all so-called Rights of Man without losing his essential quality as man, his human dignity. Only the loss of a polity itself expels him from humanity.

The right that corresponds to this loss and that was never even mentioned among the human rights cannot be expressed in the categories of the eighteenth century because they presume that rights spring immediately from the "nature" of man – whereby it makes relatively little difference whether this nature is visualized in terms of the natural law or in terms of a being created in the image of God, whether it concerns "natural" rights or divine commands. The decisive factor is that these rights and the human dignity they bestow should remain valid and real even if only a single human being existed on earth; they are independent of human plurality and should remain valid even if a human being is expelled from the human community.

When the Rights of Man were proclaimed for the first time, they were regarded as being independent of history and the privileges which history had accorded certain strata of society. The new independence constituted the newly discovered dignity of man. From the beginning, this new dignity was of a rather ambiguous nature. Historical rights were replaced by natural rights, "nature" took the place of history, and it was tacitly assumed that nature was less alien than history to the essence of man. The very language of the Declaration of Independence as well as of the *Déclaration des Droits de l'Homme* – "inalienable," "given with birth," "self-evident truths" – implies the belief in a kind of human "nature" which would be subject to the same laws of growth as that of the individual and from which rights and laws could be deduced. Today we are perhaps better qualified to judge exactly what this human "nature" amounts to; in any event it has shown us potentialities that were neither recognized nor even suspected by Western philosophy and religion, which for more than three thousand years have defined and redefined this "nature." But it is not only the, as it were, human aspect of nature that has become question-able to us. Ever since man learned to master it to such an extent that the destruction of all organic life on earth with man-made instruments has become conceivable and technically possible, he has been alienated from nature. Ever since a deeper know-ledge of natural processes instilled serious doubts about the existence of natural laws at all, nature itself has assumed a sinister aspect. How should one be able to deduce laws and rights from a universe which apparently knows neither the one nor the other category?

Man of the twentieth century has become just as emancipated from nature as eighteenth-century man was from history. History and nature have become equally alien to us, namely, in the sense that the essence of man can no longer be compre-hended in terms of either category. On the other hand, humanity, which for the eighteenth century, in Kantian terminology, was no more than a regulative idea, has today become an inescapable fact. This new situation, in which "humanity" has in effect assumed the role formerly ascribed to nature or history, would mean in this context that the right to have rights, or the right of every individual to belong to humanity, should be guaranteed by humanity itself. It is by no means certain whether this is possible. For, contrary to the best-intentioned humanitarian attempts to obtain new declarations of human rights from international organizations, it should be understood that this idea transcends the present sphere of international law which still operates in terms of reciprocal agreements and treaties between sovereign states; and, for the time being, a sphere that is above the nations does not exist. Furthermore, this dilemma would by no means be eliminated by the establishment of a "world government." Such a world government is indeed within the realm of possibility, but one may suspect that in reality it might differ considerably from the version promoted by idealistic-minded organizations. The crimes against human rights, which have become a specialty of totalitarian regimes, can always be justified by the pretext that right is equivalent to being good or useful for the whole in distinction to its parts. (Hitler's motto that "Right is what is good for the German people" is only the vulgarized form of a conception of law which can be found everywhere and which in practice will remain ineffectual only so long as older traditions that are still effective in the constitutions prevent this.) A conception of law which identifies what is right with the notion of what is good for – for the individual, or the family, or the people, or the largest number – becomes inevitable once the absolute and transcendent measurements of religion or the law of nature have lost their authority. And this predicament is by no means solved if the unit to which the "good for" applies is as large as mankind itself. For it is quite conceivable, and even within the realm of practical political possibilities, that one fine day a highly organized and mechanized humanity will conclude quite democratically – namely by majority decision – that for humanity as a whole it would be better to liquidate certain parts thereof. Here, in the problems of factual reality, we are confronted with one of the oldest perplexities of political philosophy, which could remain undetected only so long as a stable Christian theology provided the framework for all political and philosophical problems, but which long ago caused Plato to say: "Not man, but a god, must be the measure of all things."

These facts and reflections offer what seems an ironical, bitter, and belated confirmation of the famous arguments with which Edmund Burke opposed the French Revolution's Declaration of the Rights of Man. They appear to buttress his assertion that human rights were an "abstraction," that it was much wiser to rely on an "entailed inheritance" of rights which one transmits to one's children like life itself, and to claim one's rights to be the "rights of an Englishman" rather than the inalienable rights of man.[20] According to Burke, the rights which we enjoy spring "from within the nation," so that neither natural law, nor divine command, nor any concept of mankind such as Robespierre's "human race," "the sovereign of the earth," are needed as a source of law.[21]

The pragmatic soundness of Burke's concept seems to be beyond doubt in the light of our manifold experiences. Not only did loss of national rights in all instances entail the loss of human rights; the restoration of human rights, as the recent example of the State of Israel proves, has been achieved so far only through the restoration or the establishment of national rights. The conception of human rights, based upon the assumed existence of a human being as such, broke down at the very moment when those who professed to believe in it were for the first time confronted with people who had indeed lost all other qualities and specific relationships – except that they were still human. The world found nothing sacred in the abstract nakedness of being human. And in view of objective political conditions, it is hard to say how the concepts of man upon which human rights are based – that he is created in the image of God (in the American formula), or that he is the representative of mankind, or that he harbors within himself the sacred demands of natural law (in the French formula) – could have helped to find a solution to the problem.

The survivors of the extermination camps, the inmates of concentration and internment camps, and even the comparatively happy stateless people could see without Burke's arguments that the abstract nakedness of being nothing but human was their greatest danger. Because of it they were regarded as savages and, afraid that they might end by being considered beasts, they insisted on their nationality, the last sign of their former citizenship, as their only remaining and recognized tie with humanity. Their distrust of natural, their preference for national, rights comes precisely from their realization that natural rights are granted even to savages. Burke had already feared that natural "inalienable" rights would confirm only the "right of the naked savage,"[22] and therefore reduce civilized nations to the status of savagery. Because only savages have nothing more to fall back upon than the minimum fact of their human origin, people cling to their nationality all the more desperately when they have lost the rights and protection that such nationality once gave them. Only their past with its "entailed inheritance" seems to attest to the fact that they still belong to the civilized world.

If a human being loses his political status, he should, according to the implications of the inborn and inalienable rights of man, come under exactly the situation for which the declarations of such general rights provided. Actually the opposite is the case. It seems that a man who is nothing but a man has lost the very qualities which make it possible for other people to treat him as a fellow-man. This is one of the reasons why it is far more difficult to destroy the legal personality of a criminal, that is of a man who has taken upon himself the responsibility for an act whose consequences now determine his fate, than of a man who has been disallowed all common human responsibilities.

Burke's arguments therefore gain an added significance if we look only at the general human condition of those who have been forced out of all political communities. Regardless of treatment, independent of liberties or oppression, justice or injustice, they have lost all those parts of the world and all those aspects of human existence which are the result of our common labor, the outcome of the human artifice. If the tragedy of savage tribes is that they inhabit an unchanged nature which they cannot master, yet upon whose abundance or frugality they depend for their livelihood, that they live and die without leaving any trace, without having contributed anything to a common world, then these rightless people are indeed thrown back into a peculiar state of nature. Certainly they are not barbarians; some of them, indeed, belong to the most educated strata of their respective countries; nevertheless, in a world that has almost liquidated savagery, they appear as the first signs of a possible regression from civilization.

The more highly developed a civilization, the more accomplished the world it has produced, the more at home men feel within the human artifice – the more they will resent everything they have not produced, everything that is merely and mysteriously given them. The human being who has lost his place in a community, his political status in the struggle of his time, and the legal personality which makes his actions and part of his destiny a consistent whole, is left with those qualities which usually can become articulate only in the sphere of private life and must remain unqualified, mere existence in all matters of public concern. This mere existence, that is, all that which is mysteriously given us by birth and which includes the shape of our bodies and the talents of our minds, can be adequately dealt with only by the unpredictable hazards of friendship and sympathy, or by the great and incalculable grace of love, which says with Augustine, "*Volo ut sis* (I want you to be)," without being able to give any particular reason for such supreme and unsurpassable affirmation.

Since the Greeks, we have known that highly developed political life breeds a deep-rooted suspicion of this private sphere, a deep resentment against the disturbing miracle contained in the fact that each of us is made as he is – single, unique, unchangeable. This whole sphere of the merely given, relegated to private life in civilized society, is a permanent threat to the public sphere, because the public sphere is as consistently based on the law of equality as the private sphere is based on the law of universal difference and differentiation. Equality, in contrast to all that is involved in mere existence, is not given us, but is the result of human organization insofar as it is guided by the principle of justice. We are not born equal; we become equal as members of a group on the strength of our decision to guarantee ourselves mutually equal rights.

Our political life rests on the assumption that we can produce equality through organization, because man can act in and change and build a common world, together with his equals and only with his equals. The dark background of mere givenness, the background formed by our unchangeable and unique nature, breaks into the political scene as the alien which in its all too obvious difference reminds us of the limitations of human activity – which are identical with the limitations of human equality. The reason why highly developed political communities, such as the ancient city-states or modern nation-states, so often insist on ethnic homogeneity is that they hope to eliminate as far as possible those natural and always present differences and differentiations which by themselves arouse dumb hatred, mistrust, and discrimination because they indicate all too clearly those spheres where men cannot act and change at will, i.e., the limitations of the human artifice. The "alien" is a frightening symbol of the fact of difference as such, of individuality as such, and indicates those realms in which man cannot change and cannot act and in which, therefore, he has a distinct tendency to destroy. If a Negro in a white community is considered a Negro and nothing else, he loses along with his right to equality that freedom of action which is specifically human; all his deeds are now explained as "necessary" consequences of some "Negro" qualities; he has become some specimen of an animal species, called man. Much the same thing happens to those who have lost all distinctive political qualities and have become human beings and nothing else. No doubt, wherever public life and its law of equality are completely victorious, wherever a civilization succeeds in eliminating or reducing to a minimum the dark background of difference, it will end in complete petrifaction and be punished, so to speak, for having forgotten that man is only the master, not the creator of the world.

The great danger arising from the existence of people forced to live outside the common world is that they are thrown back, in the midst of civilization, on their natural givenness, on their mere differentiation. They lack that tremendous equalizing of differences which comes from being citizens of some commonwealth and yet, since they are no longer allowed to partake in the human artifice, they begin to belong to the human race in much the same way as animals belong to a specific animal species. The paradox involved in the loss of human rights is that such loss coincides with the instant when a person becomes a human being in general – without a profession, without a citizenship, without an opinion, without a deed by which to identify and specify himself – *and* different in general, representing nothing but his own absolutely unique individuality which, deprived of expression within and action upon a common world, loses all significance.

The danger in the existence of such people is twofold: first and more obviously, their ever-increasing numbers threaten our political life, our human artifice, the world which is the result of our common and co-ordinated effort in much the same, perhaps even more terrifying, way as the wild elements of nature once threatened the existence of man-made cities and countrysides. Deadly danger to any civilization is no longer likely to come from without. Nature has been mastered and no barbarians threaten to destroy what they cannot understand, as the Mongolians threatened Europe for centuries. Even the emergence of totalitarian governments is a phenomenon within, not outside, our civilization. The danger is that a global, universally interrelated civilization may produce barbarians from its own midst by forcing millions of people into conditions which, despite all appearances, are the conditions of savages.

NOTES

1 By S. Lawford Childs, "Refugees – a Permanent Problem in International Organization" in *War is not Inevitable. Problems of Peace*. 13th Series, London, 1938, published by the International Labor Office.

2 Kurt Tramples. "Völkerbund und Völkerfreiheit," in *Süddeutsche Monatshefte*, 26. Jahrgang, Juli 1929.

3 The struggle of the Slovaks against the "Czech" government in Prague ended with the Hitler-supported independence of Slovakia; the Yugoslav constitution of 1921 was "accepted" in Parliament against the votes of all Croat and Slovene representatives. For a good summary of Yugoslav history between the two wars, see *Propyläen Weltgeschichte. Das Zeitalter des Imperialismus*, 1933, Band 10, 471 ff.

4 Mussolini was quite right when he wrote after the Munich crisis: "If Czechoslovakia finds herself today in what might be called a 'delicate situation,' it is because she was not just Czechoslovakia, but Czech-Germano-Polono-Magyaro-Rutheno-Rumano-Slovakia...." (Quoted from Hubert Ripka, *Munich: Before and After*, London, 1939, p. 117.)

5 This term was first coined by Otto Bauer, *Die Nationalitätenfrage und die österreichische Sozialdemokratie*, Vienna, 1907.

6 It has been estimated that prior to 1914 there were about 100 million people whose national aspirations had not been fulfilled. The population of minorities was estimated approximately between 25 and 30 millions. The actual situation in Czechoslovakia and Yugoslavia was much worse. In the former, the Czech "state people" constituted, with 7,200,000, about 50 per cent of the population, and in the latter 5,000,000 Serbs formed only 42 per cent of the total.

7 P. de Azcarate, *op. cit.*: "The Treaties contain no stipulations regarding the 'duties' of minorities towards the States of which they are a part. The Third Ordinary Assembly of the League, however, in 1922, ... adopted ... resolutions regarding the 'duties of minorities.'..."

8 Wilson notably, who had been a fervent advocate of granting "racial, religious, and linguistic rights to the minorities," "feared that 'national rights' would prove harmful inasmuch as minority groups thus marked as separate corporate bodies would be rendered thereby 'liable to jealousy and attack'" (Oscar J. Janowsky, *The Jews and Minority Rights*, New York, 1933, p. 351).

9 In 1933 the chairman of the Congress expressly emphasized: "One thing is certain: we do not meet in our congresses merely as members of abstract minorities; each of us belongs body and soul to a specific people, his own, and feels himself tied to the fate of that people for better or worse. Consequently, each of us stands here, if I may say so, as a full-blooded German or full-blooded Jew, as a full-blooded Hungarian or full-blooded Ukrainian." See *Sitzungsbericht des Kongresses der organisierten nationalen Gruppen in den Staaten Europas*, 1933, p. 8.

10   Twenty-five years after the Soviet regime had disowned one and a half million Russians, it was estimated that at least 350,000 to 450,000 were still stateless – which is a tremendous percentage if one considers that a whole generation had passed since the initial flight, that a considerable portion had gone overseas, and that another large part had acquired citizenship in different countries through marriage.

It is true that the United States has placed stateless immigrants on a footing of complete equality with other foreigners, but this has been possible only because this, the country *par excellence* of immigration, has always considered newcomers as prospective citizens of its own, regardless of their former national allegiances.

11   The *American Friends Service Bulletin* (General Relief Bulletin, March, 1943) prints the perplexed report of one of their field workers in Spain who had been confronted with the problem of "a man who was born in Berlin, Germany, but who is of Polish origin because of his Polish parents and who is therefore . . . Apatride, but is claiming Ukrainian nationality and has been claimed by the Russian government for repatriation and service in the Red Army."

12   Lawrence Preuss, "La Dénationalisation imposée pour des motifs politiques," in *Revue Internationale Française du Droit des Gens*, 1937, vol. IV, nos. 1, 2, 5.

13   The first law of this type was a French war measure in 1915 which concerned only naturalized citizens of enemy origin who had retained their original nationality; Portugal went much farther in a decree of 1916 which automatically denaturalized all persons born of a German father. Belgium issued a law in 1922 which canceled naturalization of persons who had committed antinational acts during the war, and reaffirmed it by a new decree in 1934 which in the characteristically vague manner of the time spoke of persons *"manquant gravement à leurs devoirs de citoyen belge."* In Italy, since 1926, all persons could be denaturalized who were not "worthy of Italian citizenship" or a menace to the public order. Egypt and Turkey in 1926 and 1928 respectively issued laws according to which people could be denaturalized who were a threat to the social order. France threatened with denaturalization those of its new citizens who committed acts contrary to the interests of France (1927). Austria in 1933 could deprive of Austrian nationality any of her citizens who served or participated abroad in an action hostile to Austria. Germany, finally, in 1933 followed closely the various Russian nationality decrees since 1921 by stating that all persons "residing abroad" could at will be deprived of German nationality.

14   The only guardians of the right of asylum were the few societies whose special aim was the protection of human rights. The most important of them, the French-sponsored Ligue des Droits de l'Homme with branches in all democratic European countries, behaved as though the question were still merely the saving of individuals persecuted for their political convictions and activities. This assumption, pointless already in the case of millions of Russian refugees, became simply absurd for Jews and Armenians. The Ligue was neither ideologically nor administratively equipped to handle the new problems. Since it did not want to face the new situation, it stumbled into functions which were much better fulfilled by any of the many charity agencies which the refugees had built up themselves with the help of their compatriots. When the Rights of Man became the object of an especially inefficient charity organization, the concept of human rights naturally was discredited a little more.

15   Only the Russians, in every respect the aristocracy of the stateless people, and the Armenians, who were assimilated to the Russian status, were ever officially recognized as "stateless," placed under the protection of the League of Nations' Nansen Office, and given traveling papers.

16   A circular letter of the Dutch authorities (May 7, 1938) expressly considered each refugees as an "undesirable alien," and defined a refugee as an "alien who left his country under the pressure of circumstances." See "L'Emigration, Problème Révolutionnaire," in *Esprit*, 7e année. no. 82, July, 1939, p. 602.

17 Lawrence Preuss, *op. cit.*, describes the spread of illegality as follows: "The initial illegal act of the denationalizing government...puts the expelling country in the position of an offender of international law, because its authorities violate the law of the country to which the stateless person is expelled. The latter country, in turn, cannot get rid of him ... except by violating...the law of a third country.... [The stateless person finds himself before the following alternative]: either he violates the law of the country where he resides...or he violates the law of the country to which he is expelled."

18 In practical terms, any sentence meted out to him will be of small consequence compared with an expulsion order, cancellation of a work permit, or a decree sending him into an internment camp. A West Coast Japanese-American who was in jail when the army ordered the internment of all Americans of Japanese ancestry would not have been forced to liquidate his property at too low a price; he would have remained right where he was, armed with a lawyer to look after his interests; and if he was so lucky as to receive a long sentence, he might have returned righteously and peacefully to his former business and profession, even that of a professional thief. His jail sentence guaranteed him the constitutional rights that nothing else – no protests of loyalty and no appeals – could have obtained for him once his citizenship had become doubtful.

19 This was by no means only a notion of Nazi Germany, though only a Nazi author dared to express it: "It is true that a refugee question will continue to exist even when there is no longer a Jewish question; but since Jews form such a high percentage of the refugees, the refugee question will be much simplified" (Kabermann, "Das internationale Flüchtlingsproblem," in *Zeitschrift für Politik*, Bd. 29, Heft 3, 1939).

20 Edmund Burke, *Reflections on the Revolution in France*, 1790, edited by E. J. Payne, Everyman's Library.

21 Robespierre, *Speeches*, 1927. Speech of April 24, 1793.

22 Introduction by Payne to Burke, *op. cit.*

3

The Good, the Bad, and the Intolerable: Minority Group Rights

Will Kymlicka

Ethnocultural minorities around the world are demanding various forms of recognition and protection, often in the language of "group rights." Many commentators see this as a new and dangerous trend that threatens the fragile international consensus on the importance of individual rights. Traditional human rights doctrines are based on the idea of the inherent dignity and equality of all individuals. The emphasis on group rights, by contrast, seems to treat individuals as the mere carriers of group identities and objectives, rather than as autonomous personalities capable of defining their own identity and goals in life. Hence it tends to subordinate the individual's freedom to the group's claim to protect its historical traditions or cultural purity.

I believe that this view is overstated. In many cases, group rights supplement and strengthen human rights, by responding to potential injustices that traditional rights doctrine cannot address. These are the "good" group rights. There are cases, to be sure, where illiberal groups seek the right to restrict the basic liberties of their members. These are the "bad" group rights. In some cases, these illiberal practices are not only bad, but intolerable, and the larger society has a right to intervene to stop them. But in other cases, liberal states must tolerate unjust practices within a minority group. Drawing the line between the bad and the intolerable is one of the thorniest issues liberal democracies face.

I want to look at the relationship between group and individual rights in the context of the claims of indigenous peoples in North America. In both the United States and Canada, these peoples have various group rights. For example, they have rights of self-government, under which they exercise control over health, education, family law, policing, criminal justice, and resource development. They also have legally recognized land claims, which reserve certain lands for their exclusive use and

Originally published in *Dissent*, 43: 3 (1996), 22–30.

provide guaranteed representation on certain regulatory bodies. And in some cases, they have rights relating to the use of their own language.

The situation of indigenous peoples is a useful example, I think, for several reasons. For one thing, they have been at the forefront of the movement toward recognizing group rights at the international level – reflected in the Draft Universal Declaration on Indigenous Rights at the United Nations. The case of indigenous peoples also shows that group rights are not a new issue. From the very beginning of European colonization, the "natives" fought for rights relating to their land, languages, and self-government. What has changed in recent years is not that indigenous peoples have altered their demands, but rather that these demands have become more visible, and that the larger society has started to listen to them.

Reflecting on this long history should warn us against the facile assumption that the demand for group rights is somehow a byproduct of current intellectual fashions, such as postmodernism, or of ethnic entrepreneurs pushing affirmative action programs beyond their original intention. On the contrary, the consistent historical demands of indigenous peoples suggests that the issue of group rights is an enduring and endemic one for liberal democracies.

Group rights, as I will use the term, refer to claims to something more than, or other than, the common rights of citizenship. The category is obviously very large and can be subdivided into any number of more refined categories, reflecting the different sorts of rights sought by different sorts of groups.

Two Kinds of Group Rights

For my purposes, however, the most important distinction is between two kinds of group rights: one involves the claim of an indigenous group against its own members; the other involves the claim of an indigenous group against the larger society. Both of these can be seen as protecting the stability of indigenous communities, but they respond to different sources of instability. The first is intended to protect a group from the destabilizing impact of internal dissent (that is, the decision of individual members not to follow traditional practices or customs), whereas the second is intended to protect the group from the impact of external decisions (that is, the economic or political policies of the larger society). I will call the first "internal restrictions" and the second "external protections."

Both are "group rights," but they raise very different issues. Internal restrictions involve intra-group relations. An indigenous group may seek the use of state power to restrict the liberty of its own members in the name of group solidarity. For example, a tribal government might discriminate against those members who do not share the traditional religion. This sort of internal restriction raises the danger of individual oppression. Group rights in this sense can be invoked by patriarchal and theocratic cultures to justify the oppression of women and the legal enforcement of religious orthodoxy.

Of course, all forms of government involve restricting the liberty of those subject to their authority. In all countries, no matter how liberal and democratic, people are required to pay taxes to support public goods. Most democracies also require people to undertake jury duty or to perform some amount of military or community service, and a few countries require people to vote. All governments expect and sometimes require a minimal level of civic responsibility and participation from their citizens.

But some groups seek to impose much greater restrictions on the liberty of their members. It is one thing to require people to do jury duty or to vote, and quite another to compel people to attend a particular church or to follow traditional gender roles. The former are intended to uphold liberal rights and democratic institutions, the latter restrict these rights in the name of orthodoxy or cultural tradition. It is these latter cases that I have in mind when talking about internal restrictions.

Obviously, groups are free to require respect for traditional norms and authorities as terms of membership in private, voluntary associations. A Catholic organization can insist that its members be Catholics in good standing, and the same applies to voluntary religious organizations within indigenous communities. The problem arises when a group seeks to use *governmental* power, or the distribution of public benefits, to restrict the liberty of members.

On my view, such legally imposed internal restrictions are almost always unjust. It is a basic tenet of liberal democracy that whoever exercises political power within a community must respect the civil and political rights of its members, and any attempt to impose internal restrictions that violate this condition is unjust.

External protections, by contrast, involve *inter*-group relations. In these cases, the indigenous group seeks to protect its distinct existence and identity by limiting its vulnerability to the decisions of the larger society. For example, reserving land for the exclusive use of indigenous peoples ensures that they are not outbid for this resource by the greater wealth of outsiders. Similarly, guaranteeing representation for indigenous peoples on various public regulatory bodies reduces the chance that they will be outvoted on decisions that affect their community. And allowing indigenous peoples to control their own health care system ensures that critical decisions are not made by people who are ignorant of their distinctive health needs or their traditional medicines.

On my view, these sorts of external protections are often consistent with liberal democracy, and may indeed be necessary for democratic justice. They can be seen as putting indigenous peoples and the larger society on a more equal footing, by reducing the extent to which the former is vulnerable to the latter.

Of course, one can imagine circumstances where the sorts of external protections demanded by a minority group are unfair. Under the apartheid system in South Africa, for example, whites, who constituted less than 20 per cent of the population, demanded 87 per cent of the land mass of the country, monopolized all the political power, and imposed Afrikaans and English throughout the entire school system. They defended this in the name of reducing their vulnerability to the decisions of other larger groups, although the real aim was to dominate and exploit these groups.

However, the sorts of external protections sought by indigenous peoples hardly put them in a position to dominate others. The land claims, representation rights, and self-government powers sought by indigenous peoples do not deprive other groups of their fair share of economic resources or political power, nor of their language rights. Rather, indigenous peoples simply seek to ensure that the majority cannot use its superior numbers or wealth to deprive them of the resources and institutions vital to the reproduction of their communities. And that, I believe, is fully justified. So, whereas internal restrictions are almost inherently in conflict with liberal democratic norms, external protections are not – so long as they promote equality between groups rather than allowing one group to oppress another.

The Group Rights of Indigenous Peoples

Which sorts of claims are indigenous peoples making? This is not always an easy question to answer. Self-government rights can be used either to secure external protections or to impose internal restrictions, and some indigenous groups use these rights in both ways.

But most indigenous peoples seek group rights primarily for the external protections they afford. Most groups are concerned with ensuring that the larger society does not deprive them of the resources and institutions necessary for their survival, not with controlling the extent to which their own members engage in untraditional or unorthodox practices. Under these circumstances, there is no conflict between external protections and individual rights. Groups that have these external protections may fully respect the civil and political rights of their own members. Indeed, many indigenous groups have adopted their own internal constitutional bills of rights, guaranteeing freedom of religion, speech, press, conscience, association, and a speedy and public trial.

In these cases, group rights supplement, even strengthen, standard human rights. Far from limiting the basic civil and political rights of individual Indians, they help to protect the context within which those rights have their meaning and efficacy. The long history of European–indigenous relations suggests that even if indigenous peoples have citizenship rights in the mainstream society, they tend to be politically impotent and culturally marginalized.

Some readers might think that I am underestimating the illiberal tendencies of indigenous groups. I have argued that many Indian communities are committed to respecting the rights of their individual members. Why then are most indigenous peoples in the United States opposed to the idea that their internal decisions should be subject to judicial review under the U.S. Bill of Rights?

This is an important question, which goes to the heart of the relationship between group and individual rights, and which is worth exploring in some depth. As part of their self-government, tribal councils in the United States have historically been exempted from the constitutional requirement to respect the Bill of Rights. Various efforts have been made by federal legislators to change this, most recently the 1968 Indian Civil Rights Act. According to this act, which was passed by Congress despite vociferous opposition from most Indian groups, tribal governments are now required to respect most (but not all) constitutional rights. However, there are still limits on judicial review of the actions of tribal councils. If a member of an Indian tribe feels that her rights have been violated by her tribal council, she can seek redress in a tribal court, but she cannot (except under exceptional circumstances) seek redress from the Supreme Court.

Indian groups remain strongly opposed to the 1968 Act, and would almost certainly resist any attempt to extend the jurisdiction of federal courts over Indian governments. Similarly, Indian bands in Canada have argued that their self-governing councils should not be subject to judicial review under the Canadian Charter of Rights and Freedoms. They do not want their members to be able to challenge band decisions in the courts of the mainstream society.

These limits on the application of constitutional bills of rights suggest that individuals or subgroups within Indian communities could be oppressed in the name of group solidarity or cultural purity. For example, concern has been expressed that Indian women in the United States and Canada might be discriminated against under certain systems of self-government, if these communities are exempt from the constitutional requirement of sexual equality. Demanding exemption from judicial review in the name of self government, for many people, is a smokescreen behind which illiberal groups hide their oppressive practices.

Before jumping to this conclusion, however, we should consider the reasons why groups that believe in individual rights would nonetheless be distrustful of judicial review. In the case of indigenous peoples, these reasons are, I think, painfully obvious. After all, the federal courts have historically accepted and legitimated the colonization and dispossession of Indian peoples and lands. Why should Indians trust the federal courts to act impartially now?

But there are other, more specific concerns. Many Indians argue that their self-government needs to be exempt from the Bill of Rights, not in order to restrict the liberty of women or religious dissidents, but to defend the external protections of Indians vis-à-vis the larger society. Their special rights to land, or to hunting, or to group representation, which reduce their vulnerability to external economic and political decisions, could be struck down as discriminatory under the Bill of Rights. Such protections do not, in my view, violate equality. On the contrary, a powerful case could be made that they promote equality, by protecting Indians from unjust majority decisions. But Indians rightly worry that the Supreme Court could take a different and more formalistic view of equality rights.

Indian leaders also fear that white judges might interpret certain rights in culturally biased ways. For example, traditional Indian forms of consensual political decision making could be seen as denying democratic rights. These traditional procedures do not violate the underlying democratic principle of the Constitution – namely, that legitimate authority requires the consent of the governed, subject to periodic review. However, they do not use the particular method for securing consent envisioned by the Constitution – namely, periodic election of representatives. Rather, they rely on time-honored procedures for ensuring consensual decision making. Indian leaders worry that white judges will impose their own culturally specific form of democracy, without considering whether traditional Indian practices are an equally valid interpretation of democratic principles.

It is often difficult for outsiders to assess the likelihood that self-government for an indigenous minority will lead to the suppression of basic individual rights. The identification of oppression requires sensitivity to the specific context, particularly when dealing with other cultures, and so it is not surprising that Indians would want these questions settled in a forum where judges are familiar with the situation.

Hence many Indian leaders seek exemption from the Bill of Rights, but at the same time affirm their commitment to basic human rights and freedoms. They endorse the principles, but object to the particular institutions and procedures that the larger society has established to enforce these principles. They seek to create or maintain their own procedures for protecting rights, specified in tribal constitutions (some of which are based on the provisions of international protocols).

Of course, not all Indian groups accept the commitment to respect individual rights. One example of internal restrictions concerns freedom of religion on the Pueblo reservation. Because they are not subject to the Bill of Rights, tribal governments are not required to obey its strict separation of church and state. The Pueblo have, in effect, established a theocratic government that discriminates against those members who do not share the tribal religion. For example, housing benefits have been denied to members of the community who have converted to Protestantism. In this case, self-government powers are being used to limit the freedom of members to question and revise traditional practices.

The Pueblo also use sexually discriminatory membership rules. If female members marry outside the tribe, their children are denied membership. But if men marry outside the tribe, the children are members. Here again, the rights of individuals are being restricted to preserve a communal practice (although there is some debate about whether this membership rule is in fact the "traditional" one, or whether it was adopted by the Pueblo at the behest of the American government, which hoped thereby to minimize its financial obligations).

In other cases, tribal governments have become profoundly undemocratic, governed by strongmen who ignore traditional ideals of consensus and govern by a combination of intimidation and corruption.

In these cases, not surprisingly, members of the Indian community often seek some form of outside judicial review. These cases put liberals on the horns of a serious dilemma. This is no longer a case of whites imposing "our" norms on Indians, who would prefer to live by "their" norms. The problem, rather, is that Indians themselves are deeply divided, not only about their traditional norms, but also about the ability of their traditional decision-making procedures to deal with these divisions. In some cases, reformers seeking federal judicial review may form a sizable minority, if not a majority, within their community. For example, the Native Women's Association of Canada, worried about the danger of sexual discrimination on their reserves, has demanded that the decisions of Aboriginal governments be subject to the Canadian Charter.

The Limits of Toleration

How should liberal states respond in such cases? It is right and proper, I think, for liberals to criticize oppressive practices within indigenous communities, just as we should criticize foreign countries that oppress their citizens. These oppressive practices may be traditional (although many aren't), but tradition is not self-validating. Indeed, that an oppressive practice is traditional may just show how deep the injustice goes.

But should we intervene and impose a liberal regime on the Pueblo, forcing them to respect the religious liberty of Protestants and the sexual equality of women? Should we insist that indigenous governments be subject to the Bill of Rights, and that their decisions be reviewable by federal courts?

It's important here to distinguish two questions: (1) Are internal restrictions consistent with liberal principles? and (2) Should liberals impose their views on minorities that do not accept some or all of these principles? The first is the question of *identifying* a defensible liberal theory of group rights; the second is the question of *imposing* that theory.

The first question is easy: internal restrictions are illiberal and unjust. But the answer to the second question is less clear. That liberals cannot automatically impose their principles on groups that do not share them is obvious enough, I think, if the illiberal group is another country. The Saudi Arabian government unjustly denies political rights to women or non-Muslims. But it doesn't follow that liberals outside Saudi Arabia should forcibly intervene to compel the Saudis to give everyone the vote. Similarly, the German government unjustly denies political rights to the children and grandchildren of Turkish "guest-workers," born and raised on German soil.

But it doesn't follow that liberals outside Germany should use force to compel Germany to change its citizenship laws.

What isn't clear is the proper remedy for rights violations. What third party (if any) has the authority to intervene in order to force the government to respect those rights? The same question arises when the illiberal group is a self-governing indigenous community within a single country. The Pueblo tribal council violates the rights of its members by limiting freedom of conscience and by employing sexually discriminatory membership rules. But what third party (if any) has the authority to compel the Pueblo council to respect those rights?

Liberal principles tell us that individuals have certain claims that their government must respect, such as individual freedom of conscience. But having identified those claims, we now face the very different question of imposing liberalism. If a particular government fails to respect those claims, who can legitimately step in and force compliance? (By "imposing" liberalism, I am referring to forcible intervention by a third party. Noncoercive intervention is a different matter, which I discuss below.)

The attitude of liberals toward imposing liberalism has changed over the years. In the international context, they have become increasingly skeptical about using force to compel foreign states to obey liberal principles. Many nineteenth-century liberals thought that liberal states were justified in colonizing and instructing foreign countries. Woodrow Wilson defended the American colonization of the Philippines in 1902 on the grounds that "they are children and we are men in these matters of government and justice." Contemporary liberals, however, have abandoned this doctrine as both imprudent and illegitimate, and sought instead to promote liberal values through persuasion and financial incentives.

In the case of self-governing indigenous minorities, however, liberals have been much more willing to endorse coercive intervention. Many American liberals assume that the Supreme Court has the legitimate authority to overturn any decisions of the Pueblo tribal council that violate individual rights. They commonly assume that to have a "right" means not only that legislators should respect one's claim, but also that there should be a system of judicial review to ensure that respect. Moreover, this judicial review should occur at a country-wide level. That is, in addition to the various state and tribal courts that review the laws of state and tribal governments, there should also be a Supreme Court to which all governments within the country are answerable. Indeed, many American liberals often talk as if it is part of the very meaning of "rights" that there should be a single court in each country with the authority to review the decisions of all governments within that country.

This is a very particularist understanding of rights. In some liberal countries (for example, Britain), there is a strong tradition of respecting individual rights, but there is no constitutional bill of rights and no basis for courts to overturn parliamentary decisions that violate individual rights. (The same was true in Canada until 1982.) In other countries, there is judicial review, but it is decentralized – that is, political subunits have their own systems of review, but there is no single bill of rights and no single court to which all levels of government are answerable. Indeed, this was true in the United States for a considerable period of time. Until the passage of the Fourteenth Amendment, state legislatures were answerable to state courts for the way they respected state constitutions, but were not answerable to the Supreme Court for respecting the Bill of Rights.

It's easy to see why American liberals are committed to giving the Supreme Court such wide authority. Historically, this sort of judicial review, backed up by federal troops, was required to overturn the racist legislation of Southern states, which state courts had upheld. Given the central role federal courts have played in the struggle against racism, American liberals have developed a deep commitment to centralized judicial review. So when a question is raised about self-governing indigenous peoples, many liberals automatically support centralized review, even though these peoples were historically exempt from any such external intervention.

In short, contemporary liberals have become more reluctant to impose liberalism on foreign countries, but more willing to impose liberalism on indigenous minorities. This, I think, is inconsistent. Both foreign states and indigenous minorities form distinct political communities, with their own claims to self-government. Attempts to impose liberal principles by force are often perceived, in both cases, as a form of aggression or paternalistic colonialism. And, as a result, these attempts often backfire. The plight of many former colonies in Africa shows that liberal institutions are likely to be unstable when they are the products of external imposition rather than internal reform. In the end, liberal institutions can work only if liberal beliefs have been internalized by the members of the self-governing society, be it an independent country or an indigenous minority.

There are, of course, important differences between foreign states and indigenous minorities. Yet, in both cases, there is relatively little scope for legitimate coercive interference. Relations between the majority society and indigenous peoples should be determined by peaceful negotiation, not force. This means searching for some basis of agreement. The most secure basis would be agreement on fundamental principles. But if the two groups do not share basic principles, and cannot be persuaded to adopt the other's principles, they will have to rely on some more minimalist modus vivendi.

The resulting agreement may well exempt the indigenous minority from the Bill of Rights and judicial review. Indeed, such exemptions are often implicit in the historical treaties by which the minority entered the larger state. This means that the majority will sometimes be unable to prevent the violation of individual rights within the minority community. Liberals have to learn to live with this, just as they must live with illiberal laws in other countries.

It doesn't follow that liberals should stand by and do nothing. An indigenous government that rules in an illiberal way acts unjustly. Liberals have a right, and a responsibility, to speak out against such injustice. Hence, liberal reformers inside the culture should seek to promote their principles through reason and example, and liberals outside should lend their support. Since the most enduring forms of liberalization are those that result from internal reform, the primary focus for liberals outside the group should be to support liberals inside.

Moreover, there is an important difference between coercively imposing liberalism and offering incentives for liberal reforms. Again, this is clear in the international arena. For example, the desire of former communist countries to enter the European Community (EC) has provided leverage for Western democracies to push for liberal reforms in Eastern Europe. Membership in the EC is a powerful, but noncoercive, incentive for liberal reform. Similarly, many people thought that negotiations over the North American Free Trade Agreement provided an opportunity for Canada and the United States to pressure the Mexican government into improving its human rights record.

There are many analogous opportunities for a majority to encourage indigenous peoples, in a noncoercive way, to liberalize their internal constitutions. Of course there are limits to the appropriate forms of pressure. Refusing to extend trade privileges is one thing, imposing a total embargo or blockade is quite another. The line between incentive and coercion is not a sharp one, and where to draw it is a much-debated point in the international context.

Finally, and perhaps most important, liberals can push for the development and strengthening of international mechanisms for protecting human rights. Some Indian tribes have expressed a willingness to abide by international declarations of rights, and to answer to international tribunals about complaints of rights violations within their communities. They accept the idea that their governments, like all sovereign governments, should be accountable to international norms. Indeed, they have shown greater willingness to accept this kind of review than many nation-states, which jealously guard their sovereignty in domestic affairs. Most Indian tribes do not oppose all forms of external review. What they object to is being subject to the constitution of their conquerors, which they had no role in drafting, and being answerable to federal courts composed entirely of non-Indian justices.

This shows, I think, that the assumption of American liberals that there must be one court within each country that is the ultimate defender of individual rights is doubly mistaken, at least in the case of indigenous peoples. History has proven the value of holding all governments accountable for respecting human rights. But the appropriate forum for reviewing the actions of self-governing indigenous peoples may skip the federal level, as it were. Many indigenous groups would endorse a system in which their decisions are reviewed in the first instance by their own courts and then by an international court. Federal courts, dominated by the majority, would have little or no authority over them.

These international mechanisms could arise at the regional as well as global level. European countries have agreed to establish their own multilateral human rights tribunals. Perhaps North American governments and Indian tribes could agree to establish a similar tribunal, on which both sides are fairly represented.

This isn't to say that federal intervention to protect liberal rights is never justified. In cases of gross and systematic violation of human rights, such as slavery, genocide, torture, or mass expulsions, there are grounds for intervening in the internal affairs of an indigenous group. A number of factors are relevant here, including the severity of rights violations within the community, the degree of consensus on restricting individual rights, and the ability of dissenting members to leave the community if they so desire. For example, whether intervention is justified in the case of an Indian tribe that restricts freedom of conscience surely depends on whether it is governed by a tyrant who lacks popular support and prevents people leaving the community or whether the tribal government has a broad base of support and religious dissidents are free to leave.

I should note that my arguments here do not just apply to indigenous peoples. They also apply to other national minorities – that is, other nonimmigrant groups whose homeland has been incorporated into a larger state through conquest, colonization, or the ceding of territory from one imperial power to another. Non-indigenous national minorities include the Québécois in Canada and Puerto Ricans in the United States. These groups differ from indigenous peoples in many ways, but in all these cases, the role of the federal courts in reviewing the decisions of self-governing minorities should be settled by negotiation, not imposition.

Cases involving immigrant groups are quite different. It is more legitimate to compel respect for liberal principles. I do not think it is wrong for liberal states to insist that immigration entails accepting the state's enforcement of liberalism, so long as immigrants know this in advance, and nonetheless choose to come.

Thinking Creatively about Rights

I've argued that the group rights sought by indigenous peoples need not conflict with human rights, and that the relationship between the two must be assessed carefully on a case-by-case basis. Even when the two do conflict, we cannot assume automatically that the courts and constitutions of the larger society should prevail over the self-governing decisions of the indigenous group. Indigenous peoples have good reasons, and sound legal arguments, to reject federal review of their self-government.

We should, however, think creatively about new mechanisms for enforcing human rights that will avoid the legitimate objections indigenous peoples have to federal courts. My aim is not to undermine human rights but rather to find fairer and more effective ways to promote them.

As Joseph Carens puts it, "People are supposed to experience the realization of principles of justice through various concrete institutions, but they may actually experience a lot of the institution and very little of the principle." This is exactly how many indigenous peoples perceive the supreme courts of Canada and the United States. What they experience is not the principle of human dignity and equality, but rather a social institution that has historically justified their conquest and dispossession.

Moreover, to focus exclusively on the danger of internal restrictions is often to miss the real source of injustice. The fact is that many indigenous groups feel compelled to impose internal restrictions because the larger society has denied them legitimate external protection. As Denise Réaume has noted, part of the "demonization" of other cultures is the assumption that they are naturally inclined to use coercion against their members. But insofar as some groups seem regrettably willing to use coercion to preserve traditional practices, this may be due, not to any innate illiberalism but to the fact that the larger society has failed to protect them. Unable to get protection for its lands and institutions, the minority turns to the only people it does have some control over, namely, its own members. This tendency does not justify internal restrictions, but it suggests that before we criticize a minority for imposing restrictions on its members, we should first make sure we are respecting its legitimate group rights.

Our goal, therefore, should be to find new mechanisms that will protect *both* the individual and group rights of indigenous peoples. We need to think about effective mechanisms, acceptable to indigenous peoples, for holding their governments accountable for the way individual members are treated. But we need simultaneously to think about effective mechanisms for holding the larger society accountable for respecting the group rights of indigenous peoples. Focusing on the former while neglecting the latter is counterproductive and hypocritical.

Many indigenous peoples have looked to the United Nations, and its draft declaration on indigenous rights, as a possible forum for pursuing these twin forms of accountability. Unfortunately, both the Canadian and U.S. governments have been reluctant to give any international body jurisdiction over the treaty rights, land claims, or self-government rights of indigenous peoples. Viewed in this light, the real obstacle to a more satisfactory balance of individual and group rights is not the refusal of indigenous peoples to accept external review, but rather the refusal of the larger society to accept restrictions on its sovereignty.

4

Toward a Cross-Cultural Approach to Defining International Standards of Human Rights: The Meaning of Cruel, Inhuman, or Degrading Treatment or Punishment

Abdullahi Ahmed An-Na'im

An intelligent strategy to protect and promote human rights must address the underlying causes of violations of these rights. These violations are caused by a wide and complex variety of factors and forces, including economic conditions, structural social factors, and political expediency. For the most part, however, human rights violations are due to human action or inaction – they occur because individual persons act or fail to act in certain ways. They can be the overlapping and interacting, intended or unintended, consequences of action. People may be driven by selfish motives of greed for wealth and power, or by a misguided perception of the public good. Even when motivated by selfish ends, human rights violators normally seek to rationalize their behavior as consistent with, or conducive to, some morally sanctioned purpose. Although their bid to gain or maintain public support may be purely cynical, such an attempt is unlikely unless they have reason to believe that their claim of moral sanction is plausible to their constituency.

It is not possible in this limited space to discuss the multitude of factors and forces that contribute to the underlying causes of human rights violations in general. I maintain that the lack or insufficiency of cultural legitimacy of human rights standards is one of the main underlying causes of violations of those standards.

Originally published in *Human Rights in Cross-Cultural Perspectives: A Quest for Consensus*, ed. Abdullahi Ahmed An-Na'im. Philadelphia: University of Pennsylvania Press, 1992, pp. 19–43.

In this chapter, I argue that internal and cross-cultural legitimacy for human rights standards needs to be developed, while I advance some tentative ideas to implement this approach. The focus of my supporting examples will be the right not to be subjected to cruel, inhuman, or degrading treatment or punishment. Insiders may perceive certain types of punishment, for example, as dictated or at least sanctioned by the norms of a particular cultural tradition, whereas to outsiders to that culture, such measures constitute cruel, inhuman, or degrading treatment. Which position should be taken as setting the standards for this human right? How can the cooperation of the proponents of the counter-position be secured in implementing the chosen standards?

My thesis does not assume that all individuals or groups within a society hold identical views on the meaning and implications of cultural values and norms, or that they would therefore share the same evaluation of the legitimacy of human rights standards. On the contrary, I assume and rely on the fact that there are either actual or potential differences in perceptions and interpretations of cultural values and norms. Dominant groups or classes within a society normally maintain perceptions and interpretations of cultural values and norms that are supportive of their own interests, proclaiming them to be the only valid view of that culture. Dominated groups or classes may hold, or at least be open to, different perceptions and interpretations that are helpful to their struggle to achieve justice for themselves. This, however, is an *internal* struggle for control over the cultural sources and symbols of power within that society. Even though outsiders may sympathize with and wish to support the dominated and oppressed groups or classes, their claiming to know what is the valid view of the culture of that society will not accomplish this effectively. Such a claim would not help the groups the outsiders wish to support because it portrays them as agents of an alien culture, thereby frustrating their efforts to attain legitimacy for their view of the values and norms of their society.

Cross-Cultural Perspectives on Human Rights

The general thesis of my approach is that, since people are more likely to observe normative propositions if they believe them to be sanctioned by their own cultural traditions, observance of human rights standards can be improved through the enhancement of the cultural legitimacy of those standards.[1] The claim that all the existing human rights standards already enjoy universal cultural legitimacy may be weak from a historical point of view in the sense that many cultural traditions in the world have had little say in the formulation of those standards. Nevertheless, I believe not only that universal cultural legitimacy is necessary, but also that it is possible to develop it retrospectively in relation to fundamental human rights through enlightened interpretations of cultural norms.

Given the extreme cultural diversity of the world community, it can be argued that human rights should be founded on the existing least common denominator among these cultural traditions. On the other hand, restricting international human rights to those accepted by prevailing perceptions of the values and norms of the major cultural traditions of the world would not only limit these rights and reduce their scope, but also exclude extremely vital rights. Therefore, expanding the area and quality of agreement among the cultural traditions of the world may be necessary to provide the foundation for the widest possible range and scope of human rights.

I believe that this can be accomplished through the proposed approach to universal cultural legitimacy of human rights.

The cultural legitimacy thesis accepts the existing international standards while seeking to enhance their cultural legitimacy within the major traditions of the world through internal dialogue and struggle to establish enlightened perceptions and interpretations of cultural values and norms. Having achieved an adequate level of legitimacy *within* each tradition, through this internal stage, human rights scholars and advocates should work for *cross-cultural* legitimacy, so that peoples of diverse cultural traditions can agree on the meaning, scope, and methods of implementing these rights. Instead of being content with the existing least common denominator, I propose to broaden and deepen universal consensus on the formulation and implementation of human rights through internal reinterpretation of, and cross-cultural dialogue about, the meaning and implications of basic human values and norms.

This approach is based on the belief that, despite their apparent peculiarities and diversity, human beings and societies share certain fundamental interests, concerns, qualities, traits, and values that can be identified and articulated as the framework for a common "culture" of universal human rights. It would be premature in this exploratory essay to attempt to identify and articulate these interests, concerns, and so on, with certainty. Major theoretical and methodological issues must first be discussed and resolved so that the common culture of universal human rights may be founded on solid conceptual and empirical grounds. At this stage, I am concerned with making the case for internal and cross-cultural discourse on the subject, raising some of the questions and difficulties that must be faced and generally describing the process that should be undertaken. Neither concrete results nor guarantees of success can be offered here, only a promising approach to resolving a real and serious issue.

Concern with the implications of cultural diversity has been present since the earliest stages of the modern international human rights movement. In 1947, UNESCO carried out an inquiry into the theoretical problems raised by the Universal Declaration of Human Rights. This was accomplished by inviting the views of various thinkers and writers from member states,[2] and organizing subsequent conferences and seminars on this theme. Other organizations have also taken the initiative in drawing attention to the dangers of ethnocentricity and the need for sensitivity to cultural diversity in the drafting of international human rights instruments.[3] Individual authors, too, have addressed these concerns.

My approach draws upon these earlier efforts and supplements them with insights from non-Western perspectives. Some Western writers have highlighted conflicts between international human rights standards and certain non-Western cultural traditions, without suggesting ways of reconciling them.[4] Despite their claims or wishes to present a cross-cultural approach, other Western writers have tended to confine their analysis to Western perspectives. For example, one author emphasizes the challenge of cultural diversity, saying that it would "be useful to try to rethink the normative foundations of human rights and consider which rights have the strongest normative support."[5] Yet, the philosophical perspectives he actually covers in his discussion are exclusively Western. Another author calls for taking cultural diversity seriously, yet presents arguments based exclusively on Western philosophy and political theory.[6]

Alison Renteln is one of the few human rights scholars sensitive to issues of cultural legitimacy. She suggests a cross-cultural understanding that will shed light on a common core of acceptable rights.[7] Her approach seems to be content with the existing least common denominator, however, a standard I find inadequate to assure sufficient human rights throughout the world. In my view, a constructive element is needed to broaden and deepen cross-cultural consensus on a "common core of human rights." I believe that this can be accomplished through the internal discourse and cross-cultural dialogue advocated here.

Cultural relativity and human rights

Culture is defined in a variety of ways in different contexts.[8] A wide array of definitions is available in the social sciences.[9] In this chapter, culture is taken in its widest meaning – that of the "totality of values, institutions and forms of behavior transmitted within a society, as well as the material goods produced by man [and woman]...this wide concept of culture covers *Weltanschauung* [world view], ideologies and cognitive behavior."[10] It can also be defined as "an historically transmitted pattern of meanings in symbols, a system of inherited conceptions expressed in symbolic form by means of which men [and women] communicate, perpetuate and develop their knowledge and attitudes towards life."[11]

Culture is therefore the source of the individual and communal world view: it provides both the individual and the community with the values and interests to be pursued in life, as well as the legitimate means for pursuing them. It stipulates the norms and values that contribute to people's perception of their self-interest and the goals and methods of individual and collective struggles for power within a society and between societies. As such, culture is a primary force in the socialization of individuals and a major determinant of the consciousness and experience of the community. The impact of culture on human behavior is often underestimated precisely because it is so powerful and deeply embedded in our self-identity and consciousness.

Our culture is so much a part of our personality that we normally take for granted that our behavior patterns and relationships to other persons and to society become the ideal norm. The subtlety of the impact of culture on personality and character may be explained by the analogy of the eye: we tend to take the world to be what our eyes convey to us without "seeing" the eye and appreciating its role.[12] In this case, the information conveyed by the eye is filtered and interpreted by the mind without the individual's conscious awareness of this fact. Culture influences, first, the way we see the world and, further, how we interpret and react to the information we receive.

This analogy may also explain our ethnocentricity, the tendency to regard one's own race or social group as the model of human experience. Ethnocentricity does not mean there is no conflict and tension between a person and his or her own culture, or between various classes and groups within a society. It rather incorporates such conflict and tension in the ideal model, leading us to perceive the conflict and tension we have within our own culture as part of the norm. For example, some feminists in one cultural tradition may assume that women in other cultures have (or ought to have) the same conflicts and tensions with their societies and are seeking (or ought to seek) the same answers.

A degree of ethnocentricity is unavoidable, indeed indispensable. It is the basis of our acceptance of the validity of the norms and institutions of our culture, an acceptance that ultimately is a matter of material and psychological survival.[13] Even the most radical "dissidents" rely on their culture for survival. In fact, their dissent itself is meaningful to them only as the antithesis of existing cultural norms and institutions. Rigid ethnocentricity, however, breeds intolerance and hostility to societies and persons that do not conform to our models and expectations. Whether operating as initial justification or as subsequent rationalization, the tendency to dehumanize "different" societies and persons underlies much of the exploitation and oppression of one society by another, or of other classes within a society by one class of persons in the same society.

The appreciation of our own ethnocentricity should lead us to respect the ethnocentricity of others. Enlightened ethnocentricity would therefore concede the right of others to be "different," whether as members of another society or as individuals within the same society. This perspective would uphold the equal human value and dignity of members of other societies and of dissidents within society. In sociological terms, this orientation is commonly known as cultural relativism, that is to say, the acknowledgment of equal validity of diverse patterns of life.[14] It stresses "the dignity inherent in every body of custom, and...the need for tolerance of conventions though they may differ from one's own."[15]

Cultural relativism has been charged with neutralizing moral judgment and thereby impairing action against injustice.[16] According to one author, "[It] has these objectionable consequences: namely, that by limiting critical assessment of human works it disarms us, dehumanises us, leaves us unable to enter into communicative interaction; that is to say, unable to criticize cross-culturally, cross-sub-culturally; intimately, relativism leaves no room for criticism at all...behind relativism nihilism looms."[17] Some writers on human rights are suspicious of a cultural relativism that denies to individuals the moral right to make comparisons and to insist on universal standards of right and wrong.[18]

As John Ladd notes, however, relativism is identified with nihilism because it is defined by its opponents in absolute terms.[19] I tend to agree with Clifford Geertz that the relativism/antirelativism discourse in anthropology should be seen as an exchange of warnings rather than as an analytical debate. Whereas the relativists maintain that "the world being so full of a number of things, rushing to judgment is more than a mistake, it's a crime," the antirelativists are concerned "that if something isn't anchored everywhere nothing can be anchored anywhere."[20] I also agree with Geertz's conclusion:

> The objection to anti-relativism is not that it rejects an it's-all-how-you-look-at-it approach to knowledge or a when-in-Rome approach to morality, but that it imagines that they [these approaches] can only be defeated by placing morality beyond culture and knowledge beyond both. This...is no longer possible. If we wanted home truths, we should have stayed at home.[21]

In my view, the merits of a reasonable degree of cultural relativism are obvious, especially when compared to claims of universalism that are in fact based on the claimant's rigid and exclusive ethnocentricity. The charge that it may breed tolerance of injustice is a serious one, however. Melville J. Herskovits, one of the main proponents of cultural relativism, has sought to answer this charge by distinguishing between absolutes and universals:

> To say that there is no absolute [not admitted to have variations] criterion of value or morals...does not mean that such criteria, in differing *forms*, do not comprise universals [least common denominators to be extracted from the range of variations] in human culture. Morality is a universal, and so is enjoyment of beauty, and some

standard of truth. The many forms these concepts take are but products of the particular historical experience of the societies that manifest them. In each, criteria are subject to continuous questioning, continuous change. But the basic conceptions remain, to channel thought and direct conduct, to give purpose to living.[22]

Although this statement is true, it does not fully answer the charge. Morality may be universal in the sense that all cultures have it, but that does not in any way indicate the *content* of that morality, or provide criteria for judgment or for action by members of that culture or other cultures. The least common denominator of the universality of morality must include some of its basic precepts and not be confined to the mere existence of some form of morality. Moreover, in accordance with the logic of cultural relativism, the shared moral values must be authentic and not imposed from the outside. As indicated earlier, the existing least common denominator may not be enough to accommodate certain vital human rights. This fact would suggest the need to broaden and deepen common values to support these human rights. This process, however, must be culturally legitimate with reference to the norms and mechanisms of change within a particular culture.

Another author has sought to respond to the charge that cultural relativism impairs moral judgment and action by saying that, although it is appropriate to distinguish between criticism corresponding to standards internal to the culture and that corresponding to external ones, the theory of cultural relativism does not block either.[23] This observation holds true of a reasonable degree of cultural relativism but not of its extreme form.[24] Moreover, we should not only distinguish between criticism corresponding to standards internal to a culture and that corresponding to external ones, but also stress that the former is likely to be more effective than the latter.

I would emphasize that, in this age of self-determination, sensitivity to cultural relativity is vital for the international protection and promotion of human rights. This point does not preclude cross-cultural moral judgment and action, but it prescribes the best ways of formulating and expressing judgment and of undertaking action. As Geertz states, morality and knowledge cannot be placed beyond culture. In intercultural relations, morality and knowledge cannot be the exclusive product of some cultures but not of others. The validity of cross-cultural moral judgment increases with the degree of universality of the values upon which it is based; further, the efficacy of action increases with the degree of the actor's sensitivity to the internal logic and frame of reference of other cultures.

Cultural universality and human rights

Although human rights require action within each country for their implementation, the present international human rights regime has been conceived and is intended to operate within the framework of international relations. The implications of culture for international relations have long been recognized. For example, as Edmund Burke has said:

> In the intercourse between two nations, we are apt to rely too much on the instrumental part. We lay too much weight on the formality of treaties and compacts.... Men [and women] are not tied to one another by paper and seals. They are led to associate by resemblances, by conformities, by sympathies. It is with nations as with individuals. Nothing is so strong a tie of amity between nation and nation as correspondence in

laws, customs, manners and habits of life. They are obligations written in the heart. They approximate men [and women] to one another without their knowledge and sometimes against their intentions. The secret, unseen, but irrefragable bond of habitual intercourse holds them together even when their perverse and litigious nature sets them to equivocate, scuffle, and fight about the terms of their written obligations.[25]

This bonding through similarities does not mean, in my view, that international peace and cooperation are not possible without total global cultural unity. It does mean that they are more easily achieved if there is a certain minimum cultural consensus on goals and methods. As applied to cooperation in the protection and promotion of human rights, this view means that developing cross-cultural consensus in support of treaties and compacts is desirable. Cultural diversity, however, is unavoidable as the product of significant past and present economic, social, and environmental differences. It is also desirable as the expression of the right to self-determination and as the manifestation of distinctive self-identity. Nevertheless, I believe that a sufficient degree of cultural consensus regarding the goals and methods of cooperation in the protection and promotion of human rights can be achieved through internal cultural discourse and cross-cultural dialogue. Internal discourse relates to the struggle to establish enlightened perceptions and interpretations of cultural values and norms. Cross-cultural dialogue should be aimed at broadening and deepening international (or rather intercultural) consensus. This direction may include support for the proponents of enlightened perceptions and interpretations within a culture. This effort, however, must be sensitive to the internal nature of the struggle, endeavoring to emphasize internal values and norms rather than external ones.

One of the apparent paradoxes of culture is the way it combines stability with dynamic continuous change.[26] Change is induced by internal adjustments as well as external influences. Both types of change, however, must be justified through culturally approved mechanisms and adapted to preexisting norms and institutions. Otherwise, the culture would lose the coherence and stability that are vital for its socializing and other functions.

Another feature of the dynamism of culture is that it normally offers its members a range of options or is willing to accommodate varying individual responses to its norms. As Herskovits observes, "culture is flexible and holds many possibilities of choice within its framework...to recognize the values held by a given people in no wise implies that these values are a constant factor in the lives of succeeding generations of the same group."[27] Nevertheless, the degree of flexibility permitted by a culture, and the possibilities of choice it offers its members, are controlled by the culture's internal criteria of legitimacy.

A third and more significant feature of cultural dynamism is the ambivalence of cultural norms and their susceptibility to different interpretations. In the normal course of events, powerful individuals and groups tend to monopolize the interpretation of cultural norms and manipulate them to their own advantage. Given the extreme importance of cultural legitimacy, it is vital for disadvantaged individuals and groups to challenge this monopoly and manipulation. They should use internal cultural discourse to offer alternative interpretations in support of their own interests. This internal discourse can utilize intellectual, artistic, and scholarly work as well as various available forms of political action.

Internal cultural discourse should also support cross-cultural dialogue and set its terms of reference. It should encourage good will, mutual respect, and equality with other cultural traditions. This positive relationship can be fostered, for example, by enlisting the support of what I would call the principle of reciprocity, that is to say, the rule that one should treat others in the same way that he or she would like to be treated. Although this is a universal rule, most traditions tend to restrict its applications to "others" from the same or selected traditions rather than all human beings and societies. Internal discourse should propagate a broader and more enlightened interpretation of the principle of reciprocity to include all human beings.

It is vital for cross-cultural dialogue that internal cultural discourse along these lines be undertaken simultaneously in all cultural traditions. As a matter of principle, it should be admitted that every cultural tradition has problems with some human rights and needs to enhance the internal cultural legitimacy of those rights. From a tactical point of view, undertaking internal cultural discourse in relation to the problems one tradition has with certain human rights is necessary for encouraging other traditions to undertake similar discourse in relation to the problematic aspects of their own culture.

The object of internal discourse and cross-cultural dialogue is to agree on a body of beliefs to guide action in support of human rights in spite of disagreement on the justification of those beliefs. Jacques Maritain, a French philosopher, explained this idea more than forty years ago:

> To understand this, it is only necessary to make the appropriate distinction between the rational justifications involved in the spiritual dynamism of philosophic doctrine or religious faith [that is to say, in culture], and the practical conclusions which, although justified in different ways by different persons, are principles of action with a common ground of similarity for everyone. I am quite certain that my way of justifying belief in the rights of man and the ideal of liberty, equality and fraternity is the only way with a firm foundation in truth. This does not prevent me from being in agreement on these practical convictions with people who are certain that their way of justifying them, entirely different from mine or opposed to mine, in its theoretical dynamism, is equally the only way founded upon truth.[28]

Total agreement on the interpretation and application of those practical conclusions may not be possible, however, because disagreement about their justification will probably be reflected in the way they are interpreted and applied. We should therefore be realistic in our expectations and pursue the maximum possible degree of agreement at whatever level it can be achieved. This approach can be illustrated by the following case study of the meaning of the human right "not to be subjected to cruel, inhuman or degrading treatment or punishment."

Cruel, Inhuman, or Degrading Treatment or Punishment

Some international human rights instruments stipulate that "no one shall be subjected to torture or to cruel, inhuman or degrading treatment or punishment."[29] There is obvious overlap between the two main parts of this right, that is to say, between protection against torture and protection against inhuman or degrading treatment or punishment. For example, torture has been described as constituting "an aggravated and deliberate form of cruel, inhuman or degrading treatment or punishment."[30] Nevertheless, there are differences between the two parts of the right. According to the definition of torture adopted in United Nations instruments, it "does not include pain or suffering arising only from, inherent in or incidental to lawful sanctions."[31] As explained below, this qualification is not supposed to apply to the second part of the right. In other words, lawful sanctions can constitute "cruel, inhuman or degrading treatment or punishment."

The following discussion will focus on the meaning of the second part of the right, that is to say, the meaning of the right not to be subjected to cruel, inhuman or degrading treatment or punishment. In particular, I will address the question of how to identify the criteria by which lawful sanctions can be held to violate the prohibition of cruel, inhuman or degrading treatment or punishment. The case of the Islamic punishments will be used to illustrate the application of the cross-cultural perspective to this question.

The meaning of the clause in United Nations sources

Cruel or inhuman treatment or punishment is prohibited by regional instruments, such as the European Convention for the Protection of Human Rights and Fundamental Freedoms, as well as under the international system of the United Nations. While regional jurisprudence is applicable in the regional context, and may be persuasive in some other parts of the world, it may not be useful in all parts of the world. For example, the jurisprudence developed by the European Commission and Court of Human Rights under Article 3 of the European Convention would be directly applicable in defining this clause from a European point of view, and may be persuasive in North America. It may not be useful, however, when discussing non-Western perspectives on cruel, inhuman, or degrading treatment or punishment. The following survey will therefore focus on UN sources because they are at least supposed to reflect international perspectives.

The early history of what is now Article 7 of the Covenant on Civil and Political Rights indicates that drafters and delegates were particularly concerned with preventing the recurrence of atrocities such as those committed in concentration camps during World War II.[32] Thus, the Commission on Human Rights proposed in 1952 that the Article should read: "No one shall be subjected to torture or to cruel, inhuman or degrading treatment or punishment. In particular, no one shall be subjected without his free consent to medical or scientific experimentation involving risk, where such is not required by his state of physical or mental health."[33] At the 13th Session of the Third Committee in 1958, however, most discussion centered on the second sentence. Some delegates felt that the sentence was unnecessary and also weakened the Article in that it directed attention to only one of the many forms of cruel, inhuman, or degrading treatment, thereby lessening the importance of the general prohibition laid down in the first sentence. Others insisted on retaining the second sentence as complementing the first sentence rather than being superfluous.[34] Although several suggestions were made to meet the objection that the second part of the Article was emphasized at the expense of the first, the second sentence was retained and eventually adopted, as amended, by the General Assembly.[35]

Whether because of preoccupation with this issue or due to the belief that the first sentence of the Article was self-explanatory, there is little guidance from the history of the Article on the meaning of "cruel, inhuman or degrading treatment or punishment." It was generally agreed early in the drafting process that the word "treatment" was broader in scope than the word "punishment." It was also observed that the word "treatment" should not apply to degrading situations that might be due to general economic and social factors.[36] In 1952, the Philippines suggested before the Third Committee that the word "unusual" should be inserted between the words "inhuman" and "or degrading." Some delegates supported the addition of the word "unusual" because it might apply to certain actual practices that, although not intentionally cruel, inhuman, or degrading, nevertheless affected the physical or moral integrity of the human person. Others opposed the term "unusual" as being vague: what was "unusual" in one country, it was said, might not be so in other countries. The proposal was withdrawn.[37]

It is remarkable that the criticism of vagueness should be seen as applying to the word "unusual" and not as applying to the words "cruel, inhuman or degrading." Surely, what may be seen as "cruel, inhuman or degrading" in one culture may not be seen in the same light in another culture. Do other UN sources provide guidance on the meaning of this clause and criteria for resolving possible conflicts between one culture and another regarding what is "cruel, inhuman or degrading treatment or punishment?"

A commentary on Article 5 of the UN Code of Conduct for Law Enforcement Officials of 1979 states: "The term 'cruel, inhuman or degrading treatment or punishment' has not been defined by the General Assembly, but it should be interpreted so as to extend the widest possible protection against abuses, whether physical or mental."[38] Decisions of the Human Rights Committee under the Optional Protocol provide examples of treatment or punishment held to be in violation of Article 7 of the covenant by an official organ of the UN.[39] Although these examples may be useful in indicating the sort of treatment or punishment that is likely to be held in violation of this human right, they do not provide an authoritative criteria of general application.[40]

When the Human Rights Committee attempted to provide some general criteria, the result was both controversial and not particularly helpful. For example, the committee said of the scope of the protection against cruel, inhuman, or degrading treatment or punishment:

> [It] goes far beyond torture as normally understood. It may not be necessary to make sharp distinctions between various forms of treatment and punishment. These distinctions depend on the kind, purpose and severity of the particular treatment...the prohibition must extend to corporal punishment, including excessive chastisement as an educational and disciplinary measure.[41]

This statement is not particularly helpful in determining whether a certain treatment or punishment is cruel, inhuman, or degrading; and the example it cites is controversial. In the majority of human societies today, corporal punishment is not regarded as necessarily cruel, inhuman, or degrading. It may be even more debatable whether this characterization applies to what might be considered by some as excessive chastisement but which is routinely used for educational and disciplinary purposes in many parts of the world. This example clearly shows the dangers and difficulty of providing generally accepted criteria for defining the concept. Nevertheless, such criteria are necessary to implement this human right. Would a cross-cultural approach be helpful in this regard?

Again, this discussion focuses on the question of how lawful sanctions can be held to violate the prohibition of cruel, inhuman, or degrading treatment or punishment. It is important to address this question because such sanctions have been excluded from the definition of torture under Article 1 of the Convention Against Torture and Other Cruel, Inhuman or Degrading Treatment or Punishment of 1984. Does this give the state a free hand to enforce whatever treatment or punishment it deems fit, so long as it is enacted as the lawful sanction for any conduct the state chooses to penalize? Does the international community have the right to object to any lawful sanction as amounting to cruel, inhuman, or degrading treatment or punishment?

Article 16 of the 1984 Convention provides for the obligation to prevent "other acts of cruel, inhuman or degrading treatment or punishment which do not amount to torture." Unlike Article 1, however, which defines torture in detail, Article 16 neither defines the clause "cruel, inhuman or degrading treatment or punishment," nor excludes pain or suffering arising only from, inherent in, or incidental to lawful sanctions. This phrasing means that States Parties to the Convention may not enforce lawful sanctions which constitute cruel, inhuman, or degrading treatment or punishment. But this obligation cannot be implemented or enforced in accordance with provisions of the Convention unless there is agreement on the definition of this clause.

Cross-cultural perspectives on the concept

Some predominantly Muslim countries, such as Afghanistan and Egypt, have already ratified the 1984 Convention; others may wish to do so in the future. The meaning of cruel, inhuman, or degrading treatment or punishment in Islamic cultures, however, may be significantly, if not radically, different from perceptions of the meaning of this clause in other parts of the world.

Islamic law, commonly know as Shari'a, is based on the Qur'an, which Muslims believe to be the literal and final word of God, and on Sunna, or traditions of the Prophet Muhammad. Using these sources, as well as pre-Islamic customary practices of the Middle East which were not explicitly repudiated by Qur'an and Sunna, Muslim jurists developed Shari'a as a comprehensive ethical and legal system between the seventh and ninth centuries AD. To Muslim communities, however, the Qur'an and Sunna were always believed to be absolutely binding as a matter of faith and were applied in individual and communal practice from the very beginning. Shari'a codes were never formally enacted, but the jurists systematized and rationalized what was already accepted as the will of God, and developed techniques for interpreting divine sources and for supplementing their provisions where they were silent.[42]

Due to the religious nature of Shari'a, Muslim jurists did not distinguish among devotional, ethical, social, and legal aspects of the law, let alone among various types of legal norms. The equivalent of penal or criminal law would therefore have to be extracted from a wide range of primary sources. For the purposes of this discussion, Islamic criminal law may be briefly explained as follows.[43] Criminal offenses are classified into three main categories: *hudud*, *jinayat*, and *ta'zir*. *Hudud* are a very limited group of offenses which are strictly defined and punished by the express terms of the Qur'an and/or Sunna. These include *sariqa*, or theft, which is punishable by the amputation of the right hand, and *zina*, or fornication, which is punishable by whipping of one hundred lashes for an unmarried offender and stoning to death for a married offender. *Jinayat* are homicide and causing bodily harm, which are punishable by *qisas*, or exact retribution (an eye for an eye) or payment of monetary compensation. The term *ta'zir* means to reform and rectify.

Ta'zir offenses are those created and punished by the ruler in exercising his power to protect private and public interests.

It is important to emphasize that the following discussion addresses this question in a purely theoretical sense and should not be taken to condone the application of these punishments by any government in the Muslim world today. The question being raised is: Are Muslims likely to accept the repudiation of these punishments *as a matter of Islamic law* on the ground that they are cruel, inhuman, or degrading? This question should not be confused with the very important but distinct issue of whether these punishments have been or are being applied legitimately and in accordance with all the general and specific requirements of Islamic law.

Islamic law requires the state to fulfill its obligation to secure social and economic justice and to ensure decent standards of living for all its citizens *before* it can enforce these punishments. The law also provides for very narrow definitions of these offenses, makes an extensive range of defenses against the charge available to the accused person, and requires strict standards of proof. Moreover, Islamic law demands total fairness and equality in law enforcement. In my view, the prerequisite conditions for the enforcement of these punishments are extremely difficult to satisfy in practice and are certainly unlikely to materialize in any Muslim country in the foreseeable future. Nevertheless, the question remains, can these punishments be abolished as a matter of Islamic law?

Shari'a criminal law has been displaced by secular criminal law in most Muslim countries. Countries like Saudi Arabia, however, have always maintained Shari'a as their official criminal law. Other countries, such as Iran, Pakistan, and the Sudan, have recently reintroduced Shari'a criminal law. There is much controversy over many aspects of the criminal law of Shari'a that raise human rights concerns, including issues of religious discrimination in the application of Shari'a criminal law to non-Muslims.[44] To the vast majority of Muslims, however, Shari'a criminal law is binding and should be enforced today. Muslim political leaders and scholars may debate whether general social, economic, and political conditions are appropriate for the immediate application of Shari'a, or whether there should be a preparatory stage before the reintroduction of Shari'a where it has been displaced by secular law. None of them would dispute, at least openly and publicly, that the application of Shari'a criminal law should be a high priority, if not an immediate reality.

Although these are important matters, they should not be confused with what is being discussed here. For the sake of argument, the issue should be isolated from other possible sources of controversy. In particular, I wish to emphasize that I believe that the Qur'anic punishments should *not* apply to non-Muslims because they are essentially religious in nature. In the following discussion, I will use the example of amputation of the right hand for theft when committed by a Muslim who does not need to steal in order to survive, and who has been properly tried and convicted by a competent court of law. This punishment is prescribed by the clear and definite text of verse 38 in chapter 5 of the Qur'an. Can this punishment, when imposed under these circumstances, be condemned as cruel, inhuman, or degrading?

The basic question here is one of interpretation and application of a universally accepted human right. In terms of the principle Maritain suggests – agreement on "practical conclusions" in spite of disagreement on their justification – Muslims would accept the human right not to be subjected to cruel, inhuman, or degrading treatment or punishment. Their Islamic culture may indicate to them a different interpretation of this human right, however.

From a secular or humanist point of view, inflicting such a severe permanent punishment for any offense, especially for theft, is obviously cruel and inhuman, and probably also degrading. This may well be the private intuitive reaction of many educated modernized Muslims. However, to the vast majority of Muslims, the matter is settled by the categorical will of God as expressed in the Qur'an and, as such, is not open to question by human beings. Even the educated modernized Muslim, who may be privately repelled by this punishment, cannot risk the consequences of openly questioning the will of God. In addition to the danger of losing his or her faith and the probability of severe social chastisement, a Muslim who disputes the binding authority of the Qur'an is liable to the death penalty for apostasy (heresy) under Shari'a.

Thus, in all Muslim societies, the possibility of human judgment regarding the appropriateness or cruelty of a punishment decreed by God is simply out of the question. Furthermore, this belief is supported by what Muslims accept as rational arguments.[45] From the religious point of view, human life does not end at death, but extends beyond that to the next life. In fact, religious sources strongly emphasize that the next life is the true and ultimate reality, to which this life is merely a prelude. In the next *eternal* life, every human being will stand judgment and suffer the consequences of his or her actions in this life. A religiously sanctioned punishment, however, will absolve an offender from punishment in the next life because God does not punish twice for the same offense. Accordingly, a thief who suffers the religiously sanctioned punishment of amputation of the right hand in this life will not be liable to the much harsher punishment in the next life. To people who hold this belief, however severe the Qur'anic punishment may appear to be, it is in fact extremely lenient and merciful in comparison to what the offender will suffer in the next life should the religious punishment not be enforced in this life.

Other arguments are advanced about the benefits of this punishment to both the individual offender and society. It is said that this seemingly harsh punishment is in fact necessary to reform and rehabilitate the thief, as well as to safeguard the interests of other persons and of society at large, by deterring other potential offenders.[46] The ultimately *religious* rationale of these arguments must always be emphasized, however. The punishment is believed to achieve these individual and social benefits because God said so. To the vast majority of Muslims, scientific research is welcome to confirm the empirical validity of these arguments, but it cannot be accepted as a basis for repudiating them, thereby challenging the appropriateness of the punishment. Moreover, the religious frame of reference is also integral to evaluating empirical data. Reform of the offender is not confined to his or her experience in this life, but includes the next life, too.

Neither internal Islamic reinterpretation nor cross-cultural dialogue is likely to lead to the total abolition of this punishment as a matter of Islamic law. Much can be done, however, to restrict its implementation in practice. For example, there is room for developing stronger general social and economic prerequisites and stricter procedural requirements for the enforcement of the punishment. Islamic religious texts emphasize extreme caution in inflicting any criminal punishment. The Prophet said that if there is any doubt (*shubha*), the Qur'anic punishments should not be imposed. He also said that it is better to err on the side of refraining from imposing the punishment than to err on the side of imposing it in a doubtful case. Although these directives have already been incorporated into definitions of the offenses and the applicable rules of evidence and procedure, it is still possible to develop a broader concept of *shubha* to include, for example, psychological disorders as a defense against criminal responsibility. For instance, kleptomania may be taken as *shubha* barring punishment for theft. Economic need may also be a defense against a charge of theft.

Cross-cultural dialogue may also be helpful in this regard. In the Jewish tradition, for instance, jurists have sought to restrict the practical application of equally harsh punishment by stipulating strict procedural and other requirements.[47] This theoretical Jewish jurisprudence may be useful to Muslim jurists and leaders seeking to restrict the practical application of Qur'anic punishments. It is difficult to assess its practical viability and impact, however, because it has not been applied for nearly two thousand years. Moreover, the current atmosphere of mutual Jewish–Muslim antagonism and mistrust does not make cross-cultural dialogue likely between these two traditions. Still, this has not always been the case in the past and need not be so in the future. In fact, the jurisprudence of each tradition has borrowed heavily from the other in the past and may do so in the future once the present conflict is resolved.

I believe that in the final analysis, the interpretation and practical application of the protection against cruel, inhuman, or degrading treatment or punishment in the context of a particular society should be determined by the moral standards of that society. I also believe that there are many legitimate ways of influencing and informing the moral standards of a society. To dictate to a society is both unacceptable as a matter of principle and unlikely to succeed in practice. Cross-cultural dialogue and mutual influence, however, is acceptable in principle and continuously occurring in practice. To harness the power of cultural legitimacy in support of human rights, we need to develop techniques for internal cultural discourse and cross-cultural dialogue, and to work toward establishing general conditions conducive to constructive discourse and dialogue.

It should be recalled that this approach assumes and relies on the existence of internal struggle for cultural power within society. Certain dominant classes or groups would normally hold the cultural advantage and proclaim their view of the culture as valid, while others would challenge this view, or at least wish to be able to do so. In relation to Islamic punishments, questions about the legitimate application of these punishments – whether the state has fulfilled its obligations first and is acting in accordance with the general and specific conditions referred to earlier – are matters for internal struggle. This internal struggle cannot and should not be settled by outsiders; but they may support one side or the other, provided they do so with sufficient sensitivity and due consideration for the legitimacy of the objectives and methods of the struggle within the framework of the particular culture.

Conclusion: Toward a Cross-Cultural Approach

I have deliberately chosen the question of whether lawful sanctions can be condemned as cruel, inhuman, or degrading punishment or treatment in order to illustrate both the need for a cross-cultural approach to defining human rights standards and the difficulty of implementing this approach. The question presents human rights advocates with a serious dilemma. On the one hand, it is necessary to safeguard the personal integrity and human dignity of the individual against excessive or harsh punishments. The fundamental objective of the modern human rights movement is to protect citizens from the brutality and excesses of their own governments. On the other hand, it is extremely important to be sensitive to the dangers of cultural imperialism, whether it is a product of colonialism, a tool of international economic exploitation and political subjugation, or simply a product of extreme ethnocentricity. Since we would not accept others' imposing their moral standards on us, we should not impose our own moral standards on them. In any case, external imposition is normally counterproductive and unlikely to succeed in changing the practice in question. External imposition is not the only option available to human rights advocates, however. Greater consensus on international standards for the protection of the individual against cruel, inhuman, or degrading treatment or punishment can be achieved through internal cultural discourse and cross-cultural dialogue.

It is unrealistic to expect this approach to achieve total agreement on the interpretation and application of standards, whether of treatment or punishment or any other human right. This expectation presupposes the existence of the interpretation to be agreed upon. If one reflects on the interpretation she or he would like to make the norm, it will probably be the one set by the person's culture. Further reflection on how one would feel about the interpretation set by another culture should illustrate the untenability of this position. For example, a North American may think that a short term of imprisonment is the appropriate punishment for theft, and wish that to be the universal punishment for this offense. A Muslim, on the other hand, may feel that the amputation of the hand is appropriate under certain conditions and after satisfying strict safeguards. It would be instructive for the North American to consider how she or he would feel if the Muslim punishment were made the norm. Most Western human rights advocates are likely to have a lingering feeling that there is simply no comparison between these two punishments because the Islamic punishment is "obviously" cruel and inhuman and should never compete with imprisonment as a possible punishment for this offense. A Muslim might respond by saying that this feeling is a product of Western ethnocentricity. I am not suggesting that we should make the Islamic or any other particular punishment the universal norm. I merely wish to point out that agreeing on a universal standard may not be as simple as we may think or wish it to be.

In accordance with the proposed approach, the standard itself should be the product of internal discourse and cross-cultural dialogue. Moreover, genuine total agreement requires equal commitment to internal discourse and equally effective participation in cross-cultural dialogue by the adherents or members of different cultural traditions of the world. In view of significant social and political differences and disparities in levels of economic development, some cultural traditions are unlikely to engage in internal discourse as much as other cultural traditions and are unable to participate in cross-cultural dialogue as effectively as others. These processes require a certain degree of political liberty, stability, and social maturity, as well as technological capabilities that are lacking in some parts of the world.

The cross-cultural approach, however, is not an all-or-nothing proposition. While total agreement on the standard and mechanisms for its implementation is unrealistic in some cases, significant agreement can be achieved and ought to be pursued as much as possible. For example, in relation to cruel, inhuman, or degrading treatment or punishment, there is room for agreement on a wide range of substantive and procedural matters even in relation to an apparently inflexible position, such as the Islamic position on Qur'anic punishments. Provided such agreement is sought with sufficient sensitivity, the general status of human rights will be improved, and wider agreement can be achieved in relation to other human rights. We must be clear, however, on what can be achieved and how to achieve it in any given case. An appreciation of the impossibility of the total abolition of the Qur'anic punishment for theft is necessary for restricting its practice in Muslim societies as well as for establishing common standards, for instance, in relation to punishments that are, from the Islamic point of view, the product of human legislation.

NOTES

1 See generally Abdullahi Ahmed An-Na'im, "Problems and Prospects of Universal Cultural Legitimacy for Human Rights," in *Human Rights in Africa: Cross-Cultural Perspectives*, ed. A. An-Na'im and F. Deng (Washington, DC: Brookings Institution, 1990), 331–67.

2 For the results of this questionnaire see UNESCO, *Human Rights: Comments and Interpretations* (London: Allan Wingate, 1949), Appendix I.

3 See, for example, Executive Board of the American Anthropological Association, "Statement on Human Rights," *American Anthropologist* 49 (1947): 539.

4 See, for example, Jack Donnelly, "Human Rights and Human Dignity: An Analytic Critique of Non-Western Conceptions of Human Rights," *American Political Science Review* 76 (1982): 303; Rhoda Howard and Jack Donnelly, "Human Dignity, Human Rights and Political Regimes," *American Political Science Review* 80 (1986): 801.

5 James W. Nickel, "Cultural Diversity and Human Rights," in *International Human Rights: Contemporary Issues*, ed. Jack L. Nelson and Vera M. Green (Stanfordville, NY: Human Rights Publishing Group, 1980), 43.

6 A. J. M. Milne, *Human Rights and Human Diversity: An Essay in the Philosophy of Human Rights* (Albany, NY: State University of New York Press, 1986).

7 Alison D. Renteln, "The Unanswered Challenge of Relativism and the Consequences for Human Rights," *Human Rights Quarterly* 7 (1985): 514–40; and "A Cross-Cultural Approach to Validating International Human Rights: The Case of Retribution Tied to Proportionality," in *Human Rights Theory and Measurements*, ed. D. L. Cingranelli (Basingstoke, Hampshire, and London: Macmillan, 1988), 7. See generally her recent book, *International Human Rights: Universalism versus Relativism* (Newbury Park, Calif., London, and New Delhi: Sage Publications, 1990).

8 See, for example, T. S. Eliot, *Notes toward the Definition of Culture* (London: Faber and Faber, 1948); Raymond Williams, *Keywords: A Vocabulary of Culture and Society* (New York: Oxford University Press, 1976), 76–82.

9 See generally, for example, A. L. Kroeber and C. Kluckhohn, eds., *Culture: A Critical Review of Concepts and Definitions* (New York: Vintage Books, 1963).

10 Roy Preiswerk, "The Place of Intercultural Relations in the Study of International Relations," *The Year Book of World Affairs* 32 (1978): 251.

11 Clifford Geertz, *Interpretation of Culture* (New York: Basic Books, 1973), 89.

12 I am grateful to Tore Lindholm for suggesting this useful analogy.

13 Melville J. Herskovits, *Cultural Dynamics* (New York: Knopf, 1964), 54.

14 See generally, Ruth Benedict, *Patterns of Culture* (Boston: Houghton Mifflin, 1959); Herskovits, *Cultural Dynamics*, chap. 4.

15 Melville Herskovits, *Man and his Works* (New York: Knopf, 1950), 76.

16 Elvin Hatch, *Culture and Morality: The Relativity of Values in Anthropology* (New York: Columbia University Press, 1983), 12.

17 I. C. Jarvie, "Rationalism and Relativism," *British Journal of Sociology* 34 (1983): 46.

18 Rhoda E. Howard and Jack Donnelly, "Introduction," in *International Handbook of Human Rights*, ed. R. E. Howard and J. Donnelly (Westport, Conn.: Greenwood Press, 1988), 20.

19 John Ladd, "The Poverty of Absolutism," *Acta Philosophica Fennica* (Helsinki) 34 (1982): 158, 161.

20   Clifford Geertz, "Distinguished Lecture: Anti Anti-Relativism," *American Anthropologist* 86 (1984): 265.

21   Ibid. 276.

22   Herskovits, *Cultural Dynamics*, 62.

23   Alison D. Renteln, "Relativism and the Search for Human Rights," *American Anthropologist* 90 (1988): 64.

24   I find Jack Donnelly's classification of radical relativism and universalism as extreme positions in a continuum, with varying mixes of (strong or weak) relativism and universalism in between, useful in this connection. While a radical (extreme) relativist would hold that culture is the sole source of validity of a moral right or rule, a radical universalist would hold that culture is irrelevant to the validity of moral rights or rules that are universally valid. See his article "Cultural Relativism and Universal Human Rights," *Human Rights Quarterly* 6 (1984): 400–1. He argues that "weak" cultural relativism is acceptable and even necessary for the implementation of human rights.
      For a critique of Donnelly's position see Renteln, "The Unanswered Challenge of Relativism," 529–31.

25   Edmund Burke as quoted in R. J. Vincent, "The Factor of Culture in the Global International Order," *Year Book of World Affairs* 34 (1980): 256.

26   Herskovits, *Cultural Dynamics*, 4, 6.

27   Ibid. 49–50.

28   In his Introduction to UNESCO, *Human Rights*, 10–11.

29   Article 5 of the Universal Declaration of Human Rights of 1948 and Article 7 of the International Covenant on Civil and Political Rights of 1966. The latter adds that "In particular, no one shall be subjected without his free consent to medical or scientific experimentation." For the texts of these instruments see *Basic Documents on Human Rights*, ed. Ian Brownlie, 2nd edn (Oxford: Clarendon Press, 1981), 21 and 128, respectively.

30   Article 1.2 of the Declaration on the Protection of All Persons from being Subjected to Torture and Other Cruel, Inhuman or Degrading Treatment or Punishment of 1975. United Nations General Assembly Resolution 3452 (XXX), 30 UN GAOR, Supp. (No. 34) 91, UN Doc. A/100 (1975).

31   Ibid., Article 1.1 and Article 1 of the Convention against Torture and Other Cruel, Inhuman or Degrading Treatment or Punishment. United Nations General Assembly Resolution 3946 (1984). This convention came into force in June 1987. For the text of the convention, see *International Commission of Jurists Review* 39 (1987): 51.
      It is interesting to note that whereas the 1975 Declaration requires such pain and suffering to be consistent with the United Nations Standard Minimum Rules for the Treatment of Prisoners, the 1984 Convention omitted this requirement. This was probably done in order to encourage countries that do not comply with the Minimum Rules for the Treatment of Prisoners to ratify the Convention.

32   M. J. Bossuyt, *Guide to the "Travaux Preparatoires" of the International Covenant on Civil and Political Rights* (Dordrecht: Martinus Nijhoff, 1987), 151. See the review of early work of the Drafting Committee, 1947–8, ibid. 147–9; and discussions at meetings of the Commission on Human Rights, 1949–52, ibid. 151–4.

33   UN Doc. E/CN.4/SR.312, 13.

34   Bossuyt, *Guide*, 155.

35   Ibid. 155–8. In its final version, the sentence ends with the word "experimentation," and does not include the phrase "involving risk."

36   The 5th and 6th Sessions of the Commission on Human Rights, 1949 and 1950. Ibid. 150.

37   Ibid. 151.

38   United Nations General Assembly Resolution 3469 (1979), cited in Amnesty International, *Human Rights: Selected International Standards* (London: Amnesty International Publications, 1985), 27.

39   By virtue of Article 1 of the Optional Protocol to the International Covenant of Civil and Political Rights of 1966, a State Party to the Covenant may recognize the competence of

the Human Rights Committee established under the Covenant to receive and consider communications from individuals subject to the state's jurisdiction who claim to be victims of a violation by that state. The protocol provides for the admissibility and processing of such communications, which may culminate in the communication of the committee's views to the state party concerned and to the individual and the inclusion of those views in the annual report of the committee. Thus this procedure may bring moral and political pressure to bear on a state which elected to ratify the Optional Protocol by publicizing its human rights violations, but it does not provide for direct enforcement.

For the text of the protocol *see* Brownlie, ed., *Basic Documents on Human Rights*, 146.

40   In the context of the Optional Protocol, the Human Rights Committee is restricted by its terms of reference to making specific findings on the case rather than stating general principles and guidelines. See CCPR/C/OP/1, *International Covenant on Civil and Political Rights: Human Rights Committee, Selected Decisions under the Optional Protocol (Second to Sixteenth Sessions)* (New York: United Nations, 1985), for examples of the sort of treatment which, according to the committee, constituted violations of Article 7 of the Covenant, see 40, 45, 49, 57, 72, 132, and 136. All the communications relating to Article 7 published in this report involve very similar situations in a single country, Uruguay, over a short period of time, between 1976 and 1980. It would have been more helpful if the report had covered a wider variety of situations from more countries.

41   UN Doc. A/3740, at 94–5 (1982).

42   On the sources and development of Shari'a see generally, Abdullahi A. An-Na'im, *Toward an Islamic Reformation: Civil Liberties, Human Rights and International Law* (Syracuse: Syracuse University Press, 1990), chap. 2.

43   For fuller explanations see, generally, ibid., chap. 5; Mohamed S. El-Awa, *Punishment in Islamic Law* (Indianapolis: American Trust Publications, 1982); Safia M. Safwat, "Offenses and Penalties in Islamic Law," *Islamic Quarterly* 26 (1982): 149.

44   An-Na'im, *Toward an Islamic Reformation*, 114–18, 131–3.

45   Rationality is also relative to the belief system or frame of reference. What may be accepted as rational to a believer may not be accepted as such by an unbeliever, and vice versa.

46   Mahmoud Mohamed Taha, *The Second Message of Islam*, trans. Abdullahi A. An-Na'im (Syracuse: Syracuse University Press, 1987), 74–5.

47   *Encyclopedia Judaica* (Jerusalem: Keter 1971), vol. 5, 142–7; vol. 6, 991–3.

5

Human Rights
and Capabilities

Amartya Sen

Introduction

The moral appeal of human rights has been used for varying purposes, from resisting torture and arbitrary incarceration to demanding the end of hunger and of medical neglect. There is hardly any country in the world – from China, South Africa and Egypt to Mexico, Britain and the United States – in which arguments involving human rights have not been raised in one context or another in contemporary political debates.

However, despite the tremendous appeal of the idea of human rights, it is also seen by many as being intellectually frail – lacking in foundation and perhaps even in coherence and cogency. The remarkable co-existence of stirring appeal and deep conceptual scepticism is not new. The American Declaration of Independence took it to be 'self-evident' that everyone is "endowed by their Creator with certain inalienable rights", and 13 years later, in 1789, the French declaration of 'the rights of man' asserted that "men are born and remain free and equal in rights". But it did not take Jeremy Bentham long to insist, in *Anarchical Fallacies*, written during 1791–2, that "natural rights is simple nonsense: natural and imprescriptible rights [an American phrase], rhetorical nonsense, nonsense upon stilts" (Bentham, 1792/1843, p. 501). That division remains very alive today, and there are many who see the idea of human rights as no more than "bawling upon paper" (to use another of Bentham's barbed descriptions).

The concepts of human rights and human capabilities have something of a common motivation, but they differ in many distinct ways. It is useful to ask whether considering the two concepts together – capabilities and human rights – can help the understanding of each. I will divide the exercise into four specific questions. First, can human rights be seen as entitlements to certain basic capabilities, and will this be a good way of thinking about human rights? Second, can the

Originally published in *Journal of Human Development*, 6: 2 (2005), 151–66.

capability perspective provide a comprehensive coverage of the content of human rights? Third, since human rights need specificity, does the use of the capability perspective for elucidating human rights require a full articulation of the list of capabilities? And finally, how can we go about ascertaining the content of human rights and of basic capabilities when our values are supposed to be quite divergent, especially across borders of nationality and community? Can we have anything like a universalist approach to these ideas, in a world where cultures differ and practical preoccupations are also diverse?

Human Rights as Entitlements to Capabilities

It is possible to argue that human rights are best seen as rights to certain specific freedoms, and that the correlate obligation to consider the associated duties must also be centred around what others can do to safeguard and expand these freedoms. Since capabilities can be seen, broadly, as freedoms of particular kinds, this would seem to establish a basic connection between the two categories of ideas.

We run, however, into an immediate difficulty here. I have argued elsewhere that 'opportunity' and 'process' are two aspects of freedom that require distinction, with the importance of each deserving specific acknowledgement.[1] While the opportunity aspect of freedoms would seem to belong to the same kind of territory as capabilities, it is not at all clear that the same can be said about the process aspect of freedom.

An example can bring out the *separate* (although not necessarily independent) relevance of both *substantive opportunities* and *freedom of processes*. Consider a woman, let us call her Natasha, who decides that she would like to go out in the evening. To take care of some considerations that are not central to the issues involved here (but which could make the discussion more complex), it is assumed that there are no particular safety risks involved in her going out, and that she has critically reflected on this decision and judged that going out would be the sensible – indeed the ideal – thing to do.

Now consider the threat of a violation of this freedom if some authoritarian guardians of society decide that she must not go out ('it is most unseemly'), and if they force her, in one way or another, to stay indoors. To see that there are two distinct issues involved in this one violation, consider an alternative case in which the authoritarian bosses decide that she must – absolutely *must* – go out ('you are expelled for the evening – just obey'). There is clearly a violation of freedom even here though Natasha is being forced to do exactly what she would have chosen to do anyway, and this is readily seen when we compare the two alternatives 'choosing freely to go out' and 'being forced to go out'. The latter involves an immediate violation of the *process aspect* of Natasha's freedom, since an action is being forced on her (even though it is an action she would have freely chosen also).

The opportunity aspect may also be affected, since a plausible accounting of opportunities can include having options and it can *inter alia* include valuing free choice. However, the violation of the opportunity aspect would be more substantial and manifest if she were not only forced to do something chosen by another, but in fact forced to do something she would not otherwise choose to do. The comparison between 'being forced to go out' (when she would have gone out anyway, if free) and, say, 'being forced to polish the shoes of others at home' (not her favourite way of spending time, I should explain) brings out this contrast, which is primarily one of the opportunity aspect, rather than the process aspect. In the incarceration of Natasha, we can see two different ways in which she is losing her freedom: first, she is being forced to do something, with no freedom of choice (a violation of her process freedom); and second, what Natasha is being obliged to do is not something she would choose to do, if she had any plausible alternative (a violation of her substantive opportunity to do what she would like to do).[2]

It is important to recognise that both processes and opportunities can figure powerfully in the content of human rights. A denial of 'due process' in being, say, sentenced without a proper trial can be an infringement of human rights (no matter what the outcome of the fair trial might be), and so can be the denial of opportunity of medical treatment, or the opportunity of living without the danger of being assaulted (going beyond the exact process through which these opportunities are made real).

The idea of 'capability' (i.e., the opportunity to achieve valuable combinations of human functionings – what a person is able to do or be) can be very helpful in understanding the opportunity aspect of freedom and human rights.[3] Indeed, even though the concept of opportunity is often invoked, it does require considerable elaboration, and capability can help in this elucidation. For example, seeing opportunity in terms of capability allows us to distinguish appropriately between (i) whether, a person is actually able to do things she would value *doing*, and (ii) whether she possesses the *means or instruments or permissions* to pursue what she would like to do (her actual ability to do that pursuing may depend on many contingent circumstances). By shifting attention, in particular, towards the former, the capability-based approach resists an overconcentration on means (such as incomes and primary goods) that can be found in some theories of justice (e.g. in the Rawlsian Difference Principle). The capability approach can help to identify the possibility that two persons can have very different substantial opportunities even when they have exactly the same set of means: for example, a disabled person can do far less than an able-bodied person can, with exactly the same income and other 'primary goods'. The disabled person cannot, thus, be judged to be equally advantaged – with the same opportunities – as the person without any physical handicap but with the same set of means or instruments (such as income and wealth and other primary goods and resources).

The capability perspective allows us to take into account the parametric variability in the relation between the means, on the one hand, and the actual opportunities, on the other.[4] Differences in the capability to function can arise even with the same set of personal means (such as primary goods) for a variety of reasons, such as: (1) *physical or mental heterogeneities among persons* (related, for example, to disability, or proneness to illness); (2) *variations in non-personal resources* (such as the nature of public health care, or societal cohesion and the helpfulness of the community); (3) *environmental diversities* (such as climatic conditions, or varying threats from epidemic diseases or from local crime); or (4) *different relative positions vis-à-vis others* (well illustrated by Adam Smith's discussion, in the *Wealth of Nations*, of the fact that the clothing and other resources one needs "to appear in public without shame" depends on what other people standardly wear, which in turn could be more expensive in rich societies than in poorer ones).

I should, however, note here that there has been some serious criticism of describing these substantive opportunities (such as the capability to live one kind of a life or another) as 'freedoms', and it has been argued that this makes the idea of freedom too inclusive. For example, in her illuminating and sympathetic critique of my *Development as Freedom*, Susan Okin has presented arguments to suggest that I tend "to overextend the concept of freedom".[5] She has argued: "It is hard to conceive of some human functionings, or the fulfilment of some needs and wants, such as good health and nourishment, as freedoms without stretching the term until it seems to refer to everything that is of central value to human beings" (Okin, 2003, p. 292).

There is, certainly, considerable scope for argument on how extensively the term freedom should be used. But the particular example considered in Okin's counter-argument reflects a misinterpretation. There is no suggestion whatever that a functioning (e.g. being in good health or being well nourished) should be seen as freedom of any kind, such as capability. Rather, capability concentrates on the *opportunity* to be able to have combinations of functionings (including, in this case, the opportunity to be well nourished), and the person is free to make use of this opportunity or not. A capability reflects the alternative combinations of functionings from which the person can choose one combination. It is, therefore, not being suggested at all that being well-nourished is to be seen as a freedom. The term freedom, in the form of capability, is used here to refer to the extent to which the person is free to choose particular levels of functionings (such as being well-nourished), and that is not the same thing as what the person actually decides to choose. During India's struggle for independence from the Raj, Mahatma Gandhi famously did not use that opportunity to be well fed when he chose to fast, as a protest against the policies of the Raj. In terms of the actual functioning of being well-nourished, the fasting Gandhi did not differ from a starving famine victim, but the freedoms and opportunities they respectively had were quite different.

Indeed, the *freedom to have* any particular thing can be substantially distinguished from actually *having* that thing. What a person is free to have – not just what he actually has – is relevant, I have argued, to a theory of justice.[6] A theory of rights also has reason to be involved with substantive freedoms.

Many of the terrible deprivations in the world have arisen from a lack of freedom to escape destitution. Even though indolence and inactivity had been classic themes in the old literature on poverty, people have starved and suffered because of a lack of alternative possibilities. It is the connection of poverty with unfreedom that led Marx to argue passionately for the need to replace "the domination of circumstances and chance over individuals by the domination of individuals over chance and circumstances".[7]

The importance of freedom can be brought out also by considering other types of issues that are also central to human rights. Consider the freedom of immigrants to retain their ancestral cultural customs and lifestyles. This complex subject cannot be adequately assessed without distinguishing between *doing* something and being *free* to do that thing. A strong argument can be constructed in favour of an immigrant's having the freedom to retain her ancestral lifestyle, but this must not be seen as an argument in favour of her pursuing that ancestral lifestyle whether she herself chooses that pursuit or not. The central issue, in this argument, is the person's freedom to choose how she should live – including the *opportunity* to pursue ancestral customs – and it cannot be turned into an argument for that person specifically pursuing those customs in particular, irrespective of the alternatives she has.[8] The importance of capability – reflecting opportunities – is central to this distinction.

The Process Aspect of Freedom and Information Pluralism

In the discussion so far I have been concentrating on what the capability perspective can do for a theory of justice or of human rights, but I would now like to turn to what it *cannot* do. While the idea of capability has considerable merit in the assessment of the opportunity aspect of freedom, it cannot possibly deal adequately with the process aspect of freedom, since capabilities are characteristics of individual advantages, and they fall short of telling us enough about the fairness or equity of the processes involved, or about the freedom of citizens to invoke and utilise procedures that are equitable.

The contrast of perspectives can be brought out with many different types of illustrations; let me choose a rather harsh example. It is, by now, fairly well established that, given symmetric care, women tend to live longer than men. If one were concerned only with capabilities (and nothing else), and in particular with equality of the capability to live long, it would have been possible to construct an argument for giving men more medical attention than women to counteract the natural masculine handicap. But giving women less medical attention than men for the same health problems would clearly violate an important requirement of process equity, and it seems reasonable to argue, in cases of this kind, that demands of equity in process freedom could sensibly override a single-minded concentration on the opportunity aspect of freedom (and on the requirements of capability equality in particular). While it is important to emphasise the relevance of the capability perspective in judging people's substantive opportunities (particularly in comparison with alternative approaches that focus on incomes, or primary goods, or resources), that point does not, in any way, go against seeing the relevance also of the process aspect of freedom in a theory of human rights – or, for that matter, in a theory of justice.

In this context, I should comment briefly also on a misinterpretation of the general relevance of the capability perspective in a theory of justice. A theory of justice – or more generally an adequate theory of normative social choice – has to be alive both to the fairness of the processes involved and to the equity and efficiency of the substantive opportunities that people can enjoy.[9] In dealing with the latter, capability can indeed provide a very helpful perspective, in comparison with, say, the Rawlsian concentration on 'primary goods'. But capability can hardly serve as the sole informational basis for the *other* considerations, related to processes, that must also be accommodated in normative social choice theory.

Consider the different components of Rawls's (1971) theory of justice. Rawls's 'first principle' of justice involves the priority of liberty, and the first part of the 'second principle' involves process fairness, through demanding that 'positions and offices be open to all'. The force and cogency of these Rawlsian concerns (underlying his first principle and the first part of the second principle) can neither be ignored nor be adequately addressed through relying only on the informational base of capabilities. We may not agree with Rawls's own way of dealing with these issues, but these issues have to be addressed, and they cannot be sensibly addressed within the substantive boundaries of capability accounting.

On the other hand, the capability perspective comes into its own in dealing with the *remainder* of the second principle; namely, 'the Difference Principle' – a principle that is particularly concerned with the distribution of advantages that different people enjoy (a consideration that Rawls tried to capture, I believe inadequately, within the confines of the accounting of 'primary goods'). The territory that Rawls reserved for primary goods, as used in his Difference Principle, would indeed, I argue, be better served by the capability perspective. That does not, however, obliterate in any way the relevance of the rest of the territory of justice (related to the first principle and the first part of the second principle), in which process considerations, including liberty and procedural equity, figure.

A similar plurality of informational base has to be invoked in dealing with the multiplicity of considerations that underlie a theory of human rights. Capabilities and the opportunity aspect of freedom, important as they are, have to be supplemented by considerations of fair processes and the lack of violation of people's right to invoke and utilise them.

Listing Capabilities

I turn now to the controversial question of the listing of capabilities. In its application, the capability approach allows considerable variations in application. Martha Nussbaum has discussed powerfully the advantages of identifying an overarching 'list of capabilities', with given priorities. My own reluctance to join the search for such a canonical list arises partly from my difficulty in seeing how the exact lists and weights would be chosen without appropriate specification of the context of their use (which could vary), but also from a disinclination to accept any substantive diminution of the domain of public reasoning. The framework of capabilities helps, in my judgement, to clarify and illuminate the subject matter of public reasoning, which can involve epistemic issues (including claims of objective importance) as well as ethical and political ones. It cannot, I would argue, sensibly aim at displacing the need for continued public reasoning.

Indeed, I would submit that one of the uses of the capability perspective is to bring out the need for transparent valuational scrutiny of individual advantages and adversities, since the different *functionings* have to be assessed and weighted in relation to each other, and the opportunities of having different *combinations* of functionings also have to be evaluated.[10] The richness of the capability perspective broadly interpreted, thus, includes its insistence on the need for open valuational scrutiny for making social judgements, and in this sense it fits in well with the importance of public reasoning. This openness of transparent valuation contrasts with burying the evaluative exercise in some mechanical – and valuationally opaque – convention (e.g. by taking market-evaluated income to be the invariable standard of individual advantage, thereby giving implicit normative priority to institutionally determined market prices).

The problem is not with listing important capabilities, but with insisting on one pre-determined canonical list of capabilities, chosen by theorists without any general social discussion or public reasoning. To have such a fixed list, emanating entirely from pure theory, is to deny the possibility of fruitful public participation on what should be included and why.

I have, of course, discussed various lists of capabilities that would seem to demand attention in theories of justice and more generally in social assessment, such as the freedom to be well nourished, to live disease-free lives, to be able to move around, to be educated, to participate in public life, and so on. Indeed, right from my first writings on using the capability perspective (for example, the 1979 Tanner Lecture

'Equality of what?'; Sen, 1980), I have tried to discuss the relevance of specific capabilities that are important in a particular exercise. The 1979 Tanner lecture went into the relevance of "the ability to move about" (I discussed why disabilities can be a central concern in a way that an income-centred approach may not be able to grasp), along with other basic capabilities, such as "the ability to meet one's nutritional requirements, the where-withal to be clothed and sheltered, the power to participate in the social life of the community". The contrast between lists of capabilities and commodities was a central concern in *Commodities and Capabilities* (Sen, 1985a). The relevance of many capabilities that are often neglected were discussed in my second set of Tanner Lectures, given at Cambridge University under the title *The Standard of Living* (Hawthorn, 1987).

My scepticism is about fixing a cemented list of capabilities that is seen as being absolutely complete (nothing could be added to it) and totally fixed (it could not respond to public reasoning and to the formation of social values). I am a great believer in theory, and certainly accept that a good theory of evaluation and assessment has to bring out the relevance of what we are free to do and free to be (the capabilities in general), as opposed to the material goods we have and the commodities we can command. But I must also argue that pure theory cannot 'freeze' a list of capabilities for all societies for all time to come, irrespective of what the citizens come to understand and value. That would be not only a denial of the reach of democracy, but also a misunderstanding of what pure theory can do, completely divorced from the particular social reality that any particular society faces.

Along with the exercise of listing the relevant capabilities, there is also the problem of determining the relative weights and importance of the different capabilities included in the relevant list. Even with a given list, the question of valuation cannot be avoided. There is sometimes a temptation not only to have one fixed list, but also to have the elements of the list ordered in a lexicographic way. But this can hardly work. For example, the ability to be well-nourished cannot in general be put invariably *above* or *below* the ability to be well-sheltered (with the implication that the tiniest improvement of the higher ranked capability will always count as more important than a large change in the lower ranked one). The judgement must take into account the extent to which the different abilities are being realised or violated. Also, the weighting must be contingent on circumstances. We may have to give priority to the ability to be well-nourished when people are dying of hunger in their homes, whereas the freedom to be sheltered may rightly receive more weight when people are in general well-fed, but lack shelter and protection from the elements.

Some of the basic capabilities (with which my 1979 Tanner Lecture was particularly concerned) will no doubt figure in every list of relevant capabilities in every society. But the exact list to be used will have to take note of the purpose of the exercise. There is often good sense in narrowing the coverage of capabilities for a specific purpose. Jean Drèze and I have tried to invoke such lists of elementary capabilities in dealing with 'hunger and public action', and in a different context, in dealing with India's economic and social achievements and failures (Drèze and Sen, 1989, 2002). I see Martha Nussbaum's powerful use of a given list of capabilities for some minimal rights against deprivation as being extremely useful, in the same practical way. For another practical purpose, we may need quite a different list.

For example, when my friend Mahbub ul Haq asked me, in 1989, to work with him on indicators of human development, and in particular to help develop a general index for global assessment and critique, it was clear to me that we were involved in a particular exercise of specific relevance. So the 'Human Development Index' was based on a very minimal listing of capabilities, with a particular focus on getting at a minimally basic quality of life, calculable from available statistics, in a way that the Gross National Product or Gross Domestic Product failed to capture (United Nations Development Programme, 1990). Lists of capabilities have to be used for various purposes, and so long as we understand what we are doing (and, in particular, that we are getting a list for a particular reason, related to assessment, evaluation, or critique), we do not put ourselves against other lists that may be relevant or useful for other purposes.

All this has to be contrasted with insisting on one 'final list of capabilities that matter'. To decide that some capability will not figure in the list of relevant capabilities at all amounts to putting a zero weight on that capability for every exercise, no matter what the exercise is concerned with, and no matter what the social conditions are. This could be very dogmatic, for many distinct reasons.

First, we use capabilities for different purposes. What we focus on cannot be independent of what we are doing and why (e.g. whether we are evaluating poverty, specifying certain basic human rights, getting a rough and ready measure of human development, and so on).

Second, social conditions and the priorities that they suggest may vary. For example, given the nature of poverty in India as well as the nature of available technology, it was not unreasonable in 1947 (when India became independent) to concentrate on elementary education, basic health, and so on, and to not worry too much about whether everyone can effectively communicate across the country and beyond. However, with the development of the internet and its wide-ranging applications, and the advance made in information technology (not least in India), access to the web and the freedom of general communication has become a very important capability that is of interest and relevance to all Indians.

Third, even with given social conditions, public discussion and reasoning can lead to a better understanding of the role, reach and the significance of particular capabilities. For example, one of the many contributions of feminist economics has precisely been to bring out the importance of certain freedoms that were not recognised very clearly – or at all – earlier on; for example, freedom from the imposition of fixed and time-honoured family roles, or immunity from implicit derogation through the rhetoric of social communication.

To insist on a 'fixed forever' list of capabilities would deny the possibility of progress in social understanding, and also go against the productive role of public discussion, social agitation, and open debates. I have nothing against the listing of capabilities (and take part in that activity often enough), but I have to stand up against any proposal of a grand mausoleum to one fixed and final list of capabilities.

Public Reasoning, Cultural Diversity and Universality

I turn now to the final question. If the listing of capabilities must be subject to the test of public reasoning, how can we proceed in a world of differing values and disparate cultures? How can we judge the acceptability of claims to human rights and to relevant capabilities, and assess the challenges they may face? How would such a disputation – or a defence – proceed? I would argue that, like the assessment of other ethical claims, there must be some test of open and informed scrutiny, and it is to such a scrutiny that we have to look in order to proceed to a disavowal or an affirmation. The status that these ethical claims have must be ultimately dependent on their survivability in unobstructed discussion. In this sense, the viability of human rights is linked with what John Rawls has called 'public reasoning' and its role in 'ethical objectivity'.[11]

Indeed, the role of public reasoning in the formulation and vindication of human rights is extremely important to understand. Any general plausibility that these ethical claims – or their denials – have is, on this theory, dependent on their ability to survive and flourish when they encounter unobstructed discussion and scrutiny (along with adequately wide informational availability). The force of a claim for a human right would be seriously undermined if it were possible to show that they are unlikely to survive open public scrutiny. But contrary to a commonly offered reason for scepticism and rejection, the case for human rights cannot be discarded simply by pointing to the possibility that in politically and socially repressive regimes, which do not allow open public discussion, many of these human rights are not taken seriously at all.

Open critical scrutiny is essential for dismissal as well as for defence. The fact that monitoring of violations of human rights and the procedure of 'naming and shaming' can be so effective (at least, in putting the violators on the defensive) is some indication of the wide reach of public reasoning when information becomes available and ethical arguments are allowed rather than suppressed.

It is, however, important not to keep the domain of public reasoning confined to a given society only, especially in the case of human rights, in view of the inescapably universalist nature of these rights. This is in contrast with Rawls's inclination, particularly in his later works, to limit such public confrontation within the boundaries of each particular nation (or each 'people', as Rawls calls this regional collectivity), for determining what would be just, at least in domestic affairs.[12] We can demand, on the contrary, that the discussion has to include, even for domestic justice (if only to avoid parochial prejudices and to examine a broader range of counterarguments), views also from 'a certain distance'. The necessity of this was powerfully identified by Adam Smith:

> We can never survey our own sentiments and motives, we can never form any judgment concerning them; unless we remove ourselves, as it were, from our own natural station, and endeavour to view them as at a certain distance from us. But we can do this in no other way than by endeavouring to view them with the eyes of other people, or as other people are likely to view them.[13]

Questions are often raised about whether distant people can, in fact, provide useful scrutiny of local issues, given what are taken to be 'uncrossable' barriers of culture. One of Edmund Burke's criticisms of the French declaration of the 'rights of man' and its universalist spirit was concerned with disputing the acceptability of that notion in other cultures. Burke argued that "the liberties and the restrictions vary with times and circumstances, and admit of infinite modifications, that cannot be settled upon any abstract rule".[14] The belief that the universality that is meant to underlie the notion of human rights is profoundly mistaken has, for this reason, found expression in many other writings as well.

A belief in uncrossable barriers between the values of different cultures has surfaced and resurfaced repeatedly over the centuries, and they are forcefully articulated today. The claim of magnificent uniqueness – and often of superiority – has sometimes come from critics of 'Western values', varying from champions of regional ethics (well illustrated by the fuss in the 1990s about the peerless excellence of 'Asian values'), or religious or cultural separatists (with or without being accompanied by fundamentalism of one kind or another). Sometimes, however, the claim of uniqueness has come from Western particularists. A good example is Samuel Huntington's (1996) insistence that the "West was West long before it was modern", and his claim that "a sense of individualism and a tradition of individual rights and liberties" are "unique among civilized societies". Similarly, no less a historian of ideas than Gertrude Himmelfarb has argued that ideas of 'justice', 'right', 'reason' and 'love of humanity' are "predominantly, perhaps even uniquely, Western values" (1996, pp. 74–5).

I have discussed these diagnoses elsewhere (for example Sen, 1999). Contrary to cultural stereotypes, the histories of different countries in the world have shown considerable variations over time as well as between different groups within the same country. When, in the twelfth century, the Jewish philosopher Maimonedes had to flee an intolerant Europe and its Inquisitions to try to safeguard his human right to stick to his own religious beliefs and practice, he sought shelter in Emperor Saladin's Egypt (via Fez and Palestine), and found an honoured position in the court of this Muslim emperor. Several hundred years later, when, in Agra, the Moghal emperor of India, Akbar, was arguing – and legislating – on the government's duty to uphold the right to religious freedom of all citizens, the European Inquisitions were still going on, and Giordano Bruno was burnt at the stake in Rome, in 1600.

In his autobiography, *Long Walk to Freedom*, Nelson Mandela (1994, p. 21) describes how he learned about democracy and individual rights, as a young boy, by seeing the proceedings of the local meetings held in the regent's house in Mqhekezweni:

> Everyone who wanted to speak did so. It was democracy in its purest form. There may have been a hierarchy of importance among the speakers, but everyone was heard, chief and subject, warrior and medicine man, shopkeeper and farmer, landowner and laborer.

Not only are the differences on the subject of freedoms and rights that actually exist between different societies often much exaggerated, but also there is, typically, little note taken of substantial variations *within* each local culture – over time and even at a point of time (in particular, right now). What are taken to be 'foreign' criticisms often correspond to internal criticisms from non-mainstream groups.[15] If, say, Iranian dissidents are imprisoned by an authoritarian regime precisely because of their heterodoxy, any suggestion that they should be seen as 'ambassadors of Western values' rather than as 'Iranian dissidents' would only add serious insult to manifest injury. Being culturally non-partisan requires respecting the participation of people from any corner of the earth, which is not the same thing as accepting the prevailing priorities, especially among dominant groups in particular societies, when information is extremely restricted and discussions and disagreements are not permitted.

Scrutiny from a 'distance' may have something to offer in the assessment of practices as different from each other as the stoning of adulterous women in the Taliban's Afghanistan and the abounding use of capital punishment (sometimes with mass jubilation) in parts of the United States. This is the kind of issue that made Smith insist that "the eyes of the rest of mankind" must be invoked to understand whether "a punishment appears equitable".[16] Ultimately, the discipline of critical moral scrutiny requires, among other things, "endeavouring to view [our sentiments and beliefs] with the eyes of other people, or as other people are likely to view them" (*The Theory of Moral Sentiments*, III, 1, 2; in Smith, 1976, p. 110).

Intellectual interactions across the borders can be as important in rich societies as they are in poorer ones. The point to note here is not so much whether we are *allowed* to chat across borders and to make cross-boundary scrutiny, but that the discipline of critical assessment of moral sentiments – no matter how locally established they are – *requires* that we view our practices *inter alia* from a certain distance.

Both the understanding of human rights and of the adequacy of a list of basic capabilities, I would argue, are intimately linked with the reach of public discussion – between persons and across borders. The viability and universality of human rights and of an acceptable specification of capabilities are dependent on their ability to survive open critical scrutiny in public reasoning.

Conclusions

To conclude, the two concepts – human rights and capabilities – go well with each other, so long as we do not try to subsume either entirely within the other. There are many human rights for which the capability perspective has much to offer. However, human rights to important process freedoms cannot be adequately analysed within the capability approach.

Furthermore, both human rights and capabilities have to depend on the process of public reasoning, which neither can lose without serious impoverishment of its respective intellectual content. The methodology of public scrutiny draws on Rawlsian understanding of 'objectivity' in ethics, but the impartiality that is needed cannot be confined within the borders of a nation. We have to go much beyond Rawls for that reason, just as we also have to go beyond the enlightenment provided by his use of 'primary goods', and invoke, in that context, the more articulate framework of capabilities. The need for extension does not, of course, reduce our debt to John Rawls. Neither human rights nor capabilities would have been easy to understand without his pioneering departures.

NOTES

1 See Sen (2002a), particularly the Arrow Lectures ('Freedom and Social Choice') included there (essays 20–2).
2 An investigation of more complex features of the opportunity aspect and the process aspect of freedoms can be found in the Arrow Lectures ('Freedom and Social Choice') in Sen (2002a), essays 20–2.
3 On the concept of capability, see Sen (1980, 1985a, 1985b), Nussbaum and Sen (1993), and Nussbaum (2000). See also the related theories of substantial opportunities developed by Arneson (1989), Cohen (1989), and Roemer (1996), among other contributions.
4 The relevance of such parametric variability for a theory of justice is discussed in Sen (1990).
5 See Okin (2003, p. 293). On related issues see also Joshua Cohen (1994, especially pp. 278–80), and G. A. Cohen (1995, esp. pp. 120–5).
6 See Sen (1980, 1985a, 1985b). In contrast, G. A. Cohen has presented arguments in favour of focusing on achieved functionings – related to his concept of 'midfare' – rather than on capability (see Cohen, 1989, 1993).

7   See Marx (1845–6/1977, p. 190).
8   There is a substantial difference between: (1) valuing multiculturalism because of the way – and to the extent that – it enhances the freedoms of the people involved to choose to live as they would like (and have reason to like); and (2) valuing cultural diversity *per se*, which focuses on the descriptive characteristics of a social pattern, rather than on the freedoms of the people involved. The contrast receives investigation in the *Human Development Report 2004* (United Nations Development Programme, 2004).
9   On the plurality of concerns that include processes as well as opportunities, which is inescapably involved in normative social choice (including theories of justice), see Sen (1970, 1985b). Since I have often encountered the diagnosis that I propound a "capability-based theory of justice", I should make it clear that this could be true only in the very limited sense of naming something according to one *principal* part of it (comparable with, say, using England for Britain). It is only one part of the informational base of a theory of justice that the capability perspective can expect to fill.
10 I cannot emphasise adequately how important I believe it is to understand that the need for an explicit valuational exercise is an advantage, rather than a limitation, of the capability approach, because valuational decisions have to be explicitly discussed, rather than being derived from some mechanical formula that is used, without scrutiny and assessment. For arguments *against* my position on this issue, see Beitz (1986) and Williams (1987). My own position is more fully discussed in Sen (1999, 2004).
11 See Rawls (1971, 1993, especially pp. 110–13).
12 See particularly John Rawls (1999). See also Rawls's formulation of the original position in *Political Liberalism* (Rawls, 1993, p. 12): "I assume that the basic structure is that of a closed society: that is, we are to regard it as self-contained and as having no relations with other societies.... That a society is closed is a considerable abstraction, justified only because it enables us to focus on certain main questions free from distracting details."
13 See Smith (1759/1790, III, 1, 2), Smith (1976, p. 110). I have tried to discuss and extend the Smithian perspective on moral reasoning in Sen (2002b).
14 Quoted in Lukes (1997, p. 238).
15 On this see Nussbaum and Sen (1988).
16 Smith (1978/1982, p. 104).

REFERENCES

Arneson, R. (1989) 'Equality and Equal Opportunity for Welfare', *Philosophical Studies*, 56, pp. 77–93.
Beitz, C. (1986) 'Amartya Sen's resources, values and development', *Economics and Philosophy*, 2, pp. 282–90.
Bentham, J. (1792) *Anarchical Fallacies; Being an Examination of the Declaration of Rights Issued during the French Revolution* [Republished in J. Bowring (ed.) (1843), *The Works of Jeremy Bentham*, volume II, William Tait, Edinburgh].
Cohen, G. A. (1989) 'On the currency of egalitarian justice', *Ethics*, 99, pp. 906–44.
Cohen, G. A. (1993) 'Equality of what? On welfare, resources and capabilities', in M. Nussbaum and A. Sen (eds.), *The Quality of Life*, Clarendon Press, Oxford.
Cohen, G. A. (1995) 'Review: Amartya Sen's unequal world', *New Left Review*, January, pp. 117–29.
Cohen, J. (1994) 'Review of Sen's *Inequality Reexamined*', *Journal of Philosophy*, 92, pp. 275–88.
Drèze, J. and Sen, A. (1989) *Hunger and Public Action*, Clarendon Press, Oxford.
Drèze, J. and Sen, A. (2002) *India: Participation and Development*, Oxford University Press, Delhi.

Hawthorn, G. (ed.) (1987) *Amartya Sen et al., The Standard of Living*, Cambridge University Press, Cambridge.

Himmelfarb, G. (1996) 'The illusions of cosmopolitanism', in M. Nussbaum with respondents (ed.), *For Love of Country*, Beacon Press, Boston.

Huntington, S. (1996) *The Clash of Civilizations and the Remaking of World Order*, Simon and Schuster, New York.

Lukes, S. (1997) 'Five fables about human rights', in M. Ishay (ed.), *The Human Rights Reader*, Routledge, London.

Mandela, N. (1994) *Long Walk to Freedom*, Little, Brown & Co., Boston.

Marx, K. (1845–6) *The German Ideology*, with F. Engels [Republished in D. McLellan (ed.) (1977), *Karl Marx: Selected Writings*, Oxford University Press, Oxford].

Nussbaum, M. (2000) *Women and Human Development: The Capabilities Approach*, Cambridge University Press, Cambridge.

Nussbaum, M. and Sen, A. (1988) 'Internal criticism and Indian rationalist traditions', in M. Krausz (ed.), *Relativism: Interpretation and Confrontation*, University of Notre Dame Press, Notre Dame.

Nussbaum, M. and Sen, A. (eds.) (1993) *The Quality of Life*, Clarendon Press, Oxford.

Okin, S. (2003) 'Poverty, well-being and gender: what counts, who's heard?', *Philosophy and Public Affairs*, 31, pp. 280–316.

Rawls, J. (1971) *A Theory of Justice*, Harvard University Press, Cambridge, MA.

Rawls, J. (1993) *Political Liberalism*, Columbia University Press, New York.

Rawls, J. (1999) *The Law of Peoples*, Harvard University Press, Cambridge, MA.

Roemer, J. E. (1996) *Theories of Distributive Justice*, Harvard University Press, Cambridge, MA.

Sen, A. (1970) *Collective Choice and Social Welfare*, Holden-Day, San Francisco [Republished by North-Holland, Amsterdam].

Sen, A. (1980) 'Equality of what?', in S. McMurrin (ed.), *Tanner Lectures on Human Values*, volume I, Cambridge University Press, Cambridge.

Sen, A. (1985a) *Commodities and Capabilities*, North-Holland, Amsterdam.

Sen, A. (1985b) 'Well-being, agency and freedom: the Dewey Lectures 1984', *Journal of Philosophy*, 82, pp. 169–221.

Sen, A. (1985/1987) *The Standard of Living*, Tanner Lectures, Cambridge University Press, Cambridge.

Sen, A. (1990) 'Justice: means versus freedoms', *Philosophy and Public Affairs*, 19, pp. 111–21.

Sen, A. (1999) *Development as Freedom*, Knopf, New York; Oxford University Press, New York.

Sen, A. (2002a) *Rationality and Freedom*, Harvard University Press, Cambridge, MA.

Sen, A. (2002b) 'Open and closed impartiality', *Journal of Philosophy*, 99, pp. 445–69.

Sen, A. (2004) 'Elements of a theory of human rights', *Philosophy and Public Affairs*, 32(4), pp. 315–56.

Smith, A. (1759/1790/1976) *The Theory of Moral Sentiments*, revised edition 1790 [Republished by Clarendon Press, Oxford].

Smith, A. (1776/1979) *An Inquiry into the Nature and Causes of the Wealth of Nations*, Clarendon Press, Oxford [Reprinted by Liberty Press, 1981].

Smith, A. (1978/1982) in R. L. Meek, D. D. Raphael, and P. G. Stein (eds.), *Lectures on Jurisprudence*, Clarendon Press, Oxford [Reprinted by Liberty Press, Indianapolis].

United Nations Development Programme (1990) *Human Development Report 1990*, Oxford University Press, Oxford.

United Nations Development Programme (2004) *Human Development Report 2004*, Oxford University Press, Oxford.

Williams, B. (1987) 'The standard of living: interests and capabilities', in G. Hawthorn (ed.), *Amartya Sen et al., The Standard of Living*, Cambridge University Press, Cambridge.

Part II
Anthropology and Human Rights Activism

6

Declaration on Anthropology and Human Rights (1999)

Committee for Human Rights, American Anthropological Association

Adopted by the AAA membership June 1999

This Declaration on Anthropology and Human Rights defines the basis for the involvement of the American Anthropological Association, and, more generally, of the profession of Anthropology in human rights. Comments and queries from members regarding the Declaration's content are welcome.

Preamble

The capacity for culture is tantamount to the capacity for humanity. Culture is the precondition for the realization of this capacity by individuals, and in turn depends on the cooperative efforts of individuals for its creation and reproduction. Anthropology's cumulative knowledge of human cultures, and of human mental and physical capacities across all populations, types, and social groups, attests to the universality of the human capacity for culture. This knowledge entails an ethical commitment to the equal opportunity of all cultures, societies, and persons to realize this capacity in their cultural identities and social lives. However, the global environment is fraught with violence which is perpetrated by states and their representatives, corporations, and other actors. That violence limits the humanity of individuals and collectives.

Anthropology as a profession is committed to the promotion and protection of the right of people and peoples everywhere to the full realization of their humanity, which is to say their capacity for culture. When any culture or society denies or

Retrieved from www.aaanet.org/stmts/humanrts.htm, on August 29, 2007. American Anthropological Association.

permits the denial of such opportunity to any of its own members or others, the American Anthropological Association has an ethical responsibility to protest and oppose such deprivation. This implies starting from the base line of the Universal Declaration of Human Rights and associated implementing international legislation, but also expanding the definition of human rights to include areas not necessarily addressed by international law. These areas include collective as well as individual rights, cultural, social, and economic development, and a clean and safe environment.

Declaration on Anthropology and Human Rights

The American Anthropological Association has developed a Declaration that we believe has universal relevance:

> People and groups have a generic right to realize their capacity for culture, and to produce, reproduce and change the conditions and forms of their physical, personal and social existence, so long as such activities do not diminish the same capacities of others. Anthropology as an academic discipline studies the bases and the forms of human diversity and unity; anthropology as a practice seeks to apply this knowledge to the solution of human problems.
>
> As a professional organization of anthropologists, the AAA has long been, and should continue to be, concerned whenever human difference is made the basis for a denial of basic human rights, where "human" is understood in its full range of cultural, social, linguistic, psychological, and biological senses.

Thus, the AAA founds its approach on anthropological principles of respect for concrete human differences, both collective and individual, rather than the abstract legal uniformity of Western tradition. In practical terms, however, its working definition builds on the Universal Declaration of Human Rights (UDHR), the International Covenants on Civil and Political Rights, and on Social, Economic, and Cultural Rights, the Conventions on Torture, Genocide, and Elimination of All Forms of Discrimination Against Women, and other treaties which bring basic human rights within the parameters of international written and customary law and practice. The AAA definition thus reflects a commitment to human rights consistent with international principles but not limited by them. Human rights is not a static concept. Our understanding of human rights is constantly evolving as we come to know more about the human condition. It is therefore incumbent on anthropologists to be involved in the debate on enlarging our understanding of human rights on the basis of anthropological knowledge and research.

7

Anthropology, Human Rights, and Social Transformation

Ellen Messer

The twentieth century has witnessed the creation of more states in more places than ever before. In the process of state formation, the rights of individuals and groups have been severely curtailed.... During the next century, basic human rights probably will be generally agreed upon by the states, in many cases the very states that violate human rights. If anthropologists are to have any influence over the standards that are adopted, they must begin to raise the issues increasingly and in more visible arenas.

Jason Clay (1988a)

Anthropology has had no impact on human rights.

Ana-Magdalena Hurtado (1990)

Since the close of World War II the United Nations (UN) has been assembling declarations, legislation, and enforcement mechanisms to promote human rights. Both the ongoing efforts to establish a global community and to base membership on a universal but evolving standard of values constitute perhaps the greatest social transformation of this century and a process in which the leaders and societies of emerging industrializing nations have played no small part. Representatives of many different national and religious traditions have met together to promulgate human rights by consensus. They have affirmed that there must be some basic standard of human rights, although they have disagreed on what specific rights, or protections against violations, entail. Cultural values diverge around even the central question of who is counted as a human being. In view of such fundamental misunderstandings many question how universal standards can be promoted (see, e.g., Adegbite 1968,

Originally published in *Transforming Societies, Transforming Anthropology*, ed. Emilio F. Moran. Ann Arbor: University of Michigan Press, 1996, pp. 165–210.

for an example of Third World views; Clay 1988a, b, for a critical anthropological appraisal).

Both human rights activists and legal experts (e.g., Tomasevski 1989; Alston 1990a) and UN agencies charged with implementing human rights policies, such as the UN Economic, Social, and Cultural Organization (UNESCO), demand more information on pluralistic conceptualizations of "universal" human rights, in order to improve formulations, instruments, and reporting. As the UN expands to include Third World and newly independent states, the urgency grows to learn more about moral norms and civil standards of behavior in different cultural contexts, so that national, regional, community, and religious leaders can be brought into discussions of evolving human rights standards. Further investigation is needed of the contexts in which rules and standards are applied, especially which individuals are counted as full human beings or persons and who are outcasts and why. A principal limitation of the UN human rights documents and machinery has been their failure to penetrate below, or to look outside, the level of the state to identify human rights notions as well as sources of violation. The role for anthropologists in clarifying human rights would seem to be obvious.

Anthropologists and Human Rights

Why anthropologists seem to have been uninvolved in human rights

In view of anthropologists' contributions to formulating these human rights questions and answers, anthropologists should have been integrally involved and interested in human rights. Two reasons are often cited for their apparent uninvolvement: (1) the burden of cultural relativism (see, e.g., Downing and Kushner 1988); and (2) their greater interest in indigenous rights and the rights of collectivities over and against the rights of the individual specified in the original human rights concept and documents. Both are evident in the official statement of the American Anthropological Association (AAA) in 1947, which rejected the notion of (universal) human rights. This statement, with these sentiments, then contributed to the impression both inside and outside of anthropology that anthropologists have been uninterested in human rights (e.g., Downing and Kushner 1988a, b; Renteln 1988a, b). Another reason, cited by the editors of *Human Rights and Anthropology*, for anthropologists' disinterest in human rights (a view contradicted at least in part by the extensive bibliography of the volume) is the political sensitivity of doing fieldwork. Anthropologists reporting human rights abuses implicitly or explicitly question the political legitimacy of sovereign states and national notions of progress. In so doing, they imperil the continued fieldwork of anthropologists in particular political contexts and locations and their behind-the-scenes advocacy on behalf of the peoples they study.

Even with such constraints anthropologists still must explain why we have published so few comparative studies of human rights formulations or the ways different societies establish guidelines for conduct. How do concepts of "rights" and "obligations" translate into codes of behavior? Or how do notions of "personhood" and "human being" create categories of privileged or underprivileged, respectively protected or denied protection under law at multiple levels in plural societies? Anthropologists could be contributing to better international legislation and monitoring instruments (Downing and Kushner 1988) in a world that human rights legal experts recognize to be increasingly pluralistic and marked by the need to protect collective as well as individual rights (e.g., Crawford 1988; Alston 1990a).

Reciprocally, constraints of cultural relativism and national politics do not explain why anthropologists do not refer more to the human rights framework in theoretical or policy-oriented analyses of social transformation. And anthropologists are only beginning to draw on human rights rhetoric and instruments in their advocacy for particular economic, social, and cultural rights to land, to food, to health, and to self-determination. Anthropologists could be contributing to international formulations and reporting mechanisms that might help make such rights enforceable (see Zalaquett 1984). In this case constraints lie not only with anthropologists but also with the existing reporting mechanisms of the UN and nongovernment organizations (NGOs) that up until the present have preferred to deal mainly or exclusively with civil and political rights of individuals and not to incorporate socioeconomic, development, or indigenous rights into their reporting framework.

Where anthropologists have contributed or might contribute to human rights

Alternatively, the viewpoint that anthropologists have been uninterested in human rights may mask the considerable involvement of anthropologists, and adoption of anthropological principles, in the evolving human rights debate. Boas and Durkheim, along with the students they educated, demonstrated utmost concern over definitions of human beings, how sociocultural units defined individual and group identities, and the behaviors that followed from such classifications. Margaret Mead was centrally involved in the construction and signing of the 1948 Universal Declaration of Human Rights (Newman 1989). Individual anthropologists, both prior to and following the declaration, have been active in promoting the rights of indigenous peoples, the rights of workers, the rights of women, and the rights of other oppressed groups (e.g., Kuper 1982, 1986; Stavenhagen 1990).

As a discipline, anthropology continually has pressed for better cognizance and appreciation of the multiple human rights standards existing in different cultures and the utilization of these understandings to improve global conceptualizations and implementation (e.g., Schirmer, Renteln, and Weisberg 1988; UNESCO 1987). Promoting awareness of the value of cultural diversity as a prerequisite for the survival of the global community and the human species has been a separate but related human rights task (Lévi-Strauss 1952; Barnett 1988).

Anthropologists also have shaped human rights rhetoric and instruments as, drawing on cross-cultural studies, they question whether particular moral concepts or rights and obligations are universal or culturally relative and further explicate the dimensions of inequality by which states or groups exclude individuals or collectivities from human rights protections on the basis of race, language, or other cultural grouping. They also help formulate the special human rights protections needed by those groups that are especially vulnerable to abuses, such as indigenous peoples, migrants, refugees, women, children, and the elderly. They assist also in clarifying the rights to health, land, water, food, and freedom from all types of violence, including genocide, ethnocide, torture, and slavery (Schirmer, Renteln, and Weisberg 1988). In sum, the alternative viewpoint accepted here is: anthropologists have been very active in human rights but could be even more active.

In view of past activities this chapter considers additional areas in which anthropologists might contribute to human rights policy, planning, and implementation.

A first challenge is to formulate more precisely the concepts of "human" and "person," in order to raise awareness of the dynamics by which exclusion and violence prevail in situations of ethnic polarization. These anthropological understandings of human classification might well be used to predict and redress the political, economic, and sociocultural dimensions of human rights abuses.

A second concern is to promote the implementation of economic, social, and cultural rights, along with the so-called solidarity, people's, or third generation *collective* rights to development, clean environment, and peaceful existence, which emerged in discussions by Third World nations in the 1980s (see Crawford 1988).

A third issue is to explicate the linkages among institutions and values that tie together ideas and instruments of human rights at various social and institutional levels. Political philosophers (e.g., Falk 1980, 1988) tend to see human rights as growing out of either "statist" or "indigenous" frameworks, but these often prove mutually contradictory or at best incongruous. States legislate certain rights, such as the right to food through food security legislation, only to be contradicted at the local level, where regional officials may not implement policies fully or equitably or where indigenous norms may lead to neglect of certain social outcasts. Anthropologists offer frameworks and data to systematize discussions of how rights are conceptualized and obligations assumed or abrogated at different social levels or by different social institutions.

A fourth and overarching issue is to analyze the evolution of human rights rhetoric and institutions. Human rights constitutes the world's first universal ideology (see Weissbrodt 1988:1), but the words and concepts keep changing over time. How has the existence of a body of human rights literature contributed to formulations of human rights concepts and expressions at local, regional, religious, and national levels? How can human rights rhetoric be formulated so as to enable local people to voice common concerns? In sum, how can rhetoric be transformed into action? What is the process by which values, rights, and obligations are translated into action across social levels?

To place such transformations in context, I begin the discussion by tracing the development of human rights legislation historically, against a 1940s background of cultural relativism. I then proceed to consider notions of human being and personhood, as these are expressed in collective and individual rights and obligations. The final sections suggest the various ways in which anthropologists continue to be involved in human rights policy; in the formulation of plural cultural understandings relating to definitions of rights and definitions of human beings; and in the international efforts to secure certain rights, such as a universal right to freedom from hunger.

The United Nations and Human Rights

By human rights we refer here to the Universal Declaration of Human Rights (1948), the International Covenants on Civil and Political Rights, and on Economic Social, and Cultural Rights (1966), additional UN Conventions against all forms of discrimination (racist and cultural); protocols for protection of rights of the especially vulnerable migrant, refugee, and besieged populations; stated protections for the rights of indigenous, minority, or other culturally threatened groups; and attempts to formulate universal protections for women and children. We include the standards of human rights promoted through various UN agencies: the right to work and freedom of association (the International Labor Organization [ILO]), the right to culture (UNESCO), the right to health (World Health Organization [WHO]), and the right to freedom from hunger (Food and Agriculture Organization [FAO]; World Food Programme [WFP]), etc. Also included are a set of solidarity rights related to peace, socioeconomic security, and environment, which are implemented by additional legal instruments and agencies (Zalaquett 1984), and rights of indigenous peoples.

Drafting of a common set of human rights standards began in 1946, in the aftermath of World War II and the Holocaust. The Nuremberg trials in particular intensified a desire by Western philosophical and legal scholars to reaffirm concepts of natural rights and the rights of man and citizen, which had been legal beacons in the history of emancipation in Western parliamentary democracies (Zalaquett 1981). Representatives from the many non-Western or nondemocratic nations that were to become the United Nations accepted the initiative on human rights as an outgrowth of a universal tradition or an international set of standards to which they might contribute.

Three generations of rights

Professionals working in the human rights fields, principally scholars and activists in international law and political philosophy, have always seen themselves as creating a universal moral standard, a system of values, on which all can agree (Zalaquett 1981; UN 1988). As a result of plural contributions into international rights constructions, human rights notions and covenants generally are viewed as having evolved in three stages: (1) civil and political rights; (2) economic, social, and cultural rights; and (3) special human development issues relating to human rights. A fourth stage of indigenous rights is currently evolving.

The first set of rights sought to guarantee all human beings political freedom of expression, movement, and person. Civil and political rights drew on the liberal tradition of Western parliamentary democracies and the universal traditions of rights expressed in some fashion in all societies and governments. The second set of rights formulated guarantees to employment and fair working conditions, a standard of living that would ensure health, well-being, and social security, education, participation in the cultural life of the community, and the special rights of motherhood and childhood. These economic, social, and cultural rights drew on the distinct Marxist-socialist and welfare state conception of rights – namely, that citizens have rights in a state, rather than against it. Strictly speaking, socialist governments never accepted the notion of natural rights, although they signed the documents. They instead promoted the notion of economic, social, and cultural rights, the legal instruments for which the United States, among other nations, signed but never ratified (Alston 1990b).

The third generation of emerging rights addressed: (1) peace and disarmament; (2) protection of the environment and natural resources; (3) the search for a just economic order; and (4) freedom from extreme want. African national leaders who rejected the so-called universalism of civil-political rights as ethnocentrically Western (e.g., Zvogbo 1979; Legesse 1980)[1] interpreted these alternative rights (to development) as a logical corollary to political rights of self-determination, while international lawyers, promoting the human rights framework, pragmatically interpreted the formulation of such a third generation of rights to be a logical corollary of the diversity and dynamics of international law and society that is part of the UN human rights system (e.g., Alston 1990a). Notwithstanding some initial protest that such derivative rights compromise and gut the human rights concept (e.g., Donnelly 1984), this third generation of so-called solidarity rights has gradually received formalization in regional and finally international UN treaties. Moreover, the rhetoric of human rights has changed in recent years from clarifying how the three "generations" are conceptually distinct to orchestrating their harmonics (Mayor 1990). Indigenous rights constitute yet a fourth generation, which certifies people's and community rights alongside those of the individual. All these discussions of "what are rights?" and which rights take precedence in any society also raise serious discussion of who is included in the category "human" modifying the rights concept.

Human rights and human classification

Discussions over the derivation, legitimacy, or universality of human rights argue over whether there exists a universal concept of individual and natural man, or human beings as human beings apart from their social context. A twenty-year perspective on human rights in 1966 mentions that, ultimately, notions of human rights can be compared cross-culturally by evaluating what are the duties of the more fortunate to improve conditions of the underprivileged (Glean 1966; Raphael 1966). Of particular concern is how value systems affect who is counted as a person and, therefore, a beneficiary of legal rights and privileges. But there has been curiously little discussion specifically on issues of human classification within the societies (global, national, community) that must accept and implement those rights. Few discussants mention that the enlightened civil and political tradition of Western parliamentary democracies excluded initially at least women, slaves, and non-property-owning males as full members of the dominant society and that some of the most vocal proponents of human rights declarations were from South African nations, which excluded blacks, and Near Eastern nations, which excluded members of minority religious or ethnic groups from citizenship (Adegbite 1968). Throughout the history of human rights implementation national governments flagrantly abused human rights, although they had signed the treaties and covenants, and the institutions and nations that had agreed to protect human rights failed to intervene (e.g., Adegbite 1968; Kuper 1977, 1982; Jacobs 1984).

Beyond political expediency the reasons for such omissions can be found also in the international legal framework. International legal scholars did not deal with the thorny issue of how personhood and citizenry might be defined within nations. Instead, they formulated possible abuses against various classes of persons in the international arena and left internal human classification issues (at least initially) to national governments. Human rights formulations drew on three traditions in international law: the abolition of slavery;[2] humanitarian law, specifically, how to protect the human rights of prisoners and noncombatants held captive in war zones;[3] and statutes on the Protection of Minorities.[4] Provisions against genocide and the violation of cultural rights and for protection of migrants and refugees that dealt with the rights of those who might be abused as nonpersons within the statist framework constituted additional innovative legislation by separate commissions. Codes singled out Gypsies, ethnic Slavs, females, and minors for protection and suggest how, by international mandate, the UN was trying to create the terms for social inclusion. Demands for minority rights eventually coalesced into demands for solidarity rights, cultural rights, and indigenous rights. Separate legislation has also promoted the rights of women, children, and the elderly. But these international compromises have been worked out in contexts of considerable debate, disagreement, and strife – and there are few mechanisms for enforcement beyond moral persuasion, sanctions, or embarrassment.

In sum, questions of personhood have been dealt with as conventions or statements of specialized commissions or agencies – i.e., as additions – to what might be termed the nature and content of the universal human rights framework. Debates centered on the character and legitimacy of these rights in relation to the first-generation political and civil rights but they eschewed discussions of personhood that might have suggested that certain individuals or collectivities were denied rights because they were not classified as full human beings. In the aftermath of the Holocaust the victorious states desired to enshrine human rights in a legal framework. Legal experts found the anthropological discourse about social exclusion from rights based on particular cultural frameworks of human classification counterproductive. In their view, if a right is human, then it must be universally applicable; if only the privileged enjoy the right, then one is talking more about elite entitlements than human rights, and the concept is destroyed.

The American Anthropological Association was invited to contribute a professional perspective on universal rights. Philosophers were sponsored to deliberate on the same topic. Both concluded that notions of human rights might not be universal and certainly were not to be entrusted exclusively to state government authority (Maritain 1943) if universal adherence to human rights was the goal. But the international human rights commissions rejected both the anthropological and the philosophical framework (on jurisdictional grounds) as inimical to their desired goal: of lawyers drafting a universalistic framework and diplomats debating it. As a result, the relevance of the anthropological discourse on cultural relativism for human rights formulation, implementation, and monitoring was never carefully explored.

Anthropologists, Human Rights, and the United Nations

The 1940s context of cultural relativism

Early in its deliberations the Human Rights Commission(s) formulating the Universal Declaration solicited inputs by anthropologists. They perhaps were looking for answers to questions such as: (1) whether or not other cultures have a concept of human rights and if these might resemble that of the proposed Universal Declaration (and proposed covenants), or (2) whether the values of elites who were to ratify the human rights declarations and covenants correspond to the traditional value systems in the countries they represent and what implications these might have for global comprehension and compliance.[5] American cultural anthropologists, still heavily immersed in cultural relativism, consistently recognized that all societies have some basis for evaluating and enforcing what may be deemed correct or permissible behavior. Moreover, both individuals and societies refer to some superhuman or legal authority (national constitution or international treaty) as the basis for behavioral norms. But, rather than respond to these questions, and thus contribute from the perspective of cultural relativism to the activities of formulating rights, the AAA officially opposed the enterprise.

The official AAA statement insisted that rights are culturally relative and issued a statement of advocacy for the rights and autonomy of indigenous peoples, in opposition to any universal formulations. Foreseeing the violation of tribal peoples, the AAA Executive Board, in its Report of the AAA for the year ending 1944, expressed "the hope that in the settlement of this present world war the rights of so-called primitive peoples to their way of life and the possession of property be respected." Specifically, the AAA Executive Board, in a "Statement on Human Rights" drafted by Melville Herskovits in 1947, went on record against formulations of universals in human rights. The statement made three major points: (1) it demanded respect for cultural differences along with individual differences; (2) it validated this position by insisting that there had not yet been discovered a technique for *qualitatively* evaluating cultural differences; and (3) it emphasized that "standards and values are relative to the culture from which they derive" (AAA 1947:539–43). This position effectively ruled out any accord of the AAA with the commission drafting a Universal Declaration. Thus, the UN Universal Declaration was constructed against a background of official, although controversial, AAA opposition.

As its critics were quick to point out, however, this position is indefensible both emotionally and intellectually. Anthropologists who advocated tolerance for all cultural values tend to be intolerant of cultural norms of intolerance, and if they are intolerant of intolerance, then the position is a sham. This paradox had already appeared in Boas and was replicated in Herskovits. Additionally, it can be (and was) argued that there are social, technical, and biological measures of culture and human well-being, even if one rejects moral valuations.

Curiously, the defensible elements of the document that had implications for human rights formulation and implementation were neither debated nor elaborated. The statement notes that all human beings biologically are *human* beings and deserve basic human rights. This same message had already been delivered in a more elaborate and eloquent form by American physical anthropologists as their contribution to the UN position papers on race. But there appears to have been no communication between physical and cultural anthropologists about their respective documents nor emphasis that this is a central lesson and principle that anthropology has to offer the public. The document also stresses a hard core of *similarities* among cultures that consistently has been overlooked (ibid., 541). Anthropologists might have pursued the question of how a particular "universal" right is developed in other cultures and how a particular cultural formulation of a right relates to any universal. But it was many years before anthropologists pursued these questions systematically (see, e.g., Renteln 1988a; Na'im 1992).

As a corollary, the statement asserts "the aims that guide the life of every people are self-evident in their significance to that people." But the statement and subsequent discussions never looked beyond the status quo into the historical contexts in which distinctive cultural notions of human rights were developed – or the contexts in which they might change. In their debates over universals vs. cultural relativism, anthropologists never questioned what happens to those goals, the corresponding norms, and behaviors as the human ecology or human relations to the political environment change. Customs such as infanticide, underfeeding of children and women, and abandonment of the elderly, which cultural relativists sought to rationalize and nonrelativists sought to condemn, might cease to be of self-evident utility under conditions of improved health and food resources. The goals the Universal Declaration and the accompanying human rights treaties assumed, or aimed to bring about, were conditions of plenty, or at least adequacy, in which hard choices of who should eat and who must die would be unnecessary. Even in Herskovits' terms, one could argue that, if conditions could be changed to increase access to resources, some of the "less benevolent" practices of particular cultures might be abandoned. But Herskovits and other anthropologists *who were asked*[6] forewent such possible discussion. Herskovits remained firm in his support of cultural difference, insisting that all cultures are "selective" and rely on internal forces of cultural change in changed cultural contexts to bring about a more benevolent way of life (1951:30).[7]

Finally, while the anthropologists' Statement on Human Rights deplored the attempt to provide a qualitative moral or legal standard for evaluating cultures, it did not rule out a quantitative standard for evaluating the consequences of culture – i.e., the consequences of living a culture pattern can be measured (evaluated) by nutrition, health, homicide or violence rates or profiles, or other objective criteria. Such evaluations are different from statements of preference, application, or advocacy of any particular standard as good or adequate for judging culture (see Barnett 1948). Subsequent contributions by anthropologists (e.g., Mead 1950; see Messer 1993) explored these directions.

Subsequent contributions to Human Rights Commissions

After experiencing rejection, anthropologists (and philosophers) largely abandoned the philosophical and legal discussion within the Human Rights Commission, even as they continued to advocate political, economic, and cultural rights for indigenous groups, for minorities, and for other oppressed groups, whose needs for protection evolved along with the emergence of states. Under the sponsorship of UNESCO they contributed to cross-cultural discussions of rights (see *Human Rights Teaching*). They also participated in human rights debates as part of their crusade (sometimes shared with philosophers) against the common "enemy" of modernization and their defense of "the victims of progress" (e.g., Bodley 1975). Additionally, anthropologists worked within UN commissions on special aspects of human rights, such as genocide and apartheid. They spearheaded efforts to understand the etiology of intergroup hostilities that result in such atrocities for the purpose of preventing them (e.g., Kuper 1977, 1982, 1986). Additionally, they have continued to be involved in efforts to achieve human rights for indigenous peoples and for traditional communities more generally (Stavenhagen 1990; Messer 1993).

Anthropologists have also contributed to UN efforts to conceptualize the conditions under which women, children, the elderly, and "involuntary migrants" might enjoy human rights. These as well as all of the human rights issues mentioned previously are related to the issue of human classification and cultural classification and to fundamental socio-cultural questions of notions of persons, rights, and obligations.

Human Classification

Both social and cultural anthropology provide conceptual frameworks to structure human rights understandings, especially cultural privileges of inclusion and exclusion. Inequality, definitions of ingroup (or outgroup), ethnic conflict, and genocide are all topical areas explored by anthropologists that have implications for predicting and modifying human rights behaviors. They also provide arenas for exploring the relevance of anthropological concepts and methods to human rights policies and protections.

Human beings or persons have rights to demand and expect certain behaviors from others who share their common moral community. Each constitutes a bio-logical or sociocultural category, which can be analyzed from both native and observers' points of view. Human rights activists assume a universal definition of *human being* deserving universal rights on the basis of a shared "humanity." But in most cultures, including those informing Western human rights doctrine, not all individuals are considered to be complete members of humankind or full social persons. Those considered by some criteria to be defective, or not to have the full set of characteristics, include in certain cultural contexts: (1) women; (2) children; (3) the disabled, the ill, and the elderly; and (4) those with "other" physical, linguistic, cultural, or behavioral characteristics.[8] In addition, strangers of different genealogical, geographic, linguistic, or cultural background may be denied full social personhood and civil rights.

Such classifications of groups or individuals as not fully human remains a chief excuse for human rights abuses. American, British, and French anthropological studies offer insights on customs and behaviors of inclusion versus exclusion that follow from such classifications; principles extend as well to relationships of com-munities to states and of states within the world order. In examining "the dilemma of cultural diversity and equivalency in universal human rights standards," Schirmer (1988), for example, evokes the truism that classification of individuals as "other" or nonhuman allows violence and killing of otherwise fellow humans at any socio-political level. The other, to cite some particular contexts, may be an unnamed Eskimo child, not yet human according to their classification, who is allowed to die from neglect; a victim caught by Borneo headhunters, who consider those outside their boundaries to be nonhuman and fair game for attack; or indigenous peoples and poor *ladinos*, denied personhood by Guatemalan military leaders, landowners, or industrialists, who thereby justify denying them basic rights. War-time provides another special context in which it has proven easy to slip into dehumanizing the other – and into human rights abuses – as did Americans during the Vietnam War (Polgar 1968).

Beyond describing dehumanization and its consequences, anthropologists offer at least three conceptual frameworks for describing the dynamics and, in certain cases, preventing or remedying the resulting human rights abuses: the ingroup–outgroup distinction, pluralism and ethnicity, and genocide.

Ingroup–outgroup

Boas provides our first (dual) legacy on human classification and its consequences through a comparative study of peoples, classified on the basis of race, language, and culture, and a cross-cultural study of what he found to be universal tendencies to classify humans as of one's own group or others and human tendencies to include or exclude in one's own cultural terms.

> Among many primitive people, the only individuals dignified by the term human beings are the members of the tribe. It even happens in some cases that the language will designate only tribal members as "he" or "she," while all foreigners are "it" like animals. (1943:161)

Although all groups have certain standards – such as prohibitions against lying, theft, and murder – Boas noted that these standards seemed not to be applied to those outside of one's own social unit:

The one outstanding fact is that every human society has two distinct ethical standards, the one for the in-group, the other for the outgroup. Everybody has close associations with some group, however constituted, and as such has certain duties to other members of the group.... We do not observe any progress in the standards of human society. We only recognize a softening of the hostility between the conflicting groups, at least in times of peace. (1939:22)

Simply put, moral law was obligatory when acting toward members of one's own community; the same obligation did not extend to those of other communities. Moreover, Boas encountered among technologically and historically diverse groups what seemed to be a universal human tendency to classify ingroup versus outgroup, from which followed the practice not to make human rights of the ingroup extend to the outgroup.

While seeking to describe the diversity in human races, languages, and cultures, Boas tried to learn also how people acquire negative stereotypes of other groups. He attempted to discern how people acquire the notion that only the members of one's own tribe are fully human and that others are not automatic recipients of the same rights accorded to fellow kin, community, or nation. All of this work carries with it a critique of "progress," as such human tendencies to discriminate appeared in technologically advanced as well as in primitive societies. Another dimension that he might have probed, but did not, was the role competition over political or economic resources played in generating intergroup hostilities and dehumanization. Instead, he focused on cultural criteria and, on the basis of American data, demonstrated that the tendency to preserve the purity of the group through discrimination against out-siders was not biological in origin and was therefore preventable, if not reversible. In the new socioeconomic environment of America immigrant national "types" tended to assimilate.

Boas therefore was also sure that discrimination could be eliminated and focused on education and assimilation as possible remedies. Youth, early on in life, would have to be indoctrinated by outstanding individuals in their own culture to be citizens of the world rather than of their more insular and particular cultures. But on the basis of recent historical observations, and his recognition that everyone must first be taught to be a member of some particular culture, he despaired of this ever occurring (Messer 1986). He also proposed assimilation by intermarriage as a way to eliminate physical and behavioral indicators of difference.

Many fellow anthropologists even at that time disagreed with his assimilationist position. Voices for cultural relativism recognized that "every society has values and imposes restraints" but remained silent on Boas's observation that ingroups treat members of outgroups by different rules. Cultural relativism stressed universal values such as "right...justice...and beauty" variously interpreted. Proponents agreed that objective indices of cultural inferiority or superiority cannot be established (Herskovits 1951:22), but did not rule out quantitative or qualitative measures of violence (Williams 1947). They hoped "by starting from relativism and its toleration...to work out a new set of absolute values and standards, if such are attainable at all or prove to be desirable" (Kroeber 1949:320). And even Boas argued that indigenous populations and cultures should be preserved. What the Boasian legacy provides for the human rights discourse, then, is a direction for investigating where abuses are likely to occur through an analysis of ingroup–outgroup distinctions in particular cultures and a positive directive to use human rights teaching as an approach to minimizing outgroup stigmatization.

Ethnicity and pluralism

Alternatively, anthropologists study human classification, personhood, rights, and obligations within a framework of ethnicity and cultural pluralism. This framework examines interethnic dynamics, the circumstances under which states emerge, and persistent ethnic hostilities within states (see, e.g., Guideri, Pellizzi, and Tambiah 1988). Key issues within this vast literature are the dynamism, flexibility, and resilience of ethnic identity in pluralistic state contexts that may also involve regional organizations, intergovernmental organizations, and NGOs. Ethnic dimensions of human rights and Third World state policies can be studied by region, religion, and also gender (see Messer 1993).

The circumstances under which an ethnic group or state assimilates rather than distances or violates strangers constitute a special case for understanding human rights and social obligations. Colson (1970), monitoring the absorption of immigrants into Zambian Tongan society over several decades, raises the general question of "what factors encourage people to deal with aliens as potential recruits to their own order rather than as representatives of opposing interests or bearers of a unique and different heritage who must receive special status." She concludes that absorption rather than marginalization or rejection of aliens seems to depend on the political structure, especially the presence of state authority. States tend to define different status groups based on different modes of livelihood; accordingly, component groups tend to maintain and emphasize differences. Nonstate societies, "those lacking differentiated authority systems," by contrast, "show a homogeneity which belies the actual history of their recruitment"; they tend to assimilate strangers and to de-emphasize differences. Prior to the penetration of the Zambian state Tongans usually tried to recruit aliens into their social organization via patron–client relations, quasi-kinship modes, and personal relations that did not treat others as foreigners. In the face of state authority, by contrast, Tongans more and more tend to view themselves as one ethnic identity in opposition to others. They also tend to see foreigners as agents of alien communities who do not come to merge and contribute but, rather, maintain their distinctiveness and deprive locals of resources.

Such social transformations constitute part of the larger process by which states or their surrogates (multinational corporations, intergovernmental organizations, or nongovernmental organizations) engender interethnic conflict and violence and interfere with the absorption or tolerance of involuntary migrants by host groups. Understanding these intergroup-state dynamics provides a framework for anticipating abridgments of human rights norms (and legislation) by *ethnic* communities and peoples within states.

Violence and genocide

Combining Boas's concerns with their investigations of interethnic violence, anthropologists have focused also on human classification and genocide, or on who can be attacked with impunity because they are not of one's group and therefore not worthy of full moral consideration. Kapferer (1988), in a carefully documented account of ethnic violence in Sri Lanka, demonstrated how violence by the state, Buddhist monks, and ordinary citizens against those they identified as ethnically different was rationalized and built on a nationalist Sinhalese myth. Ethnic Tamils, perceived as threatening to the Sinhalese Buddhist state order, were classified as evil, outside of that order, and expungeable. State, monk, and citizen condoned their violence against Tamils with reference to a founding myth. In this myth Dutugenmunu, "a righteous Buddhist king" suffering over the knowledge that he has sent millions to slaughter in the process of founding and defending the Buddhist Sinhalese state, is comforted by Buddhist monks, who declare, "'only one and a half human beings had been slain.... One had come into the [three] refuges, and the other had taken on himself the five precepts.'... All the others are stated to be 'not more esteemed than beasts' as they are not Buddhists" (1988:69–70). Kapferer captures the sense of violence, domination, and exclusion that characterizes Buddhist epic traditions relating to state culture and does not necessarily offer a very hopeful outlook.[9]

Genocide more generally falls within this pattern of excluding the other from human status by mythic or other rationalization and then killing, massacring, enslaving, raping, annihilating by scorched earth, arbitrary imprisonment, or any other treatment prohibited against citizens (Fein 1984:5; cited in Doughty 1988). These behaviors create a self-fulfilling proposition; they literally dehumanize their victims and leave them without the protections of a common humanity. By conforming to forced inhuman conditions, the others, such as black Africans in South Africa, materialize white notions and actions of inhumanity; analogously, Jews, bestialized in Nazi concentration camps, became living testimony to German brutality that systematically aimed to destroy their human spirits as well as bodies. Analysts of genocide, as well as lesser forms of discrimination, argue that dehumanization is commonly part of the dominant group's strategy to separate, segregate, socially isolate, and deny others membership in the wider community.

As in less severe forms of interethnic violence, the anthropological approach has been to spotlight ethnic rivalries and try to negotiate peaceful solutions before full-fledged conflict erupts. Unfortunately, since rivalries tend to be predicated not only on some mythic or symbolic past but also on competition for resources, prevention of human rights abuses usually entails well-reasoned cultural analyses as well as some transformation in political-economic structure and underlying conditions.

Policy implications of anthropological studies of human classification

Inequality, ingroup–outgroup discrimination, and ethnic conflict all restrict definitions of who is counted human, but definitions of rights and persons are not static. They expand or contract under different circumstances. A developing role for anthropologists is to analyze the structural determinants of discrimination and human rights violations and also to identify and encourage the contexts that favor the expansion of human rights protections or a widening notion of human community. The foregoing sections suggest at least four approaches to research and related policy action.

The first is that of Boas, who studied the plasticity of human "types" and favored public policies that would remove differences via biological and cultural assimilation. He relied on education to create national "citizens of the world" and teach antidiscrimination. He also advanced research to demonstrate the physical and behavioral plasticity of human types. Put together, they were aimed to reduce prejudice and discrimination, at least among educated persons.

Evolutionary studies in anthropology suggest a second approach, which is to characterize the circumstances under which independent sociocultural groups are merged (assimilated, co-opted, coerced, or contracted) into a more integral social order, based on religious, political, or economic criteria (e.g., Johnson and Earle 1986). Such studies tend to emphasize as prime movers population growth and technoeconomic factors over political or cultural ones. They use these factors to account for the emergence of states and new national or international social orders, but they hardly describe the dynamics and resilience of ethnic identity or interethnic hostilities that continually threaten the stability of states. Nor do they offer plans of action for prevention or alleviation of ethnic tensions.

A third, and complementary, evolutionary approach is to study processes of interethnic and political-economic relations in relation to the emergence of states (see, e.g., Watts 1983; Guideri, Pellizzi, and Tambiah 1988). Such works again offer theoretical and practical insights but no plan of action to resolve abuses. In his overview of a collection of essays on interethnic relations and states, for example, Tambiah suggests that major transformations in political, economic, religious, and communications relations are all involved in the social transformations from kinship, caste, and local group loyalties to national and transnational (panhuman) identities. All contributed to the opening up of parochial to more inclusive social identities in particular historical periods. A case in point is the Western European nation-state, which involved subjugation by the emergent state government of more petty component identities, the expansion of capitalism and international trade, the rise of mass communication via the printing press, and the decline of power in the Catholic Church. Tambiah (1988) cautions that we probably should not anticipate that Third World nations will follow the same paths to democracy and secular humanism as did medieval to modern European states and their derivatives. These Third World societies, particularly those that are Islamic or Buddhist, are based on very different traditions that link people to land. Nevertheless, he suggests that any widening of rights and greater inclusiveness in the human community likely awaits similarly great social transformations.

A fourth approach is to learn from and apply previous experience through careful historical analysis of ethnic violence. Kuper (1977, 1982, 1986) provides probably our best example of how an anthropologist who studies human classification can translate analytical and academic research into policy. Drawing on studies of ethnic violence in Rwanda, Burundi, Zanzibar, and Algeria, Kuper analyzes how the process of ethnic polarization occurs and what opportunities potentially exist to transform oppressive social systems without violence. In points that correspond inversely to Tambiah's prerequisites for a more inclusive social order, Kuper notes in each instance how denials of economic structural transformations, political participation, and more open educational opportunities, plus the destruction of a "middle ground" of less polarized leadership, prevented advancement by deprived groups, which then pressed political-economic and sociocultural cleavages toward rupture. He suggests three measures of prevention, albeit none of them cures. One is for outside interventionists to manipulate political-economic ties to create or maintain a middle ground and a social fabric of greater complexity. This middle ground would render it less likely that the social simplification that accompanies the exaggeration of ethnic cleavages could occur. A second is for outside aid to be tied to improving the lots of deprived groups. A third and final dimension is to rely on interventions from outside the society (in political terms, the UN; in indigenous terms, God or religious authority) to end certain cycles of violence and human rights abuses. He exhorts UN agencies to ensure more equitable participation in plural societies and not to miss opportunities to prevent violence. In his view the UN Convention against genocide has proved obviously insufficient and unenforceable; the only solution is therefore prevention (Kuper 1977).

Anthropologists might contribute also their insights on how certain multiethnic Third World states have managed to minimize conflict, further human rights, and achieve a sense of national identity and community. Universal education, mass communication, and opportunities for all groups to participate in national economic improvement programs are undoubtedly elements – as demonstrated in the case of Tanzania (Shimkin 1990). Yet even such seeming success stories are qualified by their persistent failures to extend universal (national) rights and privileges to women. The very young and the very old also may find themselves deprived of official succor, especially under circumstances of dearth. We turn next to analyses of their classifications and deprivations.

Deprivation by gender

Women, either all of the time or in specific contexts, may be viewed as different from men – a separate category of person or nonperson that never totally belongs to the social unit's category of person – or some fraction of full adult human status. Undergoing their own separate rites of passage, eating separately, and in some cases even consuming different foods, women may never be counted or treated as full persons within social groups dominated by males (Strathern 1972).

The political, economic, and sociocultural structures that deny women full personhood may also deny them human rights, such as rights to representation or rights to food, either all of the time or in certain contexts (e.g., McLaughlin 1974). Although most of the anthropological literature analyzing women's rights and personhood derives from nonindustrialized societies, women are also excluded from full social participation in modern states as well as international organizations. Economic development and modernization programs usually directed by and toward males often bypass female farmers, merchants, and entrepreneurs at all social scales. Even "women-in-development" programs that seek to improve the lot of women by singling them out for assistance tend to reinforce social structures that count women as partial persons. The process of trying to redress some of the material abuses that stem from the structure may fulfill the content while leaving women's social marginality intact. Programs such as the Bangladesh Rural Advancement Committee that manage to entitle and empower women at the same time are rare exceptions (see Chen 1986). National and international organizations also perpetuate patterns of gender discrimination by establishing "normal" standards that count women as some fraction of a male consumption unit.

In these national and international structures and organizations, as in local communities, definitions of personhood are embedded in cultural values that set women apart. The rights of women as human beings then come into conflict with cultural norms and attitudes that deny women full rights. Indian cultures provide a case in point, and anthropologists, such as Papanek (1989), have suggested a comparative regional approach for measuring the extent of human rights abuses stemming from local categories of gender difference affecting, for example, access to food. She advises the researcher to describe first the actual behaviors by which females get less of available (food) resources than males; second, the material consequences of differential resource allocations (e.g., skewed survivorship ratios); and, third, what ideas underlie such inequalities.

Especially relevant to the valuation of, and behaviors toward, categories of persons labeled "female" are their ascribed biological or cultural characteristics. In local cultural terms women may be categorized as needing less or less high-quality food. Foods may, in turn, be classified in local parlance as "hot" versus "cold," so that high-quality foods are interpreted as actually damaging to females. Alternatively, food self-deprivation may be construed to be of spiritual value especially for females. Women's self-restraint additionally may be understood to be tied to a biological ability to accept pain without cost. Women and men may have differences of opinion on such matters, and so a further issue in monitoring the damage resulting from gender-based (or other) allocation rules is whether the victims themselves feel violated or deprived. More "objective" accounts often leave out this critical subjective judgment of deprivation. A case in point is when economists insist that Third World populations are not hungry or malnourished but, rather, "small but healthy," without asking their sample members to report how they feel or, for that matter, checking with medical colleagues to see whether those who are small in fact are healthy (see Messer 1989a). Anthropologists thus potentially play a dual role: (1) establishing the objective terms by which "deprivation" is defined; and (2) offering subjects' judgments on analogous dimensions. Both offer policy makers additional information on who is hungry or deprived and at what levels actions need to be targeted to improve the situation.

Deprivation by age

Age constitutes yet another criterion for denying full human status and access to resources. In many societies personhood, with its attendant rights and duties, is linked to full productive status; in situations in which resources are in short supply, those who cannot contribute to their own or the collective subsistence often find themselves deprived. In many cases the very young or old find themselves marginalized as customary socioeconomic patterns change. Anthropologists analyzing intergenerational work patterns report such social, structural, occupational, and resource changes and resulting human rights abuses. Pagezy (1988), in the course of ecological investigation in Zaire, discovered (to her obvious dismay) the formerly foraging Twa, now settled, abandoning their elderly to malnutrition or starvation as the young struggled for their own subsistence. The history of such neglect is not clear – that is, whether such disdain for the needs of the elderly was less the case under conditions of foraging or simply less obvious.

Hemmings-Gapihan (1985), in her study of changing social mores and labor organization by gender in Gourma, Upper Volta (Burkina Faso), argued that elderly women in that society traditionally controlled both land and labor; as they aged, they worked less without threat of loss to subsistence. But such customs of caring for elderly women appeared to be overturned by increasing emphasis on cash crops and male control of younger women's and men's labor. Although in each of these cases a simplifying analysis might interpret the erosion of rights entirely in political-economic terms (e.g., Watts 1983), the loss of respect for the old or infirm, who as a consequence lose land rights, food rights, and the right to subsistence and social security, is also a cultural judgment about which (partial) human beings are no longer included in the community or household that works together and shares provisions.

On the opposite pole marked age or gender categories can alternatively signal extra cultural protection or access to resources. Both women and children are favored in life and death situations in Western culture. The extra cultural value placed on children is especially evident within the ideologies and behaviors of the UN agencies, such as UNICEF, in which children are singled out for special allocations of food, health care, and protection from violence (e.g., Grant 1990). The rights of children, UNICEF insists, take precedence over national rights of sovereignty. To protect children's rights UNICEF advocates intervening in the internal affairs of states – the only circumstance under which this happens.

Additionally, much of famine relief aims explicitly at "saving the children," whether or not children are especially imperiled. Legesse (1990), for example, reports that eastern African pastoralists customarily protect their children's well-being in times of food shortage more so than neighboring farming populations. A happy scenario is where international relief agencies reinforce the benefits for children of pastoralists and add to the benefits for farmers' children. A not-so-happy scenario is where the need to intervene to feed hard-pressed East African adult pastoralists is judged to be unnecessary because the children, who have already been favored, appear to be well nourished. This can result in unrelieved hardship and suffering for adults.[10]

As is the case with gender-related access to food, anthropologists' community-based understandings of subjective and objective dimensions of preference can improve preventive and ameliorative food and health policies.

Summary

Better understandings of human classification and personhood make it possible to carry out predictive as well as after-the-fact analyses. Anticipating what categories of people defined by ethnic identity, gender, or age are likely to be denied access to critical resources such as food or health care, at all times or in times of dearth, by households, communities, states, or social agencies, can help identify groups and individuals vulnerable to rights abuses and help aid rapid response to their plight. Better understandings of human classification also can help pinpoint where political-economic structures do violence to human rights at community or national levels. Understanding the circumstances under which women, children, or the elderly lose basic subsistence entitlements assists those who might intervene to construct and use a human rights framework to identify vulnerable groups, both to constrain abuses and to create obligations.

Issues of human classification also enter into the understanding of who enjoys particular categories of social, economic, and cultural rights, another arena for anthropological contributions.

Economic, Social, and Cultural (ECOSOC) Rights

Political-economic as well as sociocultural structures deprive people of rights such as rights to adequate food and nutrition, health, a sustainable environment, and other essential prerequisites for livelihood. Although both theoretical and applied anthropologists study these issues, very little of their work has been tied explicitly to the human rights framework. As indicated earlier, one reason for this omission is that anthropologists have focused mainly on indigenous or collective rights. They have devoted less attention to documenting the socioeconomic and cultural rights of individuals, although the UN framework is based on individual rights. But, together with Third World critics of the UN international human rights framework, who share these critical views that it is ethnocentrically Western, anthropologists support the universal rights to be free from hunger, to enjoy health (or health care), and to earn a decent livelihood under humane conditions, even as they disagree on the numbers or procedures for defining acceptable levels or standards (e.g., Cohen 1993).

Anthropologists contribute to enlarging this ECOSOC framework of human rights through theory, practical reporting, and policy-related activities. Marxist interpretations offer one framework for examining the causes of ill health, hunger, and other abuses. The human rights framework offers anthropologists another global platform on which to voice concerns about political-economic institutions interpreted in particular contexts as interfering with human rights. To move from rhetoric to action, anthropologists also participate in practical programs and projects. Marchione (1984) offers several methodological approaches for examining the right to food; Clay, with colleagues at Cultural Survival, critiques the food relief work of governments and NGOs (1988b; Clay and Holcomb 1986; Clay et al. 1988); and Horowitz (1990) elaborates on structural causes of human rights abuses in the global food economy. Leading advocates of indigenous and other human rights are now employed at institutions such as the World Bank, where they draft guidelines to protect the rights of peoples affected by development projects (e.g., Cernea 1991). Carrying out predictive as well as post hoc analyses of how political-economic structures violate human rights at local to state levels, anthropologists can use a human rights framework not only to analyze the structural contexts but also to contribute to actions to constrain abuses and to create obligations. The anthropologists just cited are already drawing into the human rights arena cases of economic discrimination, which have their root causes in the inequities of the political economy. Additional examples can be found in Huss-Ashmore and Katz (1989, 1990) and Downs, Kerner, and Reyna (1991).

Institutions and Linkages

Explorations of sociocultural, political, and economic dimensions also raise the issue of linkages and levels in human rights reporting, compliance, and fulfillment. Until recently human rights research and advocacy had largely failed to conceptualize human rights formulation or implementation at any level between the state and the individual. More recently the human rights literature by anthropologists (e.g., Kuper 1977, 1981; Stavenhagen 1990) and scholars of religion (e.g., Rouner 1988) increasingly presents rights issues from the viewpoints of indigenous and minority groups and the different world religious traditions, especially as these other notions interfere with universal acceptance (Alston 1990a). Analysis of rights at local or intermediate social levels remains scarce, however, for both conceptual and methodological reasons. First, as already mentioned, some human rights scholars interpret what might be termed cross-cultural analysis of rights to obviate the principle of universality. Second, cross-cultural analysis leading to action entails new skills of conceptualization and negotiation (Na'im 1992).

Linking levels to connect theoretical notions of what rights are and who enjoys them to practical programs to fulfill rights or report abuses involves both sociocultural theory and also applied anthropology. Certainly, distinctive cultures hold distinctive notions of rights and duties. But in certain arenas rights conceived by distinctive cultures or religions might be rendered congruent if proponents focused on potential points of agreement rather than conflict with those of the international doctrines. With respect to the right to food, as a case in point, Islamic law and international UN human rights share the identical intent to protect people from hunger. How might the Muslim obligation to provide charity and to feed the hungry reinforce the international human rights principle? How might community organizations, local and regional food security mechanisms, including grain storage and hospitality customs, facilitate an implementation of the right to food through mediation among differing, but not necessarily antagonistic, cultural notions of rights to food and obligations to feed? How might anthropologists apply their sociocultural knowledge of the competing, but not always antagonistic, demands of multiple legal and human rights traditions to achieve a superior outcome for both the hungry and for those donating food? Analysis of human rights can emphasize mutually congruent and reinforcing traditions about food even where principles and other rights, such as freedom of religion, differ and where Islamic jurists insist Islamic law takes precedence over international doctrine (Farhang 1988).

Anthropology, Human Rights, and the State

Cultural understandings of rights principles and practices below the level of the state also offer new opportunities for human rights conceptualization, reporting, and achievement. The international legal codes presuppose state organization, political will, and values to create or bolster compliance. In clarifying the concept, Eide notes:

> the notion of human rights is intimately linked to the notions of "state." Only in the context of an organized society with public authorities does the notion of "human rights" make sense. "Human rights" refers to norms concerning the relationship between individuals (sometimes groups of individuals) and the state. (Eide 1984:152)

UN doctrine insists that human rights be monitored and addressed from the top down, but in practical terms rights are conceptualized and met at various levels. A challenge for anthropologists is to envision and then design strategies for meeting human rights that might better coordinate international, state, and local efforts.

Subsistence rights offer one illustration. Historical studies of land rights, water rights, community grain storage customs, and kinship and social organization all indicate how prestate communities protected subsistence rights and promoted social security. Ethnographic studies demonstrate, in addition, a range of coping strategies at the household level and also their demise under changing conditions. In particular, they report what role the state played in transforming local subsistence and risk-averse practices and the gaps between the breakdown of traditional modes of risk avoidance and the buildup of state capacity to assume responsibility for social security (e.g., Colson 1979; Moris 1989).

Such studies suggest both negative and positive implications: what states ought not to do, in order to preserve traditional local to regional mechanisms for securing subsistence rights, and what states ought to do to create new institutions to meet rights where the old have atrophied. They also suggest that states, in their current form, often are not able or choose not to meet the subsistence rights of all. Therefore, anthropologists (among others) might begin to investigate ways for local or crosscutting (e.g., religious) sociocultural groups to demand and secure rights. What might be ways to combine top-down (UN) with bottom-up "grassroots" strategies for rights?

For anthropologists linking elite or official with local levels involves paying more attention to the culture of bureaucrats and of those who protect and enforce human rights. One of the weaknesses of anthropologists' human rights reporting up to this point in time is that we tend to focus almost exclusively on the unempowered and the abusers. We do not give sufficient weight to the cultural characteristics of the empowered and the potential protectors or advocates. Nor has there been much attention directed toward cross-cultural analyses that illuminate how notions of rights and persons create categories of privileged and under-privileged at many levels in plural societies (e.g., Downing and Kushner 1988). Anthropologists might also contribute more to the ideas and instruments of international human rights in a world that anthropologists and human rights advocates increasingly recognize to be pluralistic and marked by the need to protect collective as well as individual rights (e.g., Crawford 1988; Alston 1990a). Human rights reporting instruments should include provisions for self-reporting by communities and individuals, not only the top-down monitoring of compliance by states according to human rights codes. Anthropologists are already contributing to the design and implementation of conceptual and reporting mechanisms (e.g., Stavenhagen 1990) but might contribute further.

An additional theoretical and practical concern is to analyze the meaning of human rights within the statist framework. How does the doctrine of universal human rights relate to national mores and rules of behavior? How have state governments behaved with respect to the universal framework? Whether or not states accept them in their entirety, nations sign onto the UN Charter and Universal Declaration of Human Rights because signing is a rite of passage for joining the UN and for recognition of sovereign status within the community of nations. Nations may later express divergence from the codes and refuse to ratify the legal instruments that are meant to implement them or to behave in accordance with the legal codes once ratified. Understanding the socio-cultural as well as political-economic rationales, and responding to such discrepant behaviors, are also potential items for the anthropologists' agenda.

Asian nations, as a case in point (see Yamane 1982), show great diversity in legal and moral traditions at the local, state, and crosscutting religious levels. Only India, Japan, and Sri Lanka have ratified both international covenants on human rights; the Philippines has ratified the International Covenant on Economic, Social and Cultural Rights (as of 1980). Ratifications of the ILO resolutions on human rights are much lower in Asia than in other regions of the world. Notions of human rights therefore appear not to be widely shared among Asian cultural traditions.

There are several reasons for this seeming lack. The first is that rights and obligations in Asian traditions are viewed as more communal than individual, and, thus, demands for what the international framework construes to be individual rights may be made on the basis of family or community values, rather than individual rights in a state. Asian peoples additionally have found that collective rights may prove to be the most important route for gaining access to justice, since denials are often based on group membership. Reform of the justice system may also be a prerequisite for action on human rights. Second, many Asian individuals are so poor that any notion of human rights that does not refer to economic development and fulfillment of essential subsistence rights appears meaningless. Third, many violations are tied to the abusive conduct of transnational corporations, which control and constrain individuals' rights to work and earn a decent standard of living and furthermore often control access to land and to natural resources. Technically, they can be made to adhere to human rights codes via government regulations. But in practice governments often are either reluctant or too weak to do so.

All of these factors indicate that human rights, as defined in the international sphere, are widely abused in Asia, but formulaic human rights covenants do not offer a solution. Significant human rights abusers occur among nations that have and have not ratified the UN covenants. To advance human rights practice individuals must first be apprised of their rights, and gain the consciousness to protest repression and arbitrary disciplinary actions. NGO, government, and IGO actions must then establish the frameworks and channels for human rights reporting. A further possibility is for Asian nations to join together to form either NGO or intergovernmental organization (IGO) regional human rights associations between the level of the global international community and the state.

Nongovernmental organizations

Dissatisfaction with human rights as the exclusive domain of governments potentially leads to new institutional forms of nongovernmental as well as intergovernmental organizations. Human rights-monitoring NGOs, such as the regional Human Rights Watch Committees and Amnesty International, evaluate standards, government compliance, and mechanisms for meeting obligations. These organizations, with anthropologists in staff and leadership positions, report by region, country, and issue (e.g., women's rights) and rally public sentiment to embarrass and change the behaviors of abusers.

The Independent Commission on International Humanitarian Issues (ICIHI) is another investigative think tank. Its mandate is to address humanitarian issues that are dealt with inadequately by existing international mechanisms, to suggest possible new mechanisms, and to raise international public consciousness about the causes of human suffering (Aga Khan 1988:156). ICIHI evaluates state compliance with human rights standards, where and why behaviors do not conform to standards, and what the international community might do to improve universal human rights performance. Their human rights concerns include especially famine (the right to food) (ICIHI 1985; Messer 1989b) and indigenous rights (ICIHI 1988). ICIHI also suggests what concerned citizens and NGOs might do to circumvent the inadequacies or perfidies of governments to reach the people who are suffering deprivations.

Nongovernmental organizations set policies and practices at the local level, with activities that come under scrutiny by anthropologists, much the same as the activities of governments come under scrutiny. Their activities are complementary to the inadequacies or unwillingness of governments, and they constitute yet another aspect of the social-political-economic environment with which individuals, households, and local communities must contend in making a living, producing and reproducing their biological and sociocultural beings. Smith (1996) raises one possible limitation of this NGO bypass-government approach: it may interfere with the legitimate efforts of indigenous or other local communities to negotiate more lasting (or sometimes revolutionary) solutions to immediate problems of rights and longer-term obligations. The particular programs of NGOs (referring here to NGOs in general rather than human rights NGOs in particular) may be just as intrusive and destructive to the aspirations of local political leaders and cultures as those of a domineering national state. Sometimes the NGOs that enter communities have little understanding of the historical context of suffering that they are trying to end and have no long-term commitment to action. NGOs have also been known to interfere with the day-to-day functioning of national governments and the course of their negotiations with municipalities or local governments for programs and power sharing.

As is the case with other participants in the development process, the raison-d'être of NGOs is in part humanitarian but also self-interested. Their ideologies, motivations, and activities contribute to the overall process of economic development and human rights but in their own cultural terms. The culture and organizational structure of NGOs therefore constitute one other contrasting level and linkage in the definition and practice of human rights, especially in the struggle by indigenous communities for self-determination and protections of their collectivity against outside interference.

Transformations in Human Rights Rhetoric and Institutional Structure

The rights of collectivities

Overall reviews of the human rights literature of the past forty years, and especially the summaries appearing in 1988 on the fortieth anniversary of the Universal Declaration of Human Rights (e.g., Crawford 1988; Berting et al. 1990), emphasize how the world has changed. There are new international institutional actors in the guise of UN agencies, multilateral banks, and transnational corporations. The hegemony of the old superpowers is challenged by more than 150 newly independent nations, whose needs for economic development at times appear to overwhelm themselves and potential donors. NGOs, alongside governments, provide an extensive network of international, national, and local development and human rights agencies that since 1948 also have grown in numbers and activities.

Most human rights advocates[11] (e.g., Baehr 1990; Burger 1990; VanderWal 1990) recognize that human needs and demands, expressed through collective organization and action, have changed since 1948. Human rights, evolving along with these institutional changes, now include solidarity rights and the rights of collectivities, indigenous rights, and rights to a cultural identity (Berting et al. 1990). Expanding concepts and dimensions of rights do not negate earlier Western cultural inspiration; national constitutions of the new states almost without exception enshrine both civil-political and socioeconomic rights in their founding declarations. But cultural and collective rights emphasize that individuals achieve human dignity through cultural as well as biological survival and that cultural groups are entitled to a sustainable, peaceful, and enabling natural and socioeconomic environment. In other words, cultural groups must be protected, or individual rights to survival are at risk.

Advocates have slowly come to accept what have always been the anthropologists' understandings of indigenous rights: that threats to native lands and livelihoods, languages and societies, constitute abuses to human dignity and human rights.[12] Cultural identity may be as important as health for human dignity and self-confidence. Cultural pluralism, rather than threatening humankind, is in itself of value (Kamenka 1988:134). Translated into human rights parlance, efforts to eliminate cultural distinctiveness must be constrained, and conditions to further cultural survival must be obligated.

Other new categories of rights include "people's rights," which are interpreted by Third World leaders to be a logical outgrowth of the right to self-determination. Collectivities of Third World states demand their right to exist in a peaceful, prosperous, environmentally sustainable world (Marks 1980; Crawford 1988; Baehr 1990). Human rights rhetoric now also recognizes as legitimate the demands of indigenous groups to be protected within states (Falk 1988). Overcoming the threat to indigenous survival is interpreted as an "emergency," an imperative for the survival of the human species, even though indigenous groups and rights often challenge fundamental notions of economic "progress" and state sovereignty.

The need for protection of human rights is also evident where ethnic groups come into conflict in the process of state formation and disintegration. Government efforts at control and subordination generate demands for ethnic autonomy and rights, over and against government attempts to create an assimilative sociocultural order (Guideri, Pellizzi, and Tambiah 1988). As Stavenhagen summarized so succinctly, "The idea of a right usually arises when we have to face a situation in which violations of rights occur" (1990:256).

Cross-cultural formulations of rights

The changing world order also encourages international human rights activists to explore more widely multiple cultural perspectives on human rights and their implications for standards and compliance. National governments, especially religious leaders, that are neither secular (humanist) nor Western continually must choose whether to comply with or disregard the 1948 Universal Declaration on Human Rights and subsequent instruments. To win their support for both legislation and adherence, evolving human rights standards need to resonate with these different traditions of religious and community law (e.g., Alston 1990a).

Although soliciting cultural and religious opinions on human rights is not new (see 1966 UNESCO conference reported in the *International Social Science Journal*, especially Glean 1966; Raphael 1966; and review in Robertson 1982), understanding their various points of view is much more urgent. Rallying Islamic and Buddhist principles on limits to violence and warfare, or obligations to feed the hungry or provide medical care to the sick are instances in which multicultural contributions might improve human rights performance. While rendering different value systems congruent is not easy, at least human rights lawyers and philosophers are taking the problem seriously. They accept the reality of differing concepts of rights held by different collectivities in a plural world. They also take note of the different concepts of persons who enjoy rights in different legal traditions or customary law.

The human rights commissions promulgating legal rights for a plural, international, global society then face the choice of whether to try to incorporate the distinctive viewpoints into a united but pluralistic whole or to homogenize the disparate viewpoints into a uniform whole (see, e.g., Kammerer 1988:279). The documents appear to follow the first model, incorporation of regional and indigenous human rights formulations into the expanding "whole" of international human rights. In consequence, the international (UN) human rights doctrine is "united" as a series of documents passed by the UN, but principles and practices continue to evolve in response to the "smoking mirrors" in the perennial struggle to create postimperial and new or postnational orders (Guideri, Pellizzi, and Tambiah 1988). The legal experts still wonder how to create and implement a universal human rights standard that will limit all forms of violence, including the quiet violence of hunger. Individuals, communities, NGOs, and religious and cultural groups suffering human rights abuses maintain a hope that the human rights framework can assist them in overcoming oppression.

The multiplying number of rights now recognized within the human rights framework testifies to the actions following on such hopes and the evolution of the human rights concept through debate. They also suggest an influential role for anthropologists.

Where anthropology prevailed

Although anthropologists, with a few exceptions (Stavenhagen 1990), maintain low profiles, anthropological concepts and concerns are well represented in this evolving human rights field. International human rights now incorporate notions of indigenous rights, cultural rights, and the rights of collectivities more generally. UNESCO and the ILO clarify and champion the rights of indigenous and minority peoples to enjoy their cultural heritage, including their natural resources. The Organization of African Unity has championed "Human and Peoples' Rights" (1981), the World Conference of Indigenous Peoples has issued its own "Declaration of Principles of Indigenous Rights" (1984), and the UN General Assembly has voted a "Declaration on the Right to Development" (1986) (see Crawford 1988, for commentaries on these documents). The ILO "Convention 107 concerning the Protection and Integration of Indigenous and other Tribal and Semi-Tribal Populations in Independent Countries" (1957) has been revised to strip it of assimilationist, integrationist, and paternalistic sentiments, to bring it more into line with the desires of indigenous groups to remain separate and sovereign (Burger 1988). Leaders of indigenous rights movements, moreover, have learned to frame their own human rights demands, outside of the dominance of Western academic culture (Varese 1988; Wright 1988, Wright and Ismaelillo 1982), thus changing the roles of anthropologists from torchbearers to consultants and advocates.

Ten years ago Legesse accurately described this process of change in the following terms: human rights are universal in intent but not in derivation (1980:123). UN delegates representing widely varying cultural traditions usually agree that there exists a universal concern for human rights, although they question the universality of any particular human rights notion. Over time representatives from different nations and cultures participate in a universalizing process in which all contribute to the expanding framework of human rights. Although some philosophers (e.g., Donnelly 1990) continue to define the logic of human rights in a strict sense as excluding collective rights or alternative non-Western notions of human rights (e.g., Howard 1992), others (e.g., Alston 1990a) accept the need to consider alternative formulations. While these latter also worry that alternative conceptions of human rights might water down their stature, they insist that pluralistic notions can be accommodated to retain and even strengthen the possibility of establishing universal standards with moral force, and practical enforcement mechanisms.

Indigenous rights are universally recognized to be imperative in today's world (see Stavenhagen 1990). Anthropologists, accordingly, have discarded the method of describing cultures by trait lists that proposed to measure cultural survivals versus assimilations (e.g., Tax 1952) as well as the tendency to analyze "other" cultures according to their degree of assimilation (see Guideri, Pellizzi, and Tambiah 1988:27). Instead, they are describing the processes by which rights and cultural identities are negotiated among states, peoples, and individuals and strengthening human rights advocacy in the areas of economic, social, and cultural rights with fact-finding that potentially contributes to human rights, development, and environmental policy. Cultural identity now is presented and demanded by indigenous representatives who are affirming their own biological and cultural superiority, rather than an identity "validated" (after being questioned) by the other, dominant culture (Varese 1988). In the process of indigenous peoples assuming their own voices, anthropologists also have moved from cultural analyses of "communities" to "regional" systems, including more in-depth analysis of ethnicities vis-à-vis states.

Conclusions

As anthropologists, we have questioned the units by which development and well-being are measured; the impact of development strategies on health; the intrusions of authoritarian state regimes (usually propped up by international aid); the well-being of indigenous populations; and the complex religious, political, philosophical, and economic factors that influence vulnerability to hunger and ill health. We have tried to analyze the new UN and NGO participants in development strategies and the linkages among them, communities, and governments and to connect these linkages to more conventional anthropological analyses of political economy, human and cultural ecology, and cultural and class identities. Along with other anthropologists we have debated the impacts of social transformations and tried to clarify the forces that limit human freedom and dignity and, where possible, tried to change them or mitigate their negative impact.

In total these efforts demonstrate a critical involvement in human rights concerns. Anthropologists also have been active in describing and comparing different cultural standards of behavior and how social mores and behaviors are transformed under changing material and ideological conditions. The definition of social person, or the relationship of the individual to the sociocultural group, has also been an anthropological concern (Harris 1989). Notwithstanding, anthropologists in the past have often been excluded from discussions of human rights because we are viewed as opposed to universalizing approaches and to the assimilationist, pro-development, or modernization, values that they seemed to entail. Anthropologists who argued for protection of collective, over and against individual rights, erected a barrier that kept this anthropological discourse from influencing the initial formulation of rights. This adversarial stance ostensibly was matched by the unwillingness of international legal scholars to take seriously different sociocultural definitions of human beings as these modify rights within a group, state, or human community. Such scholars have felt, rightly or wrongly, that entertaining possible exclusionary definitions of human beings does violence to the intellectual notion that certain basic rights *are* universal, which means that they are universally accepted and applied. Anthropologists in the human rights field also have asked different questions, about cultural survival and cultural diversity, and have scrutinized different units – particularly those below but also beyond the state level – in approaching human rights policies.

Despite these differences of opinion and approach, humans rights now incorporate anthropologists' notions of indigenous and collective rights (even if nonanthropologists have not been moved so far as to celebrate diversity as a virtue to the extent that anthropologists do). Moreover, the data suggest that anthropologists' alleged lack of participation in human rights activities lies more in the precision and narrowness of philosophical and disciplinary rhetoric and the connections between anthropologists and the human rights system. While marginalized in the conceptual debate, anthropologists never failed to address and try to expand the basic subject matter. Now others are beginning to address human rights from the bottom-up perspective. Some may even recognize that local definitions of personhood may be more important for realizing rights than the formula contained in some abstract legal document.

Since the 1940s anthropologists have largely moved away from the philosophical debate on whether universal rights are possible and have pressed for the rights of collective, oppressed, and vulnerable groups – all of which relate to various dimensions of human classification and discrimination. Our additional efforts try to clarify demands of the particular peoples pressing for rights and to monitor response. The most important arena for anthropologists remains a monitoring-reporting-advocacy role that also clarifies at what social levels rights are denied or fulfilled. As anthropologists, we continue to point out the discrepancies between human rights rhetoric and ratifications and human rights abuses. We provide evidence and approach the root causes of ongoing human rights abuses in political, economic, and sociocultural terms, as we champion the aspirations of indigenous peoples to maintain their cultures while protecting an adequate standard of living. All this means that the subject matter of anthropology extends beyond analyses of ethnic, class, and race relations, to notions of human rights in cross-cultural perspective. For conceptualization, strategic policy engagement, and action, this constitutes an expanded, although not a new, agenda for anthropologists.

NOTES

1 Algerian (Fanon 1963) and Senegalese (Senghor n.d.) critiques of French "universalism" dramatize how tyrannical Western powers could be in their love of man.

2 An international legal position on the abolition of slavery evolved over the 150-year period 1807–1957 and included such milestones as British colonial law (1807), the antislavery act in Brussels (1890), the League of Nations International Convention on the Abolition of Slavery and the Slave Trade (1926), the proclamation against slavery in the United Nations Universal Declaration (1948), and the United Nations Covenants against the slave trade (1957–8). Antislavery declarations notwithstanding, some form of slavery had clearly persisted over this period, especially in the European colonies. British interests in Nigeria through the early twentieth century, for example, were willing to tolerate customs of indigenous slavery, although colonial documents clarify that this was not condoned to be respectable behavior, and British interests expected that modern state landholding and other practices would gradually cause slavery to disappear.

3 The Red Cross, other humanitarian organizations, and the League of Nations were involved in extending nutritional and health services to prisoners of war and bringing relief into zones of armed conflict or other disasters since the nineteenth century (Messer 1991). Subsequent UN treaties and associated protocols furthered such humanitarian efforts to protect the victims of violent conflict. UN agencies, including the Food and Agriculture Organization (FAO), World Health Organization (WHO), United Nations' Children and Education Fund (UNICEF), and World Food Programme (WFP) designed special programs to deliver humanitarian supplies; a special UN High Commissioner on Refugees was created to deal with growing demands by refugees.

4 International organizations after World War I sought to protect minority individuals in multinational states. Official statements expressed the principle or desire that all peoples should enjoy human rights but included no provisions for enforcement. Nowhere do the documents clarify how "peoples" are linked to "persons" and actions within international law.

5 Renteln (1988a:10) has formulated these questions with respect to measuring human rights, with a specific focus on principles of violence or retaliation.

6 This small controlling group, however, did not speak for all anthropologists, most of whom were never asked for their opinion (Dimitri Shimkin notes, pers. comm., July 1990).

7 This defense of cultural relativism, coming immediately after the atrocities of World War II, appears odd, even wrongheaded.

8   Harris's review (1989:602) distinguishes among the categories of individual (the human organism as a psychological experience) and person (standing in a social order as an agent-in-society). Persons, for example, have judgmental capacities, social entitlements, and mystical capacities (connections with superhumans) depending on their positions in the social order. Beings who lack such capacities lack full status. Which concerns dominate and define full human or personal status vary according to culture. The significance of such definitions for human rights formulation and fulfillment awaits further cross-cultural clarification.

9   For an alternative and more hopeful viewpoint, see Tambiah 1992.

10 UNICEF and NGO consultants, familiar with such allegations, insist they are false (Mary Anderson, pers. comm., January 1991).

11 Some political philosophers continue to argue the precise points of logic for individual rights in the face of changing concepts, attitudes, and interpretations (see, e.g., Donnelly 1990).

12 What culture means in the development context constitutes yet another debate. Legal experts entertain varying images of "development" and a more or less dynamic concept of culture. Certain international lawyers interpret the political momentum behind people's rights as due to the failure of Western lawyers to deal seriously with Third World needs and demands. "I suspect that much of the distaste of Western international formulations of international rights conceals a complacent commitment to the interests of Western States" (Prott 1988:106).

REFERENCES

Adegbite, L. O.
    1968   African Attitudes to the International Protection of Human Rights. In *International Protection of Human Rights*, ed. A. Eide and H. Shue, 69–81. New York: Interscience.
Aga Khan, S.
    1988   Forty Years On: And So Much Left To Do. In *Human Rights*, ed. P. Davies, 155–63. New York: Routledge.
Alston, P.
    1990a   Introduction. *Human Rights in a Pluralist World: Individuals and Collectivities*. Westport, Conn.: Meckler.
    1990b   U.S. Ratification of the Covenant on Economic, Social, and Cultural Rights: The Need for an Entirely New Strategy. *American Journal of International Law* 84:865–93.
American Anthropological Association (AAA)
    1947   Statement on Human Rights. *American Anthropologist* 49:539–43.
Baehr, P. R.
    1990   Human Rights as People's Rights. In *Human Rights in a Pluralist World: Individuals and Collectivities*, ed. J. Berting et al., Westport, Conn.: Meckler.
Barnett, C.
    1988   Is There a Scientific Basis in Anthropology for the Ethics of Human Rights? In *Human Rights and Anthropology*, ed. T. E. Downing and G. Kushner, 21–6. Cambridge, Mass.: Cultural Survival.
Barnett, H. G.
    1948   On Science and Human Rights. *American Anthropologist* 50:352–5.
Berting, J., P. R. Baehr, J. H. Burger, C. Flinterman, B. de Klerk, P. Kroes, C. A. van Minnen, and K. van der Wal, eds.
    1990   *Human Rights in a Pluralist World: Individuals and Collectivities*. Westport, Conn.: Meckler.
Boas, F.
    1939   Autobiography. In *I Believe: The Personal Philosophies of Certain Eminent Men and Women of Our Time*, ed. C. Fadiman, 19–29. New York: Simon and Schuster.

1943 Individual, Family, Population, and Race. *Proceedings of the American Philosophical Society* 87(2): 161–4.

Bodley, J.
1975 *Victims of Progress*. Mountain View, Calif.: Mayfield.

Burger, J.
1988 Indigenous Peoples: New Rights for Old Wrongs. In *Human Rights*, ed. P. Davies, 99–110. New York: Routledge.

Cernea, M.
1991 *Putting People First: Sociological Variables in Development*, 2nd edn. New York: Oxford University Press.

Chen, M.
1986 *The Quiet Revolution: Women in Transition in Rural Bangladesh*. Cambridge, Mass.: Schenkman.

Clay, J.
1988a Anthropologists and Human Rights. Activists by Default? In *Human Rights and Anthropology*, ed. T. E. Downing and G. Kushner, 115–24. Cambridge, Mass.: Cultural Survival.
1988b Ethiopian Famine and the Relief Agencies. In *The Moral Nation: Humanitarianism and U.S. Foreign Policy Today*, ed. R. Nichols and G. Loescher, 232–77. Notre Dame, Ind.: University of Notre Dame Press.

Clay, J., and B. Holcomb
1986 *Politics and the Ethiopian Famine, 1984–85*. Cambridge, Mass.: Cultural Survival.

Clay, J., S. Steingraber, and P. Niggli
1988 *The Spoils of Famine: Ethiopian Famine Policy and Peasant Agriculture*. Cambridge, Mass.: Cultural Survival.

Cohen, R.
1993 Endless Teardrops: Prolegomena to the Study of Human Rights in Africa. In *Human Rights and Governance in Africa*, ed. R. Cohen, G. Hyden, and W. Nagen. Gainesville: University of Florida Press.

Colson, E.
1970 The Assimilation of Aliens among Zambian Tonga. In *From Tribe to Nation in Africa: Studies in Incorporation Processes*, ed. R. Cohen and J. Middleton, 35–54. Scranton, Pa.: Chandler.
1979 In Good Years and Bad: Food Strategies in Self-Reliant Societies. *Journal of Anthropological Research* 35:18–29.

Crawford, J.
1988 *The Rights of Peoples*. Oxford: Clarendon Press.

Donnelly, J.
1984 The Right to Development: How Not to Link Human Rights and Development. In *Human Rights and Development in Africa*, ed. C. Welch and R. Meltzer, 261–84. Albany, NY: SUNY Press.
1990 In *Human Rights in a Pluralist World: Individuals and Collectivities*, ed. J. Berting et al. Westport, Conn.: Meckler.

Doughty, P.
1988 Crossroads for Anthropology: Human Rights in Latin America. In *Human Rights and Anthropology*, ed. T. E. Downing and G. Kushner, 43–72. Cambridge, Mass.: Cultural Survival.

Downing, T. E. and G. Kushner
1988a Human Rights Research: The Challenge for Anthropologists. In *Human Rights and Anthropology*, ed. T. E. Downing and G. Kushner, 9–20. Cambridge, Mass.: Cultural Survival.
1988b Introduction. In *Human Rights and Anthropology*, ed. T. E. Downing and G. Kushner, 1–8. Cambridge, Mass.: Cultural Survival.

Downs, R. E., D. Kerner, and S. P. Reyna, eds.
1991 *The Political Economy of African Famine*. Philadelphia: Gordon and Breach.

Eide, A.
  1984   The International Human Rights System. In *Food as a Human Right*, 152–61.
  Tokyo: United Nations University Press.
Falk, R.
  1980   Theoretical Foundations of Human Rights. In *The Politics of Human Rights*, ed.
  P. R. Newberg, 65–110. New York: New York University Press.
  1988   The Rights of Peoples (in Particular, Indigenous Peoples). In *The Rights of Peoples*,
  ed. J. Crawford, 17–37. Oxford: Clarendon Press.
Fanon, F.
  1963   *The Wretched of the Earth*. Trans. C. Farrington. New York: Grove.
Farhang, M.
  1988   Fundamentalism and Civil Rights in Contemporary Middle Eastern Politics.
  In *Human Rights and the World's Religions*, ed. L. S. Rouner, 63–75. Notre Dame,
  Ind.: University of Notre Dame Press.
Fein, H.
  1984   Scenarios of Genocide: Models of Genocide and Critical Responses. In *Toward an
  Understanding and Prevention of Genocide*, ed. I. W. Charney, 1–23. Proceedings of the
  International Conference on the Holocaust. Boulder, Colo.: Westview Press.
Glean, M.
  1966   Introduction to Human Rights in Perspective. *International Social Science Journal*
  18(1):7–10.
Grant, J.
  1990   *The State of the World's Children: 1990*. New York: UNICEF.
Guidieri, R., F. Pellizi, and S. Tambiah, eds.
  1988   *Ethnicities and Nations: Processes of Interethnic Relations in Latin America, South-
  east Asia, and the Pacific*. Houston: Rothco Chapel.
Harris, Grace
  1989   Concepts of Individual, Self, and Person in Description and Analysis. *American
  Anthropologist* 91:599–612.
Hemmings-Gapihan, G.
  1985   Women and Economy in Gourma, 1919–1978: A Study of Economic Change in
  Burkina Faso (Upper Volta). Ph.D. diss., Department of Anthropology, Yale University.
Hersch, J.
  1969   *Birthright of Man*. New York: UNESCO.
Herskovits, M.
  1951   Tender and Tough-Minded Anthropology and the Study of Values in Culture.
  Southwestern Journal of Anthropology 7:22–31.
Horowitz, M.
  1990   Victims of Development. *Development Anthropology Network* 7(2):1–8.
Howard, R.
  1992   Dignity, Community, and Human Rights. In *Human Rights in Cross-Cultural Perspec-
  tive: A Quest for Consensus*, 81–102. Philadelphia: University of Pennsylvania Press.
Hurtado, A.-M.
  1990   Anthropology Has Had No Impact on Human Rights. *Anthropology Newsletter*
  31(3):3.
Huss-Ashmore, R., and S. Katz, eds.
  1989   *African Food Systems in Crisis*, Part 1: *Microperspectives*. New York: Gordon and
  Breach.
  1990   *African Food Systems in Crisis*, Part 2: *Contending with Change*. New York:
  Gordon and Breach.
Independent Commission on International Humanitarian Issues (ICIHI)
  1985   *Famine: A Man-Made Disaster?* New York: Vintage.
  1988   *Indigenous Peoples: A Global Quest for Justice*. London: Zed.
Jacobs, D.
  1984   *The Brutality of Nations*. New York: Alfred A. Knopf.

Johnson, A., and T. Earle
 1987 *The Evolution of Human Society: From Foraging Group to Agrarian State*. Stanford, Calif.: Stanford University Press.
Kamenka, E.
 1988 Human Rights: People's Rights. In *The Rights of Peoples*, ed. J. Crawford, 127–40. Oxford: Clarendon Press.
Kammerer, C.
 1988 Territorial Imperatives: Akha Ethnic Identity and Thailand's National Integration. In *Ethnicities and Nations: Processes of Interethnic Relations in Latin America, Southeast Asia, and the Pacific*, ed. R. Guideri, F. Pellizzi, and S. Tambiah, 259–92. Houston: Rothco Chapel.
Kapferer, Bruce
 1988 *Legends of People, Myths of State. Violence, Intolerance, and Political Culture*. Washington, DC: Smithsonian.
Kroeber, A. L.
 1949 An Authoritarian Panacea. *American Anthropologist* 51:320.
Kuper, L.
 1977 *The Pity of It All: Polarisation of Racial and Ethnic Relations*. London: Duckworth.
 1982 *Genocide: Its Political Use in the Twentieth Century*. New Haven, Conn.: Yale University Press.
 1986 *The Prevention of Genocide*. New Haven, Conn.: Yale University Press.
Legesse, A.
 1980 Human Rights in African Political Culture. In *The Moral Imperatives of Human Rights: A World Survey*, ed. E. Thompson, 123–38. Washington, DC: American University Press.
 1990 Personal communication.
Lévi-Strauss, C.
 1952 *Race and History*. Paris: UNESCO.
Marchione, T.
 1984 Approaches to the Hunger Problem: A Critical Overview. In *Food as a Human Right*, ed. A. Eide, W. B. Eide, S. Goonatilake, J. Gussow, and W. Omawale, 117–40. Tokyo: United Nations University Press.
Maritain, J.
 1943–71 *The Rights of Man and Natural Law*. New York: Gordon and Breach.
Marks, S.
 1980 Emerging Human Rights: A New Generation for the 1980s. *Rutgers Law Review* 33:435.
Mayor, F.
 1990 Preface. In *Human Rights in a Pluralist World: Individuals and Collectivities*, ed. J. Berting et al. Westport, Conn.: Meckler.
McLaughlin, B.
 1974 Mediation of Contradiction: Why Mbum Women Do Not Eat Chicken. In *Women, Culture, and Society*, ed. L. Lamphere and M. Rosaldo, 301–19. Stanford, Calif.: Stanford University Press.
Mead, M.
 1950 *Food and the Family*. New York: UNESCO.
Messer, E.
 1986 Franz Boas and Kaufmann Kohler: Anthropology and Reform Judaism. *Jewish Social Studies* 48(2):127–40.
 1989a Small But Healthy? Some Cross Cultural Perspectives. *Human Organization* 38(1):39–52.
 1989b The Ecology and Politics of Food Availability. In *African Food Systems in Crisis*, Part 1: *Microperspectives*, ed. R. Huss-Ashmore and S. Katz, 189–202. New York: Gordon and Breach.

1991 Food Wars: Hunger as a Weapon of War in 1990. Research Report RR-91-3, World Hunger Program, Brown University, Providence, RI.

1993 Anthropology and Human Rights. *Annual Review of Anthropology* 22:221–49.

Moris, J.
1989 Indigenous versus Introduced Solutions to Food Stress in Africa. In *Seasonal Variability in Third World Agriculture*, ed. D. Sahn, 209–34. Baltimore: Johns Hopkins University Press.

Na'im, A. A. A.
1992 Toward a Cross-Cultural Approach to Defining International Standards of Human Rights: The Meaning of Cruel, Inhuman, or Degrading Treatment or Punishment. *Human Rights in Cross-Cultural Perspective: A Quest for Consensus*, 19–43. Philadelphia: University of Pennsylvania Press.

Newman, L.
1989 Personal communication.

Newman, L., ed.
1990 *Hunger in History: Food Shortage, Poverty, and Deprivation*. London: Basil Blackwell.

Pagezy, H.
1988 Coping with Uncertainty in Food Supply among the Oto and the Twa Living in the Equatorial Flooded Forest near Lake Tumba. In *Coping with Uncertainty in Food Supply*, ed. I. de Garine and G. A. Harrison, 176–209. New York: Oxford University Press.

Papanek. H.
1989 Socialization for Inequality: Issues for Research and Action. *Samya Shakti*. New Delhi: Center for Women's Development Studies.

Polgar, S.
1968 General Discussion. In *War: The Anthropology of Armed Conflict and Aggression*, ed. M. Fried, M. Harris, and R. Murphy, 81–2. New York: Natural History Press.

Prott, L. V.
1988 Cultural Rights as Peoples' Rights in International Law. In *The Rights of Peoples*, ed. J. Crawford, 93–106. Oxford: Clarendon Press.

Raphael, D. D.
1966 The Liberal Western Tradition of Human Rights. *International Social Science Journal* 18(1):22–30.

Renteln, A. D.
1988a A Cross-Cultural Approach of Validating International Human Rights: The Case of Retribution Tied to Proportionality. In *Human Rights: Theory and Measurement*, 7–40. New York: St. Martin's.

1988b Relativism and the Search for Human Rights. *American Anthropologist* 90:56–72.

Robertson, A. H.
1982 *Human Rights in the World: An Introduction to the International Protection of Humans Rights*, 2nd edn. New York: St. Martin's.

Rouner, L. S.
1988 *Human Rights and the World's Religions*. Notre Dame, Ind.: University of Notre Dame Press.

Schirmer, J.
1988 The Dilemma of Cultural Diversity and Equivalency in Universal Human Rights Standards. In *Human Rights and Anthropology*, ed. T. Downing and G. Kushner, 121–97. Cambridge, Mass.: Cultural Survival.

Schirmer, J., A. Renteln, and L. Weisberg
1988 Anthropology and Human Rights: A Selected Bibliography. *Human Rights and Anthropology*, 121–97. Cambridge, Mass.: Cultural Survival.

Sengor, L. S.
N.d. *Liberté 1: Negritude et Humanisme* 1:98. Paris: Editions du Seuil.

Smith, C. A.
1996 Development and the State: Issues for Anthropologists. In *Transforming Societies, Transforming Anthropology*, ed. E. F. Moran, 25–56. Ann Arbor: University of Michigan Press.

Stavenhagen, R.
1990 Indigenous Rights. In *Human Rights in a Pluralist World: Individuals and Collectivities*, ed. J. Berting et al. Westport, Conn.: Meckler.

Strathern, M.
1972 *Women in Between*. New York: Seminar Press.

Tambiah, S.
1988 Foreword. In *Ethnicities and Nations: Processes of Interethnic Relations in Latin America, Southeast Asia, and the Pacific*, ed. R. Guidieri, F. Pellizzi, and S. Tambiah, 1–6. Houston: Rothco Chapel.
1992 *Buddhism Betrayed? Religion, Politics, and Violence in Sri Lanka*. Chicago: University of Chicago Press.

Tax, S., ed.
1952 *Heritage of Conquest*. Glencoe, Ill.: Free Press.

Tomasevski, K.
1989 *Development Aid and Human Rights: A Case Study for the Danish Center*. New York: St. Martin's.

United Nations
1988 Human Rights. *UN Chronicle* 25(1): 47–50.

UNESCO
1987 Anthropology and Human Rights. *Human Rights Teachings* 6.

VanderWal, K.
1990 Collective Human Rights: A Western View. In *Human Rights in a Pluralist World: Individuals and Collectivities*, ed. J. Berting et al. Westport, Conn.: Meckler.

Varese, S.
1988 Multi-Ethnicity and Hegemonic Construction: Indian Plans and the Indian Future. In *Ethnicities and Nations: Processes of Interethnic Relations in Latin America, Southeast Asia, and the Pacific*, ed. R. Guidieri, F. Pellizzi, and S. Tambiah, 57–77. Houston: Rothco Chapel.

Watts, M.
1983 *Silent Violence: Food, Famine and Peasantry in Northern Nigeria*. Berkeley: University of California Press.

Weissbrodt, D.
1988 Human Rights: An Historical Perspective. In *Human Rights*, ed. P. Davies, 1–20. New York: Routledge.

Williams, E.
1947 Anthropology for the Common Man. *American Anthropologist* 49:84–90.

Wright, R. M.
1988 Anthropological Presuppositions of Indigenous Advocacy. In *Annual Review of Anthropology* 17:365–90.

Wright, R. M., and Ismaelillo
1982 *Native Peoples in Struggle: Cases from the Fourth Russell Tribunal*. Bombay: ERIN.

Yamane, H.
1982 Human Rights for the People of Asia. *Human Rights Teaching* 3:18–22.

Zalaquett, José
1981 *The Human Rights Issue and the Human Rights Movement* [Back-ground Information]. Geneva: Commission of the Churches on International Affairs of the World Council of Churches.
1984 The Relationship between Development and Human Rights. In *The Human Right to Food*, ed. A. Eide et al., 141–51. Tokyo: United Nations University Press.

Zvogbo, E. J. M.
1979 A Third World View. In *Human Rights and American Foreign Policy*, ed. D. P. Kommers and G. D. Lescher, 90–107. Notre Dame, Ind.: Notre Dame University Press.

8

Excavations of the Heart: Healing Fragmented Communities

Victoria Sanford

The people that walked in darkness have seen a great light. They walk in lands of shadows but a light has shone forth.

Isaiah 9:1–2

"To Feel Good in the Heart"

In Plan de Sánchez, we were excavating eighteen mass graves. This meant we were unearthing a tremendous number of artifacts and clothing associated with each skeleton. On one occasion, local villagers sorted through artifacts found in a grave of burned skeletons. The bones were so badly burned and contorted from the fire that though we could count that there had been at least sixteen victims, we had no complete skeletons and were unable to associate any of the artifacts with individual skeletons. Survivors asked us if they could examine the artifacts. We laid them out above the grave in an orderly and respectful manner on top of flattened paper bags. Then the survivors surrounded the artifacts spread out before them. With great tenderness, they began to look through burned bits of clothing, necklace beads, and half-melted plastic shoes, trying to recognize something of their relatives who had been killed in the massacre. A few of the men recognized their wives' wedding necklaces and asked us if it might be possible for them to have the necklaces after the investigation was completed. There was no dissension in the community about which necklaces had belonged to which wives. Those who couldn't find the necklaces of their wives, sisters, and daughters asked if they might be able to have some of the stray beads because "surely some of those beads must have fallen

Originally published in *Buried Secrets: Truth and Human Rights in Guatemala*. New York: Palgrave Macmillan, 2003, pp. 232–47.

from our relatives' necklaces." Then, they said something I was to hear repeated in every other exhumation in which I have participated, "*Si no tiene dueño, entonces es mío*" (If it doesn't have an owner, then it is mine).

In Panzós, in the late evening after the church mass and public gathering, we moved the boxed remains to the community center. We placed the bones in small coffins and the artifacts on top of the closed coffins. We had only been able to name two of the thirty-five skeletons exhumed based on positive scientific identification. Because the greatest desire of family members is to carry the remains of their loved ones in the burial procession, we give them an opportunity to look at the artifacts to fulfill their desire to identify their lost loved one – "*para sentir bien en el corazón*," to feel good in the heart (what we might call closure). Though not considered positive scientific identifications, when a survivor recognizes artifacts, we mark the coffin so that they may carry it in the burial procession. Sometimes, there is nothing concrete in the identification, but other times it is emotionally overwhelming. One elderly man had passed nearly half of the coffins. He passed those with women's clothing and stopped at each that had men's boots. He would pick up the boots and swiftly review the instep. In front of one of the coffins, as those in line pushed forward to look at the next set of artifacts, he remained frozen in place, gripping the heel of a plastic boot. I walked over to him. He said, "This is my son. These are his boots. Look here. See that stitching? That is my stitching. I sewed his boot together the morning before he was killed. This is my son." As other survivors reached the end of the row of coffins without immediately recognizing anything, they would return and start over. During the second round, they began to stand by different coffins. When I approached them to find out what they had identified, each said, "*Si no tiene dueño, entonces es mío.*"

The Widows of Xococ

Every day I spent in Plan de Sánchez, campesinos from other villages – elderly women, elderly men, young women and men, children, entire families – came to witness the excavation of the graves. First, they would watch from a distance. As the morning wore on, they would move closer and closer. Whether alone or a part of a group, they were silent, occasionally whispering to one another. Usually after lunch, they would move right up to the edge of the grave, positioning themselves close to me and other working forensic team members. Usually, it was a woman crouched down as close as she could get without actually entering the grave. After a deep breath and brief pause, she would say, "You know, we need an exhumation, too. We also suffered a massacre." I would always ask how many people died and the response was always the same: "*Casi todos*," nearly everyone. Sometimes they meant all the men in their family. Sometimes they meant all the women. Sometimes, they meant nearly everyone in their village had been killed.

Just one week after I began working with the forensic team in Plan de Sánchez, a delegation of some forty women and one elderly man arrived to our work site in the late morning of June 28. Doña Soledad appeared to be the leader of the group, though her father, the elderly Don Miguel, was treated with great deference by all the women. They came from Xococ, a village on the other side of the mountain, in the valley, much closer to Rabinal than Plan de Sánchez. They came to report that on June 26 Xococ civil patrollers had damaged several sites of clandestine cemeteries in their village. Doña Soledad feared the civil patrol had removed the bones in an effort to destroy any evidence that might subsequently be uncovered should an exhumation take place in Xococ in the future. This delegation had walked six hours to request our intervention. They wanted the forensic team to determine if the bones of their loved ones had been taken. And they specifically wanted the judge to place an official sign, like the one we had in Plan de Sánchez, over each of the graves in Xococ. Over our work site stood a hand-painted sign on a rusting piece of metal that read: "Do Not Touch. Site of Legal Investigation By Order of the Justice of the Peace Under Protection of the National Police."

That same morning, I accompanied several members of the forensic team, the local justice of the peace, and the Xococ delegation to Xococ to survey the grave sites. Plants used by survivors to mark the graves had been cleared and the superficial layer of earth (ranging from one to two inches) had been dug and loosened. At one grave, fragments of a human rib were found mixed in the top soil. It was, however, determined that while the graves had been disturbed, the skeletons had not been removed.

The women were relieved to learn that the skeletons were still in the graves. They reiterated to the judge the need for an official "Do Not Touch" sign. The judge explained that these signs were issued by the court after an exhumation had been approved. He also commented on the conspicuous absence of men from the village. The women explained that the men were absent because of the civil patrol. Doña Soledad said, "Some of the men want the graves exhumed, but the military commissioner does not. So none of the patrollers are here. The thing is that those who don't oppose the exhumation are afraid of those who do."[1]

The women wanted a speedy exhumation for fear of the civil patrol stealing the bones of their dead sons and husbands. We recommended that they might be able to speed up the bureaucratic process by personally petitioning the national human rights ombudsman, Jorge Mario García La Guardía, who would be making a site visit to Plan de Sánchez the following Monday.

Two vans full of national Guatemalan press accompanied García La Guardía to Plan de Sánchez that Monday. He was greeted by the villagers of Plan de Sánchez and those from surrounding communities, the forensic team, and the delegation from Xococ. Before the national print, television, and radio reporters, these bold women from Xococ denounced the 1981 massacre of their sons and husbands and the recent actions of the civil patrol. They presented their personal petition to the ombudsman, who publicly promised to move the paperwork as quickly as possible. He also reproached the civil patrol for disturbing the graves. The women of Xococ were satisfied and thanked García La Guardía for listening to their petition.

I was fascinated by the independence and courage displayed by these women, who lived in what was widely regarded throughout the region as the most militarized community in Rabinal. In Xococ, the PAC (Patrullas Autodefensa Civil – Civil Patrol) had always been armed with Winchester rifles. Particularly interesting to me was this very public expression of the fragmented social relations of a community. On the one hand, the consent and coercion of the army's hegemonic control of Xococ was manifested by the continuation of an armed civil patrol in which all men in the community participated at a time when most communities in Rabinal had simply stopped patrolling, either by intentional noncompliance, passive resistance, or incremental neglect. On the other hand, a significant number of women from Xococ had seized, if not created, a public space from which to assert their demands for justice. When I mentioned my interest in interviewing the Xococ widows to Doña Soledad, she enthusiastically supported the idea. She invited me to visit Xococ.

She told me that I could go any day. "Just go to the village plaza and use the megaphone," she said. "Say, '*Que vengan las viudas*,'" (Widows come here). She assured me that they would all respond.[2]

When I spoke with Father Luís in Rabinal later that same Monday, he told me that he did not believe that Doña Soledad was sincere. "This story of the widows of Xococ is some kind of trick to sabotage the work of the forensic team. Most likely, it is an army plot," he said. "Her father, Don Miguel, is with the army. He cannot be trusted. He is a leader of the civil patrol and he likes it. He opposes the guerrilla." Father Luís went on to explain that these organized visits to Plan de Sánchez had to be part of an army trap for the forensic team; that in the past there had been some armed confrontations between the army and guerrilla in Xococ. He was convinced that the pressure to exhume quickly in Xococ was a plot to trick the forensic team into exhuming civilians killed by the guerrilla or guerrilla combatants killed in battle – either of which would have supported army claims of armed confrontations with the guerrilla rather than massacres of unarmed civilians. "Moreover," Father Luís reminded me, "the civil patrol from Xococ committed the massacre in Río Negro. This is a trap. Believe me. I know these people."

For the priest's interpretation of these events to be correct, the Xococ civil patrol, as well as the many women who traveled to Plan de Sánchez and accompanied us in our survey work in Xococ, would have all had to have been in collusion with the army in the orchestration of a huge lie to the forensic team, the local judge, the human rights ombudsman, and the villagers of Plan de Sánchez and other Rabinal communities.

"Que Vengan las Viudas"

While I was not convinced of the priest's interpretation, it was present in my thoughts ten days later as Kathleen Dill and I prepared to visit Xococ to interview the widows. Initially, we had scheduled our trip for that day in order to go with the judge and departmental human rights ombudsman, who already had arranged a visit. Our plans were cut short when the ombudsman failed to arrive with his vehicle. Kathleen and I went to the Rabinal plaza and hired a driver with a vehicle. The justice of the peace declined our offer to accompany us in the vehicle because he deemed it unsafe to travel to Xococ without benefit of the ombudsman's armed security guard.

Forensic team members were divided about our plans. One told us not to go. He said, "Look, they think gringas are stealing their babies for organs all over the country. The patrollers there will use that as their excuse to hang you. Don't go."[3] Another said, "No, they should go. They know what they're getting into." Then they all began to give us conflicting suggestions about how to ensure our security. "Go alone." "Go as part of a group." "Act like tourists." "Don't act like tourists."

We were relieved to discover that July 14 was the day of the livestock fair in Xococ. We decided to take advantage of the presence of the Achí from all over Rabinal who would be attending the fair. Though we knew that we would most likely be the only gringas, at least there would be people from other communities visiting. As we drove to Xococ, we invited the driver to pick up additional fares – this helped us stand out a little less when we arrived. To ensure he would not leave us stranded, we told him that we would pay him at the end of the day. We decided to take lots of photographs and act like wayward tourists. The women of Xococ had invited me and I wanted to honor their invitation.

While we were not necessarily expecting to be welcomed by everyone in Xococ, we had expected the festive atmosphere of a fair. Thus, we were taken aback when people leaving the fair ignored and avoided us. Women with whom I had waded through a river in Xococ only ten days earlier fixed their gaze upon the ground as they passed us silently. As we reached the plaza, we immediately knew their reason. Xococ was occupied by the army. Soldiers in camouflage with grenades hanging at their waists and machine guns in hand were everywhere.

Kathleen and I began to photograph horses and cows. When we reached the center of the plaza, we photographed the masked children in the dance competition. We were concerned about endangering anyone in Xococ and agreed that we would stay just long enough to show an interest in the fair (for anyone who might have been watching us) and then quietly return to Rabinal. After we had been there for about thirty minutes, Doña Soledad caught my attention and motioned for us to follow her outside of the sight and earshot of the soldiers. She invited us back to her house. She directed us to take a path through the cornfields to the back of her house. She walked home alone through the street. We met her at her back door.

In Doña Soledad's House

Though it was late morning, we sat in darkness with all doors and windows closed. She told us that the soldiers had been in her village since the day of the ombudsman's visit to Plan de Sánchez when the Xococ widows had presented their petition. Her village was occupied when the delegation returned that day from Plan de Sánchez. Fearing intervention from the ombudsman, the Xococ civil patrol had gone to the local army base to request the troops in hope of discouraging the women from pursuing the exhumation. Doña Soledad was overcome with fear. She told us that local villagers were blaming her for the occupation. If she had not pursued the exhumation, the soldiers would not be in Xococ. Everyone was scared. People were saying that something was going to happen to her father, Don Miguel. They said it would be Soledad's fault for convincing him to lead the delegation. Don Miguel was one of the oldest principales in Xococ. People were saying, "If they kill Don Miguel, then the civil patrol can kill anyone."

Though the soldiers had thus far not directly threatened anyone in the community, their mere presence was enough to terrify everyone. Doña Soledad was crying, "All I wanted was my husband's bones for a proper burial. I don't want my father to die. What should I do?"

We spent more than an hour discussing her options: denouncing the occupation to the national and international press; seeking support from CONAVIGUA (Coordindora Nacional de las Viudas de Guatemala – National Coordinator of Guatemalan Widows), withdrawing the petition for the exhumation, leaving Xococ to visit relatives in Guatemala City, thinking about these options for a few days in Xococ or in Guatemala City. Knowing she had options and feeling no pressure to make any immediate decisions calmed her significantly. Then, she began to tell her story, not in the form of an interview, but as an unloading of pain to someone who seemed to understand.

In March 1981, while her husband and fourteen other men were working in their fields, a blue Toyota full of judiciales raced into Xococ. They drove through the fields rounding up the men, accusing them of being guerrillas and killing them. Local villagers quickly buried them at the sites of their deaths. Doña Soledad wanted a proper burial for her husband. After she told me this, she said, "I feel better now. If you want to interview me, you can." I told her that an interview was unnecessary. I did not want her to feel that she owed me something because I had listened to her. She asked me how to get in touch with CONAVIGUA.[4]

Later that day, I spoke with Father Luís. While he was clearly concerned about the army occupation of Xococ, he maintained his initial interpretation that still, somehow, this all had to be some kind of conspiratorial army plot.

Testimony and Healing

For massacre and torture survivors, and other victims of extreme state terror, testimony has meaning beyond its implications for individual agency, community action, and challenging repressive state practices. Psychologists and other mental health professionals have found testimony, as a therapeutic model, to be an effective method for survivors to process and come to terms with the extreme traumas they have suffered. Though grounded in Western psychological training, which seeks to categorize individuals and all manifestations of psychological trauma into quantifiable and identifiable diagnostic concepts related to an assumed baseline of individual autonomy, experienced trauma researchers and practitioners have further sought to develop interventions that better address survivors' needs and recognize cross-cultural differences. The therapeutic testimonial model is one such intervention.[5]

Just as the landscape of contemporary anthropology is marked by debates about its theory and practice, the discipline of psychology and the mental health field have ongoing debates about the clinical efficacy and limitations of diagnostic concepts – which are the cornerstone of therapeutic practice. The realities of lived experiences of survivors have presented significant challenges and controversy regarding traditional Western models of labeling (and treating) individual survivors and their traumas. One example of this is post-traumatic stress disorder (PTSD), one of the many categories of psychiatric disorders defined and operationalized in the *Diagnostic and Statistical Manual of Mental Disorders* (DSM).[6] The DSM is the near-universal tool used in the United States for diagnosis and treatment of mental disorders. The therapeutic testimonial model challenges the core assumptions of homogenized culture underlying the very concept of universal diagnosis (and its emphasis on individual autonomy) and in particular the relevance of PTSD (which is based on symptoms and treatment of individuals) to cultures in which individual personhood is based more in the identity of community culture than in that of the individual. Still, when PTSD became a category of the DSM-III in 1980, its inclusion was significant in that it was the first time a collection of symptoms resulting from an environmental stress were specified and classified as a disorder.

As the mental health community sought to come to terms with the common collection of trauma symptoms present in vast numbers of Vietnam veterans, PTSD gained currency with both clinical researchers and practitioners. These symptoms later came to be recognized as a syndrome.[7] The timing for categorizing the trauma of Vietnam veterans as PTSD coincided with significant increases in immigration of traumatized refugee populations to the United States, Australia,

New Zealand, and Europe. Patrick McGorry notes that mental health services to these refugee populations were a categorical failure in the 1970s and early 1980s due to a lack of appreciation of the unique needs of traumatized refugees.[8] Despite existing literature offering new insights to the treatment of trauma,[9] PTSD swiftly became the diagnosis of choice for identifying and addressing the traumas of war and torture survival. By the 1990s, significant studies of mental health treatment models for Bosnian, Guatemalan, Chilean, Salvadoran, and Cambodian trauma survivors offered new treatment frameworks and challenged the relevance of PTSD, as well as many standard practices in psychotherapeutic treatment. Many of these new treatment models were the direct result of researchers and mental health practitioners working directly with trauma survivors in community health programs serving affected refugee populations, or explicitly involved in the provision of mental health services through new centers established for the treatment of torture survivors. Thus, their development of new models of intervention and their research on the efficacy of these models was driven by clinical experience with the inadequacies of DSM categories and treatment.[10]

Testimony became a key tool recognized for its efficacy in healing both public and private domains.[11] Drawing on psychotherapeutic models of treatment developed in the Southern Cone during the state repression of the 1970s, therapists in the United States, Europe, Australia, and New Zealand began to set aside the "neutrality" that had always been one of the basic tenets of therapeutic practice. Argentine psychiatrist Tato Pavlovsky explained his own experience with the inevitable necessity of this shift in therapeutic practice:

> Lots of people were dying and it was impossible to be objective in this period.... The issue of neutrality was dead along with the dying.... I tried to be as neutral as possible in order to understand the nature of the more irrational conflicts that a patient might be suffering. But, given the conditions we were living through, sometimes the therapy provided the important function of helping patients with the difficult task of developing a language with which to articulate their experience of terror. In retrospect, I realize that often the therapy group provided the only space in which people could put into words the fear, the panic. It was the only space in which to speak.[12]

Likewise, North American, Australian, and European therapists learned from experience that in order to establish an effective therapeutic relationship with trauma survivors, therapists needed to take explicit positions on the side of the survivors. These included an open commitment to human rights,[13] a "partisan" position,[14] and an acknowledgment of professional responsibility for the prevention of acts of state terror by encouraging "appropriate opposing actions."[15] This shift from neutrality to partisanship reflected a growing awareness of prevalent thematic conflicts common among trauma survivors. Recurring themes included:

> fear of destroying others, such as relatives and therapists, by relating the trauma; fear of loss of control over feelings of rage, violence, and anxiety; shame and rage over the vulnerability and helplessness evoked by torture; rage and grief at the sudden and arbitrary disruption of individual, social, and political projects, and at the violation of rights; guilt and shame over surviving and being unable to save others; guilt over bringing distress on self and family and over not protecting them...; fear and rage at the unpredictability of and lack of control over events; grief over the loss of significant others, through both death and exile; and loss of aspects of the self, such as trust and innocence.[16]

By transforming the therapist's role from neutral observer to partisan witness, the survivors are given the opportunity to "understand the impossible nature of the situation to which they had been exposed" and are then able to begin transferring "the burden of responsibility" to the perpetrators of violence and to the repressive structures that fomented their traumas.[17] The research experiences of the forensic team and my own fieldwork experiences reaffirm the necessity of recognizing our professional obligations as anthropologists to contribute to the prevention of human rights violations and support survivor efforts for justice by establishing solidarity with survivors of trauma.

The testimonial therapy model, as developed in the Southern Cone and now practiced in the United States, Australia, Europe, and other parts of Latin America, has much in common with the theory and practice of testimonial literature. It also resonates with the FAFG (Fundación de Antropología Forense de Guatemala – Guatemalan Forensic Anthropology Foundation) model of collecting testimonies. In each case, the testimony of survivors reflects their individual and community experiences as a part of a larger national history. In their work with Bosnian survivors of "Ethnic Cleansing," Stevan Weine and Dóri Laub write that the historical narrative of therapeutic testimony is "one dimension of the survivors' struggle to reassert their connectedness to the threatened collective entities of community, ethnicity and nationality."[18] A written record of the testimony is produced in the therapeutic process. In addition to the possibilities of catharsis and closure presented by the therapeutic model of testimony, the survivor, who plays an active therapeutic role by giving testimony, also participates in the production of the written record, which can later be used in individual and community attempts to provide evidence of human rights violations and seek justice.[19]

Community Healing

When Rolando Alecio completed his fieldwork as a contributing author for *Las Masacres en Rabinal*,[20] he was convinced that massacre survivors were in great need of psychotherapeutic intervention. A long-time human rights activist trained as an anthropologist and with extensive fieldwork in the Achí communities of Rabinal, Alecio was well-aware of the debates of cultural relativism in psychotherapy as well as the doubts about the relevance of the PTSD model. Seeking to learn from similar experiences with state repression in other countries, he immersed himself in trauma therapy literature from all over the world. With psychologists Olga Alicia Paz and Felipe Sartí, he founded the Equipo de Estudios Comunitarios y Acción Psicosocial (ECAP – Psycho-Social Community Studies and Action Team) to develop a pilot community healing project in Rabinal. Recognizing the cultural importance of community identity for the Achí, ECAP transformed the individual testimony model to a community model. Like the individual testimony model, ECAP's community healing project breaks the binary that counterpoises justice and healing, further challenging Western constructs of both politics and therapeutic healing.

The community-articulated support groups for widows, widowers, and orphans, which grew out of the exhumations, and other human rights activities in Rabinal became the base of ECAP's community work. Though ECAP was initiated in 1996 as a pilot project limited to only a few communities in Rabinal, the popular response was so great that by the end of the first year, ECAP was working in nineteen Rabinal communities at the request of local residents.[21]

Conscious of the instability of NGO (nongovernmental organization) funding, from the outset ECAP sought to develop community skills in mental health promotion. Indeed, when Alecio, Paz, and Sartí began the project, they did so with their own funds and made a collective commitment to go without salaries for six months.[22] "We began ECAP with our own funds and we always worked with the assumption that in six months or a year, we might not have any funding," explained Alecio. "So, we always sought to develop community-based mental health promotion so that community healing would continue even if ECAP collapsed."[23]

To these ends, ECAP community participants received training in responsible listening techniques, participatory healing techniques, and the development of community mental health safety nets. In addition to community participation in workshops and support groups addressing these themes, ECAP developed three low-literacy training publications and other educational tools for community use. ECAP's organizational philosophy resonates with Francesca Polleta's research on the United States civil rights movement, which emphasized development of local community leadership, "standing up" (speaking publicly), consensus decision making, and an emphasis on the collective process as a part of emancipation.[24]

I had the privilege of accompanying ECAP in their community work on numerous occasions, both formally and informally, from 1996 to 2002. Village support groups meet in their communities and at the ECAP office in Rabinal. Frequently, collaborative intercommunity meetings are held to share experiences and plan joint community projects. The following is a brief composite sketch of my observations of some of ECAP's healing techniques in action.

At community support groups, a near life-size drawing of an Achí man and/or woman is displayed (depending upon the gender composition of the group). The Achís represented in these drawings are seated in chairs with their bodies slumping forward and sad facial expressions. The group begins by describing how the person in the drawing is feeling. Nearly everyone comments that the person is "very sad," and some say the person is "angry." When asked by ECAP or local community facilitators why they describe the person in the drawing as sad or angry, support group participants identify the body language and facial expressions as those of "pain." When asked why the person might feel pain, sadness, or anger, the responses are profound. "She is sad because her eyes dried from crying so many tears," explained one woman. "He has pain because his heart has fallen into his stomach," said a man. "Her head hurts from being filled with so much pain for so long. She has no room for good thoughts," explained a woman. "His bones hurt because the weight of his pain pulls him to the ground," said a man.

These initial discussions in support groups provide an opening for community therapy to begin. ECAP points out that community healing reaffirms Maya community values and practices of cooperation, equilibrium, and respect. ECAP's goals of community healing include creating: (1) a space where community members can express themselves and be heard; (2) a space of trust and acceptance; and (3) a space for solidarity to nurture new relations of mutual support. Through the collective creation of this space, and with the assistance of ECAP facilitators, support groups themselves identify their existing community resources and new resources that arise out of group discussion. Additional goals of the community healing project are the development of: (1) local capacity to collectively sustain community healing; (2) a sense of belonging; (3) validation of community experiences; (4) community empowerment for local action; (5) the group's ability to put forth solutions for community problems; and (6) local skills in conflict resolution to reduce community divisions and antagonisms resulting from internal village disputes.[25]

After the exhumation, Juan Manuel Gerónimo participated as a local researcher/ organizer in the archbishop's *Nunca Más* (REHMI – Proyecto Interdiocesano de Recuperación Histórico – Interdiocesene Project for the Recuperation of Historical Memory) human rights project. Now, he participates in ECAP's community healing project in Plan de Sánchez and in other communities throughout Rabinal. I asked Don Juan Manuel why he decided to dedicate a significant amount of his time to ECAP meetings and workshops. He explained: "I believe the work of REHMI needs to continue in the communities. The same people who worked in REHMI can collaborate with ECAP to help the poor people who suffered these massacres talk about what happened and how it happened. This needs to be done and it needs to be done formally so that as our children and families grow, they will have clarity about our history and so there will be a space to continue to declare the truth."[26]

In their efforts to develop safe community spaces of mutual emotional support, those who participate in community healing in Rabinal have strengthened practices of solidarity, trust, communication, participation, integration, support, and tolerance grounded in Achí community practices. ECAP's methodology and practice of community healing recognized and elaborated community experiences of traumas suffered. By creating safe collective spaces for individuals to speak and be heard, individuals and communities are able to recuperate and redefine collective identity in the aftermath of violence. It is this nascent collective identity that offers hope for the recovery of human dignity and the reconstruction of the social fabric so damaged by political violence. Like the exhumations, this process of collective recovery of psycho-social community identity also establishes the community as the conduit from the individual to the nation.

"Now There is More Freedom"

Following the public burials of massacre victims in Rabinal, survivors sought the healing of space and community by building monuments to commemorate the victims. In Plan de Sánchez, survivors requested support from the Catholic Church and NGOs to raise funds to purchase materials for the community construction of a memorial chapel at the site of their new, legal cemetery. The chapel in Plan de Sánchez was constructed in keeping with Maya religious burial practices. Massacre victims are buried under the chapel floor, making the chapel a large monumental marker and facilitating Maya religious practices of communicating with the ancestors at the altar within the chapel. A chiseled marble plaque entitled "It is not possible to cover the sun with just one finger" tells the history of the army massacre in Plan de Sánchez. Local residents frequently visit the chapel, leave flowers, light candles, and pray to the ancestors. Each year on the anniversary of the massacre, the residents of Plan de Sánchez invite friends, relatives, neighbors, government officials, the press, national and international NGOs, and all of Rabinal to participate in a religious commemoration for the victims.

In 1997, more than 500 people attended the event, where both Catholic mass and Maya costumbre were celebrated. The community provided all in attendance with an impressive feast of tamales, meat, beans, tortillas, coffee, and sodas. While Achí from Rabinal and other villages, as well as many NGO representatives, attended the commemoration, the only Rabinal ladinos attending were two elderly women. I asked them why they came to Plan de Sánchez. Doña Sonia responded,

"Doña Angela is very religious. She attends every mass for the dead. La Violencia really affected her. So, now she is very religious." I asked Doña Sonia if she too was "very religious." "Not really," she responded as she drank her second beer purchased from the Plan de Sánchez *tienda*. "These people are my friends. They are human beings. I have always known that. After the massacres, I tried to help them. But, what can one widow do?" she asked. Then she went on to explain, "When they were in the mountains, if they came to my house, I would give them food, candles, and some clothing, because they had nothing. They were wearing rags. They are my friends. They always came to my store before [La Violencia]. So I couldn't turn my back on their needs."

When I asked why other ladinos from Rabinal were absent, she said, "Some are embarrassed because they did nothing. Others are scared because of what they did. Bad people became rich from the massacres. They stole the livestock from the villages. They became rich as butchers selling the meat of the animals they stole." I asked her if these men were always bad or if the violence had made them bad. After thinking for a few minutes, she said, "I think they were always bad. What happened is that La Violencia gave them the power to do bad things with impunity. So they became worse."[27]

While much of the distance remains between the ladinos and the Achí of Rabinal, there are notable changes in the town. Windows and doors that, in the past, were locked shut in the daytime are now left open into the early evening. People no longer rush through the streets to reach their destination. At night, Achí and ladina women stroll the streets arm in arm, visiting friends and neighbors, buying an ice cream in the park; children play games and cruise the streets on their bicycles. While some might think that these changes are due simply to the passage of time, this comfortable freedom of movement is hard to find in other municipalities where truth of La Violencia remains locked in silence.

An Achí professional in Rabinal commented, "The exhumations changed the way people understand themselves in this community. Now, people are living better lives. They're not afraid to leave their homes."[28]

"Now there is more freedom," explained Don Juan Manuel. "The ex-authorities, the ex-commissioners, these people aren't threatening to us anymore. If someone declares their reality, there aren't threats like there were before the exhumation."[29]

Don Pablo described his feelings about the changes:

We are grateful for the exhumations and we are grateful to Juan Manuel for his example. He struggled for the community. Now, there is liberty. Now, our lives are a little better. Some of the fear is gone. We can walk on the paths, we can go to our fields to work without fear. We can go to Rabinal to make our purchases in the market without worries. There are still some bad people there. But now, all they have are words and their words don't hurt us.

Even though we are still very poor, we can live without fear. We are tranquil in our homes. We are grateful to all of you internationals who have taken our declarations because the government had to take account of our case, take account of what happened here.

It is our hope that what happened here never happens again and that the army officials who are responsible go to jail. Now, we go on with our lives: taking care of the land, growing our crops, and trying to give our children some schooling, trying to improve the lives of our families.

As I have said to you before, and maybe others have also told you in their testimonies, it isn't just that we heard it, it isn't just that we saw it. We lived La Violencia and it is written in our hearts. Thanks to God, we have reached an equilibrium. Perhaps now peace will come. This is my testimony. Thank you for listening.[30]

NOTES

1   Xococ testimony no. 1, 28 June 1994.

2   Xococ testimony no. 2, 4 July 1994.

3   1994 was the year of the *Roboniños* national panic in Guatemala. Several North American women were attacked and severely beaten in rural communities. They were accused of stealing babies to sell their organs. Like other international women, Kathleen and I were frequently viewed with suspicion, and parents would spirit their children out of our paths, sometimes saying, "*Vienen las lobas*" (Here come the wolves). For more on roboniños, see Abigail Adams, "Word, Work and Worship: Engendering Evangelical Culture between Highland Guatemala and the United States" (Ph.D. diss., University of Virginia, 1999), and Diane Nelson, *A Finger in the Wound* (Berkeley: University of California Press, 1999). On worldwide organ-stealing rumors, see Nancy Scheper-Hughes, "Theft of Life: The Globalization of Organ Stealing Rumors," *Anthropology Today* 12, no. 3 (June 1996): 3–11.

4   Xococ testimony no. 3, 14 July 1994.

5   For more on the therapeutic testimonial model, see Yael Fischman and Jaime Ross, "Group Treatment of Exiled Survivors of Torture," *American Journal of Orthopsychiatry* 60, no. 1 (January 1990): 135–41; Patrick Morris, Derrick Silove, Vijaya Manicavasagar, Robin Bowles, Margaret Cunningham, and Ruth Tarn, "Variations in Therapeutic Interventions for Cambodian and Chilean Refugee Survivors of Torture and Trauma: A Pilot Study," *Australian and New Zealand Journal of Psychiatry* 3 (September 1993): 429–35; Patrick McGorry, "Working with Survivors of Torture and Trauma: The Victorian Foundation for Survivors Perspective," *Australian and New Zealand Journal of Psychiatry* 29, no. 3 (September 1995): 463–72; Ronan McIvor and Stuart Turner, "Assessment and Treatment Approaches for Survivors of Torture," *British Journal of Psychiatry* 166 (1995): 705–11; Maritza Thompson and Patrick McGorry, "Psychological Sequelae of Torture and Trauma in Chilean and Salvadoran Migrants: A Pilot Study," *Australian and New Zealand Journal of Psychiatry* 29, no. 1 (March 1995): 84–95; Stevan Weine and Dori Laub, "Narrative Constructions of Historical Realities in Testimony with Bosnian Survivors of 'Ethnic Cleansing,'" *Psychiatry* 58 (August 1995): 246–61; Howard Waitzkin and Holly Magaña, "The Black Box in Somatization: Unexplained Physical Symptoms, Culture, and Narratives of Trauma," *Social Science and Medicine* 45, no. 6 (September 1997): 811–25.

6   See Thomas Gavagan and Antonio Martinez, "Presentation of Recent Torture Survivors to Family Practice," *Journal of Family Medicine* 44, no. 2 (February 1997): 209.

7   Patrick McGorry, "The Clinical Boundaries of Posttraumatic Stress Disorder," *Australian and New Zealand Journal of Psychiatry* 29, no. 3 (September 1995): 385.

8   McGorry, "Working with Survivors of Torture and Trauma," 463.

9   See, for example, Jerzy Krupinski, "Psychiatric Disorders of East European Refugees Now in Australia," *Social Science and Medicine* 7 (1973): 31–49; Elizabeth Lira, "Sobrevivir: Los Limites de la psicoterapia," in E. Lira and E. Weistein, eds., *Psicoterapía y represión política* (Mexico City: Sigo Veintiuno Editores, 1984); A. J. Cienfuegos and C. Monelli, "The Testimony of Political Repression as a Therapeutic Instrument," *American Journal of Orthopsychiatry* 53 (1983): 43–51.

10 See, for example, Fischman and Ross, "Group Treatment of Exiled Survivors of Torture"; Morris et al., "Variations in Therapeutic Interventions"; McGorry, "Working with Survivors of Torture and Trauma"; Thompson and McGorry, "Psychological Sequelae of Torture and Trauma"; Weine and Laub, "Narrative Constructions"; Harvey Weinstein, Laura Dansky, and Vincent Iacopino, "Torture and War Trauma Survivors in Primary Care Practice," *Western Journal of Medicine* 165, no. 3 (September 1996): 533–8.

11 Weine and Laub, "Narrative Constructions of Historical Realities," 246.

12 Nancy Caro Hollander, *Love in a Time of Hate – Liberation Psychology in Latin America* (New Brunswick: Rutgers, 1997), 85.

13 McIvor and Turner, "Assessment and Treatment Approaches for Survivors of Torture."

14 McGorry, "Working with Survivors of Torture and Trauma."

15 Weine and Laub, "Narrative Constructions," 260.

16 Fischman and Ross, "Group Treatment of Exiled Survivors of Torture," 137.

17 Fischman and Ross, "Group Treatment of Exiled Survivors of Torture," 137.

18 Weine and Laub, "Narrative Constructions of Historical Realities," 247.

19 McIvor and Turner, "Assessment and Treatment Approaches for Survivors of Torture," 706.

20 FAFG, *Las Masacres de Rabinal* (Guatemala City: FAFG, 1995). Other contributing authors included Fernando Moscoso and Ronaldo Sánchez. At the time of the publication of *Las Masacres en Rabinal* in 1995, it was still considered safer for the security of the authors that the publication carry no names other than the institutional name of the FAFG.

21 In 1997, ECAP replicated the Rabinal healing project in Nebaj and began to accompany the FAFG during exhumations.

22 This is not an uncommon occurrence within human rights NGOs. Without salaries, FAFG staff continued exhumations for nearly six months between 1996 and 1997. Sometimes funding agencies change their funding priorities or funding schedules without notice, and sometimes the NGOs are too overwhelmed with work and/or lack sufficient staff to keep track of application deadlines. The decision to continue to work without salaries was made at great personal and familial sacrifice. All the staff members of the FAFG and ECAP as well as their families depend upon their modest NGO salaries for their livelihoods.

23 Rolando Alecio, interview with author, Guatemala City, 28 August 1997.

24 Francesca Polletta, *Freedom is an Endless Meeting: Democracy in American Social Movements* (Chicago: University of Chicago Press, 2002).

25 See ECAP, *Técnicas de Escucha Responsable. Cuadernos de Salud Mental No. 1* (Guatemala City: ECAP, September 1998); ECAP, *Nuestras Molestias – Técnicas Participativas de Apoyo Psicosocial. Cuadernos de Salud Mental No. 2* (Guatemala City: ECAP, October 1998); ECAP, *El Sistema de Vigilancia de la Salud Mental Comunitaria. Cuadernos de Salud Mental No. 3* (Guatemala City: ECAP, November 1998); ECAP, *Psicología Social y Violencia Política* (Guatemala City: ECAP, 1999). An interesting and unexpected outcome of this process has been that parties in conflict often request arbitration by ECAP staff when they are unable to independently reach agreement. In such cases, the parties in conflict further develop their skills by resolving the real-life dispute and laying a framework for peaceful resolution of future village conflicts.

26 Rabinal testimony no. 6–3, 6 June 1997.

27 Plan de Sánchez interview no. 3, 18 July 1997.

28 Rabinal interview no. 1, 19 July 1997.

29 Rabinal testimony no. 6–3, 6 June 1997.

30 Rabinal testimony no. 6–4, 17 June 1997.

9

Rethinking Health and Human Rights: Time for a Paradigm Shift

Paul Farmer and Nicole Gastineau

From the perspective of a preferential option for the poor, the right to health care, housing, decent work, protection against hunger, and other economic, social, and cultural necessities are as important as civil and political rights and more so.
Leigh Binford, The El Mozote Massacre

Medicine and its allied health sciences have for too long been peripherally involved in work on human rights. Fifty years ago, the door to greater involvement was opened by Article 25 of the Universal Declaration of Human Rights, which underlined social and economic rights: "Everyone has the right to a standard of living adequate for the health and well-being of himself and his family, including food, clothing, housing, and medical care and necessary social services, and the right to security in the event of unemployment, sickness, disability, widowhood, old age or other lack of livelihood in circumstances beyond his control."[1]

But the intervening decades have seen too little progress in the push for social and economic rights, even though we may point with some pride to gains in civil and political rights. That these distinctions are crucial is made clear by a visit to a Russian prison. With its current political and economic disruption, Russia's rate of incarceration – 644 per 100,000 citizens are currently in jail or prison – is second only to that of the United States, where there are 699 prisoners per 100,000 in the population. Compare this to much of the rest of Europe, where the figure is about one-fifth as high.[2]

In the cramped, crammed detention centers where hundreds of thousands of Russian detainees await due process, many fall ill with tuberculosis. Convicted prisoners who are diagnosed with tuberculosis are sent to one of more than fifty

Originally published in *Journal of Law, Medicine & Ethics*, 30: 4 (2002).

"TB colonies." Imagine a Siberian prison in which the cells are as crowded as cattle cars, the fetid air thick with tubercle bacilli. Imagine a cell in which most of the prisoners are perpetually coughing and all are said to have active tuberculosis. Let the mean age of the inmates be less than 30 years old. Finally, imagine that many of these young men are receiving ineffective treatment for their disease – given drug toxicity, worse than receiving placebo – even though they are the beneficiaries of "directly observed therapy" with first-line antituberculous agents, delivered by European humanitarian organizations and their Russian colleagues.

If this seems hard to imagine, it shouldn't be. I have seen this situation in several prisons; there are still prisoners receiving directly observed doses of medications that cannot cure them. For many of these prisoners, the therapy is ineffective because the strains of tuberculosis that are epidemic within the prisons are resistant to the drugs being administered. Various observers, including some from international human rights organizations, have averred that these prisoners have "untreatable forms" of tuberculosis, and few have challenged this claim even though treatment based on the standard of care used elsewhere in Europe and in North America can cure the great majority of such cases.[3] "Untreatable," in these debates, really means "expensive to treat." For this and other reasons, tuberculosis has again become the leading cause of death among Russian prisoners – even among those nominally receiving treatment. Similar situations may be found throughout the former Soviet Union.

Are human rights violated in this dismal scenario? If we look only at civil rights without taking social and economic rights into consideration, we would focus on a single violation: prolonged pretrial detention. Those arrested are routinely detained for up to a year before making a court appearance. In many documented cases, young detainees have died of prison-acquired tuberculosis before their cases ever went to trial. Such detention clearly violates not only Russian law, but several human rights charters to which the country is signatory. Russian and international human rights activists have focused on this problem, demanding that all detainees be brought quickly to trial. An impasse is quickly reached when the underfunded Russian courts wearily respond that they are working as fast as they can. The Ministry of Justice agrees with the human rights people, and is now interested in amnesty for prisoners and alternatives to imprisonment. But these measures, helpful though they may prove, will not save those already sick.

What of social and economic rights violations? Examining these yields a far longer list of violations – but, importantly, also a longer list of possible interventions. Prison conditions are deplorable; the directors of the former gulag do not dispute this point. The head of the federal penitentiary system, speaking to Amnesty International, described the prisoners as living in "conditions amounting to torture."[4] Detainees are subjected to conditions that guarantee increased exposure to drug-resistant strains of M. tuberculosis, and to make matters worse, they are denied adequate food and medical care. In the words of one physician: "I have spent my entire medical career caring for prisoners with tuberculosis. And although we complained about shortages in the eighties, we had no idea how good we had it then. Now it's a daily struggle for food, drugs, lab supplies, even heat and electricity."[5]

These prisoners are dying of ineffectively treated multidrug-resistant tuberculosis (MDRTB). Experts from the international public health community have argued that it is not necessary to treat MDRTB – the "untreatable form" in question – in this region. These experts have argued that all patients should be treated with identical doses of the same drugs and that MDRTB will disappear if such strategies are adopted.[6] Cost-efficacy arguments against treating drug-resistant tuberculosis almost always fail to note that most of the drugs necessary for such treatment have been off-patent for years. And it is simply not true that MDRTB is untreatable – Partners In Health has done work in Peru and Haiti showing that MDRTB can be cured in resource-poor settings.[7] All the prison rights activism in the world will come to naught if prisoners are guaranteed the right to treatment but given the wrong prescriptions. A civil and political rights perspective does not allow us to grasp the full nature of these human rights violations, much less attempt to fix all of them.

So what does a focus on health bring to the struggle for human rights? A narrow legal approach to health and human rights can obscure the nature of violations, thereby enfeebling our best responses to them. Casting prison-based tuberculosis epidemics in terms of social and economic rights offers an entry point for public health and medicine, an important step in the process that could halt these epidemics. Medicine enters the picture and can respond to the past-neglected call for action. Conversely, of course, failure to consider social and economic rights can prevent the allied health professions and the social sciences from making their fullest contribution to the struggle for human rights.

Pragmatic Solidarity: A Synergy of Health and Human Rights

Public health and access to medical care are social and economic rights. They are at least as critical as civil rights. One of the ironies of our global era is that while public health has increasingly sacrificed equity for efficiency, the poor have become well-informed enough to reject separate standards of care. In our professional journals, these subaltern voices have been well-nigh blotted out. But snatches of their rebuke have been heard recently with regard to access to antiretroviral therapy for HIV disease. Whether we continue to ignore them or not, the destitute sick are increasingly clear on one point: Making social and economic rights a reality is the key goal for health and human rights in the twenty-first century.

Although trained in anthropology, I, like most anthropologists, do not embrace the rigidly particularist and relativist tendencies popularly associated with the discipline.[8] That is, I believe that violations of human dignity are not to be accepted merely because they are buttressed by local ideology or long-standing tradition. But anthropology – in common with sociological and historical perspectives in general – allows us to place both human rights abuses and the discourses (and other responses) they generate in broader contexts. Furthermore, these disciplines permit us to ground our understanding of human rights violations in broader analyses of power and social inequality. Whereas a purely legal view of human rights tends to obscure the dynamics of human rights violations, the contextualizing disciplines reveal them to be pathologies of power. Social inequalities based on race or ethnicity, gender, religious creed, and – above all – social class are the motor force behind most human rights violations. In other words, violence against individuals is usually embedded in entrenched structural violence.

In exploring the relationships between structural violence and human rights, I draw on my own experience serving the destitute sick in settings such as Haiti and Chiapas and Russia, where human rights violations are a daily concern (even if structural violence is not always seen as a human rights issue). I do this not to make over-much of my personal acquaintance with other people's suffering, but rather to ground a theoretical discussion in the very real experiences that have shaped my views on health and human rights. Each of these situations calls not only for our recognition of the relationship between structural violence and human rights violations, but also for what we have termed "pragmatic solidarity": the rapid deployment of our tools and resources to improve the health and well-being of those who suffer this violence.

Pragmatic solidarity is different from, but nourished by, solidarity – the desire to make common cause with those in need. Solidarity itself is a precious thing: people enduring great hardship often remark that they are grateful for the prayers and good wishes of fellow human beings. But when sentiment is accompanied by the goods and services that might diminish unjust hardship, surely it is enriched. To those in great need, solidarity without the pragmatic component can seem like abstract piety. The goal of our partnerships with sister organizations in Haiti, Peru, Mexico, Russia, and the United States is neither charity nor development. Rather, these relationships reflect a commitment to struggle alongside the poor, and against the economic and political structures that create their poverty. We see pragmatic solidarity as a means to synergize health and human rights – when the destitute sick can fulfill their human right to health, the door may be opened to more readily achieve other economic, social, cultural, and political rights?[9] One telling example comes from Haiti, where HIV-positive patients placed on antiretroviral therapy repeatedly inform us that they can now return to daily life and caring for their children.[10] When we move beyond sentiments to action, we incur risks, and these deter many. But it is possible, clearly, to link lofty ideals to sound analysis. This linkage does not always occur in human rights work, in part because of a reluctance to examine the political economy of suffering and brutality.

I will not discuss, except in passing, the covenants and conventions that constitute the key documents of the human rights movement here. The goal of this article is to raise, and to answer, some questions relevant to health and human rights; to explore the promise of pragmatic solidarity as a response to structural violence; and to identify promising directions for future work in this field. It is my belief that the conclusions that follow are the most important challenges before those who concern themselves with health and human rights.

How Far has the Human Rights Movement Come?

The field of health and human rights, most would agree, is in its infancy. Attempting to define a new field is necessarily a treacherous enterprise. Sometimes we appear to step on the toes of those who have long been at work when we mean instead to stand on their shoulders. Human rights law, which focuses on civil and political rights, is much older than human rights medicine. And if vigor is assessed in the typical academic style-by length of bibliography – civil and political rights law is the more robust field, too. That legal documents and scholarship dominate the human rights literature is not surprising (note Steiner and Alston), given that the human rights movement has "struggled to assume so law-like a character."[11]

But even in legal terms, the international human rights movement is essentially a modern phenomenon, beginning, some argue, with the Nuremberg trials. It is this movement that has led, most recently, to the creation of international tribunals to judge war crimes in the Balkans and in Rwanda. Yet 50 years after the Universal Declaration of Human Rights, and 50 years after the four Geneva Conventions, what do we have to show for these efforts? Do we have some sense of outcomes? Aryeh Neier, former executive director of Human Rights Watch, recently reviewed the history of various treaties and covenants from Nuremberg to the Convention against Torture and Other Cruel, Inhuman or Degrading Treatment or Punishment. He said, "Nations have honored these obligations largely in the breach."[12]

Few could argue against Neier's dour assessment, but the past few years have been marked by a certain amount of human rights triumphalism. The fiftieth anniversary of the Universal Declaration has led to many celebrations, but to few careful assessments of current realities. Even those within the legal community acknowledge that it would be difficult to correlate a steep rise in the publication of human rights documents with a statistically significant drop in the number of human rights abuses. Rosalyn Higgins says pointedly:

> No one doubts that there exists a norm prohibiting torture. No state denies the existence of such a norm; and, indeed, it is widely recognized as a customary rule of international law by national courts. But it is equally clear from, for example, the reports of Amnesty International, that the great majority of states systematically engage in torture. If one takes the view that noncompliance is relevant to the retention of normative quality, are we to conclude that there is not really any prohibition of torture under customary international law?[13]

Whether these laws are binding or largely hortatory constitutes a substantial debate in the legal literature, but such debates seem academic in the face of overwhelming evidence of persistent abuses.

When we expand the concept of rights to include social and economic rights, the gap between the ideal and reality is even wider. Local and global inequalities mean that the fruits of medical and scientific advances are stockpiled for some and denied to others. The dimensions of these inequalities are staggering, and the trends are adverse. To cite just a few examples – in 1998, Michael Jordan earned from Nike the equivalent of 60,000 years' salary for an Indonesian footwear assembly worker; Haitian factory workers, most of them women, made 28 cents per hour sewing Pocahontas pajamas, while Disney's US-based chief executive officer made $97,000 for each hour he toiled.[14]

The pathogenic effects of such inequality are now recognized.[15] Many governments, including our own, refuse to redress inequalities in health, while others are largely powerless to address them.[16] But although the reasons for failure are many and varied, even optimists allow that human rights charters and covenants have not brought an end to – and may not even have slowed – egregious abuses, however they are defined. States large and small violate civil, economic, and social rights, and inequality both prompts and covers these violations. In other words, rights attributed on paper are of little value when the existing political and social structures do not afford all individuals the ability to enjoy these rights, let alone defend them.

There are, of course, exceptions; victories have been declared. But not many of them are very encouraging on close scrutiny. Haiti, the case I know best, offers a humbling example. First, the struggle for social and economic rights – food, medical care, education, housing, decent jobs – has been dealt crippling blows in Haiti. Such basic entitlements, the centerpiece of the popular movement that in 1990 brought the country's first democratically elected president to power, were buried under an avalanche of human rights violations after the military coup of 1991. And although human rights groups were among those credited with helping to restore constitutional rule in Haiti, this was accomplished, to a large extent, by sacrificing the struggle for social and economic rights.[17] In recent years, it has sometimes seemed as if the steam has run out of the movement to bring to justice those responsible for the murder and mayhem that have made Haiti such a difficult place to live. There are notable exceptions – for instance, the sentencing of military officials responsible for a 1994 civilian massacre – but both the legal and socio-economic campaigns have slowed almost to a standstill.[18]

Or take Argentina. The gruesome details of the "dirty war" are familiar to many.[19] Seeking what Aryeh Neier has chillingly termed "a better mousetrap of repression," the Argentine military government began "disappearing" (as Latin Americans said in the special syntax crafted for the occasion) people it identified as leftists.[20] Many people know, now, about the death flights that took place every Wednesday for two years. Thousands of citizens the government deemed subversive, many of them students and most of them just having survived torture, were flown from a military installation out over the Atlantic, stripped, and shoved out of the plane. A better mousetrap, indeed.

What happened next is well-documented, although it is a classic instance of the half-empty, half-full glass. Those who say the glass is half full note that an elected civilian government subsequently tried and convicted high-ranking military figures, including the generals who shared, in the fashion of runners in a relay, the presidential office. Those who say the glass is half empty note that the prompt pardoning and release of the criminals meant that, once again, no one has been held accountable for thousands of murders.[21] Similar stories abound in Guatemala, El Salvador, the state of Chiapas in Mexico, and elsewhere in Latin America.[22]

These painful experiences are, of course, no reason to declare legal proceedings ineffective. On the contrary, they remind us that some of what was previously hidden away is now out in the open. Disclosure is often the first step in the struggle against impunity, and human rights organizations – almost all of them nongovernmental – have at times forced unwilling governments to acknowledge what really happened. These efforts should serve as a rallying cry for those who now look to constitute international criminal tribunals.

Still, the results to date suggest that we would be unwise to place all our hopes on the legal-struggle approach. This approach has proved insufficient in preventing human rights abuses, and all the civil and political rights ever granted will provide little comfort to the starving and the sick if they are not enforced by the state, as they so often are not. Complementary strategies and new openings are critically needed. The health and human rights "angle" can provide new opportunities and new strategies at the same time that it lends strength and purpose to a movement sorely in need of buttressing.

Can One Merely Study Human Rights Abuses?

A few years ago, the French sociologist Pierre Bourdieu and his colleagues pulled together a compendium of testimonies from those the French term "the excluded" in order to bring into relief la misere du monde. Bourdieu and colleagues qualified their claims for the role of scholarship in addressing this misery: "To subject to scrutiny the mechanisms which render life painful, even untenable, is not to neutralize them; to bring to light contradictions is not to resolve them."[23] It is precisely such humility that is needed, and rarely exhibited, in academic commentary on human rights.

It is difficult merely to study human rights abuses. We know with certainty that rights are being abused at this very moment. And the fact that we can study, rather than endure, these abuses is a reminder that we too are implicated in and benefit from the increasingly global structures that determine, to an important extent, the nature and distribution of assaults on dignity.

Ivory-tower engagement with health and human rights can, often enough, reduce us to seminar-room warriors. At worst, we stand revealed as the hypocrites that our critics in many parts of the world have not hesitated to call us. Anthropologists have long been familiar with these critiques; specialists in international health, including AIDS researchers, have recently had a crash course.[24] It is possible, usually, to drown out the voices of those demanding that we stop studying them, even when they go to great lengths to make sure we get the message. But social scientists with more acute hearing have documented a rich trove of graffiti, songs, demonstrations, tracts, and broadsides on the subject. A hit record album in Haiti was called International Organizations. The title cut includes the following lines: "International organizations are not on our side. They're there to help the thieves rob and devour... International health stays on the sidelines of our struggle."

In the context of long-standing international support for sundry Haitian dictatorships, one can readily see the gripe with international organizations. But "international health"? The international community's extraordinary largesse to the Duvalier regime has certainly been well-documented.[25] Subsequent patterns of giving, addressed as they were to sundry Duvalierist military juntas, did nothing to improve the reputation of US foreign aid or the international organizations, though they helped greatly to arm murderous bands and line the pockets of their leaders. Haitians saw international health, if not from within institutions such as the United States Agency for International Development (USAID), then as part of the same dictator-buttressing bureaucracy. Such critiques are not specific to Haiti, although Haitians have pronounced them with exceptional frankness and richness of detail. Their accusations have been echoed and amplified throughout what some are beginning to call the global geoculture.[26] A full decade before the recent AIDS research debates,[27] it was possible to collect a bookful of such commentary.[28]

It is in this context of globalization, "mediatization," and growing inequality that the new field of health and human rights emerges. Contextual factors are particularly salient when we think about social and economic rights, as Steiner and Alston have noted: "An examination of the concept of the right to development and its implications in the 1990s cannot avoid consideration of the effects of the globalization of the economy and the consequences of the near-universal embrace of the market economy."[29] This context defines our research agenda and directs our praxis. We are leaving behind the terra firma of double-blind, placebo-controlled studies, of cost effectiveness, and of sustainability. Indeed, many of these concepts end up looking more like strategies for managing, rather than challenging, inequality.

What, then, should be the role of the First World university, of researchers and health-care professionals? What should be the role of students and others lucky enough to be among the "winners" in the global era? We can agree, perhaps, that these centers are fine places from which to conduct research, to document, and to teach. A university does not have the same entanglements or constraints as an international institution such as the United Nations, or as organizations such as Amnesty International or Physicians for Human Rights. Universities could, in theory, provide a unique and privileged space for conducting research and engaging in critical assessment.

In human rights work, however, research and critical assessment are insufficient – analysis alone cannot curb human rights violations. No more adequate, for all their virtues, are denunciation and exhortation, whether in the form of press conferences or reports or harangues directed at students. To confront, as an observer, ongoing abuses of human rights is to be faced with a moral dilemma: Does one's action help the sufferers or the system? The increasingly baroque codes of research ethics generated by institutional review boards will not help us out of this dilemma, nor will medical ethics, which are so often restricted to the quandary ethics of the individual. But certain models of engagement are not irrelevant. If the university-based human rights worker is in a peculiar position, it is not entirely unlike that of the clinician researcher. Both study suffering; both are bound to relieve it; neither is in possession of a tried-and-true remedy. Both the human rights specialist and the clinician researcher have blind spots, too.

To push the analogy further, it could be argued that there are, in both lines of work, obligations regarding the standard of care. Once a reasonably effective intervention has been identified, it – and not a placebo – is considered the standard against which a new remedy must be tested. In the global era, is it wise to set, as policy goals, double standards for the rich world and the poor world, when we know that these are not different worlds but in fact the same one? Can we treat the rich with the "gold standard," while offering the poor an essential "placebo"? Are the acrid complaints of the vulnerable necessary to remind us that they invariably see the world as one world, riven by terrible inequality and injustice? A placebo is a placebo is a placebo.

That we have failed to meet high goals does not imply that the next step is to lower our sights, although this has been the default logic in many instances. The next step is to try new approaches and to hedge our bets with indisputably effective interventions. Providing pragmatic services to the afflicted is one obvious form of intervention. But the spirit in which these services are delivered makes all the difference. Service delivery can be just that, or it can be pragmatic solidarity, linked to the broader goals of equality and justice for the poor. Again, my own experience in Haiti, which began in 1983, made this clear. The Duvalier dictatorship was then in power, seemingly immovable. Its chief source of external financial aid was the United States and various international institutions, many of them ostensibly charitable in nature. The local director of USAID at the time had often expressed the view that if Haiti was underdeveloped, the causes were to be sought in Haitian culture.[30] The World Bank and the International Monetary Fund seemed to be part of the same giant blur of international aid organizations that Haitians associated, accurately enough, with US foreign policy.

Popular cynicism regarding these transnational institutions was at its peak when my colleagues and I began working in Haiti, and that is precisely why we chose to work through nascent community-based organizations and for a group of rural peasants who had been dispossessed of their land. Although we conducted research and published it, research did not figure on the wish list of the people we were trying to serve. Services were what they asked for, and as people who had been displaced by political and economic violence, they regarded these services as a rightful remedy for what they had suffered. In other words, the Haitian poor themselves believed that social and economic rights were central to the struggle for human rights. As the struggle against the dictatorship gathered strength in the mid-eighties, the language was explicitly couched in broad human rights terms. *Pa gen lape nan tet si pa gen lape nan vant*: There can be no peace of mind if there is no peace in the belly.[31] Health and education figured high on the list of demands as the Haitian popular movement began to swell.

The same has been true of the struggle in Chiapas. The Zapatista rebellion was launched on the day the North American Free Trade Agreement was signed, and the initial statement of the rebellion's leaders put their demands in terms of social and economic rights:

> We are denied the most elementary education so that they can use us as cannon fodder and plunder our country's riches, uncaring that we are dying of hunger and curable diseases. Nor do they care that we have nothing, absolutely nothing, no decent roof over our heads, no land, no work, no health, no food, no education. We do not have the right to freely and democratically elect our own authorities, nor do we have peace or justice for ourselves and our children.[32]

It is in settings such as these that we are afforded a rare clarity about choices that are in fact choices for all of us, everywhere. There's little doubt that discernment is a daily struggle. We must decide how health professionals might best make common cause with the destitute sick, whose rights are violated daily. Helping governments shore up failing public health systems may or may not be wise. As mentioned earlier, pragmatic solidarity on behalf of Russian prisoners with tuberculosis included working with their jailors. But sometimes we are warned against consorting with governments. In Haiti in the eighties, it made all the difference that we formed our own nongovernmental organization far from the reach of the governments of both Haiti and the United States. In Chiapas, the situation was even more dramatic, and many poor communities simply have refused to use government health services. In village after village, we heard the same story. In some "autonomous zones," the Mexican Army – again, as many as 70,000 troops are now stationed in Chiapas – entered these villages and destroyed local health records and what meager infrastructure had been developed. To quote one health worker: "The government uses health services against us. They persecute us if they think we are on the side of the rebels." Our own investigations have been amply confirmed by others, including Physicians for Human Rights:

> At best, [Mexican] Government health and other services are subordinate to Government counterinsurgency efforts. At worst, these services are themselves components of repression, manipulated to reward supporters and to penalize and demoralize dissenters. In either case, Government health services in the zone are discriminatory, exacerbate political divisions, and fail utterly to address the real health needs of the population.[33]

It's not acceptable for those of us fortunate enough to have ties to universities, and to be able to do research, to throw up our hands and bemoan the place-to-place complexity. Underlying this complexity are a series of very simple first principles regarding human rights, as the liberation theologians remind us. Our commitments, our loyalties, have to be primarily to the poor and vulnerable. As a reminder of how unique this commitment is, remember that the international agencies affiliated with the United Nations, including the World Health Organization, are called to work with governments. Think, once again, of Chiapas. The individual member of any one of these international institutions may have loyalties to the Zapatistas, but have no choice in his or her agency's primary interlocutor: This will be the Mexican government. Membership in a university (or hospital or local church) permits us more flexibility in making allegiances. This flexibility is a gift that should not be squandered by mimicking mindlessly the choices of the parastatal international organizations. Close allegiance with suffering communities reminds us that it is not possible to merely study human rights abuses. But part of pragmatic solidarity is bringing the real story to light.

Merely telling the truth often calls for exhaustive research. In the current era, human rights violations are usually both local and global. Telling who did what to whom and when becomes a complicated affair. The chain of complicity, I have learned, reaches higher and higher. At the time of the Haitian military coup, US officialdom's explanation of human rights abuses in Haiti, including the torture and murder of civilians, focused almost exclusively on local actors and local factors. One heard of the "culture of violence" that rendered this and other similarly grisly deaths comprehensible. Such official analyses, constructed through the conflation of structural violence and cultural difference, were distancing tactics.

Innumerable immodest claims of causality, such as attributing a sudden upsurge in the torture of persons in police custody to long-standing local custom, play into the convenient alibi that refuses to follow the chain of events to their source, that keeps all the trouble local. Such alibis obscure the fact that the modern Haitian military was created by an act of the US Congress during our 20-year occupation (1915–34) of Haiti. Most official analyses did not discuss the generous US assistance to the post-Duvalier military: over $200 million in aid passed through the hands of the Haitian military in the 18 months after Jean-Claude Duvalier left Haiti on a US cargo plane in 1986. Bush administration statements, and their faithful echoes in the establishment press, failed to mention that many of the commanders who issued the orders to detain and torture civilians were trained in Fort Benning, Georgia. At this writing, human rights groups in the United States and Haiti have filed suit against the US government in order to bring to light over 100,000 pages of documents revealing links between Washington and the paramilitary groups that held sway in Haiti between 1991 and 1994.[34]

The masking of the mechanisms of human rights violations has occurred elsewhere. In El Salvador, the massacres of entire villages could not in good conscience be considered unrelated to US foreign policy, since the US government was the primary funder, advisor, and supporter of the Salvadoran government's war against its own people. Yet precisely that fiction of deniability was maintained by officialdom, even though we were also the primary purveyors of armaments, as physical evidence was later to show. It was years before we could read accounts, such as that by Mark Danner, who, on investigating the slaughter of every man, woman, and child in one village, concluded: "of the two hundred and forty-five cartridge cases that were studied – all but one from American M16 rifles – '184 had discernable headstamps, identifying the ammunition as having been manufactured for the United States Government at Lake City, Missouri.'"[35] The fiction of local struggles ("ethnic," "religious,...historical," or otherwise picturesque) is exploded by any honest attempt to understand. Paramilitary groups linked tightly with the Mexican government were and are responsible for the bulk of intimidation and violence in the villages of Chiapas. But, as in Haiti, federal authorities have insisted that such violence is due to "local inter-community and interparty tension" or to ethnic rivalries.[36]

Immodest claims of causality are not always so flagrantly self-serving as those proffered to explain Haiti's agony, or the violence in El Salvador and Chiapas.

But only careful analysis allows us to rebut them with any confidence. Physicians, when fortunate, can alleviate the suffering of the sick – but explaining the distribution and causes of suffering requires many minds and resources. To explain each individual's suffering, one must embed individual biography in the larger matrix of culture, history, and political economy. We cannot merely study human rights abuses, but we must not fail to study them.

What can a Focus on Health Bring to the Struggle for Human Rights?

Scholarship is not always readily yoked to the service of the poor. Medicine, I have discovered, can be. At its best, medicine is a service much more than a science, and the latest battery of biomedical discoveries, in which I rejoice, has not convinced me otherwise. Medicine and public health, and also the social sciences relevant to these disciplines, have much to contribute to the great, often rancorous debates on human rights. But what, precisely, might be our greatest contribution? Rudolph Virchow saw doctors as "the natural attorneys of the poor."[37] A "health angle" can promote a broader human rights agenda in unique ways. In fact, the health part of the formula may prove critical to the success of the human rights movement. The honor in which public health and medicine are held affords us openings – again, a space of privilege – enjoyed by few other professions. For example, it is unlikely that my colleagues and I would have been welcomed so warmly into Russian prisons if we were social scientists or human rights investigators. We went instead as TB specialists, with the expectation that a visiting group of doctors might be able to do more for the rights of these prisoners than a delegation from a conventional human rights organization. It is important to get the story straight: the leading cause of death among young Russian detainees is tuberculosis, not torture or starvation. Prison officials were opening their facilities to us, and asking for pragmatic solidarity. (In Haiti and Chiapas, by contrast, we were asked to leave when we openly espoused the cause of the oppressed.)

Medicine and public health benefit from an extraordinary symbolic capital that is, so far, sadly underutilized in human rights work. No one made this point more clearly and persistently than the late Jonathan Mann. In an essay written with Daniel Tarantola, Mann noted that AIDS "has helped catalyze the modern health and human-rights movement, which leads far beyond AIDS, for it considers that promoting and protecting health and promoting and protecting human rights are inextricably connected."[38]

But have we gone far beyond AIDS? Is it not a human rights issue that Russian prisoners are exposed, often during illegally prolonged pretrial detention, to epidemic MDRTB and then denied effective treatment? Is it not a human rights issue that international expert opinion has mistakenly informed Russian prison officials that treatment with second-line drugs is not cost-effective or just plain unnecessary? Is it not a human rights issue that, in wealthy South Africa, where participants at the XIIIth International AIDS Conference were reminded in the glossy program that "medical care is readily available in South Africa," antiretroviral therapy that could prolong millions of (black) lives is declared "cost ineffective"? Is it not a human rights issue that villagers in Chiapas lack access to the most basic medical services, even as government medical facilities stand idly by? Is it not a human rights issue that thousands of Haitian peasants displaced by a hydroelectric dam end up sick with HIV after working as servants in Port-au-Prince?

Standing on the shoulders of giants – from the authors of the Universal Declaration to Jonathan Mann – we can recognize the human rights abuses in each of these situations, including epidemic tuberculosis within prisons. But what, precisely, is to be done? Russian penal codes already prohibit overcrowding, long pretrial detention, and undue risk from malnutrition and communicable disease. Prison officials already regard the tuberculosis problem as a top priority; that's why they have let TB specialists in. In a 1998 interview, one high-ranking prison official told me that the ministry saw their chief problems as lack of resources, overcrowding, and tuberculosis.[39] And the piece de resistance might be that Boris Yeltsin had already declared 1998 "the year of human rights."

Passing more human rights legislation will not be a sufficient response to these human rights challenges, because many of the (nonbinding, clearly) instruments have already been disregarded by those in charge. The Haitian military coup leaders were beyond the pale. But how about Chiapas? Instruments to which Mexico is already signatory include the Geneva Conventions of 1949; the International Covenant on Civil and Political Rights; the International Covenant on Economic, Social and Cultural Rights; the International Labor Organization Convention 169; the American Convention on Human Rights; the Maastricht Guidelines on Violations of Economic, Social and Cultural Rights; and the Convention on the Elimination of All Forms of Discrimination Against Women. Each one of these is flouted every day in Chiapas.

As the Haitians say, "Laws are made of paper; bayonets are made of steel." Law alone is not up to the task of relieving such immense suffering. Louis Henkin has reminded us that international law is fundamentally a set of rules and norms designed to protect the interests of states, not their citizens. "Until recently," he observed in 1989, "international law took no note of individual human beings."[40] And states, as we have seen, honor human rights law largely in the breach – sometimes through intention, and sometimes through sheer impotence. This chief irony of human rights work – that states will not or cannot obey the treaties to which they are signatory – can lead to despair or to cynicism, if all of one's eggs are in the international law basket.[41]

Laws are not science; they are normative ideology and tightly tied to power? Biomedicine and public health, though also vulnerable to ideological deformations, serve different imperatives, ask different questions. Physicians practice triage and referral daily. What suffering needs to be taken care of first and with what resources? Medicine and public health do not ask whether an event or process violates an existing rule; they ask whether that event or process can be shown to have ill effects on a patient or on a population. They ask whether such events can be prevented or remediated. Thus medicine and public health, so directly tied to human outcomes, give us an immediate sense of impact and a means of measuring progress – because health fields are well-versed in marrying the analysis of problems with practical solutions. And when medicine and public health are explicitly placed at the service of the poor, there is even greater insurance against their perversion.

To return to the case of prisoners with MDRTB, the best way to protect their rights is to cure them of their disease. And the best way to protect the rights of other prisoners, and of those who take care of them, is to prevent transmission by treating the sick. Thus, after years of equivocation, all parties involved are being forced to admit that the right thing to do in Russia's prisons is also the human rights thing to do. A variety of strategies, from human rights arguments to epidemiologic scare tactics, have been used to make headway in raising the funds necessary to treat these and other prisoners. In the end, then, the health angle on human rights may prove more pragmatic than approaching the problem as one of penal reform alone, in part because the health angle focuses less on public blame and more on finding solutions. This is not to say that human rights advocates should not strive for policy reform, but rather that we need a fast, non-controversial solution that attacks the root of many human rights violations. Previously closed-door institutions have invited international collaboration designed to halt prison epidemics. This approach – pragmatic solidarity – may, in the end, lead to penal reform as well.

New Agendas for Health and Human Rights

Is it grandiose to seek to define new agendas? When one reads the powerfully worded statutes, conventions, treaties, and charters stemming from international revulsion over the crimes of the Third Reich, it seems pointless to call for better instruments of this sort. More recent events in the former Yugoslavia and in Rwanda serve as a powerful rebuke to undue confidence in these legalistic approaches: "That it should nevertheless be possible for Nazi-like crimes to be repeated half a century later in full view of the whole world," remarks Aryeh Neier, "points out the weakness of that system – and the need for fresh approaches."[42] Steiner and Alston, similarly, call for "heightened attention to the problems of implementation and enforcement of the new ideal norms. The old techniques," they conclude, "simply won't work."[43]

A corollary question is whether a coherent agenda springs from the critique inherent in the answers to the questions presented here. If so, is this agenda compatible with existing approaches and documents, including the Universal Declaration of Human Rights? To those who believe that social and economic rights must be central to the health and human rights agenda, the answers to these questions are "Yes." This agenda, inspired by the notion of a preferential option for the poor, is coherent, pragmatic, and informed by careful scholarship. In large part because it focuses on social and economic rights, this agenda, though novel, builds on five decades of work within the traditional human rights framework: Articles 25 and 27 of the Universal Declaration inspire the vision of this emerging agenda, which could rely on tighter links between universities, medical providers, and both non-governmental and community-based organizations. The truly novel part of the alliance comes in subjugating these networks to the aspirations of oppressed and abused people.

How might we proceed with this effort if most reviews of the effects of international laws and treaties designed to protect human rights raise serious questions of efficacy, to say the least? What can be done to advance new agendas of health and human rights? In concluding, we offer six suggestions, which are intended to complement ongoing efforts.

Make health and healing the symbolic core

If we make health and healing the symbolic core of a new agenda, we tap into something truly universal – concern for the sick – and, at the same time, engage medicine, public health, and the allied health professions, including the basic sciences. Put another way, we need to throw the full weight of the medical and scientific communities behind a noble cause. The growing outcome gap between the rich and the poor constitutes

both a human rights violation and a means of tracking the efficacy of our interventions. In brief, reduction of the outcome gap will be the goal of our pragmatic
solidarity with the destitute sick.

Make provision of services central to the agenda

We need to listen to the sick and abused and to those most likely to have their rights
violated. They are not asking for new centers of study and reflection. That means we
need new programs in addition to the traditional ventures of a university or research
center. We need programs designed to remediate inequalities of access to services
that can help all humans lead free and healthy lives. If everyone has a right "to share
in scientific advancement and its benefits," where are our pragmatic efforts to
improve the spread of these advances? How can we make the rapid deployment of
services to improve health – pragmatic solidarity – central to the work of health and
human rights programs? Our own group, Partners In Health, has worked largely
with community-based organizations in Haiti, Peru, and Mexico, with the express
goal to remediate inequalities of access. This community of providers and scholars
believes that "the vitality of practice" lends a corrective strength to our research and
writing.[44] The possibilities for programmatic collaboration range, we have learned,
from Russian prison officials to peasant collectives in the autonomous zones of
Chiapas. Novel collaborations of this sort are certainly necessary if we are to address
the increasing inequalities of access here in wealthy, inegalitarian countries such
as the United States. Relying exclusively on nation-states' compliance with a
social-justice agenda is naive at best.

  Fifteen years of work in the most difficult field conditions have taught our group
that it is hard – perhaps impossible – to meet the highest standards of health care
in every situation. But it is imperative that we try to do so. Projects striving for
excellence and inclusiveness – rather than, say, "cost-effectiveness" or "sustainability," which are often at odds with social justice approaches to medicine and public
health – are not merely misguided quests for personal efficacy. Such projects respond
to widespread demands for equity in health care. The din around AIDS research in
the Third World is merely the latest manifestation of a rejection of low standards as
official policy. That such standards are widely seen as violating human rights is no
surprise for those interested in social and economic rights. Efficiency cannot trump
equity in the field of health and human rights.

Establish new research agendas

We need to make room in the academy for serious scholarly work on the multiple
dynamics of health and human rights, on the health effects of war and political-
economic disruption, and on the pathogenic effects of social inequalities, including
racism, gender inequality, and the growing gap between rich and poor. By what
mechanisms, precisely, do such noxious events and processes become embodied as
adverse health outcomes? Why are some at risk and others spared?

  We require a new level of cooperation between disciplines ranging from social
anthropology to molecular epidemiology. We need a new sociology of knowledge that
can pick apart a wide body of commentary and scholarship: complex international
law; the claims and disclaimers of officialdom; postmodern relativist readings of
suffering; clinical and epidemiologic studies of the long-term effects of, say, torture
and racism. But remember, none of the victims of these events or processes are asking

us to conduct research. For this reason alone, research in the arena of health and human rights is necessarily fraught with pitfalls:

> Imperiled populations in developing countries include extraordinarily vulnerable individuals ripped from their cultures and communities and victimized by myriad forms of abuse and violence. Public health research on violence and victimization among these groups must vigilantly guard against contributing to emotional and social harm.[45]

The fact that research is and should remain a secondary concern does not mean that careful documentation is not critical to both our understanding of suffering and our ability to prevent or allay it. And because such research would be linked to service, we need operational research by which we can gauge the efficacy of interventions quite different from those measured in the past.

Assume a broader educational mandate

If the primary objective is to set things right, education is central to our task. We must not limit ourselves to teaching a select group of students with an avowed interest in health and human rights, nor must we limit ourselves to trying to teach lessons to recalcitrant governments. Jonathan Mann signaled to us the limitations of the latter approach: "Support for human rights-based action to promote health... at the level of declarations and speeches is welcome, and useful in some ways, but the limits of official organizational support for the call for societal transformation inherent in human rights promotion must be recognized."[46] A broader educational mandate would mean engaging students from all faculties, but also, as noted, engaging the members of these faculties. Beyond the university and various governmental bodies lies the broader public, for whom the connections between health and human rights have not even been traced. It is doubtful that the destitute sick have much to learn from us about health and human rights, but there is little doubt that, as their students, we can learn to better convey the complexity and historicity of their messages.

Achieve independence from governments and bureaucracies

We need to be untrammeled by obligations to powerful states and international bureaucracies. A central irony of human rights law is that it consists largely of appeals to the perpetrators. After all, most crimes against humanity are committed by states, not by rogue factions or gangs or cults or terrorists. That makes it difficult for institutions accountable to states to take their constituents to task. None of this is to say that international organizations have little to offer to those seeking to prevent or assuage human rights abuses. Rather, we need to remember that their supposed "neutrality" comes at a great cost, and that cost is usually paid by people who are not represented by official advocates in places like New York, Geneva, Washington, DC, London, or Tokyo. Along with the efforts of nongovernmental organizations, university- and hospital-based programs have the potential to be independent, well-designed, pragmatic, and feasible. The imprimatur of medicine and public health would afford even more weight and independence. And only a failure of imagination has led us to ignore the potential for collaboration with community-based organizations and with communities in resistance to ongoing violations of human rights.

Although we must maintain independence from powerful institutions, this is not to say that collaboration should never happen. If these institutions team up with health and human rights practitioners to facilitate the pragmatic delivery of services, substantial gains can be made. While policy reform is certainly worth striving for, and can be an extraordinary tool, we cannot necessarily rely on institutional bodies to enforce the policies they may adopt under pressure. In short, pragmatic solidarity should be our goal – and any collaborations among health professionals, human rights activists, and governing bodies should strive toward this end.

Secure more resources for health and human rights

Of course, it's easy to demand more resources, harder to produce them. But if social and economic rights are acknowledged as such, then foundations, governments, businesses, and international financial institutions – many of them now awash in resources – may be called to prioritize human rights endeavors that reflect the paradigm shift advocated here.

Regardless of where one stands on the process of globalization and its multiple engines, these processes have important implications for efforts to promote health and human rights. As states weaken, it is easy to discern an increasing role for nongovernmental institutions, including universities and medical centers. But it's also easy to discern a trap: states' withdrawal from the basic business of providing housing, education, and medical services usually means further erosion of the social and economic rights of the poor. Our independent involvement must be quite different from current trends, which have nongovernmental organizations relieving the state of its duty to provide basic services, thus becoming witting or unwitting abettors of neoliberal policies that declare every service and every thing to be for sale.

The experience of Partners In Health suggests that ambitious goals can be met even without a large springboard. Over the past decade and against a steady current of naysaying, we have channeled significant resources to the destitute sick in Haiti, Peru, Mexico, and Boston. We didn't argue that it was "cost-effective," nor did we promise that such efforts would be replicable. We argued that it was the right thing to do. It was the human rights thing to do.

Conclusion

Some of the problems born of structural violence are so large that they have paralyzed many who want to do the right thing. But we can find resources, and we can find them without sacrificing our independence and discernment. We will not do this by adopting defensive postures that are tantamount to simply managing inequality with the latest tools from economists and technocrats. Utopian ideals are the bedrock of human rights. We must set our sights high and reject a double standard between rich and poor.

Claims that we live in an era of limited resources fail to mention that these resources happen to be less limited now than ever before in human history. Arguing that it is too expensive to treat MDRTB among prisoners in Russia sounds nothing short of ludicrous when this world contains roughly 497 billionaires.[47] Arguments against treating HIV in precisely those areas in which it exacts its greatest toll warn us that misguided notions of cost-effectiveness have already trumped equity. Arguing that nominal civil and political rights are the best we can hope for will mean that members of the healing professions will have their hands fled. In implementing a paradigm shift that focuses on solidarity with victims of structural violence, and the provision of pragmatic services to those in need, we can begin to address these large problems of inequality and human rights violations. Otherwise, we will be forced to stand by as the rights and dignity of the poor and marginalized undergo further sustained and deadly assault.

NOTES

1 Universal Declaration of Human Rights, GA Res. 217 A (III), UN Doc. A/810 (1948): at Article 25, available at http://www.un.org/Overview/rights.html.

2 The Sentencing Project, "U.S. Continues to be World Leader in Rate of Incarceration," at http://www.Sentencingproject.org/news/usnol.pdf (revised August 2001).

3 E. E. Telzak et al., "Multidrug-Resistant Tuberculosis in Patients Without HIV Infection," *N. Engl. J. Med.*, 333 (1995): 907–11; C. Mitnick et al., "Treatment Outcomes in 75 Patients with Chronic Multidrug-Resistant Tuberculosis Enrolled in Aggressive Community-Based Therapy in Urban Peru," *International Journal of Tuberculosis and Lung Disease*, 5, no. 11, suppl. 1 (2001): S156; P. E. Farmer et al., "Preliminary Results of Community-Based MDRTB Treatment in Lima, Peru," *International Journal of Tuberculosis and Lung Disease*, 2, no. 11, suppl. 2 (1998): S371; P. E. Farmer et al., "Responding to Outbreaks of MDRTB: Introducing 'DOTS-Plus,' " in L. B. Reichman and E. S. Hershfield, eds., Tuberculosis: A Comprehensive International Approach, 2nd edn. (New York: Marcel Dekker Inc., 1999): 447–69; K. Tahaoglu et al., "The Treatment of Multidrug-Resistant Tuberculosis in Turkey," *N. Engl. J. Med.*, 345 (2001): 170–4.

4 Amnesty International, *Torture in Russia: "This Man-Made Hell"* (London: Amnesty International, 1997): at 31.

5 Dr Natalya Vezhina, Medical Director, TB Colony 33, Mariinsk, Kemerovo, Russian Federation; interview by author (Farmer), Mariinsk, September 1998.

6 A. Alexander, "Money Isn't the Issue; It's (Still) Political Will," *TB Monitor*, 5, no. 5 (1998): 53.

7 See Farmer et al. (1998), supra note 3.

8 See D. Campbell, "Herskovits, Cultural Relativism and Metascience," in M. Herskovits, ed., *Cultural Relativism: Perspectives in Cultural Pluralism* (New York: Random House, 1972): 289–315; C. Geertz, "Anti-Anti-Relativism," *American Anthropologist*, 86 (1984): 263–78; E. Hatch, *Culture and Morality: The Relativity of Values in Anthropology* (New York: Columbia University Press, 1983); A. D. Renteln, "Relativism and the Search for Human Rights," *American Anthropologist*, 90 (1988): 56–72; P. E. Schmidt, "Some Criticisms of Cultural Relativism," *Journal of Philosophy*, 70 (1955): 780–91.

9 The Right to the Highest Attainable Standard of Health: General Comment 14, United Nations, Economic and Social Council, E/C 12/2000/4 (2000), available at http://www.unhchr.ch/tbs/doc.nsf/MasterFrameView/40d009901358b0e2c125691500 5090be?Opendocument.

10 See P. E. Farmer et al., "Community-Based Approaches to HIV Treatment in Resource-Poor Settings," *Lancet*, 358 (2001): 404–9.

11 H. Steiner and P. Alston, *International Human Rights in Context: Law, Politics, Morals* (New York: Oxford University Press, 1996): at vi.

12 A. Neier, *War Crimes: Brutality, Genocide, Terror, and the Struggle for Justice* (New York: Times Books, 1998): at 75.

13 Cited in Steiner and Alston, supra note 11, at 141 (emphasis in the original).

14 J. V. Millen and T. H. Holtz, "Dying for Growth, Part I: Transnational Corporation and the Health of the Poor," in J. Y. Kim et al., eds., *Dying for Growth: Global Inequality and the Health of the Poor* (Monroe, ME: Common Courage Press, 2000): 177–223, at 185.

15 See P. E. Farmer, "Cruel and Unusual: Drug Resistant Tuberculosis as Punishment," in V. Stern and R. Jones, eds., *Sentenced to Die? The Problem of TB in Prisons in East and Central Europe and Central Asia* (London: International Centre for Prison Studies, 1999): 70–88; R. G. Wilkinson, *Unhealthy Societies: The Afflictions of Inequality* (London: Routledge, 1997); I. Kawachi et al., "Social Capital, Income Inequality, and Mortality," *American Journal of Public Health*, 87 (1997): 1491–8; A. Leclerc et al., eds., *Les Inegalites Sociales de Sante* (Paris: Editions la Deouverte et Syros, 2000).

16 See M. Whitehead et al., "Setting Targets to Address Inequalities in Health," *Lancet*, 351 (1998): 1279–82.

17 P. E. Farmer, "The Significance of Haiti," in North American Congress on Latin America, ed., *Haiti: Dangerous Crossroads* (Boston: South End Press, 1995): 217–30.

18 See B. Concannon, "Beyond Complementarity: The International Criminal Court and National Prosecutions, A View from Haiti," *Columbia Human Rights Law Review*, 32, no. 1 (2000): 201–50.

19 See Oficina los Derechos Humanos del Arzobispado de Guatemala (ODHAG), *Guatemala: Nunca Mas* (Guatemala: Informe Proyecto Interdiocesano de Recuperacion de la Memoria Historica, 1998).

20 See Neier, supra note 12, at 33.

21 See A. Neier, "What Should be Done about the Guilty?," *New York Review of Books*, February 1, 1990, at 32–5.

22 See A. Guillermoprieto, *The Heart that Bleeds: Latin America Now* (New York: Alfred A. Knopf, 1994); N. Chomsky, *Turning the Tide: U.S. Intervention in Central America and the Struggle for Peace* (Boston: South End Press, 1985); W. LaFeber, *Inevitable Revolutions: The United States in Central America* (New York: W. W. Norton, 1984).

23 P. Bourdieu, ed., *La Misere du Monde* (Paris: Seuil, 1993): at 944.

24 See T. Asad, ed., *Anthropology and the Colonial Encounter* (London: Ithaca Press and Humanities, 1975); D. Hymes, "The Uses of Anthropology: Critical, Political, Personal," in D. Hymes, ed., *Reinventing Anthropology* (New York: Random House, 1974): 3–79; G. D. Berreman, "Bringing It All Back Home: Malaise in Anthropology," in D. Hymes, ed., *Reinventing Anthropology* (New York: Random House, 1974): 83–98.

25 See P. E. Farmer, *The Uses of Haiti* (Monroe, ME: Common Courage Press, 1994); G. Hancock, *The Lords of Poverty: The Power, Prestige, and Corruption of the International Aid Business* (New York: Atlantic Monthly Press, 1989).

26 See I. Wallerstein, "The Insurmountable Contradictions of Liberalism: Human Rights and the Rights of Peoples in the Geoculture of the Modern World-System," *South Atlantic Quarterly*, 46 (1995): 1161–78.

27 T. Quinn et al., "Viral Load and Heterosexual Transmission of Human Immunodeficiency Virus Type 1," *N. Engl. J. Med.*, 342 (2000): 921–9; M. S. Cohen, "Preventing Sexual Transmission of HIV – New Ideas from Sub-Saharan Africa," *N. Engl. J. Med.*, 342 (2000): 970–2; M. Angell, "Investigators' Responsibilities for Human Subjects in Developing Countries," *N. Engl. J. Med.*, 342 (2000): 967–9; D. Greco, "The Ethics of Research in Developing Countries," *N. Engl. J. Med.*, 343 (2000): 362.

28 P. E. Farmer, *AIDS and Accusation: Haiti and the Geography of Blame* (Berkeley: University of California Press, 1992).

29 See Steiner and Alston, supra note 11, at 1110.

30 L. Harrison, "Voodoo Politics," *Atlantic Monthly*, 271, no. 6 (1993): 101–8.

31 Haitian proverb.

32 S. Marcos and the Zapatista Army of National Liberation, *Shadows of Tender Fury: The Letters and Communiques of Subcomandante Marcos and the Zapatista Army of National Liberation* (New York: Monthly Review Press, 1995): at 54.

33 Physicians for Human Rights, *Health Care Held Hostage: Human Rights Violations and Violations of Medical Neutrality in Chiapas, Mexico* (Boston: Physicians for Human Rights, 1999): at 4.

34 See Concannon, supra note 18.

35 M. Danner, "The Truth of El Mozote," *New Yorker* (December 6, 1993): 50–133, at 132. Danner quotes from the Truth Commission's report, "From Madness to Hope: The Twelve-Year War in El Salvador."

36 See Physicians for Human Rights, supra note 33, at 4.

37 R. L. K. Virchow, *Die Einheitsrebungen in der Wissenschaftlichen Medicin* (Berlin: Druck und Verlag yon G. Reimer, 1849); L. Eisenberg, "Rudolf Ludwig Karl Virchow, Where Are You Now That We Need You?," *American Journal of Medicine,* 77 (1984): 524–32.

38 J. Mann and D. Tarantola, "Responding to HIV/AIDS: A Historical Perspective," *Health and Human Rights*, 2, no. 4 (1998): 5–8, at 8.

39 Ivan Nikitovich Simonov, Chief Inspector of Prisons (now with the Chief Board of Punishment Execution), Ministry of Internal Affairs, Russian Federation; interview by author (Farmer), Moscow, June 4, 1998.

40 L. Henkin, *International Law: Politics, Values and Functions: General Course on Public International Law* (Boston: M. Nijhoff, 1990): at 208.

41 See O. Schachter, *International Law in Theory and Practice* (Boston: M. Nijhoff, 1991): at 6.

42 See Neier, supra note 12, at xiii.

43 See Steiner and Alston, supra note 11, at viii.

44 See P. E. Farmer, *Infections and Inequalities: The Modern Plagues* (Berkeley: University of California Press, 1999): at 18.

45 R. Neugebauer, "Research on Violence in Developing Countries: Benefits and Perils," *American Journal of Public Health*, 89, no. 10 (1999): 1473–4, at 1474.

46 J. Mann, "AIDS and Human Rights: Where Do We Go From Here?," *Health and Human Rights*, 3, no. 1 (1998): 143–9, at 145–6.

47 L. Kroll and L. Goldman, "The World's Billionaires" (February 28, 2002), at http://www.forbes.com/home/2002/02/28/billionaires.html.

10

Rotten Trade: Millennial Capitalism, Human Values and Global Justice in Organs Trafficking

Nancy Scheper-Hughes

Amidst the neo-liberal readjustments of societies, North and South, we are experiencing today a rapid depletion, an 'emptying out' even, of traditional modernist, humanist and pastoral ideologies, values and practices. New relations between capital and labor, bodies and the state, belonging and extra-territoriality, and between medical and biotechnological inclusions and exclusions are taking shape. But rather than a conventional story of the lamentable decline of humanistic social values and social relations, our discussion is tethered to a frank recognition that the material grounds on which those modernist values and practices were based have shifted today almost beyond recognition.

What the Comaroffs (2001) refer to as millennial or 'second coming' capitalism has facilitated a rapid dissemination to virtually all corners of the world of advanced medical procedures and biotechnologies alongside strange markets and 'occult economies'. Together, these have incited new tastes and desires for the skin, bone, blood, organs, tissue and reproductive and genetic material of others. Nowhere are these processes more transparent than in the field of organ transplant, which now takes place in a transnational space with both donors and recipients following new paths of capital and medical technology in the global economy.

The spread of transplant capabilities created a global scarcity of transplantable organs at the same time that economic globalization released an exodus of displaced persons and a voracious appetite for foreign bodies to do the shadow work of production and to provide 'fresh' organs for medical consumption. The ideal conditions of an 'open' market economy have thereby put into circulation mortally sick bodies traveling in one direction and 'healthy' organs (encased in their human

Originally published in *Journal of Human Rights*, 2: 2 (2003), 197–226.

packages) in another direction, creating a bizarre 'kula ring' of international body trade. The emergence of strange markets, excess capital, renegade surgeons,[1] local 'kidney hunters' with links to an international Mafia (Lobo and Maierovitch 2002) (and thereby to a parallel traffic in slave workers, babies, drugs and small arms) has produced a small but spectacularly lucrative practice of transplant tourism, much of it illegal and clandestine.

This confluence in the flows of immigrant workers and itinerant kidney sellers who fall into the hands of ruthless brokers and unscrupulous, notorious, but simultaneously rewarded, protected and envied outlaw transplant surgeons is a troubling sub-text in the story of late twentieth and early twenty-first century globalization, one that combines and juxtaposes elements of pre- and postmodernity. These new transplant transactions are a strange blend of altruism and commerce; consent and coercion; gifts and theft; science and sorcery; care and human sacrifice.

On the one hand, the phenomenal spread of transplant technologies, even in the murky context of black markets in medicine, has given the possibility of new, extended or improved quality of life to a select population of mobile kidney patients from the deserts of Oman to the rain forests of the Amazon Basin.[2] On the other hand, new developments in 'transplant tourism' have exacerbated older divisions between North and South, core and periphery, haves and have-nots, spawning a new form of commodity fetishism in demands by medical consumers for a quality product: 'fresh' and 'healthy' kidneys purchased from living bodies. In these radical exchanges of body parts and somatic information, life-saving measures for the one demands a bodily sacrifice of self-mutilation by the other. And one man's biosociality (Rabinow 1996) is another woman's biopiracy, depending on whether one is speaking from a Silicon Valley biotech laboratory or from a sewage-infested *banguay* in Manila.

Commercialized transplant, a practice that trades comfortably in the domain of postmodern biopolitics with its values of disposability, individuality, free and transparent circulation, exemplifies better than any other biomedical technology the reach and the limits of economic liberalism. In transplant gifts of life and death (Parsons et al. 1969) promise to surpass all previous 'natural' limits and restrictions. And the uninhibited circulation of purchased kidneys exemplifies the neo-liberal episteme, a political discourse based on juridical concepts of the autonomous individual subject, equality (at least equality of opportunity), radical freedom, accumulation and universality (the expansion of medical rights and medical citizenship[3]). The commodified kidney is, to date, the primary currency in transplant tourism; it represents the gold standard of organ sales worldwide. In the past year, however, markets in part-livers and single corneas from living vendors are beginning to emerge in Southeast Asia.

This paper continues my discussion (Scheper-Hughes 2000b, 2001a, 2001b, 2002) of the darker side of transplant practice. In all, three crucial points about the organs trade have emerged. The first is about invented scarcities and artificial needs within a new context of highly fetishized 'fresh' organs. The scarcity of cadaver organs has evolved into an active trade in 'surplus' organs from living 'suppliers' as well as in new forms of 'biopiracy'. The second point concerns the transplant rhetoric of altruism masking real demands for human sacrifice. The third point concerns surplus empathy and the relative visibility of two distinct populations – excluded and invisible organ givers and included and highly visible organ receivers. We have found almost everywhere a new form of globalized 'apartheid medicine' that privileges one class of patients, organ recipients, over another class of invisible and unrecognized 'non-patients', about whom almost nothing is known – an excellent place for a critical medical anthropologist (Scheper-Hughes 1990) to begin.

Here I will focus on the networks of organized crime (and so called 'body mafia') that are putting into circulation ambulatory organ buyers, itinerant kidney hunters, outlaw surgeons, medical technicians, makeshift transplant units and clandestine laboratories in what economist Jagddish Bhagwati (2002) refers to as 'rotten trade'. By this Bhagwati means all kinds of trade in 'bads' – arms, drugs, stolen goods, hazardous and toxic products as well as traffic in babies, bodies and slave labor – as opposed to ordinary and normative trade in 'goods'. In this instance, the rotten traffic in human organs brings together buyers and sellers from distant locations for fleeting, intimate and illicit bodily exchanges occasioned by a dual waiting list, one formed by mortal sickness, the other by human misery.

Like any other business, the kidney trade is driven by a simple market calculus of supply and demand. For example, in the Middle East, from the Gulf states to Israel, transplantable cadaver organs are extremely scarce owing to religious reservations, both Jewish and Islamic, about the ontological status of the brain-dead donor, and to the elaborate religious protocol for the proper treatment and burial of the dead. Both orthodox Judaism and Islam permit organ transplantation, however, and their religious scholars and ethicists generally treat *living* donation as a meritorious act, even if the donor has been paid (Steinberg 1996). Consequently, one solution to the problem of long waiting lists of frustrated kidney patients in this region was found in transplant abroad, in some cases (as in Israel) with the support of government-sponsored medical insurance. For the last twenty years organized programs have carried affluent patients from Israel, Saudi Arabia, Oman and Kuwait initially to India for transplant and later to Turkey, Iran and Iraq and, most recently, to Russia, Romania and Moldova where kidney sellers are recruited (sometimes coercively) from army barracks, prisons, unemployment offices, flea markets, shopping malls and bars. So we can even speak of organ-donor vs. organ-recipient nations.

In India, trading a kidney for a dowry has become a common strategy for parents to arrange marriage for an otherwise economically disadvantaged daughter (Cohen 1999). And, 'one-kidney' shantytowns have sprung up in the peripheries of Manila and Thailand to service the needs of Saudi and Japanese transplant patients and, in recent years, a growing number of North Americans (Jimenez and Bell 2001). Indeed, the commodified kidney has become the poor man's and woman's ultimate collateral against debt and penury in many parts of the world. Meanwhile, trans-plant package tours are arranged in Europe, North America and Japan, to take transplant patients to China where their surgery is arranged, with the complicity of Chinese doctors and surgeons, to coincide with public executions that provide the primary source of highly lucrative transplant organs. Condemned prisoners are reportedly intubated and surgically prepped for 'harvesting' minutes before execution.[4]

'Transplant tourism' has become a vital asset to the medical economies of rapidly privatizing hospitals and clinics in poorer countries struggling to stay afloat. The 'global cities' (Sassen 1991) in this nether economy are not London, New York and Tokyo but Istanbul, Lima, Lvov, Tel Aviv, Chisenau, Bombay, Johannesburg and Manila. In general, the circulation of kidneys follows the established routes of capital from South to North, from poorer to more affluent bodies, from black and brown bodies to white ones, and from females to males, or from poor males to more affluent males. Women are rarely the recipients of purchased or purloined organs anywhere in the world.

Biosociality or Bio-Sociopathy? The Kidney Sellers

New forms of 'social kinship' and biosociality are invented to link strangers, even political 'enemies' from distant locations, described by the operating surgeons as 'a perfect match – like brothers', while the pair are normally prevented from seeing, let alone speaking, to each other.[5] If and when these 'kidney kin' meet at all, it will be by accident and like ships passing in the night as they are wheeled, heavily sedated, on hospital gurneys into their respective operating rooms where one surgeon *removes* and the other *inserts* the seller's kidney of despair, his or her kidney of last resort now magically transformed into the buyer's precious organ of opportunity.

Who, for example, would imagine that in the midst of the longstanding religious and ethnic hostilities and an almost genocidal war in the Middle East, one of the first 'sources' of living donors for Israeli kidney transplant patients would be Palestinian guest workers,[6] or that, as recently as March 2002, Israeli patients would be willing to travel to Istanbul to be transplanted in a private clinic by a Moslem surgeon who decorates his waiting room with photos of Ataturk and a plastic glass eye to ward off evil (Jimenez and Scheper-Hughes 2002a)? Or that the transplanted kidneys would be taken from impoverished Eastern Orthodox peasants from Moldova and Romania who came to Turkey to sell smuggled cigarettes until they ran into the famous kidney brokers of Istanbul's Askary flea market (Jimenez and Scheper-Hughes 2002b)?

In some parts of the world, especially in rural Eastern Europe (Romania and Moldova in particular) naïve villagers looking for work and to make their fortunes in seemingly wealthy cities like Istanbul are tricked and coerced into parting with a kidney by knife- and gun-wielding Russian and Turkish small-time Mafia.

Figure 10.1   Banon Lupa slum in Manila: site of active kidney selling (photo by Nancy Scheper-Hughes).

Afterwards the kidney sellers return home to face ridicule and ostracism. While young men in Moldova are targeted by brokers as fair game for the kidney business in Istanbul, village women in the same economic straits are recruited to work abroad in more conventional forms of body selling. But *both* itinerant kidney sellers and female sex workers of Moldova are held in contempt at home as shameless prostitutes. 'No', corrected Viorel, a 27-year-old unemployed kidney seller from Moldova's capital city, Chisenau. 'We [kidney sellers] are *worse* than prostitutes because what we have sold we can never get back. We have given away our health, our strength, and our lives.' Months and even years later the young men suffer from deep shame and regret. Nicolae, a 26-year-old former welder from the village of Mingir, broke down during a meeting in his small home in December 2000, calling himself 'a disgrace to my family and to my country'.

Figure 10.2 Vladimir, a stigmatized kidney seller from Minger, Moldova, who was recruited by a local broker and trafficked to Turkey where he was paid $2,700 for his organ. Today Vladimir is unemployed and ridiculed as a 'one kidney' in his home community. He is alienated from his father and ashamed to be seen in the village. At the age of 19 he is both bitter and self-hating (photo by Nancy Scheper-Hughes).

But in Turkey one actually finds a diverse population of kidney sellers, some of whom gather at weekends on the sidelines of a minibus station and flea market in Aksaray, a dilapidated immigrant section of Istanbul. Among them are indigent Turks, small-time criminals and recently arrived immigrants from Eastern Europe. Negotiations are conducted over a cup of Turkish tea in a café across the street from the 'suitcase market' and away from the disapproving stares of the more conventional venders of smuggled cigarettes, Russian vodka, Pokamon chocolates and imitation French perfumes. And like the carpet sellers and gold merchants at the famous Covered Bazaar of Istanbul, they haggle furiously over the price of their wares but are always willing to agree to less.

In March 2002 I sat across from Satilmis K., a 40-year-old former baker with dirt-stained fingers, a deeply lined forehead and a defeated air. 'I never thought it would come to this', he said of his desperate decision to enter the kidney market. Originally from a small village on Turkey's Black Sea coast, Mr K. lost his job and now shares a one-room flat with a friend. He now lives on the $2 a day he earns as a junkman, wheeling his wooden cart past the cheap hotels and discount leather shops in Aksaray, collecting scrap metal and old pop cans. It was in the flea market that he first heard about the brokers in suits who arrive at the weekend looking for sellers. He felt lucky to have run into our 'broker' (actually a Turkish journalist in disguise) and was anxious to begin the negotiation. Mr K.'s opening price for one of his kidneys ('left or right, your choice') was $50,000. In the space of a few minutes he reduced his price to $20,000.

Mr K. believes he is a 'perfect match' for a kidney transplant patient with AB blood type. When questioned about it, he dismissed the two badly infected sores on his hand as superficial wounds. 'I have had a tetanus shot', he assured us, though he could not afford the antibiotic he was prescribed. 'But I am clean', he insisted, while unraveling the tattered blood and pus-stained cloth bandage on his right hand. 'And I am healthy. I've only ever had the flu.' Mr. K. was unafraid of the surgery because his own brother had lost a kidney as a result of untreated kidney disease and manages to make do without it. Mr K.'s only requirement was that the operation take place in a 'good hospital'.

Mr K. had his requirements and he realized that the sale of his kidney was a radical and risky act, one for which he believed he should be well compensated ('My final offer', he said definitively, as we rose to leave,[7] 'is $10,000'). To the 'guest workers' from Romania and Moldiva, however, the sale of a kidney seemed an unholy and unnatural act, comparable to rape, and 'theft' was the term most commonly employed by them, even in cases where initial consent had been given to the operation. But for those living in parts of the world that have been subjected to centuries of colonization, forced labor and peonage, as in the Philippines, the idea of selling a spare body part seems as natural and ordinary as any other form of indentured labor. In the extensive shantytown of Banon Lupa, Manila, for example, the majority of young men are willing, even anxious, to sell a kidney, and they express few regrets afterwards, except for the natural limits imposed on other saleable body parts. ('Can I sell a testicle?', a former kidney seller from the shantytown asked me. 'Filipino men', he boasted, 'are very potent, very fertile'.)

In the same *banguey* of unemployed stevedores I encountered an unanticipated 'waiting list', which comprised angry and 'disrespected' kidney sellers who had been 'neglected' and 'overlooked' by the medical doctors at Manila's most prestigious private hospital, St Luke's Episcopal Medical Center. Perhaps they had been rejected, the men surmised, because of their age (too young or too old), their blood (difficult to match) or their general medical condition. Whatever the reason, they had been judged as less valuable kidney vendors than some of their lucky neighbors who now owned new VCRs, karioke machines and expensive tricycles. 'What's wrong with me?', a 42-year-old man asked, thinking I must be a North American kidney hunter. 'I registered on "the list" over six months ago, and no one from St Luke's has ever called me', Mr S. complained. 'But I am healthy. I can still lift heavy weights. And my urine is clear.' Moreover, he was willing, he said, to sell below the going rate of $1,300 for a 'fresh' kidney.

Indeed, a great many eager and willing kidney sellers wait outside transplant units; others check themselves into special wards of surgical units that resemble 'kidney motels' where they lie on mats or in a hospital bed for days, even weeks, watching color television, eating chips and waiting for the 'lucky number' that will turn them into the day's winner of the kidney transplant lottery. Such macabre scenes can be found in hospitals and clinics in India, Iraq, Iran, South Africa,

Figure 10.3 'Willie P.', an eager kidney seller in Bangon Lupa slum, Manila (photo by Nancy Scheper-Hughes).

the Philippines and Turkey. Entire neighborhoods, cities and regions are known
in transplant circles as 'kidney belts' because so many people there have found
a temporary niche in the kidney trade. One large extended family in a Philippine
slum can and often does supply a steady stream of sold kidneys, borrowing strength
from across the generations as first father, then son, and then daughter-in-law each
stepped forward to contribute to the family income.

The eager kidney sellers of Banon Lupa shantytown are helped by the many
new 'donors for dollars' transplant programs that are sponsored by enterprising
hospital administrators. Dr B. Clemente, Medical Director of Capitol Medical
Center in Manila, saw no conflict in advertising to foreigners (especially to patients
from the USA and Canada) the availability of modern transplant services at her
modest hospital and of fresh kidneys procured from local donors for whom (she
said) 'a few hundred dollars or even a large sack of rice is payment enough'. When
asked why cadaver kidneys were not generally used, Dr Clemente replied that the
Philippines was a very Catholic country in which a great many people still had
strong feelings about 'the proper disposal of the dead'. As for the living? They were
free to dispose of themselves as they saw fit, the good doctor replied. Donating an
organ for a small compensation – 'Remember, we are not talking about *sales*' – was
consistent, she said, with Catholic beliefs: 'They would be acting like the Good
Samaritan, saving the life of a stranger.'

Bioethics: The Handmaiden of Free-Market Medicine

What goes by the wayside in these new medical transactions is longstanding
modernist and humanist conceptions of bodily holism, integrity and human dignity,
let alone cultural and religious beliefs in the 'sacredness' of the body. And, it might
fair to ask if 'the life' that is teased out of the body of the one and transferred into
the body of the other bears any resemblance to the ethical life of the free citizen
(*bios*) or whether it more closely resembles the bare or naked life of the slave? Here,
I am referring to the distinction made by Giorgio Agamben (1998), drawing on
Aristotle's *Politics*, between *bios*, the proper life of the citizen, and *zoe* – the mere,
brute life of the species. Thomas Aquinas would later translate these ancient Greek
concepts into medieval Christian terms that distinguished the natural life from
the good life.[8]

But neither Aristotle nor Aquinas is with us. Instead, we are asked to take counsel
from the new discipline of bioethics, which has been finely calibrated to meet the
needs of advanced biomedicine/biotechnologies and the desires of postmodern
medical consumers.[9] Even as conservative a scholar as Francis Fukuyama (2002)
refers to the 'community of bioethhicists' as having 'grown up in tandem with the
biotech industry...and [at times] nothing more than sophisticated (and sophistic)
justifiers of whatever it is the scientific community wants to do' (ibid.: 204).

Not surprisingly, bioethics has offered little resistance to the growing markets in
humans and body parts. And today the 'right' to buy or sell human organs is
increasingly defended in the world's premier medical journals, including the *Lancet*
and *Journal of the American Medical Association*, among others. Recently, a highly
respected transplant professional defended the patient's 'right to buy' an organ as a
'mellowing' and 'maturing' of medical ethics (Friedlaender 2002). This maturation
process to which he refers is the attempt to thoroughly rationalize transplant
medicine, stripping it of its early religious trappings (see below) and of its humanist

biases so as to bring it into alignment with neoliberal conceptions of the human, the body, labor, value, rights and economics.

In effect, the corrective field of bioethics and the profession of transplant medicine have both capitulated to the dominant market ethos.[10] Growing numbers of transplant doctors now argue that the real problem lies with outdated laws, increasingly irrelevant national regulatory agencies (such as UNOS), and archaic medical professional norms that are out of touch with transplant realities today and with the 'quiet revolution' of those who have refused to face a premature death with equanimity and 'dignity' while waiting patiently on an official waiting list for a cadaver organ. Some argue for a free trade in human organs; others argue for a regulated market.

In the meantime, however, the rupture in medical norms and the disconnect between practice and the law can be summarized as follows: While commerce in human organs is illegal according to the official legal codes of virtually all nations where transplant is practiced, nowhere in the world are the renegade surgeons (who are well known to their professional colleagues), organs brokers or kidney buyers (or sellers) pursued by the law, let alone prosecuted. It is easy to understand why kidney buyers and sellers would not be the focus of prosecution under the law. Compassion rather than outrage is the more appropriate response to their desperate acts. But the failure on the part of governments, ministries of health and law-enforcement agencies to interrupt the activities of international transplant outlaws, their holding companies, money-laundering operations and Mafia connections can only be explained as an *intentional* oversight. Indeed, some of the most notorious outlaw transplant surgeons are the medical directors of major transplant units, and serve on prestigious international medical committees and ethics panels. None has been cast out or even censored by their own profession, though a few have been investigated, and some are socially isolated by some of their dissenting colleagues. All practice their illicit trade freely, though the outlaw surgeons move their bases of international operations frequently so as to avoid medical or police surveillance.

One of the world's leading transplant outlaws, Dr Zaki Shapira of Bellinson Medical near Tel Aviv, served with me on the prestigious international 'Bellagio Task Force' on transplant ethics and traffic in organs (Rothman et al. 1997). In one of his subsequent trips to Italy he was the recipient of a prestigious human service award. Meanwhile, one of Dr Shapira's recovering transplant patients in Jerusalem gave me copies of his medical documents that led me to the fraudulent medical society in Bergamo, Italy to whom the patient was told to forward the $180,000 that his illicit transplant (in Turkey) had cost. But when I called the 'medical society' in Bergamo I was told that it was only a clearinghouse for medical encyclopedias.

The impunity of these transplant outlaws concerns more than governmental lassitude and medical professional corruption, though these exist. In no small part the surgeons are protected by their extraordinary privilege over life, death and the bodies of their patients and by the charisma that accompanies their seemingly miraculous powers. As much as his younger colleagues worry about Dr Shapira's ethics, with few exceptions they continue to praise his surgical technique, his 'courageous', if reckless, disregard of medical convention, and the service he is providing to Israeli citizens, even if at the expense of other citizens of the world. The same holds true for Dr Yusef Somnez, the notorious 'Doctor Vulture' of Istanbul. The head of the Turkish medical ethics committee lamented that 'Somnez is one of our very best transplant surgeons. He is the man who single-handedly put transplant on the map in Turkey.'

Transplant surgeons do sometimes see themselves as 'above the law'. In the early years of transplant famous surgeons such as Christian Bernard in South Africa and Thomas Starzel in the United States had to battle against the 'irrationality' (as they saw it) of those who resisted transplant's necessary redefinition of death as brain death. Barnard, for example, refused to respond seriously to his critics, silencing them with his proverbial arrogant reply that the patient was dead 'when the doctor says he is dead'. That same 'independent' tradition continues today among the younger generation of transplant doctors who often still see and describe themselves as societal mavericks breaking down 'old taboos' standing in the way of advancing technological capabilities. In the face of illicit transplants with paid donors, a great many kidney transplant surgeons simply look the other away. Some actively facilitate an informal sale that will save or improve the life of one of their patients. Others prepare and counsel kidney patients for transplant trips overseas and admire the initiative of those who have returned having purchased a kidney from a hapless women in a Lima slum or from a Chinese executed prisoner, as the case may be. Patient autonomy, individual freedom, the right to choose and a vague (though unexamined) commitment to a utilitarian ethos of 'greatest good for the greatest number' guide a great many transplant surgeons' sense of 'the ethical'.

In the rational choice language of contemporary medical ethics the conflict between non-malfeasance ('do no harm') and beneficence (the moral duty to perform good acts) is increasingly resolved in favor of the libertarian and consumer-oriented principle that those able to broker or buy a human organ should not be prevented from doing so. Paying for a kidney 'donation' is viewed as a potential 'win–win' situation that can benefit both parties (see Richards 1998). Individual decision making and patient autonomy have become the final arbiters of medical and bioethical values. Social justice and notions of the 'good society' hardly figure at all their discussions.

In the late or postmodern, consumer-oriented context, the ancient prescriptions for virtue in suffering and grace in dying can only appear patently absurd. But the transformation of a person into a 'life' that must be prolonged or saved at any cost has made life into the ultimate commodity fetish. And an insistence on the absolute value of a single human life saved, enhanced or prolonged ends all ethical or moral inquiry and erases any possibility of a global social ethic. Meanwhile, the traffic in kidneys reduces the human content of all the lives it touches.

Justice in Transplant – Scarcity for Whom?

The 'demand' for human organs, tissues, and body parts – and the desperate search among wealthy transplant patients to purchase them – is driven, above all, by the medical discourse on scarcity. The specter of long transplant 'waiting lists' – sometimes only virtual lists with little material basis in reality[11] – has motivated and driven questionable practices of organ harvesting with blatant sales alongside 'compensated gifting', doctors acting as brokers, and fierce competition between public and private hospitals for patients of means.

But the very idea of organ 'scarcity' is what Ivan Illich (1970) would call an artificially created need, invented by transplant technicians and dangled before the eyes of an ever-expanding sick, aging and dying population. The resulting artificially created organs scarcity is 'misrecognized' (Bourdieu 1977) as a natural medical phenomenon. In this environment of 'survivalist' utilitarian pragmatics, the ethics of transplantation is modeled after classical 'lifeboat' ethics (Koch 2001). With ethical presumptions of scarcity, there appear to be clear choices to be made, namely who gets into the lifeboat ('getting on the waiting list'); who will be shoved off the boat when it gets overcrowded (getting triaged while on the waiting list); and who will, in the end, be 'eaten' so that others may live (race and class disparities in organs procurement and distribution practices)?

There is little consciousness of the vulnerability of some social classes and ethnic groups who can be described as the 'designated donor' populations, both living and brain dead. In the United States, for example, where cadaver transplant continues to be supported as the norm for donation (if not so, increasingly, in practice), the brain dead are drawn from a population that is disproportionately poor – including whites, Latinos and African-Americans. The poor and minorities are over-represented in the intensive care centers (ICUs) of large urban hospitals, due to their over-exposure to urban violence, higher rates of homicide, suicide and vehicular death, as well as the cumulative effects of societal and medical neglect. The great irony is that those lacking public insurance (44 million citizens) also comprise the greatest number of those whose family members are asked to behave altruistically and to donate the organs and tissues of loved ones. That a great many of these poor, African-American and Latino families refuse to donate should come as no surprise. They are being asked to support with the bodies of their loved ones a social and medical system that excludes them and within which they have a lower probability of receiving an organ, should that need arise. One needs to be relatively affluent and otherwise healthy and well looked after to be recommended for organ transplant. The much commented upon refusal of African-Americans to donate organs should be seen as a political act of considered resistance.

As for living, paid donation, the social inequities are more transparent. Those who sell a kidney are normally from social and economic strata where access to basic medical care and necessary aftercare are most often lacking. But to date the only dissident voices raised against the dominant transplant narrative of life-saving come from far afield and are generally expressed in unpalatable forms that are all too easily dismissed and discredited. These alternative bioethical positions are often expressed 'primitively' and from the social margins in the form of rumors and moral panics of body theft and organ stealing, some of which turns out not to be so groundless after all. To a great many of those living on the fringes of the new global disorder, the scramble for 'fresh' organs and tissues increases their profound sense of ontological insecurity in a world that values their bodies as a reservoir of spare parts (Scheper-Hughes 1996). While popular resistance in Mexico and Brazil led to revoking new and progressivist laws of presumed consent for the purposes of harvesting organs, such resistance has been ineffectual or lacking with respect to the growth of the international organs market, as those on all sides of the transplant equation have began to accept as normal and routine these nonetheless still largely covert transactions protected by transplant medicine's coyly averted gaze.

Throughout these radical transformations, the voice of anthropology has been muted while the high-stake debates have been waged among transplant professionals, bioethicists, legal scholars and economists. But what other human science and discipline is better suited than anthropology to interrogate values and practices from a position of epistemological openness and to offer radical alternatives to the limited pragmatic utilitarianism that dominates medical bioethical thinking today?

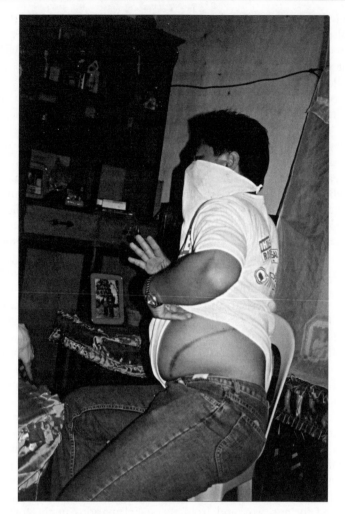

Figure 10.4   Ray, a Manila-based kidney seller turned kidney hunter and broker for a local hospital's "donors for dollars" program (photo by Nancy Scheper-Hughes).

Founding Organs Watch – an Anthropology of Organs

In the face of this ultimate, late modern dilemma – this 'end of the body' as we see it – the task of anthropology seems relatively straightforward: the recovery of our discipline's still unrealized radical epistemological promise, its abiding commitment to basic strangeness and to radical otherness, whilst maintaining a commitment to the critically examined ethical life, while simultaneously risking practical and political involvements in the murky, sometimes criminal and occasionally dangerous field sites under consideration.

To this end my colleague Lawrence Cohen and I co-founded Organs Watch in November 1999 as a temporary stop-gap measure in the absence of any other organization of its kind. We set as our initial task some basic, but necessary, first questions: How does the human organs market function? Who are the key players? How are the relations between organized crime and illicit transplant medicine structured? As for the patients, whose needs are privileged? What invisible sacrifices are demanded? What 'noble lies' are concealed in the tired transplant rhetoric of gifting, scarcities and human needs?

The resulting, collaborative[12] multi-sited field research project has investigated and documented dimensions of the organs and transplant trade in nine countries focusing on the medical and social effects on transplant patients and their providers, who constitute some of the most vulnerable citizens of the new world order. Additionally, we have observed the processes through which human tissues – cornea, bone, skin, heart valves, pituitary glands – are taken, without consent, from the dead bodies in the morgues of public hospitals and police mortuaries (from Brazil to Israel to South Africa and the United States) and sent to the tissue banks, eye banks, university research labs and biotech companies where these human parts are processed – often for sale.

In the course of this research we have followed kidney patients from dialysis clinics to meetings with their intermediaries in suburban shopping malls, and from there to illicit surgery conducted in rented operating rooms of public and private hospitals, some of these resembling the old clandestine back alley abortion clinics of the 1940s and 1950s.

We have interviewed dozens of kidney buyers or kidney seekers in their homes, in dialysis clinics and in their hospital beds to try to understand the conditions of their suffering. We have tracked down petty organ brokers only to discover that many of them, like Ray A. were originally kidney sellers themselves who were subsequently hired by their transplant surgeons as kidney hunters in their home communities. My associates and I have met with local kidney sellers in township *shabeens* in Soweto, in squatter camps in Manila, in shantytowns in Brazil, in jails in Israel, in smoke-filled bars in Chosen and in wine cellars of Mangier, both in Moldova.

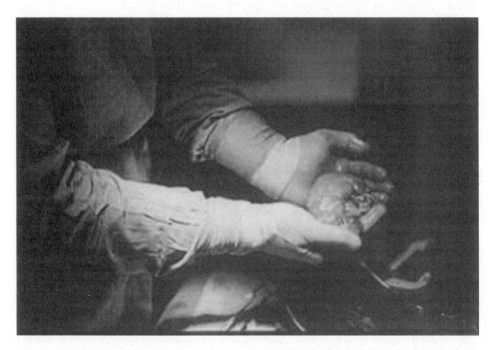

Figure 10.5 Kidney transplant in Cape Town, South Africa: 'Whose kidney?' Organs Watch keeps an eye on the traffic in human organs (Organs Watch, photo by Vivian Moos).

In short, we have gone to the places where the economically and politically dispossessed – including refugees, undocumented workers, prisoners, AWOL soldiers, aging prostitutes, cigarette smugglers, petty thieves and other marginalized people – are lured into selling their organs. And, we have followed, observed and interviewed international surgeons practicing or facilitating illicit surgery, their lawyers and representatives of their medical ethics boards, and we have attempted to map the international medical and financial connections which make their work possible. Though I am not proud to reveal it, I posed during fieldwork in Turkey in February 2002 as a buyer desperately seeking a kidney for a family member, in order to meet with hopeful sellers at a 'Russian suitcase market' in a run-down, immigrant section of Istanbul.

In its odd juxtapositions of ethnography, documentation, surveillance, and human rights work, the Organs Watch project blends genres and transgresses longstanding distinctions between anthropology, political journalism, scientific report, moral philosophy and human rights advocacy. These new ethnographic engagements require us to enter spaces and into conversations where nothing can be taken for granted and where a hermeneutics of suspicion replaces earlier fieldwork modes of bracketing and suspension of disbelief. How does one investigate covert and criminal behavior as an anthropologist? To whom does one owe one's divided loyalties? In traveling incognito, as I did when investigating allegations of illegal organs and tissues harvesting at the Argentine asylum, Montes de Oca, for the profoundly mentally retarded, I had only Laud Humphreys (1970) and his highly questionable, later roundly condemned, observational study of impersonal sex in public bathrooms as a shaky reference point. But how else, except in disguise, could one learn of the hidden suffering of an invisible population? How can the mute and the profoundly mentally retarded possibly speak for themselves? What alternative methods of investigation are appropriate? This kind of work requires a certain militancy[13] as well as a continuous and relentless form of self-criticism and a constant rethinking of anthropological (as well as medical) ethics and practice.

From Priceless Gift to Pricey Commodity – a Question of Value

Organ transplant is arguably the most intensely social, one might even say sociable, of all medical practices. The origins of transplantation depended on forging a new social contract and a social trust based on the willingness of people to share the body parts of a brain-dead relative, a new and periodically contested diagnosis, with a closely matched mortally sick stranger. Organ transplantation is, as Renee Fox so famously put it, both life-saving and death-ridden. Under traditional cadaver donation, the 'gift' of life simultaneously demands a 'gift of death' by grieving family members willing to accept, often counter-intuitively, the end of the life of a 'brain dead' but heart-beating loved one.

Consequently, from the outset the language of organ sharing and transplantation was highly idealistic, ethical and to a degree (mostly subliminal) very Christian.

While exhortations to altruism and to heroic acts are found in *all* the world's religions, the emphasis in organ donation on bodily self-sacrifice, anonymous gifting and charity toward strangers resonates with explicitly Christian values. The benevolent 'mixing' and sharing of body parts in transplantation evokes deeply Catholic notions of the Mystical Body and the Communion of Saints as well as images of medieval churchyards and their ossuaries where bones collected and mingled and where death itself was collectivized so as to erase all invidious social and individual markers of earthly difference (see Aries 1974). Indeed, the Last Supper and the Crucifixion offer the living a divine model of self-sacrifice and bodily sharing which to this day motivates some extraordinary acts of organ sharing, as captured in the popular film *Jesus of Montreal*.

It is no doubt because of these strong symbolic equivalencies between transplant ethics and a sacramental approach to life and to the care of the human body as 'borrowed' but not 'owned' that Rome readily accepted the technology of organ transplant and 'blessed' the new definition of brain death that transplantation required. More recently, the tacit acceptance of brain death for the purposes of organ harvesting was made explicit by Pope John Paul II in his brief address delivered to the 18th International Congress of the Transplantation Society on 29 August 2000. At the same time, the Pope reinforced the original transplant ethic of altruism and empathy for strangers that provides the bedrock for the gifting of cadaveric organs and he condemned commerce in human organs:

> Every organ transplant has its source in a decision of great ethical value: the decision to offer without reward a part of one's own body for the health and well-being of another person. Here precisely lies the nobility of the gesture, a gesture which is a genuine act of love. It is not just a matter of giving away something that belongs to us but of giving something of ourselves, for by virtue of its substantial union with a spiritual soul, the human body cannot be considered as a mere complex of tissues, organs and functions.
> ..rather it is a constitutive part of the person who manifests and expresses himself through it. Accordingly, any procedure which tends to commercialize human organs or to consider them as items of exchange or trade must be considered morally unacceptable, because to use the body as an 'object' is to violate the dignity of the human person.

Obviously, the pope is at least minimally aware that the ethic of the 'gift' is under assault in many parts of the world where the sale of kidneys has become a lucrative business for doctors (if not for kidney sellers) and for public and private transplant clinics, some of these Church linked, catering to wealthy foreign patients. Consequently, both anonymous cadaveric donation and living related-kidney donation are rapidly being supplanted by transplants with kidneys purchased from strangers.

The present scenario began over two decades ago with the realization by transplant professionals in the USA and elsewhere that cadaver organs, for many complex social reasons (Lock 2002) would never supply the growing demand for a steady supply of transplantable organs. Meanwhile, advances in immunology and the development of powerful new anti-rejection drugs such as cyclosporin made close tissue matching between donor and recipient unnecessary. The positive outcomes for kidney transplant patients who have purchased kidneys from impoverished vendors in various parts of the world where basic blood- but not tissue-matching procedures are followed, in clandestine commercialized transactions, lead to a growing realization that an excellent HLA tissue match is no longer required to achieve a successful transplant outcome. Today almost any person willing to be an organ donor, ideally medically suited *or not*, can do so. And living donor organs – one kidney, half a liver and lobe of one lung – are becoming the organs of choice to supply the growing demands for transplant from ever expanding waiting lists. Meanwhile, living donor organs are also preferred by surgeons and their patients to increase the longevity and viability of transplants. In 2001, for the first time, in the United States live donor kidney transplant accounted for 50% of all transplants, and living donor liver transplants rose to 10% (Delmonico 2002).

The Consumers: The Body and Commodity Fetishism

Transplant procedures are astronomically expensive (in the United States a heart transplant costs more than $300,000) and are frequently hindered by so-called shortages in organs. The media, prompted by organs procurement organizations, produce frequent references to the numbers of people who will die each year waiting for an organ. (There is no system to track or record the health, medical problems, or deaths of those who have donated organs.) In the United States over 70,000 people appear on organs waiting lists. Every year the demand for organs increases as transplant organizations, transplant professionals and patients' rights groups demand that new (and marginal) categories of people become eligible for organ transplants.

For example, at their annual meetings in Leiden, The Netherlands, in September 2000, members of Eurotransplant actively and enthusiastically supported new experiments that expanded transplant waiting lists to include the medical margins – those over 70 years, infants, those with hepatitis C and HIV seropositivity, and those proven to be immunologically prone to organ rejection. There was no consciousness or recognition that these experiments would inflate the demand for organs and promote desperate means, including the black market, to obtain them. Instead, these programs were defended as democratic in their inclusiveness and as a service to medical consumers demanding the right to any and all advanced medical procedures now *available*.

Similarly, kidney and transplant patient advocacy groups in many parts of the world – from Brazil to Israel to Iran to the United States – have articulated a new medical consumers bill of rights, one that includes a patient's right to transplant and even to unobstructed access to the life-saving and healthy spare organs of 'the other', for which patients are willing to travel great distances and to pay a negotiable, market-based price. In continuing to articulate the current dilemma of transplant, under these new social conditions, in terms of scarcity, supply and demand – when the precious 'commodities' in question are increasingly attached to living bodies – serious ethical dilemmas are created for the patients and for their doctors who find themselves in the position of passively and inadvertently or actively creating a medically protected space for the kidney commerce.

'Who am I to second guess, let alone to judge, my patients?', asked Michael Friedlaender,[14] kidney transplant specialist at Hadassah Hospital, with reference to the growing numbers of patients in his hospital-based practice who have returned from overseas having purchased a kidney. Later, he was to write (2002: 971–2): 'Here began my conversion from fierce objection to kidney marketing to passive acquiescence in this trade. We could not prevent our patients travelling to Iraq [later to Turkey, Romania, and the USA]. We gave patients who asked our advice all the information I have presented here, and warned them that we could not help them outside our national boundaries, but assured them that we would immediately assist them on their return.' Part of the information that is given to his dialysis patients is the differential survival rates for *living donor* kidneys vs. cadaveric kidneys, based on research by Wolfe and his colleagues (1999) – a median (50%) graft survival of 21.6 years (living donor kidney) compared with 13.8 years for a cadaver kidney. 'If my own kidneys failed I would opt for a transplant from a living donor', Dr Friedlaender has said on more than one public occasion. The data on differential survival rates are circulated widely among kidney transplant surgeons around the world, and are frequently cited by their patients and directly contribute to the decision to abandon conventional cadaver organ waiting lists in pursuit of 'fresh' kidneys from living people.

Antother consumer-based stimulus behind the occult economy in living donor kidneys (and part livers) is the growing rejection of hemo-dialysis by increasingly sophisticated kidney patients. Dialysis treatment for any period of time, even as a bridge while waiting for transplant, is increasingly viewed by kidney activists as unacceptable suffering, as time on the cross. In September 2000 a young man I will call Amatai, a 23-year-old university student from Jerusalem, flew to New York City for a kidney transplant with an organ purchased from a local 'donor' arranged through a broker in Brooklyn. Most of the cost of the surgery ($200,000) was paid for by his Israeli 'sick funds' (medical insurance that is guaranteed to all Israeli citizens). Particularly noteworthy in his narrative was the almost seamless natural-ization of living donation and the rejection of the artificiality of the dialysis machine:

> Kidney transplant from a living person is the most natural solution because you are free of the [dialysis] machine. With transplant you don't have to go to the hospital three times a week to waste your time for three or four hours. And after each dialysis you don't feel very well, and you sleep a lot, and on weekends you feel too tired to go out with your friends. There are still a lot of poisons left in the body and when you can't remove them, you feel tired. Look, dialysis isn't a normal life. And also you are limited to certain foods. You are not allowed to eat a lot of meat, salt, fruits, vegetables. Every month you do tests to see that the calcium level is OK, and even if so your skin becomes yellow. Aesthetically, dialysis isn't very nice. A kidney transplant from a living donor is the very best, and the most natural solution.

At the same time many kidney patients resist the idea of conventional 'waiting lists' for cadaver organs as archaic vestiges or residues of wartime triage and rationing or worse as reminiscent of socialist bread lines and petrol 'queues'. In the present climate of biotechnological optimism and biomedical triumphalism, the very idea of a shortage, even an organs shortage, suggests a basic management, market or policy failure. The ideology of the global economy is one of unlimited and freely circulating goods. And those new commodities are evaluated, like any other, in terms of their quality, durability and market value.

The cadaver kidney has been consigned to the dustbins of surgical history by those with the ability to get a living donor, like 71-year-old Avirham, a retired lawyer with end-stage kidney disease for whom time was running out and for whom neither a spectral waiting list nor a dead man's kidney seemed like reasonable options. So, in 1999 Avraham took the decisive step to fly with Dr Zaki Shapira and several other Israeli and Italian kidney patients to an undisclosed location in Eastern Europe where they were all transplanted with kidneys purchased from displaced rural workers. The entire venture was, Avriham admits, an enormous risk. 'You have no idea how poor where we went to was!' he said. 'The hospital was like something you would expect maybe in a third world country.' But it was a risk he was willing to take to avoid the queue at home for a cadaveric kidney transplant:

> Why should I have to wait months and years for a kidney from someone who was in a traffic accident, pinned under the car for many hours, then in miserable condition in the ICU [intensive care unit] for weeks and only after all that trauma, have that same organ put inside me? It's really a disgusting idea to think about putting that dead man's organ inside you. That organ is not going to be any good! His kidney is practically dead. After it was kept on ice for several hours, how can you expect it to go right back to work for

me? Or worse, I could get the kidney of an elderly person, or an alcoholic, or a person who died of a stroke. That kidney is all used up. No, it is far better to get a kidney from a healthy man or woman who can also benefit from the money I can afford to pay. Where I went for my transplant the people were so poor they did not even have bread to eat. Do you have any idea what one thousand, let alone five thousand dollars means to a peasant? The money I paid was a gift equal to the gift that I received.

Obviously, free-market medicine requires a divisible body with detachable and demystified organs seen as ordinary and 'plain things', simple material for medical consumption. But these same 'plain' objects have a way of reappearing and returning like the repressed, when least expected, almost like medieval messengers and gargoyles from the past in the form of highly spiritualized and fetishized objects of desire. As Veena Das once wryly observed: 'An organ is *never* just an organ.'

And the fetishized or 'designer' kidney purchased from a living donor conjures up primitive beliefs in human immortality, transcendence and magical energy. As Averham explained his frantic and dangerous search for a living kidney donor: 'I chose the better way. I was able to see my donor [in a small town in Eastern Europe]. My doctor pointed him out to me. He was young, strong, healthy – everything that I was hoping for!' Here, the symbolic equations between kidney market, slave market and brothel come to the surface.

Meanwhile, international Internet brokers prey on consumer prejudices and on the anxieties of transplant candidates. For example, 'Livers-4-You', until a few weeks ago when it was forced off cyberspace, advertised the following via kidneysurgery@s-s-net.com: 'Want a healthy living donor next week, or a morgue organ in five years? We are a new organization with a New York City phone number and unique experience in locating the overseas pathway for those *waiting too long* for a transplant.'

Brokers, Kidney Hunters and Outlaw Surgeons

Obviously, finding an available supply of organ vendors was only a partial solution to the new scarcities produced by transplant technologies. Even Jesus knew that 'the poor we would always have with us.' In fact, the real scarcity in organ transplant is of patients, like Avriham, of sufficient economic means to pay for these astronomically expensive operations (between $100,000 and $200,000 depending on location) as well as sufficiently 'courageous' or foolhardy to travel to the locations where people are desperate enough to self-mutilate in the interests of short-term survival. Here was a classic problem in microeconomics – one of supply- and demand-side sources separated by vast geographies, different cultures, and even by fierce religious and political hostilities. 'I think my donor was an Iraqi soldier', an Israeli transplant patient told me, admiring the organizational skills and the chutzpah of the doctors and brokers who had pulled such a feat off.

Indeed, the new transplant transactions are exceedingly complex, requiring extensive and expert teamwork among medical professionals, from lab technicians to nursing staff, to nephrologists and blood and tissue laboratories, to the surgical teams who operate in tandem. Surgical units must be rented, passports, visas and air travel arranged, and immigration officials must be dealt with. The entire process is facilitated by a new international network of body Mafia ranging from the sleazy (and sometimes armed and dangerous) underworld 'kidney hunters' of Istanbul and Cesenau, Moldova to the sophisticated but clandestine 'medical tourism' bureaux of

Tel Aviv and Manila to the medical intermediaries posing as religious or charitable trusts and 'patient's advocacy organizations' found in downtown Philadelphia, Brooklyn, and Chinatown, New York City.

The 'Livers-4-You' brokers (cited above) had 'joined with medical professionals in the Philippines and "nearby countries" (including Thailand) to help "fill the gap" between the supply and demand for organs'. For Americans who might be nervous about traveling to a developing country for transplant surgery, the website reassured them that medical schools in the Philippines are 'carbon copies' of US schools and that Philippine transplant surgeons are all trained in the United States. Those in doubt about the quality of advanced medical care in the Philippines were told to contact the US consulate in Manila, the Manila office of multinational corporations, or the Philippine Catholic Church. All are willing, the website assured the wary Internet transplant shopper, to provide positive references on the practice of transplant surgery in the Philippines. While the cost for a live liver donor is considerably 'higher than for a cadaver organ' it was still 'less than half the current cost of a liver transplant in the United States'. The payment mechanics – through bank wire transfers – would be discreetly handled by the Livers-4-You online staff. Medical arrangements would be supervised by the organization's head surgeon, a US-trained and licensed doctor who has performed 'many operations' in the United States.

In addition to the faceless Internet brokers who try to match desperate North American patients[15] to kidney sellers in the Third World, locally based brokers have appeared in ethnic enclaves of Los Angeles, Baltimore, New York City and Philadelphia where they recruit new immigrants and undocumented workers as kidney sellers and assist wealthy foreign transplant patients to find the doctors, hospitals and even the hotel accommodation that they need. In the last two years transplant tourism packages arranged mostly in the Middle East have brought scores of kidney patients to US transplant centers, both public and private, for surgery conducted with both cadaveric and living donor purchased kidneys.

One such active group, United Lifeline, began in Israel as a charitable organization to help Israeli children get expensive cancer treatments in the United States. Over time, United Lifeline developed into a larger organization with many representatives in east and west coast cities of the USA who have helped to facilitate transplant surgery for Israeli citizens who tire of waiting for a cadaver organ at home. But this service contributes to the paradox of US transplant centers accepting and even actively recruiting wealthy foreign patients to receive organs that are otherwise described as painfully scarce.[16] The University of Maryland Medical Center, for example, advertised (until recently, and under criticism from Organs Watch) its kidney transplant program in Arabic, Chinese, Hebrew and Japanese on its website.[17] The United States is extremely democratic in at least one sense: anyone, regardless where they come from, with enough cash can become a 'medical citizen' of the USA and receive a bona fide 'Made in the USA' organ. Local representatives of 'United Lifeline' (though linked to the international transplant tourism business of the Middle East) are often unpaid and religiously motivated volunteers who would resist strongly any hint of 'brokering' for patients or for transplant organs. Like many of the surgeons they deal with, these patient advocates either deny the origins of the purchased organs or suggest that existing laws restricting sales are out of touch with reality.

In other parts of the world, the necessary intermediaries and organ brokers are small-time criminals in the employ of highly sophisticated Mafia involved in all

Figure 10.6 Viorel, a 27-year-old kidney seller from Chisenau, Moldiva, is still angry at Nina, the broker who trafficked him to Turkey, and at Dr Sonmez, the surgeon who took his right kidney. 'How can that man call himself a doctor? That son of a bitch left me an invalid', he told me (photo by Nancy Scheper-Hughes).

kinds of trafficking in human bodies. The brokers who approached the naïve young men of Mingir and Chisenau in Moldova were themselves former prostitutes and kidney sellers who had subsequently developed lucrative ties to larger networks of human traffickers spread among cities in Russia, Turkey, Israel and Italy. The infamous Nina Ungureanu of Mingir village in Moldova made no pretenses about the financial motives that got her deeply involved in the Middle Eastern kidney trade. Despite 'police harassment' Ms Ungureanu remains uncontrite. When asked by an undercover reporter[18] why she had engaged in the entrapment of young village men in Mingir, Nina Ungureanu replied:

> We needed the business.... We had a hard life. We could not quite stand on our own feet [financially]. But now we've built this house, we've sorted ourselves out.... And the police are not going to do anything to us and they are certainly not going to do anything to the [big shots] in this trade [i.e. Nina Sobiola and her co-workers]. But they should at least make them pay us the money they owe us. But where are they going to find them? I imagine they all live somewhere in America.... The police are never going to find them. Especially the main guys [behind this business].... I think I could settle for what I've made so far, but they (the police) come here to the village, take me off to Chisinau.... They abuse you – if you don't want to talk, they slap you. Yes, they slapped me once! Me, a woman!... But at least I've made some money in this business. Thanks be to God! I need it badly enough! We were in dire straits. But now we have had to stop. The police are going to make us sweat a little and than they are going to let it all go.

Meanwhile, the outlaw surgeons, like Dr Zaki Shapira of Tel Aviv, and his partner Yusef Sonmez of Istanbul, practice their illicit operations in rented, makeshift clinics or, when political conditions allow, in the operating rooms of some of the best public or private medical centers in Israel, Turkey, Romania, Iraq and, Sonmez for one has boasted,[19] 'even in Europe'. They perform their illicit operations under the frank gaze of local and national governments, ministries of health, international regulatory agencies, professional medical associations. They are quite clearly protected. In short, the illegal practice of transplant tourism, relying on an extensive network of competitive markets in patients, bodies and organs, is a public secret and one that involves some of the world's leading transplant surgeons and some of the most prestigious academic hospitals and medical centers around the world. And transplant crimes – even when they explode into gunfire and leave a trail of blood as they do from time to time – go officially undetected and unpunished.[20] In large part, this is because of fear and intimidation on all sides. And even the most aggressive transplant surgeons can find themselves trapped and more deeply involved in 'the business' than they had anticipated.

Medicine, Mafia and the Military: The Biopolitical Terrorism of Free Trade Transplant

In addition to the involvement of organized crime in the international organs business, military interests and military governments, particularly during periods of intense internal conflict and war, have played a role in protecting and even in organizing illegal organ harvesting from those considered enemies or from those considered social garbage.

The emergence of death camps, torture camps, and tissue- and organ-harvesting camps came together at certain junctures in the late twentieth century. Our research has uncovered what can only be called 'fascist' military and 'dirty war' tactics used on the bodies and the organs of the enemy. A footnote and subtext to the story of military terrorism during (and following) the 'dirty war' in Argentina, the apartheid state in South Africa and the dictatorship years in Brazil is the role that doctors played in providing not only children (as in the Argentine case) but also the blood, bones, heart valves and organs needed for transplant, taken from the bodies of the politically and the socially 'disappeared'. During the Argentine Dirty War (of the 1970s) and during the military state years of Brazil (1964–84), forensic and state pathologists and transplant doctors were at times under orders to produce quotas of usable organs and tissues needed for shoring up the defenses of the social body and the military state.[21]

In addition to stripping organs and tissues from the bodies of the politically disappeared, state doctors in Argentina helped themselves to the bodies of captive and socially despised populations, such as the mentally retarded, warehoused – as they are to this day – in massive state institutions, such as Montes de Oca and Open Door in Lujan, Buenos Aires province, Argentina. There inmates were routinely used, dead and alive, as a convenient source of blood, cornea and other valuable tissues and organs throughout the decades of the 1970s and 1980s. Even today blood is routinely taken from the hapless inmates without their consent and given to public blood banks while cornea are harvested at death from patients who are mentally incapable of giving (or denying) their consent.[22] There are indications, as yet unverified, that the organ-trafficking business in Eastern Europe began amidst the chaos and utter dehumanization of the death camps during the genocidal war in the former Yugoslavia.

A highly militarized Israel is today a major player in the global market for organs, a market that began in the West Bank and then moved to nearby Arab countries. According to well-placed Israeli medical sources,[23] Israel's citizens purchase, proportionally, the largest number of organs per capita in the world. Caught between a highly educated and medically conscious public and a very low rate of organ donation owing to religious pressures operating in a secular society, the Israeli Ministry of Health permitted the expansion of transplant tourism by allowing Israeli patients to use their national insurance programs to pay for transplants conducted elsewhere, even if illegally. Several large 'business corporations' (including the firm of Coby Dyan) developed necessary links with transplant surgeons and medical centers in Turkey, Russia, Moldova, Estonia, Georgia, Romania and (most recently) the United States.

In Israel, the cost of the transplant 'package' increased from $120,000 in 1998 to $200,000 in 2001. The package, as patients call it, includes the air travel, bribes to airport and customs officials, the 'double operation' (kidney extraction and kidney transplant), rental of private operating and recovery rooms, and hotel accommodation for accompanying family members. The donor's fee of between $3,000 and $15,000 (depending on the donor source) is included. With pressure from transplant candidates to develop links in more developed countries, the cost is still rising. The specific sites of the illicit surgery are normally kept secret from transplant patients until the day of travel, and the locations are continually rotated to maintain a low profile. The surgery is performed in secret between midnight and the early morning hours. In the most common scenario, Israeli patients and doctors (a transplant surgeon and a nephrologist) fly to Istanbul or to a small town in Turkey where the kidney donors are AWOL Iraqi soldiers or Eastern European guest workers. In another scenario, the Israeli and Turkish doctors travel in tandem to a third site in

Eastern Europe, where the organ sellers are unemployed locals or guest workers from elsewhere.

The refusal of the Israeli Ministry of Health to crack down on this multi-million dollar business, which is making Israel something of a pariah in the international transplant world, is troubling. But in the absence of a strong culture of organ donation and under pressure from well-organized and demanding transplant candidates, every person transplanted abroad is one less angry client with which to contend at home. More disturbing still, however, is the support and involvement of the Ministry of Defense in the illicit transplant tourism. Several Israeli patients who traveled on a transplant junket to Turkey and Eastern Europe noted the presence of military personnel accompanying the flights or participating in the transplants.

Meanwhile, medical human rights workers in the West Bank complained of medical violations of Palestinian bodies by Israeli pathologists at the National Legal Medical Institute in Tel Aviv.[24] An official investigation committee appointed by the Minister of Health in 2001 confirmed the suspicions of Palestinian health workers. Harvested organs and tissues were distributed by the Institute to hospitals and medical centers for surgical procedures, research and medical teaching. A special squad of surgeons on military reserve duty perform the harvesting. This practice was first established by the head of the national skin bank, who was formerly Chief Medical Officer of the Israeli Defense Forces. Relying on 'presumed consent' the staff of the Forensic Institute and the surgeons who illegally harvested skin and organs defended themselves by saying that they were saving lives, and that this imperative was more important than procuring the consent of ill-informed and grieving (Palestinian) family members. In this instance the tissues and organs of the dead were regarded as detachable objects that could be medically transformed into something valuable. Some bodies, however, were exempt from this practice, specifically the bodies of Israeli soldiers, which are always returned intact to their families for burial.

Beyond Bioethics

If a living donor can do without an organ, why shouldn't the donor profit and medical science benefit?

Janet Ratcliffe-Richards

For most bioethicists the 'slippery slope' in transplant medicine begins with the emergence of an unregulated market in organs and tissue sales. But for the anthropologist the ethical slippery slope occurred the first time one ailing human looked at another living human and realized that inside that other living body was something that could prolong his or her life.

Dialysis and transplant patients are highly visible and their stories are frequently reported by the media. Their pain and suffering are palpable. But while there is empathy – even a kind of surplus empathy – for transplant patients, there is an absence of empathy for the donors, living and brain dead. Their suffering is hidden from the general public. Few organ recipients know anything about the impact of a transplant procedure on the donor's body. If the medical and psychological risks, pressures and constraints on organ donors and their families were more generally known, transplant patients might want to consider opting out of procedures that demand so much of the other.

From an exclusively market-oriented perspective the problem of unsavory and dangerous black markets in human organs can be resolved by regulation rather than by prohibition. The human and ethical dilemmas are thereby reduced to a simple problem in management. The problems with this rational solution are many. The argument for 'regulation' is out of touch with the social and medical realities operating in many parts of the world but especially in Second and Third World nations. The medical institutions created to 'monitor' organ harvesting and distribution are often dysfunctional, corrupt or compromised by the power of organ markets and the impunity of the organ brokers and of outlaw surgeons willing to violate the first premise of classical medical bioethics: Above all, do no harm.

To date only kidneys, bone marrow and liver lobes can be taken from living donors and transplanted into ailing patients. Living donation remains a risky procedure and obviously cannot supply the 'demand' for hearts, lungs and other irreducible or irreplaceable body parts. There is minimal attention in the medical literature on the risks and complications living donors often suffer in the First World let alone in countries where living donors are operated on and sent packing within a few days by bus, car or train to their home communities, their futures uncertain and their medical destinies unrecorded. In the USA two kidney donors have died during the past 18 months and another is in a persistent vegetative state as a result of donation.[25] The fact that many living donors have either died immediately following the surgical procedure, or are themselves in dire need of a kidney transplant at a later date, sounds a cautionary note about living donation and serves as a reminder that nephrectomy is not a risk-free procedure.[26] The unnecessary and brutal death of Mike Hurewitz, 57, following the removal of part of his liver transplanted to his brother at Mt Sinai Medical Center in New York City this past January underscores the dangers of treating live organ donation in a cavalier and reckless fashion.

The problems multiply when the buyers and sellers are unrelated because the sellers are likely to be extremely poor and trapped in life-threatening environments where the everyday risks to their survival are legion, including exposure to urban violence, transportation and work-related accidents, and infectious disease that can compromise their kidney of last resort. And when that spare part fails, kidney sellers often have no access to dialysis – let alone to organ transplant. While poor people in particular cannot 'do without' their 'extra' organs, even affluent people need that 'extra' organ as they age and when one healthier kidney can compensate for a failing or weaker kidney.

Transplant surgeons have disseminated an untested hypothesis of 'risk-free' live donation in the absence of *any* published, longitudinal studies of the effects of nephrectomy (kidney removal) among the urban poor living anywhere in the world. The few available studies of the effects of neprectomy on kidney sellers in India (Goyal et al. 2002) and Iran (Zargooshi 2001) are unambiguous. Even under attempts (as in Iran) to regulate and control systems of 'compensated gifting' by the Ministry of Health, the outcomes are devastating. Kidney sellers suffer from chronic pain, unemployment, social isolation and stigma, and severe psychological problems. The evidence of strongly negative sentiments – disappointment, anger, resentment and even seething hatred for the doctors and the recipients of their organs – reported by 100 paid kidney donors in Iran strongly suggests that kidney selling there represents a serious social pathology.

My qualitative research among dozens of kidney sellers in Moldova and the Philippines, which included diagnostic follow-up medical exams and sonograms, found that kidney sellers frequently face medical problems, including hypertension and even subsequent kidney insufficiency, without access to medical care or necessary medication. On returning to their rural villages or urban shantytowns kidney sellers often find themselves both sick and unemployed, unable to sustain the demands of heavy agricultural or construction work, the only labor available to men of their skills and backgrounds. Kidney sellers are often alienated from their families and co-workers, excommunicated from their churches, and if single they are even excluded from marriage. The children of kidney sellers are ridiculed as 'one-kidneys'.

In Moldova I was able to document the ill health, social disability and subsequent unemployment faced by young male kidney sellers. Not one among the kidney sellers had seen a doctor or been treated at a medical clinic following their illicit operations in Istanbul. Moreover, I had to coax the young men to agree to a basic clinical exam and sonogram at the expense of Organs Watch. Some said they were ashamed to appear in a public clinic as they had tried to keep the sale a secret; others said they were fearful of learning negative results from the tests. All said that if serious medical problems were discovered they were unable to pay for follow-up treatment or necessary medication. Above all, they said, they feared being labeled as 'weak' or 'disabled' by employers and co-workers, as well as (for single men) by potential girlfriends and brides. 'No young woman in the village will marry a man with the tell-tale scar of a kidney seller', the father of a village kidney seller said sadly. 'They believe that he will be unable to support a family.' Sergei, a married man from Chisenau, revealed that his mother was the only person who knew the reason for the large, saber-like scar on his abdomen. Sergei's young wife believed that he had been injured in a construction accident while he was away in Turkey.

In any case, how can a national government set a price on a healthy human being's body part without compromising essential democratic and ethical principles that guarantee the equal value of all human lives? Any national regulatory system would have to compete with global black markets which establish the value of human organs based on consumer-oriented prejudices, such that in today's kidney market an Indian kidney fetches as little as $1,000, a Filipino kidney $1,300, a Moldovan or Romanian kidney yields $2,700, while a Turkish seller can command up to $10,000 and an urban Peruvian can receive as much as $30,000. The circulation of kidneys transcends national borders and international markets will coexist and compete aggressively with any national, regulated systems. Putting a market price on body parts – even a fair one – exploits the desperation of the poor, turning their suffering into an opportunity. And the surgical removal of non-renewable organs is an act in which medical practitioners, given their ethical standards, should not be asked to participate. Surgeons whose primary responsibility is to provide care should not be advocates of paid self-mutilation even in the interest of saving lives.

Bio-ethical arguments about the right to sell an organ or other body part are based on Euro-American notions of contract and individual 'choice'. These create the semblance of ethical choice (e.g., the right to buy a kidney) in an intrinsically unethical context. The social and economic contexts make the 'choice' to sell a kidney in an urban slum of Calcutta or in a Brazilian *favela* or Philippine shantytown anything but a 'free' and 'autonomous' one. The idea of consent is problematic with 'the executioner' – whether on death row or at the door of the slum resident – looking over one's shoulder and when a seller has no other option left but to sell an organ. Putting a market price on body parts – even a fair one – exploits the desperation of the poor, turning their suffering into an opportunity. Asking the law to negotiate a fair price for a live human kidney goes against everything that contract theory stands for. When concepts like individual agency and autonomy are invoked in defending the 'right' to sell an organ, anthropologists might suggest that certain 'living' things are not alienable or proper candidates for commodification. And the surgical removal of non-renewable organs is an act in which medical practitioners, given their ethical standards, should not be asked to participate.

The demand side of the organ scarcity problem also needs to be confronted. Part of the current scarcity derives from expansions of organ waiting lists to include very small infants and patients over 70 years, a practice that needs to be questioned. Liver and kidney failure often originate in public health problems that could be treated more aggressively preventively. Ethical solutions to the chronic scarcity of human organs are not always palatable to the public but also need to be considered. Foremost among these are systems of educated, informed 'presumed consent' in which *all* citizens are assumed to be organ donors at brain death unless they have officially stipulated their refusal beforehand. This practice, widespread in Europe, preserves the value of organ transplant as a social good in which no one is included or excluded based on the ability to pay.

Conclusion: A Return to the Gift

The material needs of my neighbor are my spiritual needs.
    Immanuel Levinas, Nine Talmudic Readings, *quoted in Donoghue 1996: 39*

This essay ends with a return to the radical ethical challenge implied in organ sharing in which the body is understood as a gift, meaning also a gift to the self. The body and its parts remain inalienable from the self because in the most simple Kantian or Wittgen-steinian formulation, the body provides the grounds of certainly for saying that one has a self and an existence at all. Humans both *are* and *have* a body. For those who view the body in more collectivist terms (whether following Judeo-Christian, Buddhist or animistic beliefs and values) as a gift, the body cannot be sold, while it can be re-gifted and recirculated in humanitarian acts of caritas.

From its origins transplant surgery presented itself as a complicated problem in gift relations and gift theory, a domain to which sociologists and anthropologists from Marcel Mauss to Claude Lévi-Strauss to Pierre Bourdieu have contributed mightily. The spread of new medical technologies and the artificial needs, scarcities and the new commodities that they demand have produced new forms of social exchange that breach the conventional dichotomy between gifts and commodities and between kin and strangers. While many individuals have benefited enormously from the ability to get the organs they need, the violence associated with many of these new transactions gives reason to pause (see Lock 2001). Are we witnessing the development of biosociality or the growth of a widespread bio-sociopathy?

In his 1970 classic, *The Gift Relationship*, Richard Titmuss anticipates many of the dilemmas now raised by the global human organs market. His assessment of the negative social effects of commercialized blood markets in the USA could also be applied to the global markets in human organs and tissues.

> The commercialism of blood and donor relationships represses the expression of altruism, erodes the sense of community, lowers scientific standards, limits both personal and professional freedoms, sanctions the making of profits in hospitals and clinical laboratories, legalizes hostility between doctor and patient, subjects critical areas of medicine to the laws of the marketplace, places immense social costs on those least able to bear them – the poor, the sick, and the inept – increases the danger of unethical behavior in various sectors of medical science and practice, and results in situations in which proportionately more and more blood is supplied by the poor, the unskilled and the unemployed, Blacks and other low income groups. (Titmuss 1970: 314)

The goal of our project is to bring broader social and *social justice* concerns to bear on global practices of organs procurement and transplant. This essay has been an attempt to delineate some of the contradictions inherent in a market-driven solution to the problem of 'scarcity' of human organs as well as a frank attempt to recapture the original biosociality inherent in the daring proposal to circulate organs as a radical act of fraternity and, finally, to bring a critical medical anthropological sensibility into the current debates on the commodification of the body.

Amidst the tension between organ givers and organ recipients, between doctors, patients and non-patients, between North and South, between the illegal and the 'merely' unethical, clarity is needed about whose values and whose notions of the body and embodiment are being represented. Are the frank concerns, expressed here, for bodily integrity and human dignity merely a residue of the Western enlightenment? In fact, these modernist values, so embattled and under multiple assaults in the postmodern, postindustrial world, are nonetheless intensely defended in many pockets of the Third and Fourth worlds. Deeply held beliefs in bodily integrity and in human dignity lie behind the demands 'of First Peoples' for the repatriation and reburial of human remains now warehoused in museum archives (see Scheper-Hughes 2000a). They lie behind the demands of the wretchedly poor for dignified death and burial (Scheper-Hughes 1992). And they certainly lie behind the fears of organ theft, and the deep anger expressed in Eastern European villages today toward the medical 'vultures' and 'mafia dogs' who have turned them into 'communities of half-men and -women'. Indeed, the division of the world into organ buyers and organ sellers is a medical, social and moral tragedy of immense and not yet fully recognized proportions. We hope that this project will help to establish a new ethical blueprint for anthropology and for medicine in the twenty-first century.

NOTES

1 See Jimenez and Scheper-Hughes (2002), part 1 of a three part series in the *National Post* (Toronto), Saturday 30 March, B1, B4–5.
2 Ferreira and Scheper-Hughes (n.d.). Dr Ferreira and I interviewed Domba recovering at the famous Hospital das Clinicas in Sao Paulo following a kidney transplant that the middle-aged, traditional shaman faced with enormous equanimity in comparison with the anxious Sao Paulo businessman in the hospital bed next to him who approached his own kidney transplant surgery with mortal dread. The relative ease with which Brazil's indigenous people face elective surgery is captured in the recently reported story of

Sapaim, shaman and spiritual leader of the Camaiura tribe in the southern Amazon, who underwent plastic surgery after a spirit directed him in a dream to 'change his face'. Sapaim reported afterwards that the operation made his face feel 'like new', as if he were a young boy again. See 'Shaman gets facelift after dream', Monday 29 April 2002, Brasilia, Brazil (Reuters).

3   By medical citizenship I mean the growing awareness and claims made by patients and by organized patient advocacy groups of their rights as citizens and as medical consumers to free access to medical information, including the latest cutting-edge research, to participation (or not) in experimental drug-testing procedures, to control over the conditions of one's treatment regime, and ultimately over the management of one's sickness and death.

4   See 'Organs for Sale: China's Growing Trade and Ultimate Violation of Prisoner's Rights'. Hearing before the Subcommittee on International Operations and Human Rights of the Committee on International Relations House of Representatives, One Hundred Seventh Congress, First Session, 27 June 2001.

5   One exception to this rule is Iraq where Arab kidney patients from various countries, including the West Bank, are introduced to their paid kidney donors – poor Arabs from Iraq and Jordan (for the most part) – before the dual surgery and the pair are encouraged to bond with each other so as to prevent subsequent 'rejection', understood there to have a psychological as well as a physiological component.

6   Source: Interviews with Prof. Shamoye Cotev, anesthesiologist at Assota Hospital, Tel Aviv and chairman of the ethics committee established by the Israeli Ministry of Health to investigate charges of criminal behavior by Dr Zaki Shapira of Bellinson Medical Center, regarding his involvement in kidney commerce in Israel in the mid-1990s. Dr Shapira was cleared on the grounds that even if he did transplant organs purchased from poor Palestinians, the law was vague and at most the committee could only 'slap Shapira's hand' for medical mischief.

7   Before ending the conversation we revealed to Mr K. that we were not kidney hunters but two journalists and an anthropologist looking to understand the situation that brought people to this decision. We made a donation toward his most immediate necessities and explained the risks and dangers of neprectomy. Mr K. was not too disappointed and neither was he particularly dissuaded by my cautionary arguments. 'Tell me another way', he said, 'I could earn so much money so quickly. How many used soda pop cans do you think I would have to resell?'

8   Both Agamben (1998: 2–3), and Hannah Arendt (1958: 12–49) treat the translation from ancient Greek to Church Latin in slightly different ways.

9   As bioethicists become more of a force in public policy, they are coming under scrutiny with respect to the bargains they strike with medical scientists and with biotech companies and their independence is being questioned. See, for example, 'Bioethicists find themselves the ones being scrutinized', *New York Times*, 1 August 2001, 1, A-14.

10   'Offering money for organ donation ethical, HHS Committee says', *AP/Nando Times*, 3 December 2001.

11   In Sao Paulo, Brazil the head of a kidney patients' advocacy network has tirelessly tracked the regional waiting list there to discover that hundreds of transplant candidates were dropped from the list without their knowledge and that powerful transplant doctors always find ways to transfer 'public' cadaver organs to their 'private' patients. While Neide B. does not recommend that patients stranded on dialysis try to find a paid living donor, she understands the frustration of those who have been deceived by falsified and readily corruptible waiting lists. 'Those with only basic [national] insurance', she said, 'are just "decorating" the waiting list'. Nonetheless, thanks to SUS, Brazil's national insurance program, dialysis treatments are available to most citizens there who need it.

12   Lawrence Cohen is the co-founder of this project. Associate field researchers and summer interns have included Aslihan Senal (Turkey), Limor Saminian (Israel), Juan Obarrio (Argentina), Maria Epele (Argentina), Mariana Ferreira (Brazil), Monga Mehlwani (South Africa), among others.

13   See Nancy Scheper-Hughes, 'The primacy of the ethical: towards a militant anthropo-
     logy, *Current Anthropology*, 1995. In one of his last major public lectures, delivered in
     Athens in the summer of 2000, Pierre Bourdieu embraced the life of the 'engaged and
     militant intellectual' which for him implied a direct and political engagement in new
     social movements (including the anti-globalization forces organizing against generically
     altered foods) and with more traditional labor movements in a united struggle against
     globalization recognized as a particular theory of the world and not as a description of
     that same world.

14   Interview with author, March 2001, Jerusalem.

15   Canadian patients are also actively recruited by transplant brokers. See 'Transplant
     patients wait years – or they can pay this man', an investigative report by Lisa Priest
     and Estanislao Oziewicz, *Globe and Mail* (Metro), 1 June 2001. The article reports on
     the practice of a Vancouver-area businessman, Walter Klak, who has ventured into the
     shadowy world of transplant tourism, putting desperate patients on a faster track for
     fresh Chinese kidneys for a $5,000 (US) down-payment. Klak said that as of June 2001
     more than 100 patients were inscribed on his waiting list for a transplant operation in a
     Shanghai hospital. He revealed that he and his Shanghai partner were using China for
     transplants because 'we found that to be the largest supply of organs that are available'.

16   The United Network for Organ Sharing (UNOS) allows 5% of organ transplants in US
     transplant centers to be allotted to foreign patients. However, only those centers
     reporting more than 15% foreign transplant surgery patients are audited.

17   See, for example, the Arabic (as well as Hebrew and Japanese) version of the university's
     advertisement at http://www.umm.edu/transplant/arabic.html.

18   Transcription of an interview in Mingir, Moldova in July 2001, courtesy of Ian O'Reilly,
     BBC.

19   Interview in June 2000 with a representative of Berkeley Organs Watch.

20   The local mafia that controls the traffic in organs in the Philippines is, for example, held
     responsible for the murder of the daughter of a former director of the National Kidney
     and Transplant Institute in Manila. The 22-year-old daughter was shot down in June
     1999 in front of her home by unknown assailants. The murderers, believed to have been
     engaged in an act of vengeance against the victim's father, were never discovered or
     brought to justice, although an investigation was launched by the Ministry of Health and
     the Philippine government responded by ordering a moratorium on organs donated by
     non-relatives. But both the investigation and the moratorium are over and the present
     director of the National Kidney Institute has no interest in reopening the case or even
     discussing the tragic event.

21   This theme is elaborated on in my article, 'Theft of Life' (Scheper-Hughes 1996).

22   Author's interview with nursing staff of Montes de Oca asylum in January 2000.

23   This statistic is cited by many transplant doctors including those charged with the
     unsuccessful official Israeli transplant harvesting program. It also appears in the writings
     of Prof. Meira Weiss, medical anthropologist, Hebrew University, Jerusalem, author of
     The Chosen Body 2002.

24   See 'Israel kills Palestinian boys, steals their organs for transplants', *Jerusalem Post*,
     9 January 2002 (IAP News). The article reports that Israeli government officials tacitly
     admitted that doctors at the Israeli forensic institute at Abu Kabir in Tel Aviv had
     extracted the vital organs of three Palestinian teenage children killed by the Israeli
     army in late December 2001. The Israeli Minister of Health, Nessim Dahhan, said in
     response to a question by Arab Knesset Member Ahmed Teibi that he could not deny that
     organs of Palestinian youths and children, killed by the Israeli forces, were taken out for
     transplant or scientific research. Teibi said he had received evidence proving that Israeli
     doctors at the forensic institute extracted such vital organs as the heart, kidneys and liver
     from the bodies of Palestinian youths and children killed by the Israeli army in Gaza and
     the West Bank. In June 2000 I was given the photo of a murdered Palestinian youth
     returned to his family following dissection at the Forensic Institute.

25 'Man keeps vigil for comatose wife who gave him kidney, life', *Holland Sentinel*, 15 February 2001.
26 'The live donor consensus conference', *Journal of the American Medical Association*, 284 (2000), 2919–26.

REFERENCES

Agamben, G. (1998) *Homo Sacer: Sovereign Power and Bare Life* (Stanford, CA: Stanford University Press).

Arendt, H. (1958) *The Human Condition* (Chicago: University of Chicago Press).

Aries, P. (1974) *Western Attitudes toward Death: From the Middle Ages to the Present* (Baltimore and London: Johns Hopkins University Press).

Bhagwati, J. (2002) Deconstructing rotten trade. *SAIS Review*, 22(1), 39–44.

Bourdieu, P. (1977) *Outline of a Theory of Practice* (Cambridge: Cambridge University Press).

Bourdieu, P. (2002) Pour un savoir engage: un texte inedit de Pierre Bourdieu. *Le Monde Diplomatique* (fevrier), 3.

Cohen, L. (1999) Where it hurts: Indian material for an ethics of organ transplantation. *Daedalus*, 128(4), 135–68.

Comaroff, J., and Comaroff, J. (eds) (2001) *Millennial Capitalism and the Culture of Neoliberalism* (Durham, NC: Duke University Press).

Delmonico, F., Arnold, R., Scheper-Hughes, N. et al. (2002) Organ donation by ethical incentives – not by sale. *New England Journal of Medicine* (April).

Donoghue, D. (1996) The philosopher of selfless love. *New York Review of Books*, 21 March, 37–40.

Ferreira, M., and Scheper-Hughes, N. (n.d.) Domba's kidney: Shamanism and organ transplant in Xingu Park, Brazil. Manuscript.

Friedlaender, M. (2002) Viewpoint: the right to sell or buy a kidney: are we failing our patients? *Lancet*, 359 (16 March), 971–3.

Fukuyama, F. (2002) *Our Postmodern Future* (New York: Farrar, Straus & Giroux).

Goyal, M., Mehta, R., Schneiderman, L. and Sehgal, A. (2002) Economic and health consequences of selling a kidney. *JAMA* 288(13), 2 October, 1589–93.

Humphreys, L. (1970) *Tearoom Tarde: Impersonal Sex in Public Places* (Chicago: Aldine).

Illich, I. (1976) *Medical Nemesis* (New York: Pantheon Books).

Jimenez, M., and Bell, S. (2001) Organ trade: anatomy of a deal. How a wealthy Canadian businessman bought a new kidney in a Manila slum. *National Post* (National Edition), Saturday 23 June, B1.

Jimenez, M., and Scheper-Hughes, N. (2002a) Doctor vulture – the unholy business of kidney commerce. *National Post* (Toronto), Saturday 30 March, B1, B4–5.

Jimenez, M., and Scheper-Hughes, N. (2002b) Europe's poorest sell their kidneys. *National Post*, 29 March, 1.

Koch, T. (2001) *Scarce Goods: Justice, Fairness and Organ Transplantation* (Westport, CT: Praeger).

Lobo, F., and Maierovitch, W. F. (2002) O mercado dos desperados. *CartaCapital*, 16 January, 30–4.

Lock, M. (2001) The quest for organs and the violence of zeal. In V. Das, A. Kleinman, M. Rampele and P. Reynolds (eds), *Violence and Subjectivity* (Berkeley: University of California Press), 271–95.

Lock, M. (2002) *Twice Dead: Organ Transplants and the Reinvention of Death* (Berkeley and Los Angeles: University of California Press).

Parsons, T., Fox, R., and Lidz, V. (1969) The 'gift of life' and its reciprocation. *Daedalus*.

Rabinow, P. (1996) Artificiality and enlightenment: from sociobiology to biosociality. In P. Rabinow, *Essays on The Anthropology of Reason* (Princeton, NJ: Princeton University Press).

Richards, J. (1998) The case for allowing kidney sales. *Lancet*, 351, 1950–2.

Rothman, D., et al. (1997) The Bellagio Task Force Report on Global Traffic in Human Organs. *Transplantation Proceedings*.

Sassen, S. (1991) *The Global City: New York, London, Tokyo* (Princeton, NJ: Princeton University Press).

Scheper-Hughes, N. (1990) Three propositions for a critically applied anthropology. *Social Science and Medicine*, 30(2), 189–97.

Scheper-Hughes, N. (1992) *Death without Weeping: The Violence of Everyday Life in Brazil* (Berkeley: University of California Press).

Scheper-Hughes, N. (1995) The primacy of the ethical: towards a militant anthropology. *Current Anthropology*, 3693 (June), 409–20.

Scheper-Hughes, N. (1996) Theft of life: globalization of organ stealing rumors. *Anthropology Today*, 12(3), 3–11.

Scheper-Hughes, N. (2000a) Ishi's brain, Ishi's ashes. *Anthropology Today*, 17(1), 12–18.

Scheper-Hughes, N. (2000b) The global traffic in organs. *Cultural Anthropology*, 41(2), 191–224.

Scheper-Hughes, N. (2001a) Commodity fetishism in organs trafficking. *Body & Society*, 7(2–3), June–September, 32–62.

Scheper-Hughes, N. (2001b) Neo-cannibalism: the global traffic in human organs. *Hedgehog Review*, 3(2), 79–99.

Scheper-Hughes, N. (2002) The ends of the body: commodity fetishism and the global traffic in organs. *SAIS Review: A Journal of International Affairs*, 22(1), 61–80.

Scheper-Hughes, N. (2003) Keeping an eye on the traffic in human organs. *Lancet*, 361, 10 May, 1645–8.

Steinberg, A. (1996) Ethical issues in nephrology – Jewish perspectives. *Nephrology, Dialysis and Transplant*, 11, 961–3.

Titmuss, R. (1970) *The Gift Relationship: From Human Blood to Social Policy* (London: Allen & Unwin).

Weiss, M. (2002) *The Chosen Body: The Politics of the Body in Israeli Society* (Stanford, CA: Stanford University Press).

Wolfe, R. A., Ashby, V. B., Milford, E., et al. (1999) Comparison of mortality in all patients on dialysis, patients awaiting transplantation, and recipients of a first cadaver transplant. *New England Journal of Medicine*, 341, 1725–30.

Zargooshi, J. (2001) Iranian kidney donors: motivations and relations with recipients. *Journal of Urology*, 165, 386–92.

11

Anthropology and Human Rights: Do Anthropologists Have an Ethical Obligation to Promote Human Rights? An Open Exchange

Terry Turner, Laura R. Graham, Carolyn Fluehr-Lobban, and Jane K. Cowan

Between April and October 2006, the journal *Anthropology News* hosted a four-part series entitled "Anthropology and Human Rights: An Open Exchange." Each month a different question was put to a diverse group of scholars and practitioners that was intended to take the measure of current opinion on the relationship between anthropology and human rights. The final question invited respondents to consider whether or not anthropologists had an ethical obligation to serve as advocates for human rights. The following is a selection of responses to this question.

The Special Relationship between Anthropology and Human Rights
Terry Turner

"Do anthropologists have an ethical obligation to promote human rights?" The question implies that there may be a special relationship between anthropologists and human rights. Such a relationship would in turn imply a conception of human rights framed in terms of specifically anthropological principles or ideas. The AAA,

Retrieved from www.aaanet.org/press/an/1006/human_rights_oct.html#goodale, on August 29, 2007. American Anthropological Association.

in its Declaration on Anthropology and Human Rights, adopted by a vote of the membership in 1999, restated a broad working definition of human rights first drafted and adopted by the AAA Commission for Human Rights in 1993:

> Anthropology as an academic discipline studies the bases and the forms of human diversity and human unity; anthropology as a practice seeks to apply this knowledge to the solution of human problems. As a professional organization of anthropologists, the AAA has long been, and should continue to be, concerned whenever human difference is made the basis for a denial of rights – where "human" is understood in its full range of cultural, social, linguistic and biological senses. *Anthropology Newsletter* 34(3): 1, 5; March 1993

On "Human Difference"

In the terms of the document, "human difference" is a criterion of human rights because it comprises the concrete specificity of what humans, individually and collectively, have made of themselves, evolutionarily, socially and culturally. As used in the text, "difference" refers to specific cultural, social, linguistic or biological features, which are contrasted, as variable and contingent products, to the universal human capacities that enabled their production: in familiar anthropological terms, the human capacities for culture, evolutionary adaptation and social change. "Difference," as a principle of human rights, denotes the concrete products of the realization of these generic powers: specific cultural forms, social relations, physical bodies and personal identities.

While difference is explicitly cited in the statement only as an invalid basis for denying rights, rather than a positive principle of right in itself, the implication is that the right to difference may constitute a positive, trans-cultural ground for specific human rights. "Difference" thus figures in the statement as a general anthropological basis of "rights." Rights are more specific claims against the potential or actual denial or abuse of individual or group relations, properties or identities.

This set of propositions, I believe, is consistent with the understanding of human nature at which anthropology as a scientific project has arrived, and corresponds to the consensus of the great majority of anthropologists. It is not in itself a set of ethical norms, but it does have ethical implications. In asserting that people become fully human through the process of transforming their potential capacities for culture, social relations and biological adaptation into specific (different) forms, and that all people possess such capacities (though not necessarily in equal degrees), this scientific consensus constitutes a definition of what humanity is that also implies a principle of what that ought to be: namely, a species whose individual members are able to develop and realize their capacities for the creation of cultural, social, linguistic and physical forms to the limits of their potential, so long as it does not prevent others from doing the same.

On Moral and Intellectual Responsibility

When cultural, social or political systems or situations seek to prevent, devalue or inhibit some or all of their individual members or constituent groups from doing this, for example by stigmatizing the differences between their cultural forms, social practices, personal identities or bodily forms and those of the hegemonic group, this anthropological imperative is implicated as the basis for a claim of violation of human rights by the disadvantaged group.

In such situations, I would argue that anthropology as a collective project and individual anthropologists as participants in it are implicitly concerned by virtue of the fundamental principles of their professional project and calling. This concern implicitly confers a responsibility to speak and/or act against the abuses of the human right in question, although violations of human rights are so many, and so deeply entrenched in all social and political systems, that it is realistically a responsibility that can only be very selectively exercised. There are of course many human rights issues that lack the specifically anthropological aspect of stigmatized human difference I have sought to identify, with which anthropologists will be concerned simply as ordinary citizens or moral persons.

The specifically anthropological concern with certain human rights issues I have suggested, together with the implied responsibilities it entails, is not primarily ethical in character, although it clearly figures as a principle of professional ethics. Rather, it is more broadly a matter of moral and intellectual principle, and includes a sense of reciprocal obligation to and solidarity with those other human beings of different culture, social practices and physical traits whose differences anthropologists have made the subjects of their scientific careers. It is of course these very differences that have so often been made the pretexts for prejudicial treatment and violations of human rights.

Helping to combat abuses of the human rights of our research subjects becomes, in this wider perspective, not merely a narrow matter of ethical obligations but a question of the courage of our theoretical convictions and our sense of the reciprocal obligations developed in fieldwork, and ultimately of commitment to the anthropological idea of humanity as an open-ended process of realization of capacities common to all, which makes it ultimately as much a political as an ethical question.

Anthropologists are Obligated to Promote Human Rights and Social Justice especially among Vulnerable Communities
Laura R. Graham

Anthropologists who research and study people suffering human rights abuses and forms of social injustice have an ethical obligation to seek ways to improve these conditions. And as a humanistic field, the discipline of anthropology has an obligation to promote social justice.

Unlike anthropologists who research subjects of equal or higher prestige or socio-economic status, anthropologists who work with vulnerable indigenous and other marginal communities have a special responsibility to engage in support of these groups, or advocate on their behalf.

Scholarship and Advocacy

Members of communities whom anthropologists study facilitate access to the culturally specific knowledge and understanding anthropologists seek. Anthropologists transform this information into scholarly and professional dissertations, articles, books, encyclopaedia articles and films, and use these products to advance their individual professional careers. While these scholarly products may, and sometimes do, effect positive change, anthropologists should not fool themselves into thinking their scholarship in itself has the potential to bring about significant social benefits for communities they write about.

Sharing the skills, knowledge and information we possess, or have the ability to access, with communities we study is one of, if not the most important way that anthropologists can compensate those we rely upon for professional advancement. Indeed, among anthropologists' most useful skills is our ability to broker information and knowledge. This and our ability to publicly and broadly disseminate information are tremendous resources that the communities and people we research who suffer injustices can use for social empowerment.

Local Support and Broad Advocacy

Ethnographers routinely engage in local support activities. These efforts range from helping individuals open bank accounts, translating, providing medication or literacy education, to helping with grant proposals or procuring legal advice on matters such as rights to, or defense of, indigenous land. While many anthropologists may not conceive of some of these as "activist" or "advocative," no matter how small or seemingly "apolitical" these sorts of activities may appear to an outsider, within the local community they are inherently acts of advocacy. They promote, if even in very small ways, subordinate peoples' efforts to attain better service (such as healthcare), to achieve greater independence (as in banking) or rights (land claims, for instance).

The degree to which anthropologists become overtly involved in advocacy or "activism" is something that varies according to local needs, the researcher's disposition and other situational factors. Overt advocacy or "activism" involves working to advance the interests of a group or community within a broader social arena than that of the local context; for instance, in national, regional or international policy, through the institutional support of NGOs, or through linkages that extend outside the immediate locale.

As anthropologists we are well aware that social justice and human rights are cultural constructions that are constantly subject to redefinition. Our training makes us uniquely sensitive to this issue and to complicated questions regarding culturally appropriate ways in which these may be specifically defined, including in state and international policymaking.

Anthropologists Aren't Neutral

Each anthropologist must carefully consider how her or his skills will be most suitable to advancing social justice among the research community at any given moment. An anthropologist who has a PhD degree may be a more effective advocate in certain situations than one who is doing doctoral fieldwork, for example. Or someone may be a more useful advocate after having left the field.

Anthropologists' participation in efforts to improve conditions for or within communities they research does not contaminate anthropological knowledge or the ethnographic endeavour as some have argued, most recently in debates surrounding the *Darkness in El Dororado* controversy. Such activities do not necessarily compromise an investigator's ability to conduct sound research.

Whether anthropologists like it or not, conducting anthropological research is a political and *privileged* endeavour. As many have pointed out, the less *privileged* communities that anthropologists study inevitably apprehend anthropologists – be they explicitly activist or not – within networks of power. Since neutrality and observational objectivity do not exist, anthropologists must thus embrace and come to terms with the political nature of our work.

Openly Discuss Advocacy

Instead of attempting to construct the appearance of neutrality, anthropologists should openly discuss ways their support and advocacy activities unfold and especially how these affect emergent ethnographic encounters and knowledge. Work that promotes human rights and social justice, in whatever small or explicitly activist ways, like other features of the ethnographic encounter, influences our and future anthropologists' access to information and ways that ethnographers understand individuals, social relationships and communities.

Since support and advocacy are integral to anthropological research with vulnerable populations, it is imperative that anthropologists consider their advocacy as a legitimate component of their scholarly work. Moreover, advocacy and activism should be subject to discussion and reflection within anthropological scholarship. Recent "engaged anthropology" is a positive turn. It invites anthropologists to frankly discuss, consider and reflect upon in their scholarly writing the advocacy and activism that we do. This honesty renders the conditions of research more transparent and ultimately strengthens the quality of anthropological documentation and knowledge generally.

When anthropologists carry out research among vulnerable individuals, we insert ourselves into webs of social relations in which we are also social actors. Our privileged position, specialized training, unique skills (and sometimes relatively large grant budgets) carry with them specific ethical obligations that compel us to promote the well-being of the people who, after all, are collaborators in our anthropological research and in the production of anthropological knowledge.

Advocacy is a Moral Choice of "Doing Some Good" but not a Professional Ethical Responsibility
Carolyn Fluehr-Lobban

In 1996, as a member of the commission that drafted the present AAA Code of Ethics, I collaborated in crafting the language that "anthropologists may choose to move beyond disseminating research results to a position of advocacy. This is an individual decision, but not an ethical responsibility" (CoE, III.C.2).

Although the world of politics and research has changed in some fundamental ways, I continue to hold this view. However, today I would add that while advocacy may not be a professional ethical responsibility, it is a moral responsibility that anthropologists can choose to exercise if they are so moved. Recalling that the Code of Ethics is an educational and not a legislative document, advocacy as a moral responsibility can only be suggested as a course of action appropriate to anthropological practice. Advocacy as a professional choice is necessarily limited to issues arising from anthropological research, not from those that bear upon the lives of anthropologists as citizens, as religious practitioners, or any other non-professional role they may fill.

Choices for Professional Advocacy

For example, anthropologists with expertise on American Indian culture may choose to advocate in favor of a casino in a state that has historically opposed Indian gaming. The same anthropologist may be asked – by the Indian tribe, or by the state – to give objective expert testimony about Indian lands and tribal sovereignty. In that role the anthropologist would offer professional expert testimony, but not necessarily be acting as an advocate. However, if the same anthropologist is hired by the state or by the tribe, or chooses to offer his or her service without compensation to produce statements or testimony in their favor, that testimony intended to benefit one or the other side would be an example of advocacy.

My own experience as an expert witness in political asylum cases is a choice I make that I view as advocacy. However, I do not see this as an ethical responsibility for anthropologists, nor would I criticize a colleague who averred this role. However, I understand that it is my credentials as a professional anthropologist with expertise in Africa and the Middle East that are often convincing factors that favor positive outcomes. My professional credentials are why my testimony is sought, yet I do not see this as a professional responsibility, and anecdotal information suggests that few scholars do, in fact, offer their expertise in this way.

Giving expert testimony is not always an unmitigated good. Anthropologists and other experts can only testify on the basis of the asylum seeker's claims that harm will result if the seeker is returned to the country of origin. Cases with credible affidavits of suffering or loss in the country of origin are easy to accept, however some testimonies belie credibility. Expert witnesses can be compensated, making financial gain an added incentive to that of advocacy.

The Notion of Harm

Some anthropologists are strong believers and advocates for a variety of human rights initiatives. Others, myself included, have argued that universal human rights trump traditional ideas about cultural relativism, and they advocate for social change away from harmful cultural practices, such as domestic violence, or female circumcision, in my own case.

I argued that it is the notion of harm to individuals or groups that is critical in making moral choices between universal rights and cultural relativism. "When reasonable persons from different cultural backgrounds agree that certain institutions or cultural practices cause harm," I wrote in a 1998 *AnthroNotes* article, "then the moral neutrality of cultural relativism must be suspended." Diverging from traditional cultural relativism the anthropologist advocates for the amelioration or withdrawal of the harmful practice.

Complex Choices and Actors

Advocacy is, of course, highly contextual and personal. Moreover, human rights advocacy is complex. International human rights movements have broad, highly differentiated moral and political agendas. Many anthropologists would find themselves in broad agreement with advocacy groups, such as Amnesty International (AI) or Human Rights Watch. They have gained both high international credibility and legitimacy, and are often seen as needed supra-state watchdog groups for violators of human rights that do not respond to pressure from individual states that are criticized. Thus, AI universally criticizes the state application of the death penalty, whether in the US, South Africa or China. Religiously based human rights groups, such as "Save the Children," have a religious as well as humanitarian agenda.

The UN Commission on Human Rights has broad, although not universal political legitimacy, for its positions, such as recent stands on the humanitarian crisis in Darfur. However, political and human rights groups were not unanimous in their use of the term "genocide" to describe the conflict in Darfur, and the politics of genocide made the human rights response more complicated as a result leaving advocates with a complex set of choices.

Ethical discourse to "do no harm" predominates in medicine, and in the physical and social sciences, including anthropology. This core principle lies at the heart of professional ethical responsibility. Rather than "doing no harm," advocacy may be described as a moral choice of "doing some good," a choice that anthropologists may increasingly adopt as they engage more proactively with those whom they study.

An Obligation to "Support Human Rights" Unconditionally is Misguided Moralism
Jane K. Cowan

In both mischief and seriousness, somewhat against my own instincts but to provoke debate, my answer to the question whether anthropologists have an ethical obligation to promote human rights is "no." I am not advocating disengagement from human rights politics in pursuit of an objective, apolitical description, nor am I encouraging indifference to injustice, suffering and inequality.

To the contrary: my concern is with the ways a hegemonic human rights model crowds out alternative ethical visions, such as those based on need, well-being, care or responsibility, that may more effectively help us diagnose, comprehend and work towards ameliorating specific social wrongs. Rather than taking it as an unquestioned virtue, anthropologists need to keep open the question whether "supporting human rights" is always an ethically adequate or even pragmatically effective response.

Human Rights as Complex

Empirical studies of rights processes are revealing the wide appeal of human rights discourse, its multiple reinterpretations and the myriad goals to which it is directed. Rights are not emancipatory in themselves; everything depends on who uses them, how, for which purposes, for and against whom, in which contexts. Rights are simultaneously enabling and constraining; moreover, their pursuit and implementation frequently entails unforeseen and unintended consequences. Given the ambiguous character of rights processes, as well as the indeterminacy of outcomes, an obligation to "support human rights" unconditionally is misguided moralism.

Human rights have been subjected to vigorous and varied criticism, even from those passionately committed to them. Let me elaborate just three points I find especially compelling.

First, in addressing disadvantage, the human rights model focuses too narrowly on the state as primary duty-bearer. It encourages claimants to demand recognition and resources from the state without acknowledging, given always-limited state resources, that choices must constantly be made over *whose* rights and *which* rights are privileged over others, and that this prioritization requires serious public debate on rights and needs within the larger collectivity.

Focusing energies on legal formalization of rights and the state's obligations also diverts attention from other domains, like the economy, that may influence people's lives equally profoundly. Rights are notoriously poor instruments for challenging invidious practices and power arrangements in the private sphere, whether in families or the workplaces of multinational corporations.

Shift to Human Responsibility

A legacy of their origin as protection of the individual from the state, human rights construe harm through a tripartite structure of victim (passive, innocent), violator (active, deviant) and witness/advocate (active, heroic). Aimed at galvanizing public opinion, human rights representations elide facts and silence experiences which do not support this model. Yet few conflicts are so morally unambiguous.

Where both sides in a conflict perceive themselves as righteous and beleaguered, the human rights model rings false. Its strident moral absolutism may enrage and alienate those labelled, rightly or wrongly, as violators, who see their own legitimate concerns denied or misunderstood. It can prove counter-productive to long-term efforts to rebuild societies on a basis of peace and justice, in as much as these require less self-righteous modes of relating that are also more attuned to moral complexity: listening, compromise and the creation of new solidarities and practices of co-existence based on recognition of an imperfect, shared humanness.

Finally, an "ethical obligation to support human rights" demands too little from "us" in the position of witness/advocate/concerned citizen. It encourages moral laziness, guiding us toward an undemanding morality tale where victim and violator are clearly distinguished and where others are to blame. It absolves us from examining structural aspects of injustice and suffering and how we are implicated, through our practices of consuming, our political choices, the governments we elect. It diverts us from a more difficult but more creative politics which would examine global and local power relations and privilege, seek redistribution of power, authority and resources, and forge new alliances.

Rather than an obligation to support human rights, I would advocate a shift toward human responsibility. In this historical moment of ecological crisis, we need an ethical discourse that propels us toward our obligations to each other, to our children and to all of planetary life. Rights discourse is premised on the sovereign individual as passive, entitled recipient. Cultivating a more inclusive ethical imagination and an attitude of responsible agency beyond the self is now urgent.

Part III

The Ethnography of Human Rights Practices

12

Representing Human Rights Violations: Social Contexts and Subjectivities

Richard A. Wilson

Legalism in Human Rights Reporting

... whatever it is that the law is after it is not the whole story.

Geertz 1983: 173

This essay examines the genre of human rights reporting with reference to two cases of murder in Guatemala. It is argued that the category of 'human rights violation' does not exist independently of its representation in human rights reports. The process by which an event becomes textualised is highly selective, organising signs in such a way as to codify an event according to an universal template. The language in which most cases are represented is generally realist and legalistic, and it engages in a decontextualisation of events. Accounts of human rights violations are characterised by a literalism and minimalism which strip events of their subjective meanings in a pursuit of objective legal facts. Such observations have been made of law, though not yet to my knowledge of human rights law, by anthropologists such as Clifford Geertz (1983: 170–4) who has referred to the 'skeletonization' and 'sterilization' of fact in legal processes.

Although human rights organisations constantly review their policy on the language used in their publications, there seems to be nothing like the debate about representation that exists for depictions of the Nazi Holocaust.[1] Those such as LaCapra (1992: 111) have argued that conventional techniques of historiography are not sufficient to capture the 'reality' of the Holocaust: 'Nowhere more than with reference to the Holocaust do positivism and standard techniques of narrowly

Originally published in *Human Rights, Culture and Context: Anthropological Perspectives*, ed. Richard A. Wilson. London and Sterling, VA: Pluto Press, 1997, pp. 134–60.

empirical-analytic inquiry seem wanting.' Many literary works on the Holocaust eschew documentary realism in preference for an 'allusive' or 'distanced' realism, where reality is presented through the filter of memory.

These issues are not only of relevance for academic commentary on human rights texts, since they parallel debates that human rights organisations have had internally for years. Discussions about the content and style of reports have become more acute recently – for instance Amnesty International's present General Secretary has advocated a shift in Amnesty's policy towards a greater degree of contextualisation in AI reports. In the last few years, Amnesty International Council Meetings have passed resolutions calling for more context in reports. I would like to see this essay as a contribution to the debate between the 'legalists', who advocate the narrow circumscribing of information to that which is relevant for the prosecution of violations and the 'contextualists', who argue for the inherent value of including a wider scope of social and contextual material. This essay suggests that part of the brief of anthropology is to restore to accounts of political violence both the surrounding social relations and an associated range of subjective meanings.

An objection might be raised on the grounds that legal rhetoric prevails in human rights reporting precisely because its intended audience is governments and inter-national bodies such as the UN, and law is the dominant language of national and international governance. At least formally, states and transnational institutions are only willing to take seriously knowledge produced according to a 'culture of scientism' and represented in a universally classified and usually quantified manner. I seek to challenge this 'pragmatist' adherence to legalism and positivism on two grounds; that it inherently displaces questions of ethics and values from what is claimed to be an ethical endeavour (human rights reporting); and that since govern-ments are not the sole recipients of human rights reports, a wider range of reporting styles is both defensible and necessary.

Chronicle of a Death Retold

I originally had no intention of studying human rights in Guatemala, but instead focused on religious conversions and ethnic identities in the department of Alta Verapaz (see Wilson 1995). Yet I was repeatedly placed in the position of bystander – witnessing or hearing personal testimonies of violent expressions of state power within my immediate social network. One such case occurred late on a Sunday afternoon on 20 March 1988, while I was watching a local football game with a friend in the highland town of Cobán.

March is a comfortable month in the Guatemalan highlands, when the rains are far away and the summer heat is not yet intense, and the football pitches are full of local teams competing for prestige. A few minutes before the final whistle, I heard several loud bangs, but disregarded them as the common sounds of a mis-firing truck. After the game, the crowd began to aimlessly drift off home, but then it rapidly gathered around a street corner only 50 yards from the football ground. My companion went to find out what had happened, and he returned shocked and agitated. He told me that a local member of the elite, a certain Waldemar Caal Rossi, had just been murdered. Rossi had also been watching the game and while on his way home, had been shot repeatedly at point-blank range in the head. My friend urged us to leave quickly before the army arrived to disperse the crowd by force.

In the days after the murder I sought out local people's views on Waldemar Rossi's death in private discussions, and encountered a bewildering plethora of responses. Instead of a common consensus, there were five main theories about who had carried out the murder:

1. *Military repression thesis*: The extreme right and/or the army had killed him for being a prominent civilian politician in order to destabilise the electoral process which had replaced over 20 years of army rule. Rossi was on the executive board of the centre-right UCN party and had stood for mayor in the local elections two years previously. The evidence put forward for this view was that a 9 mm revolver was used, which was the conventional instrument of extra-judicial murder. I was told that this handgun was standard army issue. Also, in the local lexicon of violence, shots to the head suggested a political assassination rather than a common crime.

2. *Party political explanation*: The ruling Christian Democrat government had killed Rossi for being a leader of the UCN, the party due to win the upcoming local elections in the department of Alta Verapaz. The government had been accused of procedural irregularities and harassment of opposition parties during the run-up to the local elections in March. For instance, the legal papers and other municipal election materials sent by the Supreme Electoral Tribunal to another centre-right party, the PR, were robbed from the bus station in Cobán. Shrill complaints had appeared in the national paper *El Grafico*, which was owned at the time by the leader of Rossi's UCN party, Jorge Carpio Nicolle, who was himself assassinated in 1993. Proponents of this theory also pointed out that Rossi's assailant drove off speedily to the capital in a car. It was said that this proved that the government was involved instead of just the army, which would have used a local agent and not worried unduly about hiding him.

3. *Intra-state rivalry theory*: Rossi was killed by the ruling civilian government for being an agent of the army. Little evidence was offered for this view except to point out that the civilian and military authorities had clashed on repeated occasions. However, such pronouncements proved to be somewhat prophetic, as a few months later, in May 1988, hardline army factions rolled towards the capital in tanks and armoured personnel carriers in an attempt to oust the civilian president.

4. *Inter-elite rivalry hypothesis*: Rossi had been killed in a family feud, for simply being a Rossi, by one of the other prominent elite families of the area. Rossi was a key member of one of the few families which historically dominated the local economy, political party system and government bureaucracy. Rossi himself held a high position in the national electricity company, INDE. With names like Rossi, Leal, Hempstead and Deisseldorff, most of the local elite had originally descended from German, Italian and British entrepreneurs who built a coffee agro-export economy at the end of the nineteenth century. Yet like the Rossi family, most of them had intermarried with the local Maya-Q'eqchi' population and also had indigenous surnames. Thus Rossi was an Italian 'Rossi', but also a Q'eqchi' 'Caal'. The stability of traditional elite power had started to waver in the 1970s when the cardamom export industry generated a new class of entrepreneurs. In the late 1980s, this fragmentation was accelerated as Cobán became a centre for drug smuggling and the financial laundering of illicit profits.[2]

5. *Moral economy explanation*: The members of the house I was staying in at the time disagreed with all of the above views and stated simply that he was killed for being rich, by someone who was poor, perhaps a disgruntled employee, a thief who wanted to rob him, or simply someone who was jealous of his wealth. The Q'eqchi'

matriarch who sold tortillas to supplement her household budget said, 'See! It's better to be poor and not have all that envy around you.' The father, a retired craftsman, replied quickly, 'Ah...but it is the poor who get killed most!' And so the family commentary on the local moral economy went on, with the implicit view that there are webs of social reciprocity at work in the community which only the rich can hope to escape from, but sometimes at the cost of their lives.

Some responses are not included in this orderly catalogue of accounts since they were highly idiosyncratic to the point of being bizarre. A few were completely incomprehensible and I felt that some people, when faced with stressful questions, spoke without any intention of making sense.

My own view at the time was that the 'military repression' or 'party-political' explanations were the most probable accounts of the murder. In contrast, local views tended overwhelmingly towards the last two theories of inter-elite rivalry and the moral economy, that is, which reproduced the traditional language of local politics with its emphasis on patron–client relations and reciprocity. It could be of course, that most people did not trust me enough to make an explicit denunciation of the army or government. Yet my feeling is that in Cobán, local discourses on Rossi's death prevailed over the national ones. The people I knew best, who had in the privacy of their home often derided the army, perceived the event through the prism of local class politics.

As I discovered in the days after the death of Waldemar Rossi, each murder draws on a heterogeneous field of interpretations and memories, in a social space where meaning is contested, assertions are vague and polysemous, and where anyone and everyone could have had a motive. Narratives on murder then serve to crystallise social relations and feed off perceived tensions and discordance. As in the television murder mystery genre, the message is usually that, despite apparently calm external appearances, something is rotten in Denmark.

In such situations, a social researcher is much more likely to doubt the search for definitive lines of determinacy than a human rights researcher, and instead seek to contextualise an event rather than codify it. In the local reporting of a death, reliability becomes problematic, since individuals' statements are often more indexical than true or false. In the context of murder of a prominent local politician in Cobán, this means that some people are trying to express their position in relation to an overall situation of elite rule, death squad murders, militarisation and guerrilla war. Others, however, lose themselves behind a smoke screen of incomprehensible utterances in order to avoid taking a position at all.

Several weeks later, while on a short break in Mexico, I communicated my tentative understanding of the Rossi murder to a small international human rights agency. Without even apportioning blame to one of the parties, the mere appearance of the murder on a human rights report would have indicated that it was not a 'common crime' but that it was somehow related to the political process. In the Guatemalan context, the finger of suspicion would point towards governmental institutions – especially the security apparatus. Yet I have not come across any report on this case by a major human rights organisation; Amnesty International for instance has no record of the killing. Somehow, the fate of Waldemar Caal Rossi did not become an item of information flowing through the networks of human rights agencies.

This exclusion led me to contemplate in more depth how an event becomes a publicised human rights violation. The most obvious reason for Rossi's exclusion was that social life in Alta Verapaz is thoroughly militarised, and at the time of the event there were no human rights offices or agency workers. National and international agencies receive reports through established networks of local people who are considered reliable sources; including their own staff, journalists and occasionally church workers and local development organisations. Perhaps the place-bound explanations of Rossi's murder won out, their centripetal force confining the information to a small area.

In remote areas of rural Latin America, the absence of individual contacts means that much information derives from secondary sources. Often human rights agencies can only respond quickly to events they learn about through press reports, and therefore are bound to reproduce their language. It is possible to see this replication in a quick assessment of the content of the first line of denunciation; Amnesty International's 'Urgent Action' – a 1–2-page document which is released within hours or days of a murder or kidnapping. In Latin America this usually means that the offending agents are referred to as *desconocidos*, or 'unknown persons'. The reports mention briefly what the assailants were wearing, but there is little space for contextual information on each case.

These deliberations led me to consider in more detail how human rights violations are constructed – not in the sense that the Rossi murder did not actually happen, nor that we can never know that it happened, nor that political assassinations are not a regular occurrence in Guatemala. Instead, my meaning is that human rights agencies have to piece together contradictory fragments of information and act on the basis of already formulated criteria about what kind of murder victim, and manner of murder, is likely to constitute a human rights violation. The indeterminacy of the event and the heterogeneous nature of bystanders' narratives hamper the coherence of a single integrated plot, which is highly disconcerting for those seeking actionable certainties.[3] Human rights reports must therefore impose meaning on the chaos and incoherence of events. Further, occurrences are universalised, that is, they are represented in human rights reports in such a way that the event can be comprehended by readers on the other side of the globe.

The complexities of the Rossi case have not been presented in order to contend that human rights claims for epistemological concreteness are false and unwarranted. Nor do I want to echo the claims of governments that the language of human rights is being used by other nations to slander them, or more usually in Latin America, as part of a phantom international communist conspiracy. Instead, I have explored the contingency around one act of violence in order to examine the limitations generally on representations of 'human rights violations'. In my view, there is a need to examine the powerful representational claims articulated within human rights discourses, so as to drag them down from the rarefied epistemological and moral high ground, and include them in more sociological debates about the interpretation, understanding and explanation of empirical evidence and the limits of its representation.

The Category of 'Human Rights Violation'

The whole concept of human rights violation is constructed around state involvement, in opposition to the category of 'common crime'. Human rights organisations recognise both the difficulty of establishing culpability, and the blurred nature of the boundary between state and criminal acts. Amnesty International (1989: 8) often writes in its reports: 'In many cases, for example, it is not possible to establish precisely who carried out a particular killing, although circumstantial evidence and a pattern of similar killings by government forces often appears clearly to indicate official responsibility.'[4]

Despite the recognition of the difficulties of establishing official responsibility,[5] accusations of state involvement rest upon a clear distinction between the 'state' and 'civil society' which is not the way that either society or violence are organised. In some instances, there is direct evidence of state involvement in a violation, such as that of the murder of seven members of a Jesuit household in El Salvador in November 1989. As in the Jesuit case, most death squads in Latin America are made up of regular police and military officials operating in plain clothes under orders from their superiors. Yet not all groups involved in extra-judicial acts of violence are under such direct orders from the security apparatus. They can also be para-statal, *ad hoc* groupings of ultra-right political parties and members (or – ex-members) of the security forces. In Guatemala, human rights organisations tend to attribute responsibility to the state for acts of violence or intimidation carried out by para-statal civil defence patrols. Civil patrols were set up by the army in highland villages in the early 1980s and are made up of local men, many of whom perform their role due to coercion or neutral acquiescence. Others, however, are utterly convinced that they are protecting their village from the guerrillas and communism.[6]

Some writers have argued that regimes are repressive precisely because they are 'weak' and lack the more sophisticated surveillance and control techniques of industrialised states (see Giddens 1985; Asad 1992). In such 'weak states', acts of violence may be carried out independently by landowners or private security forces, often against employees involved in trade union activities. In countries where the administrative apparatus does not permeate the whole territory (for example, Brazil, Nicaragua, Guatemala), non-state adjudication is meted out at the 'frontier' by the patrimonial authorities of economic enclaves. In these contexts, violence emerges from both inside and outside state institutions, and these forms can be organised relatively independent from each other.

In all of these cases, the category of human rights violation is constructed in opposition to the category of 'common crime'. This is not an unproblematic distinction either, since these binary categories are not hermetically sealed, static or universal, but are overlapping and are mutually constitutive. As Jennifer Schirmer (1997) has shown, the Guatemalan military has historically both conflated and maintained the boundaries between 'criminals' and 'subversives', and intertwined emergency counter-insurgency legal measures with the conventional criminal justice system.

The categories of ordinary crime and state crime share a common semiotics of violence, and draw upon the same lexicon of conventional signs. Human rights organisations have come to recognise that political killings are often made to look like common homicides. Amnesty International (1989: 8) has written that in Guatemala: 'perpetrators of political killings were now apparently resorting to stabbing, machetes, or even poison to conceal their political motives and make it appear that those killed were the victims of common crime'. Conversely, it has been noted that 'criminals' in Guatemala have plagiarised from the stock symbolism of politically motivated murders, and one report refers to how 'many common homicides may be committed with shots to the back of the head'.[7]

At the risk of echoing standard government evasions of responsibility, it must be recognised that for a variety of reasons, it is problematic to discern a 'criminal' from a 'political' murder in many cases. In a similar vein, Judith Zur (1994: 12) argues that in a context of legal impunity, juridical 'concepts of innocence and guilt lose their meaning'. Generalised fear and violence dissolve narratives around justice. Normative juridical distinctions are the distinctions of established liberal democracies which do not have recent traditions of habitual political murder or mass criminal violence. As such, liberal categories, however desirable, may have little bearing on the experiences of punishment and surveillance during decades of militarised state rule. Where terror rules, normative categories of justice are abolished, undermining frameworks designed to conceptualise them, much less act upon them.

Since state-directed murders often operate in a context of extreme epistemological doubt, human rights organisations operate more or less reflexively with a set of criteria of what profile of person and what kind of murder is likely to be 'indicative of security force involvement'. In so doing, the discourse of human rights constructs its subjects as much as it reacts to events, since these criteria promote a selective process which screens out certain cases and homes in on others. In particular human rights texts construct the category of 'victim', and many Amnesty International country reports list violations against trade unionists, students, refugees or political activists under the umbrella heading of 'The Victims'.

Like the discourse of development, the human rights literature draws upon Manichean dualisms (violated/violator; powerless/powerful) to construct its subjects as innocent victims. Both share similar images of their subjects as in 'need' and inhabiting a social or global position of marginality. References to the 'poor, uneducated, and relatively defenceless' are readily found in both genres.[8] Human rights organisations draw a great deal of their rhetorical power from how they represent themselves as campaigning on behalf of weak innocents against powerful and violent governments in the pursuit of justice, truth and the rule of law. This could be one reason why Waldemar Rossi's case was not picked up by human rights agencies, since he was neither weak, poor, uneducated, nor, according to many from his own community, entirely an 'innocent'. As a relatively wealthy politician representing a local elite, Rossi was in the wrong category of self.

There is an acute tension in human rights reporting between recognising the blurred and constructed nature of the category of human rights violation and the desire to assert the veracity of information. On one hand many reports recognise the pitfalls of documentation, as one stated: 'the source of any particular act of violence is not always apparent, and there is often insufficient evidence on which to make a credible allegation'.[9] Yet there is a contrary process whereby cases are documented in a way which drops in 'relevant criteria' about the profile of the victim and the style of the violation. Amnesty International reports usually have only a few cases which are described in detail, and they are mostly a grisly succession of short case profiles. Usually, these only include several lines, with a standard formula including the date, name, category of victim (for example, student or trade unionist) and manner of murder (for example, with signs of torture) and occasionally a description of the assailants (for example, heavily armed men, wearing plain clothes, in a van with darkened windscreens, etc.). The usual meaningful characteristics are listed without any discussion, which has the effect of making their inclusion seem realistic, natural and unquestionable. Instead of a documentary style which recognises the indeterminacy of a case (which human rights organisations generally recognise at a different level) and the limitations of any media of representation, the facts in the main text of human rights reports simply speak for themselves.

The Murder of an Anthropologist

In this section I consider another case of a political assassination in Guatemala which, unlike the Rossi incident, was actually reported, followed through in the courts and became one of the major tests of judicial reform facing successive civilian regimes – that of Myrna Mack Chang.

Myrna Mack was one of the first Guatemalan social scientists I met on beginning fieldwork in 1987. She had studied social anthropology in the UK at Durham University and had returned to join one of the few independent and critical research institutes, AVANCSO, set up in the mid-1980s. She was helpful in finding a place for me to do fieldwork and after a few months began her own research on the internally displaced in the same locale, Cobán, Alta Verapaz. She would come up to Cobán for a few weeks at a time, carry out her interviews with internal refugees and then return to be with her daughter in the capital. We worked only a few minutes by bus from one another. I lived with a local family near one of the town's main markets and she shared a convent with Catholic nuns on the outskirts of town in a *barrio* made up of refugees who had invaded private lands after the scorched earth policies of the early 1980s. We attended a language course in Q'eqchi' together which was run by the Catholic Church.

Over time we shared ideas but I always felt that our intellectual discussions were restrained, perhaps due to an unstated professional rivalry, or perhaps a resentment of foreign researchers. Yet one area where Myrna was particularly helpful was in negotiating the delicate politics of doing ethnography in a militarised society. I remember clearly her advice when I asked what information I should and should not publish – how I should begin to define what was sensitive and what was not. She replied that although a writer should be careful about names, all of the 'broad picture' about life in Guatemala could be included in the account. She said: 'There's nothing of any importance that an ethnographer could know that the military doesn't already know. They have their own sources everywhere, so we're not going to tell them anything new.'

After I left fieldwork in Guatemala in 1988, we remained in contact and exchanged research papers, until one morning in September 1990, when I was rung by a member of staff of a London-based human rights organisation and told that Myrna had been killed the day before by an assailant armed with a knife as she left her office at AVANCSO. His account was personalised and highly emotional and subjective. My reaction was one of stunned silence – I think I only managed a few hollow-sounding expletives – but the human rights worker concerned had already moved onto a set of emotions which I would reach later that day – indignation, anger and utter disgust.

The legal investigation into the murder of Myrna Mack became a classic illustration of the struggle over the categorising and representation of human rights violations between the government, elements of the judiciary and police force, the family of a victim and human rights organisations themselves. Within hours of the event, the government's response was that this was a criminal, not a political, murder. The official version asserted that Myrna Mack was killed as she was changing money on the black market, in an ideological attempt to divert blame and reduce sympathy for the victim, by portraying her as involved in shady criminal dealings. Local and international human rights organisations countered that Myrna was killed because of the nature of her social science research into the internally displaced population at a time when the government was seeking large amounts of foreign aid for their resettlement.

These immediately contradictory stances were exacerbated by an increasingly bungled and obstructed legal investigation. The forensic evidence at the scene was either ignored or later 'lost' by police. The judicial investigation was characterised by delays, and involved over nine courts and eleven judges. Several judges and key witnesses withdrew after repeated death threats. Almost a year after the event, two police officers filed a report implicating the security forces and identifying a suspect, Noél Jesús Beteta Alvarez, who was a low-ranking member of the Security Director-ate of the Presidential Guard at the time of the murder. Shortly after filing the report, one of the investigating police officers was shot dead in the park across from police headquarters, after having received repeated death threats. The other then fled the country shortly thereafter.

In February 1992, the civilian court referred the case to a military court, but the private prosecutor, Helen Mack (Myrna Mack's sister) was successful in her appeal and the case was returned to the civilian court system.[10] In the end, Beteta was sentenced to 30 years in prison. It was argued that he was a lowly scapegoat, but the appeals court closed the case against Beteta's military superiors. Some time later, the President of the Constitutional Court, Epaminondas Gonzalez Dubón, was assassinated. One likely explanation was that the Court was about to rule on the constitutionality of closing the Mack case without investigating the 'intellectual authors' of the crime.[11]

Decontextualisation in Human Rights Reporting

Meanings exist in a force field of other meanings. You could not talk about the meaning of an action without connecting it to a narrative (including other actions) if you want to interpret its meaning.

Inglis 1993: 144

If meanings can only be understood in terms of surrounding narratives, then many human rights reports impede the interpretation of meaning by their radical acts of exclusion. Instead of narratives and 'force fields of other meanings', what the reader gets is a pared down and frozen stream of action. The gelatinous thickness of local life, as intimated in my retelling of the Rossi case, is thinned down to a watery consistency. Here, we must make a distinction between reports and narratives. Documenting human rights violations is about reporting evidence, not creating a narrative, since it is incomplete and is abstracted from the motivation and intention-ality of actors. Reports begin and usually end within a more narrow time-span than narratives; that is, with the culminating event (the death or attack). Only the evidence from the event can be used to speak about anything before or after. A narrative, on the other hand, starts with actors' intentions, at a point much earlier than the report, which puts the event into a wider context.

This process of delimiting narratives began early on in human rights reporting,[12] as one worker from a major international organisation told me:

When we first arrived in Guatemala in the late 70s, and early 80s, no one even knew who we were, and they started blurting out everything. We had to say to them, 'Just give us the facts.' This probably shaped how people came to talk about the abuses because now they tell us more directly.

This 'just give us the facts' approach inherently implies, among other things, an excising of personal biographies, the filter of memory and the performative dimensions of the speech act. Over time, it appears that private narratives on abuse have themselves transformed according to how human rights workers textualise them. The exclusion of individual interpretations and social context in human rights modes of emplotment has worked its way back through the process whereby life becomes text becomes genre and has transformed survivor's own representations (in public, at least) of human rights abuses.

Turning now to Myrna Mack's case, I increasingly felt while reading reports on her case that, due to their lack of contextualisation of Myrna's circumstances, her case became about an abstract right that had been violated. Like others on the receiving end of violence, Myrna Mack was represented by a monochromatic profile of her age and occupation, rather than as a full social person with a biographical narrative. For instance, very seldom was her daughter mentioned in any reports, which seems to be a general pattern.[13] Human rights accounts often extract 'victims' from their family and class background.[14] Like Waldemar Rossi, Myrna Mack belonged to an elite family. She was of Chinese-Guatemalan descent, and her family has significant economic interests and are large landowners on the Pacific Coast. She moved easily within powerful social networks and counted on connections which reached to the top of national society and government.

Her family's status is also important in fully understanding why this case was subjected to more thorough investigative process than others. The Mack family was able to consult a number of legal advisers and mount its own private prosecution led by Myrna's sister, Helen. Helen Mack was effective in pressuring for the resignation of two judges whom she thought were biased or incompetent. In early 1992, Helen Mack travelled to Geneva to testify before the UN Commission on Human Rights, which generated pressure on the Guatemalan government to prosecute the case with greater vigour. It is much more difficult for the family of a murdered Mayan peasant to respond in a similar fashion. As with property and citizenship rights, the wealthy and educated are more likely to be able to secure and defend the human rights of their members.

The decontextualisation of Myrna Mack's case also operated at another level. Just as there is little to nothing in human rights reports about a wider community's interpretations of events (as I offered for the Rossi case), there was very little about the daily conditions of social researchers in Guatemala. Of course there are lists of how many have been threatened, disappeared or killed in recent years, but one learns nothing of the climate in which intellectual activity is undertaken. From reading human rights reports, one remains ignorant of what it is like to think and research in a context of violence and impunity.

Before joining the research institute AVANCSO, Myrna worked for the associated press agency INFORPRESS which survived by relying on outside press reports and not sending its own agents into the 'field'. However, after the civilian government of Vinicio Cerezo was installed in 1985, AVANCSO began to tentatively undertake original field research. Myrna was constantly aware of the ambiguity and immanent danger of her situation. She struggled with her own perceptions of the political limits of research, continually pushing at the boundaries of what it seemed possible to research and report. To my knowledge, no human rights report has attempted to portray her situation as a professional social researcher before her murder. Nor is there any follow-up on the institutional response of AVANCSO, which suspended its investigation into the internally displaced, and for a time severely curtailed other projects.

It may be argued, especially by human rights activists themselves, that I have ignored the multiplicity of different organisations and documents produced by them, some of which place a strong emphasis on contextual analysis. It might be obvious that the 1-page AI Urgent Action decontextualises, since it seldom discloses more than the name, age and occupation of the victim, the place and nature of the violation, and a description of the assailants. Other documents such as the AI country reports and special reports, on the other hand, do include more analysis. Yet this is usually little more than a survey of the recent economic and political history which reads like a 'fact file'. The special report on *Guatemala: Extrajudicial Executions and Human Rights Violations against Street Children* (Amnesty International 1990) has 4 pages of general discussion on street children followed by nearly 30 pages of grim accounts of individual cases. Similarly, AI's 1989 report on Guatemala consisted of 1 page of 'political context', and over 40 pages of individual cases of human rights violations. The most in-depth section of this report was an exploration of the legal system, where it discussed the intricacies of magistrates' investigations under the Napoleonic Code.

Amnesty International is arguably the organisation which puts the greatest emphasis on the limited documentation of individual cases. Other organisations, such as the US-based Watch Committees, offer much more analysis of ongoing conditions. During the 1980s, the reports and photographs of Americas Watch representative, Jean-Marie Simon, were renowned for the degree to which they captured the prevailing social conditions in Guatemala. So one cannot simply say that all human rights documents are devoid of contextual interpretations. Yet there is a crucial separation between organisations and forms of documentation which detail individual cases and those which explore structural conditions. The importance of this distinction lies in how it separates the individual from the social, facts from interpretations, all in an effort to preserve an unassailable and legalistic regime of truth.

What are the consequences of the tendencies towards decontextualisation found in many human rights reports? First, they can depoliticise human rights violations by drawing attention away from structural processes of class or ethnic power, and reduce violations to a set of technical problems concerning the functioning of the legal system. Second, the gory semiology of human rights abuses, and particularly torture and mutilation, remain incomprehensible except as irrational outbursts devoid of meaning. It is as if the maxim 'To understand is to forgive' has been taken too literally. By under-emphasising the structural and transnational dimensions of violence, human rights reports render such acts universal. Yet increasingly, anthropologists have argued that violence, like any other social process, is expressed and interpreted according to sets of metaphors about the nature of power, gender relations and human bodies. This communicative dimension means that violence is never 'meaningless'.[15]

Finally, the removal of victims from their social and family contexts belies an ethnocentric basis to representations of human rights abuses. By disengaging an agent from their socio-historical circumstances, what we are left with is a universal decontextualised individual which is the basic unit of liberal political, economic and legal theory. We could contrast this with the dominant discourse in anthropology on the 'social person' and the view that it is not possible to refer to 'the individual' outside of a concrete historical context. As opposed to a universal maximising individual with a natural set of rights, there are social persons who are engaged in the making and remaking of complex interconnected social processes, and whose rights in those contexts are not natural, but are the result of historical struggles for power between persons and corporate groups.

As this chapter will explore more fully later on, decontextualisation is part of a human rights paradigm which generally tries to maintain as close a likeness as possible with legal texts. The criteria of judgement of human rights organisations are not solely the result of a textual genre for representing violations of rights, but derive from a radical conception of the nature of rights themselves. As Stan Cohen has commented:

> neither decontextualisation nor the exclusion of biographical narratives is a mere artefact of human rights reporting. They are the deliberate results of the human rights credo that no context (circumstances, motives, etc.) can ever justify the violations of universal prohibitions. This exclusion is even more radical than in the case of the criminal law.[16]

The Exclusion of Subjectivity

After hearing the news of Myrna's murder, I was struck by the disjuncture between the language deployed in official human rights reports and the emotionally charged language which human rights workers use to discuss events between themselves. The worker who reported to me personally spoke in a tentative language full of subjectivity, interpretation and uncertainty. He expressed anger and his doubt that it was actually a human rights violation – at the time we did consider the possibilities of it being a 'criminal' murder, given the high levels of street crime in the capital. All of this contrasts with the arid texts produced after the event, which sought to codify the jumbled signs into a clear statement, and one which was devoid of subjectivity. A strange kind of schizophrenia lurks in the space between the emotional lives of those involved in human rights activities and the way human rights texts represent violations.

Once an item is selected for inclusion in the human rights network, it is then conveyed with an aura of authority and legitimacy. Reports engage in an unemotional skeletonising of local narratives which strips subjectivity from the representation of events, in order to construct a version apparently free of distortion. Since perpetrators of abuses do all in their power to efface any record of crimes, there is an obligation both to bear witness and not to distort the record of events. Implicit here is the idea that any departure from a minimalist style is distorting. Correspondingly, human rights reports are written with an unflinching realism which bluntly recounts one fact after another in an unmitigated and relentless barrage of short case summaries. Only a literalist chronicle passes the twin test of authenticity and authority, leading to a suppression of the authorial voice and the deployment of a language purged of all tropes, metaphors and figurative elements.

Few entries are dealt with in the detail that Myrna Mack's case was, and these are generally ones which symbolise a set of violations against a targeted group, or are test cases which demonstrate the limits of the judicial process. Instead, most cases only receive a few short sentences, which are regular and have a simple subject–predicate–object form. The text makes concise and clean use of the declarative and employs few adjectives. All meaning is on the surface, and the confidence of the assertions is expressed in their lack of elaboration. Local words are seldom deployed, nor are interpretations of translated words particularly in evidence. For example, *La violencia* is the term often used by locals to refer to political violence in Guatemala. Yet like the term 'The Troubles' in Northern Ireland, it has a set of political meanings which human rights reports do not delve into or even allude to (cf. Warren 1993). The main categories used in reports are left unexamined, since they are understood to be universal and therefore not in need of interpretation.

At the same time as blunt realism and hard facts are delivered up comes the recognition that:

> the data obtained by Amnesty International from human rights workers and others is necessarily fragmented, incomplete and variable. Amnesty International is also aware that the reporting categories used by the various groups collecting such data in Guatemala and elsewhere do not necessarily conform to the organisation's own classifications of 'disappearances' and extra-judicial executions. (Amnesty International 1989: 8)

This recognition of provisionality usually occurs in the preface of a document, yet the style of the main body of the text remains unblemished by contingency apart from the references to 'unknown persons', which the reader must assume are state-directed agents, or why would the account qualify as a 'human rights violation'?

This lack of reflexivity makes it impossible to search for answers in the text to pedestrian but vital questions on particular cases, such as: what is the evidence and the counter-evidence and how was it collected (from press reports? key informants? missions of inquiry?). The rough edges of the methods which lead to knowledge in human rights reports are lost in the seamless web of text. Epistemological security is underpinned by transparent facts, not by a self-conscious awareness that knowledge emerges from creative insight, the interpretation of partial connections and in the act of representation itself.

The lack of stated authors in almost all human rights agency reports is characteristic of a desubjectified genre, of a discourse deprived of an author-function. This leads to an extreme polarisation where the de-individualisation of the author clashes with both the highly individualised content of reports and individualistic conception of rights. In contrast, I constructed my accounts of the cases of Myrna Mack and Waldemar Rossi with myself as part of the narrative. My subjectivity, memories and imputed meanings were inseparable from the events themselves, but in most human rights reports, the only documentors present and named are the photographers. The protection of workers and informants might justify this exclusion, but this cannot explain a blanket policy. Amnesty International reports are likely to have been primarily written by one of a handful of desk officers,[17] whose names are public. Similarly, governments are always aware when they are in the country on a 'mission of inquiry' and they largely know who they talk to.

Evacuating the author serves not only as a protective device, but also creates an aura of objectivity and neutrality by wiping the stain of subjectivity off the surface of the text. The simple recounting of a truthful narrative sets up human rights organisations as honest brokers, who dispassionately dispense disturbing information. Author-evacuated texts, whether human rights reports, scientific texts or legal contracts, are an established literary strategy to convey value-free information devoid of individuality and opinion. The presence or absence of the author has historically defined the binary line between the literary, figurative and expressive from the scientific, literal and realist.

In 'What is an Author?,' Michel Foucault (1979: 149) refers to how:

> A reversal occurred in the seventeenth or eighteenth century. Scientific discourses began to be received for themselves, in the anonymity of an established or always redemonstrable truth; their membership in a systematic ensemble, and not their reference to the individual who produced them, stood as their guarantee.

Similarly, the reliability of human rights reports rests not upon a reflexive mode of emplotment, but in the trustworthiness of the genre itself, and the organisations which produce it. The reports are reliable because Amnesty International or Americas Watch are reliable institutions. The validity of the report rests upon reputation and rhetoric, and the reader is forced to choose between either believing or disbelieving. When presented with a seamless style of representation, healthy scepticism has no place to take hold.

The interpreting gaze of the bystander is similarly dissipated. One seldom reads openly recognised eyewitness reports of who saw what and under what conditions. This is partly to protect bystanders from reprisals from security forces, but in many cases the security forces know exactly who is denouncing human rights abuses. For instance, in Latin America, violent actions or threats against trade unionists are regularly denounced by trade union confederations in the national press. Again, in my account of Rossi's murder, the 'bystander effect' was an important basis of my attempt to persuade you the reader that something did actually happen. Although I did not see the body, I heard the shots, saw the milling crowd, and heard the immediate description of an ashen-faced bystander. The rhetorical power of these statements is both more forceful and more directly questionable than the Olympian view-from-nowhere which characterises human rights reports.

Although the authorial interpretation of often contradictory information is an inevitable aspect of producing human rights documents, this is not acknowledged in order to preserve their status as legal fact. The fact/value distinction is refracted throughout the human rights project, for example, in the already mentioned cleavage between reports and organisations which take a restricted brief to document the bare 'facts' of a case and those which provide more systematic analysis and subjective testimony.

Another example lies in the distinction between desubjectified texts and wholly subjectified public meetings which feature testimony from victims of abuses. Here the audience is exposed to a direct and emotional experience unavailable in reports. Such testimonies do not break down the binary distinction between fact and value, instead they preserve it. Subjectivity belongs only to victims, whereas the organisations hosting them preserve their objectivity. The subjectivity of victims is harnessed in fund-raising letters: one Amnesty International letter of the early 1990s featured a Guatemalan street child with the caption, 'This boy wants to kiss you', accompanied by a testimony as to the effectiveness of Amnesty International's intervention.[18]

It is now commonly accepted that there is no neat distinction between facts and interpretations, where the former is a bedrock of truth and the latter is constructed artifice. Instead, the two are bound up in one another, where every 'fact' is an act of interpretation resulting from the critical judgement of a documentor about what constitutes valuable evidence. Further judgements are then made about the overall development of the narrative in which 'facts' are embedded, and the style and authorial voice to be used. Human rights organisations operate with a false opposition between literal versus figurative speech, since every attempt to represent a human rights violation is a narrative with a plot (however circumscribed), and every emplotment is a kind of figuration. Once it is recognised that all narratives are the result of artifice and design, then rather than hide any reference to this process, it might be preferable to place the interpretative filter in the foreground of the account, to convey something of the conditions in which knowledge is formulated and represented.

Law and the Language of State Power

The argument thus far has been to understand the genre of human rights reports with reference to their legalistic epistemology: the facts they contain are legal facts which could stand up in a court of law. Their intended aim is not just to assert truth but to demand justice through urging governments to prosecute individuals. Human rights 'missions' go to countries to 'verify and expand the information'[19] which will be instrumentally marshalled to construct a case against a government. That which matters is that which is universal, documentable through reference to 'hard' facts and relevant to rationalist legal inquiry. Subjectivity and information not immediately relevant to the prosecution of the individual case are dismissed.

It could be countered to my line of argument that human rights reporting is not an anthropological study of the local knowledge in which political violence is embedded, nor is it a fictional account of the experiential dimensions of terror. 'Pragmatists' might pose a number of rejoinders; that human rights organisation are not trying to change global systems of inequality, but have had to confine their campaigns to ensuring that international and national laws are upheld; that we have to remember that human rights reports are designed to be a persuasive assertion of truths in order to alter governmental policy or public opinion; and that governments are generally averse to human rights reporting on their own country and seek to undermine the validity of such reports in any way possible.

I recognise the importance of many of these arguments. Without a doubt, the effective deployment of human rights information can and does influence government policy. Further, information presented as legal fact based upon universal criteria of truth in the present global context carries much greater rhetorical power than interpretations made by contextualised individuals relying on a creative subjectivity. Of course, power resides not only in the fact that one genre is more faithful to local truths than another, but in the style of assertion of the same truths.

Returning to Guatemala, it could easily be argued the symbolic capital of human rights, expressed in films and reports had an impact on the legal process in the Myrna Mack case. This was one of the highest profile cases in recent Guatemalan legal history and generated condemnations not only from non-governmental organisations but also from the UN special expert and the US State Department. Helen Mack's testimony at the UN produced a plethora of international denunciations of the Guatemalan government. Helen Mack's request as prosecutor for records from army files is believed to be the first time that the military have been asked for such evidence. The trial directly led to the disbanding of the Presidential Guard to which the murderer Beteta pertained and to the removal of military advisers from police departments.

The Mack trial contributed to a wider reform of the Guatemalan criminal justice system; a reform which had been foreseen in the 1985 Constitution, but had not been implemented until July 1994, with the advent of the New Criminal Code.[20] In broad terms, this meant a move away from an inquisitorial model where the trial stage consists of a sentencing judge reading a written file during private court proceedings. In this model, the judge sentences or acquits often without listening to the testimony of witnesses. The reformed legal process gives the Public Ministry a role in the initial investigation, and introduces live oral testimony with indigenous interpreters and public hearings at the trial stage. It also makes provision for a special procedure in case habeas corpus is not filed within the allotted time.[21]

Although human rights discourses cannot claim all the credit for the recent changes of the Guatemalan judicial process, it is clear that they have influenced the pace of reforms. The power of human rights is exerted in courts of law, but also through the rhetorical form of human rights documents, and particularly through the legalism of their accounts. The knowledge produced by human rights agencies is part of the exercise of power insofar as it creates subjects and defines a context of injustice which demands to be put right. Since it is opposed to the use of power through control or coercion, the only power of human rights organisations lie in their discourse of denunciation. Since their only resource is the symbolic capital created by the ability to generate certain types of information, then it matters a great deal how that information is constructed.

The language of human rights reports mirrors the language of the modern nation-state, and the texts must engage in that discourse to influence state policy. Thus the effectiveness of human rights agencies' legalistic language lies in the fact that it speaks the language that state agents can understand. Were it to speak outside that discourse, then it presumably would have no effect.[22] Yet there is a tension here in aims, since human rights texts are directed at a heterogeneous audience, made up of other professional campaigners, local groups of non-professional activists, journalists, development workers and the general public, as well as politicians, bureaucrats and official state/UN policy-makers. This variegated community of end users could conceivably merit a differentiated body of publications of differing styles.

Yet the most powerful argument against the constrained style of human rights reporting concerns the implications it has for the conceptualisation of human rights. By situating social persons in communities and contexts, and furnishing thick descriptions of acts of the violent exercise of power, it can be seen how rights themselves are grounded, transformative and inextricably bound to purposive agents rather than being universal abstractions. The exalting of a legal/technical rationality above history and experience is ironically self-defeating, since despite its dedication to ethical ends, its method itself is denuded of ethics, having displaced value distinctions from its own operation.

Human rights are saturated with what Habermas (1971: 112–13) refers to as a 'technocratic consciousness' which engages in a displacement of values, norms and what he terms 'action-motivating meanings': 'The technocratic consciousness reflects not the sundering of (particular) ethical situations but the repression of ethics as a category of life.' It is this assimilation of ethics into scientific, technological and legal categories, which entails decontextualisation and the eradication of subjectivity. By embracing a technocratic language, human rights reporting lays itself open to the same critique as could be made of the devalued, dehumanised language of abusive forms of governance. Desubjectification, after all, is the chosen *modus operandi* of the torturer, and it hardly seems appropriate to employ a desubjectified narrative in order to represent abusive acts.

Concluding Remarks

What are the implications of the argument so far for the writing of human rights reports? My intention has not been to undermine their effectiveness, but to raise questions about the manner in which they are produced. What I would maintain is that human rights organisations could afford to adopt a greater range of styles of representing human rights abuses. As mentioned in the introduction, Amnesty International is one of many organisations which are engaged in an ongoing internal debate (or rather, struggle) on this issue. While International Council Meetings advocate greater inclusion of contextual material, and Amnesty International workers write reports with more and more social comment, the internal 'Standing Committee on the Mandate', which is made up mostly of lawyers, acts in a vigilant manner to excise what it sees as extraneous information.

The debate about the 'limits of representation' of gross violations of human rights has a long history in writings on the Holocaust. It has been pointed out by Christopher Browning (1992) that the Holocaust was not a legal or philosophical abstraction, instead it was a set of events that actually occurred. A key problem in representing the Jewish 'Shoah' results from an 'experiential gap' and the short-comings of all forms of representation. Generally historians or social scientists and their readers have nothing in their biographical experience which remotely compares with the Holocaust. Likewise, writers of human rights texts usually know nothing in a personal experiential sense about their subject (for example, torture, mutilation, etc.). It could be concluded that one way of leaping across the experiential gap would be to try to capture the nature of the subject matter through engaging with the existential circumstances of the victims, bystanders, even the perpetrators. What were the choices they faced, the emotions they felt, their coping mechanisms and ensuing changes in personality?

This experiential tack has been preferred over an arid abstract literalism by Jewish writers on the Holocaust. In his latest book, *Operation Shylock*, Philip Roth interviews the writer Aharon Appelfeld, who at the age of 9 survived the Holocaust, by escaping an extermination camp and wandering alone in Ukrainian woods. He has yet to write about the period as a direct experience or as a survivor's tale in as direct a fashion as Primo Levi's depiction of his Auschwitz incarceration. Instead, he writes fiction, and in the novel *Tzili*, retells the events of a young Jewish girl wandering among Ukrainian peasants, and the text is infused with the subjectivity of a sovereign author. In explaining why he used this genre instead of a 'factual' one, Appelfeld replied: 'The reality of the Holocaust surpassed any imagination. If I remained true to the facts, no one would believe me.'

One possible objection to the line my argument has taken could be that it leads towards a soggy relativism where any representation is as good as another. There is a general tendency for debates about modalities of representation and relativism to merge, but this need not necessarily be so. It should be possible to extend the limits of representation to include more modes of emplotment than are conventionally deployed at present in documenting human rights violations without collapsing into absolutist forms of perspectivism. I am not arguing that there exist a multiplicity of equally valid approaches, which could conceivably encourage an ethically dubious lurch into aesthetic fantasy. It could be argued successfully when comparing concrete examples that one mode of emplotment offers a more plausible rendition of the available evidence than another. As Perry Anderson (1992) has asserted, narratives are bounded both by exterior limits set by the evidence and by interior limits of the genre itself; for instance, it would be inappropriate for the Holocaust to be written about in the genres of comedy or pastoral romanticism.

Yet the main thrust of my argument is directed more towards social researchers, since human rights organisations will probably be committed to a legalistic framework at least for the foreseeable future. I would urge us to think more about the relationship between social research (and particularly anthropology) and human rights reporting, so that the texts of researchers might restore local subjectivities, values and memories as well as analysing the wider global social processes in which violence is embedded. Alex de Waal's (1994) comments are applicable here, insofar as he deliberates on what anthropologists can contribute to human rights and media reports of events like the mass ethnic violence in Rwanda. He concludes that ethnographers can complement other genres with studies that introduce history, local knowledge and an understanding of how identities are constructed, so violence is not only seen as a result of age-old animosities between primordial groups. This contextualisation is needed in order to compensate for the individualised, a-cultural, deracinated and therefore universalistic nature of most human rights accounts.

NOTES

1 See especially Saul Friedlander's (1992) edited volume, where there is a discussion of whether aesthetic experimentation is more justified when faced with events which challenge the usual categories of representation. For instance, accounts of the Holocaust by authors such as Ida Fink and David Grossman are both allegories and realistic novels, including enough references to 'real events' to prevent too much distance. Debates on representations of colonialism have gone in a similar direction; for example, James Clifford (1988) locates the genius of Joseph Conrad in his ability both to penetrate the veil of colonialism and yet to maintain a sense of its hallucinatory quality.

2 The imposing *Banco Imperial* was built in 1991 on the town square in Cobán by a drug-smuggling cartel for the purpose of money laundering and investment, but its function was discovered by law enforcement officials before it ever opened.

3 Christopher Browning (1992) arrives at similar conclusions in his reconstruction of perpetrators' testimonies of a massacre of Jews in the Polish village of Jozefów in 1942.

4 Note the use of legalistic language ('circumstantial evidence') and the equivocal statement which combines a tentative assertion ('appears'), with a confident qualification ('clearly').

5 Since direct state involvement is difficult to ascertain, Amnesty International also uses wider criteria which are not predicated on direct state involvement, by referring to cases 'where Amnesty International believes the available evidence suggests official complicity'. Complicity here means that state officers have not intervened while a crime took place, or they failed to fully pursue an investigation, suggesting official acquiescence.

6 Orin Starn (1992) reports a similar situation in highland Peru, where some community vigilante groups, or *rondas campesinas*, are military-directed counter-insurgency organisations, whereas others were inspired by the Catholic Church in order to facilitate local protection from cattle rustlers.

7 National Academy of Sciences (NAS) (1992: 39).

8 NAS (1992: 29).

9 NAS (1992: 21).

10   At the time, Guatemala's legal system operated under the Napoleonic Code, where magistrates uncovered both exculpatory and incriminatory facts, with no provision for jury trial.

11   As ever, this view competes with other explanations, including the theory that the murder may have been linked to the Court's approval to extradite a Guatemalan army officer to the US for drug smuggling. My thanks to David Stoll for pointing this out.

12   Although it is beyond the scope of this essay, there is a need for more historical studies of human rights reporting, which look at the emergence and transformation of certain languages of denunciation and the conditions under which such reports are produced. In Latin America, one might start in the early colonial period with Bartolomé de las Casas and Guaman Poma and move into the early twentieth century with Roger Casement's report to the British Foreign Office on the Putumayo rubber atrocities.

13   Children and spouses are only referred to if a person is attacked or abducted in front of them, and it is suggested that this adds to the gravity of the human rights violation, since the bystanders' rights to be free of intimidation are violated as well.

14   Human rights reports did actually include more of Myrna Mack's biography and background than the vast majority of cases due to the importance the case assumed in the legal system.

15   See Kapferer (1988) and Scott (1990) for a heated debate on violence as communication in Sri Lanka.

16   Personal communication.

17   Although they are checked by an internal monitor as well.

18   One Amnesty International desk officer referred to this specific letter as 'maudlin'.

19   NAS (1992: 37).

20   See Costello and Seider (1996).

21   However, the implementation of the new penal code is not widespread and has been hampered by a lack of funds and corruption.

22   See Richard Rorty's (1979) discussion of normal and abnormal discourses in *Philosophy and the Mirror of Nature*.

REFERENCES

Amnesty International. 1989. *Guatemala: Human Rights Violations under the Civilian Government*. London: AMR 34/07/89.

—— 1990. *Guatemala: Extrajudicial Executions and Human Rights Violations against Street Children*. London: AMR 34/37/90.

Anderson, Perry. 1992. 'On Emplotment: Two Kinds of Ruin', in S. Friedlander (ed.) *Probing the Limits of Representation: Nazism and the Final Solution*. Cambridge, MA: Harvard University Press.

Asad, Talal. 1992. 'Conscripts of Western Civilization', in Christine Ward Gailey (ed.) *Civilization in Crisis: Anthropological Perspectives*. Gainesville: University of Florida Press.

Browning, Christopher. 1992. 'German Memory, Judicial Interrogation, and Historical Reconstruction: Writing Perpetrator History from Postwar Testimony', in S. Friedlander (ed.) *Probing the Limits of Representation: Nazism and the Final Solution*. Cambridge, MA: Harvard University Press.

Clifford, James. 1988. *The Predicament of Culture: Twentieth-Century Ethnography, Literature and Art*. Cambridge, MA: Harvard University Press.

Costello, Patrick and Rachel Seider (1996) 'Judicial Reform in Central America: Prospects for the Rule of Law', in R. Seider (ed.) *Central America: Fragile Transition*. London: Macmillan/ILAS.

Foucault, Michel. 1979. 'What is an Author?' in J. Harari (ed.) *Textual Strategies: Perspectives in Post-Structuralist Criticism*. Ithaca, NY: Cornell University Press.

Friedlander, Saul. (ed.) 1992. *Probing the Limits of Representation: Nazism and the Final Solution*. Cambridge, MA: Harvard University Press.

Geertz, Clifford. 1983. 'Local Knowledge: Fact and Law in Comparative Perspective', in *Local Knowledge*. New York: Basic Books.

Giddens, Anthony. 1985. *The Nation-State and Violence*: Vol. 2 of *A Contemporary Critique of Historical Materialism*. Cambridge: Polity Press.

Habermas, Jürgen. 1971. *Towards a Rational Society*, trans. J. J. Shapiro. London: Heinemann.

Inglis, Fred. 1993. *Cultural Studies*. Oxford: Blackwell.

Kapferer, Bruce. 1988. *Legends of People, Myths of State*. Washington, DC: Smithsonian Institute Press.

LaCapra, Dominick. 1992. 'Representing the Holocaust: Reflections on the Historians' Debate', in S. Friedlander (ed.) *Probing the Limits of Representation: Nazism and the Final Solution*. Cambridge, MA: Harvard University Press.

National Academy of Sciences (NAS) Committee on Human Rights and Institute of Medicine Committee on Health and Human Rights. 1992. *Scientists and Human Rights in Guatemala: Report of a Delegation*. Washington, DC: National Academy Press.

Rorty, Richard. 1979. *Philosophy and the Mirror of Nature*. Princeton, NJ: Princeton University Press.

Schirmer, Jennifer. 1997. 'Universal and Sustainable Human Rights?' in Richard A. Wilson (ed.), *Human Rights, Culture, and Context: Anthropological Perspectives*. London: Pluto Press.

Scott, David. 1990. 'The Demonology of Nationalism: On the Anthropology of Ethnicity and Violence in Sri Lanka', *Economy and Society* 19(4): 491–510.

Starn, Orin. 1992. '"I Dreamed of Foxes and Hawks": Reflections on Peasant Protest, New Social Movements, and the *Rondas Campesinas* of Northern Peru', in A. Escobar and S. Alvarez (eds) *The Making of Social Movements in Latin America: Identity, Strategy and Democracy*. Boulder, CO: Westview Press.

Waal, Alex de. 1994. 'Editorial: Genocide in Rwanda', *Anthropology Today* 10(3): 1–2.

Warren, Kay. 1993. *The Violence Within*. Boulder, CO: Westview Press.

Wilson, Richard A. 1995. *Maya Resurgence in Guatemala: Q'eqchi' Experiences*. Norman: University of Oklahoma Press.

Zur, Judith. 1994. 'The Psychological Impact of Impunity', *Anthropology Today* 10(3).

13

Gendered Intersections: Collective and Individual Rights in Indigenous Women's Experience

Shannon Speed

The women sat in the dark front room of a house in Nicolás Ruiz. They had gathered to discuss with me their experience with social movement participation, as base supporters or as *milicianas* (militia members) of the Zapatista National Liberation Army (EZLN). The talk wound through various topics before finally making its way to the conflict among women in the community that had surged the previous year. I was worried about the topic. "What happened?" I asked uneasily. The talk became suddenly animated, leaving behind the reserved decorum of our earlier discussion. The women talked over each other, anxious to add details or elaborate their perspectives. Finally, one woman's voice rose above the others, who fell silent. "*Lo que pasa*," she said with emphasis, "is that in this community, we don't want *protagonistas* [those who assert themselves forcefully in a certain situation, usually for personal gain of prestige or power]." "We women want to organize for our rights," she said, "but we want to do it collectively."[1]

"Rosalina's" words spoke directly to the theoretical questions I had been struggling with as a feminist, an activist, and a researcher, regarding the presumed contradiction between indigenous communities' collective rights to maintain their culture and the rights of individual community members (in particular, women) that might be violated by those cultural norms and practices. Taking the women's conflict in Nicolás Ruiz as a starting point, in this essay I examine the tension between individual and collective human rights and the specific issues raised by gender and ethnicity in that tension. I argue that resolving this tension is not possible and that focusing our analytic efforts on establishing whether individual or collective rights

Originally published in *Rights in Rebellion: Indigenous Struggle and Human Rights in Chiapas*. Stanford, CA: Stanford University Press, 2008, pp. 118–36.

should have primacy is unproductive and obscures as much as it clarifies. In fact, the conceptual dichotomy individual/collective often serves to deny many women's – especially indigenous women's – lived experience of oppression and resistance. Further, I suggest that indigenous women's gender demands, constructed in active engagement with discourses at the intersection of individual and collective rights, contributes to an alternative way of thinking about rights that is consistent with local understandings and underpins local forms of resistance.

The Individual and the Collective: Theory and Practice in the Neoliberal Context

That is the Mexico we Zapatistas want ... one where respect for difference is balanced with respect for what makes us equals.

Comandanta Esther (2001)

As we have seen, the Zapatista uprising began at a key moment in Mexico's history in which relations between the state and civil society were shifting dramatically as the corporatist state gave way to the neoliberal multicultural model. This shift had been set in motion two years earlier with the changes to the Mexican Constitution that ended agrarian reform and other nationalist and corporatist policies while simultaneously recognizing its population for the first time as "pluriethnic."

This process was not unique to Mexico but was under way in a number of Latin American countries in the 1990s. Legal and constitutional reforms implemented to "neoliberalize" states – shrinking state functions and giving priority to ensuring stability and the free market – were regularly accompanied by legal recognition of indigenous populations and, to differing degrees, their rights (Assies, van der Haar, and Hoekema 2000; Postero and Zamosc 2004; Van Cott 2000; Yashar 2005). In the "neoliberal multiculturalism" (Hale 2002) model, recognition is a part of the new logics of governance that predominate in the neoliberal state.

However, it was not the reforms but the Zapatista uprising that put indigenous rights on the national radar screen and in the process drew out the tensions and contradictions with which this shift was fraught. The reform of Article 4 had acknowledged Mexico's multicultural makeup, but it did not recognize indigenous peoples as "peoples," nor did it provide indigenous groups with any specific rights. Such a move would have implied a more dramatic break with the past, as Mexico's Constitution of 1917 is founded on liberal concepts of the equality of each individual Mexican before the law. However, Mexico might have gone forward with a broader recognition of collective rights, as did countries such as Colombia, Bolivia, and Ecuador, were it not for the uprising and the emergent national indigenous movement, which called into question the terms of such reform. The Zapatistas did so in several important and interrelated ways; they are the subject of this and the following chapters. Here, I want to highlight one: a refusal to accept either modern liberal individual rights or state-defined multicultural recognition of collective rights as the unitary model for the exercise of their rights. This has been particularly clear in the case of indigenous women.

The tension between collective and individual rights was a thorny one both for the state and for the Zapatistas. With the uprising, it was not just indigenous people who stepped onto the national stage to assert their rights but also, quite prominently, indigenous women. From the start, the EZLN highlighted the presence of women in their leadership and elaborated a strong rhetoric of indigenous women's rights. Women constituted 30 percent of the Zapatista Army. Karen Kampwirth (2002) notes this is similar to the percentage of women involved in the Central American guerrilla movements of the 1980s, but the fact that the women participating in the Chiapas uprising were almost exclusively indigenous made this level of participation notable and distinct, because the subordinated position of women in indigenous communities and the hardship of their lives were well-known. For example, women in indigenous communities disproportionately suffer illiteracy, lack adequate access to medical care, have a life expectancy two years shorter than their male counterparts, and experience the highest maternal death rate in Mexico (Kovic and Eber 2003). Their personal autonomy, including the ability to choose when and whom to marry and when to bear children, the ability to travel freely outside the community, and the ability to inherit property and participate in political decisions concerning the community are frequently limited by community norms (Kovic and Eber 2003; Rovira 1996). The Revolutionary Women's Law, made public immediately after the uprising, represented a clear and systematic elaboration of the movement's support for "women's just demands of equality." These included the right to choose their partners, decide the number of children they will have, hold positions of authority in the community, and be free from rape and violence.[2]

Some feminists criticized what they viewed as the Zapatistas' "masculinist" approach to resistance. For example, Rojas (1995) and other contributors to her edited volume questioned, from their own feminist perspectives, Zapatismo's libratory effects for women. In particular, Bedregal (1994) argues that women are inherently more peaceful than men and that by taking up arms and inserting themselves into male hierarchical structures (such as that of an army) women concede too much from the start. These same authors also suggested that the women's laws were limited and did not constitute feminist demands because they did not contain a critique of patriarchal social relations. In the terms of the feminist debates of the day, they were seen as "practical" demands for bettering women's lives rather than "strategic" ones for challenging and altering unequal relations of power between men and women (Molyneux 1985; and see Stephen 1997 for a discussion of this debate). Others feminists, even while noting that in many communities little had changed for women on the ground, nevertheless argued that the Zapatista movement contributed to creating a cultural climate in which gender relations could be renegotiated and opened spaces in which new forms of women's participatory citizenship could flourish (Eber and Kovic 2003; Garza Caligarís 2002; Hernández Castillo 1998; Olivera 1997). What the Zapatistas have made clear is that the presence of women in their ranks and the demands put forward by the movement are the result of women's active struggle within the movement for a position equal to that of men. Undeniably, this remains an ongoing struggle within Zapatista communities, which has had uneven results from community to community and region to region (Speed, Hernández Castillo, and Stephen 2006). Comandanta Yolanda highlighted this ongoing process in a speech on International Women's Day in 2003:

> The men are struggling to totally understand what we are asking for as women. We are asking to have rights and for the men to give us liberty, and for them to understand that we have to fight for that along with them. For them to learn to not take our participating here badly, because, before, we never went to meetings. Now there's just a few of us

who go, but the path is opening up in all ways. There's more freedom. The men now take our words into consideration, and they understand that we, as women, have a place where we can present everything we feel and everything we are suffering.[3]

Few would deny that in the decade since the uprising, Zapatista women have made a vital contribution to the advancement of the indigenous women's movement (Hernández Castillo 2006). They have made it clear to all that while the Mexican Constitution established equality, including women's equality, in legal practice and everyday life, some people – like indigenous people and women – enjoy "real" equality considerably less than others. In Comandanta Esther's words:

> I would like to explain to you the situation of the indigenous women who are living in our communities, considering that respect for women is supposedly guaranteed in the Constitution. The situation is very hard.[4]

Comandanta Esther's speech, made in the context of the legislature's consideration of the Law on Indigenous Rights and Culture, reiterated two important points that organized indigenous women had been making for some time. The first is the inseparability of indigenous women's experience as women and as indigenous people, an inseparability ignored by many in the debates about women's individual rights. Another point was made by her lament of the futility of rights established in law, such as the right to equality that could not in fact be exercised.

The tension between individual and collective rights, rendered highly visible and contentious by the Zapatista uprising, was one that Mexico, like other neo-liberalizing states, had to grapple with. Theorists of multicultural recognition such as Kymlicka (1995) suggest that states must grapple with the antagonism between the concept of individual equality and collective claims in the interests of doing justice to the individuals who make up those groups (though individual rights trump collective ones in the final instance). But as we have seen, other theorists have suggested that the increasing prevalence of a state recognition model and associated multicultural reforms is a trend that signals a shift away from democratic states' focus on the pursuit of democracy per se and in fact may serve to manage and limit the force of collective indigenous demands (Gustafson 2002; Hale 2002; Postero 2001). In other words, in the recent Latin American context, in implementing multicultural policies the state is engineering a program that entails much more than trying to be fair to all its citizens. The limited recognition of collective rights for particular groups is an integral part of neoliberal subject formation and the construction of neoliberal rule.

The flourishing of demands for indigenous community autonomy and women's personal autonomy combined with the shifting terrain of governance and public policy to generate a national debate about collective and individual rights, about equality and cultural difference. The demand for autonomy in Mexico – as elsewhere in Latin America – has been built on the concept of *usos y costumbres*. *Usos y costumbres* usually refers to consensus decision making, local administration of justice, and the election of authorities through traditional means, but it can also encompass virtually anything a community or its leaders define as "tradition." In the autonomy debate, government officials, as well as some prominent jurists and intellectuals, argued that indigenous peoples' *usos y costumbres* served to justify local power relations and that collective norms frequently violated individuals' rights. Some argued that the state should not allow indigenous people any measure of autonomy based on their *usos y costumbres* because they had antidemocratic tendencies and would almost certainly violate the basic human rights of individuals in the community (Bartra 1997; Krauze 1999). One prominent jurist went so far as to express his concern that respecting indigenous peoples' *usos y costumbres* could lead to accepting "some ethnic groups that engage in the human sacrifice of babies."[5]

This is a thorny issue because, of course, there are many instances in which the individual's ability to act autonomously is subordinated to collective norms in the community context. The specter of extreme cases that resulted in violence, such as the expulsion of politico-religious dissenters in the highlands community of San Juan Chamula (CNDH 1995; Kovic 2005), was often raised in the public debate. Yet in many cases the arguments made relied on essentialized and static notions of indigenous *usos y costumbres*, suggesting the Indians were inherently antidemocratic and that this was an unchanging and unchangeable part of their culture. Such ideas were relatively easy to "sell" to the public, since the assimilationist national discourse had long cast Indians as culturally backward, in need of modernization and integration to the national culture.

These perspectives were manifested in government policies and actions. This often went beyond the state's defense of liberal individual rights, reflecting a more utilitarian use by the state of individual rights protections as a tool to limit indigenous rights (see Speed and Collier 2000). I have already mentioned some cases of this, such as use of individual rights as limiting language in agreements on indigenous autonomy, such as the Chiapas state law on indigenous rights, which in Article 10 states that "uses, customs, and traditions will be applied within the limits of their habitat, as long as they do not constitute violations of human rights." This dynamic was further evident in the rhetorical strategies of the government in justifying its attacks against autonomous municipalities, as in Interim Governor Albores's declaration prior to the raid on Nicolás Ruiz that tied "radical" and "primitive" to *usos y costumbres*, then suggested that they "trample individual rights."[6] So widespread was this brandishing of individual rights to limit collective ones that indigenous people in many areas – even those who supported the ruling party – began to understand human rights as a potential limit to their local autonomy (Speed and Collier 2000).

It was not infrequent in the public debate to hear women's rights serve as primary examples of the dangers of the collective violating the rights of individuals. *Usos y costumbres* such as arranged marriage, exclusion of women from political participation, and male-line inheritance were cited as examples of practices that violated women's rights to personal autonomy, civic participation, and economic sustenance. The legislators who drafted the COCOPA law, for example, included the following limiting language regarding the enjoyment of indigenous autonomy: "respecting individual constitutional guarantees, human rights and, *in particular, the dignity and integrity of women*" (emphasis mine). While few would debate the importance of respect for women's dignity and integrity, the inclusion of this phrase both reflects the prevalence of and perpetuates the notion that indigenous culture, when not restrained by the protective state, will violate individual rights and that women are in need of special protection.

These arguments echoed debates in the literature on gender and human rights, which has, as a recent article stated, a "central concern" regarding the struggle for cultural rights "when respect for customary law or traditional customs and practices violates the individual rights of women" (Deere and Leon De Leal 2002:76; see also

Okin 1999). In the theoretical realm, such debates are between cultural relativists who believe that "culture is the principal source of validity of right and rule" and feminists concerned that such a position requires accepting the subordination of women and negating indigenous women's individual human rights (Deere and Leon De Leal 2002:76; Okin 1999). In this framing, given the direct contradiction between collective claims to culture and women's individual human rights, one is forced to side with one position or the other. Thus cultural rights are positioned against gender rights in the many academic writings and in public discourse.

In Mexico, such arguments were made by a broad range of people, from feminists to conservative constitutionalists. Some critiques were made by people with a long-established commitment to women's rights. Others highlighted certain gender practices only to substantiate their claims about the authoritarian and undemocratic nature of indigenous communities. But while the actors making these arguments are diverse, they are nevertheless united by an underlying adherence to notions of liberal individualism inscribed in both the Mexican constitution and popular consciousness of much of Mexico: that the rights and equality of individuals should always have primacy and that these rights are always inherently put at risk by the collective.

This position, while consistent with liberal principles of individual equality that underpin human rights and women's rights claims, nevertheless runs the risk of paternalism and ethnocentricity. No matter how that argument is made, it is difficult to escape the implicit notion that indigenous communities (that is, the individuals within them) are in need of external protection from the civilized Mexican state to keep the "collective" from running amok.[7] The state, in this view, is posited as the legitimate enforcer of liberal discipline on illiberal cultures. Further, while often mobilized to limit the struggle for indigenous rights, this is far from being an anti-multicultural position. It is in fact consistent with classic liberal multicultural "politics of recognition" (see, for example, Kymlicka's 1995 position on the need for "external protections" by the state over "internal restrictions" on individual liberties imposed by the collective). I'll return to these issues later in this analysis, but what I want to suggest here is that what we can see in the Mexican case, and especially in the debate at the intersection of gender and ethnic rights, is the manner in which during the neoliberal moment, the hegemonic premises of liberal individualism get mobilized to limit any collective rights that might be implied by an ascendant multiculturalism.

But indigenous women, rather than accepting the designation of individual rights-bearer in need of protection from the liberal (or neoliberal) state against the illiberal collective, have instead constructed a distinct position for themselves, which articulates both the collective and the individual aspects of their experience into their social struggle on various terrains: in the community, in their organizations, and with the state. Drawing in part on the arguments of indigenous women themselves, some recent writings have argued that culture is continually changing and that indigenous groups are capable of both defending their culture and transforming it from within (toward better gender equality). This position rejects the dichotomy between relativism and women's rights and interrogates the definition of culture that underlies both the relativism and universalism stances (Engle 2005; Hernández Castillo 2002; Kapur 2002; Merry 2006; Sierra 2001). Below, I explore these questions in the context of one community's experience, focusing my discussion on the difficulties of separating out distinct realms of individual and collective experience for many women and the implications of their integration into a unified struggle for women's rights that are not formulated, arbitrated, and enforced exclusively by the state.

Nicolás Ruiz: The Multiplicity of Local Experience

The community of Nicolás Ruiz has lived the effects of the recent social dynamics in the state. Today in Nicolás Ruiz there is some reassertion of indigenous identity and the community's right to govern itself based on its *usos y costumbres*. Like many other communities in rural Mexico, Nicolás Ruiz went from identifying as "Indian" to identifying primarily as "peasant," and more recently authorities have begun to more strongly forefront the community's indigenous identity.

These shifting subjectivities reflect the fact that community identity is a fundamentally relational concept, historically constructed in dialogue with external social actors and groups. During the period in which the state's relationship to rural peoples was formulated through agrarian reform and "campesinist" assistance policies, Nicolás Ruiz's Tzeltal identity gave way to campesino identity. As the Chiapas conflict brought Nicolás Ruiz into dialogue with new interlocutors, giving them increased interaction with the discourse of human and indigenous rights, and as the discourses of the state shifted from agrarian corporatism and toward the indigenous as a basis for rights claims, people in Nicolás Ruiz reinterpreted their history and their practices in ways that altered their community identity.

Nicolás Ruiz does have traditional customs and practices, whether or not they have been defined in the recent past as indigenous. Since the community's formation, land has been held communally. Decisions about community political life are made in the community assembly by consensus, in which all *comuneros* participate. Leaders, even municipal officials, are chosen through the *usos y costumbres* of the community and then ratified through the official electoral process. Those who are elected are expected to carry out – not to make – the decisions that affect the community. That is, decisions are made in the assembly, then implemented through the elected officials. Consensus is crucial to the community's understanding of itself.

Violation of these *usos y costumbres* is considered serious enough that community members are quickly punished. One example is the revocation of the land rights of the *priísta* community members, that is, those in support of the PRI, who were refusing to participate in the assembly. Those arrested in the subsequent military-police raid in defense of the ruling-party loyalists articulated a legal defense similar to that of authorities in several other Zapatista autonomous municipalities that were raided in the same period. They argued that they were acting based on their *usos y costumbres*, which they had a right to do. By "*usos y costumbres*," they were referring to their traditional practice of decision by consensus and the concomitant responsibility to participate in the assembly, both of which had been violated by the dissenting members.[8]

It is worth noting that in Nicolás Ruiz, as in most rural communities in Chiapas, there is some internal differentiation – in class position (this is limited in Nicolás Ruiz and is more evident in some highlands communities, where *caciques* have enriched themselves, creating greater social divides), in political and religious stances, and, of course, along gender lines. In situations of internal discord, all sides are likely to legitimate their actions based on "customs and traditions," rendering the debate, in many cases, one over which "traditions" are the legitimate ones. In Nicolás Ruiz, the dissenters argued that the community tradition was to be *priísta*.

Las Mujeres: Life at the Intersection

In Nicolás Ruiz, as in many communities, consensus means consensus of the men. Women do not hold land and therefore do not participate in the community assembly. Nevertheless, women in Nicolás Ruiz have a history of organizing that predates the Zapatista uprising. This has been especially notable in times of conflict, when women organized to support the men, but also on occasion to wrest benefits from the state, such as a corn mill that reduced the labor involved in producing tortillas.[9]

After the community became Zapatista, women began to have new types of interactions with people from outside the community. Some became involved directly in "the organization" as *milicianas*, actively training with and responding to Zapatista leadership. Others became involved with "civil society" activists – generally pro-Zapatista but not tied directly to the organization. Several of these activists were feminists with long histories of activism in the region.

The work of women with civil society groups had a high profile, whereas that of the women with the organization was of necessity more clandestine. The women formed two committees: a health committee that studied and practiced herbal medicine and a "political committee" that did political support work, such as providing a presence at political events in other communities. A prominent figure among these women was "Doña Matilde," coordinator of the health committee. Over the course of several years, "Doña Matilde" became something of a spokesperson for the community and was often seen at rallies with a microphone or megaphone. An ode to "Doña Matilde's" strength and courage circulated on the Internet.

Not surprisingly, as women became increasingly organized and had increased interaction with outside actors with a women's rights orientation, some began to question and challenge their lack of political voice in the community. A women's assembly was formed, parallel to the men's assembly. Though they did not have the power to make decisions affecting the community as a whole, they could address the men's assembly on certain issues and try to sway opinion there. The women I spoke with at the time expressed their preference for a women's assembly over joining the men's assembly. In the words of one woman, "We have too much work to do to sit in there day and night," referring to the notoriously long assembly meetings. "We have little ones to take care of."[10] "Yes," agreed another woman, "It's better to have our own meetings, in agreement with our own schedules."[11] Whether all agreed with their position, I don't know. In the course of my work in the community, I did not find women who expressed interest in participating regularly in the men's assembly. But women from both the organization and civil society groups participated in the assembly, and it seemed a big step forward in women's right to political participation. "Doña Matilde" was the president of the women's assembly.

After being away for a period of several months, I returned to the community to find that the women's assembly had been officially dissolved, the committees were no longer meeting, and "Doña Matilde" was all but censured by community authorities. I was shocked by this turn of events, and it took me some time to piece together a picture of what had happened from the various and distinct versions. There had been a split among the women, along lines that could be divided roughly into those affiliated with "civil society" and those affiliated with the Zapatistas. A variety of reasons were mentioned for the rift. One that was raised often by the Zapatista-affiliated women was their resentment over "Doña Matilde's" insistence that women who did not attend the assembly pay a fine. This practice mirrored that of the men's assembly, where rules state that a fine can be levied against *comuneros* who fail to participate without good reason. But the Zapatista-aligned women complained that they had family and organizational commitments that made occasional absences necessary. They resented the fines and felt that "Doña Matilde" was wielding power over them. Tensions grew into open rupture, and the issue was brought into the general assembly. During a very tense session, "Matilde" addressed the assembly. She defended herself and in anger pointed out members of the assembly and accused them of being Zapatistas. In the context of the open conflict with the *priístas* in the community and of low-intensity warfare in general, this act was perceived by some as a threat to denounce them to the authorities. At the petition of the Zapatista-aligned women, the male authorities of the community voted to discontinue the women's assembly.

This was clearly an unhappy episode for the women involved – one that affected women's solidarity and their advances in political participation within the community. As an activist and individual involved in the social dynamics, I was personally affected by some of the fallout associated with this conflict. Nevertheless, I deeply respect women in both camps, including "Doña Matilde," and owe all a debt of gratitude for the time they spent answering my questions, telling me about their own lives and that of the community. There were many conflicting versions of events and it would be fruitless to attempt to establish whose account was right and whose was wrong. The outline constructed above is a portrayal that all (more or less) agree upon, though interpretations of the events differ. For the purposes of this analysis, it is more important to examine how the issues were perceived and interpreted by the different actors and why.

Both the male authorities and the Zapatista-aligned women accused "Matilde" of *protagonismo* – of asserting her own agenda, wielding power over others, and flaunting the community's norms and collective will. For her part, "Doña Matilde" and her supporters felt that the other women were jealous of her strong position, that the male authorities were threatened by her, and that the community's response was little more than an attempt to keep an assertive and capable woman "in her place."

One can clearly see the outlines of a classic collective culture versus individual gender rights debate in this conflict. A fairly straightforward argument could be made – and in fact was made quite cogently by a feminist sociologist close to "Doña Matilde" – about the violation of an individual's rights based on claims to the collective. The reassertion of indigenous identity and the mobilization of a discourse of *usos y costumbres* in Nicolás Ruiz was, from this perspective, functioning to maintain relations of power within the community, especially gendered relations of power.

I felt uncomfortable with the interpretation, as I often do with the form *usos y costumbres* critiques take, and this is why I was so worried about the subject of the conflict when it came up in the conversation with the Zapatista women. It was not that I doubted that the male authorities of Nicolás Ruiz are capable of exerting their power to maintain patriarchal relations, and in fact they do this to differing degrees in a myriad of ways on a daily basis. Yet I kept returning to the fact that the conflict erupted between women, and to the intuitively illogical fact that it was the Zapatista-aligned women who requested that the male authorities cancel the women's assembly. Were the Zapatista women caught in the all-too-familiar bind of subverting their own gender demands to the greater struggle of the community (organization, movement)? I gingerly tried to broach this with the women and got little response. But the question continued to gnaw at me: had my query been too vague, or had they purposefully avoided it? I decided to be more direct. Had it ever been suggested to them – by men in the organization or in the community – that they put aside or on hold their own struggle for gender equality because it might be divisive at a time when a unified front was needed in the struggle? The three women with whom I was talking looked thoughtful. After a few moments of reflection, one of them said, "I think the opposite is true. It was through the organization that we began to organize, that we began to become conscious of our rights as women."[12] The others agreed. But, I asked, what about the male authorities of the community? They thought about that for a few more moments, and then another woman spoke. "Some men are more *consciente* [enlightened] than others," she said, "but they also know that a community, to advance, must work as a collective, both men and women. That's why they supported us."[13] Undoubtedly, other women would have had a different interpretation. But I found it interesting that, again, the Zapatista women framed the issue as one of individual versus collective.

Nicolás Ruiz's particular insertion into the dynamics of social conflict in Chiapas had a variety of results. One was the separation of the women of the community into distinct groups: one aligned with civil society and one aligned with the organization (and a third, for that matter, aligned with the PRI). The division between these groups is not insignificant, since it brought them into engagement with somewhat distinct discourses regarding women's rights: the civil society version, which, while diverse itself, was strongly influenced by feminist individualism; and the Zapatista version, also uneven across various terrains, but in which women's rights were tied continuously to the collective. The latter perspective, I believe, resonated more strongly with notions of collectivity and consensus that prevailed in Nicolás Ruiz prior to the events narrated here. This was notable in the fact that, at least in my discussions with community members, it was more often women than men who raised the issue of community norms of non *protagonismo* being violated, in their view, by "Matilde's" increasingly public activism. In other words, it was not a straightforward matter of men mobilizing this discourse in order to subvert women's organizing. Women, of course, also participate in reproducing oppressive gender roles. But the fact that it was Zapatista women who were potentially playing this role seemed counterintuitive. In any case, given the community's historical privileging of the consensus model, particularly its heightened sensitivity to the issue in light of the current conflict between pro-Zapatistas and *priístas*, it is perhaps not surprising that the view prevailed that individuals need to conform to community consensus and community norms. The stakes were high, and "Matilde's" pointing to Zapatistas in the assembly brought the women's conflict into the context of the larger conflict in the minds of those present, who felt she had gone too far and was acting without regard for "the common good."[14] In this context, the individual women's rights perspective was more easily discredited, marked by many men and women as an "outsider" perspective.

Rethinking Women's Oppression and Resistance: Toward an Embrace of the Intersection

We resist hegemonic dominance of feminist thought by insisting that it is a theory in the making, that we must necessarily criticize, question, re-examine and explore new possibilities.... The formation of a libratory feminist theory and praxis is a collective responsibility, one that must be shared.

hooks 1984:5

US Third World feminists have long warned us of the dangers of essentializing all women as a homogeneous group, pointing out that women in different cultural contexts have distinct experiences and understandings of gender (Anzaldúa 1987; Bhavnani 2000; hooks 1984; Lorde 1984; Moraga and Anzaldúa 2002 [1989]). It should be clear that even in the localized context of one community, women's experience differed, and for that reason they had differences of opinion and took distinct positions regarding gender rights. "Rosalina's" statement about wanting to struggle for women's rights collectively suggests that liberal notions of individual rights are not necessarily usefully applied to all women and are not inevitably the principal element of all struggles for women's rights. Overcoming the "feminist ethnocentrism" inherent in applying liberal individual feminist notions of rights to all women and reconceptualizing women's rights in ways that encompass other experiences, such as collective identities, is critically necessary at this juncture.[15]

Feminist legal scholars and other analysts have developed the notion of inter-sectionality in order to theorize precisely that multiple and multiply constituted experience. Intersectionality theorists argue that race, class, and gender work together as "interlocking axes" to create an "overarching structure of domination" that is distinct from the subordination suffered on any of these axes alone (Collins 1991:222). They suggest that efforts to study just one of these axes at a time can only result in inadequate understandings of the way that that social hierarchy is created and maintained and of the way inequality and oppression are experienced (Carbado 1999; Collins 1991; Crenshaw 1991; Wing 2000). Intersectionality works as more than description of women's reality – it is a theoretical tool to understand multiple oppressions and discuss rights through them. From this perspective, it becomes vital to approach women's experience of oppression and resistance to that oppression from a complex place where they are not first individual women, then members of an indigenous community, or first indigenous, then women. Prioritizing one over the other in seeking to strengthen women's rights does unintended violence to all women's struggles by imposing the notion that one aspect of our identity is more significant than others, and by undermining our ability to understand and resist oppression by sectioning it off into fragments of experience that are not individually comprehensible.

This does not mean that one must be resigned to women's oppression in cultural contexts in which the collective is a significant aspect of women's experience (see Merry 2003). Such arguments are based on notions of culture as static and bounded: collective norms are "traditional" and therefore unchanging. But collect-ively held norms, like individually held ideas, are in a state of continual change forged in dialogue both with external social actors and between members of the community who challenge hegemonic configurations of power. Nicolás Ruiz's culture and identity are constantly being reshaped in relation to changing social forces, and there is no particular reason to think that gender norms and relations cannot be altered as part of that process. Looking at the multiple axes of oppression indigenous women suffer might move us beyond blaming local culture as the culprit and open a panorama in which we can understand how gendered power in the collectivity is articulated with gendered power in a broader context to create and reproduce women's and indigenous peoples' oppression in one process.

Though it seemed counterintuitive at the time, I have come to understand that it makes sense that it was the Zapatista women in Nicolás Ruiz who emphasized the need to struggle for women's rights in the collective context of the community. They have been vocal in drawing attention to the multiple oppressions suffered by indigenous women – typified by Comandanta Esther's statement, "We have to struggle more, because we are triply looked down on: because we are indigenous, because we are women, and because we are poor" (Comandanta Esther 2001).[16] Zapatista women have been among the leading voices expressing rejection of arguments that would make them – indigenous women – the reason their communities are denied autonomy. This is not a position unique to the Zapatistas. Women in many indigenous communities are facing the challenges of renegotiating gender relations in the context of the movement that they support and in the communities they call home. These women struggle to change gendered relations of power in the cultural context of their communities while simultaneously defending the right of the community to define for itself what that cultural context is and will be (see Hernández Castillo 2006).

Binaries such as individual/collective rights or cultural rights/women's rights, while they exist on a conceptual and definitional level, are not always so clearly defined in women's lived experience. Focusing instead on how women in a particular social context understand their rights, variously and differentially, may be the best way to think about women's rights and how to gain them. This does not mean, necessarily, accepting all practices and traditions of a culture as valid. We can disagree with some practices without calling the entire culture into question (Merry 2003). And we can, as many indigenous women in Mexico now are doing, call on the male authorities of indigenous communities to alter their cultural understandings and community norms to include women's rights. But those of us who are elaborating a discourse of women's rights from outside the community also need to adjust our own historically and culturally specific notions of the individual nature of those rights, so that we may encompass the experience of women throughout the world who understand themselves and their rights as existing and being defined largely in a collective context.

Challenges at the Intersection: Neoliberalism, Zapatismo, and Indigenous Women

Avoiding theoretical binaries is crucial, not just because it should be our goal to fairly represent the women involved in such struggles and not entrap them in dichotomies foreign to their experience, but also because it may be in this assertion of such multiple and intersecting experiences that resistance may be located. Gender provides us with a key site for exploring the challenges presented by the Zapatista uprising to the neoliberal state. Some analysts have argued that indigenous women's demands, at the intersection of gender and ethnicity, are fundamental to the imagining and the mapping of a multicultural Mexico (Hernández Castillo, Paz, and Sierra 2004). While this useful perspective counters the assertion of indigenous women as a barrier to indigenous rights, I want to suggest something different here – that they actually present a challenge to state multiculturalism. That is, to the extent that Zapatista indigenous women are imagining or positing a multicultural Mexico, it is a very distinct one from the "politics of recognition" model pursued, in sporadic and limited fashion, by the Mexican state.

The neoliberalizing Mexican state has not effectively harnessed multiculturalism to the project of rule. The initial "multicultural moves" gave way to a serious government reticence to institute multicultural policies, notably in its refusal to implement the San Andrés Accords on Indigenous Rights and Culture signed in

1996 by the EZLN and the government and in the failed Law of Indigenous Rights and Culture of 2001. This law was originally proposed as the implementing legislation of the San Andrés Accords. The version approved by the Congress actually set indigenous rights back by limiting indigenous jurisdiction, by denying rights to territory and to natural resources, and by passing the definition of indigenous peoples and what rights pertain to them on to the individual state-level governments. While multiculturalist rhetoric predominates, it is nevertheless clear that the Mexican government is not prepared to cede rights to indigenous peoples to the extent that some other Latin American countries have.

One important reason for the Mexican state's reticence is undoubtedly the Zapatista uprising, which raised the stakes on indigenous rights substantially. This was not simply because it generated fears of out-of-control primitive collectivities that made ceding indigenous rights and creating a multicultural state seem too dangerous. The real risk posed by the Zapatista uprising was in their refusal to accept the categories of neoliberal multiculturalism, including that of the *indio permitido* (Hale 2004): the state-defined subject of multicultural policies. One aspect of it that I want to explore here is in indigenous women's refusal to accept formulations of rights that limit them to one aspect of their experience.

The line between individual and collective rights is one of the most difficult for neoliberalizing states to negotiate. After the Zapatista uprising, Mexico halted the process it had undertaken with the 1992 constitutional reforms toward a politics of recognition of collective rights and strongly reasserted the primacy of the individual. Perhaps the clearest and most evident response against the Zapatistas' autonomy project was waged, both by government officials and in public discourse, on the sanctified terrain of individual rights. While gender issues were not the only site where individual rights and collective ones were said to clash, it was certainly among the most prominent in public debates. Indigenous women, put forward as the standard bearers for the primacy of individual rights, refused this position and reaffirmed their commitment to collective goals and to maintaining the conjunction of the individual and the collective as central to their struggle.

Once again, I do not wish to suggest that "the collective" is always inherently progressive or contestatory. It is precisely at the intersection of gender and collective rights that the inaccuracy of such a claim is made clear, when "the collective" is marshaled to justify and defend practices that are harmful to specific members or groups within that collective. What I do want to suggest is that the Zapatistas' refusal to separate them makes the state, whose judicial system is premised on this separation, extremely uneasy.

Through their "double activism" (Hernández Castillo 2006) that refuses to conceptualize women's rights outside their collective context, women present a double challenge to oppressive relations of power. The first challenge is to men within their communities and organizations to recognize women's rights and change traditional gender norms; this challenge is strengthened because it is not a product of paternalistic external protections and because it cannot be discounted as the discourse of outsiders. The second challenge, which arises by their refusal to disarticulate their struggle for women's equality within their communities from their struggle for rights based on cultural difference, is to the multiculturalism of the neoliberal state in Mexico, drawing the contradictions to the fore and offering an alternative logic.

Mexico has not "multiculturalized" in the manner that some other Latin American countries have for a variety of reasons. One of them, I have suggested, is that indigenous challenges from within made the internal contradictions of such an undertaking too difficult to overcome. Zapatismo and the indigenous women's movement that has gained force since the Zapatista uprising are a part of that internal challenge. Indigenous women, due to their location at the juncture of multiple identities of race, class, and gender, may well be at the forefront of contributing to a new multicultural Mexico. However, the one they advocate is not only different from but also challenging to that of the neoliberal state.

Conclusions

In this discussion of women's rights in one community, we have seen that local appropriations, even in the context of one community, may be diverse, depending on the differing subjectivities of groups of actors within the community and the types of external actors and discourses with which they are in dialogue. In the context of this conflict in Nicolás Ruiz, it made a significant difference for the two groups of women whether they were interacting primarily with the Zapatistas, who as a movement were mobilizing a collective rights discourse, or with activists from civil society, who were more likely to have a Western feminist notion of women's rights. Though these are generalizations of both groups of actors, it is nevertheless clear that the perspectives of the women involved were influenced by the dialogues they were engaged in with their primary interlocutors. The women's different interpretations of gender rights forged in dialogic interaction with outsiders are then brought into dialogue inside the community, itself a complex space of interaction within which continual struggles over meaning, culture, and power are always present.

All of these dialogisms take place in the larger context of conflict, counterinsurgency, and the renegotiation of power relations with the state. It was the uprising and social struggle that brought these particular external actors and discourses through the porous boundaries of the community. This was also what created the cultural climate in which gender rights could be and were debated and new interpretations were forged.

In Nicolás Ruiz, as in many other communities, these interpretations are still being struggled over, among women and between women and men. But even on this uneven and shifting topography, there is more, I want to suggest, at the intersection of gender and ethnicity than the collision of individual and collective rights. By overcoming "feminist ethnocentrism" (Hernández Castillo 2006) and thinking beyond these binaries to their multiply constituted meanings, we may see many indigenous women fostering potentially powerful new ways of conceptualizing rights and of resisting oppressive power relations.

NOTES

1 "Rosalina," interview with the author, July 2001.
2 The Women's Revolutionary Law is republished in Speed, Hernández Castillo, and Stephen 2006.
3 Available in English online at http://www.infoshop.org/news_archive/mex_woman.html. Last accessed April 2006.
4 Available in English online at http://www.zmag.org/chiapas1/estmar28.htm. Last accessed April 2006.

5 Ignacion Burgoa, cited in Jaime Avilés, "Burgoa: Los acuerdos de San Andrés, in existentes," *La Jornada*, March 4, 1997.
6 *Cuarto Poder*, June 2, 1998.
7 It is worth noting that the state has done very little until now to protect individual indigenous women from suffering violations of their rights implied by particular customs, such as those I have mentioned. Moreover, it is not at all clear that the judicial system of the Mexican state is entirely willing or able to protect any women's rights, even those established in law (see Azaola 1996).
8 Other cases are discussed in Speed and Collier 2000.
9 "Doña Matilde," interview with the author, June 1999.
10 "Francisca," conversation with the author, 2000.
11 "María," conversation with the author, 2000.
12 Conversation with the author, August 2001.
13 Conversation with the author, August 2001.
14 Interview with *comunero*, September 2001.
15 Hernández Castillo (2006) notes that this perspective has been accepted by some Mexican academic feminists (as it has by many academic feminists in other parts of Latin America and in the United States). However, in both the United States and Latin America, academic or "hegemonic" feminism has remained focused largely on the specific goals of reproductive rights and domestic violence. While these issues are relevant to indigenous women, their dominance continues to marginalize and exclude indigenous women's specific demands from the feminist agenda.
16 Comandanta Esther's complete speech of March 8, 2001, is available at www.infoshop. org/news_archive/mex_woman.html. Also reprinted in Speed, Hernández Castillo, and Stephen 2006.

REFERENCES

Anzaldúa, Gloria. 1987. *Borderlands/La Frontera: The New Mestiza*. San Francisco: Spinsters/Aunt Lute.
Assies, Willem, Gemma van der Haar, and Andre Hoekema, eds. 2000. *The Challenge of Diversity: Indigenous Peoples and Reform of the State in Latin America*. Amsterdam: Thela Thesis.
Azaola, Elena. 1996. *El delito de ser mujer*. Mexico, DF: CIESAS and Plaza y Valdes.
Bartra, Roger. 1997. "Violencias indígenas," *La Jornada Semanal* 130:8–9.
Bedregal, Ximena. 1994. "Reflexiones desde nuestro feminismo," in *Chiapas, y las mujeres, qué?* 1:43–56. Rosa Rojas, ed. Mexico, DF: La Correa Feminista.
Bhavnani, Kum Kum. 2000. *Feminism and "Race."* New York: Oxford University Press.
Carbado, Devon W., ed. 1999. *Black Men on Race, Gender, and Sexuality: A Critical Reader*. New York: New York University Press.
Collins, Patricia Hill. 1991. *Black Feminist Thought: Knowledge, Consciousness, and the Politics of Empowerment*. Boston: Unwin Hyman.
Comandanta Esther. 2001. "Speech before the Congress of the Union." Available at: fzlnnet.org. Last accessed March 24, 2005. Also reprinted in Shannon Speed, Rosalva Aída Hernández Castillo, and Lynn Stephen, eds. 2006. *Dissident Women: Gender and Cultural Politics in Chiapas*. Austin: University of Texas Press.
Comisión Nacional de Derechos Humanos (CNDH). 1995. *El problema de las expulsiones en las comunidades indígenas de Chiapas y los derechos humanos*. Mexico, DF: CNDH.
Crenshaw, Kimberle. 1991. "Mapping the Margins: Intersectionality, Identity Politics, and Violence against Women of Color," *Stanford Law Review* 43(6):1241–99.
Deere, Carmen Diana, and Magdalena Leon De Leal. 2002. "The Gender Asset Gap: Land in Latin America." Paper prepared for Latin America Regional Workshop on Land Issues, 19–22 (May), Pachuca, Hidalgo, Mexico.

Engle, Karen. 2005. "International Human Rights and Feminisms: When Discourses Keep Meeting," in *International Law: Modern Feminist Approaches*. Doris Buss and Ambreena Manji, eds. Oxford: Hart Publishing.

Gustafson, Bret. 2002. "Paradoxes of Liberal Indigenism: Indigenous Movements, State Processes, and Intercultural Reform in Bolivia," in *The Politics of Ethnicity: Indigenous Peoples in Latin American States*, 267–306. David Maybury-Lewis, ed. Cambridge, MA: Harvard University Press.

Hale, Charles R. 2002. "Does Multiculturalism Menace? Governance, Cultural Rights and the Politics of Identity in Guatemala," *Journal of Latin American Studies* 34(3):485–524.

——. 2004. "Rethinking Indigenous Politics in the Era of the 'Indio Permitido,'" *NACLA* 38(2):16–21.

Hernández Castillo, Rosalva Aída. 1998. "Construyendo la utopia: Esperanzas y desafios de las mujeres Chiapanecas de frente al siglo XXI," in *La otra palabra: Mujeres y violence en chiapas antes y después de acteal*. Aída Hernández, ed. Mexico: CIESAS.

——. 2002. "Indigenous Law and Identity Politics in Mexico: Indigenous Men's and Women's Struggles for a Multicultural Nation," *Political and Legal Anthropology Review (PoLAR)* 24(2):90–109.

——. 2006. "Between Feminist Ethnocentricity and Ethnic Essentialism: The Zapatistas' Demands and the National Indigenous Women's Movement," in *Dissident Women: Gender and Cultural Politics in Chiapas*, 57–74. Shannon Speed, Rosalva Aída Hernández Castillo, and Lynn Stephen, eds. Austin: University of Texas Press.

Hernández Castillo, Rosalva Aída, Sarela Paz, and María Teresa Sierra, eds. 2004. *El estado y los indígenas en tiempos del PAN: Neoindigenismo, legalidad e identidad*. Mexico DF: CIESAS-Porrúa.

hooks, bell. 1984. *Feminist Theory from Margin to Center*. Boston, MA: South End Press.

Kampwirth, Karen. 2002. *Women and Guerrilla Movements: Nicaragua, El Salvador, Chiapas, Cuba*. University Park: Pennsylvania State University Press.

Kapur, Ratna. 2002. "The Tragedy of Victimization Rhetoric: Resurrecting the 'Native' Subject in International/Post-Colonial Feminist Legal Politics," *Harvard Human Rights Journal* 15 (Spring):1–37.

Kovic, Christine. 2005. *Mayan Voices for Human Rights: Displaced Catholics in Highland Chiapas*. Austin: University of Texas Press.

Kovic, Christine, and Christine Eber. 2003. "Introduction," in *Women of Chiapas: Making History in Times of Struggle and Hope*. London: Routledge.

Krauze, Enrique. 1999. "Chiapas: The Indians' Prophet," *New York Review of Books* (December 16):65–73.

Kymlicka, W. 1995. *Multicultural Citizenship: A Liberal Theory of Minority Rights*. Oxford: Clarendon Press.

Lorde, Audre. 1984. *Sister/Outsider*. Freedom, CA: Crossing Press Books.

Merry, Sally Engle. 2003. "Human Rights Law and the Demonization of Culture (and Anthropology along the Way)," *Political and Legal Anthropology Review (PoLAR)* 26(1):55–77.

——. 2006. *Human Rights and Gender Violence: Translating International Law into Local Justice*. Chicago: University of Chicago Press.

Molyneux, Maxine. 1985. "Mobilization without Emancipation?: Women's Interests, State and Revolution in Nicaragua," *Feminist Studies* 2(2):227–54.

Moraga, Cherie, and Gloria Anzaldúa. 2002 (1989). *This Bridge Called My Back: Writings by Radical Women of Color*. Berkeley, CA: Third Woman Press.

Okin, Susan Moller. 1999. *Is Multiculturalism Bad for Women?* Princeton, NJ: Princeton University Press.

Olivera, Mercedes. 1997. "Acteal: Los efectos de la guerra de baja intensidad," in *La otra palabra: Mujeres y violencia en Chiapas, antes y despues de Acteal*. Rosalva Aída Hernández Castillo, ed. Mexico, DF: CIESAS, COLEM, CIAM.

Postero, Nancy Grey. 2001. "Constructing Indigenous Citizens in Multicultural Bolivia." Available at: geocities.com. Last accessed February 2005.

Postero, Nancy, and Leon Zamosc, eds. 2004. *The Struggle for Indian Rights in Latin America*. London: Sussex Academic Press.

Rojas, Rosa, ed. 1995. *Chiapas, y las mujeres, qué?* Vols. 1 & 2. Mexico, DF: La Correa Feminista.

Rovira, Guiomar. 1996. *Mujeres de maíz*. Mexico: Era.

San Andrés Accords on Indigenous Rights and Culture. 1999. Lynn Stephen and Jonathan Fox, trans. *Cultural Survival Quarterly* 12(1):33–8.

Sierra, María Teresa. 2001. "Human Rights, Gender and Ethnicity: Legal Claims and Anthropological Challenges in Mexico," *PoLAR* 23(2):76–92.

Speed, Shannon, and Jane Collier. 2000. "Limiting Indigenous Autonomy: The State Government's Use of Human Rights in Chiapas," *Human Rights Quarterly* 22(4):877–905.

Speed, Shannon, Rosalva Aída Hernández Castillo, and Lynn Stephen, eds. 2006. *Dissident Women: Gender and Cultural Politics in Chiapas*. Austin: University of Texas Press.

Stephen, Lynn. 1997. *Women and Social Movements in Latin America: Power from Below*. Austin: University of Texas Press.

Van Cott, Donna Lee. 2000. *The Friendly Liquidation of the Past: The Politics of Diversity in Latin America*. Pittsburgh: University of Pittsburgh Press.

Wing, Adrien Katherine. 2000. *Global Critical Race Feminism: An International Reader*. New York: New York University Press.

Yashar, Deborah. 2005. *Contesting Citizenship in Latin America: The Rise of Indigenous Movements and the Postliberal Challenge*. Cambridge Studies in Contentious Politics. Cambridge, UK: Cambridge University Press.

14

Human Rights and Moral Panics: Listening to Popular Grievances

Harri Englund

Toward the end of 2003, several primary schools in Lilongwe became the sites of a moral panic. Parents rushed to collect their children and take them back home, ordered them not to attend school at all, or demanded that the schools' management provide greater security. The reason was a perceived rise in the abductions and abuse of children in the capital. Strangers had been reported to wait for children outside schools to entice them away. Further rumors quickly provided a context for the scare. The abducted children were said to be killed, their body parts sold during President Bakili Muluzi's frequent trips abroad. This trade sustained Muluzi's and his cabinet ministers' infinite riches while it gave raw material to wealthy nations for their own pursuit of affluence. Human flesh was needed as a bait to attract a certain fish species in the Indian Ocean. The fish ate sand found in the bottom of the sea, and the sand transformed into gold while inside the fish. Some countries produced their unrivaled wealth through processing gold, and the leaders of poor countries secured their personal comfort through the provision of human body parts as raw material.

These rumors, easily dismissed as superstition by those who do not live under the conditions in which they emerge, open up an alternative perspective on democracy and human rights. Activists and politicians proclaimed a particular interpretation of human rights during Malawi's first decade of neoliberal democracy. The poor were asked to assume responsibility for their poverty, to embrace "participation" even if their resources remained as depleted as ever, and to face their exploitative employers as mere individuals seeking legal redress. Docility was often an obvious feature of this human rights regime. Yet perhaps it was too obvious, masking the many contentious discourses and subversive practices that actually informed the

Originally published in *Prisoners of Freedom: Human Rights and the African Poor*. Berkeley: University of California Press, 2006, pp. 170–92.

everyday experiences of being poor. The entrenched habits of elitism ensured orderly crowds during civic-education sessions and submissive clients seeking legal aid, only exceptionally replaced with direct challenges to activists' chosen framework of human rights. Collective outbursts of anger inevitably seemed, to activists and authorities alike, equally exceptional diversions from the real project of consolidating democracy. No NGO was prepared to analyze these outbursts in the context of inconsequential civic education or ineffective legal aid. Neoliberal governance, despite NGOs' best efforts, secured only a very uneasy peace.

This essay examines the above-mentioned rumors and the circumstances around their emergence in order to highlight some of the channels for expressing popular discontent in democratic Malawi. Although the diversity of views among the populace presents a problematic standpoint for studying popular discontent, a moral panic reveals commonly felt frustrations, a predicament that can be juxtaposed with the preoccupations of human rights activists. The moral panic of 2003 directs our attention to impoverished parents' desire to provide their children with quality education, it forces us to consider the moral and material conditions of these parents' livelihoods, and it brings into focus popular ideas of Malawi's place in the world. An examination of these circumstances can lead to an enriched understanding of the kinds of claims that Malawians made in spite of human rights activists' best efforts to inculcate neoliberal values and attitudes. The predominance of individual freedoms, asserted in the human rights discourse of activists and politicians, risked eclipsing the actual diversity of claims and concerns. Ethnographic witnessing uncovers in popular concerns intellectual resources, "modes of thinking which help us think" (Strathern 2004, 203). Crucially, the aim of this essay is less to give a voice to the voiceless than to lend ears to the earless. The Malawian poor were just as opinionated as their civic educators, sometimes to the point of being vociferous. Their problem was not a lack of voice; the problem was that so few listened to them.

The bulk of my observations comes from several years of fieldwork in the capital's Chinsapo Township. By the end of the 1990s, the township hosted some thirty thousand residents, the vast majority of whom were migrants from rural areas (see Englund 2002b). An "unplanned" area built on the land of old Chewa villages, Chinsapo had grown to become the largest residential area in Lilongwe. Plots in its congested neighborhoods, allocated by local chiefs, lacked basic amenities, such as running water, and while access to electricity greatly improved during the late 1990s, the majority of households were still unable to afford it in 2003. Located some five kilometers from the capital's commercial center in Old Town, Chinsapo was the home of small-scale traders and vendors, low-ranking civil servants, self-employed service providers, and semiskilled laborers. Their involvement in the moral panic of 2003 was, however, more than a simple reaction to their miseries. A remarkable emphasis on civil virtues coexisted with harrowing impoverishment. Just as Yamikani Chikondi sought to observe proper procedures in the administration of justice, so too did Chinsapo residents pursue their livelihoods in the context of moral considerations. They were not abstract subjects whose victimhood would have justified human rights activists' interventions and intellectual leadership. By the same token, the intellectual challenge also applies to the ethnographic description of Chinsapo residents' situation. While the injustices of their situation were obvious enough, how does the ethnographer find a descriptive language that is not a version of the human rights discourse it interrogates, including its particular idea of freedom?

Bombs of the Poor

"Moral panic" refers, in widespread academic usage, to extraordinary collective actions that seek to counter perceived threats to fundamental values (La Fontaine 1998, 19–21). Mass hysteria or psychosis is not at issue, because the subjects of a moral panic are able to analyze the causes of their distress and are adamant about the values they seek to defend. The class position of those who are gripped by a moral panic is not constant. Whereas the moral panic of 2003 in Malawi tormented the urban poor, South Africa has provided examples of middle-class citizens' moral panic over crime and disorder (see Samara 2005).

The challenge to ethnographic description becomes apparent, as in a host of recent studies from Africa (see especially J. Comaroff and J. L. Comaroff 1999 and Geschiere 1997),[1] when beliefs in witchcraft and the occult are observed as recurring expressions of moral panic. The perceived rise in witchcraft accusations has been related, in this cited literature, to the unevenly distributed profits of neoliberalism, seen as "occult economies," in which some seem capable of gathering inexplicable wealth with the smallest effort. When the chances of the Malawian poor to initiate public debates about their exploitation were preempted by their official status as "partners" in development, few secular or recognizably rational counterdiscourses were at their disposal. However, the academic focus on witchcraft discourses, while welcome as an effort to reach beyond official rhetorics, can create its own virtual reality in which, as studies of the occult multiply, generalizations begin to gloss over the actual range of situations. Not only can beliefs in witchcraft and the occult appear as the most potent, if not the only, popular modes of critique and subversion, but also the variable significance and scope of these beliefs in moral panic may be overlooked. The moral panic of 2003 in Lilongwe arose from entirely rational concerns over the safety and success of schoolchildren. Beliefs in the occult appeared to be of secondary importance, expressed as fears over Satanism among prominent entrepreneurs.[2]

Residents in Lilongwe had long believed that certain entrepreneurs and politicians in the city engaged in Satanic rituals involving the consumption of human body parts. Popular reflections often referred to a particular building in the low-density Area 3, where the most prominent Satanic worshippers were thought to gather. The building was white and windowless, and it had been used by the Freemasons during the colonial era.[3] Ministerial vehicles, along with the cars of Lilongwe's business class of Asian origin, were rumored to have brought people to the building even before the democratic transition. Initiation into the group was thought to involve murder, and a major activity inside the building was said to be the comparison and sale of human body parts. A principal source of these rumors was born-again Christians, even among those who did not belong to Christian churches.[4] In 1999, for example, a letter signed by Lucifer Satan was intercepted by pentecostal pastors in Lilongwe. It contained a reminder to Satanists of forthcoming meetings in the General Assembly Headquarters, understood as the building in Area 3. However, even though such rumors were long-standing and widespread in the city, one would too hastily conclude that the moral panic of 2003 was about Satanism as such. Lilongwe residents understood some abductors and suppliers of body parts to be mere criminals taking orders from high-level authorities, who in turn participated in transnational trade. Insofar as Satanism and the occult appeared in popular discourses during this moral panic, they were related to the new constitutional provision that granted Malawians the freedom of worship (*ufulu wachipembedzo*). This freedom, residents in Chinsapo Township told me, had facilitated Satanism and expanded its networks.

Parents' concerns during this moral panic were less about witchcraft than about trade in human body parts. The concerns appeared to resonate with widespread fear over bodies becoming commodities, items that could be bought and sold in a transnational market (see Sharp 2000; Scheper-Hughes and Wacquant 2002). Studies of these scares elsewhere have demonstrated that illicit trade in human body parts does take place and that, in its particularly insidious form, the organs of healthy poor people in the South have been exported to the North, appropriated to enhance the condition of ailing millionaires. On the other hand, in Malawi as elsewhere in the region, human body parts, particularly the genitals and eyes, have long been thought to provide potent items to witches. Scares over organ thefts can, therefore, draw on a variety of issues, and they need not arise from similar cosmologies of the body. What the rumors in Lilongwe appeared to emphasize was, again, not so much witchcraft as a transnational division of labor. I discuss this view of transnationalism toward the end of this chapter, but it is already worth mentioning that the rumor about the use of Malawians' flesh in rich countries' production of wealth evoked Malawi's historical role as a labor reserve. When the large-scale export of male labor to mines and plantations in southern Africa ended in the 1980s, it had lasted for several decades, making a profound impact on the social life of many areas of Malawi. The highly unequal exchange that underlay this labor migration occasionally raised Malawian concerns over, for example, the theft of their blood.[5] For the participants in the moral panic of 2003, many of whom were too young to have personal experience of labor migration, the rumors expressed the continuing subservient status of Malawi in the world.

The historical resonances of scares over trade in body parts indicate, therefore, that these scares can be more than simple responses to neoliberal injustices. In point of fact, historians and anthropologists have traced the origins of such scares and associated beliefs in the occult much further in history, from extractive labor regimes under late colonialism (White 2000) to the transcontinental slave trade (Shaw 2002). Exact chronologies remain a moot point, established with great difficulty, if at all, because rumors take on new meanings and forms as they travel through history. An illuminating example is the fault that Maia Green (2003) has found with Luise White's account of white Catholic priests and blood stealing in colonial Zambia (White 2000, 175–207). "The origins of tales of blood stealing for sale," Green writes, "lie in the legacy of the slave trade rather than Catholic ritual, hence the widespread association of blood thieves with 'Arabs' as stereotypical representatives of the trade in people" (2003, 73).

The precise history of the rumors inciting the 2003 moral panic is beyond the scope of this book. More pertinent here are two other issues: one, that generally such scares are indeed historical and, two, the ways in which they gripped the imagination of impoverished township dwellers. White's comment that the "generic qualities" of rumors assume efficacy only when they are "locally credible" goes to the heart of the matter (2000, 6, 83). Rumors must be adjusted to particular landscapes and relationships in order to appear plausible. Moreover, once credibility is achieved, rumors cease to inspire contemplation but find their force in the lived experience of those who believe in them. As such, although unscrupulous opposition politicians may manipulate popular discontent by launching such rumors, much more than the mere gullibility of the populace is at issue. Subjective experience under harrowing conditions determined the veracity of these rumors, and authorities found themselves compelled to comment on them. As a "poor man's bomb" (Mbembe 2001), rumor contested official discourses and had the potential of affecting the conduct of those who wielded political, economic, and spiritual power (see Ellis 1993; Ellis and ter Haar 2004).

In Malawi at the turn of the millennium, the thefts of body parts and human blood appeared to occur with alarming frequency. The reaction of the United Democratic Front was to deny ruling politicians' involvement in this trade and to issue warnings through the state media that anyone found spreading such rumors would be arrested. As in White's study of colonial Africa, "published denunciations of rumor were often thought to prove its truth" (2000, 57). Far from extinguishing the flames of popular discontent, the official denunciations, especially when broadcast on the national radio, only served to circulate elements of the rumors to even wider audiences. Human rights NGOs, in turn, demonstrated their detachment from popular concerns either by failing to consider the cases at all or by condemning the outbursts of violence as "mob justice." While also keen to condemn mob justice, the mass media were somewhat more attuned to popular discourses. Articles about the abuse of children by witches in both Malawi and other African countries were published by *The Nation*, Malawi's biggest daily, when the moral panic rocked Lilongwe.[6] The same period also witnessed letters to the editor demanding a "witchcraft law," which would assist in prosecuting witches rather than merely proscribing witchcraft accusations.[7] Although the vast majority of residents in Chinsapo Township could not afford to buy newspapers, their stories were widely known and discussed. Many township dwellers visited the city every day and came back with accounts of what the newspapers had said.

The events and rumors that culminated in the moral panic of 2003 were preceded by several incidents that, while not directly linked to the predicament of schoolchildren in Lilongwe, influenced their parents' sense of impending tragedies. Toward the end of the 1990s, Chiradzulu, a rural district in southern Malawi, was the scene for brutal attacks on women. At least twenty women were killed, their corpses – usually without genitals, eyes, breasts – found near roads, flimsily hidden in the bush. Popular rumors in Lilongwe claimed that Gwanda Chakuamba, then the leader of the Malawi Congress Party, had implicated the UDF in these hideous crimes, promptly countered by Muluzi's visit to the area and his efforts to console the bereaved at the Sanjika Palace. UDF officials became the targets of direct assaults soon afterward, when the famine of 2001–2 devastated many areas in the country. The government was believed to receive relief maize in return for its citizens' blood. Victims emerged to tell terrifying tales of nocturnal attacks by unknown blood suckers, and local leaders of the UDF were beaten in some areas. This crisis occasioned the official denouncements mentioned above.

These dramatic incidents were only the most high-profile disturbances in a series of events. Locally known entrepreneurs who owned refrigerators became particularly vulnerable to popular suspicions and rumors. A number of related rumors in Malawi's urban centers suggested that fridges were used to store human body parts. In one case in Blantyre, for example, the house of a businessman and his family was attacked by angry residents in the city's Zingwangwa Township. Rumors claimed that he was in possession of seven human heads and other body parts and that he was personally responsible for killing people, particularly children, in order to sell their organs. When the angry crowd started to pelt stones at the house, swearing to kill the businessman if found, the police arrived to protect his house and property.

Two aspects of the police's behavior were reported to have intensified the crowd's fury.[8] First, the businessman was thought to have been arrested earlier, but the police had released him on bail. How could, members of the crowd asked the reporters, a murderer be allowed to return home? Second, the crowd's observations would have seemed sarcastic if they had not touched on the very core of insecurity and injustice in the township. Whenever the poor majority had reported cases of theft and other crimes to the police, people in the crowd said, the police had explained their inertia as a result of their lack of vehicles. Now that a prominent businessman came under attack, the police suddenly appeared with vehicles and in force.

Distrust of the police was also common in Lilongwe, and the ownership of refrigerators was also a key issue in the rumors there. One notable case implicated the founder of the Miracle Church of God, a pentecostal preacher who had also gained some popularity as a singer. This man of God shocked the capital by becoming embroiled in a scandal in which human body parts were said to have been stored in his fridge. When he emerged to protest his innocence on the national radio, popular opinion began to entertain the possibility that the real culprit was the preacher's second-in-command, who had taken advantage of his leader's fridge. In the meantime, incidents involving schoolchildren appeared to multiply. A ten-year-old girl, who had been on her way to the Assemblies of God church in her neighborhood in a high-density area in Lilongwe, disappeared, her abused corpse subsequently found in Lilongwe River. Another girl also disappeared from her residential area and was later found in a different area several miles away. Crying and confused, the girl refused to talk about her ordeal. A common explanation suggested that her abductors had pitied her and decided to abandon her. Even schools were seen to be unsafe when, at the end of September 2003, a large tree suddenly fell and crushed the young primary school pupils studying under it. This fatal accident prompted popular reflections on the government's failure to construct enough school buildings, leaving children to learn outdoors. The impending moral panic gained momentum from this perceived lack of order and safety in schools, with children coming under threat not only from old trees but also from abductors.

The Conditions of a Moral Panic

Mphekesera, the Chichewa word for "rumors" or unverified stories, did not appear in Chinsapo residents' reflections on the above-mentioned incidents. The incidents were considered news (*nkhani*), something that had happened (*zimene zidachitika*), amply verified by eyewitness testimony, even if heard through second- or thirdhand sources. After all, women actually had been found mutilated and killed in Chiradzulu, and the abused corpse of a schoolgirl had been sighted in Lilongwe River. The other stories contributed to a popular understanding of a pattern, to a gradual realization of the horrifying circumstances of poor people in general coming under attack. The stories were more than mere stories – they condensed aspects of commonly felt threats and crises. It is, therefore, essential to reach beyond the stories to the conditions that made them appear compelling to many Chinsapo residents. Understanding those conditions brings us one step closer to understanding the limited relevance of Malawi's human rights discourse.

The township offers a wide range of schools, but most of them are privately owned, following liberalization in Muluzi's Malawi. As elsewhere in Malawi, it soon became apparent that insufficient mechanisms were in place to monitor the quality of education in these private institutions, many operating without an official license and overcharging for their teaching. Some private schools did have a policy of recruiting teachers with diplomas or degrees, thus contributing to the lack of qualified teaching staff in government schools. The prospect of having a five- to tenfold increase in salary was irresistible to teachers in government primary schools, who earned well under two thousand kwacha (twenty US dollars) per month in 2003.[9] Teachers' public image was not improved by the scandals and rumors that implicated them, which involved incidents ranging from teachers having written exams on behalf of students for a fee to sexual misconduct, as publicized in, among other venues, the popular news program *Nkhani za m'maboma* (News from the Districts) on the national radio.

Such incidents and the rumors they helped to stimulate did little justice to the many committed teachers who continued to pursue their vocation under difficult circumstances. Government schools were virtual megaschools in Chinsapo, in which the majority of children came from families unable to pay for private education. The largest primary school in the township was a source of pride to both its political and its "traditional" leaders. Funded by the World Bank, the United Nations Children's Fund had supervised the construction of several buildings equipped with electricity and enclosed by a brick wall. It would have been a triumph of development, an oasis of education amid searing poverty, if the school had not been rendered inadequate as soon as it was completed. Some seven thousand pupils studied there at the turn of the millennium, their number far exceeding what some sixty teachers could possibly manage. The number of teachers had been almost halved, through deaths and resignations, since the new premises were inaugurated in 1998. Yet the number of classes continued to grow, because in the following year the school assumed the status of a full primary school offering eight grades, known as standards in Malawi. During the first standards, one lone teacher would face a class of some three hundred pupils. Worse still, despite the imposing new buildings, only a minority of classes could be accommodated in them. All pupils from the first through the sixth standards studied outside, sitting on the ground under trees or, if all shaded space had been taken, under the scorching sun. Whether the children remained seated was, of course, often beyond any teacher's control. The school, praised by UDF politicians when they held their meetings there on the weekends, was reduced to a scene of pandemonium during the school hours.

It was painfully clear to most parents that their children appeared to learn nothing in a school like Chinsapo Full Primary School. Many parents complained to me that children "only played" (*amangosewera*) at school and failed to read and write properly even after several years of schooling. Added to these frustrations over academic performance – and to the crushed expectations of personal advancement through education – was the popular understanding of the township's schools as sites of criminal activities. Not only were many private schools established by dubious entrepreneurs, operating without an official permission, but also government schools were deprived of their scarce resources by thefts, sometimes perpetrated by their own members of staff. The new primary school lost large amounts of donated exercise books and other learning materials when its teachers allegedly sold them to private schools. The new buildings also attracted armed burglars, who either overpowered the school's unarmed guards or, as rumors suggested, were actively assisted by them. More learning materials were thereby lost, together with other items that could be removed, including the main switch for electricity. Despite the efforts of some church-based and humanitarian well-wishers to replace these lost items, burglars kept coming back to steal the main switch, leaving the school without electricity for long periods of time.

These dismal material conditions and illegitimate activities had created the conditions for a moral panic when rumors suggested the arrival of more insidious criminals. One remarkable feature of these rumors was that they consistently focused on the low-income, high-density areas of the capital, with parents, pupils, and teachers in Kawale, Chilinde, Mchesi, Area 24, Area 23, and Area 22 becoming gripped by fears similar to those of their counterparts in Chinsapo. In Area 24, pupils fled their school in panic when the word spread that strangers had entered the school to abduct children.[10] Their parents were quick to come on the scene, and they searched the school for remaining children. In Chinsapo as in many other areas, the moral panic involved confrontations between parents and the school management. When the rumors of abductions were at their height, a group of parents stormed into a headmaster's office in Chinsapo. They demanded greater security at school, achieved, among other measures, through a policy of releasing children only to those whom they recognized as their parents or guardians. Pupils were also expected to be escorted by these parents and guardians between home and school.

I observed that teachers were often quite as distraught as parents when the rumors about abductions and the sale of human body parts circulated in the capital. The focus of these rumors on the schools could only increase teachers' personal sense of failure. Not only had the conditions for academic achievement been ruined, but also teachers were powerless when their students' lives came to be at risk. As a consequence, some parents withdrew their children from school. I also witnessed parents in Chinsapo instructing their children to shun strangers, particularly those who attempted to persuade children to go into their cars. Chinsapo parents often pointed out that, because they did not know anyone who had a car, their children should not trust such strangers.

It was, in the end, these private instructions that appeared more efficient than the measures the school management could devise in collaboration with parents' representatives and local leaders in school committees. The resolutions at these meetings ranged from the provision of escort services to the recruitment of additional guards to the issuing of identity cards, all rather substantial initiatives beyond the actual means of government schools. Local UDF leaders and Chinsapo's headmen were eager to represent the threat of abductions as an isolated and passing danger, probably committed by an ill-defined gang of marijuana (*chamba*) smokers. Yet they could not distract the popular attention from the lived reality of primary education, offered free of charge by the Muluzi administration but woefully inadequate to equip children with knowledge and skills. It was as if the rumors about life-threatening abductions gave a form to grievances, which had intensified over the years since the democratic transition.

From Injustice to Mob Justice

The moral panic in 2003 inevitably extended the popular attention from the management of schools to the conduct of other authorities. Although Chinsapo's headmen settled disputes involving both "those who were born" (*obadwa*) and "those who had arrived" (*obwera*) in the township, their jurisdiction did not encompass criminal offenses. The rumors about trade in human body parts brought into focus what the police did in response to them. As was seen above in the case of popular uproar in Blantyre's Zingwangwa Township, the alleged atrocities by an evil businessman created a context for remembering how inaction by the police had often obstructed the pursuit of justice in the township. The arrival of police officers to protect the house and property of this businessman appeared to confirm their complicity in crime. The crowd resorted to direct action in order to punish the businessman, a mode of intervention condemned by the police, the media, and human rights NGOs alike as "mob justice."

The incidents of violence against wealthy and powerful individuals unleashed by otherwise docile subjects raise the question of the full extent of grievances that this moral panic evoked. Chinsapo residents also had ample reason to doubt the integrity of the police force when the rumors about abducted schoolchildren and trade in body parts provoked their moral panic. Again, eyewitness testimony and personal experience played a part in launching rumors. A major incident in Chinsapo involved the realization that a prominent shopkeeper appeared to be a participant in the trade in human body parts. He was one of those few individuals who had been able to make full use of electricity by buying a refrigerator for his store. When township residents were becoming increasingly alarmed by child abductors, burglars broke into his store at night. They wanted to take the fridge, but it was too heavy to be carried very far. Assuming that the fridge was full of beer, the burglars opened it to remove the drinks, only to be shocked to find it packed with human body parts. Horrified by their finding, the burglars forgot their own criminal pursuit and rushed to the police. The police came to inspect the fridge at dawn, the township already bustling with life. Their vehicle attracted considerable attention, and a large crowd witnessed the police driving away with the fridge and its owner. Both returned the next day, with the police issuing a warning against "mob justice." Anyone found inciting hatred against the shopkeeper, the police proclaimed, would be arrested – the man was innocent.

Because the information offered by the police was as implausible as it was minimal, rumors quickly answered the popular demand for explanations. According to rumor, the reason the police denied that anything criminal had taken place, not only in this case but in *every* case, was that the highest political authorities in the country were implicated. Rumor explained that when abductors and traders in human body parts had been taken to a police station, they had pointed out that they were not working alone. After the suspects named the cabinet ministers for whom they had acquired human body parts, the police had allegedly called these ministers to ascertain the veracity of the claims. The cabinet ministers, in turn, had explained that they themselves had received orders from their *bwana*, President Muluzi. The ministers had directed the police to release the detainees and to issue denials that anything criminal was at issue.

The plausibility of such rumors derived from the reality of township dwellers' situation. The frustrations and fears over schools were the immediate reasons for the speed with which rumors about high-profile perpetrators of trade in body parts assumed currency in the township. Yet, so too had township dwellers' trust in the police evaporated over a long period of time. The police force, one of the clenched fists of the one-party state, had gained little popular credibility after the democratic transition. Township dwellers considered both the police and the army corrupt, and both were seen to collaborate with criminals. Armed criminals acquired their guns from these apparent custodians of law and order, the deal stipulating that the owners of the weapons were entitled to a share in the loot. Thieves who had not struck a deal with the police could buy their way back to freedom by giving them the money they had stolen. Such rumors were consistent with what some township dwellers were able to witness in the city. Roaming the streets as hawkers, they had ample opportunity to observe how uniformed police officers collected bribes from known criminals in backstreets. The most distressing, if not absurd, practice was familiar to any township dweller who had attempted to deliver a thief to a police station. If they wanted the culprit to stay for investigation, the police had told them, they had to provide food. There could hardly be a more potent example of the injustice of the formal justice system from the point of view of impoverished township dwellers. What was the purpose of catching a thief, I was often asked, if one was obliged to forget food shortages in one's own house and give the thief a bag of maize?

Under these circumstances, the notion of mob justice would seem to obscure impoverished Malawians' grievances. The police, journalists, and human rights NGOs deployed the notion with little regard to the actual conditions in which people were expected to trust the police. The condemnations of mob justice viewed the poor through the usual elitist lenses as ignorant and impulsive masses, all too eager to commit murders if not restrained by civic education. Not only did such views bypass the question of why poor Malawians distrusted the police; they also assumed that popular modes of delivering justice were brutal and, in a word, unjustified. Excessive violence was certainly the fate of many captured thieves and other criminals in the townships and villages of Malawi, but vigilante groups in many villages and townships were overseen by locally elected committees. In Chinsapo as in many other locations, such a group was known as Inkatha, its name evoking the ferocious warriorhood of South African Zulus. Armed with clubs, the men representing Inkatha patrolled the township especially at night, interrogating those who were found outdoors at unusual hours. Like other vigilantes, Inkatha trod a tightrope in seeking to keep violence against potentially violent offenders to a minimum. The task was to bring these offenders before a committee of elders, often led by a headman, who decided on the punishment. Rather than permitting violence, Inkatha committees often made offenders perform work for those who had been their victims. Crop thefts, for example, were compensated by work in the victim's garden.[11]

The recommendations proposed in the media and the civic-education materials of NGOs, by contrast, began from the assumption that the police and formal courts delivered justice. An editorial commenting on the above-mentioned incident in Blantyre's Zingwangwa Township reprimanded people for damaging the house of the accused.[12] While admitting that murder and trade in body parts were serious offenses that made people's anger understandable, the editorial insisted that the police were not to be faulted: "The problem is not the police, they are following the laws of this country" (*Vuto si la apolisi koma nawo akutsatira malamulo a dziko lino*). The police had, the editorial pointed out, released the suspect on bail because of a law that granted this provision, and it reminded the readers that passing judgment was the task of neither Zingwangwa residents nor newspapers but of a court of law. Yet the author of the editorial was only too pleased to present the case from a particular point of view. The very reason for popular uproar was questioned when the editorial expressed doubt that enough evidence existed to prove that anyone had actually gone missing in the township. In language that was likely to sound offensive to Zingwangwa residents, the editorial referred to the issue as *mphekesera* (rumor, hearsay) and *nkhambakamwa* (chatter).

The editorial is only one example of the way in which journalists and human rights activists were unable to distinguish between different modes and rationales of so-called mob justice. The Centre for Human Rights and Rehabilitation, a provider of legal aid, was at the forefront of spreading civic education that demanded the public's compliance with the orders of the police. Its audio tape made with the popular comedians Izeki and Jacob, for example, included an episode entitled "Ufulu wokhala ndi moyo" (Freedom to Be Alive).[13] In the episode, two men who had participated in burning a thief were rebuked by a better-informed citizen. She condemned the men's action and stressed that such cases should be determined "only in a court of law" (pokhapokha pabwalo la khoti). She presented the procedure of taking a criminal to the court as a straightforward matter of "simply catching him or her and going with him or her to the police" (kungomugwira ndi kupita naye kupolisi). In a similar vein, the CHRR's leaflet on mob justice, entitled Kulanga kwa mchigulu (To Punish through a Mob), insisted that only courts had the right to deliver justice.[14] Those who took the law into their own hands must themselves be deposited at the police. "The police make sure that such people are taken to the court quickly so that they are tried and given a punishment if they are found guilty" (Apolisi awonetsetsa kuti anthu amenewa atengeredwe kukhoti mwansangansanga kuti akaweruzidwe ndi kupatsidwa chilango ngati atapezeka olakwa).

The gap between such messages of civic education and the reality of the situation described earlier does not stem from dissimilar ideas of justice. Taking someone's life is always a serious matter among Malawians who despise the world of crime. The moral panic over human body parts would hardly have sparked widespread anxiety if murder were not considered an atrocity. The discrepancy between activists' civic education and popular views was, rather, produced by the former's refusal to take the actual circumstances of impoverishment and disempowerment as a point of departure. The discrepancy was paradoxical insofar as human rights NGOs, including the CHRR, had criticized the police for their partisan approach in investigating cases of political violence. Toward the end of Muluzi's regime, the police looked the other way on several occasions when the UDF's youth wing, the Young Democrats, had descended on Muluzi's critics, such as the clergy and supporters of the opposition (see Englund 2002a). The executive officers of the CHRR were invariably outspoken in their condemnation of political bias among the police, and they were among the most prominent activists demanding the resignation of the inspector general of the police after the 2004 general elections. Yet it was precisely this focus on high-profile political cases that made activists deaf to the actual expressions of insecurity among the rural and urban poor. Much as the CHRR contributed to democracy by publicly condemning the police for turning a blind eye to the violence of the UDF's Young Democrats, its civic education represented the police as the unproblematic custodians of law and order.

In other words, while activists were fully aware of problems in the police force, their civic education proceeded from the assumption that the police could be entrusted with the investigation of the cases in which poor Malawians had been the victims. Witnesses to the bias of the police toward the rich and the powerful, who sometimes doubled as the masterminds behind crime, ordinary Malawians had learned to expect little justice from the institutions promoted by civic educators. Crippled, in turn, by their elitist assumption that the poor were prone to violence and easily excitable, civic educators were unable to listen properly to popular grievances. As such, those grievances were likely to be given little attention in the reform of justice delivery in Malawi.[15]

Trust in an Immoral Economy

Human rights activism is hardly an obvious instrument in policing the poor. By sharing the same discourse on mob justice with the police, however, some human rights activists in democratic Malawi became agents of the neoliberal order, one of the media through which popular grievances were actually erased from public discourse. It is plausible to assume that moral panics are at least partly provoked by this lack of recognition for the lived experience in actual situations. Yet a focus on moral panics may also obscure that very experience by representing extraordinary events as typical instances of people's tribulations. Distrust of the police, political leaders, and some entrepreneurs was certainly palpable during Chinsapo residents' moral panic in 2003, but distrust could not be their only reality. Along with distrust existed trust, a necessary feature of their precarious livelihoods. If the notion of trust acquires meaning only in relation to risk (see Gambetta 1988), then Chinsapo residents' daily pursuits of money and food provide perfect illustrations of this general condition. Smallscale traders and vendors, making up some 50 percent of Chinsapo's adult population (see Englund 2002b), were particularly vulnerable to fluctuations in incomes and obliged to offer goods on credit in order to cultivate their essential relationships with customers. Under such circumstances, the civil virtues of trust, courtesy, and patience were constitutive of successful entrepreneurship. It is against the background of such civil virtues that the eruptions of so-called mob justice must be understood, occasioned by an economy that, despite all the trust it appeared to demand of its participants, was never quite as moral as those virtues seemed to promise.

The moral panic of 2003 resonated not only with Malawians' historical experiences of selling their labor to companies in other countries, as mentioned, but also with contemporary changes in their livelihoods. The liberalization of the economy flooded the streets of urban centers with vendors and hawkers selling imported or smuggled goods and local foodstuffs. It was only appropriate that nightmarish rumors drew on the idioms of vending. The primary suppliers of human body parts were said to receive "orders" from more prominent entrepreneurs in this sinister commerce, "order" spoken of with the same term, *odala*, used in all vending. Vendors "ordered" their goods from wholesalers, and just as the trade in body parts involved entrepreneurs with highly disparate means, so too was street vending embedded in strikingly unequal economic relations. Secondhand clothes, for example, arrived in Malawi in large shipments, which were sold in bales to traders of various means.[16] The sizes of the bales decreased from bundles of hundreds of clothes, often acquired by entrepreneurs of Asian origin, to half a dozen items that the poorest vendors were able to "order" at any one time. Instead of being entitled even to enter the stores of Asian entrepreneurs, most vendors from Chinsapo had to deal with Malawian middlemen, who had bought bales of clothes and acted as wholesalers in their own right. The larger the initial capital, the greater the profits, with better-off vendors having the privilege to choose items from bales before their poorer peers could. The cycle of poverty thus continued, the poorest vendors selling the cheapest and least desirable clothes.

The issue of credit discloses in a particularly vivid fashion the vicissitudes of trust in an immoral economy. As was seen in chapter 4, microcredits were as generously promised by politicians in democratic Malawi as they were desired by the poor. They became, however, accessible on a much smaller scale than what the neoliberal rhetoric of private entrepreneurship had led many to expect. The vast majority of vendors and hawkers who lived in Chinsapo at the turn of the millennium had never obtained credit from formal financial institutions. At the same time, credit or "debt" (*ngongole*) was critical to the relations of trust underlying their livelihoods. At one extreme were the above-mentioned wholesalers who would not enter into debt relations with vendors who were short of money. Anyone who wished to purchase items from wholesalers had to pay cash. Vendors' access to goods reflected, therefore, the lack of trust they inspired among wholesalers, whether Malawians or Asians. At another extreme, vendors were forced to accommodate considerable uncertainty in their business because of customers who defaulted on agreed credit. Among the dozen vendors I came to know particularly well in Chinsapo, about half of their monthly income derived from payments on credit that their customers had requested, often several weeks earlier. Especially toward the end of the month before salaries were paid in civil service, the largest employer in Malawi, cash transactions were exceptional.

Considerable time in vendors' work, in other words, went into efforts to persuade their debtors to pay back their loans. Different goods entailed, of course, different kinds of relationships, with the vendors of foodstuffs, particularly those who delivered their goods to customers' homes, often developing rapport with their customers. The capacity to make conversation, "to chat" (*kucheza*), was virtually more important than the consistency in the supply and quality of goods. The vendor had little choice but to appear cheerful even when his or her customer defaulted on credit. For their part, some of these "customers" (*makastomala*) – a specific status that was earned through loyal cooperation with the same vendor – complained to me that they had to tolerate occasional poor quality in order to enjoy the privileges this status provided. Not only could they count on receiving items on credit, an unthinkable option in the city's largest stores, but also they were often treated to discounts or small amounts of free goods, known as *price* that the vendor added after an agreement on a purchase had been reached.

Trust thus joined persons with very different standings in the overall economy. Work in the office, associated with appropriate status symbols as described previously, could not completely alienate the salaried class from the poorest echelons of the neoliberal economy. Civil servants' salaries, although paid fairly regularly, were often too low to last until the end of the month, and credit arrangements had to be negotiated with vendors, service providers, and more affluent relatives and friends. The relationships of trust varied in the extent to which people of different economic means contributed to one another's lives. Many vendors retained some influence over their regular customers by granting them credit, patiently maintaining a façade of compassion when the payment of a debt was delayed. When some vendors discovered that their customers were their ethnic compatriots or members of the same church, for example, the relationship could begin to cater to other aspects of their mutual welfare. In such cases, it was not uncommon for the customer to assist the vendor when a funeral or illness occurred in the latter's household. These gestures were usually the customer's prerogative, however, which bespoke an entrenched discrepancy even in the most trusted relationships. Much as a vendor could apply moral pressure to make a customer stay loyal to him or her, in the end it was the customer who was understood by both parties to have access to regular income and the benefits it entailed. Seemingly trivial incidents in the customer's personal finances, such as unforeseen expenditures or even a simple failure to withdraw money from the bank on a particular day, could seriously affect the vendor's livelihood. I witnessed cases in which vendors awaited the payment of debts until they had depleted both their food supplies at home and their capital to start another cycle of vending. It was usually futile for a vendor to plead with his or her customer under such circumstances. A penniless customer was rarely prepared to take on another debt to settle his or her accounts with a vendor.

It may be assumed that food vendors were particularly vulnerable to the whims of their customers. As vendors of perishable goods, they had to dispose of their merchandise even when prompt payments were not forthcoming. Yet the vending of goods such as secondhand clothes was no less detached from the vicissitudes of trust. While some vendors could enter into credit arrangements with customers they met in the streets, many had to look actively for customers in offices and companies where salaried people worked. Access to the markets that these sites represented involved intricate negotiations. Vendors' first challenge was often to find their way past the security guards that most offices and companies in the city deployed at their gates and their front doors. Whether an outright bribe, a discount on goods, or a simple friendly greeting was needed varied enormously. Another hurdle awaited inside these institutions, with low-ranking office personnel often jealously guarding their own access to those with higher status and better purchasing power. In many cases, vendors had to enter into agreements whereby someone in the office took the responsibility for the actual trade. Hospitals, for example, were highly desired locations for vending, because the potential clientele included not only the adminis-trative and medical personnel but also patients and their guardians. Nurses or low-ranking administrators who sold goods on vendors' behalf required a share of the money these goods generated and the privilege to buy them at a lower price than what vendors demanded from others. Just as the relationship between a food vendor and a customer could involve expressions of concern for their mutual welfare, so too was it possible for relationships between vendors and office workers to produce long-term rapport, with vendors addressed as "brothers" (achimwene) by their business partners. Yet crises revealed, once again, the precarious position that vendors occupied in the economy. Their salaried partners could violate the agreed principles without vendors having a proper channel to settle the disputes, or their partners could abruptly lose interest in trading or be warned by their superiors against engaging in such practices. It was invariably the vendor who stood the greatest risk of losing his income.

Lest this predicament be seen as a "good-faith economy," which, according to Pierre Bourdieu, is one that devotes "as much time to concealing the reality of economic acts as it expends in carrying them out" (1977, 172), it is important to emphasize the imperatives of trust. Although money was often as scarce as it was needed, credit arrangements indicated that the monetary side of trust did not exhaust the moral considerations involved. Rather than seeking to conceal their self-interest, participants in this economy came to develop the quality of their relationship as the very foundation of their economic transactions. Jane Guyer (2004, 92) has usefully pointed out that the quality of goods also needs to be trusted when credit is negotiated. As my account has suggested, however, vendors were not always in control of the quality of the goods they obtained from wholesalers or local food producers, and their customers sometimes needed to endure con-siderable variation in quality. In this instance, quality inhered in relationships rather than in goods, with various appeals to moral considerations keeping the transaction alive despite obvious deficiencies both in goods and in customers' credit worthiness. More broadly, vendors and customers did not approach their transactions as mutually independent individuals. Both had something to gain from a relationship that evoked, among other things, kinship, ethnic, or religious affiliations and at the same time provided money and goods. As Marcel Mauss (1954) observed long ago, it is only under particular conditions that the distinction between interested and disinterested action becomes absolute. Contemporary Malawians are among the vast majority who cannot afford to alienate themselves from the moral considerations that relationships entail.

The significance of trust and debt indicates the sense of freedom under these circumstances. Subjects' potential to exercise freedom was predicated on a range of deliberate dependencies. Rather than being a necessary evil in this economy, debt was actively desired. After all, debt signified trust for both sides of the transaction, a continuing relationship in an economy of ever-present uncertainties and sudden personal bankruptcies. The contrast to the human rights discourse preferred by Malawian activists is clear. Persons sought to make their mutual dependence explicit as the ground on which transactions were built. They did not claim their dues as rights or *individual* freedoms, as if their transactions could be sustained by mutual strangers. Instead, debt generated relationships in which people owed one another not only money and goods but also the morally binding pledge to stay loyal to the relationship. The situations of conflict mentioned above emerged not so much from self-interest as from the economy remaining profoundly unequal. Too constrained to create wealth among the majority, whether salaried or self-employed, the Malawian economy constantly pushed its subjects to encounter the limits of their moral considerations. Trust was a precarious achievement, and petty traders were often the first casualties when it vanished.

Popular Perspectives on Transnational Governance

The moral dimensions of Chinsapo residents' livelihoods serve to remind us of the discursive resources in which rumors about trade in body parts came to capture their imagination. Seeking to cultivate civil virtues against considerable odds, township dwellers were horrified by the total inversion of their trading practices. "Mob justice" was, therefore, a sign of a moral panic, a consequence of a perceived assault on fundamental values. Yet the moral panic of 2003 resonated not only with the predicaments of petty trade but also with the popular understandings of Malawi's place in the world. As mentioned, rumors about blood thieves during the 2001–2 famine had suggested that the Malawi government received relief maize in exchange for its citizens' blood. The moral panic of 2003 indicated similar concerns with transnational exchange that exploited ordinary Malawians. It provided not only an explanation for the infinite riches of Muluzi and his cronies and the searing poverty of their subjects – the body parts of the poor, sold by Muluzi, were the raw material for rich countries' production of wealth – but also a basis for understanding the breathtaking affluence of "Indians" (*amwenye*) and "whites" (*azungu*), though this affluence was hardly made more acceptable.

The notion of transnational governance, in other words, finds some equivalence among popular Malawian discourses on the unequal world. Moreover, just as the rumor about trade in body parts evoked far-reaching historical and contemporary parallels, so too was its perspective on unequal transnational exchange merely an extreme version of other popular discourses on the subject. After the transition in the early 1990s, Muluzi's Muslim identity aroused suspicions, particularly among

Christians. Although only about 12 percent of Malawians were Muslims, usually associated with the Yao ethnic identity, rumors about Muluzi's desire to turn Malawi into an Islamic state had emerged soon after his ascension to power. They became particularly intense during the run-up to the 1999 parliamentary and presidential elections. The fears these rumors caused were manipulated by opposition politicians, who insisted on the need to have a Christian president in a country where the majority was Christian. The 2004 elections, in which Muluzi's chosen heir was a Catholic, were also preceded by similar arguments, fueled by a common belief that Muluzi would continue to rule the country behind the scenes. His choice of Cassim Chilumpha, an apparently devout Muslim, as the vice president only seemed to lend credence to the rumors about Islamization.

Muluzi usually played down his religious affiliation in public life, preferring greed to creed, but Malawians found evidence for impending Islamization in the arrival of new entrepreneurs from the Middle East and North Africa, in the building of new mosques across the country, and in Muluzi's fraternization with the Libyan leader Colonel Muammar Gaddafi. These developments, coupled with the arrival of Islamic charities handing out food and goods and the urban-based businesses of Lebanese entrepreneurs, often as exploitative as those of Indian and Pakistani merchants who had begun to arrive in Malawi during the colonial period, were taken to be signs of profound changes in Malawi's religious, political, and economic landscape. Perhaps the most disconcerting rumor was the one that circulated before the 1999 elections. Muluzi had allegedly sold Malawi for nine hundred million kwacha to Gaddafi, who would build oil rigs in Lake Malawi after the elections and close churches in order to build mosques in their stead. In 2002, Malawians witnessed a spectacle of Gaddafi's power. In response to his visit to Malawi, Muluzi vacated the official presidential residence in Lilongwe and moved to a hotel; the presidential residence was taken over by Gaddafi and his entourage. A more poignant example of Malawi's subservient role in world politics and economy was barely imaginable.

Whites (*azungu*), Malawi's more traditional donors, were shown equal deference by Muluzi and his cabinet ministers. Although Muluzi would occasionally assert the independent status of Malawi in a thinly veiled reference to some donor representatives' criticism, he eagerly seized on any remark or report that could be interpreted as an endorsement of his government by the *azungu*. An analysis of Malawi's forthcoming elections published in *The Economist* in 2003 predicted victory for the UDF. Muluzi made the UDF's publicity secretary read aloud an extract from the analysis at a political rally.[17] Muluzi then asked the crowd, in a triumphant voice, to tell everyone that "whites in England" (*azungu a ku Mangalande*) were saying that the UDF would win the elections. For the disillusioned majority in Chinsapo Township, such declarations could only deepen the suspicions of complicity between their national leaders and foreign agencies. If the *azungu* already knew that the UDF was going to win the elections, I heard Chinsapo residents discussing, did it not indicate their vested interests in the regime? Access to money was the long and the short of it, Chinsapo residents thought, sharing some of ruling politicians' ambivalence over foreign power. The wealth of the *azungu* was understood to be spectacular enough to attract anyone to them, including the poorest Christian congregations in Chinsapo (see Englund 2001). Yet Chinsapo residents also understood themselves to be doomed to witness the *azungu* from a distance, separated by language, lifestyle, and virtually inconceivable disparities in opportunity. Employment as the domestic servants of *azungu* rarely bridged the gap and, on the contrary, often gave the poor only more imaginative resources to make it even wider. Only those who ran the government could enjoy unmitigated access to the *azungu*, sometimes acting as their partners in sinister businesses.

Popular perspectives on transnational governance provide yet another example of how implausible the discourse of human rights activists could be from the viewpoint of impoverished Malawians. Activists' exhortations of participation located, as discussed in chapter 4, the subjects of development and democracy in individual persons or in the immediate communities where they lived. The freedoms and responsibilities of the new era were primarily attributes of individuals, the poorest of whom were deemed by activists to need civic education in order to harness the new potentials. During the first ten years of democracy in Malawi, activists' high-profile interventions in the media were not more attuned to realities beyond Malawi. Despite their own location in various transnational networks, activists portrayed the Malawi government as an independent actor, surely account-able to foreign donors but nevertheless a sovereign entity. In line with their general indifference toward economic issues, activists seldom paused to reflect on the extent to which problems in Malawi's democracy had to be understood from a trans-national perspective. In this regard, the popular perspectives described here were somewhat more enlightened, despite the moral panic that their most extreme forms incited. The alternative sense of freedom that also emerged in this essay may likewise be more compatible with Chinsapo residents' situation of human rights than with the abstractions informing activists' interventions. When the potential to exercise freedom is understood to depend on relationships with others, the objectification of the poor as ignorant masses, their redemption prompted by tacit contempt, becomes much less plausible.

NOTES

1   For an excellent review of the new and earlier anthropology of African witchcraft, see Moore and Sanders 2001.
2   By seeking to highlight the rationality of this moral panic, at least as far as its initial troubles were concerned, I do not mean to dismiss witchcraft as irrational. The rationality and irrationality of witchcraft beliefs have preoccupied anthropologists and philosophers since E. E. Evans-Pritchard's 1937 classic work. Posed as questions of relativist and universal reason, however, philosophical inquiries have often been circumscribed by a certain "elitism of doubt" (Fields 2001, 310). An ethnographic approach, by contrast, may take us beyond the problems of reason altogether, because it shows how beliefs are embedded in practical activities (see Kapferer 2002).
3   Although Freemasonry seems to have disappeared from Malawi during the postcolonial era, it is noteworthy that Kamuzu Banda took part in it during his many years abroad (Short 1974). During Banda's regime, the freedom of worship extended only to those denomin-ations and individuals who did not voice criticism of the regime. Jehovah's Witnesses faced particularly severe persecution because of their lack of allegiance to the state. Banda's relation to Freemasonry and its status in postcolonial Malawi were among the many issues that could not be discussed openly during his rule. It appears that Lilongwe residents found ways of breaking the silence by associating the Freemasons' building with Satanism. Compare also President Bongo in Gabon, who is reported to have been initiated into Freemasonry in the city and into an occult cult in the village (Geschiere 1997, 254).
4   For born-again Christians in Africa, particularly those who worship in various pentecostal and charismatic churches, the figure of Satan is virtually as important as Christ and God (see, e.g., Englund 2004 and Meyer 1999).

5 Many elderly men, former labor migrants to South Africa, have described to me their suspicions when authorities in the mines forced them to donate blood. The issue of blood tests also contributed to the Malawi government's decision to stop large-scale labor migration, because South African authorities were seen to make unreasonable demands in testing Malawians' blood for HIV.

6 See, for example, "Church Saves Children from Witchcraft Practice," *The Nation*, October 17, 2003; and "Witchcraft Rocking Societies as Children Are Targeted," *The Nation*, October 21, 2003. A story obtained from the news agency Reuters had an atypical headline: "Superstition Fuels Reports of Child Witches," *The Nation*, November 3, 2003.

7 See, for example, "Witchcraft Law Needed," *The Nation*, October 3, 2003; "In Support of Law on Witchcraft," *The Nation*, October 17, 2003. For a sympathetic, if essentialist, attempt to reconcile "African witchcraft" and "Western law," see Hund 2004.

8 See "Mitu ya anthu akufa iyambitsa phokoso," *Tikambe Supplement to Malawi News*, December 6–12, 2003.

9 The exchange rate became increasingly unfavorable to Malawi kwacha during 2001–4.

10 The incident was reported in the biggest daily along with the disappearance of one of the above-mentioned schoolgirls: "The Story of Josephine," *The Nation*, October 22, 2003.

11 Chinsapo's Inkatha was in the domain of headmen and avoided direct influence from political parties and the state. For a study of relations between vigilantism and the state, see Abrahams 1998.

12 "Zonsezi ndi chifukwa cha malamulo athu," *Tikambe Supplement to Malawi News*, December 6–12, 2003.

13 *Dziwani malamulo a dziko lanu*, an audio tape released by the Centre for Human Rights and Rehabilitation (no date).

14 *Kulanga kwa mchigulu*, a leaflet published by the Centre for Human Rights and Rehabilitation in a series entitled Dziwani ufulu wanu (no date).

15 For a discussion of Malawi's posttransition reform program for the police, see Dzonzi 2003. The CHRR embarked in 2001 on a program that sought to promote security in local communities. The program, together with the NGO's involvement in controlling access to small arms, was undoubtedly beneficial to the populace. Popular grievances against the police, however, remained underresearched.

16 For a study that carefully traces the origins and destinations of second-hand clothes in Zambia, see Hansen 2000.

17 The rally occurred on December 21, 2003, in Machinga District.

REFERENCES

Abrahams, Ray. 1998. *Vigilant Citizens: Vigilantism and the State*. Cambridge: Polity Press.

Bourdieu, Pierre. 1977. *Outline of a Theory of Practice*. Cambridge: Cambridge University Press.

Comaroff, Jean, and John L. Comaroff. 1999. Occult Economies and the Violence of Abstraction: Notes from the South African Postcolony. *American Ethnologist* 26: 279–303.

Dzonzi, Lot Thauzeni Pansipandana. 2003. The Malawi Police Reform and Human Rights. In B. Immink, S. Lembani, M. Ott, and C. Peters-Berries, eds., *From Freedom to Empowerment: Ten Years of Democratisation in Malawi*. Lilongwe: Forum for Dialogue and Peace.

Ellis, Stephen. 1993. Rumour and Power in Togo. *Africa* 63: 462–75.

Ellis, Stephen, and Gerrie ter Haar. 2004. *Worlds of Power: Religious Thought and Political Practice in Africa*. London: Hurst & Co.

Englund, Harri. 2001. The Quest for Missionaries: Transnationalism and Township Pentecostalism in Malawi. In A. Corten and R. Marshall-Fratani, eds., *Between Babel and Pentecost: Transnational Pentecostalism in Africa and Latin America*. London: Hurst & Co.

——. 2002a. Introduction: The Culture of Chameleon Politics. In H. Englund, ed., *A Democracy of Chameleons: Politics and Culture in the New Malawi*. Uppsala: Nordic Africa Institute and Blantyre: Christian Literature Association in Malawi (CLAIM).

——. 2002b. The Village in the City, the City in the Village: Migrants in Lilongwe. *Journal of Southern African Studies* 28: 137–54.

——. 2004. Cosmopolitanism and the Devil in Malawi. *Ethnos* 69: 293–316.

Evans-Pitchard, E. E. 1937. *Witchcraft, Oracles and Magic among the Azande*. Oxford: Clarendon Press.

Fields, Karen E. 2001. Witchcraft and Racecraft: Invisible Ontology in Its Sensible Manifestations. In G. C. Bond and D. M. Ciekawy, eds., *Witchcraft Dialogues: Anthropological and Philosophical Exchanges*. Athens, GA: Ohio University Press.

Gambetta, Diego, ed. 1988. *Trust: Making and Breaking Co-operative Relations*. Oxford: Blackwell.

Geschiere, Peter. 1997. *The Modernity of Witchcraft: Politics and the Occult in Postcolonial Africa*. Charlottesville: University Press of Virginia.

Green, Maia. 2003. *Priests, Witches and Power: Popular Christianity after Mission in Southern Tanzania*. Cambridge: Cambridge University Press.

Guyer, Jane I. 2004. *Marginal Gains: Monetary Transactions in Atlantic Africa*. Chicago: University of Chicago Press.

Hansen, Karen Tranberg. 2000. *Salaula: The World of Second-Hand Clothing and Zambia*. Chicago: University of Chicago Press.

Hund, John. 2004. African Witchcraft and Western Law: Psychological and Cultural Issues. *Journal of Contemporary Religion* 19: 67–84.

Kapferer, Bruce. 2002. Outside All Reason: Magic, Sorcery and Epistemology in Anthropology. *Social Analysis* 46: 1–30.

La Fontaine, Jean S. 1998. *Speak of the Devil: Tales of Satanic Abuse in Contemporary England*. Cambridge: Cambridge University Press.

Mauss, Marcel. 1954. *The Gift: Forms and Functions of Exchange in Archaic Societies*. London: Cohen and West.

Mbembe, Achille. 2001. *On the Postcolony*. Berkeley: University of California Press.

Meyer, Birgit. 1999. *Translating the Devil: Religion and Modernity among the Ewe in Ghana*. Edinburgh: Edinburgh University Press for the International African Institute.

Moore, Henrietta L., and Todd Sanders. 2001. Introduction. In H. L. Moore and T. Sanders, eds., *Magical Interpretations, Material Realities: Modernity, Witchcraft and the Occult in Postcolonial Africa*. New York: Routledge.

Samara, Tony Roshan. 2005. Youth, Crime and Urban Renewal in the Western Cape. *Journal of Southern African Studies* 31: 209–27.

Scheper-Hughes, Nancy, and Loïc Wacquant, eds. 2002. *Commodifying Bodies*. London: Sage.

Sharp, Lesley A. 2000. The Commodification of the Body and Its Parts. *Annual Review of Anthropology* 29: 287–328.

Shaw, Rosalind. 2002. *Memories of the Slave Trade: Ritual and the Historical Imagination in Sierra Leone*. Chicago: University of Chicago Press.

Short, Philip. 1974. *Banda*. London: Routledge and Kegan Paul.

Strathern, Marilyn. 2004. Losing (Out On) Intellectual Resources. In A. Pottage and M. Mundy, eds., *Law, Anthropology, and the Constitution of the Social: Making Persons and Things*. Cambridge: Cambridge University Press.

White, Luise. 2000. *Speaking with Vampires: Rumor and History in Colonial Africa*. Berkeley: University of California Press.

15

Legal Transplants and Cultural Translation: Making Human Rights in the Vernacular

Sally Engle Merry

How do transnational human rights ideas become part of local social movements and local legal consciousness? Throughout the Asia-Pacific region, transnational activists, national elites, and middle-tier educated NGO leaders are energetically appropriating global human rights frameworks and translating them to fit into particular situations. This often means *transplanting institutions and programs* such as gender training programs, domestic violence laws, counseling centers for battered women, or human rights commissions. This is at heart a process of translation across boundaries of class, ethnicity, mobility, and education. Intermediaries who translate global ideas into local situations and retranslate local ideas into global frameworks play a critical role in the process. They foster the gradual emergence of a local rights consciousness among grassroots people and greater awareness of national and local issues among global activists. These actors include national political elites, human rights lawyers, feminist activists and movement leaders, social workers and other social service providers, and academics. Although grassroots groups are the ultimate target of these efforts, they are not typically the translators.

Movement activists, NGO leaders, and government officials create programs and institutions that are a blend of transnational, national, and local elements as they negotiate the spaces between transnational ideas and local concerns. These institutions incorporate indigenous social institutions such as kinship systems, transnational models such as shelters, and human rights ideas such as the right to safety from violence. The result is a bricolage of elements in constantly

Originally published in *Human Rights and Gender Violence: Translating International Law into Local Justice*, ed. Sally Engle Merry. Chicago: University of Chicago Press, 2006, pp. 134–78.

shifting relation to one another made up of elements that do not necessarily fit together smoothly.

This essay examines the way programs and strategies are transplanted from one social context to another. Rather than providing a comprehensive view of national strategies for dealing with gender violence, it focuses on the transplanting process in five countries. Intriguingly, activists in each country are committed to developing models suited to their distinctive history and social conditions, yet the strategies they have adopted are all fairly similar. Although there is some reframing of reforms to fit local conditions, the array of programs and institutions being adopted in India, China, Fiji, Hong Kong, and the United States are roughly the same. Global processes, such as the worldwide feminist and human rights movements, account for the similarities.

Deterritorialized ethnography reveals these connections since it focuses on flows of information, funds, and personnel rather than the comparison of sites as discrete entities. Global and local are slippery terms in this process. Transplants are programs or models adapted from one local context to another, but the process of transplanting is a global one. For example, when shelters or hotlines are transplanted from one social and cultural context to another, the leaders are often feminist activists whose networks of knowledge are forged in international meetings such as global UN conferences or training programs. The programs are tailored to local contexts but arrive through paths of global circulation. Each was initially developed in some local place but is now being swept to a different local place on the currents of globalization. Transplantation is both global and local at the same time.

Transplanting institutions and programs involves appropriation and translation. Appropriation means taking the programs, interventions, and ideas developed by activists in one setting and replicating them in another setting. Appropriation is often transnational, as ideas and programs are discovered elsewhere and imported to a new set of circumstances at home. Appropriation requires knowledge of approaches in other countries and, in many cases, the ability to attract funding and political support. Successful innovations in one place feed back into global circuits and inspire other copies, arrayed in a different dress for the new location. Appropriation often depends on the availability of donors and the capacity of a program to deliver measurable change in a relatively short time period. Translation is the process of adjusting the rhetoric and structure of these programs or interventions to local circumstances. Appropriated programs are not necessarily translated, but they are more likely to be popular if they are. On the other hand, if they are translated so fully that they blend into existing power relationships completely, they lose their potential for social change.

Translation has three dimensions. First, the images, symbols, and stories through which the program is presented draw on specific local cultural narratives and conceptions. For example, domestic violence advocates in India tell stories about powerful Hindu deities to promote self-assertiveness among Hindu women while in China, feminists label abusive behavior as "feudal." Sociologists studying social movements describe this process as "framing" (Snow et al. 1986; Tarrow 1998). Frames are not themselves ideas but ways of packaging and presenting ideas that generate shared beliefs, motivate collective action, and define appropriate strategies of action. Frames can have powerful effects on the way situations are understood and on the tactics their supporters deploy (Khagram, Riker, and Sikkink 2002: 12–13). The frame is an interpretive package surrounding a core idea (Ferree 2003: 308).

Social movement theorists point out that the frame needs to be culturally resonant for the ideas to be adopted. However, Ferree argues that resonant discourses are less radical than nonresonant ones and that some movement leaders may choose the nonresonant approach in order to induce greater social change in the long run (2003:305). Indeed, resonance is a costly choice since it may limit the possibility of long-term change. Choosing resonance requires sacrificing ideals, limiting demands on authorities, and possibly excluding significant groups and their demands from the movement (Ferree 2003: 340). This is precisely the problem human rights activists confront: If they frame human rights to be compatible with existing ways of thinking, they will not induce change. It is only their capacity to challenge existing power relations that offers radical possibilities.

The second dimension of translation is adapting the appropriated program to the structural conditions in which it operates. For example, in Hong Kong, shelters focus on getting social welfare department officials to move battered women higher up on the public housing priority list. In India, which lacks significant public housing, activists focus on giving battered women the right to remain in the matrimonial home through legal reform. In urban China, there are very few shelters since most housing is assigned on the basis of one's job, and it is the man who gets the housing. The woman who leaves her batterer for a shelter has few other housing options and must sooner or later go back to him. In China, activists rely on local leaders of the quasi-governmental mass organization for women, the All-China Women's Federation (ACWF), to deal with gender violence. In India, domestic violence is often handled by special dowry-focused police stations. Each location has a distinctive set of government and private services, laws, court and police systems, and political institutions that affect how the prototype is translated.

Third, as programs are translated, the target population is also redefined. For example, in China domestic violence occurs among many family members, not just within romantic relationships between men and women. Violence is common between adults and their co-resident elderly parents and between parents and children. The definition of the problem in China has been expanded to reflect these patterns. In the United States, domestic violence is more common in intimate, romantic relationships whether or not the couple is married than in larger family networks. Laws have gradually shifted from protecting women in marriage to women in households. There is a growing recognition that violence is also common in same-sex intimate relationships and that some programs need to be tailored to these populations (Ristock 2002).

However, even though programs are translated into new contexts and framed in culturally specific ways, they are never fully indigenized. They retain their underlying emphasis on individual rights to protection of the body along with autonomy, choice, and equality, ideas embedded in the legal codes of the human rights system. Inside the culturally resonant packaging is a core that radically challenges patriarchy. Despite arguments that human rights must be translated into local webs of meaning based on religion, ethnicity, or place in order for them to appear both legitimate and appealing, such transformations take place only at a relatively superficial level (see An-Na'im 1992a, 1992b; Coomaraswamy 1994). When the Aboriginal center in Australia developed its brochure for domestic violence services using Aboriginal art images, for example, it translated the program into local artistic forms, but it still produced a brochure. Moreover, this brochure listed the same kinds of services found in other women's centers around the world. In another example, the social worker running a treatment program in

Hong Kong for men who batter sought to frame his curriculum in terms of Chinese ideas of masculinity and family headship, but he nevertheless ran a therapeutic discussion group for men whose domestic violence had been defined as a social problem. The focus on Chinese masculinity represents an adaptation to the Hong Kong context but not a complete transformation of ideas, an indigenization (Chan 2000b).

As the examples of appropriation and translation in this chapter indicate, human rights retain their fundamental meanings even as they become resources in local struggles. They grow out of a modernist understanding of the self and its capacity to act autonomously as well as an emphasis on equality and the security of the body. The power of human rights to change the way people think and act is their capacity to change existing cultural practices such as the husband's authority to discipline his wife through beating. It is not their ability to blend into preexisting cultural systems. Adopting human rights locally does not build on a preexisting similarity of cultural beliefs any more than introducing bureaucracy or traffic lights does. But proponents do dress them in familiar costumes.

Two different approaches to translating human rights concerning violence against women emerged in my research. The first was a social service approach inspired by feminists and social workers, largely middle-tier professionals and academics. Social workers and feminist activists transplanted from other countries social service programs that offered support services to victims and retraining for offenders. The second was a human rights advocacy approach led by lawyers and political elites. These groups worked to change national laws and institutions and transplanted institutions such as human rights commissions. Both social service provision and human rights advocacy are local appropriations of global ideas. The first transplants programs such as shelters, counseling, support groups, and legal aid through a transnational community of feminist social organizations. It uses sociological modes of analysis and grows out of an activist feminist community as well as NGO social service providers. It works with individual clients. The second develops mechanisms for defining human rights and responding to violations at the national level. This includes efforts to incorporate international standards into domestic law, to create human rights commissions and women's commissions, and to promote international human rights education programs. Governmental policymakers, legislators, and judges are key actors. They use legal modes of analysis and try to develop human rights complaint-handling mechanisms and enact legal reform through the legislative or judicial process.

Despite the disparate origins and fundamental differences between the two movements, there is a growing convergence between them. National interest in participating in the human rights system creates spaces for rights-based social service programs at the grassroots. As local social service programs encourage clients to frame their grievances in terms of human rights, they develop a rights-conscious local constituency that pushes governments to abide by the standards of the international system. Thus, human rights institutions benefit from the rights consciousness promoted by local social service programs and local social service programs benefit from adopting a nationally and internationally recognized rights framework. UN meetings and conferences punctuate this relationship by creating opportunities for consultation between the two tiers at international conferences, commission meetings, and during the writing of country reports for treaty bodies such as CEDAW. This essay compares and systematizes a vast array of initiatives, using the five-country comparison to unearth common strategies and their global origins. This approach lacks the deep, contextualized form of analysis that anthropologists generally provide for a single site but shows gender violence reform efforts as part of global flows of knowledge and action.[1] It focuses largely on the capital cities of these countries, except for the United States.

Feminist Social Services

Criminal law and the criminal justice system

Four basic initiatives against domestic violence have been transplanted globally in these five countries: criminalization, provision of social services, public education, and survey research. Criminalization is usually the first step. Activists develop and pass laws against gender violence, train police to arrest offenders, encourage no-drop (i.e., mandated) prosecution, and train judges to treat wife battering and sexual assault seriously. Because the implementation of laws lags well behind the passage of these laws, activists devote considerable energy to implementation strategies. The justice system is often very lenient. When a man is arrested for battering in Fiji, for example, he receives a suspended sentence and if he offends again, he receives another suspended sentence. In the United States, the battered-women's movement, confronting a failure to enforce laws by police, prosecutors, and judges, has invested heavily in training programs. Deploying the police against batterers poses problems for some communities, however. Many groups experience the criminal justice system as hostile and racist. Groups such as Australian Aboriginal people, Native Hawaiians, Native Americans, and African Americans are already disproportionately incarcerated. In India, there is concern that the police are inefficient and corrupt.

India

India's penal code covers domestic violence, defined as cruelty by a husband or relatives to his wife, in Section 498A of the Indian Penal Code. A legal aid handbook dates the law to 1983 and says it is the "first time the crime of violence specifically against a woman by her husband was recognized in law" (Lawyers' Collective 1992: 36). The term "domestic violence" was unknown until recently, according to an attorney at the Lawyers' Collective, and the term "cruelty" was used instead. It is now becoming far more widespread and the number of complaints is increasing dramatically. According to a police officer I interviewed in Delhi in 2001 who handles domestic violence cases, the sentence is a fine plus prison up to three years, and some men do actually go to jail. An activist working at Jagori, a feminist documentation and resource center in Delhi, said that the police complain that women often drop criminal charges under 498A.

So-called dowry deaths or dowry murders are a particular form of violence against women in India produced by the practice of providing substantial gifts from the bride's family to the groom's family at marriage. Quarrels over dowry gifts often last years into the marriage and contribute to abuse of the woman and possibly murder if her family fails to provide the promised dowry. This problem, along with rape of women in police custody, galvanized the women's movement in the 1970s. The Dowry Prohibition Act of 1961 made asking for dowry illegal, while amendments in 1984 and 1986 provided stringent punishments for giving and taking dowry (Poonacha and Pandey 1999: 179). Nevertheless, the practice continues. According to an amendment to the Indian Evidence Act, if a woman commits suicide within seven years of the date of her marriage and her husband or husband's relatives have subjected her to cruelty, the court may presume that the suicide is abetted by the husband or his family, and if a woman dies within seven years of marriage and she has experienced cruelty, her husband and relatives are assumed guilty unless it is proven otherwise (Lawyers' Collective 1992: 41; Jethmalani 2001: 60–1). The police officer I interviewed said that even a little harassment is enough for a criminal conviction. One consequence of the focus on dowry murders is that there is a tendency to see all incidents of domestic violence as economic struggles over dowry.

Special police stations focused on dowry conflicts were established starting in 1983 in Delhi (interview, Special Cell, 2001) and in 1989 in Bangalore as a branch of the detective units (Poonacha and Pandey 1999: 76–7). Each of the nine police districts of Delhi has such a cell. In 2001 I visited a dowry police station, called a Special Cell for Crimes against Women and Children. This station handles about 7500 cases a year and has 18 police inspectors working there. It also runs a police helpline that is available around the clock. Walking past a crowd of women and children as well as a few men waiting in the small anteroom, I was ushered into the office of the commissioner of police. This is not a police station, he told me, but a place that deals with domestic violence and dowry. After telling me that they generally reconcile couples and negotiate the terms of a settlement, he invited me to observe several cases he handled along with the social workers at the station. In 2000, 23 percent of cases were reconciled through counseling, including those resolved with the assistance of professional counselors from the Central Social Welfare Board. All the cases I observed in a two-day period were settled, often with the help of social workers, despite indications of significant violence in the relationship in several cases.

For example, in one case I heard in 2001, a young woman married for six months came to court because she was afraid of her husband's father. Her husband beat her as well. She came from a wealthier family than her husband. He offered to rent a room for her, but she did not want to live alone. She said that she could accuse him of harassment and beating, but then the marriage would fall apart. She wanted him to sign a paper so that he has something over his head if he does not treat her better. She does not really want a divorce. His parents, who attended the hearing as well, posted a notice in the newspaper saying that they have disowned him so that, if she accuses him of a dowry offense, they are not responsible. The police inspector worked out a compromise along these lines, and she stayed with her husband.

A second case involved both property and violence. A young couple, married seven years with one child, was supported by the husband who sells vegetables. He left her one month ago and his mother has taken all her jewelry. She says he beats her, but she will come back if he treats her better. The parents counter that this is a love marriage and since the couple eloped, it is not a real marriage. She insists that it is. She fled to her mother's house and he went to get her, but her brothers attacked him with a knife. He then filed a criminal complaint against her brothers. She wants to live with him but he beats her and she says she is black and blue. She would like some promise that he will not beat her and she wants her jewelry back. She cannot remain with her own parents. He insists that he never beats her, except "just to make her understand." He saw a woman of bad character going to visit her, so he beat her, he said. They left the hearing arguing with each other. It appears that the woman has little choice but to stay with him, but desperately wants him to be less violent. The hearing officer told me that his major goal in these cases is conciliation.

A third case followed a similar pattern. A woman came alone to tell her story and showed a list of goods owed to her, but the husband failed to show up. He drinks a lot and beats her. She works in a pen factory and gives all her earnings to her in-laws, but they still beat and harass her. She has left and the husband wants her to come back, but she is not persuaded. She has a list of the dowry articles she wants back, including gold chains, rings, clothes, blankets, ornaments, color TV, and washing machines. She wants to keep their child because the husband is an alcoholic. She was pregnant but lost another child because he kicked her in the stomach. The police commissioner pays little attention to the allegations of violence and works on negotiating a reconciliation.

These cases are quite similar to those handled by the *nari adalats*, or women's courts, discussed below (see Krishnamurthy 2002). Women typically seek return of their marriage goods and some reduction in violence yet need to stay with their husbands in order to have a respectable place to live. In general, it appeared that the police sought a compromise involving the exchange of money and the woman's return to her marital home. Money, rather than violence, was the focus of concern. These women seemed quite assertive, although they were not often supported by the police commissioner. I found the lack of attention to the violence quite striking. Cases were interpreted in terms of dowry and debt despite horrific stories. Reconciliation focused on the exchange of goods. The women clearly had no good alternative to returning to their violent husbands.

All-women police stations were formed in 1995 in twelve states and territories to deal with crimes against women, thus having a slightly different mandate than the dowry cells. The number has increased somewhat since then (Task Force on Women 2000: 28). They tend to be understaffed and unpopular among women police officers since they lack advancement possibilities (Poonacha and Pandey 1999: 76–7). They also tend to see violence in the home narrowly as a product of dowry claims (Sitaraman 2002). Legal aid and counseling are available at women's centers, but activists in Delhi pointed out that there are very few centers and that those that exist are only a band aid over a widespread problem. Family Courts were established about 1998, primarily in urban areas, and did not seem to have a substantial impact (UNIFEM interview, 2000).

Indian law has some provisions for civil remedies such as the right to live in the matrimonial home and protective orders to restrain a spouse from further abuse of the woman and her children available in family court or civil court, but women's rights groups are working to expand these remedies (Lawyers' Collective 1992: 13). Several NGOs in India, led by the Women's Rights Initiative of the Lawyers' Collective with funding provided by the Ford Foundation, worked from 1999 to 2001 to develop new civil domestic violence legislation. After extensive consultations with women's groups, a draft was completed in 2001. When I visited the collective in October 2001, an attorney leading the project said they had been through 150 drafts of this legislation and had consulted extensively with NGOs all over the country and translated the text into many Indian languages. Although much of the text of the bill was borrowed from other countries – primarily South Africa but also Canada, Australia, Sri Lanka, the Philippines, and some states in the United States – it has been adapted to the Indian context by taking a primarily civil law approach and by focusing on a woman's safety and her right to stay in the matrimonial home. The law is framed in rights language and emphasizes providing protection rather than punishing offenders. Section 5 of the 2001 draft contains provisions for protection orders prohibiting domestic violence as well as entering the home or workplace of the person aggrieved or making any attempt to contact that person or alienating any assets held by both parties, including a woman's *stridhan* (property a woman brings to the marriage). In a society in which divorce is extremely rare and virtually all women are married, it is not safe or desirable for a woman to live alone, so the bill protects a woman's right to reside in her home of marriage. The bill includes provisions for monetary relief for expenses and losses of the aggrieved person and any children as well as a residence order which prevents the respondent from dispossessing the aggrieved person from a shared household or for securing alternative accommodation if the shared accommodation is danger-ous, in the view of the court (Ch. III, Secs. 6 and 7). Protection orders are accom-panied by suspended arrest warrants to be executed if the order is breached (Jethmalani 2001: 73). The bill also specifies the creation of protection officers to assist the court in carrying out these provisions (Ch. IV). This officer is to investigate complaints of domestic violence, inform aggrieved persons of their rights to orders, and ensure that monetary relief is made available (Ch. IV, Sec. 20). Despite consi-derable debate about counseling for men, the Lawyer's Collective decided that a judge could require it, but it was not mandatory (interview, October 2001).

In December 2001, the government introduced its own bill on domestic violence, including provisions for protection officers and protection orders. Leading women's groups objected that the government law did not incorporate international human rights standards set by CEDAW into its definition of domestic violence and rejected this law (emails on February 27, 2002 and September 30, 2002 to the end-violence and CEDAW listserves). Indira Jaising of the Lawyers' Collective argued in February 2002 that the government bill defined domestic violence in terms of conduct that makes the aggrieved person's life miserable rather than in terms of rights, failed to specify forms of violence, and did not include the broad range of abuses identified in the UN Declaration and the Platform for Action. Most important, it did not specify that the woman has a right to remain in the shared household. Although it provides for the creation of protection officers, it includes no funding proposal to make this possible. Jaising contrasts this absence with the US Violence against Women Act of 1994, which committed substantial funds to preventing violence against women. An email posting from the Lawyers' Collective in December 2004 indicated that the law had still not been enacted (esaconf.un.org).

In Fiji, activists have been working since the mid 1980s to develop and implement laws to criminalize domestic violence. Historically the police and courts have been reluctant to prosecute violence against women and impose penalties. A 1988 study of the Suva area found that police reconcile 64 percent of reported cases of domestic violence, generally by persuading wives to drop the charges (Jalal 1988: 35–6). At the time, the police were reluctant to prosecute husbands. Between 1993 and 1997, police still reported reconciling 38 percent of cases (Fiji Women's Crisis Centre c.2000: 45). Both police and courts find these cases embarrassing and often do not support women who complain. In the 1990s, the government, police force, judiciary, and military were over-whelmingly male.

Fiji's active women's movement has focused on rape and domestic violence. The Fiji Women's Crisis Centre (FWCC), a feminist battered-women's center, was founded in 1984 with considerable initial input from overseas feminists (Anon. 1999). Its energetic leader, Shamima Ali, makes public statements critical of the police and the government. She started to work in the anti-rape movement in England during a stay of three and a half years, then volunteered at FWCC in 1985 and became its coordinator in 1986. She participated in the Center for

Women's Global Leadership in Rutgers University, New Jersey. The FWCC now operates four centers providing counseling and legal advice for battered women. I visited the main office and one of the branch offices, where counselors were busy talking to women who had come for help with their violent home situations. In 1986, the Fiji Women's Rights Movement (FWRM) developed as a sister organization to work on policy issues of women's rights, human rights education and public awareness of gender discrimination. By the 1990s these groups had separated into two quite distinct but still complementary organizations, one focusing on battered women's service and advocacy and the other on women's human rights.

Fiji now has a no-drop policy in the prosecutor's office, although some prosecutors still prefer to reconcile cases. FWCC trained police and military officers, but does not maintain batterer education programs. It initiated a Pacific network of organizations working on domestic violence, supported by the Australian government's aid program. Another feminist NGO in Fiji, the Regional Rights Resource Team (RRRT), worked for eight years to develop a new family law bill, finally passed in 2003. The Family Law Act is based on principles from the Convention on the Rights of the Child and CEDAW. It created the Family Court with mediation, a fairer distribution of matrimonial property, and greater priority for the interests of children in custody situations. The enforcement of maintenance payments is increased. NGOs are still working on a domestic violence bill.

The Fiji feminist movement was a collaborative effort among leaders from Fiji, Australia, and Canada. A workshop in 1991, early in the movement, brought together 25 activists, community leaders, and housewives with sponsorship by the Canada Fund and content developed by an Australian. At the time, the FWCC was being supported by the Australian Freedom from Hunger Campaign. The organizer of the workshop, Shamima Ali, stressed counseling as a major part of the center's function (Singh-Wendt 1991: 11). The workshop discussed the meaning of feminism, oppression, sexism, classism, and racism as different forms of oppression. Peni Moore, then head of FWRM, spoke on the antirape movement and discussed efforts to change the laws on rape (Singh-Wendt 1991: 16). Participants came from both Fijian and Indo-Fijian backgrounds and talked about the role of women in overcoming the deep ethnic divisions in the country (see Prasad 1989). Both FWCC and FWRM emphasize working across this ethnic divide.

Fiji focused on criminal justice reforms in its 1998 Women's Plan of Action 1999–2008 (Vol. II, by the Ministry for Women and Culture [Suva, Fiji], at www.unescap.org/pop/database/law_fiji/fiji_017.htm, February 2, 2001). In the section Violence against Women and Children, this plan recommends law reform, supportive services, and the training of care providers and law enforcement agencies to deal with "ingrained bias against women and the stigma attached to victims of sexual violence." The plan argues that it is important to promulgate specific laws to deal with violence against women and to improve the law and practice for child abuse. It is also important to provide victims of violence with a safe haven in urban and rural areas and to improve data collection and analytical services to assist in designing strategies beyond the legal system. Violence against women is defined as "the most pervasive violation of human rights and for women it is considered as a major impediment to their participation in development." The report focuses on the role culture plays in perpetuating this violence: "Some forms of violence against women, particularly those that occur within the family, are entrenched and not recognized by society and our institutions as they are explained as 'family discipline' and therefore ignored, condoned, or tolerated. These social attitudes perpetuate violence and it requires more than punishment of the perpetrators to change these attitudes and behaviours" (p. 8).

This report advocates law reform and criminal justice education, safety systems, attitude change education, and research as basic strategies for violence against women, the same basic package of reforms that is found around the world. This report attributes the origins of this movement to Europe and North America two decades earlier and in other parts of the world in conjunction with development issues. It stresses the contribution of the UN in its decade for women (1975–85), women and development efforts, the 1995 World Summit for Social Development at Copenhagen, and the 1995 Beijing Conference (p. 9). It makes clear that Fiji's attention to this issue was inspired by international movements and the expansion of women's human rights. In this report the government presents itself as deeply concerned with violence against women, influenced by international conferences and feminist movements, and working to ameliorate the problem using the standard set of approaches.

China

In China, domestic violence has appeared quite recently as a public issue and to a large extent in response to international interest and pressure. Until the mid 1990s, government and public awareness of the problem was very limited (Human Rights in China 1995: 25). As late as 1990, the government was able to deny that there was a problem in China (see Liu and Chan 1999, 2000). The world conference on women in Beijing in 1995 galvanized public concern about violence against women and spawned the development of hotlines, legal services clinics, and counseling centers in urban areas. The impact was far less in the rural areas. In most areas, a woman's only recourse in a battering situation is her family or the ACWF.

The ACWF is a mass governmental organization representing women's interests, although it presents itself as an NGO at international meetings. It is the main organization protecting women's rights and providing legal aid. The policy of gender equality was fundamental to the New China established by the Chinese Communist Party (Hecht 1998: 72). In 1983, rights departments were established within every Women's Federation Branch down to the county level (Hecht 1998: 79). A report by four women's NGOs to the 2000 Beijing Plus Five Conference states that 85–90 percent of all counties have set up legal counseling centers to protect women and provide legal counseling and assistance and notes that several provinces have passed legislation against domestic violence (China Working Group against Domestic Violence 2000a: 11). A survey of women's status in China in 2001 by the ACWF reported 1759 counseling centers for legal aid in the country established by the ACWF (*Women's Daily News*, November 5, 2001, trans. by Wei-Ying Lin). However, the ACWF's mandate is to implement government policies, so that it cannot represent women's interests when they conflict with those of the ruling party (Human Rights in China 1998: 8).

With a turn toward greater reliance on law to implement policy in China along with concerns about the social disruptions of the economic liberalization process since the 1980s, the government asked the ACWF along with other organizations to draft legislation on women's rights. The result, the Law of the People's Republic of China on the Protection of Women's Rights and Interests, was passed in 1992 after three years of investigation and refinement (Hecht 1998: 72–4). It was intended to bring CEDAW principles into Chinese law. Although it clearly articulates a policy of gender equality, it specifies that men and women should be treated equally, not that their conditions of life or social status should be equal. The law protects women's bodily integrity and contains considerable protective legislation for the workplace, which emphasizes women's biological differences and the need to protect maternity (Hecht 1998: 76–7). However, it does not define discrimination nor provide an enforcement mechanism (Human Rights in China 1998: 13). It prohibits violence and abuse against women but does not specifically mention violence in the family, nor are remedies provided. Instead, the language is abstract and general. A report at a domestic violence conference in Beijing in 2002 on police effectiveness said that the police are often reluctant to intervene, and neither the police nor the public is aware of the problem. Even many women police officers think the antidomestic-violence movement is too "feminist."[2]

China's 2001 Marriage Law prohibits domestic violence but does not define it nor specify any mechanisms for preventing or punishing it. However, activists recognize that it is very important that this law names domestic violence as a problem rather than as a necessary form of discipline. Some worry that the law does not expand the concept beyond hitting to threats and mental and sexual abuse (Wang Xingjuan in *China Women's News*, November 16, 2000, trans. by Wei-Ying Lin). Since it is civil law, it does not delineate punishments but offers the victim mediation and the opportunity to press criminal liability claims (Article 43, trans. by Wei-Ying Lin). The victim has the right to bring a lawsuit to the people's court. The public security division will carry out the investigation and the people's court will bring the lawsuit (Article 45). Despite the efforts of activists, the law does not include a provision for a protection order and it requires the victim to take the initiative in going to the law. A 2000 survey of 10 provinces and cities by the ACWF reported that 96 percent of respondents thought this revised Marriage Law should include regulations on domestic violence (*China Women's News*, August 3, 2000, trans. by Wei-Ying Lin).

Between 2000 and 2002, a Domestic Violence Research and Intervention Project (DVRIP) engaged in major research and intervention initiatives concerning violence against women. Funded by the Ford Foundation, NOVIB of Holland, SIDA of Sweden, and the Human Rights Center of Oslo University in Norway (Domestic Violence in China: Research, Intervention and Prevention *Newsletter* 2 [October 2001], typescript), it culminated in the first international conference on violence against women held in Beijing in 2002, which I attended. In 2001 I interviewed many of its leading researchers and the director. At the final session of the 2002 conference, the chair presented a draft bill on domestic violence prepared by the research team after two years of intensive effort and consultation of domestic violence laws collected from forty countries. The presentation of the law was the culmination of the conference. Many of the conference participants expressed the need for a strong and effective domestic violence law in China.

In addition to legal aid services provided by the ACFW, there is a prominent legal aid clinic in Beijing established in 1995 that offers legal assistance to women who are victims of violence or rape and pursues high visibility policymaking cases. I visited the center in Beijing in 2001 and 2005. It is a small two-room office, festooned with banners given by grateful beneficiaries, but hardly capable of providing services to much of populous Beijing. It does not have the resources to handle a large volume of cases. Its clients range from highly educated people to low-status women such as migrant workers, housekeepers, and peasants (Guo 2000: 3). Between 1995 and 2000, the center provided consultations to 7,000 clients through its hotline, interviews, letters, and email. These cases cover domestic violence, sexual crimes, employment discrimination, distribution of joint property after divorce, and child custody. The center has strong international connections and tries to use CEDAW in its legal work. Some of its funding comes from the Ford Foundation, and a 2001 research report on women's rights and the implementation of CEDAW was supported by the British government (Centre for Women's Law Studies and Legal Services of Peking University 2001).

Although cases of domestic violence are handled in court, they pose difficult dilemmas for victims. The DVRIP reported some of its research findings on the legal situation of domestic violence victims in its newsletter. Wang Kairong observed a case in the appeal court in Tianjin in 2000. The court of first instance had already decided in favor of the appellee, a 26-year-old housewife married to a young peasant living in Tianjin City for almost two years. She was said to be battered by her husband because she had been slow in caring for her ill mother-in-law. She filed a criminal suit and a civil claim against her husband in the Jing County People's Court with a private prosecutor. Forensic evidence confirmed that she had a fractured rib, and the court sentenced the husband to 10 months' imprisonment with one year's probation and a fine of 2,000 yuan for medical expenses, damage compensation to the plaintiff, and a lawsuit fee. The husband appealed the judgment. He claimed he did not beat his wife's chest and cause the fracture. The case was the first one heard in the Domestic Violence Criminal Collegiate Tribunal since its establishment within the intermediate court. A legal aid agency lawyer was appointed for the appellant and the Tianjin Women's Federation recommended two lawyers from its affiliated law firms for the appellee.

The appeal was witnessed by over one hundred visitors including family members, women's federation leaders, judicial administrative officials, and law school students and was broadcast live by Tianjin television. The court upheld the earlier judgment. The woman was successful because her husband confessed that he did beat his wife and the village clinic doctor and other villagers testified to the violence. Finding witnesses willing to testify would have been far more difficult in a city. The audience had some sympathy for the man, however. An older woman said, "I found the woman too aggressive and deserved beating. The husband looks really pitiable!" Even though the woman won the appeal, the fine will probably be paid out of family resources, which are jointly owned by husband and wife, so that he will use part of his wife's property to pay for the damage he has inflicted on her. Wang, the author of the newsletter article, concludes that there are still problems in the legal resolution of domestic violence cases (Wang Kairong c.2001: 4–6).

In the same newsletter, a lawyer who handles domestic violence cases in court notes the many difficulties battered women face in court: a lack of concern by law enforcement officers in comparison to other criminal cases, a lack of effort by police and court to gather evidence, and an unwillingness of other family members, neighbors, friends, coworkers, and relatives to serve as witnesses. They may be afraid of the perpetrator or reluctant to interfere in other families' business. Even brothers and sisters of the abused woman may feel intervention is inappropriate (Liu Donghua c.2001: 6–7).

Even as China eagerly examines programs for dealing with domestic violence in other countries and relies on the social science literature produced in North America for its theoretical framework, national leaders insist that their approaches have Chinese characteristics. The leaders of DVRIP as well as other domestic violence activists want to develop a Chinese model of preventing violence against women, more kin-based and less focused on spouses and romantic/sexual relationships than are Western models (see Li Hongxian 2000: 75). Because Chinese families are typically three-generational, violence is not restricted to husband–wife battering but occurs among a variety of relatives and often against elderly parents or children. In rural areas, the husband's family is very important, and if a woman sues her husband, the whole family will hate her. She has often lost ties with her natal family and has no place to go if she leaves her husband's family.

These family conditions affect patterns of violence and forms of intervention. They make recourse to shelters or the use of restraining orders very difficult. Instead, the domestic violence intervention program focuses on raising awareness among the police so that they see domestic violence as their responsibility and on working with local hospitals and women's federation workers. A Chinese NGO, the Maple Women's Psychological Counseling Center, recommended strengthening the Peoples' Mediating Committees to prevent and halt domestic violence since they are a mass organization with a long history spread all over China (China Working Group against Domestic Violence 2000b: 9). There are also neighborhood committees made up of retired people and chosen by the party who sometimes get involved. But, even though there are many local organizations such as work units, they rarely view domestic violence as a problem they must handle.

At the 2002 conference, there was little talk of "Chinese characteristics" for domestic violence reforms, however, nor of clans, lineages or even neighborhood groups as sources of support. Instead, the focus was on the institutions of the state: the police, the courts, and hospitals. Many participants spoke of the need to "catch up" and of being "behind" the United States, Canada, the Nordic countries, and Japan. Despite the desire to tailor the understanding of the problem and its solution to Chinese kinship characteristics, the focus was on state intervention and the goal was creating a more modern society. The DVRIP director pointed to the need to change traditions, such as eliminating the common Confucian proverb that a man needs to beat a woman every three days or she will climb up on the roof and destroy the house (Liu and Chan 2000: 74). The activists in this project were highly educated urban elites with significant international travel and knowledge of international human rights.

Hong Kong

Hong Kong has a specific piece of legislation for domestic violence, the Domestic Violence Ordinance. This law, passed in 1986, provides for temporary restraining orders and the possibility of arrest (Yeung 1991: 35; Man 2001: 4–5). However, by 2002 there was some concern among activists, including the executive director of the first shelter, that the law was too narrowly defined and overly restrictive since it only covered marital relationships (*South China Morning Post*, March 14, 2002, p. 15). Women's groups have trained police officers in handling domestic violence cases and prepared guidelines. In 2000, a Domestic Violence Policy Unit was established in the police department (Man 2001: 22). Nevertheless, researchers commonly observe that the police are still reluctant to intervene and consider battering simply a domestic disturbance (Yeung 1991: 35).

USA

In the United States, although the battered-women's and antirape movements of the early 1970s emphasized criminalization, by the mid 1980s there was growing interest in civil protective orders as well (Schechter 1982; Ptacek 1999; Schneider

2000). A centerpiece of the US effort has always been increasing the severity of criminal penalties, improving policing to make arrests more frequent, and developing more certain prosecution through no-drop mandates. These efforts have improved the likelihood of arrest and prosecution, but penalties are still relatively light. Significant police training has improved intervention, yet many still fail to take this offense seriously. Those who violate restraining orders are subject to criminal penalties, at least in theory. In my research in a small town in Hawai'i, I found that a woman getting a restraining order can still have contact with her violent partner, but he will probably be required to attend a psycho-educational violence control program (1995a, 1995b). If he fails to attend or violates the order, he will usually be sent back to the program. Many battered women I talked to in Hawai'i did not want criminal penalties for their partners but preferred to get a protective order and send them to a program that tries to train them not to be violent.

Thus, there are substantial similarities in the criminal justice and legal interventions being developed for men who batter in all five countries and roughly contemporaneous program and legal innovations. This is clearly a transnational social reform movement.

Social services and violence control training

Some social service initiatives seek to improve the woman's safety rather than to punish the offender. The most important of these initiatives are shelters or refuges for women fleeing from their batterers, an idea that emerged in both the UK and the United States about 1974. Although shelters have now spread through the urban areas of many countries, they are far from universal. Women's violence advocates in Beijing told me that there were very few shelters in China, with one existing for a time in Wuhan and one being developed in Tianjin (see Wang Xingjuan 1999a, 1999b). The director of a counseling center in Beijing told me she was under pressure from foreign donors to set up a shelter and asked my advice about how to do it. According to some of the people I interviewed, shelters are difficult because China lacks a civil society with NGOs who might be able to develop and run one. It is currently difficult to establish an NGO under Chinese regulations. Shelters are also expensive.

Activists in Delhi told me that there were virtually no shelters in India either. There were two shelters for the whole of Delhi in 2001. Some women's activists said shelters do not mesh well with a kinship system in which a woman must either live with her husband's family or her natal family. Accounts of incidents of domestic violence indicate that women generally flee to their natal families when violence becomes severe (Poonacha and Pandey 1999; Krishnamurthy 2002; ICRW 2002: 26). Some said it was not safe for poor women to live outside a family setting. A study of West Bengal argued that shelter homes set up by the state are not a good idea because they isolate women from their communities rather than encouraging the community to respond to such problems (ICRW 2002: 30). Some activists I talked to in India thought there was a desperate need for shelters but that there were no resources to set them up.

Fiji has only one small private shelter for its population of about 800,000, but its dynamic and high-profile women's center offers counseling and legal aid for battered women as well as considerable community education and political advocacy. This women's center attempted to set up a shelter in the early 1990s but found it too expensive and security too difficult (Fiji Women's Crisis Centre 1996: 19).

Shelters require substantial investment by governments or donors. Their absence reflects resource deficits more than kinship structures. For example, Hong Kong has four shelters, one of which was started in 1985 by an NGO, one in 1986 by the government, one by a Christian church that has since become secular, and one sponsored by the government but run by Caritas, which opened in 2002 in response to concerns about rapid increases in rates of domestic violence and demands for shelter services (*South China Morning Post*, February 16, 2002, p. 4, Ella Lee). These shelters typically offer hotlines, counseling, legal, financial, and housing assistance, and support groups plus tutorial groups for children (Yeung 1991: 35; Tang, Lee, and Cheung 1999: 50–1). The pioneer shelter, Harmony House, was started in 1985 by Americans and Britons using models from the United States and the UK. Its current executive director spent ten years in Canada working on family violence. In its early years, Harmony House was described as offering treatment and shelter for abused women rather than promoting women's human rights in order to diminish opposition, according to a social worker who worked at Harmony House at the time (interview, March 2002). Human rights sounded more Western. Only when they began to develop publicity pamphlets did they talk about family violence.

Activists in Hong Kong told me that their dilemma was that the city was now too affluent to interest international donors and they had to fund the shelters and domestic violence programs with government money. The government offers substantial subventions to many NGOs, thus guaranteeing their survival for service delivery but inhibiting innovation and advocacy. Although the directors of these programs typically emphasize their efforts to "indigenize" the program, they also rely on concepts of gender equality, understanding feelings, and the icon of a power/control wheel developed in the United States. "Chinese traditional culture" is cited as a factor contributing to the occurrence of gender violence rather than a mode of combating it (Yeung 1991: 34).

Shelters are widespread in the United States, but they too face challenges in receiving sufficient government funding. The first shelter in Hilo, Hawai'i, set up in 1978, was a rambling old house with little staff or support run by formerly battered women (Merry 2001). Like shelters elsewhere in the country, it has gradually become more established and professional, but shelters continue to run on limited government funding. Around the country, they face cutbacks when local governments run short of funds. Discussions with activists in each of these countries suggest that shelters are only feasible in urban areas where women can live outside a kin group. If a woman's only housing option is within a family, moving to a formal state institution is not a viable solution. Moreover, shelters are expensive, and even in relatively affluent nations there are constant concerns about the expense of providing a secure space and offering the broad set of services necessary to allow a woman to find housing and employment away from her violent partner.

Other widespread innovations are hotlines to receive emergency calls, counseling for women seeking to escape battering situations, legal aid if they decide to go to court or pursue a divorce, and supportive discussion groups to help women talk about their problems. There is an NGO counseling center and hotline in Beijing, but it handles relatively few cases and a wide variety of family problems, including a significant minority who are men having difficulties with the sexual aspects of their marriages. The *China Women's News*, an ACWF-affiliated newspaper, ran a hotline for a year, called Household National Defense, until the lawyer who answered calls left (interview, 2001). The first specifically anti-domestic-violence hotline was established in Shaanxi Province in 2001 by the Shaanxi Women's Federation (*People's*

Daily, May 15, 2001). The main organization for most women is the local office of the ACWF, the place they typically turn for help. As one activist told me, the ACWF is the only institution that cares about domestic violence; police, judges, and lawyers do not seem concerned. In rural areas, however, the ACWF is primarily responsible for enforcing the one-child population policy so that it may not be trusted by women for other types of problems, according to a China human rights organization based in the United States (Human Rights in China 1998: 70).

Most of the innovative programs that address women's rights are located in cities. For example, the Maple Women's Psychological Counseling Center in Beijing, established in 1992, offers counseling and a hotline. The center's hotline has increasingly focused on issues of gender violence (interview with director, 2001). About 70 percent of the phone calls about domestic violence involve husbands beating wives, while 30 percent concern children beating parents. The first in the country, it is now joined by five others in other provinces. This organization has significant transnational linkages: it is supported by the Ford Foundation (which is now pushing them to set up a shelter) and a German foundation. A few years ago, this group received training in how to handle domestic violence calls from a hotline in Korea. It was also aided by Harmony House in Hong Kong. Its director attended the Beijing Plus Five Conference and was involved in the DVRIP program.

Women's support groups, while common in the United States, are not so widespread globally. The Fiji Women's Crisis Centre offers counseling to individual women who are battered, but not in groups. While the core of the Fiji intervention is counseling, it is more concerned with jobs and legal aid than with psychological adjustments. I visited a branch center in 2003 and talked with the counselors who described talking to women who dropped in for advice or support on a regular basis. China has recently developed women's support groups that meet once a week for six weeks under the supervision of a social worker. This initiative came from the ShangXi Province Women, Marriage, and Family Counseling Center.[3] However, this process can only help a small fraction of the people in the country and there are very few social workers available to do it.

In India, some NGOs in Delhi such as Sakshi and Jagori offer counseling, but support groups are rare. Women typically turn to their families for help. However, a report on organizations that provided services to women, including domestic violence, in the Indian states of Karnataka and Gujarat found a large number of organizations, at least some of which offered shelter homes. The study identified 480 organizations working in these two states and studied 20 of these that dealt with domestic violence (Poonacha and Pandey 1999: 2). These ranged from all-women's police stations to counseling cells associated with the police or private organizations and shelter homes. Many offered legal aid as well as counseling. Most of these programs focused on helping women in general rather than just victims of domestic violence. The report found that counseling in the centers, as well as in the police stations, generally sought reconciliation between husband and wife. They found that women typically want reconciliation unless their children are being harmed. Only then, as a last resort, do they seek divorce (1999: 30, 58). Many programs also offer job training and education for women. In 1990 the Central Social Welfare Board in New Delhi began a countrywide initiative to set up Family Counseling Centers to counter family breakdown and the violence it caused, growing out of a 1980s efforts to provide "preventive, referral, and rehabilitative services to victims of domestic violence and counseling in cases of 'marital maladjustment'" (UAB Annual Report, Karnataka, 1995–6, quoted in Poonacha and Pandey 1999: 132–3).

Violence control programs for batterers were developed in the United States in the early 1980s but have not spread globally to the same extent as these other initiatives. They are fairly common in the United States, and there were several in Hawai'i. Hong Kong has had therapeutic groups for male batterers since 1995, and they are currently being run on a voluntary basis by several of the shelters. I spoke to the leader of one group in 2002. He commented that the intervention was valuable for the men but that they participated on a voluntary basis rather than under court mandate and it was very difficult to persuade men to participate at all (see Chan 2001). Their experimental treatment programs relied on anger control techniques and on changing abusers' belief systems using a US approach similar to the Duluth model, the Domestic Abuse Intervention Project (Pence and Paymar 1993; Chan 2001: 49). However, court-mandated counseling for batterers also reflects Confucian values of harmonic interpersonal relationships and reeducation (Man 2001: 14–18).

In many ways, the provision of services in Hong Kong was more similar to that in the United States than either India or China. It seems likely that the relative affluence of the government and the influence of the British expatriate community both played critical roles in generating this level of services. It is noteworthy that these differences developed despite the similarity in the culture between China and Hong Kong. Economic and political resources are as important as kinship systems and religious beliefs in explaining the differences. Fiji also had relatively more services, again inspired and funded by Australian and British expatriates and governments.

Although many of these programs copy transnational prototypes, some build on local feminist activism and forms of village political organization to a far greater extent than others. For example, in India, nari adalats, or women's courts, emerged in the mid 1990s from a government-initiated program to develop women's collectives in the villages and a long tradition of women's movement activism addressing violence against women. The parent program, called Mahila Samakhya, is a village-level women's empowerment program (ICRW 2002). Started by the Department of Education in 1989 with funding from the Dutch government, Mahila Samakhya (MS) endeavored to promote development by collectivizing and empowering poor women through knowledge and the confidence to make changes (Poonacha and Pandey 1999: 161; ICRW 2002: 32–65; Sharma 2006). Promoting women's equality was an important part of this effort, along with health, literacy and nonformal education, savings, political involvement, and community development initiatives. During the first four years of the MS program, the training in Uttar Pradesh was carried out by Jagori, a feminist resource and training center I visited in Delhi in 2001, which adopted a radical feminist approach (see Krishnamurthy 2002: 42). The philosophy of the MS program is that decision making should rest with local collectives. The program depends on a cadre of women activists, *sahyoginis*, who develop and encourage *sanghas*, or women's collectives, in each village. Each sahyogini works with a cluster of ten villages.[4]

Since violence in the home was a major concern to many of the women, the women's collectives focused on this problem. A system of nari adalats emerged from the women's cooperatives in Gujarat in 1995 and in Uttar Pradesh in 1998 (ICRW 2002: 34). These were informal courts intended to handle women's legal problems. A 2001 study reported that since they were initiated in 1995, the four adalats in the Vadodara district handled about 1200 cases of marital violence, harassment, divorce, maintenance, property, and child custody and successfully resolved a majority of these. The clients were mostly low-caste and tribal women (Krishnamurthy 2002: 3, based on MS Annual Reports).

The nari adalat consists of a core team of selected sangha women and sahyoginis, most of whom have poor literacy skills and many of whom are *dalits*, people of low-caste status (ICRW 2002: 36).[5] The members of the nari adalat tour the district, meeting at regular days and times in public places near government offices to dispense legal advice and settle marital disputes (Poonacha and Pandey 1999: 161–78). They are not paid nor is their transportation covered. They have no legal authority but rely on pressure and shaming. Like the parent MS program, they straddle the government–NGO divide, claiming either identity as it seems helpful (Sharma 2006). Krishnamurthy's ethnography describes how nari adalats move creatively between community and state to gain recognition in the villages and access to formal institutions (2002: 12, 51). The women meet in government compounds close to police and local government offices, assert their status as part of the official MS program, use state symbols such as files, stamp paper, and seals, call on the police for protection, and cite formal laws to support their decisions as they were trained to do by urban activists. At the same time, they reflect the communities they come from. They use humor and shaming to pressure litigants, adjust their meeting times to the rhythms of village life, and use their knowledge of local practices, customs, and social networks to gather evidence and negotiate agreements. They do not try to end marriages but emphasize the rights of the woman within marriage (ICRW 2002: 51). Their authority is limited, and they seem to be most successful in helping women arrange divorces and escape violent marriages, particularly among poor families. They are less successful with wealthy families and with cases of rape and molestation, which require greater evidentiary effort (2002: 99).

Nevertheless, an International Center for Research on Women (ICRW) study in 1999–2000 indicated that the operation of these courts and the closely related *mahila panch* (women's councils) made violence in the home a more open and public offense. ICRW evaluations of these programs indicate that sangha and sahyogini women and those who experienced the nari adalats were more aware of their rights and better able to speak up (ICRW 2002: 40–1, 54). This initiative claims to introduce human rights concepts to poor, illiterate women, many of whom are tribals or dalits. The goal of the MS program itself is to deal with domestic violence and to raise consciousness about women's rights (ICRW 2002: 70). A counterculture based on resisting violence in terms of the intrinsic rights of women is developing slowly, largely in local terms: "Research documented the innovative ways in which activists use their local knowledge to reshape and reinterpret community idioms, phrases and beliefs to create and persuade the community to adopt new perspectives" (ICRW 2002: 72). At the same time, they push the ideology of human rights.

In sum, this overview reveals many similarities in the repertoire of social services in these five countries although the more costly initiatives, such as shelters, are found only in richer countries. As in Hawai'i, the informal social network is the first place women turn for help and often the most important one. Women's centers of various kinds are common, some patterned after US or UK models such as those in Fiji and Hong Kong, but others more locally shaped, such as the nari adalats. These program transplants are a bricolage of local and international elements. Unlike the United States, these centers focus less on psychological support than on housing and legal problems. Gender violence was more often seen as a structural problem related to poverty, alcoholism, or patriarchy and less as a psychological issue of childhood trauma or learned behavior.

Community education and public awareness

The third initiative against domestic violence is community education. This includes public awareness campaigns in the media, curricular development in schools, gender training, and public events such as marches and demonstrations. Local adaptation is important since messages must be presented in ways that are understood, in mediums that are heard, and in places where people will notice. This may mean TV or radio spots, tee shirts or coasters, brochures with local designs, or community meetings. The medium and the message are tailored to the particular community. However, the fundamental message, that women have the right not to be beaten under any circumstances, comes from the transnational feminist movement and is grounded in rights concepts and ideas of gender equality. Moreover, the idea of doing community education is itself a transnational concept.

There are many similarities in approaches used for community education. One NGO I visited in Fiji was training Fijians to conduct street theater about domestic violence. The DVRIP program in Beijing developed street theater, a billboard campaign using media personalities, and a TV soap opera on domestic violence. Celebrities were termed "image ambassadors." Starting in 2001, a group in the rural area of Yangqing County distributed more than 45,000 publicity flyers, information sheets, and posters, while women formed a local group to perform stories on stage based on their experiences (2002 DVRIP conference). The group says that this effort reduced the frequency of domestic violence in the county. Public education and awareness campaigns have been actively pursued in Hong Kong since the war-on-rape campaign of 1977 (Tang, Lee, and Cheung 1999: 49). Community education is an important dimension of the work of the first shelter, Harmony House. Among the numerous forms of community education in India, the *Mahila Suraxa Samiti* focuses on preventive measures to curb crimes against women. It intervenes in some cases of violence that are brought to it, as well as collaborating with NGOs in performing street plays, cultural programs, workshops and classes for housewives on sex education, marriage, and family life (Poonacha and Pandey 1999: 157–8). The US battered-women's movement has worked for many years to develop music, film, and media messages about the problem.

Survey research

A fourth category of intervention is survey research. Survey data on the frequency of battering and rape along with statistics from the police and courts are used to document the extent and causes of the problem. Surveys documenting the extent of the problem in Fiji, India, China, Hong Kong, and Hawai'i as well as elsewhere in the United States helped to build political support for the movement. For example, in India, the National Family Health Survey, which is a major study done of 90,000 households, asked questions about domestic violence for the first time in the 1998/99 survey. It reported that 56 percent of ever-married women thought it was legitimate for their husbands to beat them for infractions (NFHS-2, 2000: 73). The same study reported that 21 percent of women have been beaten or mistreated since they were 15 and 19 percent of women by their husbands, although it is likely that this figure is underreported because of shame and fear

(NFHS-2, 2000: 74–5). The ICRW conducted a large empirical study in India to map out the extent of domestic violence, which researchers told me in 2001 was the first effort to create a large empirical database on domestic violence in India. It began in 1995 and was at least partially funded by USAID and included a household survey on domestic violence in seven locations involving almost 10,000 people (letter from ICRW, January 19, 2000).

The Fiji Women's Crisis Centre (FWCC) carried out a major survey on the frequency of domestic violence through 1575 survey questionnaires, qualitative research, and an examination of police statistics and FWCC data from 1993 to 1997. The research was supported by the UNIFEM Trust Fund, the Asia Foundation, and the Fiji government (Fiji Women's Crisis Centre 2000). This survey found that 65.8 percent of women with partners (1,500 people) have been hit by their partners, while 47 percent of all married male respondents said they hit their wives (2000: 16–17). Of those women who reported being hit, 30 percent said they were beaten repeatedly (2000: 24). The report found that domestic abuse is widely tolerated and is increasing in frequency and that women most commonly think they are hit for disobedience, laziness, or adultery, while men most commonly say they hit their wives because of disobedience (2000: 32).

A survey of research on domestic violence in Hong Kong notes that there was virtually no data prior to 1980, but in the early 1980s some research began to document the scope of the problem (Yeung 1991: 32–3). As early as 1984, police in Hong Kong recorded "battered wife" as a separate category, facilitating research on the problem. Several studies examined frequencies of domestic violence and sexual harassment during the late 1980s and early 1990s (Tang, Lee, and Cheung 1999: 46–7). The social welfare department also began to collect statistics (Yeung 1991: 33). A 1996 survey of 1,132 cohabiting women randomly sampled in Hong Kong revealed that two-thirds reported at least one incident of verbal abuse and a tenth one incident of physical abuse by their husbands in the past year (Tang 1999a: 180; see also Tang 1999b). More recent research has explored the impacts on children and children's perspectives (Chan 2000a, 2000b; Yeung and Lok 2001).

The earliest studies on domestic violence in China were in the 1990s (Wang Xingjuan 1999b). A 1990 nationwide ACWF survey in China reported that about 29 percent of women said they are beaten at least occasionally (Human Rights in China 1995: 23). In 1994 the Beijing Women's Federation did a survey of surrounding counties and found domestic violence in 20 percent of families surveyed (Human Rights in China 1995: 23). The DVRIP program in Beijing included in its many research projects a survey of the frequency of domestic violence. They collected 3,780 questionnaires in wealthy, middle, and poor provinces and did 30 in-depth interviews and monitored hotline calls. The survey showed that 24 percent of women reported fighting at least once a year and 38 percent of those with fighting said that there was some violence in the marriage. A survey of 2,351 households in urban and rural Shanghai by the Shanghai Women's Federation in 2002 reported 93.5 percent of urban women and 94.5 percent of rural women said they had never experienced family violence (Xinhua News Agency 2002, June 14). On the other hand, another news report said that the ACWF survey found that domestic violence occurs in 30 percent of all Chinese families (Impress Service 2000). A 2000 survey of 2,500 men and women reported that 33.9 percent of families face domestic violence, probably an underreported statistic because of the "traditional" idea of Chinese people of keeping family problems within the family (*China Women's News*,

March 25, 2000, trans. by Wei-Ying Lin). A 1999–2000 national survey of 3,323 men and women between 20 and 64 reported that 34 percent of women experienced violence by their male partners and 18 percent of men were hit by their female partners, most of the latter in the course of mutual fighting. Male on female hitting was more common in rural areas than urban (21% vs. 14%; Parish et al. 2004: 177). Statistics from ACWF showed that domestic violence increased in the late 1990s as a result of women's increasing economic dependence on men and the increase in extramarital affairs (*China Women's News*, August 3, 2000, trans. by Wei-Ying Lin).[6]

Disparities in survey data come from many sources, but one is the term used. There is no term for "domestic violence" in Chinese. One word, *bao-li*, refers to brute force, while another, *nue-dai*, refers to cruel treatment or abuse, and a third, *qin-fan*, refers to violation. A focus group in Hong Kong found that the latter terms provided a broader definition of abuse (Tang et al. 2000). The term used will clearly affect reported frequencies. A 2002 survey of 3,692 rural and urban men and women in China using the term bao-li found 2.7 percent reported violence by their spouses, 1.3 percent of men and 3.9 percent of women. However, when couples are asked if they quarrel, of the 80 percent who say they do, 35 percent said they used violence in the quarrel and 29 percent of women said that their husband verbally insults or abuses them, suggesting different patterns depending on the term used (Liu and Zhang 2002).

Most people think males cause the violence with the wife being the victim, and a quarter think that the children are also victims (*China Women's News*, March 25, 2000, trans. by Wei-Ying Lin). Over a third (38%) thought respecting and taking care of each family member were the best ways to deal with domestic violence, but 17 percent thought each family should take care of its family problems itself, 27 percent advocated resort to law, and 14 percent to other organizations such as the local women's federation.

To a significant extent, shared academic work and conferences spread ideas about domestic violence globally. There are several global Internet listserves on violence against women, sponsored by INSTRAW, UNIFEM, International Women's Rights Action Watch of Asia Pacific, the Rutgers Center for Global Leadership, Amnesty International, the CEDAW Committee, and a women's rights organization in Nigeria. UNIFEM sponsored an end-violence listserve that included perhaps 2,500 people in 130 countries and ran, more or less continuously, for about two years in 2001–2. A six-month seminar sponsored by the UN training agency INSTRAW focused on men's violence. Cedaw4change is an online discussion forum with 683 members.

Major conferences play similar roles. The Ford Foundation facilitated the development of a Chinese program on violence against women by hosting a conference for Indian and Chinese activists in Jaipur, India in 1998. Chinese activists said this meeting was the impetus for their domestic violence intervention project and that they learned a lot about developments in the United States and Britain. There was also an important training program in India on judicial attitudes toward violence in India that helped to galvanize women's rights activists in Fiji. In the early 1990s, the NGO Sakshi studied judicial attitudes toward women and violence against women by interviewing 109 judges in a project supported by the Canadian International Development Agency, finding widespread gender bias (Sakshi 1996). In 1997, Sakshi held a training session in gender equality for the judiciary with the support of the chief justice of India (Sakshi 1997). This program was attended by judiciary leaders from Bangladesh, India, Nepal, Sri Lanka, Pakistan, Fiji, Canada, Australia, and Kiribati. Judges from Canada and Australia discussed the problems of gender bias and judicial discretion in their countries. Both of the representatives from Fiji who attended this workshop have continued to work for human rights and women's rights subsequently and one of them is still very central to the movement. This is only a small fraction of the international meetings and conferences regularly attended by the leaders of the NGOs dedicated to stopping violence against women in these countries.

Comparisons

Thus, a basic set of social service strategies circulates globally. These strategies are appropriated and translated into local social and cultural conditions. Despite claims to national distinctiveness, approaches to gender violence in all of these countries take place within a shared discourse of feminism and social work. The activists who develop these strategies are part of a transnational feminist movement whose members routinely meet and exchange ideas at transnational conferences and through publications and the Internet. Transnationally educated national elites and expatriates play critical roles in the transfer of service intervention models. Expatriate communities contributed to the relatively early and extensive adoption of services in Fiji and Hong Kong. Many of the leaders of gender violence interventions in these countries traveled widely for their academic education and now journey to conferences around the world.

Despite talk about the need to indigenize these approaches, they are the same feminist ideas and techniques rephrased in local cultural terms. In Hong Kong, for example, the power and control wheel is translated into Cantonese. Examples of independent women are drawn from Chinese history and Confucianism in a process one scholar described as "Chinese packaging." Men's groups in Hong Kong empha-size Western ideas of gender equality rather than Chinese concepts of lineage solidarity or Confucian family harmony. Similarly, advocates in India draw on images from Hindu mythology of strong, independent women, but they still see gender inequality as the basic problem and understand battering as the product of social and economic conditions. While family and economic systems shape the opportunities for exit and the costs of leaving, the basic approach to controlling male violence is surprisingly similar across these broad economic, political, and social differences.

The meanings of culture

Insofar as culture is discussed in social service settings, the concept is more like contentious culture than tradition or national identity, ideas common in national and transnational human rights debates. The national and local level social service providers I talked to rarely blamed culture in any simple or essentialized way for the violence women encountered. Although activists thought that cultural beliefs sup-ported domestic violence, they focused on state indifference, a lack of services, and a failure of laws and their implementation. The inability to find a satisfactory life outside marriage was often mentioned, not as a problem of culture but as a difficulty with housing, social stigma, and economic survival. They recognized variations by religion, region, urbanism, and social class in the extent to which women experi-enced violence and could leave their family situations but did not see women trapped by culture. Female feticide is recognized as a growing problem in India, for example, but it is attributed to patriarchal views found in only some regions in the north of the country.

Sometimes culture was described as contributing to violence for minorities or people in rural areas. National minority or immigrant characteristics were raised in discussions of the Muslim community in India and the mainlanders in Hong Kong. In China, activist leaders sometimes attributed the problem in rural areas to "feudal ideologies" because there "traditional feudal concepts and customs are stronger" (Wang Xingjuan 1999a: 1502). In Hong Kong, a disproportionate number of shelter residents are women from mainland China, and their greater vulnerability to violence is understood as a product of their more traditional culture as well as their isolation from networks of family support. Chan Ko Ling, on the basis of his study of male batterers in Hong Kong, argues that it is not traditional culture that is at fault but rigid gender-role expectations in the face of rapid economic and social changes and a changing status for women (2000). He advocates a Chinese approach that emphasizes face and the man's responsibility for the family as well as gender equality.

Allowing local community control over programs is one way to help them adapt to local cultural and social conditions. For example, Merilyn Tahi has been running the Vanuatu Women's Centre for many years and, with funding from the Australian aid agency AusAID through the Fiji Women's Crisis Centre (FWCC) has set up about eighteen local committees in different parts of the country. These committees are working to develop violence intervention programs in their communities. In my interview with her and in her lectures, she stressed the importance of bringing the local chiefs or church pastors into the process, inviting them to meetings, including them in discussions with her when she comes from the capital, and getting them involved in opposing domestic violence. Several grass-roots activists have developed strategies for involving local male and female leaders. These are examples of efforts to tailor programs to local cultural conditions in a way that recognizes and works through the power relationships of the local community.

Thus, local activists doing service delivery tend to see culture not as a reified entity but as a set of resources. If donors do not allow grassroots control of programs, they may import notions of "culture" from the transnational domain rather than allowing local groups to define for themselves what culture means at that particular moment and place. There is an important difference between a top-down program seeking to be culturally sensitive in terms of an essentialized idea of culture and a locally controlled program that recognizes the complexity of local cultural ideas but allows local groups to tailor the program to the power dynamics and symbolic resources of the situation in which they work.

Human Rights Advocacy

Human rights advocates rely on the international legal system far more than local social service providers do. International treaties and principles can be incorporated into national legal systems either by legislation or by reference in judicial decisions. Human rights are also promoted by human rights commissions that handle individual complaints. It is primarily at the highest levels of government that international human rights instruments are important. National NGOs, national commissions for women, human rights commissions, and the upper layers of the judiciary are

most likely to invoke international human rights treaties. These international standards may be used to interpret the meaning of gender equality for constitutional
jurisprudence (ESCAP 1997: 14).

In contrast to the social service tier, human rights advocacy is primarily an activity
of national and transnational elites. By and large, these ideas have little resonance at
the grass roots. The major actors in human rights advocacy at the national level are
typically educated, transnational elites who are part of the same transnational world
as those who serve as experts and government representatives in UN meetings.
Many are lawyers, academics, or NGO leaders. Political and economic elites in
postcolonial societies often feel that they belong to the modern transnational world
more than the local village one. Although many retain ties to their villages, some
elites in Delhi, Beijing, and Hong Kong view the rural village as farther away than
London, Paris, and New York.

In none of the countries I studied did activists think human rights were widely
understood in poor communities. Even for countries with a British colonial legal
legacy, human rights are far less salient than national rights at the grass roots.
In India, for example, many people said that although rights language in general
was widespread, knowledge of human rights and of specific documents such as
CEDAW was limited to those working internationally. Delhi activists working on
violence against women said that the national discourse of rights is far more
important for promoting reforms in the area of gender violence than international
human rights principles. According to a leader in the Joint Women's Program in
Delhi, only women's groups are aware of CEDAW. CEDAW is good for lobbying at
high levels with government officials such as those in the Department of Women and
Child Development, but poor urban and rural people do not understand these ideas
(interview, October 2001). For most people, the Indian Constitution is the basis for
rights. A prominent feminist lawyer in Delhi, the director of the Women's Rights
Initiative of the Lawyers' Collective, said that she uses local laws rather than
international conventions in her cases, but international laws can be invoked in
support of arguments as a form of setting standards, perhaps influencing judges who
have open minds toward international treaties. A member of the Human Rights
Commission in India told me that the Indian Constitution is so strong that most
people draw their faith in rights from that document and pay little attention to the
international standards (interview, October 2001).

A central feature of human rights advocacy is generating international pressure
on one's own government. By appropriating human rights language, advocates
gain access to international expertise, funding, and political pressure that may influence decisions at home. There are symbolic, economic, and institutional pressures
on states to conform to the norms of the international community. International
pressure is important for countries concerned about international opinion and economically dependent on international trade, aid, and investment. Large and economically powerful countries, such as China with its vast markets, can more easily resist
this pressure (see Foot 2000). As CEDAW experts point out, the impact of their
concluding comments depends on the pressure that national NGOs can mobilize.
Some NGOs, such as Sakshi, in India use international law itself as a resource.[7]

International donors are as important for human rights advocates as they are for
social service providers. Advocacy organizations, human rights education programs,
and conferences where governmental and NGO leaders learn the treaty-monitoring
process, all require donors, as does NGO attendance at UN meetings. UN agencies
such as UNIFEM and UNICEF usually have national or regional offices that

develop programs and promote transnational policies and sometimes fund NGO participation in UN events. On the basis of my discussions with Ford Foundation representatives in India and other donors at UN meetings, observations of international funding procedures, and participation on the board of a regional NGO, it appears that international donors allow some flexibility in specific projects but set the general agenda. A funder may wish to support human rights education, for example, but allow local groups to determine how to carry this out. This means that the broad agendas for intervention are defined internationally although the scope of work is defined locally.

The rest of this chapter discusses four specific ways that international human rights law shapes policy toward violence against women. First, human rights ideas may be incorporated into domestic law through legislation or judicial decision-making. Second, human rights commissions and women's commissions encourage citizens to complain about their problems in human rights terms. Third, international workshops and training programs educate the judiciary about the treaty process, human rights standards, and treaties such as CEDAW. International and national donors also sponsor programs to provide human rights education and advocacy at the grass roots. And fourth, the frequent demands for country reports, NGO shadow reports, and attendance at UN meetings and conferences encourages stocktaking by governments and fosters communication between government and civil society.

Incorporation of CEDAW through legislation and judicial decisions

In most countries, particularly those that follow the UK model, ratified treaties do not automatically become state law but must be incorporated through legislation and administrative regulation or indirectly through judicial interpretations of court cases (ESCAP 1997: 12). In India, for example, ratified treaties do not have the force of law without an additional act of Parliament (interview, October 2001). A former Supreme Court justice of India, now on the Human Rights Commission, said when I interviewed her that the Indian Constitution is actually better than the international instruments since it can be enforced. But the international documents can be used to interpret the laws. A 1997 Supreme Court judgment on sexual harassment in the workplace, which this judge wrote (Vishaka v. State of Rajasthan, AIR 1997 SC 3011), provided guidelines proscribing sexual harassment in the workplace. The opinion used CEDAW in support of its decision (National Commission for Women 2001: 6–7). A UN study found that the Indian superior courts have used constitutional interpretation creatively to develop a human rights jurisprudence, providing an example for other countries in the region (ESCAP 1997: 29). New legislation can draw on international treaties. The Indian 2001 draft domestic violence law mentions CEDAW and the UN Declaration on the Elimination of All Forms of Violence against Women, while a UN document advocating a uniform civil code for personal laws in South Asia notes that international principles can serve as the standard for these new laws (ESCAP 1997: 24). Both the Family Law Act in Fiji and the Law of the People's Republic of China on the Protection of Women's Rights and Interests are based on CEDAW.

Attorneys may also refer to international law in their briefs. A former chief justice of the Indian Supreme Court, interviewed in October 2001, said that it is common for briefs to the Supreme Court to refer to international human rights treaties. For example, a case filed in the Supreme Court in 1994 by Women's Action Research and Legal Action for Women (Writ Petition [Civil] No. 684 of 1994) used CEDAW (Jethmalani 1995: 106–7). The petition asked the court to order the government to show what steps were being taken to end discrimination in the personal laws consistent with the principles of CEDAW and relied on the preliminary report of Radhika Coomaraswamy and the 1994 Protection of Human Rights Act of India. The petition suggests that initial efforts should be directed toward the personal laws of Hindus until other groups are ready to change their personal laws. It focuses on gender inequalities in Hindu laws of inheritance, adoption, and guardianship (Jethmalani 1995: 113, 114–16). When I interviewed the head of Women's Action Research in 2001, the Supreme Court had not yet acted on this petition.

In Fiji, a High Court judge said in a 2003 interview that Section 43:2 of the Fiji Constitution makes provision for applying international law in cases of human rights violations. She looks at court of appeal decisions from the Canadian, Namibian, South African (post-apartheid), and New Zealand supreme courts to see how other countries have applied these international laws. Fiji ratified CEDAW in 1995, but the judge uses conventions that Fiji has not ratified as well for issues such as that on the treatment of offenders. The Fiji Human Rights Commission also relies on international law. When the Fiji government presented its first report to CEDAW in 2002, it said it was reviewing legislation in the light of Convention on the Rights of the Child and CEDAW. A women's rights activist in Fiji said that CEDAW is helpful in rape and family law cases and has been used domestically on several occasions. Judicial decisions in Fiji sometimes rely on CEDAW, such as State v. Filipe Bechu (1999), heard in the magistrate's court.

In the run up to Hong Kong's incorporation into China in 1997, Hong Kong leaders turned enthusiastically to international human rights treaties. The 1991 Basic Law incorporated much of the International Covenant on Civil and Political Rights (ICCPR). CEDAW was ratified in 1996 and was mentioned in debates over social welfare. Hong Kong presented its first report to CEDAW in 1999 with considerable participation by women's NGOs (Erickson and Byrnes 1999: 359–61). In March 1999, the Home Affairs Panel of the Legislative Council held hearings to consider the concluding comments and the government's response to them. Although it did not accept the major recommendations of the committee, especially the creation of national machinery for women's issues, Erickson and Byrnes argue that the reporting exercise still forced government officials to engage in analysis and justification of their policies in light of the convention's requirements in front of the Legislative Council and the international community (1999: 363–4).

Although China ratified CEDAW in 1980, the government has only recently made efforts to educate the people about it. There are ongoing debates about whether or not CEDAW can be considered law (interview, May 2001). A feminist journalist in Beijing said that she finds the UN's documents and mechanisms useful for her activism and another journalist said that the national-level support for interventions in violence against women is far less than the international support (interviews, 2001). CEDAW is sometimes used by feminist lawyers in their arguments. For example, a lawyer I interviewed at the Centre for Women's Law Studies and Legal Services of Peking University in Beijing, one of the most influential centers on women's rights in China, said that the center sometimes referred to CEDAW in their complaints (interview, May 2001). In one case, CEDAW was not mentioned in the final judgment but reference to it in the briefs probably helped the center prevail.

Human rights commissions and women's commissions

National and state commissions are important institutional mechanisms for implementing international treaties. These are typically government-funded but semiautonomous institutions that advise on policy and receive and manage complaints. India and Fiji have human rights commissions and Hong Kong has an Equal Opportunity Commission. Both India and Hong Kong have National Women's Commissions. These commissions are, of course, transnational transplants. The Human Rights Commission in India was established in 1993 by the Human Rights Protection Act. It provides a forum for the investigation of human rights violations including those against women (see generally Mohapatra 2001). About 70,000 people file complaints every year at India's Human Rights Commission, mostly about police behavior. In the area of women's rights, complaints are about dowry deaths, reproductive rights, rape, and female feticide. The commission will investigate the complaint and make recommendations to the government. The number of complaints has increased dramatically from 400 in the first year to about 70,000 in the late 1990s, according to the annual reports of the commission. In 2001 I interviewed one of the five members of the commission who is a former chief justice of the Supreme Court. She said that many people from the villages complain and that this avenue of complaining is spreading. They get faxes from the villages, as well as postcards, telegrams, and letters. She thought that world conferences, such as the 1993 Vienna Conference on Human Rights, helped to generate an increasing interest in human rights. Interest in human rights seems to be spreading into the countryside. The commission makes policy proposals to Parliament and has recently pushed hard for reform of Hindu personal laws to eliminate ceilings on maintenance for women after divorce (interview, 2001). The NGO developing a new domestic violence law consulted the commission on several occasions. In 2001 the Human Rights Commission defined female feticide as a human rights violation after an investigation into the sharp disparity in numbers between boys and girls aged 0–6 in certain provinces revealed in a recent census.

Fiji established its Human Rights Commission in 1999 as an autonomous body supported by the government (interview with director, February 2002). Although its primary focus is labor relations, it also supports women's rights. It works on the prevention of sexual harassment in the workplace and does considerable education and outreach promoting human rights. Decisions of the commission frequently refer to UN treaties. The director is from Fiji, but spent 14 years in New Zealand and has both a PhD and a law degree. She is a member of a prominent family in Fiji. She travels widely internationally and knows judicial and legal leaders around the world. The commission played an important role in facilitating international scrutiny of Fiji's racial policies, cooperating with the committee monitoring the Convention on the Elimination of Racial Discrimination (CERD) in 2002. During the CERD hearings in 2003, the government published a long statement in the national paper defending itself against its international critics (*Fiji Time*, March 5, 2003: 15; see also Ecumenical Centre for Research, Education and Advocacy 2002).

Hong Kong formed the Equal Opportunity Commission instead of a Human Rights Commission. The EOC was developed in 1996 to implement the 1995 Sex Discrimination Ordinance, a law enacted in part to permit the extension of CEDAW to Hong Kong (Byrnes 1999: 13). The Equal Opportunity Commission has broad jurisdiction to review laws, policies, and practices related to gender-based violence and other forms of gender discrimination by the ordinance (Byrnes 1999: 13;

Tang, Lee, and Cheung 1999: 51). In a flagship case, the EOC demonstrated that school admissions procedures discriminated against girls and, through litigation, succeeded in changing the policy.

Hong Kong and India have national women's commissions, while the ACWF serves as the political spokesman for women's issues in China. The National Commission for Women (NCW) in India was set up in 1990 to safeguard women's interests by reviewing legislation, intervening in individual complaints, and undertaking remedial actions. It has examined laws, made recommendations, and participated in the planning process for women's socioeconomic development. It has some autonomy from the government because of its legislative basis. For the NCW, international law is very important. It uses ratified treaties to pressure the government. I interviewed a former member of the commission in 2000 and its member secretary in 2001. According to the member secretary, the commission receives about 5000 complaints a year and either calls the accused into the office and tries to sort out the problem or refers the case to state governments and state women's commissions. In 1993–4 the NCW drafted a bill on domestic violence and sent it on to the government. The NCW also established *Pariwar Mahila Lok Adalat* (Women's Family Courts) to provide speedy justice to women (NCW Annual Report 1996–7: 7, quoted in Poonacha and Pandey 1999: 179–80). A UNIFEM representative said only a few had been established by 2000, primarily in urban areas. These courts are for family disputes and use social workers instead of lawyers. They deal largely with divorce, maintenance, marriage, adoption, and dowry (NCW interview, January 2000). However, many NGOs complain that the NCW lacks power. For example, a member of the Women's Rights Initiative of the Lawyer's Collective complained on an electronic listserve that although the NCW did a report on the communal violence in Gujarat in 2002 and referred to CEDAW and other international conventions, the report was weak and did not pinpoint the police's role in this violence (May 20, 2002 posting, end-violence listserve).

The Women's Commission in Hong Kong was established by the Hong Kong Special Administrative Region in 2001 after a long period of pressure by Hong Kong women's NGOs and strong support from the CEDAW Committee. Its mandate is to advise the government on strategies for the advancement of women, review service delivery measures, initiate research, and encourage education on women's issues (Leung 2002: 2). At a major conference sponsored by the Women's Commission in 2002, CEDAW was raised as a resource for the women's movement. Yet, the Women's Commission in Hong Kong has also been criticized for its weakness. These transnational institutions operate in relatively similar ways and are clearly part of a single global network of institutions.

International human rights training

An important way that human rights ideas and activists circulate globally is through training programs. I encountered several forms of internationally supported human rights training. The UN runs training programs on treaty ratification and report writing that bring together government and NGO representatives as well as international experts such as CEDAW members. A series of workshops in both South Asia and the Pacific organized by UNIFEM and the Division for the Advancement of Women to teach about CEDAW ratification and report writing took place during the 1990s and early 2000s. In the Pacific, there was a subregional meeting on Pacific women in 1980 (Rasmussen 1980), a training program for Pacific nations on the process of ratifying CEDAW in 1991 run by the Division for the Advancement of Women (1991), and a workshop on CEDAW in 1992 (Singh 1992). In 1998, the Secretariat of the Pacific Community held a regional consultative meeting on the implementation of CEDAW (Secretariat of the Pacific Community 1998). In 2001, another workshop on CEDAW took place in Auckland, New Zealand. In 1998–9, FWRM served as the secretariat for CEDAW in Fiji and organized national workshops, local legal literacy training, and media campaigns to increase awareness of its benefits for women (ESCAP 2000: 13–19). This project culminated in a subregional meeting on CEDAW in the Pacific region in 1999 (ESCAP 2000: 63). UNIFEM and several South Pacific regional organizations sponsored a workshop for NGOs and government representatives on report writing in 2003.

A similar series of meetings took place in South Asia. In November 1999 and December 2001, UNIFEM held workshops on CEDAW report writing that brought together government representatives from India, Nepal, Sri Lanka, and the CEDAW Committee. UNIFEM also held pre- and post-reporting meetings for Nepal, India, the Maldives, and Sri Lanka.

Some UN workshops focus directly on violence against women. In 2003, the UNIFEM regional office in Fiji held a workshop inspired by a similar one for the Asian region in 2002. Some women from the Pacific attended the earlier workshop and thought that it was needed in the Pacific region. This workshop was part of a UNIFEM global scan to assess the status of violence against women world wide, a project discussed at the 2003 CSW meetings in New York.

Training is also done by national NGOs with international funding. For example, Jagori, one of the oldest women's organizations in India, provides gender training for development projects, including the MS program that produced the nari adalats. In 2001, I visited Jagori's office and resource center in Delhi, a set of small rooms packed floor to ceiling with books and resource materials, desks, and computers and a small staff of energetic young women. The director, Kalpana Vishwanathan, told me that they talk about rights and CEDAW in workshops they run. Although they have not used CEDAW extensively, they refer to the convention to indicate global support for women's rights. Jagori chose to accept donor funds to run its programs, although it recognized that this compromised its autonomy. Its busy office differed from that of other NGOs who refused external funding and achieved greater independence but were not able to maintain an office, staff, and services.

In 1997, some women activists in China approached the ACWF and offered to do training in gender awareness. They used a UNDP training manual, *Gender and Development*, that I had also seen in India to provide participatory gender-training seminars for judges, court personnel, members of the ACWF, hospital staff, police, and subdistrict leaders (interview, May 2001). Many of the participants resisted at first because they were used to a far more authoritarian style of teaching instead of sitting in a circle and talking. Over time, many came to like it. In my interview with the feminist journalist who ran these programs, she spoke Chinese to an interpreter but used the words for "facilitators" and "trainees" in English, suggesting that this training approach was originally in English. There are very few NGOs in China and those that exist are largely dependent on foreign funding.

In Fiji, the FWRM has worked since 1993 on legal literacy campaigns, focusing on CEDAW and women's rights (FWRM 2000: 2–3). It seeks to improve the socio-economic and political status of women through legislative and attitudinal change (FWRM 2000: 8). It handles complaints, provides paralegal services, and serves as an advocacy and lobbying group for women's human rights in a wide range of areas. Some of the FWRM leaders attended the Global Leadership Institute for Women's Organizations at the Center for Women's Global Leadership at Rutgers University in 1997 (FWRM 2000: 25). The Regional Rights Resource Team (RRRT) grew out of FWRM. Since 1995 it has provided grassroots human rights education focused on women's rights and CEDAW. In 2003 RRRT was working in Vanuatu, Kiribati, and Fiji with funding from the British government. In 1999, the crisis center, FWCC, received A\$2.2 million for five years from AusAID, the Australian government's aid agency, to provide counseling and community education and to develop a Pacific network of programs addressing violence against women (Fiji Women's Crisis Centre, *Pacific Women against Violence* 5 [4]: 3). Funding for Pacific human rights programs comes largely from wealthy Pacific donor countries such as Australia, New Zealand, and Japan as well as Britain and Canada.

International foundation or government funding is essential to these programs. Many of the programs I visited in Delhi, Beijing, and Fiji had international donor funding, as did the major research study on domestic violence in Beijing. I talked to Macarthur and Ford program officers in Delhi who said both foundations are interested in funding human rights and women's rights projects. Ford has a budget of about \$25 million in India and has had a program there for fifty years; in China the Ford program is a little over ten years old (interview with Ford official, October 2001). In India, 50 percent of the human rights work is on women's rights, both in funds and in proportion of grantees. The human rights program officer in Delhi said that most of these projects work on violence against women, sexual harassment, domestic violence or women's property and inheritance. Ford also supported groups going to Beijing and Beijing Plus Five. A sociology professor I interviewed in Delhi in 2001 said that since the late 1990s, human rights have become increasingly important as the basis for funding. She both welcomed the ideas and worried that NGOs often operate outside the state with little accountability.

In China, the Ford Foundation now funds community legal services and university-based programs such as legal education. My trip to China in May 2001 was funded by a grant from Ford to develop university training in the sociology of law. It provided me the opportunity to interview many activists and academics working to reduce violence against women, including those in the DVRIP research project on domestic violence. Because I heard about the DVRIP project in 2001, I was invited to attend the final conference in November 2002 as one of nine international participants. The Ford program in China defines its work as falling in the area of rule of law, governance, and judicial administration. Hong Kong, in contrast, no longer receives international funding because of its affluence. Human rights advocacy and social services are now supported by the government or by local funders, such as the Jockey Club.

According to officials at Ford, their general practice is to decide on a focus and consider proposals or look for groups that do work in this area. They may encourage groups to take up such issues. Once a project is started, they try not to direct it, although there are differences in the personalities of program officers. Program officers recognize the power imbalance between them and the recipients and that any comments they make may be taken as authoritative. In Delhi, both the Ford Foundation program officer and one of its recipients, the Lawyer's Collective, said that although the funder sets the general agenda, the recipient has considerable flexibility in how the work is carried out. Close scrutiny is reserved mostly for questions of finances and accountability. Another feminist Indian NGO said that the funders set the issues and the organization has to respond. For example, they now do a lot of gender training because all the funders insist on including gender training in their programs. Ford recipients in China said that they discussed the project with them at some length but had a free hand to work it out as they wanted. Thus, the extensive training and educational programs funded by foreign governments and foundations on behalf of human rights draw people together transnationally, promote global ideas, and reflect agendas that circulate globally.

UN events and NGO–government collaboration

UN events punctuate the exchange of information among NGOs and governments. They are fundamental to transnational consensus building, program transplants, and the localization of transnational knowledge. UN conferences and commission meetings provide NGOs opportunities to work together at the national and international level and to work with their governments in what is often a more accessible environment. When government representatives and NGOs prepare country reports and make presentations about the conditions in their countries in international forums, they are often forced to talk to each other. Writing reports together fosters interchange, even when governments and NGOs do not agree. UN training for convention ratification and report writing typically includes both NGO and government representatives.

Large meetings such as the 1995 Fourth World Conference on Women in Beijing spread human rights ideas to those who participate and beyond. These world conferences pull together large numbers of NGO representatives – about 30,000 in Beijing – plus government delegations that include both NGOs and government representatives. A large proportion of the activists and academics I interviewed had attended the Beijing meeting and many said they found it transformative. Even a woman from the tiny Pacific nation of Kiribati whom I met at the Fiji Women's Crisis Centre said she went to Beijing and was very impressed by the excitement of the event, all the marching, carrying of placards, and assertion of opinions. In India, I met a 60-year-old woman activist living in a remote rural village who described her first plane ride and her trip to Beijing with great excitement. Feminists I interviewed in Beijing all agreed that the conference had galvanized work on domestic violence and made clear the links with women's health and the enjoyment of human rights. Many of the reforms I heard about in Beijing in 2001 and 2002 dated from the 1995 conference. People I talked to throughout the Asia-Pacific region referred to the Beijing Platform for Action. In Fiji, the Platform for Action served as the basis for the government's Women's Plan of Action drawn up in 1998.

Since the late 1990s, both UNIFEM and UNICEF have incorporated more of a rights perspective in their work. UNICEF organized two conferences on violence against women and girls in South Asia in 1997 and 1999, for example (UNICEF 1999). While UNICEF supports the Convention on the Rights of the Child, UNIFEM has been increasingly active in supporting the CEDAW process. After 1998, UNIFEM put more emphasis on sending NGO representatives to CEDAW meetings, often through the International Women's Rights Action Watch of Asia Pacific, based in Malaysia. In an interview in India in 2001, a UNIFEM staff member told me that UNIFEM supported NGO participation in the CEDAW process by training governments and NGOs in report preparation and by sending NGO representatives to CEDAW hearings. When India reported to CEDAW in 2000, UNIFEM encouraged NGOs to prepare a shadow report and sent nine

NGO representatives from India. One of those who authored the report said that the experts at CEDAW used the shadow report to ask the government many pointed questions. Under the pressure, inspiration, challenge, and financial support of UNIFEM, NGOs in India brought out a shadow report for Beijing Plus Five called Task Force on Women 2000, according to one of the activists who organized the project. This 80-page report assessed the progress of the government on each of the 12 points of the Platform for Action. The task force had 25 members, but according to one of its leaders, it took considerable networking among the NGOs to get them together and, after completing its task, the task force disbanded (interview, 2001).

CEDAW reports also generate consultation between NGOs and governments. In Fiji, several women's NGOs worked with the government on the CEDAW report and also produced an independent shadow report. Three NGO representatives attended the 2002 CEDAW meetings in New York representing FWRM and RRRT. China also sent a delegation to Beijing Plus Five and organized informational meetings when the delegates returned from the conference. Two factions from Hong Kong went to Beijing Plus Five, divided between a more establishment and a more feminist group. Two working groups from China went to Beijing Plus Five, one on media and one on violence against women (interview, 2001). The working group against domestic violence, made up of four China NGOs (the Women's Legal Research and Service Center, the Female Counseling and Developing Center of the Social Work Department of the Chinese Women's College, the Maple Women's Center, and the ShanXi Women's Legal Research and Service Center) prepared two reports for Beijing Plus Five. The reports discussed government and NGO actions against domestic violence and were funded by Hong Kong Oxfam (China Working Group 2000a and 2000b). Two NGO observers watched China make its report to CEDAW in 1999 and an expert from China sits on the CEDAW Committee. However, the shadow report by Human Rights in China, a New York-based NGO, and three other NGOs outside China complained that the government's 1999 CEDAW report failed to incorporate the substantial research and publication within China on women's status. It failed to circulate the report or to allow these groups to participate in its preparation even though the report was produced by the ACWF (Human Rights in China 1998: 5, 12–13, 27).

Thus, UN events and conferences provide rich opportunities for collaboration and conversation among NGOs and governments domestically and internationally. The British Commonwealth sponsors other international collaborations such as a conference sponsored by the Commonwealth Secretariat in the mid-1990s in Hong Kong for Commonwealth countries on using CEDAW in domestic courts (Byrnes, Connors, and Bik 1996) and regular meetings among Commonwealth countries and their judiciaries.

Conclusions

Social service programs and human rights advocacy are complementary. Although human rights workers are usually transnational NGO and government elites while social service providers are more often middle-class professionals, the two initiatives support each other. The successful delivery of services, such as shelters and support groups, may create a greater rights consciousness among service recipients. Programs encourage clients to define themselves as rights-bearing individuals.

Rights-conscious clients are more willing to support other human rights projects. Moreover, leaders of social service NGOs themselves become important promoters of transnational human rights. They often attend international meetings, write shadow reports, and pressure their governments with UN documents and concluding comments. Some push governments to write more thoughtful reports to international treaty bodies. Many find that their governments are more responsive and more vulnerable to shaming at international meetings. At home, NGO leaders and their rights-conscious clientele promote human rights institutions that respond to rights claims. Thus, the provision of services framed in rights terms fosters the development of rights consciousness by middle-level social service providers and grassroots service recipients and generates pressure on governments to expand their human rights systems.

On the other side, human rights advocacy at the national level creates political space for local social service delivery focused on women's rights. Those eager to expand services for women find that nationally ratified international documents help to mobilize national support. Human rights commissions and women's commissions generate political support for rights initiatives. In countries with few social service resources, the provision of services is shaped less by domestic political agendas and more by international definitions of problems and solutions since these are the principal funders.

This essay has described how transnational feminist approaches to violence against women have been appropriated by country-based activists and tailored to specific contexts. The most striking finding is the extent to which, despite significant variation in cultural background, political power, and history of each country, the palette of reforms is similar. Domestic violence laws are developed through prototypes in other countries; shelters and other services are built on Euro-American models; community education campaigns and brochures conform to modern communication techniques; and surveys rely on shared social science methodologies. Countries develop similar commissions to support women's human rights. These are not parallel inventions but the product of transnational flows of knowledge, actors, programs, and funds. Mechanisms such as UN conferences foster circulation and exchange, drawing people from different countries together to learn about activities in other countries. The circulation is never free, however, but always channeled by global inequalities in wealth and power.

Transnational programs and ideas are translated into local cultural terms, but this occurs at a relatively superficial level, as a kind of window dressing. The laws and programs acquire local symbolic elaboration, but retain their fundamental grounding in transnational human rights concepts of autonomy, individualism, and equality. The programs are appropriated and translated but not fully indigenized. To blend completely with the surrounding social world is to lose the radical possibilities of human rights. It is the unfamiliarity of these ideas that makes them effective in breaking old modes of thought, for example, denaturalizing male privilege to use violence against women as a form of discipline. On the other hand, it is only when they take a familiar form that they are readily adopted. Like the tee shirt developed by the Aboriginal teenagers, human rights are appropriated when they draw on transnational ideas but present them in familiar cultural terms. These appropriations promote global cultural homogeneity, but the impact is greater on transnational elites and middle-level NGO activists than on people at the grass roots.

NOTES

1   In her comparative study of government responses to domestic violence and sexual ass-
    ault in 36 democratic countries, Weldon observes a similar repertoire of interventions.
    She finds that they are most extensive in Australia, Canada, and the United States (2002:
    143–54).
2   Rong Weiyi, "The interaction between the police and the community," DVRIP conference
    2002, trans. by Wei-Ying Lin.
3   "Social Work and Support for victims of Domestic Violence," presented at DVRIP
    International Conference 2002, trans. by Wei-Ying Lin, p. 4.
4   The MS program straddles the government–NGO divide, claiming either identity as it
    seems helpful (Sharma 2006). It functions in the autonomous fashion of a nongovern-
    mental organization in some contexts and as a government program in others. Personnel
    are paid by the government and sometimes emphasize their official roles, while other
    branches of government view them as relatively powerless (Sharma 2006). The full-time
    local women organizers are paid, but only slightly more than the government-stipulated
    minimum for skilled work (Sharma 2006: n. xi).
5   Seventeen women were given paralegal training by the MS program with a feminist
    critique of the legal system to develop alternate definitions of violence against women,
    divorce, and the like (ICRW 2002: 49).
6   A major study of Chinese women's social status conducted in 2001, updating a 1990
    survey, by the ACWF of 19,512 people in urban and rural areas showed that in the
    last ten years, despite improvements of women's social status and a great increase in
    consciousness of women's rights and acceptance of gender equality, the income gap
    between men and women is widening every year (*China Women's News*, September 5,
    2001, trans. by Wei-Ying Lin).
7   Sakshi offers training in addressing violence, intervention, and the law to women's
    groups, police, medial and legal personal, government functionaries, judges, parents,
    and individual women as well as conducting feminist legal research on violations of
    women's human rights (www.mnet.fr/webparticulier/a/aiindex/sakshi.html, September
    24, 2001).

REFERENCES

An-Na'im, Abdullahi Ahmed, 1992a. "Introduction." In Abdullahi Ahmed An-Na'im,
    ed., *Human Rights in Cross-Cultural Perspectives: A Quest for Consensus*, pp. 1–18.
    Philadelphia: Univ. of Pennsylvania Press.
—— . 1992b. "Toward a Cross-Cultural Approach to Defining International Standards
    of Human Rights: The Meaning of Cruel, Inhuman, or Degrading Treatment or
    Punishment." In Abdullahi Ahmed An-Na'im, ed., *Human Rights in Cross-Cultural
    Perspectives: A Quest for Consensus*, pp. 19–44. Philadelphia: Univ. of Pennsylvania
    Press.
Anon. 1999. "Fighting Violence against Women." *Tok Blong Pacific* 53 (1/2): 28.
Byrnes, Andrew. 1999. "CEDAW and Violence against Women: Implications for Hong Kong."
    A World Free of Violence against Women: Conference Proceedings. March 20, 1999.
    Hong Kong Convention and Exhibition Center.
Byrnes, Andrew, Jane Connors, and Lum Bik, eds. 1996. *Advancing the Human Rights of
    Women: Using International Human Rights Standards in Domestic Litigation*. London:
    Commonwealth Secretariat.
Centre for Women's Law Studies and Legal Services of Peking University. 2001. *Theory and
    Practice of Protection of Women's Rights and Interests in Contemporary China*. Beijing:
    Workers' Publishing House of China.

Chan Ko Ling. 2000a. "Study of the Impact of Family Violence on Battered Women and Their Children." Hong Kong: Christian Family Service Center and Department of Social Work and Social Administration, Univ. of Hong Kong, Resource Paper Series no. 38.

——— . 2000b. "Unraveling the Dynamics of Spousal Abuse through the Narrative Accounts of Chinese Male Batterers." PhD diss., Univ. of Hong Kong.

——— . 2001. *An Evaluative Study of Group Therapy for Male Batterers cum Intervention Strategies*. Hong Kong: Hong Kong Family Welfare Society.

China Working Group against Domestic Violence, ed. 2000a. *A Review of Governmental Efforts against Domestic Violence in China*. Project for Beijing + 5. Founded by Hong Kong Oxfam. 17 pp. Booklet in English and Chinese.

——— , ed. 2000b. *China: Actions Undertaking against Domestic Violence*. Project for Beijing + 5. Founded by Hong Kong Oxfam. 36 pp. Booklet in English and Chinese.

Coomaraswamy, Radhika. 1994. "To Bellow like a Cow: Women, Ethnicity, and the Discourse of Rights." In Rebecca J. Cook, ed., *Human Rights of Women: National and International Perspectives*, pp. 39–57. Philadelphia: Univ. of Pennsylvania Press.

Division for the Advancement of Women. 1991. "Report: South Pacific Seminar on CEDAW." Vienna, UN Office, April 2, 1991. SPS/CEDAW/1991/2. UN DAW reference room, New York.

——— . 2000. *Assessing the Status of Women: A Guide to Reporting under the Convention on the Elimination of All Forms of Discrimination against Women*. New York: United Nations Department of Economic and Social Affairs.

Domestic Violence in China: Research, Intervention and Prevention. c. 2001. *Newsletter*, no. 3.

Economic and Social Commission for Asia and the Pacific (ESCAP). 1997. *Human Rights and Legal Status of Women in the Asian and Pacific Region*, By Savitri Goonesekere. Studies on Women in Development 1. New York: United Nations.

——— . 2000. *Using CEDAW at the Grass Roots: Convention on the Elimination of All Forms of Discrimination against Women in the Pacific*. New York: United Nations, ST/ESCAP/2095.

Ecumenical Centre for Research, Education and Advocacy. 2002. *An NGO Report on the International Convention on the Elimination of All Forms of Racial Discrimination: Submission to the Fiji Country Report*. January. 32 pp.

Erickson, Moana, and Andrew Byrnes. 1999. "Hong Kong and the Convention on the Elimination of All Forms of Discrimination Against Women." *Hong Kong Law Journal* 29: 350–69.

Ferree, Myra Marx. 2003. "Resonance and Radicalism: Feminist Framing in the Abortion Debates of the United States and German." *American Journal of Sociology* 109 (2): 304–44.

Fiji Women's Crisis Centre. 1996. *Report on the Second Regional Meeting on Violence against Women in the Pacific*. Suva, Fiji.

——— . c.2000. *The Incidence, Prevalence and Nature of Domestic Violence and Sexual Assault in Fiji: A Research Project of the Fiji Women's Crisis Centre*. Supported by the UNIFEM Trust Fund New York, Asia Foundation, Government of Fiji, Department for Women.

Fiji Women's Rights Movement (FWRM). 2000. *Herstory: A Profile of the Fiji Women's Rights Movement*. Suva: Fiji Women's Rights Movement.

Foot, Rosemary. 2000. *Rights Beyond Borders: The Global Community and the Struggle over Human Rights in China*. Oxford: Oxford Univ. Press.

Guo Jianmei. 2000. "A Research Report of the Legal Aid Cases Undertaken by the Center for Women's Law Studies and Legal Services under the Law School of Peking University (1996–2000)." Typescript.

Hecht, Jonathan. 1998. "Women's Rights, States' Law: The Role of Law in Women's Rights Policy in China." In John D. Montgomery, ed., *Human Rights: Positive Policies in Asia and the Pacific Rim*, pp. 71–96. Hollis, NH: Hollis Publishing.

Human Rights in China. 1995. *Caught between Tradition and the State: Violations of the Human Rights of Chinese Women.* New York: Human Rights in China.

——. 1998. *Report on Implementation of CEDAW in the People's Republic of China: A Report with Recommendations and Questions for the Chinese Government Representatives.* New York: Asia Monitor Resource Centre, China Labour Bulletin, and Hong Kong Christian Industrial Committee.

ICRW (International Center for Research on Women (ICRW)): 1999–2002. *Domestic Violence in India,* vols. 1–5. Washington, DC: USAID/India.

——. 2002. *Women-Initiated Community Level Responses to Domestic Violence: Domestic Violence in India: Exploring Strategies, Promoting Dialogue 5.* Washington, DC: USAID/India.

International Women's Tribune Center. 2000. "Moving Ahead from the Final PrepCom to the Beijing Plus Five Special Session." From "300 Religious Right Representatives Attend Beijing Plus Five Preparatory Committee Meeting." By Jennifer Butler, Ecumenical Women 2000. *Preview 2000* (4 May): 1–11. New York: International Women's Tribune Center.

Jalal, Patricia. 1988. "The Urban Woman: Victim of a Changing Social Environment." In Leatuailevao Ruba Va'a and Joan Martin Teaiwa, eds., *Environment and Pacific Women: From the Globe to the Village,* pp. 30–7. Suva, Fiji: UH Manoa Library.

Jethmalani, Rani, ed. 1995. *Kali's Yug: Empowerment, Law and Dowry Deaths.* New Delhi: Har-Anand Publications.

——, ed. 2001. "Kali's Yug." *Women and Law Journal* (March), special issue: Bride Burning and Dowry. WARLAW.

Khagram, Sanjeev, James V. Riker, and Kathryn Sikkink, eds. 2002. *Restructuring World Politics: Transnational Social Movements, Networks, and Norms.* Minneapolis: Univ. of Minnesota Press.

Krishnamurthy, Mekhala. 2002. "In the Shadow of the State, in the Shade of a Tree: The Politics of the Possible in Rural Gujarat." BA thesis, Harvard University. MS on file with author.

Lawyers' Collective. 1992. *Legal Aid Handbook* 1: *Domestic Violence.* Delhi: Kali for Women.

Leung, Elsie. 2002. "Women for a Better Tomorrow." Speech by the Secretary for Justice at a Luncheon of the Women's Commission Conference 2002 on May 11, 2002.

Li Hongxiang. 2000. "Definition of Domestic Violence in Law Theory." In China Law Society et al., eds., *Research on Prevention and Control of Domestic Violence,* pp. 75–82. Beijing: Qunzhong Publishing House.

Liu Donghua. c.2001. "Five-year Consulting Report." Center for Women's Law Studies and Legal Service of Peking University.

Liu Meng and Cecelia Chan. 1999. "Enduring Violence and Staying in Marriage: Stories of Battered Women in Rural China." *Violence against Women* 5 (12): 1469–92.

—— and ——. 2000. "Family Violence in China: Past and Present." *New Global Development* 16: 74–87.

Liu Meng and Zhang Li-Xi. 2002. "Current Situation, Attitude, and Prevention Survey Report on Domestic Violence in China (National Survey subproject DVRIP)." Trans. by Wei-Ying Lin. 12 pp. on file with author.

Man Chung Chiu. 2001. "Politicising Han-Chinese Masculinities: A Plea for Court-Mandated Counselling for Wife Abusers in Hong Kong." *Feminist Legal Studies* 9: 3–27.

Merry, Sally Engle. 1995a. "Wife Battering and the Ambiguities of Rights." In Austin Sarat and Thomas Kearns, eds., *Identities, Politics, and Rights,* pp. 271–307. Amherst Series in Law, Jurisprudence, and Social Thought. Ann Arbor: Univ. of Michigan Press.

——. 1995b. "Gender Violence and Legally Engendered Selves." *Identities: Global Studies in Culture and Power* 2: 49–73.

——. 2001. "Rights, Religion, and Community: Approaches to Violence against Women in the Context of Globalization." *Law and Society Review* 35: 39–88.

Mohapatra, Arun Ray. 2001. *National Human Rights Commission of India: Formation, Functioning, and Future Prospects*. New Delhi: Radha Publications.

National Commission for Women. 2001. *Sexual Harassment at Workplace*. New Delhi: National Commission for Women.

NFHS-2. 2000. National Family Health Survey (NFHS-2), India, 1998–99. Mumbai: International Institute for Population Sciences; Calverton, MD: ORC Macro.

Parish, William L, Tianfu Wang, Edward D. Laumann, Suiming Pan, and Ye Luo. 2004. "Intimate Partner Violence in China: National Prevalence, Risk Factors and Associated Health Problems." *International Family Planning Perspectives* 30 (4): 174–81.

Pence, Ellen, and Michael Paymar. 1993. *Education Groups for Men who Batter: The Duluth Model*. New York: Springer Publishing.

Poonacha, Veena, and Divya Pandey. 1999. *Responses to Domestic Violence in the States of Karnataka and Gujarat*. Mumbai: Research Centre for Women's Studies, SNDT Women's Univ.

Prasad, Satendra, ed. 1989. *Coup and Crisis: Fiji – a Year Later*. North Carlton, Victoria, Australia: Arena Publications.

Ptacek, James. 1999. *Battered Women in the Courtroom: The Power of Judicial Responses*. Boston: Northeastern Univ. Press.

Rasmussen, Joyce. 1980. "Memorandum on Subregional Follow-up Meeting for Pacific Women of the World Conference of the UN Decade for Women." Library of the University of the South Pacific.

Ristock, Janice L. 2002. *No More Secrets: Violence in Lesbian Relationships*. New York: Routledge.

Sakshi. 1996. *Gender and Judges: A Judicial Point of View*. New Delhi: Sakshi.

——. 1997. *Report: Regional Perspectives on Gender Equality* (January 4–5). New Delhi: Sakshi.

Schechter, Susan. 1982. *Women and Male Violence: The Visions and Struggles of the Battered Women's Movement*. Boston: South End Press.

Schneider, Elizabeth M. 2000. *Battered Women and Feminist Lawmaking*. New Haven: Yale Univ. Press.

Secretariat of the Pacific Community. 1998. *Joint SPC/ESCAP/UNDP Consultative Meeting on the Implementation of the CEDAW Mechanisms in the Pacific: Nadi, Fiji, 20–23 July 1998*. Noumea, New Caledonia: Secretariat of the Pacific Community.

Secretary-General Report. 2001. "Status of Submission of Reports by States Parties under Article 18 of the Convention." CEDAW, United Nations. CEDAW/C/2001/II/2.

Sharma, Aradhana. 2006. "Cross-breeding Institutions, Breeding Struggle: Women's 'Empowerment,' Neoliberal Governmentality, and State Re(Formation) in India." *Cultural Anthropology* 21 (1): 60–95.

Singh, Debbie. 1992. "Workshop on the Convention of the Elimination of All Forms of Discrimination against Women, 3–6 March 1992." Library of the University of the South Pacific.

Singh-Wendt, Debbie, for Fiji Women's Crisis Centre. 1991. "National Workshop on Violence against Women," August 10–20, 1991, Coral Coast Christian Camp, Deuba. Funded by Canada Fund.

Sitaraman, Bhavani. 2002. "Policing Poor Families: Domestic Dispute Resolution in All-Women Police Stations." Paper presented at the Law and Society Association Meeting, Vancouver.

Snow, David, E. Burke Rochford, Jr., Steven K. Worden, and Robert D. Benford. 1986. "Frame Alignment Processes, Micromobilization, and Movement Participation." *American Sociological Review* 51 (4): 464–81.

Tang, Catherine So-Kum. 1999a. "Wife Abuse in Hong Kong Chinese Families: A Community Survey." *Journal of Family Violence* 14 (2): 173–91.

——. 1999b. "Marital Power and Aggression in a Community Sample of Hong Kong Chinese Families." *Journal of Interpersonal Violence* 14 (6): 586–602.

Tang, Catherine So-kum, Antoinette Lee, and Fanny Mui-ching Cheung. 1999. "Violence against Women in Hong Kong." In Fanny M. Cheung, Malavika Karlekar, Aurora De Dios, Juree Vichit-Vadakan, Lourdes R. Quisumbing, eds., *Breaking the Silence: Violence against Women in Asia*, pp. 38–58. Hong Kong: Equal Opportunities Commission in collaboration with Women in Asian Development and UNESCO National Commission of the Philippines.

Tang, Catherine So-Kum, Day Wong, Fanny M. C. Cheung, and Antoinette Lee. 2000. "Exploring How Chinese Define Violence against Women: A Focus Group Study in Hong Kong." *Women's Studies International Forum* 23: 197–209.

Tarrow, Sidney. 1998. *Power in Movements: Social Movements and Contentious Politics*. 2nd edn. Cambridge: Cambridge Univ. Press.

Task Force on Women 2000: India. 2000. *What Has Changed for Women and Girls Since 1995? The NGO Country Report on Beijing Plus Five from the Indian Women's Movement*. Delhi: National NGO Core Group for the Beijing Plus Five Review.

UNICEF. 1999. *Transforming Private Rage into Public Action: Strategy Meetings on Gender and Violence against Women and Girls: Perspectives on the Future Role of UNICEF in South Asia*. August 16–18, 1999, Central Godavari Resort, Kathmandu, Nepal.

United Nations. 1995. "Beijing Declaration and Platform for Action: Platform 3." *The IV World Conference on Women, 1995 – Beijing, China: Official Documents*. www.un.org/esa/gopher-data/conf/fwcw/off/a--3.en.

United Nations General Assembly. 2000. *Report of the Committee on the Elimination of Discrimination against Women: Twenty-Second Session (17 January–4 February 2000), Twenty-Third Session (12–30 June 2000)*. Supplement No. 38 (A/55/38). New York: United Nations.

Wang Kairong. c.2001. "Observation of a Court Trial over a Domestic Violence Case." *Newsletter* 3: 4–6. Domestic Violence in China: Research, Intervention, and Prevention Program, China Law Society Project Group, Beijing, China.

Wang Xingjuan. 1999a. "Why are Beijing Women Beaten by their Husbands? A Case Analysis of Family Violence in Beijing." *Violence against Women* 5: 1493–504.

—— . 1999b. "Domestic Violence in China." In Fanny M. Cheung, Malavika Karlekar, Aurora De Dios, Juree Vichit-Vadakan, and Lourdes R. Quisumbing, eds., *Breaking the Silence: Violence against Women in Asia*, pp. 13–37. Hong Kong: Equal Opportunities Commission in collaboration with Women in Asian Development and UNESCO National Commission of the Philippines.

Weldon, S. Laurel. 2002. *Protest, Policy, and the Problem of Violence against Women: A Cross-National Comparison*. Pittsburgh: Univ. of Pittsburgh Press.

Yeung, Caroline. 1991. "Wife Abuse: A Brief Historical Review on Research and Intervention." *Hong Kong Journal of Social Work* 25: 29–36.

Yeung Chan So-tuen Caroline, and David Lok Ping-pui. 2001. *An Exploratory Study on Children's Accounts of Wife Abuse in Hong Kong: A Research Monograph*. Hong Kong: Harmony House and City Univ. of Hong Kong.

Part IV

Critical Anthropologies
of Human Rights

16

Culture and Rights after *Culture and Rights*

Jane K. Cowan

In *Culture and Rights: Anthropological Perspectives* (Cowan et al. 2001a), my coeditors and I attempted to address the dramatic increase in recent decades in negotiations among various kinds of social groups, at various levels, phrased in a language of "rights." As elaborated in the book's introductory argument, we proposed that anthropologists should help to develop a forum in which theoretical debates about rights, justice, citizenship, and similar concepts could engage with empirical, contextualized studies of rights-claiming processes. With one eye on the theoretical and the other eye on the empirical, we insisted on the need to explore how universal concepts were being taken up in local struggles: how they were mobilized, vernacularized, resisted, reinterpreted, and transformed. We saw the model of rights – one historically specific way of conceptualizing entitlement and obligation – as hegemonic in our times and imbued with an emancipatory aura. Yet, as we stressed, that rights model "has had complex and contradictory implications for individuals and groups whose claims must be articulated within its terms" (Cowan et al. 2001b:1).

Within the efflorescence of rights discourse, we were particularly struck by the increasing deployment of talk about "culture," including culture as an object of rights. This was productively jarring in two senses. First, since the early 1980s, anthropologists had subjected anthropological understandings of culture to a thorough critique. Many anthropologists had railed against tendencies to treat the "culture" concept as fixed, bounded, and static, with some even wondering if the concept should be totally abandoned. No sooner had anthropology emerged from this critique than anthropologists found their informants taking up with renewed gusto just such essentialized notions of "culture" in their own political talk. This then raised a whole range of questions of why and how this was happening and what its effects might be. The second shock was the very juxtaposition of "culture" alongside "rights," given that the two concepts had historically been seen as

Originally published in *American Anthropologist*, n.s. 108: 1 (2006), 9–24.

opposed. Previously, one had been required to declare oneself as either for rights or for culture; now it was possible to be in favor of both.

In light of these two surprises, the first task for my coeditors and I was to map out the terrain of discourse, by identifying how the concepts of "rights" and "culture" had been juxtaposed, both historically and in the present. We identified four distinctive conjunctions between "rights" and "culture": (1) rights versus culture, (2) the right to culture, (3) rights as culture, and (4) culture as "analytic" to rights. Starting with the first, the predominant tendency to characterize the relationship as one of rights versus culture (a typical stance in the universalism–cultural relativism debates) articulated long-term tensions – moral, ethical, ontological, epistemological, philosophical, and political – between two antithetical currents of thought. Enlightenment universalism and liberal individualism – not least because of their association with French civilizational hegemony – had provoked their nemesis: a politically oppositional romantic particularism. As formulated by the German philosopher Johann Gottfried von Herder, that political response emphasized the holistic integrity of each distinct people, privileging the communal forms – language, traditions, and culture – through which its spirit was expressed.

A second conjunction, the right to culture, was not altogether contemporary, having long been central to the political demands of romantic nationalism; nonetheless, it reemerged with novel connotations in the late 20th century. Building on Nancy Fraser's (1997) insights on the historical shift from demands for redistribution to demands of recognition in the postsocialist moment, we identified this as, in fact, a more pervasive global phenomenon with implications for the ways that rights were conceptualized. And although many took the emancipatory character of claims to culture as given, we were more skeptical. The political implications of claims clearly could not be generalized: Culturalist claims might be used just as easily for reactionary as for progressive political projects. As we insisted, that very same notion of a "right to culture" that helped indigenous peoples to claim autonomy within nation-states was also being deployed by Ulster Protestant Orangemen marching through Catholic neighborhoods in Northern Ireland, and by repressive nation-states like Malaysia who argued that "Asian values" privileging the collective good justified censorship and restrictions of civil liberties.

The third conjunction was rights as culture. We suggested that just as anthropologists had come to look on law as culture, thereby making law an object of analysis, anthropologists could examine, and, indeed, were already examining, rights as culture. This involved seeing rights not simply as informed by certain philosophical assumptions – an orientation to individuals, a privileging of rights over needs – but as themselves defining a social and ideational space, one that entailed certain ideas of "self" and "sociality," specific modes of agency, and particular rules of the game. This conjunction encapsulated the wider claims of those like Richard Rorty (1993) and Norberto Bobbio (1996), who suggest that we can now properly speak of a "human rights culture" in the sense of an increasingly pervasive structuring discourse in the late 20th and 21st centuries that shapes how the world is apprehended. It also signaled a Foucauldian alertness to the power and knowledge relations associated with this expanding legal and political apparatus.

The fourth conjunction, culture as analytic to rights, now seems to me, in retrospect, imprecisely phrased, but it was intended to distinguish between object and method. The argument was not that rights constitute a culture, as in the third conjunction, but, rather, that rights could be grasped through methods of and orientations to cultural analysis. Thus, one can approach rights practices armed with an anthropologist's commitment to teasing out patterns and identifying rela-tionships of meaning and practice between different domains of social life without necessarily taking on rights as a total ideological–practical apparatus, or assuming that they constitute anything so coherent as a culture. In fact, using anthropological methods of analysis almost inevitably entails treating culture as a different kind of entity: not as an object in itself but as an abstraction whose exploration offers a window for seeing and understanding other relations and domains to which it is connected. This distinguishes anthropologists' more analytic use of culture from the more objectifying approach of many practitioners of other disciplines.

Since the publication of *Culture and Rights*, the terms *culture* and *rights* continue to be deployed. In this essay, I explore that deployment not so much in the rhetorics of claimants but, rather, as conceptual terms within recent analytical work. I do not undertake here a review of responses to the book (although I do include, and engage with, a few). Instead, I reflect on several selected works concerned with the political accommodation of culture, diversity, or difference authored by scholars in anthro-pology, political philosophy, and critical legal theory as well as interventions by practitioners in the UN system in both scholarly and policy documents. I am concerned, first, with how analysts understand the term *culture*. More urgently, I am keen to explore how culture and rights are used in relation to each other. My objective in scrutinizing how various authors deploy the terms *culture* and *rights* is to draw out the implicit assumptions about the social world – about persons and collectivities, agency and structure – informing those usages; I intend to identify the social theory that underpins and animates their analyses and their policy recommen-dations. Social struggles around culture and difference – and the social, political, and institutional responses to them – touch deeply on issues of justice, equality, peace, and well-being, and challenge us to find ways to reconcile apparently competing claims for recognition and redistribution (Fraser 1997; Fraser and Honneth 2003). We need to develop theorizations of these processes that are both analytically acute and sensitive to the complexities of the real world.

In *Culture and Rights*, my coeditors and I presented, albeit schematically, a critical approach both to rights, conceived as framed within larger relations of power and knowledge, and to culture, understood as contested or contestable, which also acknowledged agency and indeterminacy. Through this theorization, we drew atten-tion to the ways that (1) rights are both enabling and constraining, (2) rights are productive (of subjectivities, of social relations, and even of the very identities and cultures they claim merely to recognize), and (3) their pursuit and achievement entails unintended consequences. We insisted further that investigations into rights processes and theorization of them must pay attention to their ambiguous, contra-dictory, contingent, and unpredictable dimensions.

As many anthropologists will recognize, our approach represents a forging of theoretical insights developed within anthropology over the past four decades – particularly in the broadly defined "practice anthropology" (Ortner 1984), which has flourished in conversation with wider debates in social theory, critical theory, feminism, and history. Anthropologically grounded, this approach to culture and rights is thus animated by an interdisciplinarity integral to emerging work on culture and power and on transnational formations, among other themes. At the same time, the approach relies on deep engagement with and reflection on our experiences in the field. It entails an understanding of description and interpretation that requires a continuously oscillating movement of mutual interrogation between theory and the empirical, and a constant critical reflection on method and on conceptual terms and frameworks. I wish to argue that with respect to the matters at issue in the debate around culture, difference, and rights, the political stakes are simply too high to permit the luxury of ignoring the insights of critical social theory; this is the case equally for those working outside the social sciences. It is therefore incumbent on both anthropologists and scholars in other fields to engage much more assiduously with these conceptual issues to develop adequate theorizations of social struggles around culture and rights and of their solutions. I submit that the approach to culture and rights I have outlined here offers a sound, flexible, and theoretically subtle starting point for the issues to hand. Thus, my key aim in this essay is to consider the degree to which the recent work that I examine begins from these kinds of theoretical premises and addresses the concerns and dimensions toward which I have pointed, as well as how some of that work can take us even further in our understandings of culture and rights.

Accommodating Culture: Positions and Critiques from within Liberal Political Philosophy and Theory

How should the internal multiplicity of contemporary societies be understood, addressed, and, indeed, politically organized? Questions of culture, rights to culture, and multiculturalism – along with debates about identity and difference – have generated not only a massive corpus of publications but also a good deal of soul-searching among political philosophers, no less than other scholars.[1] What Seyla Benhabib phrases as "the claims of culture" (2002) also have profound implications for political philosophy, inasmuch as the meanings of *culture* and the nature, validity, and urgency of its claims are all matters for theoretical scrutiny. More fundamentally, these claims call into question liberalism's core premises. Political theory's "community" had always referred, although implicitly, to the national community, the republic legitimated by the popular sovereignty expressed in this national entity. Demands for recognition (and more) by groups united by some different kind of identity or commonality have compelled many political theorists to reconsider the limits and boundaries of the community that political theory assumes, and the nature of what is or is not shared within.

I turn my attention first to work in liberal political philosophy, partly because it is predominantly writers in this discipline who have defined the contours of the wider public debate on culture and multiculturalism.[2] Our common concerns on these compelling public issues justify efforts toward interdisciplinary dialogue between anthropologists and political philosophers, yet knowing how to proceed with the conversation is not straightforward; a brief parenthesis on epistemology is in order. As an avid reader of certain debates within certain strands of political theory, I have long puzzled over how to engage with these debates as an anthropologist and incorporate them into my specifically anthropological endeavors. I have also wondered to what extent it is our divergent intellectual projects that sometimes impede this potentially fruitful conversation.

Let me map, crudely, the divergences as I see them. Anthropologists, even more than other social scientists, are concerned with "what is." Our foremost task is descriptive: We address the empirical, although this cannot be grasped except through the terms of a prior social theory. There is, thus, necessarily a dynamic back-and-forth movement between theory and data, requiring incessant critical reflection on our conceptual tools. With respect to present issues, anthropologists investigate how rights and cultural claims actually operate in the real world, not how they should operate, in order to refine theorization in respect to particular questions about them. Political philosophy, in contrast, is concerned primarily with "what ought to be." Framed by a project of imagining the good society (or, in other versions, the just, decent, or well-ordered society, or the realistic utopia), political philosophy aims to identify principles, norms, and procedures that would facilitate justice, equality, freedom, or happiness – depending on what was prioritized in a given philosophical tradition – and that would guide the ways judgments could be made when persons or projects came into conflict. Yet these systematic explorations of potential political frameworks are not unaffected by the real world. Indeed, the most instructive debates are those rooted in current political controversies: Charles Taylor's (1993) and Will Kymlicka's (1998) interventions on Quebecois culture, language, and autonomy is one notable example. In the contemporary moment, political philosophers explicitly grapple with what is politically desirable and how to secure it in a context of increasing plurality and differentiation.[3]

This representation of divergence may be overdrawn: Our positions with respect to the empirical differ, yet in neither is the empirical unimportant. Such a representation of divergence also perhaps underplays the convergence between anthropologists' pronounced ethical streak – our collective self-image as advocates of the less powerful, our egalitarian commitments, and the political vision implicit in any critical analytical approach – and political philosophy's explicit normative agenda. Likewise, as mentioned above, political theorists and philosophers frame their problems in response to what they perceive as key political questions of the day. While the consequences of these epistemological divergences for our conversation should not therefore be overestimated, ultimately a more serious source of anthropologists' and political philosophers' habitual talking past each other may be incongruous assumptions about the social world – at least, between some anthropological approaches and some types of political theorizing and philosophizing. I am speaking of the assumptions, both theoretical and ontological, that provide the point of departure, and also the degree to which scholars are willing to open those assumptions to questioning.

Rights, culture, and choice

Coexisting in a certain tension with other influential models of how complexity should be conceptualized and politically addressed – notably versions of cosmopolitanism and of hybridity such as those developed by Homi Bhabha (1994) and Paul Gilroy (1995, 2000) – multiculturalism has become the primary rubric under which contemporary claims about culture are both produced and evaluated. Defining this term has proved notoriously difficult; at the very least, one has to distinguish between *multicultural* as a mere (although never self-evident) adjective, describing an objective condition of plurality, and *multiculturalism* as a political project. That project, admittedly, comes in different versions: Terence Turner (1993) has usefully differentiated the more typical essentializing and celebratory versions from a "critical multiculturalism" that incorporates fluidity, creativity, and contestation. These important distinctions notwithstanding, the indisputably dominant way of envisaging cultural plurality, as much among social movements as among theorists and policy makers across the whole political spectrum, is in terms of a "mosaic multiculturalism."

As description and as political project, multiculturalism has reopened and provoked rearticulations of long-standing debates concerning the relations between individual and society – in particular, the competing claims of individuals and collectivities. Interestingly, multiculturalism has come to be associated with a communitarian philosophical position. In one characteristic formulation, for instance, Christian Joppke and Steven Lukes define *multiculturalism* as

> a critique of Western universalism and liberalism, with affinities to post-structuralism and communitarianism. Ontologically, it posits the group over the individual. Not any group, but "social groups" defined by "cultural forms, practices or ways of life," which are not the result of choice but of some existential "thrownness" (Young 1990:42–48). Society is composed not of individuals, or systemic spheres, but of groups, each constituted by a particular way of life, or "culture." [1999:5]

Given the concept's association with communitarianism, it is ironic that arguably the best-known and most influential proponent of multiculturalism – in its mosaic version – speaks from a liberal position of moral individualism. Never consciously swerving from this philosophical commitment, in a series of publications over the past 15 years, the political philosopher Will Kymlicka has been developing an elaborate and systematic argument for "liberal multiculturalism" (most recently rephrased as "liberal culturalism" [2001] and "multicultural citizenship" (1995b). His accessible style, clear arguments, and commitment to finding pragmatic yet principled solutions to multicultural problems, as well as the sheer volume of his publications, have established Kymlicka as a primary reference point in these debates.

Distinguishing between majorities, national minorities, and ethnic groups, while conceding that some groups fall outside this model (e.g., refugees, guestworkers, and descendants of slaves), Kymlicka argues for the increased recognition of the rights of minority cultures (1995b), cultural rights (1995a), and group-differentiated citizens' rights (1996). He sees this as a means of managing ethnocultural diversity within liberal democratic, often welfare, states. Depending on the state, the group concerned, and the group's particular needs and history, such rights can include the following: (1) language rights (state support of minority or indigenous languages through funding language courses, monolingual or bilingual education, minority language broadcasting, and the provision of minority language speakers or translators in courts or state welfare agencies);[4] (2) rights to support for cultural activities; (3) rights to exemption on the basis of religious or cultural custom from certain state laws (e.g., the exemption of British turban-wearing Sikh males from the requirement to wear motorcycle helmets); and, more controversially, (4) varying degrees of group autonomy over territory (in the case of indigenous peoples) and community control of certain domains of internal affairs (such as courtship, marriage, and divorce practices; religious or customary practices; and property and inheritance). Kymlicka's overarching position is that multiculturalism not only can, but must, be undertaken – and, indeed, is best undertaken – from within a liberal political framework, one that guarantees individual freedom and autonomy. Paradoxically, Kymlicka relies on culture to ground the argument for multiculturalism no less than do communitarian proponents. In ways that partly overlap and partly diverge from those proponents' usages, however, culture is made to do very contradictory kinds of work within his model.[5]

Kymlicka's use of culture is frequently criticized, and it is not hard to see why. On the one hand, culture is that meaningful common life based on shared heritage that defines and establishes boundaries for a group – a group that always already exists, awaiting the state's recognition – and that minority rights and multicultural policies must protect. On the other hand, culture is a vague, contentless context for choice that makes few demands on, much less shapes, the individual. This contradiction can be partly unraveled when we notice that Kymlicka talks about culture differently depending on which social group he is discussing. When describing the "societal culture" – the modern public space of shared language and common institutions of a territorially based community; the majority or national culture in its gesellschaft dimension – culture is what makes possible that pick-n-mix that characterizes the daily practice of the middle-class citizen choosing between Vietnamese and Italian food before setting out in a Japanese car to see the latest Iranian film. Although Kymlicka does talk about the societal culture of a national minority like the Canadian Quebecois in much the same terms, what is stressed for indigenous groups (also classified as "national minorities") is shared language, identity, and practices as well as a common history and long-term ties to a territory. Kymlicka, in fact, does not deny internal heterogeneity, yet this is not stressed in the case of indigenous peoples, whose culture is represented – or at least, defended – in more static and preservationist terms (Benhabib 2002:67).

"Horses for courses," as the British expression goes; like any astute advocate, Kymlicka adapts his interventions to the contours of the debate at hand. Yet this involves, I think, an unacknowledged strategic essentialism smuggled into political theory, one that strategically overemphasizes a group's stable and cohesive character, in the service of a progressive, if liberal, political agenda. If "culture" is little more than consumption choices, does it really merit the protection of rights? Hemmed in by his overall advocacy of multiculturalism, Kymlicka defends the rights of indigenous peoples (as "national minorities") in the cultural terms of multiculturalism rather than the territorial terms of traditional sovereignty, even though it is as much their forcible incorporation into modern states that, for him, legitimizes whatever autonomy might be claimed.

As behoves Kymlicka the political philosopher, as well as Kymlicka the advocate, the analytical focus of his work is on the state, and the state–minority relationship; his work shows much more conceptual development around how states could accommodate "minority cultures" than around what happens within (not to mention between) those putative groups. His commitment to a focus on the state–minority relationship; to a liberal ontology, which hampers a dynamic and mutually constitutive conception of the individual, groups, society, and culture that would be theoretically adequate to his task; and to the analytical terms of liberal political philosophy all work to limit his grasp of the wider implications of claiming and receiving rights to culture for those involved "on the ground." This is evident in Kymlicka's engagement, in a thoughtful and not unappreciative review, with the issues my fellow contributors and I raised in *Culture and Rights*. Consider this excerpt of the review's final section where he lays out his major criticisms:

> The central claim of the volume – namely, that the "logic" of cultural rights is inherently essentialist – is never clearly defended. There is no sustained discussion of the concept of "rights" and how it differs from other legal concepts, such as "duties." In several places, the authors seem to equate the *right* to practice one's culture or to express one's identity with the *duty* to do so. For example, Cowan implies that granting Macedonians the right to use their mother-tongue would involve imposing a duty on them to use it, even if some or most members would prefer not to. Similarly, Gellner implies that the

modern idea of cultural rights has the same logic as the traditional Hindu idea of cultural duties. Yet a right differs from a duty precisely in that people can choose whether or not to exercise their rights: rights are voluntarist and choice-enhancing in a way that duties are not. Nor is this just a conceptual point. All the recent international declarations on cultural rights include safeguards to protect this element of choice, including principles of voluntary self-identification and democratic accountability. The authors rarely discuss these safeguards, but they are fundamental to the "logic" of cultural rights, and I believe they have often successfully solved the problems that the authors raise, at least in countries with democracy and the rule of law. [Kymlicka 2002:1097]

In characterizing as the volume's "central claim" that the logic of cultural rights is inherently essentialist, Kymlicka squeezes our concern with the implications of culturalist claims on the broad tableaux of people's lives into the narrow confines of legally recognized cultural rights. For Kymlicka, cultural rights offer choices, but the state cannot demand that an individual exercise them; in providing safeguards to protect choice, via principles of voluntary self-identification and democratic accountability, recent international declarations on cultural rights meet his acid test against state compulsion. At this formal legal level, we would agree, although such a choice-based approach to culture and identity can be decidedly dangerous for citizens in societies lacking democracy and the rule of law or – given that most civil conflict is constructed in ethnic terms – simply vulnerable to instability: Nepal, Guatemala, and Macedonia at the moment of Yugoslavia's dissolution were precisely our examples.

Kymlicka's analytical focus at the level of state–minority relations, as mediated by legal and political systems, allows him to comment sensibly on the formal legal situation of a rights holder. However, as soon as one moves into the wider social world with an interest in how rights struggles are lived and experienced in the everyday, the legal language of rights and duties becomes profoundly inadequate. Referring to my chapter (Cowan 2001) on Macedonian human rights activism in northern Greece, Kymlicka criticizes the implied argument that, in his words, "granting Macedonians the right to use their mother-tongue would involve imposing a duty on them to use it, even if some members would prefer not to" (2002:1097). This puts my contentions a little too bluntly; I would nonetheless respond that, in politicized moments, such an individual would, indeed, come under pressure – not necessarily from the state but from nationalists on both sides – to speak or not to speak her minority language. It is by no means unusual for nationalists to admonish in a language of "duty."

This said, if one wishes to register, in an anthropologically perceptive way, the nature of individual agency in minority rights struggles – indeed, in all social action – one needs a more sophisticated analytical vocabulary than simply that of rights, duties, and choices. I contend, moreover, that this vocabulary needs to be grounded in a theory of individual agency conceived as deeply shaped by and within social relations. Kymlicka is reluctant to concede the determining dimension of the social, and this gravely limits his understanding of how identity politics are mediated by – even while they challenge and alter – social relations. Whereas Janet Halley (1999) has criticized Kymlicka's "sunny story of culture" for underplaying constraint, an even more intriguing operation of the social on the individual concerns the compulsory: not in the strictly legal sense, but in the context of social forms and moral norms. As I have argued in my work on dance and sociability (1990:3–27 and passim), inspired in part by Georg Simmel (1971), engagement in social life entails being caught by, as much as caught up in, its reciprocities, such that opting out is often not an option. Speaking and not speaking, as well as taking up or not taking up particular identities, are acts framed by the imperatives of sociability. Kymlicka's methodologically individualist understanding of both rights and culture simply cannot grasp the complex, countervailing pressures, evolving situationally and historically, on individuals caught in the dynamic of minority politics or, indeed, in other social movements in which rights are on the agenda. These subtle, yet powerful, and at times destructive social pressures, leading to both constraint and compulsion, would be unlikely to register as "violations" of an individual's free choice by Kymlicka's criteria; they operate beneath his radar, as it were. Kymlicka's epistemological commitment to the liberal subject, and his analytical focus on formal rights, lead to a reading of what my coeditors and I in *Culture and Rights* preferred to call "culturalist claims" that illuminates a mere fraction of people's lived experience of political battles around culture and identity, leaving the greater part uninvestigated and thus obscured.

Kymlicka's optimism that recognizing cultural rights primarily offers options for greater choice and diversity is echoed in the influential UN Development Programme (UNDP) Human Development Report 2004, devoted to the theme "Cultural Liberty in Today's Diverse World." Although the moral philosopher Amartya Sen provided the overarching conceptual framework for this report, Kymlicka's contribution as a principle consultant was also significant; his cultural instrumentalism is grounded in the same position of moral individualism as that of Sen.[6] Strongly informed by Sen's and Kymlicka's theorizations of self and society, the collectively authored report attempts to debunk myths that recognizing diversity weakens and fragments states and undermines development, insisting to the contrary that such recognition is a necessary condition and concomitant for development.

Because scholars outside the field of development policy and practice too often read such documents naively, as merely flawed examples of familiar modes of academic writing, I must stress that this report is best understood as a strategic intervention within a very particular discursive field. The report's admirably simple and direct language indicates the authors' striving for accessibility to a diverse audience of government bureaucrats, policy makers, non-governmental organizations (NGOs), and international institutions, while the vigor with which it counters Samuel Huntington–style stereotypes about cultures and civilizations. (Huntington 1996; Huntington and Harrison 2000) indexes the perceived prevalence of such thinking within these institutions. The report's authors are clearly aware of, and frequently deploy, the recent anthropological critique of culture; they explicitly argue against "the assumption that culture is largely fixed and unchanging," pointing (as others have) to the irony that "just as anthropologists have discarded the concept of culture as a bounded and fixed social phenomenon, mainstream political interest in finding core values and traits of 'a people and their culture' is growing" (UNDP 2004:5). They insist further that "neither cultural freedom nor respect for diversity should be confused with the defence of tradition; cultural liberty is the capability of people to live and be what they choose, with adequate opportunity to consider other options" (UNDP 2004:4).

Why the conceptual focus on "cultural liberty"? The report's authors are anxious to applaud the emphasis on culture as choice as against the communitarian claim – this being, according to Michael Sandel (1998), a concomitant of its "constitutive conception" of community – that individuals discover, rather than choose, the attachments that bind them. Influenced by feminist and critical multiculturalist

analysts of difference, they are also concerned with shifting the overriding preoccupation with the ethnocultural, stressing instead the significance of other affiliations.
To neglect the role of choice and reasoning in each individual's decisions about
the relative importance of membership in any particular group, or any specific
identity, is, in the authors' view, "ethical delinquency and political dereliction of
responsibility" (UNDP 2004:17). They also wish to warn against what Anthony
Appiah (1996:84) has characterized as the "new tyrannies" of exclusive or putatively
overarching identities.

Although the argument for greater state tolerance and even the championing of
its internal diversity would be seen as commendable, in many respects, by most
anthropologists and human rights advocates, its phrasing in terms of cultural liberty
seems to me theoretically incoherent, not to say impractical. Culture is presented as
a "take it or leave it" proposition, trivializing its significance while at the same time
exaggerating its rigidity: The happenstance of being born into a particular cultural
milieu, the report insists, "becomes aligned to cultural liberty only if the person
chooses to continue to live within the terms of that culture, and does so having had
the opportunity of considering other alternatives" (UNDP 2004:16–17). Not only
does assuming the ready availability of alternatives seem poignantly wishful thinking in respect to citizens of developing countries; more seriously, it rests on a notion
of "culture" as something wholly extricable from social relations. How easy is it for,
say, a poor Hindu village woman to contest the dowry system, or to decide to marry
a Muslim? These are neither unimaginable nor impossible acts, but they carry heavy
social costs: ridicule, loss of social support, exposure to psychological or physical
pressure, and very likely, exclusion or worse.

This emphasis, moreover, throws out at least one baby with the communitarian
bathwater. Sen's and Kymlicka's unremittingly individualist approaches and the
emphasis on cultural liberty that stems from them can neither conceive of nor
look toward facilitating or protecting what Charles Taylor has called "irreducibly
social goods": objects of value that, by definition, individuals cannot possess and
which "cannot be reduced to a set of acts, choices or, indeed, other predicates of
individuals" (Taylor 1990:54–5), but which are "intrinsically valuable in the constitution of the goodness or badness of states of affairs" (Gore 1997:243). Finally, the
exhortation that states pursue "multicultural policies that recognize differences,
champion diversity and promote cultural freedoms, so that all people can choose
to speak their language, practice their religion, and participate in shaping their
culture – so that all people can choose to be who they are" (UNDP 2004, see front
cover), apart from its circularity, expresses perfectly Kymlicka's static conception
of culture as simply preexisting the political structures charged with recognizing or
denying them.

I want to conclude this interrogation of the choice model of culture and rights by
referring briefly to the extended debate within political philosophy on what John
Rawls called "nonliberal" (and others have subsequently called "illiberal") peoples
(Rawls 1993, 1999). Kymlicka sees this debate as somewhat exaggerated and
outdated given that, in his view, most conflicts between ethnocultural groups now-
adays are not over the legitimacy of liberal principles (Kymlicka 2001:60); rather,
they are best seen as "debates amongst liberals about the meaning of liberalism"
(Kymlicka 2001:20). For many other analysts, however, including the many feminist
scholars and activists who have strenuously debated the gender implications of
individual and collective rights, the issues are far from resolved.[7] Certain political
philosophers have recognized that cultures (by which they mean minority groups)

may hold to values and practices at odds with liberal equality and that this may impinge disproportionately on certain members – most notably, women.[8] How, they ask, can the right to culture of an illiberal society – one that restricts the actions and opportunities of certain of its members – be honored without sacrificing liberal commitments to equality? One of the primary solutions proposed for this dilemma has been the right to exit. Positing the individual as ontologically preexisting any association, and defining culture, pace Kymlicka, as a context of choice, liberals in this debate frequently see justice to inhere in the guarantee that the individual may leave her culture if it does not fulfill her desires and needs (e.g., Galston 1995; Kukathas 1997). They have therefore been preoccupied with the practical impediments to exit, such as lack of economic resources or knowledge of the world outside.

Major critiques of the right-to-exit solution have come from communitarian positions, whose proponents argue that the individual is not ontologically prior to but, rather, constituted by her society, community, or culture; consequently, the right to exit is deemed either ontologically destabilizing, socially devastating, or cognitively unimaginable. Indeed, according to Andrew Fagan (n.d.), if one takes seriously the communitarian argument of culture's constitutive quality, one must conclude that such an individual will not be able to question the tenets of her own culture, even when they oppress and limit her. Unfortunately, for some time the debate has foundered on the conceptually problematic premises of both sides, oscillating fruitlessly between the Scylla of liberal underdetermination and the Charybdis of communitarian overdetermination of the individual.[9] Part of the analytical problem is the assumption that an individual is inside only one culture at any one time, part of it is the conflation of consciousness with social relations, and part of it is a more generally inadequate theorization of subjectivity. Beyond this, though, the debate has revealed that "the right of exit" concept is not only impractical as a primary solution but also politically unimaginative and conservative as well as theoretically flawed, grounded as it is in a presumption of cultures as unchanging.

Rights, culture, and communication

The conundrums surrounding the "right-to-exit" concept and the unsatisfactory nature of the alternatives signal, in my view, deeper troubles in certain strands of political philosophizing. Listening closely to the key voices in this and other multiculturalism debates, I have found not infrequently that the ways problems are set up and analyzed, as well the manner of solutions proposed, reveal a remarkable innocence of the last few decades' debates in social theory, with respect (among other issues) to the following: the theorization of subjectivity; conceptions of person, society, power, and agency; the relative significance of interest, emotion, and morality in human action; and the degree to which contingency, as well as structure, should be acknowledged. Not surprisingly, I find the problems most extreme in the work of those writing from a liberal position; I am particularly critical of such work on social theoretical grounds of the atomistic individual at its center. Of course, precisely because this particular conception of the individual expresses a political and moral ontology, one that provides the very foundation of liberalism, rather than something as (in principle) revisable as a theory, the commitment of liberal political philosophers to it tends to be intransigent.

If social theory in the round – as a broader set of interlocking concepts – has yet to be addressed within mainstream political philosophy, internal critique on particular key themes is nonetheless emerging. The political philosopher Seyla

Benhabib (2002) recently published a penetrating examination of the "culture" concept as deployed "within and beyond the academy," with particular attention to the challenges these deployments pose to the theory and practice of liberal democracies. In contemporary debates, Benhabib insists, cultural preservationist arguments are being voiced by those positioned across the entire political – and presumably theoretical – spectrum. In a manifesto that could have been written by an anthropologist – and that, indeed, draws on some anthropologists' work – Benhabib takes issue with the prevailing wisdom:

> Whether conservative or progressive, such attempts [to preserve culture] share faulty epistemic premises: 1) that cultures are clearly delineable wholes; 2) that cultures are congruent with population groups and that a non-controversial description of the culture of a human group is possible; and 3) that even if cultures and groups do not stand in one-to-one correspondence, even if there is more than one culture within a human group and more than one group that may possess the same cultural traits, this poses no important problems for politics or policy. These assumptions form what I will call the "reductionist sociology of culture." In the words of Terence Turner, such a view "risks essentializing the idea of culture as the property of an ethnic group or race; it risks reifying cultures as separate entities by overemphasizing their boundedness and distinctness; it risks overemphasizing the internal homogeneity of cultures in terms that potentially legitimise repressive demands for communal conformity; and by treating cultures as badges of group identity, it tends to fetishize them in ways that put them beyond the reach of critical analysis" (1993:412). A central thesis of this book is that much contemporary debate in political and legal philosophy is dominated by this faulty epistemology, which has grave normative political consequences for how we think injustices among groups should be redressed and how we think human diversity and pluralism should be furthered. [2002:4–5]

In place of the "reductionist sociology of culture," Benhabib offers "social constructivism." This social theory begins, Bourdieu-like, by distinguishing the social observer, who attempts to represent culture from the outside, imposing unity and coherence on it, from the social agent, who along with fellow "participants in the culture experience traditions, stories, rituals and symbols, tools and material living conditions through shared, albeit contested and contested, narrative accounts" (Benhabib 2002:5). Such a narrative approach to culture dovetails nicely with the communicative ethics framework established by the philosopher Jürgen Habermas (1990) that has long grounded Benhabib's work; her analyses in this text focus on processes of narrative, dialogue, and interlocution. Influenced, as well, by the political philosopher Hannah Arendt (1973), Benhabib also emphasizes the ethical dimensions of culture: She defines *culture* not only as a "web of narratives" but as "the horizon formed by evaluative stances" on those narratives and doings, whereby events in "space-time are demarcated into 'good' and 'bad,' 'holy' and 'profane,' 'pure' and 'impure'" (Benhabib 2002:7).

Adopting a critical and analytically more powerful concept of "culture" leads Benhabib to recommend quite different strategies from those Kymlicka suggests in face of the dilemmas of multicultural coexistence. For instance, taking up the question baldly formulated by Susan Moller Okin as "Is multiculturalism bad for women?" (Okin 1999), Benhabib criticizes U.S. criminal courts for accepting "my culture made me do it" (Honig 1999) kinds of arguments from men who raped fiancées and murdered adulterous wives. Benhabib points out that this erroneously accepts a view of culture as authoritative and uncontested, allowing individual men to abdicate responsibility for their choices and actions. With respect to the vexed headscarf affair in France of recent years, Benhabib draws attention to the worrying lack of interest, from both defenders of republican principles of *laïcité* and of the rights of religious Muslims, in the girls' own reasons for donning the headscarf. She shows how the conflict is analytically and ethically reconfigured when the multiple resignifications of the scarf are taken into account: for example, when it is acknowledged that wearing the headscarf may be a gesture of religious or cultural identification, a noncoerced expression of individual piety, an act of resistance to a hegemonic state, or even a strategy to legitimize young Muslim women's appropriation of greater autonomy and mobility.[10]

At the same time, recognizing that certain groups do restrict women, Benhabib sees the solution neither in ignoring or condoning restrictive or otherwise abhorrent practices in the name of respect for cultural autonomy nor in imposing liberal freedoms but, rather, in supporting democratic deliberation internally. Thus, she argues that non-members can support minority women and other nonelites in their demands to participate fully and equally in intra-group dialogue, their contestations of illiberal practices, and their arguments for alternative interpretations. Nonmembers are justified to do so on the basis of the Rawlsian argument that within liberal society, all groups, including minority groups, need to offer "public reasons" – that is, they need to explain and defend internal practices in terms understandable and acceptable to the society at large. Drawing especially on Ayelet Shachar (2000), Benhabib also explores the solution of interlocking legal jurisdictions, an area of legal theorization that builds on ongoing work on legal pluralism, much of it by anthropologists (e.g., Merry 1997).

Benhabib's approach, like that of her frequent interlocutors Nancy Fraser (1989, 1997) and Iris Marion Young (1990), is informed by a theoretical and personal feminist engagement, building on that tradition's history of involvement in material–political struggles to criticize gender-oblivious theory and think through political philosophy's gender implications. In attempting to devise more sensitive normative solutions, she reflects on empirical cases, and her much more powerful analytical concept of "culture" shifts very considerably how new normative solutions can be imagined. There is a theoretical, as well as practical, openendedness to this conception of "deliberative democracy." Vigorous public debate within a cultural group among all kinds of persons affected by a policy – in multiple forums of public and, indeed, private space – does have the potential to transform the terms of culture – at least, its explicit terms – quite fundamentally. Such an approach is not only vastly superior analytically and theoretically but also politically more enabling than the liberal choice: to either live "according to the culture's terms" or leave.

Although Benhabib effectively challenges the dominant assumption in political philosophy that one can identify a true, authentic, and consensual version of a culture, anthropologists – who tend to work closer to events on the ground – might argue that she underestimates impediments to internal contestation. I do not mean merely the efforts, on the part of those whose interests or privileges are challenged, to block and undermine. Benhabib's is a highly rationalist, not to mention logocentric, rendering of culture that, while capturing its dialogical and disputatious character, misses other dimensions: habit, the "taken for granted," and the embodied domination and deference built into ordinary everyday forms of social exchange and reciprocity (Bourdieu 1977; Cowan 1990; Willis 1977). Culture is more than intertwining, enduring, and contesting narratives; it also includes the very significant domain of the tacit and unspoken. Although crucial, her normative project to develop principles for more inclusive forms and forums of democratic debate – which would encourage critical and reflexive discussion of culture and difference among members of culturally defined subgroups as well as in multiple sites in the broader public sphere – will not by itself fully address the ways social symbolizations are embedded in practice, in which hierarchies and exclusions are quietly and often un-reflectively reproduced. Neither can it interrogate how these symbolizations are inscribed in the structures of fantasy of the individual unconscious (Rose 1996; Žižek 1995).

Rethinking Culture and Rights: Empirically Grounded Accounts

Political philosophers, I have argued, are addressing the issues raised by cultural plurality, yet they typically do so at some remove from real-world struggles for rights to, or in the name of, culture. Moreover, in some cases (including influential ones), they are confronting the issues armed with theoretical and analytical concepts that are inadequate to the task. I turn now to three works that, although not authored exclusively by anthropologists, are grounded in an empirical engagement with rights processes, each of a quite different character and scope. I contend that theoretically informed exploration of actual contexts and situations pertaining to culture and rights can enable us to refine or reformulate theory about culture and rights. Moreover, this engagement with the empirical allows for deep investigation of the contradictions, ambiguities, and impasses arising from struggles for and responses to culture and rights, which themselves pose theoretical challenges.

Rights, culture, and cunning

In one of the most fascinating ethnographies of recent years – *The Cunning of Recognition: Indigenous Alterities and the Making of Australian Multiculturalism* – Elizabeth Povinelli (2002) considers Australia's response to Aboriginal land claims within the context of an official state policy of multiculturalism. Povinelli does not examine Australian multiculturalism cynically, instead she acknowledges its best intentions. Building on insights of Slavoj Žižek, Gayatri Spivak, and Jacqueline Rose, Povinelli understands that "the critique of liberalism does not begin with where it fails or where subjects know or do not know this failure, but rather where it seems to be succeeding" (Povinelli 2002:155). Her objective is to interrogate the profoundly ambivalent stance of European Australians to "Aboriginal culture," in relation to which Aboriginal claims must – in a multiculturalist framework – be justified. As Tom Boellstorff has remarked, Povinelli reveals that "the multiculturalist trope that asks for recognition of difference meets its limit when it encounters forms of incommensurability that refuse the sameness on which that difference depends" (Boellstorff 2005:37).

Within the turbulent reformulation of Australian national identity since the 1980s, the concept of "Aboriginal culture" figures as a contradictory symbol for sincere, well-meaning supporters of multiculturalism. Valued for its sacred and mystical qualities, it has been enthusiastically appropriated as the nation's ("our") heritage, available to all Australians. Yet, in the context of a long history of sensationalized and orientalized popular representations of certain "bizarre" Aboriginal sexual rites, which have come to be seen as emblematic, "Aboriginal culture" is for many white Australians simply beyond the pale: repugnant and irredeemable. Povinelli insightfully explores the role of feeling in confronting "the unspeakable": the strongly visceral response that founds Aboriginal abjection.

Despite such ambivalence, Australia has undertaken constitutional reform that establishes a framework for recognizing Aboriginal claims, predominantly to land. Australia's multicultural regime grounds the recognition of Aboriginal rights – in a way that other regimes, for instance, in the United States in relation to Native Americans or in Brazil in relation to indigenous peoples, do not – in "the performance of cultural continuity" (Povinelli 2002:156). The consequence, arguably unintended, of this ostensibly enlightened policy is that Aboriginal subjects are, in multiple ways, trapped by the demands of an impossible authenticity, one that is, furthermore, irremediably tainted through its association with primitivity and violence. Aboriginal legal power with respect to land claims is wholly contingent on Aboriginal claimants being judged by Australian courts as culturally authentic, yet in ways that do not offend majority sensibilities, exhibiting neither too much nor too little cultural difference.

One of Povinelli's most significant theoretical moves concerns the relation between institutions and rights-claiming persons or groups and its productive implications for the contours of culture and rights. Now, recall the ways this was conceptualized in the political philosophical works I examined earlier: Kymlicka's understanding of cultures as preexisting the structures called on to recognize them can be contrasted to Benhabib's more sophisticated grasp of the mutually constitutive dynamic between cultural–social forms and political processes in the context of claims for recognition and redistribution (Benhabib 2002:71–81). Through her richly described ethnography, Povinelli provides an extended demonstration of the Foucauldian-inspired contention – which I have also explored in the context of Macedonian rights claiming (Cowan 2001:153; see also Cowan 2003) – that the recent revision of political and legal structures to recognize "culture" and "multiculturalism" has its own transformative effects, shaping and at times creating that which it purports merely to recognize. Going beyond a simple problem of incommensurability, a call to take the relativist or the universalist side, Povinelli shows "Aboriginal culture" to be produced in the interaction between state agents, white Australian citizens, and Aboriginal citizens, all of whom are contesting memories of Australians' past and struggling to imagine and define its political future. Neither the perception of alterity nor the kind of culture founded on that perception are "interior to the forms themselves"; rather, in Georg Simmel's phrasing, they are emergent in the "sites of contact" between them (Povinelli 2002:137–8).

"Aboriginal culture" is forged through structures of white European Australian domination. As Povinelli emphasizes, "law is one of the primary sites through which liberal forms of recognition develop their disciplinary sides as they work with the hopes, pride, optimisms and shame of indigenous and other minority subjects" (2002:184). Dominant subjects, meanwhile, are protected from real alterity – from the discourses, desires, or practices of indigenous peoples – and from their possible challenge to the nation as well as to its core institutions of democracy. Citing Wendy Brown's notion of "wounded attachments" (1995), Povinelli caustically observes that "the invitation to absorption" within the multicultural project is, paradoxically, combined with the injunction on indigenous subjects.

> to stage for the nation this sublime scene – not too much and not too little alterity. In this liberal imaginary, the now recognized subaltern subjects would slough off their traumatic histories, ambivalences, incoherencies, and angst like so much outgrown skin, rather than remain for themselves or for others a wounded testament to the nation's past bad faith. [Povinelli 2002:184]

Meanwhile, lamenting its own past villainy in mistreating Aboriginal peoples, the state transforms that self critique into a form of legitimation, placing itself in position to punish harmful difference, judge cultural authenticity, and decertify the rights and resource-bearing Aboriginal identity if the alterity on which it is founded is deemed either insufficient or excessive.

Through the many twists and turns of the ethnography, Povinelli highlights Aboriginal agency, emphasizing its risks and how it is constrained. But her larger point is the coerciveness of the game of recognition or, more to the point, its "cunning": the ways it disciplines while seeming merely to grant recognition of difference and freedom of cultural expression. In this respect, Povinelli's approach shares a theoretical orientation – informed by poststructuralist and Foucauldian premises but also insights from feminism and queer theory – with certain critical legal theorists. Characteristic of this work is a skepticism of liberal institutions, and a preoccupation with the complex and contradictory consequences of being granted rights on the basis of having a culture and a cultural identity. However, the work of critical legal theorists complements rather than replicates the kind of critique that Povinelli is developing in that it addresses the essentialism not of culture but of law. For instance, in their introduction to *Left Legalism/Left Critique* (2002), Wendy Brown and Janet Halley, noting how the US Left has in recent years put its energies for social justice into engagement with the law, argue that although the Left should engage strategically with law, it must track the effects of this engagement.

Inevitably, that engagement entails unintended consequences. While denigrated or excluded subjects yearn for recognition – a yearning that itself has been interrogated by Costas Douzinas (2002), another critical legal theorist – the concern of Brown and Halley, like that of their close collaborator the philosopher Judith Butler, is with the ways that the law makes identities "a site of regulation" and thus produces identities and subjects. In doing so, as they stress, it also forecloses other possibilities – of identity, of action, of imagining the political. It is not only post-structuralists who register such objections, of course. In an important recent assessment of the current state of play in gender and development in the South, feminist scholars and activists, many of them rooted in a socialist feminist tradition, lamented the depoliticizing quality of rights-based approaches (Cornwall et al. 2004).

Rights, culture, and context (revisited)

In a recently published chapter, "Losing (Out on) Intellectual Resources," Marilyn Strathern (2004) makes a very different kind of theoretical move, which destabilizes and thus allows a potential reworking of the terms of culture and rights and the relationship between the two. Drawing on a variety of sources – court records, newspaper reports, the verbal and written accounts of several anthropologists, and her own extensive knowledge of Papua New Guinea (henceforth, PNG) – Strathern explores the case of a young PNG woman, Miriam, from the Western Highlands region. In 1996, Miriam was given – that is, in marriage – as part of a compensation payment to a clan that had lost one of its relatives through the fault of Miriam's patriclan. A human rights NGO objected to the notion that a woman might be owned by a collective group and could be traded; they "sought a series of orders from the court to enforce Miriam's constitutional rights" (Strathern 2004:204). The presiding judge of the Mount Hagen National Court, Judge Salamo Injia, "ordered the two 'tribes' to refrain from enforcing their custom" (Strathern 2004:204); in his final verdict, he described the custom as "repugnant to the general principles of humanity" (Strathern 2004:201). The case precipitated discussions in the national press, framed in a discourse of tradition and modernity, about "good" versus "bad" customs and about how countervailing imperatives of obligation and choice ought to be weighed in making such moral delineations.

Strathern elucidates the specifically PNG version of this "rights versus culture" conundrum by recourse, first, to her now-classic analysis of personhood, developed in *The Gender of the Gift* (1988). Strathern argues that in PNG, persons are understood to embody relations with multiple collectivities; they are most whole when they are seen as an image of just one relationship, yet each body is embedded in, and therefore represents, multiple webs of kinship relationships. Strathern here distinguishes analytically between the "person" and the "agent": The person is "construed from the vantage point of the relations that constitute him or her; she or he objectifies and is thus revealed in these relations" (1988:273). By contrast, "The agent is construed as the one who acts because of those relationships and is revealed in his or her actions" (Strathern 1988:273). Strathern asks us to take seriously Miriam's agency in agreeing to be exchanged; acknowledging the pressure and distress this entailed, Strathern nonetheless insists that we acknowledge Miriam's wish to fulfill her obligations to her kin (2004:225–32). The implications towards which Strathern leads are that all agents in this context are bound to diverse sets of kin, which generates obligations. No agents have unlimited free choice. By contrast, human rights as philosophy and ideology posits free and equal persons outside such relations; in PNG, such relations are the very thing that makes them persons.

Although the critique hinges on a contrast between PNG and Western forms of personhood, Strathern is not making an argument that falls within the familiar tracks of the cultural relativism versus universalism debate. This is evident from the way her analysis of the PNG compensation case regarding the ownership of Miriam proceeds in tandem with an exploration of parallels with principles being developed over the ownership of body parts (limbs, organs, tissue, sperm, and ova) in contemporary Western legal debates. The double-stranded argument confounds that simple opposition because – reading both cases through questions of law, objects, and ownership – she finds both convergences and distinctions. Contingent on this analysis, she refuses to reduce the upholding of Miriam as compensation payment to an instance of cultural imperative or the demands of tradition; according to Strathern, it is best seen as an expression of the commitment to kin relations.

This move very subtly, but unmistakably, shifts the work that culture does in the analysis. Strathern develops this point through critique of another influential anthropological position advocating analyses of rights in context: that of Richard Wilson in his groundbreaking volume, *Human Rights, Culture and Context: Anthropological Perspectives* (1997a). However, Strathern undertakes this critique in oddly circuitous fashion – by way of a review article by Nigel Rapport (1998). Rapport's enthusiastic review of the edited volume repeatedly returns to Wilson's reference to "the increasingly convincing judgement that we are moving into a 'post-cultural' world" (Wilson 1997b:10), one in which cultural relativism has little purchase. Rapport uses this reference to the postcultural to launch an exposition of Richard Rorty's vision of "postmodern bourgeois liberalism," which purports to provide a foundation for human rights without ethnocentrism by retaining a focus on the diversity of individuals as well as the diversity of cultures (Rapport 1998:386; Rorty 1986, 1992). Rapport describes the postcultural as a polity that "posits human beings as ontologically prior to the cultural milieux they create" (1998:386); drawing on the ideas of Marc Augé (1995:111), Rapport further elaborates on the desired globalized liberal polity as one that "publicly respects the right of the individual citizen to his own civil freedoms *against* cultural prejudices, *against* social statuses, and *against* the language embodied in their self-expressions" (Rapport 1998:386).

These are Rapport's words, not Wilson's, and may, indeed, be paraphrases of Rorty and Augé, yet Strathern uses all of this in building her case against Wilson's contextualism. There is irony here: Wilson's article in the volume (1997c) insists on the anthropologist's brief "to restore the richness of subjectivities and chart the complex fields of social relations, contradictory values and the emotional accompaniment to macro-structures that human rights accounts often exclude" (1997b:15). Strathern contends that this does not go far enough; social relations are interesting for Wilson, she maintains, not in their own right but primarily as phenomena that "trace local connection to macro-global processes" (Strathern 2004:231). In her view, Wilson takes concrete social relations as mere background rather than fundamentally constitutive of the person.

Although her argument is somewhat tortuous, Strathern has a point. Inasmuch as Wilson accepts the privileged and a priori theoretical category of the "individual" entailed in the liberal model of human rights, his framework for analyzing human rights practices cannot accommodate the possibility of a very different form of personhood nor fully take account of the constructed nature of social being. In the terms of such a framework, Miriam exists prior to social relations; recognizing and bestowing Miriam's rights can occur outside her embeddedness in these relations. Strathern calls for an approach to human rights analysis that would take into account "the diverse ways in which persons visualize themselves as carried by other persons and, for better or worse, by their relations to others" (Strathern 2004:233); failure to do so leads to a deficit not merely in cultural understanding but, more fundamentally, in social analysis (Strathern 2004:232). This insistence on social relations as starting point resonates with that of many communitarian analysts who see society or community as constitutive of the individual. It also echoes the analytical concerns of sociologists like Adam Seligman (2000), who sees the model of the rights-bearing individual – grounded in a conception of the autonomous and unencumbered individual, motivated by self-interest and obligated to nothing and no one beyond his or her own conscience – as unable to take into account the persuasiveness, for increasing numbers of individuals in the contemporary moment, of the moral imperatives emanating from alternative sources of authority, such as religion.

In emphasizing the significance of indebtedness for personhood, Strathern underplays contestation; a sense of the richness and contradiction of Miriam's – or anyone else's – subjectivity is not the reader's reward. Strathern, however, sacrifices thick description for a different theoretical move. She holds firmly to the importance of attention to locality, in the sense of a conjunction of time (history) and space, insisting that "only the particularity of circumstances would define what an entitlement or right might mean in those specific conditions under which people live" (Strathern 2004:232). Yet, while arguing for acknowledgment of local conditions and conceptions, she displaces culture as the privileged object or index of the local, ceding this to social relations. At the same time, her provocative conclusion leads back toward anthropology's comparative project. It does so through a disarming proposition. As she demonstrated in the case of Miriam, human rights are appealed to in order to challenge the objectification or "thingification" of the victim (even though human rights discourse itself also makes the victim "thinglike," as Wilson [1997c] persuasively showed in respect to human rights reporting). Strathern does not repudiate that objectification; rather, her argument moves laterally. The Melanesian construct of "the reified person as a thing-image," she avers, offers a different route to thinking about culture, rights, and the persons implicated: "one that dares us to begin specifying what it is as human beings we might own of each other" (Strathern 2004:233). Slipping tangentially across the well-worn tracks between opposed positions – universalism versus cultural relativism, victim versus perpetrator, and individual versus society – Strathern evades the impasse and reframes the problem to address a 21st-century dilemma that we have barely begun to conceptualize. Something like this is what I, at least, had in mind when suggesting that, in the hands of the skillful anthropologist, culture could be analytic to rights.

Rights, culture, and creative interpretation

All of my three examples demonstrate what an "on the ground" engagement with actual rights practices – often, although not always, undertaken by anthropologists – can illuminate. The final example focuses on rights practices in a context that is still greatly underinvestigated ethnographically: the international institution. In large part a response to *Culture and Rights*, the article "Reflections on Culture and Cultural Rights" (Robbins and Stamatopoulou 2004) is coauthored by the literary and cultural theorist, Bruce Robbins, former editor of *Social Text*, and Elsa Stamatopoulou, who directs the Permanent Forum on Indigenous Issues at the United Nations Secretariat in New York and who speaks and writes on human rights issues (e.g., Danieli et al. 1999). With complementary professional expertises, the authors together bring critical insights from the debates about "culture" with wisdom drawn from a long-term familiarity with indigenous organizing within one particular international organization.

Robbins and Stamatopoulou emphasize the pragmatic uses of cultural rights claims. Their reminder that questions of rights and culture are not mere academic issues but have real material import is refreshing. Commenting on my article in *Culture and Rights*, Robbins and Stamatopoulou concur with my observation that anthropologists studying struggles for rights to culture may find themselves torn between skepticism of their informants' political project, on the one hand, and empathy with their suffering and desires for recognition, on the other hand. They also endorse my conclusion that "the only tenable position for the engaged scholar [is] a paradoxical one": to support a minority's demands for recognition yet, at the same time, to problematize, not celebrate, its project and to query its emancipatory aura (Cowan 2001:171). Such a position, they argue, is "right enough" in today's context, in which, as they insist, "too much is at stake in minority and indigenous assertions of their cultural identity, at stake materially as well as spiritually, for the academic critic to begrudge due recognition on the grounds of some sort of theoretical incorrectness" (Robbins and Stamatopoulou 2004:422). According to them, analysts should remember the historical, as much as the political, contexts of the processes they are investigating: "Claims to cultural rights cannot be understood and defended...without nuanced and nimble attention both to internationally established human rights norms and the particularities of time and place" (Robbins and Stamatopoulou 2004:422). Once one specifies and considers the implications of the articulation of cultural claims within the present, historically particular, moment in the development of human rights discourse, "taking sides around these rights can perhaps come to seem less like facing a universal philosophical dilemma (as Cowan makes it seem) and more like making a reasoned, situated political choice" (Robbins and Stamatopoulou 2004:422).

The argument for more fully recognizing contingency and situated choices is extended by two additional general claims. Indigenous leaders and their constituencies, they argue, are more reflexive about their cultures than we may give them credit for, and they strategically employ essentialist views of culture. Robbins and Stamatopoulou's argument concurs, interestingly, with Kymlicka's. The latter further asserts that although many ethnic leaders do, indeed, use essentialist discourses about culture to demand a set of rights, these, in fact, and paradoxically, often "create legal spaces for choice and hybridity" (Kymlicka 2002:1097). Focusing on "the actual legal form that these rights take," Kymlicka argues, might tell us "a different story about the theory and practice of cultural rights" (2002:1097).

In Robbins and Stamatopoulou's analysis, the strategic engagement – essentialist or otherwise – on the part of activists is effective largely because it is matched by institutional flexibility at the United Nations. Minority activists may achieve considerable success in getting demands met if they avoid or repudiate the claim to self-determination that states find most threatening; the process involves a pragmatic willingness among all parties to work without agreed definitions for key terms like *minority* or *indigenous*. Indeed, working in an international legal environment of partial and not-yet-ratified agreements and declarations concerning indigenous peoples, the Human Rights Committee "has made creative and clever interpretation of the minority-related article 27 of the International Covenant on Civil and Political Rights" (Robbins and Stamatopoulou 2004:429). For instance, according to the authors, the committee has taken the liberty of interpreting the article in an extended way to cover cultural rights of noncitizens, migrant workers, and visitors, and they have used it "to stop the granting of leases for oil and gas exploration and timber development on indigenous land in Canada and to defend Maori fishing rights in New Zealand, as well as Sami practicing reindeer husbandry in Finland, which were threatened by logging interests" (Robbins and Stamatopoulou 2004:429).

The authors stress the "suppleness of the law," the scope for indigenous people's agency, and the material payoffs for less powerful constituencies that cultural claims can bring. It is not insignificant that such an argument comes from analysts witnessing rights formulation and claims making on the ground (in this case, in the meeting rooms and corridors of an international institution) by actors strategizing and pursuing interests within a political field of human rights activism that, from an actor's perspective, must seem like the only game in town. Robbins and Stamatopoulou's optimism is reminiscent of Kymlicka's and strongly contrasts with the gloomier prognosis of Povinelli, critical legal theorists, and many contemporary feminists, all of whom remain less sanguine about the emancipatory possibilities for less powerful or politically subordinated agents – primarily, ethnic minorities and indigenous peoples – encountering both national systems of multicultural recognition and the international legal apparatus of human rights.

Even though Kymlicka defines the spaces – and, thus, the possible stories – for cultural rights too narrowly (2002:1097), those legal forms that create legal spaces are certainly one aspect that anthropologists and others have yet to fully plumb. We need more empirical investigation of specific legal claims about culture, their

careers within and movements (nationally and transnationally) across social and institutional sites, and their implications within legal spaces: in judicial decisions, policy
making, and funding. Just how legal institutions might find ways of recognizing,
protecting, and promoting an "essentially contested" phenomenon, a "moving
object" (as John Bowen has described for Islam in France; see 2003:50), remain,
however, unresolved questions.

Conclusion

This essay represents an engagement with selected writers making public and
published interventions in various forums and from various disciplines, all of
whom are addressing questions of culture and rights. I have proceeded by examining
the uses of culture and rights (particularly the relationship between the two), both of
which operate as analytical concepts and, for some writers, as desired objectives in
themselves. I have also attempted to tease out the broader social theory or social
ontology that underpins these uses. My critique aims toward a more adequate
theoretical grasp of the contingency and complexity of social struggles involving
culture and rights and of the consequences, often unanticipated and sometimes
surprising, when demands are recognized or accommodated. The need will be
obvious in respect to anthropologists; but I am arguing that other scholars engaged
in questions of culture in the context of rights, law, and politics similarly need to
address what Benhabib, in her important critique from within political theory and
philosophy, has characterized as "reductionist sociology," which informs and limits
much political philosophizing and theorizing around culture.

My critique has acknowledged that the empirical figures importantly, yet differently, for anthropology and political philosophy as intellectual projects as well as
within our distinctive epistemologies. Similarly, although I have identified a kind of
division of labor between anthropology's descriptive project and political philosophy's normative one, these are neither absolute nor mutually exclusive. Scholars on
both sides of the disciplinary divide have acknowledged considerable common
ground in our aims and concerns around questions of living with diversity; my call
for rigorous interrogation of the concepts and methods we use to investigate those
questions is motivated by the hope that we can build on this common ground.
An interdisciplinary dialogue seems to me essential in the struggle for more just
and creative ways of living together. In the context of this dialogue and our – at least
partially – shared project, I have argued forcefully for the especial value of empirically grounded studies of rights and culture – when undertaken in a theoretically
informed, reflexive, and critical way. This is precisely because such studies confront
us with – and force us to grapple with – the messiness, contradiction, ambiguity,
impasses, and the unintended consequences that neither neat and tidy theory nor the
best-laid plans for political reform can ever fully anticipate.

NOTES

1   An important early trigger for this work came from feminism, some of it under the
    influence of Derridean theory, on the basis of a critique of "man" or the liberal subject.
    Feminist critics argued that this subject was not neutral and universal but, in its qualities
    of autonomy, agency, independence, and self-maximization, was instead modeled on

(as the now-hackneyed litany goes) the relatively unencumbered, able-bodied, adult, European, heterosexual, middle-class, white male. The critical project was to expose the specificity masked by the norm, its normativity being both the reflection and source of its privilege. Later tendencies of identity movements notwithstanding, the initial insight concerned the relational nature of being, meaning, and identity.

2   In the contemporary academy, the study of politics is classed under different names – political science, political theory, political philosophy, and politics – all of which may variously reflect theoretical divisions, substantive emphases, and national traditions. Most of the writers I deal with in this article call themselves "political philosophers," although US-based scholars would probably define work in this vein as *political theory*. A British colleague who holds an academic post in politics while teaching on a postgraduate program called "Social and Political Thought" (Neil Stammers, personal communication, July 15, 2005) has urged me to specify the tradition with which I am engaging as "liberal political philosophy," the strand that does, indeed, dominate – often to the extent that other forms of political philosophy are excluded from this rubric and labeled as something else (history, the study of social movements, etc.). For ease of expression, I will use primarily the term *political philosophy* to refer to that inquiry into the principles of politics, although this may include an empirical element.

3   Arguably, what we have seen in recent years, at least in the United States, is a diminution of actual cultural differences among ethnic and racial communities at the same time that claims to difference are voiced ever more vociferously and tokens of difference have become increasingly significant politically. See Appiah 1997.

4   Complex issues surrounding claims to language rights were explored in an *AA* "In Focus" debate on "Language Ideologies, Rights, and Choices: Dilemmas and Paradoxes of Loss, Retention, and Revitalization" (*American Anthropologist* 105(4):710–81).

5   Readers may wish to consult our critique of some leading political philosophers' use of the "culture" concept in *Culture and Rights* (Cowan et al. 2001b:15–20), in which we briefly addressed, among others, the work of Ronald Dworkin, the work of Will Kymlicka, and the communitarian position outlined by Charles Taylor in his seminal essay, *Multiculturalism and "The Politics of Recognition"* (1992). Although criticism concerning the role of culture in political philosophy has tended to be targeted toward communitarians, we observed that proponents of both liberal and communitarian positions may be equally guilty of reifying culture or seeing it as singular, bounded, ahistorical, overly coherent, or overly determining. In the 2001 text, we looked hopefully toward Kymlicka for a more theoretically adequate approach; my analysis here is less sanguine about Kymlicka's use of the "culture" concept and concurs with Benhabib (2002), whose critique is explored in the next section and who suggests that outmoded conceptualizations pervade a great deal of political theorizing and philosophizing.

6   The authors were guided by an external advisory panel of eminent experts as well as by principal consultants who provided background papers. Experts and consultants included a number of academic luminaries, among them Arjun Appadurai, Lourdes Arizpe, Seyla Benhabib, Nicholas Dirks, Will Kymlicka, Mahmood Mamdani, Rodolfo Stavenhagen, and Aristide Zolberg (with Amartya Sen providing the core conceptual framing).

7   Because my objective here is to outline Kymlicka's position, its concomitant implications, and the dominant responses to these, I am unable to engage at length with the fascinating, important, and creative feminist debates on the vexed relations between women's rights and cultural rights or multiculturalism, which is worthy of a long discussion in its own right. This interdisciplinary (both scholarly and activist) debate addresses issues of social, cultural, and religious restrictions for women; domestic violence; abductions and forced marriages; problems of "who defines *culture*" (typically, male elders); case studies of how women fare in countries with systems of personal law for religious communities (e.g., the well-known Shah Bano case in India) or where indigenous customary law is legally recognized; and more. See Merry 2001; Mullally 2004; and contributors to Okin 1999; Phillips 2001; Shachar 2000; Sieder and Witchell 2001; Southall Black Sisters 2003;

and Zechenter 1997. Precisely because feminist work is concerned with both theory and practice and committed to emancipatory change, yet sensitive to the difficulties and unintended consequences of policies aimed toward both gender equality and cultural respect, I expect that this area of inquiry will continue to provide some of the most fruitful interventions on issues of culture and rights. Indeed, I consider that a feminist awareness and an attention to gender dimensions are essential to an adequate grasp of the issues. Readers will notice that most of the key scholars with whom I have engaged in this essay (Benhabib, Povinelli, and Strathern) bring a strong gender-oriented or feminist perspective to their analyses.

8   The tendency of political philosophers in this debate to use the word *culture* to refer to a minority group is infuriating to anthropologists, most of whom insist on the importance of distinguishing the "culture" concept as an ideational realm – or, at least, a realm in which ideas and practices are coherently linked – instead of seeing "culture" as synonymous with "society" or "social groups" (including minority groups). It certainly creates conceptual confusion in cross-disciplinary readings. Ironically, some of the apparent reification of culture and attribution of agency to it is more comprehensible if we acknowledge this particular usage, in which *culture* is meant to refer to a collectivity of persons.

9   Interventions by feminist political philosophers, frequently nuanced and more than usually sensitive to the complexity of the issues, have mostly avoided this trap and, indeed, lay the ground-work for moving beyond the impasse. See, for example, Nussbaum 1999; Phillips 2001; and Tamir 1993.

10 Benhabib draws exclusively on references to the French debate, but I want to emphasize that feminist anthropologists have contributed major insights on precisely this issue of contestations around and resignifications of the veil or headscarf in a number of sociohistorical contexts, both inside and outside Europe. A few examples from an extensive literature include Abu-Lughod 1986, 2002; Brenner 1996; Dembour 1995, 1996; MacLeod 1991; Mahmood 2001; and Mandel 1989.

REFERENCES

Abu-Lughod, Lila
    1986   Veiled Sentiments: Honor and Poetry in a Bedouin Society. Berkeley: University of California Press.
    2002   Do Muslim Women Really Need Saving? Anthropological Reflections on Cultural Relativism and Its Others. American Anthropologist 104(3):783–90.
Appiah, Kwame Anthony
    1996   Race, Culture, Identity: Misunderstood Connections. *In* Color Consciousness: The Political Morality of Race. K. Anthony Appiah and Amy Gutmann, eds. pp. 30–105. Princeton: Princeton University Press.
    1997   The Multiculturalist Misunderstanding. New York Review of Books 44(14):30–6.
Arendt, Hannah
    1973[1958]   The Human Condition. 8th edition. Chicago: University of Chicago Press.
Augé, Marc
    1995   Non-Places. Introduction to an Anthropology of Supermodernity. London: Verso.
Benhabib, Seyla
    2002   The Claims of Culture: Equality and Diversity in the Global Era. Princeton: Princeton University Press.
Bhabha, Homi
    1994   The Location of Culture. New York: Routledge. Bobbio, Norberto
    1996   The Age of Rights. Cambridge: Polity Press.
Boellstorff, Tom
    2005   Replacing Heteronormative Views of Kinship and Marriage. American Ethnologist 32(1):37–8.

Bourdieu, Pierre
  1977   Outline of a Theory of Practice. Cambridge: Cambridge University Press.
Bowen, John
  2003   Two Approaches to Rights and Religion in Contemporary France. *In* Human Rights in Global Perspective: Anthropological Studies of Rights, Claims and Entitlements. Richard Ashby Wilson and Jon P. Mitchell, eds. pp. 33–53. London: Routledge.
Brenner, Suzanne
  1996   Reconstructing Self and Society: Javanese Muslim Women and "the Veil." American Ethnologist 23(4):673–97.
Brown, Wendy
  1995   States of Injury: Power and Freedom in Late Modernity. Princeton: Princeton University Press.
Brown, Wendy, and Janet Halley, eds.
  2002   Left Legalism/Left Critique. Durham, NC: Duke University Press.
Cornwall, Andrea, Elizabeth Harrison, and Ann Whitehead
  2004   Repositioning Feminisms in Development: Introduction. IDS Bulletin 3(4):1–10.
Cowan, Jane K.
  1990   Dance and the Body Politic in Northern Greece. Princeton: Princeton University Press.
  2001   Ambiguities of an Emancipatory Discourse: The Making of a Macedonian Minority in Greece. *In* Culture and Rights: Anthropological Perspectives. Jane K. Cowan, Marie-Bénédicte Dembour, and Richard A. Wilson, eds. pp. 152–76. Cambridge: Cambridge University Press.
  2003   The Uncertain Political Limits of Cultural Claims: Minority Rights Politics in South-East Europe. *In* Human Rights in Global Perspective: Anthropological Studies of Rights, Claims and Entitlements. Richard A. Wilson and Jon P. Mitchell, eds. pp. 140–62. London: Routledge.
Cowan, Jane K., Marie-Bénédicte Dembour, and Richard A. Wilson, eds.
  2001a   Culture and Rights: Anthropological Perspectives. Cambridge: Cambridge University Press.
  2001b   Introduction. *In* Culture and Rights: Anthropological Perspectives. Jane K. Cowan, Marie-Bénédicte Dembour, and Richard A. Wilson, eds. pp. 1–26. Cambridge: Cambridge University Press.
Danieli, Yael, Elsa Stamatopoulou, and Clarence J. Dias, eds.
  1999   The Universal Declaration of Human Rights: Fifty Years and Beyond. New York: Baywood Publishing Company for the United Nations.
Dembour, Marie-Bénédicte
  1995   Not Another Muslim Headscarf Affair, Please: The Significant Story of an Identity Photograph in Belgium. Contemporary Issues in Law 1(4):9–24.
  1996   Le foulard: un faux problème (The headscarf: A false problem). Agenda Interculturel 142:14–18.
Douzinas, Costas
  2002   Identity, Recognition, Rights or What Can Hegel Teach Us about Human Rights. Journal of Law and Society 29(3):379–405.
Fagan, Andrew
  N.d.   Challenging the "Right of Exit" Remedy in the Political Theory of Cultural Diversity. Unpublished MS, Human Rights Centre, University of Essex.
Fraser, Nancy
  1989   Unruly Practices: Power, Discourse and Gender in Contemporary Social Theory. Cambridge: Polity Press.
  1997   Justice Interruptus: Critical Reflections on the "Postsocialist" Condition. New York: Routledge.
Fraser, Nancy, and Axel Honneth
  2003   Redistribution or Recognition? A Political-Philosophical Exchange. New York: Verso.

Galston, William
  1995 Two Concepts of Liberalism. Ethics 105(3):516–34. Gilroy, Paul
  1995 Black Atlantic: Modernity and Double Consciousness. Cambridge, MA: Harvard University Press.
  2000 Against Race: Imagining Political Culture beyond the Color Line. Cambridge, MA: Harvard University Press.
Gore, Charles
  1997 Irreducibly Social Goods and the Informational Basis of Amartya Sen's Capability Approach. Journal of International Development 9(2):235–50.
Habermas, Jürgen
  1990 Moral Consciousness and Communicative Action. Cambridge, MA: MIT Press.
Halley, Janet
  1999 Culture Constrains. *In* Is Multiculturalism Bad for Women? J. Cohen, M. Howard, and M. C. Nussbaum, eds. pp. 100–4. Princeton: Princeton University Press.
Honig, Bonnie
  1999 "My Culture Made Me Do It." *In* Is Multiculturalism Bad for Women? J. Cohen, M. Howard, and M. C. Nussbaum, eds. pp. 35–40. Princeton: Princeton University Press.
Huntington, Samuel
  1996 The Clash of Civilizations and the Remaking of World Order. New York: Simon and Schuster.
Huntington, Samuel, and Lawrence Harrison, eds.
  2000 Culture Matters: How Values Shape Human Progress. New York: Basic Books.
Joppke, Christian, and Steven Lukes, eds.
  1999 Multicultural Questions. Oxford: Oxford University Press.
Kukathas, Chandran
  1997 Cultural Toleration. *In* Ethnicity and Group Rights. Ian Shapiro and Will Kymlicka, eds. pp. 69–104. New York: New York University Press.
Kymlicka, Will
  1995a Multicultural Citizenship: A Liberal Theory of Minority Rights. Oxford: Polity Press.
  1995b The Rights of Minority Cultures. Oxford: Oxford University Press.
  1996 Three Forms of Group-Differentiated Citizenship in Canada. *In* Democracy and Difference: Contesting the Boundaries of the Political. Seyla Benhabib, ed. pp. 153–70. Princeton: Princeton University Press.
  1998 Finding Our Way: Rethinking Ethnocultural Relations in Canada. Toronto: Oxford University Press.
  2001 Politics in the Vernacular. Oxford: Oxford University Press.
  2002 *Review of* Culture and Rights: Anthropological Perspectives. Ethnic and Racial Studies 25(6):1096–7.
MacLeod, Arlene
  1991 Accommodating Protest. New York: Columbia University Press.
Mahmood, Saba
  2001 Feminist Theory, Embodiment, and the Docile Agent: Some Reflections on the Egyptian Islamic Revival. Cultural Anthropology 16(2):202–35.
Mandel, Ruth
  1989 Turkish Headscarves and the "Foreigner Problem": Constructing Difference through Emblems of Identity. New German Critique 46:27–46.
Merry, Sally Engle
  1997 Legal Pluralism and Transnational Culture: The *Ka Ho'okolokolonui Kanaka Maoli* Tribunal, Hawai'i, 1993. *In* Human Rights, Culture and Context: Anthropological Perspectives. Richard A. Wilson, ed. pp. 28–48. London: Pluto Press.
  2001 Changing Rights, Changing Culture. *In* Culture and Rights: Anthropological Perspectives. Jane K. Cowan, Marie-Bénédicte Dembour, and Richard A. Wilson, eds. pp. 31–55. Cambridge: Cambridge University Press.

Mullally, Siobhan
   2004   Feminism and Multiculturalism Dilemmas in India: Revisiting the *Shah Bano* Case.
      Oxford Journal of Legal Studies 24(4):671–92.
Nussbaum, Martha
   1999   A Plea for Difficulty. *In* Is Multiculturalism Bad for Women? J. Cohen, M. Howard,
      and M. C. Nussbaum, eds. pp. 105–14. Princeton: Princeton University Press.
Okin, Susan Moller
   1999   "Is Multiculturalism Bad for Women?" *In* Is Multiculturalism Bad for Women?
      J. Cohen, M. Howard, and M. C. Nussbaum, eds. pp. 9–24. Princeton: Princeton
      University Press.
Ortner, Sherry
   1984   Theory in Anthropology since the Sixties. Comparative Studies in Society and
      History 26(1):126–66.
Phillips, Anne
   2001   Multiculturalism, Universalism and the Claims of Democracy. Democracy, Governance
      and Human Rights, Programme Paper, 7. Geneva: UNDP.
Povinelli, Elizabeth
   2002   The Cunning of Recognition: Indigenous Alterities and the Making of Australian
      Multiculturalism. Durham, NC: Duke University Press.
Rapport, Nigel
   1998   The Potential of Human Rights in a Post-Cultural World. Social Anthropology
      6(3):381–8.
Rawls, John
   1993   The Law of Peoples. *In* On Human Rights: The Oxford Amnesty Lectures. Stephen
      Shute and Susan Hurley, eds. pp. 41–82. New York: Basic Books.
   1999   The Law of Peoples. Cambridge, MA: Harvard University Press.
Robbins, Bruce, and Elsa Stamatopoulou
   2004   Reflections on Culture and Cultural Rights. The South Atlantic Quarterly 103(2–3):
      419–34.
Rorty, Richard
   1986   On Ethnocentrism: A Reply to Clifford Geertz. Michigan Quarterly Review
      25:525–34.
   1992   Contingency, Irony and Solidarity. Cambridge: Cambridge University Press.
   1993   Human Rights, Sentimentality and Universality. *In* On Human Rights: The Oxford
      Amnesty Lectures. Stephen Shute and Susan Hurley, eds. pp. 111–34. New York: Basic
      Books.
Rose, Jacqueline
   1996   States of Fantasy. Oxford: Oxford University Press.
Sandel, Michael
   1998   Liberalism and the Limits of Justice. Cambridge: Cambridge University Press.
Seligman, Adam B.
   2000   Modernity's Wager: Authority, the Self and Transcendence. Princeton: Princeton
      University Press.
Shachar, Ayelet
   2000   The Puzzle of Interlocking Power Hierarchies: Sharing the Pieces of Jurisdictional
      Authority. Harvard Civil Rights/Civil Liberties Law Review 35(2):387–426.
Sieder, Rachel, and Jessica Witchell
   2001   Advancing Indigenous Claims through the Law: Reflections on the Guatemalan
      Peace Process. *In* Culture and Rights: Anthropological Perspectives. Jane K. Cowan,
      Marie-Bénédicte Dembour, and Richard A. Wilson, eds. pp. 201–25. Cambridge:
      Cambridge University Press.
Simmel, Georg
   1971   Sociability. *In* On Individuality and Social Forms. Donald N. Levine, ed. pp. 127–40.
      Chicago: University of Chicago Press.

Southall Black Sisters
   2003   From Homebreakers to Jailbreakers: Southall Black Sisters. London: Zed Books.
Strathern, Marilyn
   1988   The Gender of the Gift: Problems with Women and Problems with Society in
          Melanesia. Berkeley: University of California Press.
   2004   Losing (Out on) Intellectual Resources. *In* Law, Anthropology, and the Constitution
          of the Social: Making Persons and Things. Alain Pottage and Martha Mundy, eds.
          pp. 201–33. Cambridge: Cambridge University Press.
Tamir, Yael
   1993   Liberal Nationalism. Princeton: Princeton University Press.
Taylor, Charles
   1990   Irreducibly Social Goods. *In* Rationality, Individualism and Public Policy.
          G. Brennan and C. Walsh, eds. pp. 45–63. Canberra: Centre for Research on Federal
          Financial Relations, The Australian National University.
   1992   Multiculturalism and "The Politics of Recognition." Amy Gutmann, ed. Princeton:
          Princeton University Press.
   1993   Reconciling the Solitudes: Essays on Canadian Federalism and Nationalism. Guy
          Leforest, ed. Montreal: McGill-Queens University Press.
Turner, Terence
   1993   Anthropology and Multiculturalism: What Is Anthropology That Multiculturalists
          Should Be Mindful of It? Cultural Anthropology 8(4):411–29.
UN Development Programme (UNDP)
   2004   Human Development Report 2004: Cultural Liberty in Today's Diverse World. New
          York: UNDP.
Willis, Paul
   1977   Learning to Labour: Why Working-Class Kids Get Working-Class Jobs. New York:
          Columbia University Press.
Wilson, Richard A.
   1997b Human Rights, Culture and Context: An Introduction. *In* Human Rights, Culture
          and Context: Anthropological Perspectives. Richard A. Wilson, ed. pp. 1–27. London:
          Pluto Press.
   1997c Representing Human Rights Violations: Social Contexts and Subjectivities.
          In Human Rights, Culture and Context: Anthropological Perspectives. Richard A.
          Wilson, ed. pp. 134–60. London: Pluto Press.
Wilson, Richard A., ed.
   1997a Human Rights, Culture and Context: Anthropological Perspectives. London: Pluto
          Press.
Young, Iris Marion
   1990   Justice and the Politics of Difference. Princeton: Princeton University Press.
Zechenter, E. M.
   1997   In the Name of Culture: Cultural Relativism and the Abuse of the Individual.
          Journal of Anthropological Research 53:319–47.
Žižek, Slavoj
   1995   The Sublime Object of Ideology. London: Verso.

17

Human Rights as Cultural Practice: An Anthropological Critique

Ann-Belinda S. Preis

Il faut suivre ce qui est commun, c'est-à-dire ce qui est universel. Car le verbe universel est commun à tous. Or bien que ce verbe soit commun à tous, la plupart vivent comme s'ils possédaient en propre une pensée particulière.

Héraclite in Moustapha Safouan 1993[1]

Introduction

Forty-eight years have passed since the American Anthropological Association (AAA) issued Melville Herskovits' now well-known rejection of "the applicability of any Declaration of Human Rights to mankind as a whole."[2] The statement explicitly emphasized that "[t]he rights of Man in the Twentieth Century cannot be circumscribed by the standards of any single culture, or be dictated by the aspirations of any single people";[3] a situation which would "lead to frustration, not realization of the personalities of vast numbers of human beings."[4] The following year, Julian H. Steward reconfirmed this position in rather undisguised terms: "[W]e are prepared to take a stand against the values in our own culture which underly [sic] such imperialism."[5] Since then, anthropologists' opposition to, or at least peripheral interest in, human rights formulations has remained somewhat commonplace both inside and outside of the discipline. Indeed, if one could point retrospectively to the major intellectual contributions of social anthropology in the twentieth century, it would consist of "[t]he observations that other people's truths are contained in their own classifications and understanding, and that our own culture offers no self-evidently privileged standard of verity...."[6] This perspective

Originally published in *Human Rights Quarterly*, 18: 2 (1996), 286–315.

has pervaded the discipline as an ethical undercurrent despite the emergence of different schools of thought and various theoretical directions.

A recent article examining the somewhat intransigent relationship between anthropology and human rights lists five major reasons why anthropologists have been largely uninvolved in human rights research and formulations. First, there has been a clear preference among anthropologists to advocate the rights of collectivities, especially "indigenous people"; the recognition of "collective rights" as an integral part of international human rights has only recently assumed importance. Second, rather than participating in political discussions of abstract rights, or processes of drafting declarations, anthropologists have involved themselves in applied or action-oriented anthropology to improve the economic conditions and political negotiating strength of smaller-scale societies. Third, due to the particular sensitivity of doing fieldwork, anthropologists have tended to avoid extensive critical questioning of the political legitimacies of sovereign states and their actions. Fourth, despite anthropologists' contributions to the rhetorics of socioeconomic, cultural, and indigenous rights, the UN human rights commissions continue to be dominated by legal discourse. Finally, anthropologists have tended to see the limitations of the UN documents and procedures which fail to penetrate below, or to look outside, the level of the state to identify human rights notions as well as sources of violation.[7]

However, the most fundamental and pertinent reason for anthropologists' restricted involvement with human rights issues can be traced directly to the theory of "cultural relativism." This is exemplified by the AAA statement's rejection of the notion of universal human rights, its emphasis on different peoples' different rights concepts, and its criticism of a universal international legal framework as ethnocentrically Western. While this position is generally seen as a major "burden" contributing to the exclusion of anthropologists from human rights research,[8] this is not the only impact of cultural relativism. For quite some time now, the theory has, in fact, been nurturing a seemingly never-ending debate among human rights researchers on the question of the "universalism" or "relativism" of human rights. The "classical" conflict is well-known: cultural relativists see the Universal Declaration on Human Rights as enumerating rights and freedoms which are culturally, ideologically, and politically nonuniversal. They argue that current human rights norms possess a distinctively "Western" or "Judeo-Christian" bias, and hence, are an "ethno-centric" construct with limited applicability. Conversely, universalists assert that human rights are special entitlements of all persons. They are grounded in human nature and as such, are inalienable. "To have human rights one does not have to be anything other than a human being. Neither must one do anything other than be born a human being," as a common phrase goes.[9] Despite various attempts to reject relativist propositions as a confusion of human rights and human dignity, or of rights and duties, the question of the "transferability" and "cross-cultural validity" of human rights continues to be a battlefield of fierce, heated, and passionate debate, with researchers making strong – and strongly varying – philosophical, political, or moral commitments. As the first sentence of a recent review article describes the situation: "Few scholarly topics more readily engender controversies than the question of the universality of international human rights norms."[10]

An interesting paradox emerges from this situation and calls for attention: during precisely the same period as cultural relativism has been an active component of human rights research and debates (from which anthropologists have been excluded to some extent), the theory has gradually, but effectively, lost its import within anthropology itself. By and large, the scenario has been the following: over the past ten to fifteen years, rapid changes in the modern world have forced anthropologists to rethink their discipline's fundamentally "relativistic" position, and most importantly, its underlying assumption of "culture" as a homogeneous, integral, and coherent unity.[11] This view has implied that anthropological analysis is no longer effectuated through "the lens of cultural relativity that...made the world appear as culture gardens separated by boundary-maintaining values – as posited essences."[12] The contemporary globalization of economic, political, and social life has resulted in cultural penetration and overlapping, the coexistence in a given social space of several cultural traditions, and in a more vivid interpenetration of cultural experience and practice due to media and transportation technologies, travel, and tourism. In order to capture this more fluid character of present-day relationships between center and peripheries and the realization that cultural flows are no longer territorially bounded, notions like "creolization," "hybridity," and "cultural complexity" have emerged in anthropological vocabulary. Culture is increasingly seen "as a network of perspectives, or as an ongoing debate."[13]

These theoretical shifts are not without significance for contemporary debates on the universality or cultural relativity of human rights. As I shall attempt to demonstrate below, the debates often take place at an abstract, and highly generalized level where "culture" is implicitly or explicitly conceptualized as a static, homogenous, and bounded entity, defined by its specific "traits." The debates, therefore, remain caught in various outdated approaches to "culture contact," within which a rigid "us" and "them" dichotomy is constantly reproduced, and from which there seems to be no apparent escape. In a world of increased mobility and intensification of cultural flows between centers and peripheries, the question is, of course, whether this theoretical perspective still reflects the reality of culture, let alone that of human rights.

This article suggests that recent anthropological reflections on the notion of culture might contribute not only to pushing the universality–relativity debate out of its present stalemate, but also to assisting in the formulation of a more promising framework for comprehending the real and symbolic dimensions of the current flows of human rights values in what we used to call "foreign cultures." In several, formerly "remote" areas of the world, different human rights discourses have now become a vehicle for the articulation of a wide variety of concerns of different people at different levels of society. Human rights increasingly form part of a wider network of perspectives which are shared and exchanged between the North and South, centers and peripheries, in multiple, creative, and sometimes conflict-ridden ways. Human rights have become "universalized" as values subject to interpretation, negotiation, and accommodation. They have become "culture."

I attempt to illustrate this point through the analysis of three empirical cases from the Southern African country of Botswana: the societal position attributed to the Basarwa or San people of the Kalahari desert, a recent event known as the Unity Dow court case, and finally, the presentation of an extract of dialogue between two researchers on the issue of "freedom of expression." The complexity of these examples suggests, in different ways and at different levels of analysis, that a more dynamic approach to culture is needed in order to capture the various ways in which human rights give meaning to, and are attributed with meaning in, the on-going life experiences and dilemmas of men and women. A theoretical shift must be made from the static view of culture to the analysis of culture as practice, a practice embedded in local contexts and in the multiple realities of everyday life. A. Belden Fields and Wolf-Dieter Narr have recently phrased the issue as follows:

> They [human rights] cannot be pulled out of the air or the mind of a thinker.... A theory of human rights must be based upon real human beings rooted in their social contexts. The theoretical postulate of the isolated and antagonistic human being is false in that it requires abstraction from the context that gives life its fullest potential meaning.[14]

The step towards the study of human rights as cultural practice demands a departure from mechanical, prefabricated, and externalist models of human behavior and social change, and the incorporation into human rights theory of the more critical 1980s poststructuralist and postmodernist work in sociology and anthropology. This is a major argument with a number of methodological consequences which I attempt to introduce at different levels of analysis in the sections that follow. Towards the end of the article, I conclude by suggesting that recent advances in the field of development research, especially its renewed focus on human agency and social actor perspectives, offer particularly stimulating methodological perspectives with a powerful potential for rethinking certain trends in contemporary human rights research. First, I consider the nature of the difficulties that the debates on the universality or relativity of human rights have so regrettably engendered.

The Impasse of Human Rights and Culture

In their well-known, and often-cited work on human rights as "A Western Construct with Limited Applicability," Adamantia Pollis and Peter Schwab engage in serious criticism of what they see as a cultural and ideological ethnocentrism in the area of human rights and human dignity. They view the Universal Declaration of Human Rights as a document with underlying democratic and libertarian values, "based on the notion of atomized individuals possessed of certain inalienable rights in nature."[15] Because of the pervasiveness of the notion of the group rather than the individual in many cultures, they conclude that "[t]he Western conception of human rights is not only inapplicable" and "of limited validity," but even "meaningless" to third world countries.[16] In a similar vein, Asmarom Legesse argues that "[d]ifferent societies formulate their conception of human rights in diverse cultural idioms,"[17] and that in the liberal democracies of the Western world "[t]here is a perpetual, and in our view obsessive, concern with the dignity of the individual, his worth, personal autonomy, and property."[18]

Using India as the basis for reflection, Raimundo Panikkar similarly proposes that most of the "assumption and implications [of Western human rights] are simply not given in other cultures."[19] He dismisses the idea of transcultural values, and hence, of universal human rights, "for the simple reason that a value exists as such only in a given cultural context."[20] According to Panikkar, the crucial question with regard to the intercultural intelligibility of human rights is "how, from the *topos* of one culture to understand the constructs of another."[21] This approach is echoed by Paulin Hountondji, who suggests that human rights scholars must increasingly ask questions such as: "[w]hat varies, not only from one culture to another... but also from one class or social group to another."[22]

Addressing the problem of cultural differentiation from a slightly different angle, Dustan M. Wai attempts to reject the Western supremacy in the area of human rights vis-à-vis Africa. He argues that "traditional African societies supported and practiced human rights," and that "traditional African attitudes, beliefs, institutions, and experiences sustained the 'view that certain rights should be upheld against alleged necessities of the state.'" Precolonial Africans not only had the right to select and depose their own leaders, but also had "methods and mechanisms for resolving issues affecting their societies as a whole." Consequently, Wai sees modern aberrations, such as attempts by African leaders to rationalize their authoritarian regimes through various defenses of cultural relativity, as having been "facilitated by colonial legacies and reinforced by the agonies of underdevelopment."[23]

In a critical response to some of the above writers, Jack Donnelly claims that their standpoints are based on outright confusion of human rights and human dignity, and between rights and duties, a position he largely shares with Rhoda Howard.[24] In Donnelly's view, "most non-Western cultural and political traditions lack not only the practice of human rights but the very concept."[25] He illustrates this through a "political culture" analysis of human rights in Islam, traditional Africa, Confucian China, Hindu India, and in the Soviet Union.[26] This permits him to draw the conclusion that "the differences between Western and non-Western approaches to human dignity certainly are large."[27] He sees the incorporation of third world views, such as the valuing of the group or the community over that of the individual, as a "great risk" to the essential character of human rights, which would come "dangerously close to destroying or denying human rights as they have been understood."[28] Donnelly sums up his argument by saying that:

> We must recognize the validity of claims of traditional values and institutions, as well as the rights of modern nations and states to choose their own destiny. At the same time, though, we feel a need to keep these choices restrained within acceptable bounds and reject an anything-goes attitude.[29]

There are many more examples, but the above examples suffice to show that the debate about the universality or relativity of human rights is not only highly antagonistic, but it also takes place at an extremely abstract level. Whether the matter is about rejecting the existence of human rights in India or Africa, or proving these rights' ethnocentric origin in Western thought, the arguments presented obviously provide us with more information about their authors than about the so-called "other cultures" in which human rights are supposed to apply. What is, for example, and more precisely, this entity called "traditional African societies" that Wai explores? The African continent is known to contain more cultural (social, economic, political) differentiation than Europe and North America taken together.[30] Furthermore, who belongs to Pollis and Schwab's category of "Third World countries" to whom (Western) human rights are meaningless? The different women's groups I worked with in Zimbabwe and Botswana during the Autumn of 1992 would certainly not be pleased to hear this. Who is this "we" authorized (by whom?) to "keep choices restrained" and reject a so-called "anything goes attitude"? Isn't this the much-debated Western hegemony discretely slipping in, yet again?

The point I wish to emphasize here is that at this metageneral level of analysis, almost all arguments become plausible, or equally true or false. One glosses over a multitude of cultural particularities such as those in Islam or traditional Africa, in a few pages, just for the sake of creating an argument about the presence or absence of human rights, an argument that can be contradicted the next moment with just as many convincing arguments. One might further ask at what analytical level the above "phenomena" – a religion, a continent, an epoch, a subcontinent, a regime – are at all comparable? Taken alone, understanding caste in India

(I deliberately avoid the term caste system) so far has been a matter of decades of anthropological inquiry based on in-depth fieldwork and subsequent analytical scrutiny, and still "caste," to a large extent, escapes our comprehension in a total sense of the term.[31] When the debate on the universalism or relativism of human rights is so radically removed from the cultural "realities" it alleges to speak about, it hardly creates anything but its own impasse.

A major reason behind this apparent stalemate is that the notion of culture is repeatedly launched, both by universalists and relativists, as if it were an unproblematic, everyday term about which there exists overall, common consent. However, expressions such as "cultures," "other cultures," and "non-Western cultures," do in fact carry with them a specific, underlying conceptualization of culture; namely, as an almost physically concrete, quantitatively measurable entity. Culture is implicitly defined as a homogenous, bounded unit, almost as if it were "a thing." At best then, the debates on the universality or relativity of human rights reveal a continued preoccupation with various outmoded approaches to "culture contact" that developed within North American anthropology in the 1930s, mostly on the basis of the "melting pot" vision or on the idea of "acculturation."[32] Hence, debaters are inclined to conceptualize "culture contacts" as if they were new or at least recent. It is doubtful that this concept could be justified at the time; in any case, another half-century later, such situations have become practically nonexistent. As a result, the universality-relativity debates seem somehow unsatisfying, despite the vigor and passion with which they are launched. It is as if larger, more important questions are lurking under the surface, but they remain unexplored and somewhat blocked, precisely because of the rigid "us" and "them" dichotomy inherent in the "culture contact" perspective.

Intermediate Positions

On several occasions, the anthropologist [*sic*], Alison Dundes Renteln, has attempted to mediate between universalists and relativists by arguing that misunderstandings and misconceptualizations surround the theory of cultural relativism.[33] In her 1988 article, Renteln claims that in the views of the earlier anthropologists such as Franz Boas, Ruth Benedict, and Melville Herskovits, relativism was a question of the extent to which relativists must tolerate intolerance. She suggests that this misunderstanding of the theory as wrongly connected with tolerance was already reflected in the original debate (launched by the United Nations Educational, Scientific and Cultural Organization (UNESCO)) surrounding the Universal Declaration of Human Rights in the 1940s. In Renteln's view, however, the core of the relativist argument ought to be "whether or not it is possible to establish cross-cultural universals,"[34] and she provides the answer herself: "relativism in no way precludes the possibility of cross-cultural universals discovered through empirical research."[35] A detailed reexamination of the concept of relativism, its origins, implications, and formulations, allows Renteln to conclude that "[i]f only [the early relativists] had realized that relativism does not imply tolerance and does not deny the possible existence of cross-cultural universals, anthropologists might have been spared much anguish."[36]

More recently, Abdullahi An-Na'im has attempted to make a step towards the formalization of a "cross-cultural approach" to human rights.[37] According to An-Na'im, the aim of this approach is to enhance the credibility of national and international human rights standards by developing more effective approaches to promoting and implementing those rights.[38] Recognizing that the ultimate theory of this approach is premature at the present stage, An-Na'im comments that "this theme has not yet received sufficient scholarly attention,"[39] and proposes that scholars ought to explore "the possibilities of cultural reinterpretation and reconstruction through internal cultural discourse and cross-cultural dialogue, as a means to enhancing the universal legitimacy of human rights."[40] In An-Na'im's view, however, the major difficulty of this endeavor lies in the "cultural biases of various nations"[41] and in the "competing cultural perspectives [which] tend to undermine each other's priorities."[42] The place thereby accorded to culture unfortunately curbs the initial promises of this cross-cultural initiative.

While one can sympathize with a proposition that strives towards greater mutual comprehension and dialogue in the world, it is nevertheless difficult to see how this approach can ever become "bottom-up," as An-Na'im wishes,[43] when it posits culture as an obstacle or as something outside human beings, their thoughts, and their actions. When culture is thus viewed as an externalized impediment to the struggle towards human rights, rather than as an integral part of the struggle itself, we are prevented from seeing the various contradictions, inconsistencies, and disagreements as culture – and perhaps the culture of human rights itself. The result is that this cross-cultural approach can hardly become more than an idealistic, programmatic suggestion, characterized, more than anything else, by self-evidence: "[t]hose of one cultural tradition who wish to induce a change in attitudes within another culture must be open to a corresponding induce-ment in relation to their own attitudes and must also be respectful of the integrity of the other culture."[44] If there is a solution in any sense of the term, we probably would not have to confront a debate about the cultural relativity of human rights at all.

In one of their "dialogues" with the relativists, Donnelly and Howard rightly suggest that more attention must be paid to the underlying conceptualization of culture in the human rights debates.[45] They suggest that "cultural relativism, as applied to human rights, fails to grasp the nature of culture,"[46] and correctly criticize the prevailing assumption that "culture is a unitary and unique whole."[47] Yet, they also conclude by falling victim to their own criticism when they depict cultural processes as a matter of people choosing "which aspects of a 'new' culture they wish to adopt and which aspects of the 'old' they wish to retain."[48] They also comment that social transformation as a "structure does affect culture" with an "amalgamation of many different ethnic groups into one nation-state."[49] Apart from the strong evolutionary bias of such statements (such as those made by modernists who believe in progress and development as a one-way street), the underlying perception of culture is too simplistic and too mechanical.

In my view, one does not escape the questions pertaining to human rights and culture by distinguishing between "radical," "strong," or "weak" relativism,[50] by renaming radical relativism "cultural absolutism,"[51] or by suggesting mediating terms like "enlightened ethnocentricity."[52] Nor is it simply a matter of "distinguishing acceptable cultural orientations from unacceptable ones,"[53] or developing models of "[t]ypes of Conflicts over Culturally Relative Practices."[54] Both technically and with regard to content, these propositions merely send us back to UNESCO's questionnaire in 1947, to Herskovits' and Steward's debate about "tolerance." Alternatively, they force us to engage in fallacious reductionism. More than anything else, these sugges-tions tend to represent rather ethnocentric Western models of social behavior based upon the assumption of the individualistic "utilitarian man," consequently ignoring the specificities of culture and context.

In sum, defining concepts this way offers no real solution to the methodological and theoretical questions pertaining to human rights and culture; at best, it reproduces them at a different, perhaps more sophisticated, level. Because there now seems to be wide agreement among various scholars, politicians, and practitioners that in the years to come some of the most crucial intellectual, moral, and ideological battles about human rights issues are likely to turn on their cross-cultural intelligibility and justifiability,[55] a radically new and far more dynamic approach to culture is needed.

Beyond the Universality–Relativity Debate?

During the past ten years or so, volumes carrying titles like "Interpretive Social Science," "The Invention of Culture," "Writing Culture," "Creating Culture," and "The Predicament of Culture," have signalled a repositioning of anthropology with regard to its object of study.[56] In the process, anthropology's conventional use of analytical concepts and theoretical tools has been critically reviewed under exotic banners like "de-construction," "reflexivity," and "experimentalism," most of which tend to converge in the broader matrix of "post-modernism." This has involved a rather self-conscious reexamination of the anthropological enterprise, from the participant-observation ideal to the natural, even "style" of (writing) the anthropological account. Many underlying assumptions, primarily the homogeneity, holism, and integrity evident in classical anthropological analysis, have been scrutinized on the basis of the recognition of an overall crisis – the erosion of classical norms – in the social sciences. As the above titles indicate, anthropologists have been forced to reevaluate such central analytical concepts in anthropology as that of culture, and by extension, the idea of "cultural difference."

The resurgence of interest in the culture concept stems directly from a particular disillusionment with social science and its aspiration for a general and material account of social life. This disillusionment fundamentally concerns the "strong commitment in Western culture to a particular notion of 'science' " – a notion that is an error for the social sciences in that it emphasizes "timeless, context-free axiomatized laws, controlled manipulation of clearly defined variables, and mathematical measurement in a quest for objective knowledge about the world."[57] The truth of objectivism – that it is absolute, universal, and timeless – increasingly has lost its monopoly status. "It now competes, on more nearly equal terms, with the truths of case studies that are embedded in local contexts, shaped by local interests, and colored by local perceptions. The agenda for social analysis has shifted to include not only eternal verities and lawlike generalizations but also political processes, social changes, and human differences. Such terms as objectivity, neutrality, and impartiality refer to subject positions once endowed with great institutional authority, but they are arguably neither more nor less valid than those of more engaged, yet equally perceptive, knowledgeable social actors."[58]

Although the classic vision of unique cultural patterns has proven merit, its limitations are seen today as serious, indeed. Most importantly, this vision emphasizes shared patterns at the expense of processes of change and internal inconsistencies, conflicts, and contradictions. In contrast with the "classic view, which posits culture as a self-contained whole made up of coherent patterns," culture, therefore, is increasingly conceived of as "a more porous array of intersections where distinct processes crisscross from within and beyond its borders."[59] One of the most well-founded rejections of the usage of culture in anthropological analysis as a sort of "sum total" of observable patterns and ideological bases was made some years ago by Frederik Barth, who convincingly demonstrated that people's realities are culturally constructed.[60] In a central passage Barth wrote that "[p]eople participate in multiple, more or less discrepant, universes of discourse; they construct different, partial and simultaneous worlds in which they move; their cultural construction of reality springs not from one source and is not of one piece."[61] A major implication of these perspectives is that ethnography is no longer defined as the interpretation of distinct, "whole" ways of life, but rather as a series of specific dialogues, impositions, and inventions. Cultural difference is no longer viewed as a stable, exotic otherness; self-other relations are increasingly considered to be matters of power and rhetoric rather than essence.[62] Modern anthropology thus attempts to overcome the rigid opposition of subjectivity and objectivity by arguing that interpretation begins from the postulate that the web of meaning constitutes human existence to such an extent that it cannot ever be reduced to constitutively prior speech, acts, didactic relations, or any predefined elements. "Culture, the shared meanings, practices, and symbols that constitute the human world, does not present itself neutrally or with one voice. It is always multivocal and overdetermined, and both the observer and the observed are always enmeshed in it.... There is no privileged position, no absolute perspective, no final recounting."[63]

Case 1: Basarwa complexities

Consider how the above perspectives relate in the case of the "Basarwa" – the "San," "Kung," or "Bushmen," as they have been called by anthropologists and others (along with a variety of different, local group names), of the Southern African Kalahari desert: they are considered to be some of the possibly best known, most intensely studied, if not over-researched, people of the world today. While knowledge of the Basarwa goes back several centuries in Southern Africa, it was not until the 19th century that observations of their ways of life began to be recorded in any depth in Botswana. For well over a century, the Basarwa have thus drawn considerable anthropological, administrative, and popular attention. They appear in the writings of explorers, hunters, and missionaries; in the last quarter of the 19th century they were the object of linguistic and ethnographic research. The first reference to Basarwa in official records came soon after the founding of Bechuanaland Protectorate in 1885; the colonial office initiated an investigation into the treatment of the Basarwa, who were rumored to be serving as the "slaves" of other groups.[64]

An overview of the vast literature on the Basarwa suggests that the understanding of this people has taken place predominantly as a series of encounters with varying ideological and political contexts. In the early 1900s Basarwa were used primarily as "anthropological specimens"; later, this interest contributed to the push for serious examinations of the status and treatment of this population. According to Isaac Schapera, who published his classic work, "The Khoisan Peoples of South Africa: Bushmen and Hottentots" in 1930, the Basarwa were dying out or at least merging with their "Bantu" neighbors. During the 1950s and 1960s, this attention changed into a wide variety of multidisciplinary research projects among the Basarwa, particularly long-term intensive anthropological research led by the famous Marshall family, who defined most of the research topics to be taken up by a host of anthropologists and other researchers in the following decades. Two decades later, the emphasis of the government's Remote Area Development Programme (RADP) was on "community development," and various forms of government assistance to the Basarwa were being provided under the label of "Villagisation," envisaged "to enable them to settle in one place."[65] Finally, in the late 1980s and early 1990s, the focus on Basarwa made yet a new turn; it increasingly conceptualized in human rights terms. As a preparation for the then forthcoming "UN International Year of Indigenous People" in 1993, attention was explicitly drawn to the government's responsibilities under international human rights conventions considered relevant to this minority population.[66]

Despite this massive amount of "knowledge" on the Basarwa, accumulated through various forms of contact between them and anthropologists, development consultants, government officials, and now also human rights experts, the Basarwa themselves have remained remarkably remote. They are still predominantly considered to belong to the "hunter-gatherer populations in Africa [who] have long endured harsh treatment from more powerful adjoining societies."[67] Additionally, they have been described as people who "preceded the settlement of black people and white people," and lived "undisturbed, together with the wildlife" until "[t]he land which they had come to know as 'theirs' was taken away from them" – an act that is viewed as fundamental in contributing to their present "alienation."[68] In a recent article, Akhil Gupta and James Ferguson correctly point out that there has been surprisingly little criticism of the eroticization implicit in such assessments.[69] They emphasize M. L. Pratt's point about the "blazing contradiction" between the portrait of primordial beings untouched by historical events and the genocidal advance of the White "Bushman conquest."[70] Yet, even in Pratt's account, the Basarwa are basically presented "as a preexisting ontological entity – 'survivors,' not products (still less producers), of history. 'They' are victims, having suffered the deadly process of 'contact' with 'us.'"[71]

What is obviously ignored in much of the work on the San-speaking people is that they "always" have been in continuous interaction with other groups; hence, the picture of the isolated "Bushman tribe" of the desert is in serious need of revision. According to the anthropologist Edwin N. Wilmsen, the Zhu (!Kung), for instance, have never been a classless society, and if they give such an impression, "it is because they are incorporated as an underclass in a wider social formation that includes Batswana, Ovaherero, and others." Furthermore, Wilmsen shows how the Bushman/San label has been produced through the "retribalization" of the colonial period, and how the "cultural conservation uniformly attributed to these people by almost all anthropologists who have worked with them until recently, is a consequence – not a cause – of the way in which they have been integrated into the modern capitalist economies of Botswana and Namibia." The conclusion is that "[t]he appearance of isolation and its reality of dispossessed poverty are recent products of a process that unfolded over two centuries and culminated in the last moments of the colonial era."[72]

Barsarwa "culture," in the sense of a unitary, homogenous, and bounded entity, thus, simply does not exist. The intent here is not to belittle or to deny that the San-speaking people occupy various positions of inequality and that such inequality might be conceived of in human rights terms. It is indeed possible to meet individuals in Botswana who do not hesitate to define the Basarwa issue as the most total accumulation of human rights abuses. What the above perspective does suggest, however, is that the Barsarwa are also, and perhaps primarily, "victims" of the shifting categorization – emanating from early anthropological, developmental, and now also human rights discourses – that have continuously (re)invented them as the "Bushmen others." The plight of the Basarwa, as real and as serious as it is, must be examined in light of these long-term constructions, a major consequence of which has been the freezing of a Bushman identity, although often in a romantically heroizing way.

One would be considerably benefitted in the attempt to "know" the Basarwa by taking these constructions seriously, by critically questioning the "otherness" of the other, and by examining the production of "cultural difference" within historical processes that are evidently characterized more by contact and interconnection than by isolation and demarcation. However, such an exercise demands more than a departure from the "world-view of the Basarwa,"[73] or other similarly inspired versions of the increasingly fashionable willingness to "listen to the people" in order to arrive at appropriate alternatives "from below." Gupta and Ferguson convincingly suggest that

> what is needed is a willingness to interrogate, politically and historically, the apparent "given" of a world in the first place divided into "ourselves" and "others." A first step on this road is to move beyond naturalized conceptions of spatialized "cultures" and to explore instead a production of difference within common, shared, and connected spaces – "the San," for instance, not as "a people," "native" to the desert, but as a historically constituted and de-propertied category systematically relegated to the desert.[74]

Case 2: Multivocality

The second example concerns the highly-published Unity Dow court case,[75] which unfolded in Botswana in the early 1990s, and became immediately significant because it was the first time in the history of the country that a woman challenged the government in court. The case, correctly known as *Dow v. State of Botswana*, has its origins in changes to the Citizenship Act that were enacted in 1984 when the government amended the Act to restrict the categories of persons who could become citizens through birth or descent. Section four said that children born to Batswana women married to foreigners no longer had the right of Botswana citizenship by virtue of their birth there. Section five dealt with citizenship by descent, and it prevented Batswana women married to foreign men from passing on Botswana citizenship to their children. Only unwed Batswana women who gave birth to children of foreigners, and all Batswana men, even those with foreign wives, were accorded that right.

Unity Dow is a prominent Gaborone lawyer, a leading member of the feminist organization Emang Basadi ("Stand Up Women"), and a participant in the Women and Law in Southern Africa Research Project, who, prior to 1984, had married a US citizen, Peter Nathan Dow. They have three children, two of whom were born after 1984, and therefore are affected by the changes to the Citizenship Act. Under the amended Act, the two children are not citizens of Botswana, even though they were born in Botswana and have lived there all their lives, and even though their mother is a citizen of Botswana. In November of 1990, Unity Dow decided to challenge sections four and five of the Citizenship Act in court. She argued that her children were denied Botswana citizenship because her husband was a noncitizen. She also contended that if it were a man who married a woman from outside Botswana, his children would have been granted citizenship without any problem; hence, sections four and five of the Act stripped away women's rights guaranteed in 1966 by Botswana's Constitution.

From the beginning, the case was viewed as a test, intended to set a precedent for future legal action on behalf of women. As Unity Dow herself explained to me in October 1992:

> [w]hat really made me go ahead with the case was that I believed that the law must be wrong. That the Citizenship Act had to be wrong and that surely the Constitution must say that there is equality between the sexes in this country. I seriously felt that I must do this case and I always believed that I was right. There must be something wrong with a law that says that my children, having been born here where I work and pay tax, cannot be permitted citizenship. For me there was something fundamentally wrong.[76]

In June 1991, Judge Horowitz delivered his twenty-four page verdict. Writing that in matters of human rights he was compelled to take a generous interpretation of the law, the Judge found for Unity Dow and declared sections four and five of the Citizenship Act "null and void." He accepted that Unity Dow had been discriminated against on the basis of her sex and had thereby been denied fundamental rights to liberty, protection from being subjected to degrading treatment, and protection from restrictions on her freedom of movement – all arguments made by Dow's lawyer. He rejected the argument of the state defense that gender discrimination is allowed, writing that "the time when women were treated as chattels or were there to obey the whims and wishes of males is long past."[77] As to the state's contention that Unity Dow and the children should just follow Mr. Dow if he decided to leave the country, the judge dismissed this as an irrelevant view, which "would have appealed to the patriarchs of Biblical times."[78]

The reaction to the verdict was swift and largely divided along gender lines. Supporters of Unity Dow hailed it as a breakthrough for women. According to the President of Emang Basadi, Ntomi Setwaelo, it demonstrated that "there was truth and justification in what we have been complaining about as women." Other prominent women echoed these sentiments, adding that they hoped that the government would now move swiftly to change all discriminatory laws. Among the very few male public figures who lauded the judgement was a leading opposition politician, Paul Rantao, the Mayor of Gaborone, who said that all laws with an inkling of sexism and feudalism should be outlawed, as "such laws are stupid and unnecessary."

Government ministers, however, who seemed to speak for the vast majority of men on this issue, vehemently attacked the decision as an unacceptable affront to Tswana culture. What the government feared was the same thing that the feminists welcomed – a major overhaul of the laws of Botswana. According to the Attorney General, Moleleji Mokama, the ruling had thrown the country into "a big constitutional crisis the like of which we have never seen before in Botswana." He said that now, "even chiefs are not safe in their positions because [they] can be challenged by their oldest sisters if they are not first born."

Two weeks after the judgment, the government published its decision to contest it, announcing that it would launch an appeal before a full five-member panel of the Court of Appeals, and that in the meantime, the relevant sections of the Citizenship Act would continue in force. The government further indicated that, should the appeal fail, it would probably move to amend the Constitution to allow gender discrimination. As a statement from the Attorney General said, it might become necessary to "ensure that the constitution reflects the popular norms of

Botswana." In December 1991, however, the appeal was heard by the full bench of the Court of Appeals, which in July 1992 upheld Justice Horowitz's judgment in the Dow case.[79] The local newspaper, *Mmegi*, subsequently triumphantly announced that

> [t]he Constitution of Botswana is against all forms of discrimination. It accords equal human rights to all Batswana irrespective of their sex, creed and religion. By ruling in favour of Unity Dow the Appeals Court has saved our Constitution from further abuse. Hundreds, even thousands, of innocent kids have been denied citizenship in this country because of an Act which is ultra vires the Constitution.[80]

By early 1993, the government of Botswana had not taken any steps to amend the Constitution. According to a widely distributed letter from International Women's Rights Action Watch, the Ministry of Labour and Home Affairs had recently advised the government to hold a national referendum with a view to amending the Constitution to permit sex discrimination. According to the news account, "most government leaders believe the women of Botswana want to be subservient." The Ministry promoting the referendum expressed the rationale for holding it in easily interpretable language: "if Arab countries can hold on to their traditions, there is no reason why Botswana should not."[81]

Nevertheless, the government shortly before the Fourth World Conference on Women in Beijing, where the President of Botswana was heading up the delegation, changed the Citizenship Act to conform to the Court of Appeals decision. Unity Dow's children are now citizens of Botswana.

The Unity Dow court case, referred to in 1992 by a Gaborone-based lawyer as the most important event in Botswana since independence, thus touches directly upon the "cultural values" and "rights" antagonism in international human rights debates. It has structural equivalents in many parts of Sub-Saharan Africa, where numerous women's movements, organizations, and networks presently place women's human rights high on the agenda, as forcefully evidenced during the 1993 World Human Rights Conference in Vienna. Unity Dow's attack on the government of Botswana also clearly and explicitly shows how "concepts such as cultural relativity…are happily adopted by those who control the state."[82] However, to conceive of this rich scenario solely in terms of an antagonism between the universality and cultural relativity of human rights would be to simplify what is going on in the Unity Dow court case. Much more is happening here than the legal category of constitutional sex discrimination or the "accountability" versus "empowerment" model of human rights struggles is capable of revealing.

First, the case exemplifies what has already been signalled with regard to the San Bushmen, but here at a different level of analysis: there is no Botswana culture in the sense of a unitary whole, a bounded entity, to which human rights may be said to apply. This culture is itself being vehemently contested, negotiated, and debated. This suggests that the numerous disagreements and conflicts within this debate are not simply unpleasant, external disturbances to an otherwise stable and harmonious "Botswana culture," but rather, constitutive of it. Disagreement and conflict are culture, and in this particular case, the culture of human rights.

Furthermore, in the process of negotiating what (women's) human rights in Botswana are, or ought to be, power is far from absent. Various knowledge, or more broadly, discursive forms are manipulated by various actors in specific contexts in the pursuit of certain ends and stereotypic positions abound. Batswana feminists, assisted by their Western sisters, generalize about "patriarchal" Botswana, just like government representatives do about the assumed "subservience" of Batswana women. Had rural women joined the debate, other interpretations perhaps would have been revealed. This, at least, was what happened in neighboring Zimbabwe when lawyers from an urban-based human rights organization went out to the villages announcing that according to the Age of Majority Act (1984), women were now granted majority status when they turned eighteen and were endowed with the right, among others, to marry without parental consent.[83] Many local people, women visibly among them, were so angry that they burned the pamphlets intended to "liberate" them once and for all from male domination and oppression.[84]

In any case, human rights as culture in action in and around the Unity Dow court case is obviously multivocal and multidimensional. It is constituted by many voices from within and outside Botswana itself. This clashes conspicuously with old perceptions of the autonomy and integrity of territorially based cultures. It simultaneously suggests that the traditional relativist view of human rights as particularly "Western" can no longer be sustained; Unity Dow and her feminist supporters certainly consider human rights to be theirs as well. Human rights clearly have become part of a much wider, globalized, cultural network of perspectives. This does not mean, however, that they simply constitute an influx of alien meaning or cultural form which enters into a vacuum or inscribes itself on "a cultural tabula rasa."[85] They enter various kinds of interactions with already existing meanings and meaningful forms; in this case, particular conceptualizations of Batswana men and women, for instance. The root metaphor of "creole culture," fashionable in contemporary anthropology, captures the fact that cultural processes, such as the Unity Dow case, are not simply a matter of constant "pressure" from the center toward the periphery, but of a much more creative interplay. The periphery indeed "talks back":

> This creolist cluster of understandings . . . stands opposed to the view of cultures as well-bounded wholes, as well as to assumptions of a replication of uniformity within them. It suggests that the the [sic] flow of culture between countries and continents may result in another diversity of culture, based more on interconnections than on autonomy. It also allows the sense of a complex culture as a network of perspectives, or as an ongoing debate. People can come into it from the diaspora, as consultants and advisors, or they can come into it from the multiform local cultures, from the bush. The outcome is not predicted.[86]

Case 3: Intersubjectivity

Indeed, the unpredictability and openendedness of cultural processes can no longer be ignored. Consider this last example of a dialogue between an "outsider" and "insider" researcher on the issue of freedom of expression in contemporary Botswana. The dialogue should be viewed against a descriptive term that constantly reappears in the writings of scholars of contemporary Botswana: "unique."[87] A general consensus seems to exist that the history, the politics, and the socio-economic constellations of that land-locked, sparsely populated, country, two-thirds of which is covered by the Kalahari desert, occupies a remarkably unique position in the African context.[88] The uniqueness is first and foremost attributed to the fact that, placed in a broader African, third world, or even global context, Botswana's human rights record has been surprisingly good.[89] Botswana is one of the few states in Africa that has maintained a multiparty electoral system since independence.[90] Electoral politics have been free, open, and held on a regular basis in 1965, 1974, 1979, 1984, and 1989.[91] In addition to genuinely competitive elections, Botswana has a parliamentary system with protection for individual rights and an independent judiciary.[92] The country's Constitution allows for freedom of association, freedom of the press, and the rule of law.[93] To date, Botswana still boasts of a record of no political prisoners.[94]

This is matched by the dramatic economic success, or "revolution," that Botswana has undergone in the past two decades, or more. This success has largely been attributable to three factors – the mining boom, foreign assistance, and beef exports. Contrary to what is happening in the majority of African economies which are either under structural adjustments of the International Monetary Fund or burdened by a deep debt crisis, Botswana presently enjoys a stable economy and a healthy balance of payments. The country has one of the "fastest growing economies in Africa" with one of the "highest growth rates in the world."[95]

While the conglomeration of these features have rightly made Botswana earn such titles as "Africa's success story" and "shining star of democracy," and have projected her as a political and economic model for many developing countries, the stability and durability of the country's liberal democracy is today being increasingly questioned by observers and scholars of different disciplinary backgrounds. The following dialogue, part of an interview with Dr. Bojosi Otlhogile at the Faculty of Law in October 1992, illustrates this essential point. The dialogue begins as Dr. Otlhogile first responds to a question of why and how Botswana is always referred to in terms of its democratic uniqueness:

OTLHOGILE: People look at Botswana in a context of a continent which has violated all democratic norms, a continent which does not respect the basics of democracy, where one-party systems are the order of the day. The comparison is between us and all these other countries, *that* made us an exception.

A.B.P.:   Some people say that this perception has allowed for some sort of ignorance of the different weaknesses inherent in the democratic system here?

OTLHOGILE: Oh, yes. If you look at the reports from Danida [the Danish International Development Agency] or from Sweden, they never talk about the right of assembly in this country. There were cases where the government did not allow the people to organise, or where they organised and there was state intervention. Until very recently – they are trying to amend the law at present – the Minister of Home Affairs could dissolve a committee and appoint his own people at any time, or even insist on having his representatives in the meetings of Trade Unions. The ILO knows about it, but the Human Rights Bulletins from the Scandinavian countries never mention it. Not even the Americans, let alone Amnesty, look into, for example, the issue of death penalty in Botswana; it simply does not appear. Or even take, for instance, the question of freedom of expression. Look at all the reports from Article 19; they never include Botswana.

A.B.P.:   But that is because your press has been free since . . . is it 1982, or . . .?

OTLHOGILE: (interrupts) Well, is it free? I don't know, but that is a different matter. The impression here is that it is not. I mean, you must have heard that there is a case against a newspaper in this country at present?

A.B.P.: Yes, against the Mmegi, isn't it?

OTLHOGILE: Yes, and it is not the first case of its kind. They have been going on for many years. And there are even cases where journalists were thrown out of the country, deported. Some have been arrested and persecuted. But we never heard anything from Article 19. We never heard anything from human rights organizations throughout the world. As I say, this is because they see us as an exception to the general picture within the African continent.

A.B.P.: Isn't this because one can speak of isolated incidents in Botswana, and not a real trend?

OTLHOGILE: I think a real trend is developing. You are free to publish as long as it does not affect the government. If it does affect the government, it will intervene. This is a trend, one cannot call it an incident. . . .

The above conversation not only reveals that there is disagreement about Botswana's human rights performance, but that the culture of human rights (its meanings, practices, and symbols) does not present itself neutrally or with one voice. This is probably the most "universal" characteristic of human rights. The conversation certainly also invites the question of why the views of Mr. Otlhogile are not reflected in the more official versions of Botswana's human rights record. Mr. Otlhogile is a well-established university researcher and a significant social actor; why is he not heard?

Perhaps an even more important fact revealed by the dialogue is that the "reality" of human rights is culturally constructed and that both the observer and the observed are enmeshed in this process. This suggests that one cannot determine, in any absolute sense of the term, whether there is freedom of expression in Botswana or not. There simply is no objective position from which human rights can be truly "measured." As Paul Rabinow and William Sullivan say, there is no privileged position, no absolute perspective, and no final recounting.[96] This ought to fundamentally challenge the current practice of establishing "human rights records" of particular states (by organizations such as Human Rights Watch, Amnesty International, and the International Commission of Jurists) because such evaluations are always inherently partial, committed, and incomplete. If, as suggested here, impersonal standards of observation and objective distance are problematic, the meaning of scientific objectivity consequently poses itself in a particularly poignant way. One might even question the possibility for human rights of having "objects" in a classical scientific sense. In any case, the above dialogue points to the fact that we can no longer presuppose a standpoint outside – looking at, objectifying, or "reading" – a given (human rights) reality. Reality is heard, invented in dialogue, or transcribed as James Clifford describes it, and it resists any final summation.[97]

In legal terminology the concept of "rights" is often referred to as an "evolving paradigm."[98] The Unity Dow court case and the above dialogue suggest that they are certainly also cultural practice. Human rights are continuously in the process of reconstituting and reformulating themselves; they are always "at work." In the (post)modern, and post-Berlin Wall world, the important issue is not any longer whether human rights are universal or relative, applicable or inapplicable, transferable or nontransferable. Human rights now form part of the multiple cultural flows between centers and peripheries in a world where "cultures have lost their moorings in particular places," and "the rapidly expanding and quickening mobility of people combines with the refusal of cultural products and practices, to 'stay put.'"[99] In this culture-play of diaspora, familiar lines between "here" and "there," center and periphery, colony and metropole have become blurred; hence, the question of the relevance or irrelevance of human rights has become strictly irrelevant.

Today, human rights are "universal" as values, as ideological vehicles, or, more precisely, as signifiers in action. This does not mean that "the crucial normative issue finally has been determined,"[100] as Fields and Narr put it with regard to the assumption that the world is progressing in a linear direction toward the universal respect for human rights. Paradoxically, the celebration of universality is always inversely proportionate to the extent of human rights abuses. What it does mean, however, is that we must attempt to renew and refocus our analytical perspectives in order to enlarge the understanding of the contemporary, globalized conditions of cultural complexity, in which human rights enter as both a defining, and a defined set of values. One way to begin is to identify more yielding ways of exploring how, when, and why human rights become attributed with meaning in various contexts, including how they are put to work in the everyday life situations of men and women. In short, we need to come to grips with the question of human rights as "cultural practice."

From Abstract Categories to Social Actors

This article has proposed that the understanding of human rights and culture begins with a reconceptualization of the notion of culture itself. In order to avoid that new debates in human rights resemble old anthropology in its "complicity with imperialism, a commitment to objectivism, and a belief in monumentalism,"[101] a paradigmatic shift is therefore needed: the critical 1980s poststructuralist and postmodernist work in sociology and anthropology must now begin to make substantial inroads into the analysis of human rights. The time has come to draw together these new theoretical insights and to eschew those models tainted by determinist, linear, and externalist views of human behavior and social change. Prefabricated solutions and quick recipes like the universalists' "[t]reat people like human beings – see attached list – and you will get truly *human* beings,"[102] or the relativists' insistence on the cultural difference in its essentialist sense, simply do not generate the knowledge that we need in order to make more valid statements about the dynamics of human rights and culture in the (post)modern world.

One way forward is to seek inspiration in the theoretical and methodological advances made over the past years within the field known as "development research." Of particular relevance to human rights is the growing interest in the notion of human agency, and in the search for a more thorough-going actor-oriented approach, as recently outlined by Norman Long and others in an excellent, thought-provoking volume.[103] The immediate importance of these perspectives for human rights lies in their obvious connection to the question of practice. Human rights researchers often make statements about the relationship between the theory and practice of human rights, but rarely, if ever, on the basis of more thorough definitions of what the practice(s) might actually, and more concretely, consist of. This problem has recently been formulated as follows:

If human rights is really a set of social practices ... what precisely are those practices? How are they legitimized as opposed to the delegitimized practices they displace? How do these practices relate to other social practices and political forms? Without adequate conceptualization, we can never be sure what human rights are and if they are indeed being respected.[104]

In order for the current impasse of the universality-relativity debate to become "a passage," the introduction of a more open-ended (ethnographic) approach is therefore needed: one that attempts to unravel the complexities of meaning and social action through the development of a conceptual framework that accords priority to the understanding of human rights in everyday life situations. This is not, I wish to emphasize, an argument against international human rights conventions and formulae; these are important as a general goal, but at the same time, they are only intelligible in situated contexts. That is, they are grounded in the meanings accorded them through the ongoing life experiences and dilemmas of men and women, and therefore do not – and cannot – in any straightforward, linear, or mechanical manner, form the basis of human rights action.

In Norman Long's definition, the essence of an actor-oriented approach is that its concepts are grounded in everyday life experiences and understandings of men and women, be they – as in the present essay – Basarwa, feminists, government representatives, politicians, or researchers.[105] More precisely, Long and his colleagues seek to develop

theoretically grounded methods of social research that allow for the elucidation of actors' interpretations and strategies, and of how these interlock through processes of negotiation and accommodation. Such an approach places actors at the centre of the stage and rejects linear, determinist and simple empiricist thinking and practice.... [A]n actor-oriented perspective entails recognizing the "multiple realities" and diverse social practices of various actors, and requires working out methodologically how to come to grips with these different and often incompatible social worlds.[106]

In general terms, the notion of agency attributes to the individual actor the capacity to process social experience and to devise ways of coping with life, even under the most extreme forms of coercion. Within the limits of information, uncertainty, and other constraints (for example, physical, normative, or politicoeconomic), social actors are knowledgeable and capable. They attempt to solve problems, learn how to intervene in the flow of social events around them, and continuously monitor their own actions, observing how others react to their behavior and taking note of the various contingent circumstances: "[A]ll forms of dependence offer some resources whereby those who are subordinate can influence the activities of their superiors."[107] In these ways they actively engage in the construction of their own social worlds, although, as Long reminds us (with Marx), the circumstances they encounter are not simply of their own choosing.[108]

In his fundamental concern to reconcile structure and actor perspectives analytically, Long argues that "development and social change are all too often seen as emanating primarily from centers of power in the form of intervention by state or international interests, and following some broadly determined developmental path, signposted by 'stages of development' or by the succession of 'dominant modes of production.'"[109] The same applies, I contend, to the more or less hidden, progressionist assumptions of many human rights texts. However, such models are tainted by determinist, linear, and externalist views of social change. Although it might be true that certain important structural changes result from the impact of outside forces (due to encroachment by the state, for instance), it is theoretically unsatisfactory to base one's analysis on the concept of external determination. As the Unity Dow court case so brilliantly illustrates, "[a]ll forms of external determination necessarily enter the existing life-worlds of the individuals and social groups affected, and in this way are mediated and transformed by these same actors and structures."[110]

This is precisely why a more dynamic approach to the understanding of human rights is needed which stresses the *interplay* and *mutual determination* of "internal" and "external" factors and relationships, and recognizes the central role played by human action and consciousness. Much human rights theory still seems to cling to a rather mechanical model of the relationship between international human rights standards, their implementation, and outcomes. However, this separation is a "gross oversimplification of a much more complicated set of processes" which involve the actual reinterpretation or transformation of human rights during the very "implementation process," such that "there is no straight line from policy to out-comes."[111] Just like the notion of development, the idea of (a) human rights practice needs "deconstructing," to use a postmodern term, so that it is "seen for what it is – an ongoing, socially constructed and negotiated process – not simply the execution of an already specified 'plan of action' with expected 'outcomes.'"[112]

If, by contrast, we accept Long's view that "we are dealing with 'multiple realities,' potentially conflicting social and normative interests, and diverse and discontinuous configurations of knowledge," then we can begin to "look closely at the issue of *whose* interpretations or models ... prevail over those of other actors and under what conditions" this takes place.[113] In the case of the Basarwa, for instance, this would imply a thorough analysis of why, and especially how, the San-speaking people have been silenced to the extent which is apparently the case, as compared to the audibility of anthropologists, development officials, human rights experts, and many other such "authoritative voices." The treatment of this question would obviously include critical scrutiny of the processes by which their "remoteness" has been constructed culturally during decades of interaction with the surrounding world.

Finally, the significance of adopting an actor perspective lies in viewing the researcher as an active agent influencing specific events and the construction of the final human rights text. Long continually stresses the central importance of treating the researcher herself as an active social agent who struggles to understand social processes by entering the life-worlds of local actors, who, in turn, actively shape the researcher's own fieldwork strategies, thus molding the contours and outcomes of the research process itself. In this sense, the dialogue with Mr. Otlhogile forces us to repudiate the existence of an objective (human rights) "reality" beyond specific people's forms of sociability, mutual understandings, and conceptual horizons. In Long's view, this perspective brings out certain parallels between power and knowledge processes: "[l]ike power, knowledge is not simply something that is possessed or accumulated. Nor can it be measured precisely in terms of some notion of quantity or quality. It emerges out of processes of social interaction and is essentially a joint product of the encounter and fusion of horizons."[114]

Introducing this methodology to human rights, thus, clearly involves much more than the simple task of "translating" the rights into different cultural idioms, as several writers on the intercultural intelligibility of human rights seem to suggest.[115] In explaining or translating human rights action, there is always the danger that we might "displace the agency or intentions of those we study by our own 'folk' notions or theoretical concepts."[116] This is indeed the case with the earlier-mentioned "tolerance" approach to human rights, the different versions of which converge in an ethnocentric view of social behavior based upon the individualism of "utilitarian man," leaving very little space for cultural and contextual differentiation. If the question of "culture" and "cultural difference" is to be addressed in a less abstract and demystifying manner, we must attempt to see, "human worlds as constructed through historical and political processes, and not as brute timeless facts of nature."[117] This seems to be all the more important in human rights research where the temptation to confuse our local culture with universal human nature has proven to be such a marvelous temptation.

In the aftermath of the 1993 World Human Rights Conference in Vienna, there seems to be a growing recognition among human rights scholars that "the human rights literature of the past fifteen years has been seriously lacking in detailed empirical analysis of even the most discussed issues," and that "[o]ne source of these empirical shortcomings is the rather shallow penetration of human rights into established social science disciplines."[118] This article has attempted to develop a set of propositions as to where and how such penetration might take off. The perspectives suggested here do not, one should hasten to say, offer a recipe for getting "human rights right," to paraphrase Long. On the contrary, they expose the unpredictable, fragmentary, and partial nature of human rights, and emphasize the important fact that human rights discourse and action essentially involve a struggle over images of human rights and "the good society." Yet, if human rights researchers wish to address large issues, such as the relationship between the theory and practice of human rights, they must also be willing to do a "big job." This job, I suggest, begins with examining the various cultural constructions of human rights in the everyday life of living and breathing social actors.

NOTES

1   Moustapha Safouan, *La Parole ou la Mort: Comment une Société Humaine est-elle Possible?* 65 (1993).
2   *Statement on Human Rights*, 49 Am. Anthropologist 539, 542 (1947). This statement was submitted to one of the commissions of the United Nations, which, as is well-known, in 1947 carried out a theoretical inquiry into the foundations of an international declaration of human rights, drawing on a large number of individual philosophers, social scientists, jurists, and writers from UNESCO member states. For details, see Tore Lindholm, Prospects for Research on the Cultural Legitimacy of Human Rights: The Cases of Liberalism and Marxism, in *Human Rights in Cross-Cultural Perspectives: A Quest for Consensus* 387 (Abdullahl Ahmed An-Na'im ed., 1992) [hereinafter *Human Rights in Cross-Cultural Perspectives*].
3   Statement on Human Rights, *supra* note 2, at 543.
4   Ibid.
5   Julian H. Steward, Comments on the Statement on Human Rights, 50 *Am. Anthropologist* 351 (1948).
6   *History and Ethnicity* 1, 10 (Elizabeth Tonkin et al. eds., 1989).
7   Ellen Messer, Anthropology and Human Rights, 22 *Ann. Rev. Anthropology* 221, 224–5 (1993).
8   Ibid. at 224.
9   Jack Donnelly, Human Rights and Human Dignity: An Analytical Critique of Non-Western Conceptions of Human Rights, 76 *Am. Pol. Sci. Rev.* 303, 306 (1982).

10 Ann Elizabeth Mayer, Book Review, 14 *Hum. Rts. Q.* 527 (1992).

11 See, e.g., Arjun Appadurai, Theory in Anthropology: Center and Periphery, 28 *Comp. Stud. Soc'y & Hist.* 356 (1986); Fredrik Barth, The Analysis of Culture in Complex Societies, 54 *Ethnos* 120 (1989); James Clifford, *The Predicament of Culture: Twentieth-Century Ethnography, Literature, and Art* (1988); Global Ethnoscapes: Notes and Queries for a Transnational Anthropology, in *Recapturing Anthropology: Working in the Present* 191 (Richard G. Fox ed., 1991).

12 Liisa Malkki, National Geographic: The Rooting of Peoples and the Territorialization of National Identity among Scholars and Refugees, 7 *Cultural Anthropology* 24, 28 (1992) (quoting Gyan Prakash, Writing Post-Orientalist Histories of the Third World: Perspectives from Indian Historiography, 32 *Comp. Stud. Soc'y & Hist.* 383, 394 (1990)).

13 Ulf Hannerz, *Cultural Complexity: Studies in the Social Organization of Meaning* 266 (1992).

14 A. Belden Fields & Wolf-Dieter Narr, Human Rights as a Holistic Concept, 14 *Hum. Rts. Q.* 1, 9–19 (1992).

15 Adamantia Pollis & Peter Schwab, Human Rights: A Western Construct with Limited Applicability, in *Human Rights: Cultural and Ideological Perspectives* 1, 8 (Adamantia Pollis & Peter Schwab eds., 1980) [hereinafter *Cultural and Ideological Perspectives*].

16 Ibid. at 13.

17 Asmarom Legesse, Human Rights in African Political Culture, in *The Moral Imperatives of Human Rights: A World Survey* 123, 124 (Kenneth W. Thompson ed., 1980).

18 Ibid.

19 Raimundo Panikkar, Is the Notion of Human Rights a Western Concept?, *Diogenes*, Winter 1982, at 86.

20 Ibid. at 87.

21 Ibid. at 77.

22 Paulin J. Hountondji, The Master's Voice – Remarks on the Problem of Human Rights in Africa, in *Philosophical Foundations of Human Rights: A World Survey* 325 (Paul Ricoeur ed., 1988).

23 Dunstan M. Wai, Human Rights in Sub-Saharan Africa, in *Cultural and Ideological Perspectives*, *supra* note 15, at 115.

24 Donnelly, *supra* note 9, at 313, 304; Rhoda E. Howard, Dignity, Community, and Human Rights, in *Human Rights in Cross-Cultural Perspectives*, *supra* note 2, at 81, 90–91; Rhoda E. Howard, Cultural Absolutism and the Nostalgia for Community, 15 *Hum. Rts. Q.* 315 (1993).

25 Donnelly, *supra* note 9, at 303.

26 Ibid. at 306–11.

27 Ibid. at 304.

28 Ibid. at 312.

29 Ibid. at 313.

30 Cindy Patton, *Inventing Aids* 77 (1990).

31 *See* Gerald D. Berreman, The Brahmanical View of Caste, 5 *Contributions to Indian Soc.* 16 (1971) (a review symposium on Louis Dumont's *Homo Hierarchicus*); E. Valentine Daniel, *Fluid Signs, Being a Person the Tamil Way* (1984); Louis Dumont, *Homo Hierarchicus: An Essay on the Caste System* (Mark Sainsburg trans., 1981) (1966); Joan P. Mencher, The Caste System Upside Down, or the Not-So-Mysterious East, 15 *Current Anthropology* 469 (1974).

32 Robert Redfield et al., Memorandum for the Study of Acculturation, 38 *Am. Anthropologist* 149 (1936); Gregory Bateson, Culture Contact and Schismogenesis, 199 *Man: Monthly Rec. Anthropological Sci.* 178 (1935).

33 Alison Dundes Renteln, The Unanswered Challenge of Relativism and the Consequences for Human Rights, 7 *Hum. Rts. Q.* 514 (1985); Alison Dundes Renteln, Relativism and the Search for Human Rights, 90 *Am. Anthropologist* 56 (1988). See also Alison Dundes Renteln, *International Human Rights: Universalism versus Relativism* (1990).

34 Renteln, Relativism and the Search for Human Rights, *supra* note 33, at 56.
35 Ibid.
36 Ibid. at 67–68.
37 *Human Rights in Cross-Cultural Perspectives*, *supra* note 2, at 1, 6.
38 Ibid. at 1.
39 Ibid. at 6.
40 Ibid. at 3.
41 Ibid. at 1.
42 Ibid.
43 Ibid. at 7.
44 Ibid. at 5.
45 *International Handbook of Human Rights* 1, 18–19 (Jack Donnelly & Rhoda E. Howard eds., 1987).
46 Ibid. at 18.
47 Ibid. at 19.
48 Ibid.
49 Ibid.
50 Jack Donnelly, *Universal Human Rights in Theory and Practice* 109–10 (1989).
51 Howard, Cultural Absolutism and the Nostalgia for Community, *supra* note 24, at 317.
52 Abdullahi Ahmed An-Na'im, Toward a Cross-Cultural Approach to Defining International Standards of Human Rights, in *Human Rights in Cross-Cultural Perspectives*, *supra* note 2, at 19, 24.
53 Richard Falk, Cultural Foundations for the International Protection of Human Rights, in *Human Rights in Cross-Cultural Perspectives*, *supra* note 2, at 44, 46.
54 Donnelly, *supra* note 50, at 115.
55 Lindholm, *supra* note 2, at 399.
56 See generally *Creating Culture* (Diane Austin-Broos ed., 1987); Clifford, *supra* note 11; *Writing Culture: The Poetics and Politics of Ethnography* (James Clifford & George E. Marcus eds., 1986); *Interpretive Social Science: A Reader* (Paul Rabinow & William M. Sullivan eds., 1979); Roy Wagner, *The Invention of Culture* (1981).
57 Michael Agar, Hermeneutics in Anthropology, 8 *Ethnos* 253, 258 (1980).
58 Renato Rosaldo, *Culture and Truth: The Remarking of Social Analysis* 21 (1989).
59 Ibid. at 20.
60 Frederik Barth, The Analysis of Culture in Complex Societies, 3–4 *Ethnos* 120 (1989).
61 Ibid. at 130.
62 Clifford, *supra* note 11, at 14.
63 *Interpretive Social Science: A Reader*, *supra* note 56, at 6.
64 Robert K. Hitchcock, Anthropological Research and Remote Area Development among Botswana Basarwa, in *Research for Development in Botswana* 285–9 (Robert K. Hitchcock & John Taylor eds., 1985).
65 Ibid. at 289–90, 295, 333.
66 Sidsel Saugestad, Comparative Perspectives on Minority Groups, National Seminar on Remote Area Development Policy, Ganzi 31 Aug.–4 Sept. (Gaborone: Ministry of Local Government, Lands and Housing, 1992) (background paper).
67 Robert K. Hitchcock & John D. Holm, Bureaucratic Domination of Hunter-Gatherer Societies: A Study of the San in Botswana, 24 *Dev. & Change* 305–6 (1993).
68 Botswana Christian Council, Who Was (T)here First? An Assessment of the Human Rights Situation of Basarwa in Selected Communities in the Gantsi District, 10 *Occasional Paper*, 5–7 (1992).
69 Akhil Gupta & James Ferguson, Beyond "Culture": Space, Identity, and the Politics of Difference, 7:1 *Cultural Anthropology* 6, 15 (1992).
70 Ibid. at 15.
71 Ibid.
72 Ibid. at 16 (quoting Edwin N. Wilmsen).

73 Botswana Christian Council, *supra* note 68, at 2.

74 Gupta & Ferguson, *supra* note 69, at 16.

75 The following account draws on Chris Brown, The Unity Dow Court Case: Liberal Democracy and Patriarchy in Botswana, Paper Presented to the Canadian Association of African Studies, 14 May 1992, and on a number of articles, mainly from newspapers in Botswana: *The Botswana Gazette*, 19 June & 8 July 1991; *Mmegi*, 14–20 June 1991 & 10–16 July 1992; *Newslink*, 14 June 1991.

76 Ann-Belinda S. Preis, *Strengthening Civil Society: Human Rights Organizations in Zimbabwe and Botswana* (1993).

77 Judgment. In the Appeal Court of Botswana Held at Lobatse. Court of Appeal Civil Appeal No. 4/91. High Court Misca. No. 124/90. In the matter between The Attorney General (Appellant) and Unity Dow (Respondent), reprinted in 13 *Hum. Rts. Q.* 614, 623 (1991).

78 Ibid. at 621.

79 *See* ibid.

80 *Mmegi*, 10–16 July 1992.

81 International Women's Rights Action Watch (IWRAW), Urgent International Action Needed to Uphold Women's Human Rights in Botswana: Government Backlash Against Unity Dow's Victory (9 Feb. 1993).

82 *International Handbook of Human Rights*, *supra* note 45, at 20.

83 Kathy Bond-Steward, Fostering Rights Awareness through Community Publishing, in *Legal Literacy: A Tool for Women's Empowerment* 313 (Margaret Schuler & Sakuntala Kadirgamar-Rajasingham eds., 1992).

84 Ibid. at 320.

85 Hannerz, *supra* note 13, at 262.

86 Ibid. at 265–6.

87 Louis A. Picard, *The Politics of Development in Botswana: A Model for Success?* 2 (1987); Patrick P. Molutsi & John D. Holm, Developing Democracy when Civil Society is Weak, 89 *Afr. Aff.* 232–340 (1990); Mpho G. Molomo, Botswana's Political Process, in *Multi-Party Democracy in Botswana* 11, 16–18 (Mpho G. Molomo & Brian T. Mokopakgosi eds., 1991).

88 Picard, *supra* note 87, at 2.

89 Molomo, *supra* note 87, at 11.

90 Picard, *supra* note 87, at 2.

91 Ibid.

92 Picard, *supra* note 87, at 2.

93 Molomo, *supra* note 87, at 16–18.

94 Ibid. at 11.

95 Molomo, *supra* note 87, at 19; Patrick P. Molutsi, The Political Economy of Botswana: Implications for Democracy, in *Multi-Party Democracy in Botswana*, *supra* note 87, at 32.

96 *Interpretive Social Science: A Reader*, *supra* note 56.

97 Clifford, *supra* note 11.

98 Virginia A. Leary, Postliberal Strands in Western Human Rights Theory: Personalist-Communitarian Perspectives, in *Human Rights in Cross-Cultural Perspectives*, *supra* note 2, at 105, 128.

99 Gupta & Ferguson, *supra* note 69, at 7, 9.

100 Fields & Narr, *supra* note 14, at 1.

101 Rosaldo, *supra* note 58, at 31.

102 Donnelly, *supra* note 50, at 19.

103 *Battlefields of Knowledge: The Interlocking of Theory and Practice in Social Research and Development* (Norman Long & Ann Long eds., 1992) [hereinafter *Battlefields*].

104 Fields & Narr, *supra* note 14, at 1.

105 *Battlefields*, *supra* note 103, at 3, 5.

106 Ibid.

107 Norman Long, From Paradigm Lost to Paradigm Regained? The Case for an Actor-Oriented Sociology of Development, in *Battlefields*, *supra* note 103, at 16, 24 (quoting A. Giddens).
108 Ibid. at 24.
109 Ibid. at 19.
110 Ibid. at 20.
111 Ibid. at 34.
112 Ibid. at 35.
113 Ibid. at 26–7.
114 Ibid. at 27.
115 *See* Donnelly, *supra* note 50, at 61; Pollis & Schwab, *supra* note 15, at 15; Rentein, Relativism and the Search for Human Rights, *supra* note 33, at 64.
116 *Battlefields*, *supra* note 103, at 42 n. 16.
117 Rosaldo, *supra* note 58, at 39.
118 Jack Donnelly, Post-Cold War Reflections on the Study of International Human Rights, 8 *Ethics & Int'l Aff.* 97, 115–16 (1994).

18

Between Universalism and Relativism: A Critique of the UNESCO Concept of Culture

Thomas Hylland Eriksen

Introduction

In a scathing attack on the classic Herderian–Boasian concept of culture and its potential for generating both relativism and chauvinism, Alain Finkielkraut (1987) notes that although the United Nations' Educational, Scientific and Cultural Organization (UNESCO) was initially founded in an Enlightenment spirit loyal to the universalist legacy of Diderot and Condorcet, it almost immediately degenerated into a tool for parochialism and relativism. Uninhibited by the possible constraints implied by detailed knowledge regarding the topics under scrutiny, Finkielkraut was able to present a powerful, coherent and, in many people's view, persuasive criticism of the widespread culturalization of politics and aesthetics in the late twentieth century. Arguing that the meaning of culture has slid from *Bildung*[1] to heritage, from universalistic thought to relativistic anti-thought, his book on 'the defeat of thinking'[2] has been widely read and translated over the past decade.

In Finkielkraut's book, UNESCO is given a central role as a chief villain (along with social anthropologists, those dangerous purveyors of relativist nonsense). In this essay, UNESCO's ideology of culture will serve as a point of departure, engaging current debates over culture and rights with the most recent and most comprehensive statement from UNESCO regarding culture in the contemporary world, namely the report on *Our Creative Diversity* (World Commission on Culture and Development 1995), a document which heroically and often skillfully attempts to manoeuvre in the muddy waters between the Scylla of nihilistic cultural relativism and the Charybdis of supremacist universalism. Fuzzier, less elegant and less

Originally published in *Culture and Rights: Anthropological Perspectives*, ed. Jane K. Cowan, Marie-Bénédicte Dembour, and Richard A. Wilson. Cambridge and New York: Cambridge University Press, 2001, pp. 127–48.

consistent than liberal critiques of the Finkielkraut type, *Our Creative Diversity*, in spite of important shortcomings, is nonetheless more complex, presenting a multi-faceted picture of the social world. While liberal critics frame the problem as being one of 'rights versus culture', the 'right *to* culture' is a stronger concern in UNESCO. However, the authors do not explicitly address the possible contradiction between the two approaches. Nor do they see rights as culture: although they emphasize the value of cultural diversity, it appears largely as an aesthetic, rather than a moral, value.

An intriguing and ultimately disquieting context for the UNESCO model of culture is the work of Claude Lévi-Strauss on cultural relativity and culture contact, which, although peripheral to his structuralist *œuvre*, has been influential in UNESCO. The vision expressed in Lévi-Strauss' programmatic work on cultural diversity illustrates some of the difficulties inherent in *Our Creative Diversity*. The two pieces commissioned by UNESCO from Lévi-Strauss, *Race et Histoire* (Lévi-Strauss 1971 [1952]) and *Race et Culture* (Lévi-Strauss 1979 [1971]) highlight some of the dilemmas associated with a partition of the world into cultures. Central insights from these works can also be invoked against over-optimistic suppositions from scholars such as Finkielkraut that specific local circumstances and politics can be effectively divorced.

These problems recur (Plato's Socrates, for one, discussed them with his contemporary relativists, Gorgias and Protagoras). These days frequently framed as communitarianism versus liberalism, or relativism versus universalism, there are some real baby-and-bathwater problems which can doubtless be dealt with eloquently and effectively, but not comprehensively, from an unreformed Enlightenment, cosmopolitan point of view. A discussion of these problems forms the substance of this contribution.

Our Creative Diversity

UNESCO has, since its foundation in 1945, planned and implemented a vast number of developmental and cooperative projects concerning education in a wide sense.[3] Cultural creativity, cultural rights and ethnic/racial discrimination have also been important concerns since the beginning – leading, *inter alia*, to its famous list of world cultural heritage sites, which recently expanded to include 'natural heritage sites' as well. Many writings supported or published by UNESCO have, over the past five decades, made important contributions to international debates about racism, ethnocentrism, cultural relativism, cultural hegemonies and quests for equal cultural rights. Although this body of work certainly has an applied perspective in common, it cannot be maintained that all, or even nearly all, the writings published under the aegis of UNESCO share a common perspective on culture, relativism and rights, despite Finkielkraut's insinuations.[4] A few publications nevertheless stand out as implicit or explicit policy documents. The most important example of the latter is clearly the report *Our Creative Diversity* (UNESCO 1995). Written by a characteristically global and interdisciplinary group,[5] the World Commission on Culture and Development (WCCD), the report was published simultaneously in several languages and later translated into yet others (thirteen at the latest count). This report seems a particularly fruitful starting point for a discussion of the global debates regarding cultural and political rights. It is a genuine intellectual contribution to the field. It can be read symptomatically as an expression of a certain 'UNESCO ideology'; its omissions are as interesting as the points it makes; it highlights – voluntarily and involuntarily – deep predicaments of culture; and last, but perhaps not least, being what it is, it will, by default, have real-world consequences of a magnitude most academics can only dream of for their scholarly work.

Like the UN report on the environment, *Our Common Future* (World Commission on the Environment 1987), *Our Creative Diversity* was a long time in the making. It was an expensive, prestigious and cumbersome project[6] and yet it has received comparatively little attention outside UNESCO's immediate sphere of influence. The reason may be that the Brundtland report was politically easier to relate to with great popular demand for its central concept – sustainable development – which elegantly embodied and concealed a kind of double-think characteristic of this risk-aware age of global capitalism. It presented a consistent description of the world and offered predictable and concrete policy advice of the kind heard from hundreds of environmentalist lobbyists for decades, including that provided by *Limits to Growth* the famous report of the Club of Rome (Meadows et al. 1974) completed a decade and a half earlier. The Brundtland report's analyses and advice were thus consistent with much of the Romantic and green autocriticism that has been inherent in modernity at least since William Blake's day. The more recent UNESCO report, by contrast, offers little by way of actual policy recommendations. It is difficult to summarize; it introduces issues that demand real intellectual engagement – and not merely the reiteration of pre-existing conceptions – to be properly understood; and finally, it must in all justice be said, it requires a considerable talent for double- and triple-think to see it as a coherent piece of work.

Reading *Our Creative Diversity* soon after it was published, I was, like many other social anthropologists, curious to discover how it related to the current academic debates over the use and misuse of concepts of culture and, in a more political vein, the still vigorous debates regarding the relationship between individual, group and state in the contemporary, post-Cold War world. These involved quibbles over multiculturalism in North America; philosophical exchanges between communitarians and liberals, moderns and postmoderns on both sides of the Atlantic and Franco-German faultlines; disagreements over the relationship between cultural rights and equal rights among immigrants in Western Europe; nationalist essentialism 'with no head' versus marketplace liberalism 'with no heart'; consumerism and identity; globalization and localization. Now, as will be evident from the critique below, the report is sensitive almost to the point of hypochondria regarding the concept of culture (which does not preclude some interesting self-contradictions). Yet identity politics hardly figures at all in the report as a topic. This omission is symptomatic of the report's shortcomings.

A very brief summary of the report's general conclusions – which are based on the statistics, anecdotal evidence, informed reasoning and humanistic ideology featured throughout – might read like this: although global cultural variation is a fact, it is necessary to develop a common global ethics, which should draw on values most religions have in common as a starting-point. Notably, respect and tolerance must be emphasized as central values. The world is culturally diverse, and it is necessary to pursue political models which maintain and encourage this diversity. Such variation functions creatively both because it stimulates the members of a culture to be creative, and because it offers impulses to others. Equality between men and women is essential, and children and adolescents must be given the opportunity to realize their creative potential on their own terms. Modern mass media must be used to strengthen local culture, not to weaken it. The cultural heritage must also be respected – and this should be taken to mean not only one's own but also the heritage of others. Ethnic and linguistic minorities, in particular, need protection, and have the right to retain their cultural uniqueness.

While these conclusions are so generally phrased that they may seem palatable to both moderate communitarians and moderate liberals, they, and the report as a whole, gloss over fundamental problems and fail to address politically volatile issues. This shortcoming, of course, makes the report less useful than it could have been. I shall deal with the most serious problems at some length, but in all fairness it should be added that some of them cannot be resolved once and for all in political practice, which is bound to tread the muddy middle ground of compromise.

Two Problems of Culture

The report is characterized by indecision regarding the use of the concept of culture. There are two separate problems here. The first, typical of work emanating from the UN Decade for Culture, concerns the relationship between culture as artistic work and culture as a way of life. At the outset of the report, Marshall Sahlins is quoted approvingly for spelling out the classic anthropological view that every human activity, including those relating to development and the economy, has a cultural component or dimension. As a result, the report periodically reads as a catalogue of human activities. There is a nevertheless strong and slightly unsettling bias in this regard towards looking at culture as *difference*: as those symbolic acts which demarcate boundaries between groups. If culture is a way of life, then buying groceries at 7-Eleven is naturally neither less nor more cultural than taking part in Tudor revivalism or teaching English history; working in a large factory or software company is no less authentic than tilling the soil or producing local crafts for tourists and anti-tourists, and so on. Being exotic or different in the eyes of the 'we' of *our* creative diversity does not qualify for being 'cultural' in an analytic sense. Besides, the penchant for locally rooted solutions in the sections dealing with development is both mysterious and empirically misleading: it has largely been through the appropriation and local adaptation of imported technologies and imported forms of organization that poor countries have become richer during the past century. In other words, even the ostensible strengthening of local culture is irretrievably a hybrid activity as it draws on organizational and technological resources of modernity.

The second definition of culture – culture seen as artistic production – is also amply represented in the report, and little effort is made to distinguish between the two perspectives. This kind of inconsistency is, perhaps, *gefundenes Fressen*[7] to many a nitpicking anthropologist, but in my view it does little harm. It may be noted as a problem, however, that the examples of artistic production mentioned in the report, like the examples taken from everyday life, highlight the uniqueness of the local, the rootedness of cultural activity and the differences between 'ours' and 'theirs'.

The second problem related to the concept of culture in the report is more serious than the exoticist bias. In most of the report, culture is conceptualized as something that can easily be pluralized, which belongs to a particular group of people, associated with their heritage or 'roots'. On the other hand, the authors are also keen to emphasize that 'impulses', external influence, globalization and creolization are also cultural phenomena. This duality corresponds to two sets of concepts of culture prevalent in contemporary anthropology, the first characteristic of cultural

relativism, structural functionalism and structuralism, the second typical of decon-
structivist trends, as well as recent 'post-structuralist' work, taking the framework of
cultural globalization as a starting-point for what are often comparative studies of
modernities.

Culture is primarily seen as tradition by the WCCD, but a secondary meaning
allows communication to be defined as cultural as well. The result is analytically
unsatisfactory, but it does not necessarily entail an empirically wrong description.
Culture can be understood simultaneously as tradition *and* communication; as roots,
destiny, history, continuity and sharing on the one hand, and as impulses, choice, the
future, change and variation on the other. The WCCD has laudably tried to incorporate both dimensions, but it remains a fact that the latter 'post-structuralist'
perspective so typical of contemporary anthropological theorizing becomes a
garnish, an afterthought, a refreshment to accompany the main course of cultures
seen as bounded entities comprising 'groups' that share basic values and customs.

Since Lourdes Arizpe, writing on behalf of UNESCO, recently (1998) expressed
incredulity in response to a similar criticism from Susan Wright (1998), I will
highlight a few quotations from the report to substantiate this claim, which is an
important premise for the rest of this piece. In Chapter 2, programmatically entitled
'No culture is an island', the authors write about 'respect for all cultures, or at least
for those cultures that value tolerance and respect for others' (p. 54). As if cultures
were social agents; pluralism is defined as 'tolerance and respect for and rejoicing over
the plurality of cultures' (p. 55); on minorities, the authors say that '[t]hese groups
share systems of values and sources of self-esteem that often are derived from sources
quite different from those of the majority culture' (p. 57); and in the subsequent
chapter, the authors write that 'most societies today are multicultural' (p. 61), meaning that they contain several cultures, implicitly assumed to be bounded. Throughout
the report, cultures are implicitly and explicitly seen as rooted and old, shared within a
group, to be treated 'with respect' as one handles aging china or old aunts with due
attention to their fragility. (Like so many elite accounts of culture tinged with
Romanticism, this report does not explicitly recognize the cultural dimension of
mainstream or modern phenomena such as urban middle-class English culture,
the culture of New York or Bombay, or the culture of contemporary Germans or
the French etc.) Although it is said explicitly that any culture's relationship with the
outside world is 'dynamic', UNESCO cultures remain islands or at least peninsulas.[8]

Global Ethics and Identity Politics

This perspective has more to recommend it than many devastating, but often
ahistorical, recent critiques from cultural studies and anthropology have been
willing to admit. For decades, anthropologists have urged development agencies to
take the cultural dimension into account, to become more sensitive towards local
conditions and to understand that successful development processes necessarily take
local conditions and local human resources seriously as factors of change. The report
gives legitimacy to such a time-honoured anthropological view. However, the insistence on cultural difference and plurality as constitutive of the social world does not
fit very well with the equally strong insistence on the need for a global ethics.
Obviously, the WCCD wants to eat its cake and have it too; it promotes a relativistic
view of development and a universalist view of ethics. Distancing itself occasionally
from the 'vocal bullies' of identity politics and the mono-ethnic model of the

nation-state, it does not, however, discuss the obvious contradictions between cultural relativism and ethical universalism, or the perils of identity politics at the sub-national level. While the Commission may defend itself successfully against academic charges of superficiality and datedness[9] by pointing out that the target group consists of ordinary educated people, not specialized and parochial scholars engaged in games of intellectual one-upmanship, the political innocence evident in the report is nothing short of stunning. In an age when nearly all armed conflicts take place within and not between states (see SIPRI 1997), and most of them could be designated as 'ethnic'; in an age when Croatian newspapers write about their successful national football team (during the 1998 World Cup) that it is genetically determined to win when notions of collective cultural rights and fear of foreign contamination direct anti-liberal or anti-secular political efforts in contexts otherwise as different as Le Pen's France, the BJP's India (or Hindustan) and the Algeria of the FIS, issues relating to cultural rights ought not to be treated lightly by a policy-oriented body such as UNESCO. To simply state, as the report does in many places and in different ways, that one is favourable to cultural rights simply will not do, whether the context is an academic one or a political one. The notion has to be circumscribed more carefully. It is not self-evident what the term means, nor how it articulates with individual human rights. The programmatic 'right to culture' may conflict with considerations of 'rights versus culture'.

The rise of identity politics at the turn of the millennium is not caused by a widespread and contagious lack of tolerance to be mitigated by the implementation of a global ethics. Rather, it draws legitimacy from a Romantic way of thinking about difference and similarity, which the UNESCO report, in spite of its humanitarian intentions, may involuntarily contribute to perpetuating. The political conclusions to be drawn from the description of the world inherent in the report are not necessarily the liberal, tolerant and universalistic ones suggested by the authors (and here, at least, one must approve of Finkielkraut's un-reformed Enlightenment universalism-cum-provincialism). Separatists, difference multiculturalists championing exclusive criteria of judgement for 'my culture', nationalists seeking stricter border controls and restrictions on the flows of meaning across boundaries, inquisitors chasing the Salman Rushdies of the world into hiding, and myriad nationalisms writ small could find a sound basis for their isolationism and political particularism in the report, notwithstanding its periodical assertions to the contrary. These assertions stand in a mechanical, external relationship to the basic view of cultures as bounded and unique. Cultures need to talk to each other, as it were, and tolerate but they remain bounded cultures nonetheless.

Probably, as Klausen (1998) remarks in a comment on the report, it would have been both better and more credible if the internal tensions and disagreements within the committee had been made explicit. In that case, one might have explored the strengths and weaknesses of the two positions (rights *above* culture and the right *to* culture), and it would have been evident that one cannot always have one's cake and eat it too.

Hybrids, Traditions, Culturalism and Modernity

Let me sum up the argument so far. *Our Creative Diversity* invokes several concepts of culture, but it is dominated by the classic view from cultural relativism – '1930s social anthropology', Wright (1998: 13) calls it dismissively – of cultures as bounded entities with their own sets of values and practices. Their 'distinctiveness should be encouraged', Wright paraphrases the report (1998: 13), 'as it is by looking across boundaries between distinct cultures that people gain ideas for alternative ways of living'. The image presented actually resembles Darwin's (1985 [1859]) distinction between artificial selection (as in pigeon-breeding) and natural selection: artificial selection is rapid and superficial; natural selection is slow and deep. Creole culture, hybrid forms, global universals such as McDonald's (and human rights discourses?) must thus be seen as superficial; while tradition, associated with 'roots' and the past, is profound. Since the report does not distinguish between culture and ethnicity, it may perhaps be inferred that the 'deep' culture of tradition is associated with ethnic identity, while the 'superficial' culture of modernity is not. As long as such a view is not supported by evidence, it must be questioned. The many passages on 'minority cultures', further, reveal a conservationist view of cultural diversity; in several places, diversity is seen as a value in itself. To whom? – the conservationists? The pluralism endorsed in the report does not seem to include post-plural hybrid forms, the millions of mixed 'neither-nor' or 'both-and' individuals inhabiting both global megacities and rural outposts in many countries. In other words, the right to an identity does not seem to entail the right *not* to have a specific (usually ethnic) identity.[10]

The report simultaneously emphasizes the right of peoples to cultural self-determination and the need for a global ethics – as if ethics and morality had nothing to do with culture. Of course, cultural self-determination may conflict with a global ethics, since morality is an important component of locally constructed worlds (see Howell 1996). Development is framed in context-sensitive, culturalist language; ethics is discussed in universalist terms. If minorities (and, presumably, majorities) share unique 'systems of values', these 'systems' may be expected to give moral instructions to their adherents; and if these 'systems of values' are to be defended from the onslaught of modern individualism, a call for global ethics seems a tall order.

At several points in the report, group rights are defended,[11] yet it is also committed to the Universal Declaration of Human Rights, which is unanimous in according rights to individuals, not groups. The obvious dilemma in this dual position – the inevitable conflict between collective minority rights and individual rights – is not discussed. Had the problem been taken seriously by the authors, surely they would also have taken on the important question of the ways in which individual human rights could be adapted to local circumstances. For example, Johan Galtung (1996) is fond of pointing out that if nomads were given a say in the formulation of the Declaration of Human Rights, the universal right to own a goat would have been high on the list; and if Indian villagers had contributed a paragraph or two, an essential human right would have been the right to die at home surrounded by family members. These suggestions show how locally embedded values may be different from, but compatible with, individual human rights.

Finally, identity politics is treated briefly and not confronted with other parts of the report, where respect and tolerance for others, tradition and change are dealt with in laudatory terms. Along with the intellectual quagmire resulting from the insistence on unspecified cultural diversity *and* global ethics, this lack is the most disquieting aspect of the report. Can groups be free? When do group rights infringe on individual rights? How can a state strike a balance between equal rights for all its citizens and their right to be different? There is a very large literature grappling with these dilemmas,[12] which are not taken into account by the WCCP, which applauds 'minority cultures' while condemning majority nationalism, generally oblivious of the fact that minority problems are not solved, but removed to another level when minorities are accorded political rights on ethnic and territorial grounds. Fighting cultural fundamentalism (as in supremacist nationalism) with cultural fundamentalism (as in minority identity politics) is usually a zero-sum game.

In sum, surprisingly little attention is granted to the phenomenon of identity politics, whereby culture is politicized and used to legitimize not just exclusiveness, but exclusion as well. An epistemology grounding an individual's quality of life in his or her 'culture' does not pave the way for tolerance, respect and a peaceful 'global ecumene' (Hannerz 1989), and it is difficult to understand how the authors of *Our Creative Diversity* have envisioned the connection between the one and the other. In a recent volume on war and ethnicity, David Turton (1997) and his contributors show precisely how globalization and intensified contacts between groups in many parts of the world pave the way for the entrenchment of boundaries and violent identity politics, provided the political leaders are able to draw popular support from culturalist rhetoric. And as the anti-immigration lobbies of European countries might argue: 'Of course we respect others, but let them remain where they are, otherwise our culture of peace, inspired by UNESCO, will not stand a chance. A culture has the right to protect itself, and we are under siege from American vulgarity and Muslim barbarism!' This may not, in a word, be the most opportune time in world history for an organization committed to global humanism to provide arguments for cultural isolationism.

Culture and Two Lévi-Strausses

It needs to be mentioned at this point that, although the previous paragraphs may have given the opposite impression, my attitude towards the UNESCO effort is largely sympathetic. Some of the short-comings and self-contradictions of the report are, perhaps, inevitable given the composition of the committee and the need for compromise, and some of them cannot be easily resolved either in theory or in practice. Traditionalism and modernism, ethnic fragmentation and global unification are complementary dimensions of political processes in the contemporary world. Yet I have argued that the main conceptualization of culture in the book is naïve, and scarcely serves the explicit political purpose of underpinning a 'culture of peace'. In dealing with the relativity of cultures versus the universality of ethics, it seems that *Our Creative Diversity* unwittingly reproduces the old German distinction between *Kultur* and *Zivilisation*, which was especially popular in the interwar years. The former, sometimes associated with Tönnies' notion of *Gemeinschaft*,[13] is local, experience-based, unique and is passed on through socialization and the unconscious assimilation of local knowledge. The latter, the *Gesellschaft*[14] variety, is global, cognitive, universal and passed on through reflexive learning. It was frequently said about the Jews in the interwar Germanic world that 'they could acquire our civilization, but never our culture'. Does our creative diversity, then, refer to 'culture' or to 'civilization'? Doubtless the former, while the global ethics refers to the latter. Finkielkraut (1987) is therefore only partly right when he asserts that UNESCO quickly moved from a universalistic Enlightenment way of reasoning to a relativistic Romantic attitude: the recent report tries to encompass both, but it glosses over the contradictions rather than attempting to resolve them. As Finkielkraut rightly argues, any universal standards contradict any unqualified cultural relativism. This point was seen clearly a century ago by conservative French intellectuals like Maurice Barrès and Gustave Le Bon, when they argued against colonialism on ethnocentric, cultural relativist grounds: colonialism and the ensuing mixing of peoples would create confusion and moral erosion on both sides of the Mediterranean, and it should therefore be avoided. Now, this kind of view was already foreshadowed in Herder's writings against French universalism-cum-provincialism, but also in Franz Boas' cultural relativism, in later anthropologists' advocacy on behalf of indigenous peoples, in Le Pen's *Front National* program and that of apartheid, and in Claude Lévi-Strauss' work. Before moving to an examination of the two texts Lévi-Strauss wrote for UNESCO, it must be stressed, in order to preclude misunderstanding, that this does not imply that Boas' and others' defense of indigenous rights, apartheid and French supremacism are judged as similar political views; only that they draw on the same ontology of culture, namely the Herderian archipelago vision (cultures are discrete and bounded, if not entirely isolated) which lies at the historical origins of both cultural relativism and nationalism.

Claude Lévi-Strauss has arguably been the most influential anthropologist in the postwar era (which could be said to encompass the period 1945–80). While Lévi-Strauss' structuralism is a universalist doctrine about the way human minds function, his position regarding culture has always been that of a classic cultural relativist. He regards cultural variation as the necessary experimental foundation for his theory of universals at the level of cognitive mechanisms. To French critics of anthropological exoticism such as Derrida, Baudrillard and Finkielkraut, Lévi-Strauss – in spite of his 'ultimate' universalism, but because of his 'proximate' relativism – is the very embodiment of *l'ethnologie*, the art of viewing natives in their natural environment in order to identify, classify and reduce them to so many laboratory specimens.

The shadow of Lévi-Strauss looms large over UNESCO ventures into culture theory. He was an honorary member of the WCCD, and he is quoted intermittently in the report. Much more importantly, UNESCO, at an early stage in its existence, commissioned a short text on ethnocentrism from him. The small book, *Race et Histoire* (Lévi-Strauss 1961 [1952]), has become a classic of anti-racism in the French-speaking world; it has been reprinted many times, and every year, he is reportedly approached by secondary school students who are obliged to write an assignment on the book and who despairingly confess that '*nous ne comprenons rien*' (Lévi-Strauss & Eribon 1988: 208).[15] The book, arguing along lines that are familiar to every contemporary anthropologist, warns against genetic determinism; reveals the fallacies of ethnocentrism and facile cultural evolutionism; defends the rights of small societies to cultural survival; and revels in the intricacies of the symbolic systems of societies unknown to the vast majority of his readers. There is a subtle irony in the fact that *Race et Histoire*, which – like the beautifully romantic '*Tristes Tropiques*' (1955) has later been invoked as politically correct *tiersmondiste*[16] literature fit for consumption by third-generation *beurs*[17] in Parisian suburbs and Senegalese university students. Lévi-Strauss has never been *tiersmondiste*.[18] On the contrary, as he explained, 'the societies which I defended [in *Tristes Tropiques*] are even more threatened by *tiersmondisme* than by colonisation' (Lévi-Strauss & Eribon 1988: 213), adding that 'I thus defend those little peoples who wish to remain faithful to their traditional way of life, outside the conflicts that divide the modern world.' This attitude makes Lévi-Strauss a strange bedfellow for UNESCO, a body tightly allied with a *tiersmondiste* outlook and whose principal *raison-d'être* lies in the dissemination of standardized, state-monitored education and modern means of communication in the so-called Third World.

Nevertheless, the main message of *Race et Histoire* went down well in the post-war decolonizing world of the early 1950s: cultures cannot be ranked according to their level of development; they are – to use a currently fashionable phrase – equal but different. Incidentally, Lévi-Strauss' universalism is a long shot from the global ethics of *Our Creative Diversity*, although it cannot be ruled out that his structuralism could, at a formal and not substantial level, form the basis of some kind of universal ethics. Nevertheless, these would hardly be recognized as such by politicians and UN officials.[19]

Nearly twenty years after the success of *Race et Histoire*, UNESCO asked Lévi-Strauss to contribute a new text on the topics of ethno-centrism, race and culture. He now wrote a shorter piece, *Race et Culture* (Lévi-Strauss 1979 [1971]), which was received with more mixed feelings than the first commissioned work. Like his earlier text, it begins with a critique of the idea of race, but instead of discarding it as irrelevant for his purposes, he shows how pervasive notions of racial difference are in human societies, and how they contribute to the integrity of the group. 'We have a tendency', he writes (1979: 441), 'to consider those "races" which are apparently the furthest from our own, as being simultaneously the most homogeneous ones; to a White, all the Yellows [*sic*] resemble one another, and the converse is probably also true'. He notes the potential consequences of population genetics for anthropology, such that large questions regarding cultural history, pre-historical migrations, differentiation and so on may at long last be answered. He also concludes, in his characteristic Copernican way, that far from it being the case that culture is the product of race, 'race – or that which one generally means by this term – is one of several functions of culture' (Lévi-Strauss 1979: 446). Racial differences are the long-term outcome of tribal fission and the ensuing isolation of the segments ('How could it be otherwise?'). Later, he writes that 'mutual tolerance presupposes the presence of two conditions that the contemporary societies are further than ever before from fulfilling: on the one hand, relative equality [in relation to other societies], on the other hand, sufficient physical distance' (458). Also arguing that intergroup hostility is quite normal in human societies, and that conflict is bound to result from culture contact, the master anthropologist adds, within brackets, that without doubt, 'we will awake from the dream that equality and brotherhood will one day rule among men without compromising their diversity' (461).[20] It is, naturally, this dream that the WCCD has not yet awoken from, despite subscribing to Lévi-Strauss' general description of a world partitioned into cultures.

Assumed Perils of Culture Contact

When this second text was published, many of Lévi-Strauss' former admirers in the French public sphere held that there was a contradiction between the two texts, the one being a humanistic charter for equality, extending the ideas of the French Revolution to include the small and oppressed peoples, as it were; the other being a concealed defence for ethnic nationalism and chauvinism, in addition to speaking warmly of that dreaded discipline, human genetics. Actually, as Lévi-Strauss remarked much later (Lévi-Strauss & Eribon 1988: 206), the Communist newspaper *L'Humanité*, in attempting to show that Lévi-Strauss' views had changed, inadvertently quoted a passage from *Race et Culture* which he had actually lifted verbatim from *Race et Histoire*. Asked by Didier Eribon to elaborate on his views regarding immigration to France, as Lévi-Strauss is widely believed to be against mass immigration (see Todorov 1989), the master anthropologist replied that insofar as the European countries were unable to preserve or animate 'intellectual and moral values sufficiently powerful to attract people from outside so that they may hope to adopt them, well, then there is doubtless reason for anxiety' (Lévi-Strauss & Eribon 1988: 213). Confronted with these contemporary complexities, in other words, Lévi-Strauss prefers the simple assimilationist model from the Enlightenment to the cultural complexity represented by unassimilated immigrants. In sum, Lévi-Strauss' perspective on culture and intergroup relations is unhelpful as a theoretical matrix for UNESCO.

Many Cultures or None?

Read closely, there is no doubt that the argument in *Race et Culture* is consistent with *Race et Histoire*. Towards the end of the earlier work, Lévi-Strauss stresses that in order to learn from each other, cultures need to be discrete; in the latter work, he reminds his readers and UNESCO that love of one's own culture, which is necessary for a strong group identity, implies a certain distance, which may easily flip into hostility *vis-à-vis* others. The seeming contradiction – which turns out to be a complementarity – between the two texts goes to the core of UNESCO's predicament. If an archipelago vision of culture is maintained, then it is easy to defend cultural rights and to support endeavours aiming at the strengthening of symbolic and social cohesion among collectivities seen as culture-bearing groups; but in that case, the notion of global ethics becomes difficult to maintain. In addition, there is no guarantee that this notion of culture will be used in a 'tolerant and respectful' way (the *Race et Histoire* perspective) and not in a hostile and defensive way (as in *Race et Culture*).

Another, related question concerns whether Lévi-Strauss' conceptualization of a world composed of small, discrete societies can offer a useful concept of culture with which to analyse the contemporary world. He seems to deny it himself, regarding our time as a period of emergency when small societies are being obliterated (not least by their 'Third World' governments – there is no unanimous North-South manicheism here), the world is becoming too small for humanity, and contacts across cultural boundaries blur distinctions and threaten not only identities but also the comparative project providing structuralism with its data. Lévi-Strauss is, and has always been, an admirably consistent critic of universalistic ambitions of modernity, and his worldview is deeply at odds with the modernizing spirit that justifies UNESCO's development endeavours. UNESCO's attempts to accommodate notions of group rights and a concept of culture modelled on a more or less chimerical pre-modern tribal world contradict its basic commitment to individual human rights, universal education and global modernity. Individual rights, as defined since Locke, are sanctioned by a state, while group rights are associated with a collectivity at the sub-state level. One can simultaneously be a member of a cultural community and a citizen, but the social contract guaranteeing the equal treatment of citizens obtains between the citizen and the state. For this reason, it is misleading to speak of group rights, or even minority rights, if the issues pertain to, say, freedom of religion or linguistic pluralism.[21]

In real life, double standards are rarely twice as good as single standards, but in studies of social life, two descriptions are usually better than one. Not least for this reason, the UNESCO committee should be praised for attempting to arrive at a multifaceted description of culture in the contemporary world. Arne Martin Klausen, an old teacher of mine and a long-time critic of, and consultant for, development projects, often comments – slightly tongue-in-cheek – on the recent scholarly confusions over definitions of culture by proposing that several distinct concepts of culture are better than none. In his brief critique of *Our Creative Diversity*, Klausen says:

> It is of course regrettable that other people [non-anthropologists], who have started to acknowledge the importance of the cultural dimension, are now operating imprecisely within one single concept of culture that is so comprehensive that it becomes meaning-less and inoperative, but we must nevertheless continue to underline the importance of between two and four different, but precise, concepts of culture as vital tools for understanding social complexities (Klausen 1998: 32).

My own conclusion is precisely the opposite of Klausen's, although it takes a similar description of the contemporary world as its point of departure. Since the concept of culture has become so multifarious as to obscure, rather than clarify, understandings of the social world, it may now perhaps be allowed to return to the culture pages of the broadsheets and the world of *Bildung*. Instead of invoking culture, if one talks about local arts, one could simply say 'local arts'; if one means language, ideology, patriarchy, children's rights, food habits, ritual practices or local political structures, one could use those or equivalent terms instead of covering them up in the deceptively cozy blanket of culture. In a continuous world, as Ingold puts it (1993: 230), 'the concept of culture . . . will have to go'.

To be more specific:

(i)   What are spoken of as cultural rights in *Our Creative Diversity*, whatever they may be, ought to be seen as *individual* rights. It is as an individual that I have the right to go to the church or mosque or synagogue or not, to speak my mother-tongue or another language of my choice, to relish the cultural heritage of my country or prefer Pan-Germanism, French Enlightenment philosophy or whatever. As an individual I have the right to attach myself to a tradition and the freedom to choose not to.

(ii) There is no need for a concept of culture in order to respect local conditions in development work: it is sufficient to be sensitive to the fact that local realities are always locally constructed, whether one works in inner-city Chicago or in the Kenyan countryside. One cannot meaningfully rank one locality as more authentic than another. What is at stake in development work is not cultural authenticity or purity, but people's ability to gain control over their own lives.

(iii) Finally, it is perfectly possible to support local arts, rural newspapers and the preservation of historic buildings without using mystifying language about 'a people's culture'. Accuracy would be gained, and unintended side-effects would be avoided, if such precise terms replaced the all-encompassing culture concept. The insistence on respect for local circumstances, incidentally, would alleviate any suspicion of crude Enlightenment imperialism *à la* Finkielkraut. And, naturally, Radovan Karadzic and Jean-Marie Le Pen would not be pleased with such a level of precision.

If the mystifying and ideologically charged culture concept can be discarded, the case for a global ethics also seems stronger. As *Our Creative Diversity* shows, there can be no easy way out. The classic Enlightenment model (surprisingly applauded by Lévi-Strauss in response to a question about immigrants) represented by post-revolutionary France and contemporary Turkey, to mention two spectacular examples, has achieved a high score regarding equality, but a lamentable record concerning the right to difference. Within this political model, homogeneity is seen as desirable for all, and the state-designated barbarians (Basques, Bretons or 'Mountain Turks' – Kurds – as the case may be) ought to be grateful, as it were, that someone bothers to integrate them into civilization. A classic Romantic model drawing on an archipelago vision of culture was evident in the apartheid system in South Africa, providing groups with 'cultural autonomy' and thereby preventing them from becoming integrated in greater society; bluntly put, it had a high score on the right to be different and a low score on the right to equality. Anyone who tried to talk about cultural rights to an ANC member before the transformation would learn a lesson or two about culturalist politics and the political pitfalls inherent in Romantic ethnology.

It is between these extremes that contemporary politics must manoeuvre, and neither notions of culture nor rigid universalisms have helped so far. It is for this reason that the unreformed Enlightenment position represented by Finkielkraut is unacceptable: A lesson from this past century of extremes must be that any imposition of homogeneity, whether from a state or from the self-appointed spokespersons of a 'group', is ultimately at odds with a notion of rights; and that, in Bauman's words (1996: 18), 'If the *modern* "problem of identity" is how to construct an identity and keep it solid and stable, the *postmodern* "problem of identity" is primarily how to avoid fixation and keep the options open'. This position does not imply that cultural creolization, flux and perpetual change are the only viable options; conservative choices are as valid as radical ones. Who, after all, is going to stand up and say that Borneo tribespeople, in the name of liberalism and universal human rights, should get a haircut and a job, start a trade union, or at least go and vote in the next elections? (Ironically, UNESCO is liable to stand up and say just that, given its positive view of state-monitored development.)

With a French thinker I began this piece, and with a French thinker I will end it. Tzvetan Todorov, in his thoughtful and beautifully written *Nous et les Autres* (1989), ends his long and winding journey through French conceptions of cultural (and racial) difference from Montaigne to Lévi-Strauss with an ambivalent conclusion, saturated with his own and others' struggles between ethnocentrism and relativism, universalism and particularism, individualism and collectivism:

> A well-tempered humanism [*un humanisme bien temperé*] can protect us against the faults of yesterday and today. Let us break up the simple connections: to respect the equal rights of all human beings does not imply the renunciation of a value hierarchy; to cherish the autonomy and freedom of individuals does not oblige us to repudiate all solidarity; the recognition of a public morality does not inevitably lead to a regression to the times of religious intolerance and the Inquisition [. . .] (Todorov 1989: 436).

Since the word culture divides but an unqualified rejection of the relevance of local circumstances oppresses, this kind of cautious and ambivalent position is the only valid starting-point for a humanistic politics that tries to achieve the impossible:

equality that respects difference, 'a sense of belonging to a community larger than each of the particular groups in question' (Laclau 1995: 105). To achieve this end, the concept of rights is more useful than the concept of culture.

NOTES

1 In English, 'formation'.
2 The English translation of *La défaite de la Pensée* is called, somewhat idiosyncratically, *The Undoing of Thought* (Finkielkraut 1988).
3 In order to exemplify the wide scope of the organisation's activities, let me mention that my father was employed by UNESCO in the 1970s to supervise and help organise a number of rural newspapers with a clear educational bent in various African countries.
4 UNESCO's current slogans read:
Strategies for development
promoting lifelong education for all;
assisting in the advancement, transfer and sharing of knowledge;
enhancing the concept of cultural heritage and promoting living cultures;
promoting the free flow of information and the development of communication.

Strategies for peace-building
encouraging education for peace, human rights and democracy, tolerance and international understanding;
promoting human rights and the fight against discrimination;
supporting consolidation of democratic processes;
encouraging cultural pluralism and dialogue between cultures;
contributing to conflict prevention and post-conflict peace-building.

(Source: http://www.unesco.org)

5 The World Commission on Culture and Development (WCCD) responsible for the report had thirteen full members with academic, political and artistic backgrounds, from Mexico, Nigeria, Pakistan, the USA, Greece, Norway/Sápmi, Senegal, Switzerland, Brazil, Egypt, Japan, Russia, Zimbabwe and Argentina. In addition it had *ex officio* observers from India and Mozambique, as well as honourary members including Burmese human rights activist Aung San Suu Kui, West Indian poet Derek Walcott, Belgian physicist Ilya Prigogine, American writer Elie Wiesel, a couple of Arab princes in succession, and Claude Lévi-Strauss. The Commission's work was led by Peruvian Javier Pérez de Cuéllar, former Secretary-General of the UN.
6 'Once the Commission was in place', explains Lourdes Arizpe, Assistant Director-General for Culture, UNESCO (Arizpe 1998), 'the three years that followed comprised nine consultations in the different continents in which some 120 speakers took the floor'.
7 In English, 'a heaven-sent opportunity'.
8 On the archipelago view of culture, see Eriksen 1993.
9 See for example Arizpe's (1998) response to Wright (1998).
10 As an exemplification of this point, the high suicide rates among youth in Finnmark county, Norway, an area associated with the formerly transhumant Sami, is often attributed locally to identity problems: the young Sami can neither fulfil the expectations of Sami traditionalists nor of Norwegian modernists; they are condemned to leading a hybrid life with no fixed identity. From the viewpoint of culture theory, it must be asked whether the problem lies in their cultural repertoire or in the local ranking of people according to their ability to fit stereotypes of bounded cultural identities.
11 For example in paragraph 3, 'The protection of minorities', in the chapter on global ethics.
12 See for example Kymlicka 1989, Taylor et al. 1992, Wilson 1997.

13 In English, 'community'.
14 In English, 'society'.
15 Literally, 'we don't understand anything'.
16 In English, 'third-worldist'.
17 French slang word for second- or third-generation immigrants from North Africa, living in the suburbs.
18 On this background, Finkielkraut's (1987) coupling of 'fourth-worldist' Lévi-Strauss with Frantz Fanon in *La défaite de la pensée* is curious, to say the least. *Tiersmondisme*, 'third-worldism', is a modernist emancipatory ideology promoting self-determination and equity for poor countries, while 'fourth-worldism' defends the traditional culture of tribal societies. Needless to say, the two do not combine well in practice, as many visitors to Sandinista Nicaragua in the 1980s discovered when they looked into the conditions for the indigenous Miskito.
19 See Lévi-Strauss 1983, ch. 12, for intimations to this effect.
20 Commenting on Lévi-Strauss, Todorov (1989:108) says: 'If one really has to choose between the two evils – cultural relativism and unilineal evolutionism – the latter is preferable, on the cognitive level as well as on the ethical level', before reassuring his readers that there are alternatives to these extremes.
21 See Eriksen 1997 for a full discussion of this dilemma in Mauritius; see Kymlicka 1989, ch. 7, for a Canadian example.

REFERENCES

Arizpe, L. 1998. UN Cultured. *Anthropology Today* 14:3, 24.
Bauman, Z. 1996. From Pilgrim to Tourist; or A Short History of Identity. In *Questions of Cultural Identity*. (Eds.) S. Hall and P. Du Gay. London: Sage.
Darwin, C. 1985 [1858]. *The Origin of the Species by Means of Natural Selection, or The Preservation of Favoured Races in the Struggle for Life*. Harmondsworth: Penguin Classics.
Eriksen, T. H. 1993. Do Cultural Islands Exist? *Social Anthropology* 1b:1.
Finkielkraut, A. 1987. *La défaite de la pensée*. Paris: Gallimard.
Galtung, J. 1996. Personal communication.
Hannerz, U. 1989. Notes on the Global Ecumene. *Public Culture* 1:2, 66–75.
Howell, S. (Ed.). 1996. *The Anthropology of Moralities*. London: Routledge.
Ingold, T. 1993. The Art of Translation in a Continuous World. In *Beyond Boundaries: Understanding, Translation and Anthropological Discourse*. (Ed.) G. Pálsson. Oxford: Berg.
Klausen, A. M. 1998. Our Creative Diversity: Critical Comments on Some Aspects of the World Report. In *Our Creative Diversity: A Critical Perspective*. Report from the International Conference on Culture and Development, Lillehammer 5–7 September 1997. Oslo: Norwegian National Commission for UNESCO.
Kymlicka, W. 1989. *Liberalism, Community and Culture*. Oxford: Clarendon.
Laclau, E. 1995. Universalism, Particularism and the Question of Identity. In *The Identity in Question*. (Ed.) J. Ratchmann. London: Routledge.
Lévi-Strauss, C. 1955. *Tristes tropiques*. Paris: Plon.
Lévi-Strauss, C. 1961 [1952]. *Race et histoire*. Paris: Denoël.
Lévi-Strauss, C. 1979 [1971]. Race et histoire. In *Claude Lévi-Strauss*. (Eds.) R. Bellour and C. Clément. Paris: Gallimard. (Originally published in *Revue internationale des sciences sociales* 23:4.)
Lévi-Strauss, C. 1983. *Le regard éloigné*. Paris: Plon.
Lévi-Strauss, C. and D. Eribon. 1990. *De près et de loin, suivi d'un entretien inédit 'Deux ans après'*. Paris: Odile Jacob.

Meadows, D. et al. 1974. *The Limits to Growth*. Report for the Club of Rome's Project on the Predicament of Mankind. London: Pan.

SIPRI. 1997. *SIPRI Yearbook 1997: Armaments, Disarmaments and International Security*. Oxford: Oxford University Press.

Taylor, C. et al. 1992. *Multiculturalism and the 'Politics of Recognition'*. (Ed.) A. Gutmann. Princeton, NJ: Princeton University Press.

Todorov, T. 1989. *Nous et les autres. La réflexion française sur la diversité humaine*. Paris: Seuil.

Turton, D. 1997. Introduction: War and Ethnicity. In *War and Ethnicity: Global Connections and Local Violence*. (Ed.) D. Turton. Woodbridge, Suffolk: University of Rochester Press.

World Commission on the Environment. 1987. *Our Common Future*. Oxford: Oxford University Press.

World Commission on Culture and Development. 1995. *Our Creative Diversity*. Paris: UNESCO.

Wilson, R. A. (Ed.). 1997. *Human Rights, Culture and Context: Anthropological Perspectives*. London: Pluto.

Wright, S. 1998. The Politicization of 'Culture'. *Anthropology Today* 14:1, 7–15.

19

Toward a Critical Anthropology of Human Rights

Mark Goodale

Histories

American anthropology and its practitioners have had a long, strange relationship with international human rights theory and practice. Although it must be hard for anthropologists of the most recent generation to imagine, there was a time when the discipline, through its representatives, was considered a source of authoritative and scientific opinion weighty enough that it was asked to issue public statements on matters of great moment. It was natural, then, that the United Nations – through the United Nations Educational, Scientific and Cultural Organization (UNESCO) – would ask a well-known member of the American Anthropological Association (AAA) to submit a statement to assist the UN Commission on Human Rights, which was in 1947 working on a draft version of what would eventually become the 1948 Universal Declaration of Human Rights.[1] By the mid-twentieth century, all three major Western sociocultural anthropological trajectories ("schools" is certainly too strong) – American cultural anthropology, British social anthropology, and French social anthropology – had firmly established themselves, taken together, as the undisputed scientific database of cross-social and cross-cultural research findings, including cultural universals. Thus, apart from the obviously political and philosophical dimensions of the Declaration both as a statement of intent by the international community that genocide would never again be tolerated and as an international ratification of the values of liberalism, its proponents were understandably confident that professional anthropologists would endorse and then publicly substantiate the Declaration's central assertions: that human beings are naturally endowed with certain rights and that these rights are, in fact, universal,

Originally published in *Current Anthropology*, 47: 3 (2006), 485–511.

coextensive with humanness irrespective of the subjectivities embedded in history and culture.[2]

But this confidence would turn out to have been misplaced. After a period of some uncertainty, the executive board of the AAA, under the guiding influence of Melville Herskovits, authorized the publication of a "Statement on Human Rights" in late 1947 and its submission to the UN Commission on Human Rights.[3] The Statement rejected the validity of a universal declaration of human rights on both empirical and ethical grounds. The executive board observed that anthropologists had amply documented a richness of diversity in moral systems and that the cross-cultural data did not support the assertion of a universal set of substantive rights. Thus it agreed that anthropology could provide objective information about the existence or not of universal normative values such as those asserted in the declaration but simply came to the opposite conclusion from the one necessary to legitimate the UN Commission's project.[4] But, as important, it opposed a universal declaration of human rights because of its imperialistic irony. No matter how well-intentioned the Commission's effort, the end result of any internationally sanctioned statement of rights would be the imposition of hegemonic moral values on less powerful groups of people whose patterns of behavior were misunderstood and reviled by Western elites. In other words, a charter that was intended to protect the powerless from the outrages of fascism and totalitarianism in their various forms would have the unintended consequence of compelling individuals and cultures outside the majestic arc of Western liberalism to bring social practices into line with what was hoped would be a set of legal rights backed up by the mechanisms of international law.[5]

Within less than a year of the Statement's publication in the *American Anthropologist*, two critiques by prominent anthropologists appeared in the same journal (Barnett 1948; Steward 1948), followed by one more short comment the following year (Bennett 1949). Tellingly, neither Barnett nor Steward actually discussed the main bases for the executive board's rejection of the legitimacy of what would become the 1948 Universal Declaration of Human Rights – what I have characterized as the empirical and the ethical critiques. Rather, their responses were almost exclusively to what I consider something of a red herring: the Statement's second proposition and related elaborations, in which it is asserted that "respect for differences between cultures is validated by the scientific fact that no technique of qualitatively evaluating cultures has been discovered" (AAA 1947, 542). In other words, (1) anthropologists are scientists, and scientists are epistemologically barred from validating moral propositions such as those contained in the Declaration; (2) therefore, anthropologists must remain forever agnostic as to the scientific truth or falsity of claims regarding universal human rights; and (3), given this, anthropologists cannot, *as anthropologists*, endorse any intellectual or political position that assumes the existence (or nonexistence) of a universal set of rights. I consider this a red herring because it does not go to the merit of the issues that are substantively addressed elsewhere in the Statement and, moreover, transforms what was in fact the promising beginning of a concrete (and critical) anthropological engagement with human rights into yet another intradisciplinary debate – and not a very important or lasting one – over epistemology.

After 1949, the phrase "human rights" did not appear in the title of any article published in the AAA's flagship peer-reviewed journal until 1987, when Wilcomb Washburn of the Smithsonian published a very brief comment on cultural relativism in which he described some of the deliberations of the AAA executive board as it drafted and revised the 1947 statement. The absence of "human rights" from the title of any full article published in *American Anthropologist* until 1988,[6] while not evidence per se, is at least symbolic of the fact that American anthropology had spent the preceding 40 years in exile from the most important debates over human rights theory and practice.

Despite what my research into this period has indicated, however, there are notable counterpositions in the historiography of American anthropology's engagement with and disengagement from human rights. In 2001 Karen Engle, a law professor, published an account of the relationship between human rights and the AAA, a relationship that she characterized as moving from "skepticism to embrace." Although her analysis of recent developments is useful, there are several difficulties with her argument. First, the history of this relationship simply does not support her assertion that anthropologists "have been embarrassed ever since" the publication of the 1947 Statement (2001, 536). As I have shown, there was virtually no formal response by members of the AAA either in support of or in opposition to the Statement after 1947, hardly what one would expect if there had been a general outcry of indignant embarrassment over a document that misrepresented the general will of the Association's members on this issue. Second, as have several others who have described this history, Engle makes the mistake of eliding the years between 1947 and the 1980s and then representing them in terms of the past 15 years. Thus, for example, she writes that "for the past fifty years, the Statement has caused the AAA great shame. Indeed, the term 'embarrassment' is continually used in reference to the Statement" (p. 541). She does not reinforce this claim with any citations that reflect this "continual reference," even if this way of describing the 1947 Statement would become commonplace during the 1990s. In a sense, Engle commits a logical fallacy – *post hoc, ergo propter hoc* – in making this argument: that the sea change during the 1990s among some anthropologists was caused by a buildup of simmering "embarrassment" during the preceding 40 years. And finally, Engle does not mention that the AAA of 1999 was a profoundly different association from the AAA of 1947; in other words, she (mis-)interprets this history by holding the nature of the AAA (its size, stated mission, composition of membership, etc.) constant, much as legal scholars hold the *institutional* nature of the US Supreme Court constant in order to track changes in its jurisprudence.[7]

During the period from 1947 to the mid-1980s, the Universal Declaration of Human Rights served as the foundation for the creation of an entire framework of international and transnational human rights discourse, within which the most important human rights instruments,[8] nongovernmental organizations,[9] and international publications[10] were established, developed, and grew in power and influence. While the withdrawal of American anthropology and anthropologists from human rights debates and practice did not exactly create a vacuum, the development and increasing hegemony of human rights were facilitated by the ongoing participation of an eclectic mix of intellectuals and nonelites dominated by international legal scholars, legal philosophers, political scientists, diplomats, social activists, career bureaucrats and civil servants, politicians, and journalists. Although this article is not the place for a full analysis of the impact of this discursive history on current human rights theory and practice and its implications for current anthropology, it is enough at this point to observe that current human rights discourse bears the traces of its genealogy's first 40 years.

Beginning in the 1980s, however, the formal relationship between American anthropology and human rights changed, and the period from about 1987[11] to the present marks the current and third distinct era in this uneasy engagement.[12] Apart from the resurrection of the earlier debates over universalism and cultural relativism, as a matter of *practice* the discipline of anthropology underwent a much more profound realignment in its orientation toward human rights. Partly on the basis of the work of the earlier cultural survival anthropologists and those involved in the emerging indigenous rights movements, the AAA began to consider ways in which it could employ anthropological knowledge to advocate for indigenous peoples who were either direct targets or indirect victims of state and multinational corporate abuses.[13] This intent was signaled by the appointment by the AAA of a special investigating commission in 1990, chaired by Terence Turner, to investigate the aggressive encroachments by the Brazilian state on traditional Yanomami territory.[14] The creation of this commission and its subsequent report (1991), which, according to the Committee for Human Rights (2001), "appears to have played a role in stopping the appropriation of all but small, isolated reserves in the Yanomami area and precipitating Brazilian agreement to a very large, contiguous Yanomami homeland," led institutionally to the establishment by the AAA executive board of a Commission for Human Rights, which was directed "to develop a human rights conceptual framework and identify relevant human rights issues, to develop human rights education and networking, and to develop and implement mechanisms for organizational action on issues affecting the AAA, its members, and the discipline."[15]

During this time period (1992–4), one of the founding members of what would become the Committee for Human Rights (the permanent standing committee created from the Commission), Ellen Messer, published in the *Annual Review of Anthropology* something of a manifesto for this latest phase in anthropology's engagement with human rights (Messer 1993). In it she made the somewhat curious argument that even though anthropologists had been largely absent from most of the political and intellectual development of human rights, this absence had actually "contributed to the expansion of the human rights concept" (1993, 222). Even though, as she admitted, a search of "computerized databases and major human rights journals such as *Human Rights Quarterly*... uncover[s] few articles by anthropologists" (pp. 223–4), the "editors and authors of some collections on human rights in cross-cultural perspective that appeared over the past decade... are predominantly political theorists, legal scholars, and philosophers" (p. 224), and "these nonanthropological disciplines also appear to dominate the ongoing UN process of defining, advocating, and advocating human rights" (p. 224), anthropology's marginalization from the core of human rights theorizing and practice had allowed it during the 1980s to research and advocate for what were either ignored issues within long-standing human rights doctrine (e.g., linguistic or ethnic rights) or issues that had not yet been accepted as human rights issues per se (e.g., cultural rights or rights of indigenous peoples).

What made Messer's article historically significant was exactly what transformed it into a call to action. In attempting to "counter" the "conventional wisdom" that anthropological knowledge and praxis had been insignificant in the development of human rights, she compressed the history of this relationship so that what I have called the second period (1950–87) was subtly elided, with the result that the events immediately prior to and including what I have described as the third and current phase (1987-present) came to represent the history of the relationship between anthropology and human rights itself. In doing this, Messer was both right and wrong. She was wrong to the extent that she created the impression that anthropological research or theorizing had had any noticeable impact on the development of international human rights theory and practice between 1950 and the early to mid-1980s; she was absolutely right that anthropology had had the impact she described – participation in the development of new categories of collective rights and the pursuit of new epistemologies that fused anthropological knowledge with human rights activism.[16]

The programmatic nature of Messer's article received ratification by the AAA itself in 1999, when a new "Declaration on Anthropology and Human Rights" was formally adopted by the general AAA membership. This Declaration was the culmination of a process that began in the mid-1980s and, in the event, marked the definitive repudiation of the 1947 Statement.[17] The Declaration is a relatively short and ambiguously worded document, but its central point is that the AAA now affirms that the weight of anthropological knowledge demonstrates that "people and groups have a generic right to realize their capacity for culture" (Committee for Human Rights 1999). Far from rejecting the validity of international human rights instruments such as the Universal Declaration of Human Rights, the AAA's declaration emphatically subsumes the putative human right to realize a capacity for culture within a set of as-yet-to-be-articulated human rights that go beyond those currently recognized in international law. As the Declaration states, this new position "reflects a commitment to human rights consistent with international principles but not limited by them." I will discuss the Declaration's allusion to the capabilities "solution" to the rights "problem" in greater detail below, but it is enough here to reiterate that practical and ethical commitments on the part of a group of anthropologists led not only to a reversal by the AAA of its earlier position on human rights but to something much more: the emergence of the AAA as a major human rights advocacy NGO in certain world regions focused on leading-edge issues in human rights practice.

Finally, in 2000 the Committee for Human Rights augmented its original set of guidelines and objectives, and this list remains the current (as of 2005) set of operating principles for the Committee: (1) promote and protect human rights; (2) expand the definition of human rights within an anthropological perspective; (3) work internally with the membership of the AAA to educate anthropologists and to mobilize their support for human rights; (4) work externally with foreign colleagues, the people and groups with whom anthropologists work, and other human rights organizations to develop an anthropological perspective on human rights and consult with them on human rights violations and the appropriate actions to be taken; (5) influence and educate the media, policy makers, NGOs, and decision makers in the private sector; and (6) encourage research on all aspects of human rights from the conceptual to the applied (Committee for Human Rights 2001).

If we divide what I have called the third phase (1987–present) into two subperiods, 1987–93 (from the late 1980s to Messer's review article) and 1994–present, it is clear that Messer's argument for the discipline's influence on human rights, which was, even in 1993, still incipient, has been strengthened over the past 15 years, partly through the direct involvement of the Committee on Human Rights[18] but also through the collective work of a small but growing group of anthropologists who have begun to study human rights as cultural practice. Nevertheless, with respect to the development of human rights theory – the expansion and deepening of what Michael Perry (1998) calls the "idea of human rights" – anthropology's contributions remain marginal at best. In other words, despite the fact that the 1992 AAA Commission of Human Rights was directed "to develop a human rights conceptual framework and identify human rights issues" and the Commission's successor is under an ongoing mandate to "expand the definition of human rights within an anthropological perspective," even a generous evaluation of the vigorous conceptual and analytical debates over the content and meaning of human rights reveals that the AAA's goals for these areas remain as yet unrealized.

As with the use of American anthropology to symbolize the anthropological engagement with human rights more generally, this is a debatable point, but a consideration of a cross section of major works in human rights theory during the past decade shows how little the definition of human rights has been expanded "within an anthropological perspective." A list of these works would include the various writings from the "capabilities" perspective (e.g., Nussbaum 2000 [law/ philosophy]; Sen 2000 [development economics]; Ignatieff 2001 [history/journalism]; Perry 1998 [legal philosophy]; and Shute and Hurley 1993 [law and philosophy]). Even more revealing, anthropologists have been absent from many of the major works in "culture and human rights" or "human rights in cross-cultural perspective," including Bell, Nathan, and Peleg (2001 [no anthropologists among 14 contributors]) and An-Na'im (1992 [2 anthropologists among 15 contributors]).[19] Other anecdotal evidence of a relative anthropological silence in the development of human rights theory includes the fact that only 2 of the 31 fellows of Harvard's Carr Center for Human Rights, a major human rights think tank, have been anthropologists; the fellowships, predictably, have overwhelmingly gone to lawyers, philosophers, historians, and political scientists. And finally, it can hardly be gainsaid that anthropology has contributed little to the much broader and older debates about rights in general – *human* rights being a category of the general – in moral philosophy and political theory. If Dworkin (1977) urged us to take rights seriously, the same cannot be said of anthropology as a source of moral or ethical theory, which is, I would argue, ironic given that anthropology remains the academic discipline best suited to understanding the human experience in its fullest terms.

In light of the above, this article is necessarily a sally from the theoretical margins of human rights debates. But in order to develop what I understand to be a critical anthropology of human rights, I will suggest several ways in which the conceptual framework of human rights can be expanded so as not merely to take account of but rather to *rely on* the peculiar anthropological blend of cultural critique, ethnography and other hybrid methodologies, and disciplinary commitment to intersubjectivity.

In this sense, the arguments in this article are meant to point to an anthropological third way in relation to human rights. Since at least Messer's 1993 article, anthropologists on both sides of the Atlantic (if not elsewhere) have sought to clear new ground on which anthropological knowledge could contribute to expanded articulations of human rights. The first move is perhaps best represented by Terence Turner's argument (1997) that anthropologists have an obligation to use their knowledge of cultural difference and richness to help form the foundation for an "emancipatory cultural politics," and his own inspired and pathbreaking writings and activities on behalf of the Kayapo are a clear expression of how an anthropologist can link anthropological knowledge with a rights-based framework within which indigenous people can advance claims.[20] The second move was to transform the social practice of human rights into an object of anthropological inquiry. An important recent example of this approach is Sally Merry's (2006) book on the regulation of violence against women through human rights, in which she employs a transnational and mobile ethnography in order to track the production and localization of human rights discourse in China, Fiji, Hong Kong, India, Switzerland, and the United States. My call for a critical anthropology of human rights is intended to complement these efforts. Although I argue for a type of anthropological engagement that is quite distinct from both the cultural/political and the ethnographic/descriptive and although the goals of the alternative orientation I develop are also directed outside of anthropology itself, my efforts here are part of a broader intellectual history, one which makes a new formulation possible and (ideally) credible.

To say this is also to ground the remaining sections in the foregoing reinterpretation of this intellectual history. In other words, any arguments I develop must be context-ualized both in relation to the particular history I describe above and in relation to broader human rights currents outside of anthropology toward which my argument for a critical anthropology of human rights is ultimately directed. A recast historiography of American anthropology's relationship with human rights is, therefore, both a necessary starting point and an epistemological resource for what follows.

Before moving to a discussion of my proposals for a critical anthropology of human rights, however, it may be useful to make explicit the way I have been employing "human rights" throughout this article. By "human rights" I do not mean exclusively a body of positive international law that forms the "starting point for a process ... intended to render certain kinds of argument successful before judges in international courts," as one reader defined "human rights" in a review of an earlier draft of this article. This is an entirely reasonable way of understanding "human rights," one that limits the usage to the narrow confines of positive law as *informed by* an analysis of this law's ability to demonstrate that (again in this reader's words) it has "acquired teeth." This way of defining and studying human rights is best left to international lawyers and others for whom the analysis of processes of justiciability is within their competence. I use "human rights" much more broadly: the phrase captures the constellation of philosophical, practical, and phenomenological dimensions through which universal rights, rights believed to be entailed by a common human nature, are enacted, debated, practiced, violated, envisioned, and experienced. When I describe "human rights discourse" I am refer-ring to the coteries of concepts, practices, and experiences through which human rights have meaning at different levels, levels which are prior to and go beyond the merely instrumental or legal, important as these levels are. My understanding of human rights is not quite as broad as Upendra Baxi's ("protean forms of social action assembled, by convention, under a portal named 'human rights'" [2002, v]), but conceiving of human rights as discourse does, obviously, broaden the referent beyond any one of its most consequential parts (e.g., international human rights law).[21]

Proposals

To begin with, what do I mean by a "critical" anthropology? It is critical in two senses, the first mundane but essential, the second more complicated and not as self-evidently necessary for reconfiguring our understanding of human rights. First, by calling it "critical" I do not mean simply to distinguish this application of anthro-pology from those that might be seen as either dogmatic or naïve, but there is an important kernel of truth in this. In other words, I do not intend this approach to signal the strategic adoption of what Andrew Collier, in discussing the "critical realism" of Roy Bhaskar, calls "a term of approval in philosophical contexts" (Collier 1994, xi), but a critical anthropology is indeed one that self-consciously creates space between itself and ideas and practices that have become coextensive with or, in fact, constitute the experience of everyday life. An anthropology that is critical in this sense is especially salient in relation to human rights, which has become, I would argue, the most (necessarily) axiomatic of (neo-)liberalism's global discourses. A critical anthropology represents a mode, a tone, an ongoing orientation which is not intended to supplant other possibilities – an intention that led to the hubristic errors made by some of the pioneering anthropological reformers in the 1980s – but is reserved, rather, for ideas that have become ideology and social practices that have come to form part of the collective habitus.

There is a second sense in which an anthropology can be critical. This is a purposive criticality whose task is to effect what Gunzelin Schmid Noerr (2002, 230), in his discussion of Horkheimer and Adorno's (2001[1944]) *Dialectic of Enlightenment*, calls a "change in function": the identification, contextualization, and, most important, practical employment of (in this case) normative principles in order to explain their "failure to be realized in existing society." For critical theorists, of course, this is the criticality that tends toward an enlightenment of the Enlightenment – the recovery of the originally progressive nature of eighteenth-century reason, which had regressed into self-destruction during the intervening years and is (apropos of human rights discourse) the "fate which has always been reserved for triumphant thought. If it voluntarily leaves behind its critical element to become a mere means in the service of an existing order, it involuntarily tends to transform the positive cause it has espoused into something negative and destructive" (Horkheimer and Adorno 2001[1944], xv). A critical anthropology of human rights, then, is one that seeks to uncover the latent progressive potential underlying their core principles, which have become repressed as human rights discourse has become reified so that all that remains is an impenetrable granite surface that blocks from view all of the "mediated conceptual moments" that actually constitute human rights.

A critical anthropology of human rights is necessarily progressive in that it assumes that (1) there is a set of potentially emancipatory principles underlying human rights discourse that (2) have become co-opted by institutional structures of power so that human rights, ironically, tend toward what a recent volume describes as "moral imperialism" (Hernández-Truyol 2002) and that (3) formal reflection on this process of co-optation and regression in some form is required before the potentials embedded in human rights theory and practice can be "realized in existing society." And a critical anthropology of human rights is progressive in another sense: its purpose is to point to the possibility of a middle space between the reified normativity of a regressive human rights and the chaos of contemporary human rights praxis, where, as with the essence of the Enlightenment itself, according to Horkheimer and Adorno, there is now a false "choice between alternatives, and the inescapability of this choice is that of power" (2001[1944], 25). In other words, a critical anthropology of human rights can explain in context why the current international and transnational human rights regimes have failed to fulfill their promise and, if anything, have been pushed into the spiral of regression described above.

Anthropologists of human rights working in this mode will use the various techniques available to them to bracket human rights – to convert into the first object of critique the processes by which the origins, development, and transnationalizion of human rights discourse are eclipsed during the discourse's passage into hypernormativity. What I propose here is not the use of anthropological methodologies to facilitate the introduction (or consolidation) of human rights discourse as it now exists (as Messer [1993], Nagengast [1997], Turner [1997], Sponsel [1995], and others argue); rather, a critical anthropology of human rights assumes that reified, hypernormative human rights cannot serve as the basis for realizing their aim, the creation of just communities committed to the full realization of both individuals and collectivities. To a certain extent, this application of a critical anthropology to human rights parallels the "diatopical hermeneutics" of Raimon Panikkar (1996 [1982]) and Boaventura de Sousa Santos (1995). As Panikkar argues, "critique does not invalidate the Declaration of Human Rights, but offers new perspectives for an internal criticism that sets limits of validity for human rights, offering...possibilities for enlarging [their] realm" (1996[1982], 92).[22]

But the real contribution of a critical anthropology for human rights theory and practice is that it proposes an alternative to the false choices described above. The pursuit of this middle space means that the alternative paradigm for human rights I am suggesting can never be *merely* either normative or descriptive but is based on what anthropologists can say comparatively: that social actors across the range of history and place seek to create meaning in their relations with others, with greater or lesser degrees of success (depending on an array of contingencies), by striving toward a *normative humanism*.[23] "Normative humanism," a central finding of legal anthropological research in particular, constitutes a central analytical framework for a critical anthropology of human rights. Normative humanism is a way of describing a basic cross-cultural fact of collective ordering: that given the right circumstances, people will organize themselves so as to establish conditions for meaningful interactions that are both patterned and prescriptive and that recognize and formally incorporate a basic set of human-centered values, values that balance the whole breadth of local cultural and social possibilities with common cognitive, physical, and emotional imperatives. A reconstituted human rights, to be effective and legitimate, would be dependent on the *capacity* of collectivities to organize themselves on these terms.

By "capacity of collectivities to organize themselves on these terms" I mean something quite different from what is meant by those who have developed the "capabilities" alternative (or, perhaps, supplement) to international human rights, most notably Amartya Sen and Martha Nussbaum. Nussbaum is not prepared to reject the idea or practice of human rights; instead, she articulates a theory of capabilities that leaves human rights where they are: as a set of international standards that at worst do no harm and at best play "an instrumental role in preventing material disaster (in particular famine)" (Nussbaum 2000, 96, referring in part to Sen 1981). She also argues that there is still a place for the *language* of rights because it (1) imbues human capabilities with normativity, (2) underscores the importance of human capabilities, (3) emphasizes that people can choose to realize their capabilities or not, and, less plausibly, (4) "preserves a sense of the terrain of agreement, while we continue to deliberate about the proper type of analysis at the more specific level" (Nussbaum 2000, 100–1).

While the central human capabilities that Nussbaum lists (2000, 78–80) may very well overlap with some of the basic human-centered values that form part of the patterned and prescriptive orderings I describe, I think it is premature to enumerate them in the way Nussbaum does. Indeed, values differ from capabilities in that they represent a second-order cultural reflection on cognitive, physical, and emotional imperatives that are actually closer to what Nussbaum means by "capabilities" even though her list contains capabilities that go beyond them (e.g., "affiliation" and "control over one's environment"). Nevertheless, the approach I develop here assumes that what is most important is not basic human functioning – important though this is – but the fact that, in the absence of constraints, collectivities will create normative systems that are based on the recognition of a set of human-centered values.

There are several dimensions to normative humanism that need underscoring. First, normative humanism does not anticipate particular results (i.e., specific types of legal, moral, or other normative orderings) except within a broad range informed by collective anthropological and other analytical experience and a general sense of the limits imposed by common cognitive, physical, and emotional imperatives. In other words, normative humanism assumes that specific "rights" or "obligations" or "duties" or "laws" cannot be predicted in advance; indeed, it can say relatively little about even the likelihood or desirability of the adoption of certain categories – rights versus duties or some combination of these or others altogether – at particular places and points in time. It is clear from this that the fact of normative humanism means a rejection of immanent or metaphysical versions of universal human rights, but this does not mean that international human rights might not be adopted as a normative system at certain places and times. Human rights *can* legitimately function as a local normative framework, but their legitimacy will be derived not from their universality – as is assumed by all of the major foundational instruments of international human rights – but from the conditions through which they emerge or are incorporated.

Second, normative humanism does not imply a radical pluralism or relativism, because the range of possible rights or duties, for example, is constrained by cognitive, physical, and emotional requirements. This is the reason normative systems – again, those able to develop without consequential constraints – are roughly patterned. Third, normative humanism does not say anything about the scale at which collectivities will organize themselves in this way or the likelihood that normative orderings will endure; in other words, it is not a theory of culture per se. Fourth, normative humanism is grounded in the assumption that human interests and desires, articulated individually but necessarily within collectivities of equally construed individuals, can be fully realized only when the socially constituted orderings that place limits on individuals are inherently dynamic, historically rich, and capable of change. Again, to this extent universal human rights in their current hegemonic forms, as both idea and practice, cannot serve as a framework in which social actors will thrive irrespective of the actions of nation-states or institutions.[24]

Fifth, normative humanism, although primarily a description of actual social practices, is also essentially progressive in that it assumes that collectivities will, in fact, create patterned humanistic orderings unless constrained from doing so. And although history, reevaluated in these terms, reads like one long catalogue of insidious constraints – military, ideological, political – on the capacity of individuals in collectivities to realize themselves through the production of ideal normative systems, when the capacity is present the necessary – though not sufficient – conditions exist for human emancipation and some approximation of social justice; indeed, the emergence of normative humanism in practice can be seen *as* emancipation. This way of describing collective ordering is admittedly optimistic. It assumes that unconstrained normative systems will reflect a balance between the individual and the collective,[25] a balance that nevertheless can have meaning only in light of local historical and cultural imperatives.[26] "Power" is thus reconceptualized to mean – in relation to normativity – the presence of constraints which prevent the striking of this balance. The ever-presence of power in these terms is evidence that normative humanism, as an ideal process of collective social ordering, is not dominant or inevitable and must struggle against other normative possibilities which lack legitimacy as I have defined it here.

Finally, despite the fact that it also functions as an alternative analytical framework to, for example, human rights, normative humanism is above all a theory of social praxis. Moreover, it very explicitly collapses the etic into the emic, not vice versa. In other words, it assumes that ordinary social actors will themselves, given the capacity to do so, construct the normative frameworks that establish the conditions for meaningful interactions, with the result that anthropological knowledge about these local processes consists partly in simply rendering these preexisting frameworks. By describing normative humanism in these terms I necessarily locate it within a much broader and older social theoretical tradition that similarly explored empirical frameworks within which moral or ethical systems could be studied and understood. The most obvious example of this earlier foundational work is Durkheim's *Ethics and the Sociology of Morals* (1993), in which he sought a break from the twin intellectual constraints of Kantian and utilitarian approaches to ethics. Like Durkheim's discussion of comparative ethics, my description of normative humanism assumes that the search for or assertion of a single dominant ethical principle is counterproductive and, even more, unnecessary for a particular normativity – for example, human rights – to achieve its purposes (freedom, emancipation, justice, etc.). Moreover, along with recent neo-Durkheimian attempts to break out of stifling and ultimately counterproductive dichotomies (e.g., Douglas and Ney 1998), normative humanism represents a way of describing certain important facts of ethical practice that avoids the two most common theoretical errors in contemporary human rights: rational individualism on the one side, and a narrow culturalism on the other.[27]

Although this is not the place for a full discussion of this, it can be said preliminarily that a reconceptualization of human rights in these terms has certain implications for political and social practice. First, human rights are preserved as a potential framework for facilitating meaningful interactions only if their legitimacy does not depend, as it does now, on their formal transcendence (i.e., their immanent universalism)[28] and their Roman ahistoricity. Rather, nation-states or institutions interested in intervening in or, at a larger scale, directing the process by which collectivities create humanistic orderings should characterize any resulting set of entitlements or duties or normative *suggestions* as ultimately provisional even if certain basic values (such as the value of life), as interpreted in "local"[29] cultural and historical terms, will almost always merit a central position among them. Second, this alternative framework for normative systems such as human rights inverts the direction from which legitimacy flows. Normative humanism's rejection of the possibility of immanent universalism entails a rejection of doctrines of political practice that repose the ultimate authority for legitimately restraining individuals or otherwise imposing restraints in an overarching sovereign. In other words, even though ideal collective orderings, given the right conditions, will achieve some measure of local predictability (social objectivity), a normative system's legitimacy is never detached from the ongoing set of cultural and historical processes that constitute it. The implication is that a sovereign, of whatever kind, can act only as a kind of facilitator by taking steps to create the conditions for the emergence of normative humanism in social practice.

Finally, the establishment of conditions for meaningful interactions, the ways in which resulting orderings change and are reconfigured, and what can be understood as "local jurisprudence" – the contextualized rationales for the emergence of certain patterned and prescriptive frameworks – all require formal understanding, and this means the study of social practice. Anthropologists can play a fundamental role in the production of knowledge about these processes, although a thoroughly intersubjective anthropology will require them to collaborate with activists, local intellectuals, and the whole range of social actors who strive to enact normative humanism. To this extent, it is more accurate to say that the kind of study of social practices that I am referring to should be *anthropological* without having to make claims about disciplinary authority (on this point, see Ferguson 1999). Besides the broader epistemological dimensions of a critical anthropology of human rights that I have already developed at some length, there are three more that must be examined in greater detail: cultural critique, ethnography (and other hybrid methodologies), and intersubjectivity.

Cultural critique

Like most productive anthropology over the past 20 years, a critical anthropology of human rights is also anthropology as cultural critique in the traditional sense (Marcus and Fischer 1986), but there are two other more specific ways in which cultural critique is essential for those studying human rights and other normative orders. First, there is a need for a critical anthropology of human rights to partici-pate in a cultural critique *of* human rights as both an international regime of legal and quasi-legal doctrine and institutional practice and a hegemonic transnational discourse, the latter being what I have described elsewhere (Goodale 2005) as an expression of the only global superliberalism. In other words, to the extent that "human rights" does not characterize the result of the localized processes I describe above but rather refers to the presence of a hegemonic normative system based on a theory of immanent universalism, a cultural critique becomes instrumental in the sense that it seeks to contrast the disciplinary tendencies that animate international human rights with the social praxis I have described as normative humanism.

But there is a second way in which cultural critique is relevant, and we can call this human rights *as* cultural critique. When collectivities organize themselves so as to create the conditions for meaningful interactions in such a way that "human rights" characterizes the prescriptions that are anchored in a basic set of human-centered values, human rights in this sense both resist attempts to constrain the capacity to alter these conditions and serve as a ongoing critique of alternatives, especially those in the service of the various transnational imperialisms.

Ethnography (and other hybrid methodologies)

In order to be effective as cultural interpreters,[30] anthropologists, alone among the scholars who study human rights as idea and social practice, can employ an ever-shifting repertoire of methods that includes focused observation, long-term interviewing, archival research (both historical and ethnohistorical), oral history, discourse analysis, film and multimedia, network analysis, cyberresearch, institu-tional ethnography, mobile ethnography, and contextualized combinations of these, as well as other techniques and strategies for collaborating in the production of cultural knowledge and knowledge about culture.

But apart from the ability to employ and adapt a wide range of methods, critical anthropologists of human rights benefit from something even more fundamental: a reliance on hybrid methodologies. If methodologies are the systems of explanation that justify the use of certain research methods and not others, then hybrid method-ologies are those that consciously blur the boundaries between otherwise discrete systems on the assumption that the practice of everyday life – if not its ideational representations – cannot realistically be objectified in the ways that rigid theories of method require. Methodological hybridity in this sense is especially important for the kind of anthropology of human rights I envision because it mirrors the social practices I have described as normative humanism in the way that local culture and history are mediated by a set of common imperatives.

To complete this discussion of the different dimensions of a critical anthropology of human rights, it is necessary to pursue the question of methodology somewhat further and reflect on the problem of knowledge as it relates to the study of human rights, because the relationship between anthropology and its purposes is also a question of epistemology.

Intersubjectivity

In my brief history of the relationship between American anthropology and human rights I indicated that the first stirrings of what would eventually become a profound shift in this relationship could be seen in the early to mid-1980s. This movement accelerated with the establishment of a distinct section concerned with human rights in the AAA and was reflected in Messer's 1993 programmatic review article. The reconstitution of anthropology's formal orientation toward human rights was most clearly (perhaps symbolically) marked by the adoption by the AAA of the 1999 Declaration on Anthropology and Human Rights. There is an important dimension to this shift that I have not examined until now but that bears directly on this recent history and on a future critical anthropology of human rights. At the same time that anthropology as a discipline was reorienting itself in relation to human rights, anthropologists were beginning to conduct research and theorize in ways that reflected new positions on the potential for anthropological knowledge. During this period (i.e., from the 1980s on) anthropologists explored the epistemological possibilities of intersubjectivity, which, though it carried somewhat different meanings in linguistics and discourse analysis, was taken to mean that the anthro-pologist-as-subject no longer carried out research *on* objects of knowledge – as the traditional scientific method assumed – but rather participated in a collaborative process in which anthropologists served as (perhaps, at times, more skilled) co-subjects *with* the social actors with whom they interacted. As is well known, the emergence of intersubjectivity as a replacement paradigm of anthropological knowledge led to parallel movements that, among other things, critiqued the subject–object conventions of traditional ethnographic writing (e.g., the absence of the anthropologist from the narrative, the abuse of the ethnographic present, and so on) and, more important for my purposes here, decentered the anthropologist from a position of intellectual and scientific privilege.

A recognition of intersubjectivity carries several implications for a critical anthro-pology of human rights. First, it avoids the problem of agnosticism first raised in the 1947 Statement: that because no techniques existed for scientifically evaluating the content or meaning of normative systems like human rights, no anthropological knowledge about them was possible. The result, as we have seen, was first a long period of anthropological absence, then a period of reengagement marked by political and social activism by individual anthropologists and eventually its largest professional association,[31] and, finally, during the past five to ten years, a reconceptualization of human rights as a cultural *process* and the beginning of research on this basis.[32] Yet intersubjectivity introduces a qualitatively different set of possibilities. Because it represents a theory of knowledge that imparts truth value to the social process of knowledge production itself (which includes the anthropologist) rather than to what results – what is understood as an "object" in a different framework – anthropologists are able to study the constitution of normativity holistically without needing to distinguish artificially between "structure" and "agency" or the "culture of human rights" and human rights themselves. This means, among other things, that the *idea* of human rights is now a central topic for anthropological inquiry (see Goodale 2006).

Second, intersubjectivity, as I understand it here, has the potential to mediate between political action and knowledge (both self- and social). This explains in part the mechanism that transforms human rights into cultural critique when human rights emerge in the absence of constraints. Anthropologists have a role to play here, again, as perhaps more skilled co-subjects or at least as professionally interested collaborators. When human rights form the basis for resistance to attempts to alter the conditions necessary for meaningful interactions, then knowledge overlaps with political action, and when human rights in practice serve as the basis for critical reflection on social conditions, then political (or legal) action actually *constitutes* knowledge.

Finally, the position on knowledge I develop here is important for a critical anthropology of human rights because it lays a theoretical foundation – for those who feel one is needed – for anthropology's formal engagement on behalf of or in collaboration with individuals and collectivities who are unable to resist. In other words, new possibilities for activism are created when anthropology moves away from a high scientific epistemology, a reliance on which framed the discipline's orientation to the practice of human rights until recently. In this sense, it is possible to view the ambivalence that all but a small group of anthropologists felt toward human rights activism not as a question of motivation (or a lack thereof) but as a problem of epistemological validity. To this extent, my appeal to intersubjectivity parallels some of the developments in action or engaged anthropology (or what Roy Rappaport [1993] calls "the anthropology of trouble" and Nancy Scheper-Hughes [1995] styles, with Guevaran relish, "militant anthropology"), though it rests on different, and, I would argue, more sustainable grounds.[33]

Loomings

There is a final dimension to human rights that I wish to examine, one that anthropology is also well placed to address. This combines a focus on what can be understood as the political economy of human rights discourse with its instrumental disciplinarity. Although the recent anthropological engagement with human rights has been limited to topics or questions considered more properly "anthropological" – the implications for culture of human rights and vice versa, human rights as a framework for cultural survival, the ethnography of human rights as social practice, the ethnography of human rights as political strategy – I would argue that, as with the type of inquiry into the practical philosophy of human rights I have outlined above, a critical anthropology of human rights should be broadened to include topics and questions that encompass the instrumental and ideological aspects that make human rights one of the most consequential of transnational regimes.

A political economy of human rights discourse is one that studies the ways in which human rights ideas and practices – which are rendered discursively inseparable in specific social contexts – have become preeminently constitutive, so that collective identity, social meanings, and personhood cannot be understood in other terms even when – perhaps *especially* when – moves are made to suggest alternatives. In their book on "writing science," Halliday and Martin (1993) employ a political economy of discourse to reveal the constitutive processes behind contemporary science education. By adapting their framework, it is possible to show how the assumptions embedded in human rights discourse are "chained together into sequences of...relations and consequences" and to recognize that "the work of [human rights] is necessarily grammatical: naming, constructing and positioning the [normative], and doing so in a way which builds social relationships of power and knowledge" (Halliday and Martin 1993, xii). In order to critically frame the processes through which human rights discourse "builds social relationships of knowledge and power" – rather than, as international human rights doctrine presupposes, *discovers* them within the natural order of things – anthropologists must consider which interests (political, economic, military) are served through the apotheosis of human rights and how a supposedly universal set of rights (and perhaps corresponding duties) derived from our supposedly universal humanness is transformed into what Laura Nader would call a "controlling process" (1997).

Understood in this way, a political economy of human rights discourse must be distinguished from several related frameworks. When Noam Chomsky and Edward S. Herman adopted a "political economy of human rights" (1979a, 1979b) as a general approach to their critique of the "Washington Connection and Third World fascism" and the print media's culpability in the mischaracterization of postwar Indochina, they meant that "justice" was an ideological mask behind which the United States exercised its often brutal policies designed to expand and protect foreign markets for private corporate interests. A political economy of human rights discourse is also not the same as an analysis of the "politics of human rights" (e.g., Evans 2001; Obrad 2002). Evans, for example, is an advocate for a strong international human rights regime and argues that the politics of globalization are a barrier to the enforceability of human rights laws because states place the highest value on open markets and international trade, even if individual rights are violated as a result.[36] Finally, there is Ignatieff's (2001) extended essay exploring the problem of human rights *as* politics, by which he means something close to Chomsky and Herman's "political economy of human rights" but much less conspiratorial. He refers to a set of failures by the United States to pursue a human rights agenda consistently, failures which result more from the vicissitudes of realpolitik than from any conscious effort to use human rights as an excuse for economic expansion or to facilitate what Chomsky and Herman call the "reconstruction of imperial ideology" (1979b).

Yet each of these important analytical approaches begins and ends at the level of structure or focuses on the broadest frame within which human rights ideas and practices are merely *impacted* – to greater or lesser degrees of both consequence and intentionality – by political-economic forces. The kind of political economy of human rights *discourse* that I have in mind is one that requires anthropologists to trace the connections between political-economic structures and the disciplinary processes that both constitute liberal citizens (and the notion of citizenship itself) and reinforce those structures. This strategy for research and analysis assumes that the rights-bearing liberal citizen is a social and historical category rather than primarily a type of social actor associated with certain political and economic developments, and this category is marked by the extent to which it is self-constituting. In other words, if the emergence of the liberal citizen is a necessary precondition for the rise, expansion, and eventual consolidation of a transnational capitalist mode of production, then a pressing area for anthropological inquiry is the way in which human (and other) rights discourses produce the thing they assume – a citizen endowed with irrevocable rights that are entailed by a universal humanness. A critical anthropology of human rights engages, therefore, in the wider debates over the relationship between human rights and the imperatives of hegemonic political-economic structures but adds a dimension that has been missing: the specific ways in which human rights discourse attracts social actors and compels them to employ their capabilities in the service of transnational capitalist networks outside of the classic "institutional architectures" that typically frame the sites that have received most of our recent attention – the prison, the hospital, the university, and so on.

Finally, what makes a political economy of human rights discourse so urgent is the same thing that lends immediacy to a critical anthropology of human rights more generally. As my recent research in Romania and Bolivia demonstrates, international human rights have become the vanguard in the global consolidation and naturalization of (neo-)liberalism, a process that most now agree has quickened because of the demise of credible alternatives. There is, therefore, a current need for an anthropological critique in the sense I have developed above. But there is also a need to pursue the possibility of a reconstituted human rights, one that does not serve as an ideological barrier to emancipation in practice but rather resists the tendency toward moral imperialism associated with immanent universalist normative theories, is able to "center" (actually "recenter") "personhood in international narrative" (Hernández-Truyol 2002), and, perhaps most important, creates a permanent framework for the realization of human capabilities.

NOTES

1   For an account of the drafting of the Declaration, see Morsink (1999); see also Roosevelt (1948).

2   Despite the antiuniversalist tendency that characterized American anthropology up through the 1930s, by mid-century a new emphasis had emerged that sought to refocus research around more generalizable or scientific purposes. The problem of cultural universals, which the early Boasians had rejected as crypto-evolutionist, was invested with greater importance. This tendency culminated in the Human Relations Area Files and the eventual rise of the neo-evolutionist schools of cultural ecology and materialism. In Europe this period (1945–55) overlapped with the growing influence of the superuniversalism of French structural anthropology (Lévi-Strauss 1949) and the continuing emphasis in British social anthropology on pursuing a "science of mankind," that is, applying scientific epistemologies to the study of human societies.

3   The full text of the Statement was printed in the *American Anthropologist* (AAA 1947). There is still some mystery surrounding the exact sequence of events of 1946 and 1947 that culminated in the AAA Statement. Following the lead of the late Wilcomb Washburn, who published the results of some of his research in 1987, I am conducting research in the AAA archives, which are housed within the National Anthropological Archives at the Smithsonian Institution's museum support center in Suitland, Maryland. Although this work is ongoing and is being used for a book-length manuscript, there have already been

some important findings. I have studied most of the presidential and executive board correspondence and the minutes of the executive board meetings for 1946, 1947, and 1948. I have not found any official correspondence between the president or the executive board and either UNESCO or the UN Commission for Human Rights or any correspondence by other parties that refers to an official request by the UN to the AAA to draft a Statement on human rights. What can be documented, however, is the following: (1) In 1945 Melville Herskovits was named chairman of the Committee on International Cooperation in Anthropology of the National Research Council, a committee made up of AAA members that acted as the Association's de facto committee for international outreach and engagement, particularly with international institutions like the UN. (2) On June 12, 1947, Herskovits sent a draft copy of the Statement, written by him without any collaboration, to the president of the AAA (Clyde Kluckhohn) with a note reading, "Here is the draft of the Statement I sent to the UNESCO Committee, revised in accordance with the idea that it would be forwarded to the Commission on Human Rights of the United Nations, from the Association." (3) In the late summer and early fall of 1947 Kluckhohn corresponded regularly with J. Alden Mason, the editor of the *American Anthropologist*, in order to ensure that the final Statement, which had been only slightly and nonsubstantively revised (by Herskovits himself), would be published as soon as possible. (4) In October 1947 Ralph Beals and Kluckhohn took steps to stop the production of Volume 49, Number 4, because Mason had mistakenly placed the Statement in the journal's "Brief Communications" section, whereas the executive board wanted it to appear as the number's lead article (which it eventually did). (5) The Statement was published at the end of 1947 without, as far as I could discover, a formal resolution (or ratification) from the AAA executive board at its 1947 meetings. Thus it appears that UNESCO approached the National Research Council and not the AAA for the "official" American anthropological view on human rights, even though Herskovits's NRC committee eventually acted for and through the AAA. It is to this extent only that it is correct to say that the UN "asked" the AAA to comment on a declaration of human rights.

4   As the Statement says in its significant third proposition: "Standards and values are relative to the culture from which they derive so that any attempt to formulate postulates that grow out of the beliefs or moral codes or one culture must to that extent detract from the applicability of any Declaration of Human Rights to mankind as a whole" (AAA 1947, 542).

5   The board's fear that a universal declaration of human rights would lead to a kind of moral imperialism was not simply prospective; it drew upon historical precedents such as the fact that "so noble a document as the American Declaration of Independence, or the American Bill of Rights, could be written by men who were themselves slave-owners, in a country where chattel slavery was a part of the recognized social order. The revolutionary character of the slogan 'Liberty, Equality, Fraternity' was never more apparent than in the struggles to implement it by extending it to the French slave-owning colonies" (AAA 1947, 542).

6   And it was a political scientist, Alison Dundes Renteln, who published the first article in the *American Anthropologist* after the 1940s to engage directly with human rights, although in this case only in order to explore the meanings of cultural relativism (Renteln 1988).

7   In fact, recent archival research shows that the AAA in 1947 would be nearly unrecognizable to AAA members today. For example, according to AAA executive board minutes from 1946, even though there were 600 professional anthropologists in the United States at that time, the association had only 200 members, and of these a "majority" (apparently more than 100) were *nonanthropologists*: "amateurs, students, [and] interested persons from other fields, and libraries" (Minutes of AAA Executive Board, March 1946–May 1954, Box 192, National Anthropological Archives). This means that the universe of professional anthropology was dramatically smaller at mid-century, and within this world the AAA played a much less significant role than it would later. This would also explain why it appears that the National Research Council, not the AAA, was approached by UNESCO.

8   For example, the Declaration of the Rights of the Child (1959), the Declaration on the Granting of Independence to Colonial Countries and Peoples (1961), the International Covenant on Economic, Social, and Cultural Rights (1966), the International Covenant on Civil and Political Rights (1966), the International Convention on the Elimination of All Forms of Racial Discrimination (1966), and the Convention on the Elimination of All Forms of Discrimination Against Women (1976).

9   For example, Amnesty International (1961), Helsinki Watch/Human Rights Watch (1978), and Peace Brigades International (1981). One important exception is the founding of Cultural Survival by David and Pia Maybury-Lewis in 1972.

10 For example, *Human Rights Quarterly* (1978).

11 The mid- to late 1980s was the time when, partly stimulated by the 1984 publication of Clifford Geertz's 1983 AAA Distinguished Lecture "Anti Anti-Relativism," the discipline suddenly rediscovered the complexities of some of the early issues surrounding anthropology and human rights, specifically the problem of universalism and cultural relativism. Other indications of this renewed intellectual interest are Washburn's 1987 article and Ronald Cohen's 1989 article in the *American Anthropologist*, in which he argues for a "new approach" to human rights from anthropology. Cohen's characterization of the period between the creation of the Universal Declaration and the time of his article reinforces my own. He asks, rhetorically, "What for instance has anthropological *research* (not simply pious pronouncements) to say about the rights described in the U.N. Charter, or the African Charter ...?" (1989, 1015). The answer, I have argued for this period, is not much.

12 Just to be clear, I see three distinct eras or phases in American anthropology's (dis-) engagement with human rights: (1) 1945–50: formal and public consideration of the Universal Declaration of Human Rights, rejection of it, denial of possibilities for engagement; (2) 1950–87: anthropological absence from important developments as an international and transnational human rights discourse emerged and became increasingly important; and (3) 1987–present.

13 Perhaps coincidentally, much of the most important early cultural survival work involved indigenous groups in Amazonia (the Yanomami, the Kayapo, the Xerente).

14 The following information is drawn from the five-year evaluation report of the AAA's Committee for Human Rights (2001).

15 In the introduction to a 1997 special issue of the *Journal of Anthropological Research*, guest editors Carole Nagengast and Terence Turner acknowledge the important role played by Patrick Morris in the creation of the permanent Committee for Human Rights.

16 Messer went on to serve as an original member of the AAA's Committee for Human Rights between 1995 and 1998 and has continued to play an important international role in efforts to have a distinct human right to food recognized and institutionalized, most recently through her directorship of the World Hunger Program at Brown University.

17 In this regard it is interesting that no mention is made of the 1947 Statement at any place on the Committee's web site, the section entitled "Documents of Historical Value" being limited to the small number of historically important documents produced by the Committee itself since 1995.

18 It is, of course, difficult to measure degrees of "influence" in this sense with any amount of certainty, but if one simply restricts the unit of analysis to the actions of the AAA through the Committee for Human Rights one can point to several cases in which anthropologists and the AAA were partly responsible for either influencing human rights practice by states or major institutions or took the lead in bringing what were considered violations of international human rights law to the attention of the global media. The most prominent example of this is the case of the Yanomami, in which the active intervention of the special commission mentioned earlier played a major role in forcing a change in policy by the Brazilian government favorable to the Yanomami nation. At the

same time, when the alleged human rights violators are not nation-states or multinational corporations but anthropologists themselves, the record of the Committee for Human Rights and the AAA is more ambiguous, as in the infamous *Darkness in El Dorado* affair (see Borofsky 2005).

19 This has begun to change (see Cowan, Dembour, and Wilson 2001; Goodale and Merry 2007; Wilson 1997; Wilson and Mitchell 2003).

20 See also Messer (1997), Nagengast (1997), and Zechenter (1997). The special issue that contains all these articles began as a panel at the 1995 AAA annual meetings in which human rights were a topic of focused interest. More recent work in the "emancipatory cultural politics" tradition can be found in Nagengast and Vélez-Ibáñez (2004), which received an endorsement from former president Jimmy Carter.

21 Conceptualizing human rights in these broader terms makes it clear why the period 1948–89 is so important, as this was the period when human rights discourse was developed and embedded conceptually and institutionally. Indeed, the post-1989 emergence of international human rights as a legal strategy with teeth would not have been possible had the discourse of human rights not already been firmly established.

22 According to Panikkar, "Diatopical hermeneutics stands for the thematic consideration of understanding the other without assuming that the other has the same basic self-understanding as I have. The ultimate human horizon, and not only differing contexts, is at stake here" (1979, 4). This provides a way of envisioning how understanding could be framed across or between different normativities, for example, between human rights and other types of normative systems that might incorporate or otherwise adapt provisions of international human rights. Christoph Eberhard is another scholar whose work on intercultural legal theory reinforces my arguments here (see, e.g., Eberhard 2001a, 2001b, 2003).

23 After I had finished this article, I discovered that the German-American psychoanalyst Erich Fromm had used the phrase "normative humanism" first in a 1954 *Dissent* article and then in his 1955 book *The Sane Society*. As used by Fromm, however, the phrase means something quite different from my development of it here. Fromm used it to refer to a set of universal criteria for measuring whether individuals were "sane" in terms of the degree to which they met their own basic needs.

24 Indeed, as I have argued elsewhere, human rights discourse in its current international and transnational forms tends toward a kind of moral imperialism that results when the disciplinary power of human rights discourse is employed in the service of transnational capitalist relations of production (see Goodale 2005 and below).

25 In saying this, I should emphasize that I conceive of the relationship between the individual and the collective differently from, for example, Michael Ignatieff, whose theorizing on this point reinforces the position of the individual within human rights practice (see Ignatieff 2001). "Normative humanism" expresses my understanding of the relationship between the individual and the collective under unconstrained circumstances in that it describes the importance of the collective in articulating normative meanings *but* assumes that these meanings will reflect a basic human-centeredness. It goes without saying that by describing the relationship between the individual and the collective in these terms I do not intend to link normative humanism with a particular moment in Western intellectual history; its use here is, in a sense, literal and intentionally ahistorical. Simply put, "humanism" is the best way to describe human-centeredness as a basic cross-cultural value.

26 I think it is obvious, however, that the assumptions underlying normative humanism are much less "optimistic" than those underlying the Universal Declaration of Human Rights, which assumes (1) that everyone is essentially the same by virtue of a common nature, (2) that this human nature can be *objectively* described in detail, (3) that this common human nature entails quite specific normative consequences (i.e., rights), and (4) that a global framework erected through law is the best mechanism for ensuring that these enumerated rights will be recognized and protected in practice.

27 Nevertheless, there are important differences between normative humanism and Durkheim's approach to ethical issues. Despite the fact that he deemphasized this in later

writings, Durkheim's sociology of morals was conceived as a way to generate empirical data that could be used for "improvement." The study of social facts was always instrumental. As I have argued, a theory of normative humanism is, rather, both a way of describing the conditions for potential emancipation through collective ordering and an explanation of how "human rights" can be reconceptualized as a legitimate normative possibility. Emancipation and legitimacy are not universally applicable "goals" in the strict sense but rather the effects of a contested, relatively uncommon, but actual type of ethical practice.

28   By "immanent universalism" I mean a theory of normativity which makes the individual, rather than culture, society, or institutions, the ultimate source of rights, obligations, duties, and so on, and these rights, obligations, etc., are immanent in all individuals, everywhere, irrevocably. International human rights doctrine is, in substantial part, on this definition, an immanent universalist normative theory. Describing human rights as an immanent universalist normativity does not mean that, from another angle, one could not also say that human rights "transcend" culture, history, society, and so on. But since what makes human rights "transcendent" is precisely their immanence, it is confusing to describe human rights as anchored in a theory of transcendence, partly because of the old debate in philosophy and religious studies over immanence and transcendence but also because such a theory rests on false ontological premises.

29   I mean to signal that I am not making an argument at this point about social scale – about the size or type of collectivity to which the idea of normative humanism applies. Scale in this sense is certainly salient, but its importance relates to matters of institutional and bureaucratic organization.

30   In describing the work of critical anthropologists of human rights as cultural interpretation, I locate the study of the social practice of normativity along the spectrum of the interpretative tradition within anthropology and, more specifically, point to anthropologists' indispensable role in articulating the orderings of collectivities so that their "lessons' can be employed in wider dialogues of economic and political consequence.

31   An activism that was, in most cases, distinguished from actual anthropological research even if it was necessarily associated with or motivated by it. In other words, until recently anthropologists did not have epistemological grounds for engaging in human rights activism as a legitimate sphere of anthropological inquiry.

32   Some good examples of research on "human rights as culture and the culture of human rights" would be, again, Merry's work (2001, 2003, 2006) and the essays in three recent edited volumes led by Richard Wilson (Wilson 1997; Cowan, Dembour, and Wilson 2001; Wilson and Mitchell 2003), who has recently been named director of an interdisciplinary human rights institute at the University of Connecticut – a development which also marks the shift in anthropology's relationship to human rights and, perhaps more important, a nascent openness on the part of non-anthropologists in the human rights community to anthropological perspectives.

33   There is an important difference, I would argue, between an alternative epistemology that is based on strongly nonrational grounds and one that continues to rely on the possibilities enabled by rationality, even if (as with intersubjectivity) the conditions under which rationality emerges in social practice – indeed, the nature of rationality itself (cf. Habermas's communicative rationality) – are critically reconceptualized.

34   In much the same way, the Dutch scholars Berma Klein Goldewijk and Bas de Gaay Fortman (who is Professor of the Political Economy of Human Rights at the University of Utrecht) study the political, economic, and social contexts within which "traditional human rights strategies are of limited effectiveness in responding to violations of economic, social, and cultural rights" (Goldewijk and Fortman 1999, vii). Their main argument is that a political economy of human rights demonstrates that articulating underlying human needs in human rights language invests these needs with social importance, which is the first step toward meeting them.

REFERENCES

AAA (American Anthropological Association). 1947. Statement of human rights. *American Anthropologist* 49:539–43.

An-Na'im, Abdullahi Ahmed. 1992. *Human rights in cross-cultural perspective: A quest for consensus.* Philadelphia: University of Pennsylvania Press.

Barnett, H. G. 1948. On science and human rights. *American Anthropologist* 50:352–55.

Baxi, Upendra. 2002. *The future of human rights.* Oxford: Oxford University Press.

Bell, Lynda, Andrew J. Nathan, and Ilan Peleg, eds. 2001. *Negotiating culture and human rights.* New York: Columbia University Press.

Bennett, John W. 1949. Science and human rights: Reason and action. *American Anthropologist* 51:329–36.

Borofsky, Robert. 2005. *Yanomami: The fierce controversy and what we can learn from it.* Berkeley: University of California Press.

Chomsky, Noam, and Edward Herman. 1979a. *The Washington connection and Third World fascism.* Cambridge: South End Press.

——. 1979b. *After the cataclysm: Postwar Indochina and the reconstruction of imperial ideology.* Cambridge: South End Press.

Cohen, Ronald. 1989. Human rights and cultural relativism: The need for a new approach. *American Anthropologist* 91:1014–17.

Collier, Andrew. 1994. *Critical realism: An introduction to Roy Bhaskar's philosophy.* London: Verso.

Committee for Human Rights, American Anthropological Association. 1999. Declaration on anthropology and human rights. http://www.aaanet.org/stmts/humanrts.htm (accessed September 22, 2004).

——. 2001. Five-year evaluation report. http://www.aaanet.org/committees/cfhr/ar95—00.htm (accessed September 22, 2004).

Cowan, Jane, Marie-Bénédicte Dembour, and Richard A. Wilson, eds. 2001. *Culture and rights: Anthropological perspectives.* Cambridge University Press.

Douglas, Mary, and Steven Ney. 1998. *Missing persons: A critique of the social sciences.* Berkeley: University of California Press.

Durkheim, Emile. 1993. *Ethics and the sociology of morals.* Buffalo: Prometheus Books.

Dworkin, Ronald. 1977. *Taking rights seriously.* Cambridge: Harvard University Press.

Eberhard, Christoph. 2001a. Toward an intercultural legal theory: The dialogical challenge. *Social and Legal Studies* 10: 171–201.

——. 2001b. Human rights and intercultural dialogue: An anthropological perspective. *Indian Socio-Legal Journal* 23: 99–120.

——. 2003. *Droits de l'homme et dialogue intercultural.* Paris: Éditions des Écrivains.

Engle, Karen. 2001. From skepticism to embrace: Human rights and the American Anthropological Association from 1947–1999. *Human Rights Quarterly* 23:536–59.

Evans, Tony. 2001. *The politics of human rights.* London: Pluto Press.

Ferguson, James. 1999. *Expectations of modernity: Myths and meanings of urban life on the Zambian Copperbelt.* Berkeley: University of California Press.

Fromm, Erich. 1954. The psychology of normalcy. *Dissent*, Spring, 139–43.

——. 1955. *The sane society.* New York: Rinehart.

Geertz, Clifford. 1983. Fact and law in comparative perspective. In *Local knowledge: Further essays in interpretative anthropology.* New York: Basic Books. [RAW]

Goldewijk, Berma Klein, and Bas de Gaay Fortman. 1999. *Where needs meet rights: Economic, social, and cultural rights in a new perspective.* Geneva: WCC Publications.

Goodale, Mark. 2005. Empires of law: Discipline and resistance within the transnational system. *Social and Legal Studies.* 14:553–83.

——. 2006. Ethical theory as social practice. *American Anthropologist* 108:25–37.

——— . In press. The anthropology of human rights: Critical explorations in ethical theory and social practice.

Goodale, Mark, and Sally Engle Merry, eds. 2007. *The practice of human rights: Tracking law between the global and the local*. Cambridge: Cambridge University Press.

Halliday, M. A. K., and J. R. Martin. 1993. *Writing science: Literacy and discursive power*. Pittsburgh: University of Pittsburgh Press.

Hernández-Truyol, Berta Esperanza, ed. 2002. *Moral imperialism: A critical anthology*. New York: New York University Press.

Horkheimer, Max, and Theodor Adorno. 2001 (1944). *Dialectic of enlightenment: Philosophical fragments*. Stanford: Stanford University Press.

Ignatieff, Michael. 2001. *Human rights as politics and idolatry*. Princeton: Princeton University Press.

Lévi-Strauss, Claude. 1949. *Les structures elémentaires de la parenté*. Paris: Presses Universitaires de France.

Marcus, George, and Michael Fischer. 1986. *Anthropology as cultural critique: An experimental moment in the human sciences*. Chicago: University of Chicago Press.

Merry, Sally. 2001. Rights, religion, and community: Approaches to violence against women in the context of globalization. *Law and Society Review* 35:39–88.

——— . 2003. Rights talk and the experience of law: Implementing women's human rights to protection from violence. *Human Rights Quarterly* 25:343–81.

——— . 2006. *Human rights and gender violence: Translating international law into local justice*. Chicago: University of Chicago Press.

Messer, E. 1993. Anthropology and human rights. *Annual Review of Anthropology* 22:221–49.

——— . 1997. Pluralist approaches to human rights. *Journal of Anthropological Research* 53:293–317.

Morsink, Johannes. 1999. *The Universal Declaration of Human Rights: Origins, drafting, and intent*. Philadelphia: University of Pennsylvania Press.

Nader, Laura. 1997. Controlling processes: Tracing the dynamic components of power. *Current Anthropology* 38:711–37.

Nagengast, Carole. 1997. Women, minorities, and indigenous peoples: Universalism and cultural relativity. *Journal of Anthropological Research* 53:349–69.

Nagengast, Carole, and Terence Turner. 1997. Introduction: Universal human rights versus cultural relativity. *Journal of Anthropological Research* 53:269–72.

Nagengast, Carole, and Carlos G. Vélez-Ibáñez. 2004. *Human rights: The scholar as activist*. Oklahoma City: Society for Applied Anthropology.

Nussbaum, Martha. 2000. *Women and development: The capabilities approach*. Cambridge: Cambridge University Press.

Obrad, Savic, ed. 2002. *The politics of human rights*. London: Verso.

Panikkar, Raimon. 1979. *Myth, faith, and hermeneutics*. New York: Paulist Press.

——— . 1996 (1982). Is the notion of human rights a Western concept? In *Human rights law*, ed. P. Alston, 161–88. Aldershot: Dartmouth.

Perry, Michael. 1998. *The idea of human rights: Four inquiries*. Oxford: Oxford University Press.

Rappaport, Roy A. 1993. Distinguished lecture in general anthropology: The anthropology of trouble. *American Anthropologist* 95:295–303.

Renteln, Alison Dundes. 1988. Relativism and the search for human rights. *American Anthropologist* 90:56–72.

Roosevelt, Eleanor. 1948. The promise of human rights. *Foreign Affairs* 26:470–77.

Santos, Boaventura de Sousa. 1995. *Toward a new common sense: Law, science, and politics in the paradigmatic transition*. New York: Routledge.

Scheper-Hughes, Nancy. 1995. The primary of the ethical: Propositions for a militant anthropology. *Current Anthropology* 36:409–40.

Schmid Noerr, Gunzelin. 2002. The position of "dialectic of enlightenment" in the development of critical theory. In *Dialectic of enlightenment: Philosophical fragments*, by M. Horkheimer and T. Adorno, 217–47. Stanford: Stanford University Press.

Sen, Amartya. 1981. *Poverty and famine: An essay on entitlement and deprivation*. Oxford: Clarendon Press.

——. 2000. *Development as freedom*. New York: Anchor/Doubleday.

Shute, Stephen, and Susan Hurley, eds. 1993. *On human rights*. New York: Basic Books.

Sponsel, Leslie. 1995. *Indigenous peoples and the future of Amazonia: An ecological anthropology of an endangered world*. Tucson: University of Arizona Press.

Steward, Julian. 1948. Comment on the statement on human rights. *American Anthropologist* 50:351–52.

Turner, Terence. 1997. Human rights, human difference: Anthropology's contribution to an emancipatory cultural politics. *Journal of Anthropological Research* 53:273–91.

Washburn, Wilcomb. 1987. Cultural relativism, human rights, and the AAA. *American Anthropologist* 89:939–43.

Wilson, Richard, ed. 1997. *Human rights, culture, and context: Anthropological approaches*. London: Pluto.

Wilson, Richard, and Jon P. Mitchell. 2003. *Human rights in global perspective; Anthropological studies of rights, claims, and entitlements*. London: Routledge.

Zechenter, Elizabeth. 1997. In the name of culture: Cultural relativism and the abuse of the individual. *Journal of Anthropological Research* 53:319–47.

Appendix: Websites on Human Rights

Networks

Human Rights Internet
www.hri.ca/index.aspx

This network, founded in 1976, is dedicated to the empowerment of human rights organizations and activists, and to the education of governmental institutions and other actors in the public and private sphere, on human rights issues and the role of civil society. It maintains contact with more than 5,000 organizations and individuals around the world working for the advancement of human rights.

Human Rights Interactive Network
www.webcom.com/hrin/intlgrps.html#list

This is a nonprofit organization based in California dedicated to the promotion of human rights worldwide. They have created a directory of international human rights advocacy groups and NGOs that monitor human rights violations.

Human Rights Education and Research Network, University of Washington
http://depts.washington.edu/hrights/index.html

Created in 1998, this research network focuses on the education and training of students, faculty, and researchers in the study of the legal, philosophical, historical, political, psychological, and cultural dimensions of human rights.

Important Documents and International Organizations

Universal Declaration of Human Rights
www.unhchr.ch/udhr/

United Nations High Commissioner for Refugees (UNHCR)
www.unhcr.org

This organization leads and coordinates international action to protect refugees and resolve refugee problems worldwide. Its main purpose is to preserve the rights and well-being of refugees and displaced people, helping them to relocate and adjust their lives in another state, seek asylum and integrate within a new country.

Office of the United Nations High Commissioner for Human Rights
http://www.ohchr.org/EN/Pages/WelcomePage.aspx

The website includes a concise database of international law and the core international human rights instruments, as well as a guide to human rights bodies in the United Nations system and those under international regulation.

Inter-American Commission on Human Rights (IACHR)
www.cidh.org/

The IACHR is an autonomous organ of the Organization of American States (OAS) dedicated to the protection of human rights in the region. The Commission carries out visits to the different countries in the Americas in order to evaluate and gather relevant information about specific human rights violations. It also recommends to the member states of the OAS the adoption of measures which would contribute to human rights protection and the adoption of "precautionary measures" to avoid human rights violations. After a careful investigation, the Commission submits cases to the Inter-American Court and appears before the Court on behalf of victims.

ILO Convention
www.unhchr.ch/html/menu3/b/62.htm

Convention 169 was adopted on June 27, 1989 by the General Conference of the International Labor Organisation with the mission to protect and respect "indigenous and tribal peoples' cultures."

International Criminal Court
www.icc-cpi.int/

This is an independent and permanent court that tries persons accused of crimes of international concern, namely genocide, crimes against humanity, and war crimes. It was established by the Rome Statute in 1998.

NGOs and Other Institutions

Human Rights Watch
www.hrw.org/

"Human Rights Watch's principal advocacy strategy is to shame offenders by gener-ating press attention and to exert diplomatic and economic pressure on them by enlisting influential governments and institutions. With the help of our significantly smaller membership base, we have also played a key role in building broad coalitions around specific human rights issues, such as the campaigns to ban landmines, to stop the use of child soldiers, and to establish the International Criminal Court."

Derechos Human Rights
www.derechos.org/

Derechos Human Rights is an international organization working for the promotion of human rights primarily in Latin America.

Amnesty International
www.amnesty.org/

The mission of Amnesty International is focused on research and political action for preventing and ending violations of human rights, promoting freedom of conscience and expression, and ending discrimination and torture, among others.

World Organization against Torture
www.omct.org/

Based in Geneva, this organization is a coalition of international organizations that provides medical, legal, and social advice to victims of torture worldwide.

International Federation of Human Rights
www.fidh.org/_news.php3

This is an international organization based in Paris that works for the prevention of human rights abuses and in the prosecution of those responsible. It advocates for victims of human rights violations, trains local partners, mobilizes the international community, and raises public awareness within the framework of the Universal Declaration of Human Rights.

Desaparecidos (in Spanish)
www.desaparecidos.org/main.html

This project was created to bring awareness to political crimes committed by different political regimes in Latin American countries. It is also a network that supports relatives and families of those who have been "disappeared" because of their political beliefs. The website contains a database of articles, publications, and links about human rights abuses and political crimes in Latin America.

Cultural Survival
http://cs.org/

This organization works to insure that indigenous peoples and their rights are being respected. Programs in training and education are carried out to insure full and effective participation of indigenous communities in the political, economic, and social life of the country in which they live.

Academic Human Rights Websites

Center for the Study of Human Rights
www.columbia.edu/cu/humanrights/

This Center, associated with Columbia University, specializes in education, training, and capacity-building for students, human rights leaders, organizations, and universities worldwide. It also fosters interdisciplinary academic research on human rights issues.

Diana
www.yale.edu/lawweb/avalon/diana/index.html

Yale University Law School has created this online human rights archive with relevant information on a range of human rights issues in the fields of law, history, economics, politics, diplomacy, and government. It also maintains links to sources of information on human rights outside the university.

Human Rights Institute, University of Connecticut
www.humanrights.uconn.edu

"The Human Rights Institute has two core missions: first, to coordinate human rights initiatives at the University of Connecticut and support faculty and students who study human rights; and second to promote a unique approach to international human rights scholarship based upon contextual and multidisciplinary research in the social sciences, humanities and law."

University of Minnesota Human Rights Library
www.umn.edu/humanrts/

This was one of the first online human rights libraries. Its web page contains links to treaties, declarations, resolutions, opinions, and decisions from international tribunals and treaty bodies.

Academy on Human Rights and Humanitarian Law
www.wcl.american.edu/pub/humright/digest/Inter-American/index.html

American University hosts the Inter-American Human Rights Database, which provides a link to annual reports, reports on sessions, and special reports of the Inter-American Commission on Human Rights, as well as different reports on the state of human rights protections in the region (by country).

Index